I0137953

The Northern School and the Formation of Early Ch'an Buddhism

KURODA INSTITUTE

STUDIES IN EAST ASIAN BUDDHISM

Studies in Ch'an and Hua-yen
Edited by
Robert M. Gimello and Peter N. Gregory

Dōgen Studies
Edited by
William R. LaFleur

STUDIES IN EAST ASIAN BUDDHISM 3

The Northern School and the Formation of Early Ch'an Buddhism

JOHN R. MCRAE

University of Hawaii Press
HONOLULU

The Kuroda Institute for the Study of Buddhism and Human Values is a non-profit, educational corporation, founded in 1976. One of its primary objectives is to promote scholarship on Buddhism in its historical, philosophical, and cultural ramifications. The Institute thus attempts to serve the scholarly community by providing a forum in which scholars can gather at conferences and colloquia. To date, the Institute has sponsored six conferences in the area of Buddhist Studies. Volumes resulting from these conferences, as well as individual studies, are planned for publication in the present series.

Library of Congress Cataloging-in-Publication Data

McRae, John R., 1947–
The Northern School and the formation of early Ch'an Buddhism.

(Studies in East Asian Buddhism ; no. 3)
Bibliography: p.
Includes index.
1. Zen Buddhism—China—History. I. Title. II. Series.
BQ9262.M36 1986 294.3'927'0951 86-4062
ISBN 0-8248-1056-2

This book is dedicated to
Reverend Eugene "Bub-In" Wagner
of the
American Buddhist Order

Contents

Part Two: Doctrine

Foreword

Many of the manuscripts found at Tun-huang contain material of special significance to the history and development of Ch'an Buddhism. While scholars such as Hu Shih and Daisetsu Suzuki contributed noteworthy studies in the period before World War II, it was not until the documents in the Stein and, later, the Pelliot Collections became generally available on microfilm that research made substantial advances.

In the forefront of the new studies, which amounted to a reassessment and rediscovery of much of early Ch'an history, were Japanese scholars in both Kyoto and Tokyo. Among these scholars, the foremost is undoubtedly Professor Yanagida Seizan of the Research Institute for Humanistic Studies, Kyoto University. Professor Yanagida, a consummate scholar and prolific writer who combines encyclopedic learning with keen insight, has published widely in all areas of Ch'an and Zen studies. Yet despite constant demands on his time, he has always been most generous in the help he has given to students from the West.

Dr. McRae, after extensive study with Professor Stanley Weinstein at Yale, went to Japan seeking the advice and guidance of Professor Yanagida. He has requited well his debt to both his mentors by providing a distinguished study of the Northern School and the formation of early Ch'an. Until the finds at Tun-huang, Northern Ch'an was a virtually unknown teaching, forgotten and relatively undocumented. Now, thanks to Dr. McRae's exhaustive studies we have a thorough and eminently lucid description of the history and thought of Northern Ch'an, and we know the teaching to have been a mature and literate form of Ch'an that played a significant role in eighth century T'ang China.

Dr. McRae has indeed made a significant contribution, one that other scholars in the field may well look to as an example of an academic competence that combines the best of Japanese scholarship with a superior command of the original materials. Dr. McRae's study well reflects the level of academic excellence which modern scholarly studies of Ch'an have attained.

PHILIP YAMPOLSKY
Columbia University

Preface

The original idea for this study was suggested by Professor Stanley Weinstein, my advisor at Yale University, who also offered useful advice and constructive criticism during the course of writing. Research was undertaken in Kyoto with the assistance of Professor Yanagida Seizan, who took time from a very busy schedule to provide individual tutoring and instruction. Professor Yanagida also gave me permission to use his own transcriptions in the preparation of the texts included at the end of this book. My original introduction to Professor Yanagida was through the kindness of Professor Philip Yampolsky of Columbia University, who has graciously consented to add a foreword to this work. I would like to express my sincere gratitude and deepest appreciation for the teaching I have received; hopefully, my own limitations have not led to errors and misinterpretations.

Research for this book was carried out with the benefit of a Fulbright Fellowship and a grant from the Concilium on International and Area Studies at Yale.

Thanks are also due to Stephen Bodian for his skillful editorial help in the preparation of the final manuscript. Last, but not least, I would like to thank Peter Gregory, Assistant Professor at the University of Illinois and Executive Director of the Kuroda Institute, who did much to make the publication of this book possible.

Princeton, New Jersey
May 15, 1985

Abbreviations and Conventions of Usage

ABBREVIATIONS

CFPC:	Ch'üan fa-pao chi
CTL:	Ching-te ch'üan-teng lu
CTW:	Ch'ing-ting ch'üan T'ang-wen
EJSHL:	Erh-ju ssu-hsing lun
H:	Hsü tsang-ching
HKSC:	Hsü kao-seng chuan
JTFM:	Ju-tao an-hsin yao fang-pien fa-men
KSC:	Kao-seng chuan
LCFJC:	Leng-ch'ieh jen-fa chih
LCSTC:	Leng-ch'ieh shih-tzu chi
LTFPC:	Li-tai fa-pao chi
SKSC:	Sung kao-seng chuan
T:	Taishō shinshū dai-zōkyō
TCL:	Tsung-ching lu
TTC:	Tsu-t'ang chi
Z:	Dai Nippon zoku-zōkyō

CONVENTIONS OF USAGE

1. Ages of individuals are given in the Chinese style.

2. Terms such as "Buddha Nature" have been rendered capitalized and without hyphenation in order to accomodate occasional abbreviated references to "Nature" alone.

3. Interlineal glosses in translated passages are indicated by the conjoint use of parentheses and italics, i.e., *(Another text says . . .)*.

4. Chapter and section headings of the text are indicated by capitalized Roman numerals and Arabic numerals, respectively, while Roman nu-

merals and capitalized English letters have been used for the chapter and section headings of translated works.

5. Citations of material in Tun-huang manuscripts are given in the following form: manuscript line number, slash, plate number, colon, plate line number, e.g., 607/26:2.

6. The annotation for the composite version of the *Wu fang-pien* included is explained in n. 224 to Section Two.

7. All citations of material from the *Zoku-zōkyō* have been cross-referenced to the Taiwan reprint, the *Hsü tsang-ching*.

Introduction

1. The Transmission of Ch'an According to the Platform Sūtra

For ancient and modern readers alike, the most common source of information about the Northern School of Chinese Ch'an Buddhism is the *Platform Sūtra of the Sixth Patriarch (Liu-tsu t'an ching).*[1] According to the narrative found at the beginning of this text, the Fifth Patriarch, Hung-jen (600–74), instructed each of his disciples to compose a "mind-verse" *(hsin-chieh)* demonstrating the level of his enlightenment. If one of these verses manifested a true understanding of Buddhism, its author would receive the Fifth Patriarch's robe and the status of Sixth Patriarch. All but one of the disciples simply ignored Hung-jen's instructions, deferring instead to the man they felt would be the next leader of the Ch'an community. This man was Shen-hsiu (606?–706), the most important figure associated with the Northern School. Shen-hsiu's reaction to Hung-jen's request is recorded in the *Platform Sūtra* as follows:

> The others won't present mind-verses because I am their teacher. If I don't offer a mind-verse, how can the Fifth Patriarch estimate the degree of understanding within my mind? If I offer my mind to the Fifth Patriarch with the intention of gaining the Dharma, it is justifiable; however, if I am seeking the patriarchship, then it cannot be justified. That would be like a common man usurping the saintly position. But if I don't offer my mind then I cannot learn the Dharma.[2]

In the end, Shen-hsiu did compose a verse, but he was so uncertain about its worth and the propriety of seeking the patriarchship that he inscribed it anonymously on a wall in one of the monastery's corridors. He did this late at night so that no one would see him. Shen-hsiu's verse read:

> The body is the *bodhi* tree.
> The mind is like a bright mirror's stand.

At all times we must strive to polish it
and must not let dust collect.[3]

Upon seeing this verse the following morning, the Fifth Patriarch canceled a previously made commission to have illustrations from the *Laṇkāvatāra Sūtra* painted on the wall, praised the verse highly, and ordered his students to recite it so that they might not suffer unfavorable rebirths in the future. To Shen-hsiu, however, he pointed out in private that the verse did not display true understanding. He counseled Shen-hsiu to write another verse in order to gain the Dharma, but in the end the future leader of the Northern School was unable to do so.

In the meantime, an uneducated layman from the far south of China named Hui-neng (638–713)[4] was at work threshing rice, completely unaware of the Fifth Patriarch's instructions about the future succession. When one day an acolyte passed by the threshing room reciting Shen-hsiu's verse, Hui-neng realized immediately that its author did not understand the "cardinal meaning" of Buddhism. The boy explained the entire matter to Hui-neng, who asked to be led to the corridor wall on which Shen-hsiu's verse was inscribed. There he dictated his own poetic statement:

Bodhi originally has no tree.
The mirror also has no stand.
The Buddha Nature is alway clear and pure.
Where is there room for dust?[5]

In public, the Fifth Patriarch denigrated Hui-neng's verse, but late that night he called the illiterate but inspired layman into the lecture hall and expounded the *Diamond Sūtra* to him. Hui-neng was immediately awakened to its profound meaning, received the transmission of the Sudden Teaching and the Fifth Patriarch's robe, and left the monastery in secrecy that very night.

2. *The* Platform Sūtra *as Historical Allegory*

The *Platform Sūtra* is one of the most imaginative and dramatically effective pieces of early Ch'an literature. Not only is it entertaining and instructive to read, but it builds upon and resolves numerous issues of eighth-century Ch'an Buddhism in a manner that is ingenious but not forced or contrived. It takes the image of an unschooled religious genius first developed in connection with Hung-jen[6] and expands it into the character of Hui-neng, who is both illiterate and inspired, déclassé but fundamentally superior. The *Platform Sūtra*'s depiction of Shen-hsiu as head monk and the originator of a very popular form of religious practice—i.e., that based on the verse attributed to him—is thus a reflection of the phenomenal success of Shen-hsiu and the "Northern School" at the beginning of the eighth century.

Similarly, in mentioning that Hung-jen publicly rejected Hui-neng's verse and that the new Sixth Patriarch spent years in hiding, the *Platform Sūtra* is acknowledging the initial obscurity of the "Southern School." Finally, the sūtra's scriptural references conform to the traditional understanding of the development of early Ch'an: Shen-hsiu's verse displaced paintings based in part on the *Laṇkāvatāra Sūtra,* but both Hui-neng's original enlightenment experience and final teachings from Hung-jen were based on the *Diamond Sūtra.* The transition from Northern to Southern School has traditionally been explained in terms of a shift from the *Laṇkāvatāra* to the *Diamond* and from the gradual to the sudden teaching.[7] In these senses, the *Platform Sūtra* narrative can be read as an historical allegory.

One critically important omission, however, indicates that the *Platform Sūtra* was not merely echoing history, but rewriting it. This is the complete absence of any reference to the role played by Shen-hui (684–758), who carried the banner of Hui-neng during an extended, energetic campaign against Shen-hsiu's disciples and the Northern School in general.[8] The whole point of the narrative, in fact, is to validate Shen-hui's claims about Hui-neng without reference to Shen-hui himself. That is, the *Plaform Sūtra* wished to adopt and build upon Shen-hui's teachings without identifying itself with his sometimes acrimonious and self-serving campaign.[9]

Although the verses and anecdote introduced earlier were evidently written after Shen-hui's death—his extant writings include no mention of them[10]—they are designed to expand on positions first articulated by him. Shen-hui attacked the Northern School for teaching an inferior, gradualistic doctrine of meditation and enlightenment. According to Shen-hui, the adherents of that school taught that one should approach Buddhism as a means to progressively purify oneself, to propel oneself further and further along the path to perfect enlightenment.

Shen-hui was particularly critical of the meditation practices of the Northern School masters, claiming that they taught their students "to freeze the mind to enter *dhyāna,* to fix the mind to view purity, to activate the mind to illuminate the external, and to concentrate the mind to realize the internal."[11] In other words, the members of the Northern School supposedly manipulated their minds in order to achieve certain specific effects, which, through a long regimen of sustained practice, eventually led to enlightenment. Shen-hui's Southern School disdained such practices because it was interested in a realm that was beyond all notions of duality—i.e., of imperfection and perfection, etc.—and in an approach to religious training that yielded attainment of the ultimate goal instantaneously, rather than gradually.

3. The Traditional Interpretation of the Platform Sūtra*'s "Mind-Verses"*

It is in the writings of Tsung-mi (780–841), a noted Ch'an and Hua-yen School theoretician who is supposed to have been a fifth-generation successor to Shen-hui, that we find the first explicit reference to and explanation of either of the *Platform Sūtra* verses. Although Tsung-mi never mentions the *Platform Sūtra* by name and does not refer to "Hui-neng's" verse,[12] he quotes "Shen-hsiu's" verse and adds his own interpretation. Although the following passage from Tsung-mi's *Ch'an-yuan chu-ch'üan chi tu-hsü (General Preface to a Collection of the Interpretations of Ch'an)* does not refer directly to the verse in question, it does include his most concise statement of his understanding of Northern School doctrine:

> The first [interpretation of Ch'an] is the School of Stopping the False and Cultivating the Mind, which teaches that, although sentient beings are in fundamental possession of the Buddha Nature, it is obscured and rendered invisible because of their beginningless ignorance. Therefore, they [suffer the] births and deaths of saṁsāra. Because the Buddhas have eradicated false thoughts [from their own persons] they have a comprehensive perception of the [Buddha] Nature, have transcended birth and death, and have attained autonomous [mastery] *(tzu-tsai)* of the supernormal powers. One should know that the abilities and functions of ordinary persons and sages are not the same and that there are distinctions between their [apprehension of] the external realms of sensory perception and the internal mind. Therefore, one must depend on the oral instructions of one's teacher, reject the realms of perception, and contemplate the mind, putting an end to false thoughts.
>
> When these thoughts are exhausted one experiences enlightenment, there being nothing one does not know. It is like a mirror darkened by dust—one must strive to polish it. When the dust is gone the brightness [of the mirror] appears, there being nothing it does not illuminate.
>
> One must also clearly understand the expedient means of entering into the realms of *dhyāna,* keeping oneself far from any disturbance and residing in a peaceful location, harmonizing body and breath, and sitting silently in the lotus position with the tongue touching the upper gums and the mind concentrated on a single object (*ching,* a "realm" of sensory perception).
>
> [Chih]-shen of the South, [Shen]-hsiu of the North, Pao-t'ang Wu-chu, Hsuan-shih, and their disciples all belong in this category. The technical details (? *chi,* "traces") of the expedient means of spiritual progress [taught by] the Ox-head and T'ien-t'ai [Schools], Hui-ch'ou (i.e., Seng-ch'ou), and

> Guṇa[bhadra] are also largely similar, although their doctrinal interpretations differ.[13]

Tsung-mi's works contain a comprehensive systematization of the various interpretations of Ch'an, within which the teachings of the Northern School are relegated to the very lowest position.[14] According to Tsung-mi, Shen-hsiu's verse and the supposed teachings of the Northern School fail to recognize the ultimate identity of enlightenment and the afflictions and illusions by which it is apparently obscured. As a result, the long years or even lifetimes of religious cultivation required to clean away those illusions were all in vain. The only achievement of any real benefit, and all that was really necessary, was the complete cessation of dualistic thinking.[15]

According to this interpretation, the Northern School teaching was inferior because it posited enlightenment as a specific goal that could be described, sought, and attained, and because it restricted the achievement of that enlightenment to those who had the energy and opportunity to engage in long years of practice. The metaphor of the mirror was thus used in the *Platform Sūtra* to describe the gradual teaching: Just as cumulative effort would result in the mirror's becoming ever brighter, so would sustained spiritual practice result in higher and higher levels of individual purification, until at last complete perfection was attained.

The Southern School's sudden teaching, in contrast, was superior in that enlightenment could be achieved by anyone—even the illiterate barbarian Hui-neng—in a sudden, instantaneous, and complete transformation. After an initial period of popularity, the Northern School was supposedly overwhelmed and driven into extinction by the Southern School, which was inherently superior because the true transmission of Ch'an had been from Hung-jen to Hui-neng rather than to Shen-hsiu.

With minor variations, this interpretation of early Ch'an history has been accepted for over a thousand years. Modern scholarship has examined much of the background to the *Platform Sūtra,* focusing chiefly on the very crucial role played by Shen-hui. Great strides have also been made in the study of the Northern School, which is now understood to have taught something other than the simple gradualism ascribed to it within Shen-hui's polemics and Tsung-mi's elaborate system. Even so, the treatment of the Northern School in modern works on Ch'an is problematic: The "mind-verses" of the *Platform Sūtra* are widely quoted and the superiority of the sudden over the gradual teaching is often discussed, but there is no unanimity on the validity or implications of the verses themselves.[16] The absence of any comprehensive study of the Northern School and the sometimes obscure and stylistically unusual writings associated with it have led most scholars to fall back on the traditional image of the school as gradualist in doctrine and secondary in historical importance to the Southern School.

Clearly, the demands of scholarly accuracy require that such inconsistencies be avoided. Citation of the *Platform Sūtra* verses is acceptable only if one distinguishes clearly between the history and legend of early Ch'an and if one is very precise about the verses' legitimate frame of reference. That is, while the *Platform Sūtra* verses and anecdote reflect one late eighth century image of Ch'an, they do not in any way resemble the history of the Ch'an School during the seventh century.[17]

4. Implications for This Study

Obviously, in strictly historical terms the *Platform Sūtra* narrative is completely inaccurate. First of all, if we follow the earliest records, Shen-hsiu and Hui-neng were never at Hung-jen's side at the same time, and neither was there during the last few years of the master's life, when a transmission might have taken place.[18] Second, the very concept of a verse competition and the selection of a single successor seems more appropriate as literary flourish than historical fact. A single successor might have been selected as the spiritual leader of the community of ordained and lay trainees at Hung-jen's monastery, rather than as the head of the Ch'an School per se, but the *Platform Sūtra* does not mention such a possibility. (Hung-jen's monastery lapsed into almost complete obscurity after his death.) The notion that only one line of transmission could be considered legitimate—i.e., that from Hung-jen to Hui-neng rather than those from Hung-jen to Shen-hsiu, Hui-neng, *et al.* —could have developed only after Shen-hui's campaign.

This being the case, we are left with the following question: Should the *Platform Sūtra*'s references to Shen-hsiu's teachings simply be ignored, or do they have some basis in fact, however distorted or incompletely presented?

In the first place, we have reason to suspect that Shen-hsiu's verse is not an entirely groundless invention. Nothing like the verse itself occurs in Northern School literature, but a few passages and some general considerations exist that may explain part of the *Platform Sūtra*'s misinterpretation. Even more intriguing is a passage suggesting that Shen-hsiu actually could have used the metaphor of the mirror exactly as it occurs in the verse attributed to him—but with a meaning completely different from that verse's traditional interpretation. In the second place, certain other details of the verses—such as the reference to the *bodhi* tree and the famous third line of Hui-neng's verse in later texts, which reads, "Fundamentally there is not a single thing"—are reminiscent of specific references in Northern School literature. The implication is that the teachings of the Northern School played some part in the formulation of the ideas attributed to Hui-neng.

Therefore, the answer to the question just posed is that the testimony of the *Platform Sūtra* must be considered—not as a guide to the seventh- or even the early eighth-century teachings of the Northern School, but as an indication of the status of that school at the end of the eighth century.

5. Ch'an's Pseudohistorical Doctrine and the Historical Study of Ch'an

Needless to say, the *Platform Sūtra* paints far too simple a picture of the development of early Ch'an. The problem is not only that the story told in this text is inaccurate, that the exchange of verses and transmission to Hui-neng could not have occurred as stated. Nor is the problem even that the gradual and sudden teachings cannot be reliably attributed to the historical figures Shen-hsiu and Hui-neng. These are all matters of historical fact, which can be verified or refuted by examining the documents at hand. The real problem engendered by the *Platform Sūtra*'s overly simplistic depiction of early Ch'an lies rather in the extremely pervasive and seldom questioned tendency of modern scholarship to view the history of Ch'an solely in terms of a succession of individual masters and disciples.

The history of Ch'an is customarily discussed in terms of the lives and teachings of a succession of individual masters. The traditional orthodoxy of the Ch'an School would have its followers believe that the only significant information about Ch'an is the body of biographical information and inspired sayings of a number of individual religious authorities, who follow each other in master-disciple relationships much like a set of beautiful pearls on a string. The status of the Ch'an School at any given time may be defined, according to this approach, by the biography and teachings of the reigning patriarch. In the case of early Ch'an, the first subject is a treatment of the biography and teachings of Bodhidharma, followed by the biography and teachings of Hui-k'o, Seng-ts'an, Tao-hsin, Hung-jen, and so on. For later periods, one would want the sum of such information for all active masters, so that the overall history of the Ch'an School is the sum total of such descriptions.

Obviously, it *is* appropriate in many cases to organize discussion of the history of Ch'an by proceeding from one generation to the next—I will follow this course of action myself in certain parts of this book. Nevertheless, an uncritical allegiance to the Ch'an orthodoxy ignores two important realities of early Ch'an history. First, except for Shen-hsiu, Shen-hui, and a few other individuals, the extant body of primary sources does not indicate one-to-one correspondences between individual masters and specific doctrines. Rather, the bulk of our doctrinal information can be identified only as having been valid in a certain general context at a certain time. I will argue in Part Two that this is especially true of two texts that have until now been used quite frequently for the elucidation of the individual teachings of Tao-hsin and Hung-jen.[19] Second, such a simplistic methodology as the "string of pearls" approach of necessity ignores major areas of potentially significant political, social, and intellectual influences upon the development of Ch'an. Hence the passive acceptance of the Ch'an position concerning the transmission from master to disciple does a disservice to our understanding of this school as a legitimate segment of human religious history.

6. The Origin of the Terms "Northern School" and "East Mountain Teaching"

The problems of distinguishing between pseudohistorical propaganda and historical reality are not limited to the study of the *Platform Sūtra.* The following is the first recorded usage in Ch'an literature of the term "Northern School":

> When Preceptor [Shen]-hsiu was alive, spiritual aspirants [all over] China referred to these great masters as "[Hui]-neng of the South and [Shen]-hsiu of the North" *(nan Neng pei Hsiu).* This was common knowledge. These references led to [the usages] of the two schools of North and South. *Dhyāna* Master P'u-chi is in reality a student of [Shen-hsiu of] Yü-ch'üan [ssu]. He actually never went to Chao-chou [to study under Hui-neng], so it is therefore impermissible for him now to declare falsely [that his teaching is] the Southern School.[20]

This passage is from the *P'u-t'i-ta-mo nan-tsung ting shih-fei lun (Treatise on the Definition of the Truth about the Southern School of Bodhidharma),* the transcript of a polemical sermon given by Shen-hui in 732.[21] The implication of Shen-hui's statement is that P'u-chi never referred to his teachings as the "Northern School" *(pei-tsung),* but actually used the term "Southern School" *(nan-tsung).* This early usage of that term to refer to Shen-hsiu's lineage is corroborated in at least one other early text. In contrast, there is no indication that Shen-hsiu or any of his immediate disciples ever used the term "Northern School" in reference to themselves.[22]

If Shen-hui was the first to call Shen-hsiu and his associates the Northern School, then how did these men refer to themselves? The following passage provides the answer to this question:

> In the first year of the Ta-tsu [period, or 701 C.E.,] *Dhyāna* Master Shen-hsiu was given an Invitation to enter the eastern capital [of Lo-yang. Thereafter he] accompanied the [imperial] chariot on its comings and goings, pro-

> selytizing within the two capitals and personally becoming the Imperial Instructor.
>
> The Great Sage Empress [Wu] Tse-t'ien inquired of him: "Whose teaching is it that you transmit?"
>
> [He] answered: "I have inherited the *East Mountain Teaching* of Ch'i-chou (i.e., Huang-mei, the location of Hung-jen's monastery)."
>
> . . . [Empress Wu] Tse-t'ien said: "In considering the cultivation of the Path, the East Mountain Teaching is unexcelled."[23]

This passage is included in a text known as the *Leng-ch'ieh jen-fa chih (Records of the Men and Teachings of the Laṇkā* [*vatāra*]; hereafter cited as *LCJFC).* This work was compiled by Hung-jen's student Hsuan-tse, probably sometime between 708 and 710.[24] The *LCJFC* does not, however, occur independently, but only as quoted in the *Leng-ch'ieh shih-tzu chi (Records of the Teachers and Disciples of the Laṇkā* [*vatāra*]; hereafter cited as *LCSTC).* This text, fortunately still extant, was written by Ching-chueh, a disciple of both Hsuan-tse and Shen-hsiu. The terms "East Mountain Teaching" *(tung-shan fa-men)* and "Pure Teaching of East Mountain" *(tung-shan ching-men)* occur elsewhere in the *LCSTC* as well as in two slightly earlier Northern School documents.[25]

We have no direct evidence as to what name, if any, Tao-hsin (580–651) and Hung-jen (600–74) used to refer to their own teachings. As the passages just quoted make clear, however, Shen-hsiu identified himself as the transmitter of Hung-jen's teaching, P'u-chi labeled his doctrines (which were inherited from Shen-hsiu) as the Southern School, and Shen-hui appropriated this latter label for his own use.

In spite of the apparent inequity of using a term first applied pejoratively,[26] I will follow modern scholarly convention in using "Northern School" to refer to Shen-hsiu and his successors. This usage presents no problem, as long as we refrain from unreservedly accepting statements by later authors (such as Tsung-mi) that the term "Northern School" refers directly to Shen-hsiu and his successors, rather than to the *image* of Shen-hsiu and his teachings within Shen-hui's writings and the *Platform Sūtra.*

Also in accord with general modern practice, I will use the name "East Mountain Teaching" to refer to Tao-hsin and Hung-jen. This usage actually presents a much more serious problem than the label "Northern School." First, its original meaning was neither so specific nor so clearly sectarian as the other term. In one epitaph dating from shortly after 750, in fact, "East Mountain Teaching" is used to refer to the teachings of the Ch'an School as a whole in juxtaposition with "the concentration and insight of T'ien-t'ai" *(T'ien-t'ai chih-kuan).*[27] Second, the primary ancient and modern referents of the name "East Mountain Teaching,"—i.e., the teachings of Shen-hsiu and his associates or, alternatively, the teachings of Tao-hsin and Hung-jen—display a temporal disconformity that is chronologically slight but potentially very misleading.

7. The Distinction Between Legend and History

The problem with the term "East Mountain Teaching" is that *all* of our information about Tao-hsin and Hung-jen is contained in sources associated with Shen-hsiu and the so-called Northern School. Tao-hsin does receive a biographical entry, in which Hung-jen is mentioned, in the *Hsü kao-seng chuan (Continued Lives of Eminent Monks;* hereafter cited as *HKSC).* Although none of the information contained in that entry is suspicious or even significant enough to warrant close deliberation, Shen-hsiu himself was the most likely source of information for this biography.[28] All the rest of the data concerning Hung-jen's biography comes from early eighth-century Northern School sources. As subsequent discussion will indicate, these works are more concerned with legend and propagandistic rationalization than with the demands of critical historical analysis. As a result, the accuracy of their assertions regarding the early Ch'an patriarchs must occasionally be called into question.

The single most important task facing the modern student of early Chinese Ch'an Buddhism is the accurate discrimination between legend and history. Each has its own distinctive value: Legend reflects the school's total creative output and is an important guide to its self-image, whereas history is the modern understanding of the dynamic cultural and intellectual realities of the school's development. The legend of the "transmission of the lamp" of the teachings from one master to another was one of the most important innovations of early Ch'an, but the statements made within the context of this legendary format cannot be taken automatically at face value as historical assertions to be judged as either true or false and correlated with other "facts." While such "historical" assertions may have bases in fact, we must not forget that they occur within a context determined by the propagandistic or polemical purposes of the given texts.

The second passage introduced in Section 6 of this Introduction is a perfect case in point. Shen-hsiu's invitation to court and his activities in the two capitals are without doubt valid historical events, but these facts and his dialogue with Empress Wu were selected from a large body of information to glorify the status of the departed Ch'an Master, to sanctify the derivation of his teaching from a certain religious predecessor, and, implicitly, to legitimize the prestige of his heirs. In this example we need not infer any gross distortion of the original historical situation for the purposes of incorporation into the *LCSTC.*

In other cases, however, statements occur that seem to idealize the character of an individual Ch'an master in the face of other directly contradictory evidence. (Hui-neng's biography, of course, is the most prominent example.) Such cases must be approached with extreme caution, since the Ch'an orthodoxy that threatens to distort our critical perspective came into existence on the basis of a series of innovations made during the very period under study. Although it is fortunate, in one sense, that the texts of the Northern School to be considered here are not so full of patent fabrications and questionable attributions as some of the slightly later texts of early Ch'an (the *Li-tai fa-pao chi* [*Records of the (Transmission of the) Dharma-treasure through the Generations; LTFPC*], is undoubtedly the most egregious of all in this respect[29]), the most difficult parts of the Ch'an legend to work with are actually those that lie somewhere between obvious fact and palpable fiction.

The assertions made about the supposed Third Patriarch Seng-ts'an, for example, are completely unusable as historical data. Only the most foolhardy or avowedly myopic student of early Ch'an would suggest that Seng-ts'an had any knowable impact on the school's historical development or any actual connection whatsoever with the text usually attributed to him, the *Hsin-hsin ming (Inscription on Relying upon the Mind).*[30] On the other hand, the lives of Shen-hsiu, P'u-chi, and other Northern School figures are well enough documented through epitaphs and other contemporary sources that we know at least the general outlines of their lives and contributions.

The cases of Tao-hsin and Hung-jen, however, are not so clear-cut. There exist valid data about their biographies and relatively early texts describing their teachings, and these two sets of information would seem to dovetail neatly and without any blatant contradictions. As I will suggest later, however, these texts cannot be reliably attributed to Tao-hsin and Hung-jen. (See Part Two, Chapter VI, Section 1.) Even though the texts in question are no doubt more representative of the teachings of these individuals than is the *Hsin-hsin ming* representative of the teachings of Seng-ts'an, their individual attributions to Tao-hsin and Hung-jen cannot be accepted without important qualifications. In other words, for the very core of the early Ch'an succession—the third, fourth, and fifth generations—specific teachings cannot be correlated with individual patriarchs.

8. The Approach Taken Here

The considerations discussed in the previous section require that all exclusively doctrinal matters be left until the second part of this study. The first task to be undertaken here will be to describe the historical development of the Northern School. In order to probe the immediate antecedants of the school, I will begin with a brief discussion of Bodhidharma and his immediate successors. Unfortunately, considerations of space make it impossible to examine in detail the larger background of Ch'an within the context of Chinese Buddhism and Buddhist meditation traditions in general.[31] The second task to be undertaken in Part One of this study will be to analyze the development of the "transmission of the lamp" texts and the evolution of the Ch'an School's sense of its own identity.

PART ONE

HISTORY

CHAPTER I

Bodhidharma, His Immediate Successors, and the Masters of the *Laṇkāvatāra Sūtra*

1. The Legend of Bodhidharma

The traditional account of the lives of Bodhidharma and Hui-k'o is perhaps the most inspired and meaningful invention of the entire body of Ch'an legends.[1] According to this version Bodhidharma was originally a South Indian prince who arrived in China as a 150-year-old monk during the reign of Emperor Wu of the Liang (r. 502–49). Emperor Wu, it should be noted, was one of the most famous imperial supporters of Buddhism in all Chinese history, a ruler who sponsored the construction of numerous temples and images, personally studied Buddhist scriptures, and scrupulously observed Buddhist religious injunctions.[2] In a famous legendary interview with Emperor Wu, Bodhidharma emphatically rejected the value of all these activities, saying that they were of "no religious merit" whatsoever. After this celebrated confrontation, Bodhidharma traveled north to live in a cave at Shao-lin ssu[3] on Mount Sung near Loyang, where he is supposed to have sat in meditation facing a wall for nine years.

During his residence at Shao-lin, Bodhidharma gained his most gifted disciple, Hui-k'o, who was absolutely convinced of Bodhidharma's importance and fiercely determined to win the Indian monk's respect. In order to prove his sincerity and thus receive the teachings, Hui-k'o stood near where Bodhidharma was meditating and waited for hour upon hour in earnest supplication. Snow began to fall from the cold winter sky, but Hui-k'o was undaunted. Over the course of the evening the snow accumulated to Hui-k'o's knees, but when Bodhidharma finally noticed the supplicant and discovered why he was waiting there, the Indian sage only warned him about the difficulty of practicing the "unsurpassable, wondrous path of the Buddhas."

Finally, in a surge of zealous desperation and with thoughts of the trials of former enlightened ones, Hui-k'o took a knife and cut off his left arm, placing it in front of Bodhidharma. Permitted at last, through this extraordinary (if macabre) demonstration of self-sacrifice, to receive the teaching, Hui-k'o asked Bodhidharma: "My mind is not at peace; please pacify it for me."

To this Bodhidharma replied: "Bring your mind here and I will pacify it for you."

Hui-k'o: "I have searched for my mind, but it is completely unobtainable (i.e., imperceptible; or "I cannot find it anywhere")."

Bodhidharma: "I have [now] completely pacified your mind for you."[4]

Although Bodhidharma's final reply might appear as a neat piece of sophistry to a modern reader, it was enough, according to the traditional account, to inspire Hui-k'o to a great realization or enlightenment experience. Hui-k'o remained under Bodhidharma's tutelage for six years. (Bodhidharma also had a few other students of lesser abilities.) After the master's death Hui-k'o propagated Bodhidharma's teaching all over North China, eventually transmitting it to Seng-ts'an and thus on to the other Chinese Patriarchs.

The complete legend of Bodhidharma and Hui-k'o, of which this account is but the bare nucleus, evolved gradually over the span of many years. All of the most important components of the legend were added in the seventh and eighth centuries, just at the time when the Ch'an School's fundamental perception of itself was being formed. As a result, the contour of this legend's evolution is a valuable indicator of the growth of the Ch'an School itself.[5] The legend's heuristic value within the context of the meditation hall can hardly be overlooked: How many sermons have been delivered on the worthlessness of Emperor Wu's pious efforts! How many trainees have been urged on to greater efforts through the example of Hui-k'o! Indeed, the question "What is the meaning of Bodhidharma's coming from the West?" has been one of the favorite subjects of Ch'an religious dialogue and contemplation for more than a thousand years.

Nevertheless, despite its religious value, this legend is entirely unreliable as a statement of historical fact. Let us now turn to the historical analysis of Bodhidharma's biography.

2. The Life of Bodhidharma

The oldest text to mention Bodhidharma is the *Lo-yang ch'ieh-lan chi (Records of the Monasteries of Lo-yang),* written by Yang Hsuan-chih in or shortly after 547. Bodhidharma is introduced as a foil to demonstrate the magnificence of the greatest of the Lo-yang establishments, Yung-ning ssu:

At the time there was Bodhidharma, a *śramaṇa* from the western region. He was a barbarian from *po-ssu* [in Central Asia (?)]. When he came from that far-off country, traveled to China, and perceived the golden plates [at the top of Yung-ning ssu] glistening in the sun, their brilliance shining past the [very] clouds, and the precious bells rung by the wind whose echo extended beyond heaven, he sang out in praise: "This is truly a spectacular accomplishment!" He said that he was 150 years old and had wandered to all the countries in the world without exception, but that this monastery was [so] exquisite [that its equal] did not exist [anywhere] in the world (*Jambu-*[*dvīpa*]). "I have gone to the very limits of things (i.e., all over the world), but I have never [seen anything like] this." He held his palms together and chanted *namo* for several days.[6]

The image of Bodhidharma in this text is that of an aged and pious pilgrim. As Professor Yanagida points out, foreign monks appearing in this text are not given individual personalities, but function as well-traveled and exotic witnesses to the grandeur of the architecture of Lo-yang.[7] This figure is fundamentally different from the Bodhidharma of the Ch'an legend, and it may be that the man referred to here only accidentally shares the name of the founder of the Ch'an School. Nevertheless, these two Bodhidharmas were linked as early as the *HKSC,* which refers to the founder of Ch'an as being 150 years old. Incidentally, as Hu Shih has pointed out, if we are to take the *Lo-yang ch'ieh-lan chi* at face value, Bodhidharma's entry into Lo-yang occurred between 516 and 526.[8]

The *HKSC* entry on Bodhidharma is relatively straightforward, although it does embody certain textual problems that will be discussed later. After Bodhidharma is introduced as being of brahmin lineage from South India and described pro forma as gifted both intellectually and spiritually, interested in the Mahāyāna, and accomplished in meditation, we read:

Feeling compassion [as a result of the decline of the True Teaching in this] obscure corner [of the world (i.e., China), Bodhidharma sought to] lead [the people here to enlightenment] by means of the Dharma. He first reached Nan-yueh within the boundaries of the Sung and later crossed north again to the Wei. Wherever he went he gave instruction in the teaching of meditation *(ch'an-chiao).* At the time the practice of lecturing [on the Buddhist scriptures] had spread across the entire country, so that [people] often slandered [Bodhidharma] upon hearing the Dharma of *samādhi (ting-fa).*

[As students of Bodhidharma] there were Tao-yü and Hui-k'o. Although younger, these two *śramaṇas* were dedicated to the lofty ideal, so that, when they first met the Dharma General (i.e., Bodhidharma), they realized that their spiritual path had reached its natural conclusion. Accordingly, they studied directly under him for four or five years. They made offerings [to him and] inquired respectfully, and he, responding to their pure sincerity, taught them the True Dharma *(chen-fa):* Such is the pacification of the mind, called "wall contemplation" *(ju shih an-hsin wei pi-kuan);* such is the development of practices *(hsing),* called the "four teachings"; such is accordance with convention and the defense against calumnification; such is the expedient means *(fang-pien)* by which one avoids attachments. [Here follows Tao-hsuan's summary of the "two entrances and four practices."]

[Bodhidhar]ma used this Dharma to convert [the people of] the land of Wei, where those who recognized the Truth followed it and were enlightened. His sayings were recorded, and the scroll(s) [containing them] are in circulation in the world [today].

[Bodhidharma] said that he was over 150 years old. He wandered about and taught, but it is not known where he died.[9]

The Bodhidharma that appears in this text has much more depth of character than the stereotyped image of the *Lo-yang ch'ieh-lan chi,* but still falls far short of the legendary figure who appears in later Ch'an texts. Hui-k'o appears as a man of great purity and dedication, but his self-dismemberment is not mentioned. In addition, it is important to note the references to the slander of Bodhidharma and his teachings by those devoted to scriptural study and lecturing, as well as the provision within Bodhidharma's teachings for averting the impact of such abuse and ill-will. Finally, the references to "pacification of the mind," "wall contemplation," and "expedient means" in this passage are actually abbreviated references to the *Erh-ju ssu-hsing lun (Treatise on the Two Entrances and Four Practices;* hereafter cited as *EJSHL)* and its preface by T'an-lin. (This treatise will be translated and analyzed in Part Two of this book.)

It is possible to construct an outline of Bodhidharma's career in China by combining information from the *Lo-yang ch'ieh-lan chi,* T'an-lin's preface to the *EJSHL,* and the *HKSC:*

1. If we are to take the *HKSC* literally, Bodhidharma arrived in South China by the maritime route in or before the year 479.[10]

2. If we identify Seng-fu's teacher, who is listed in the *HKSC* as *Dhyāna* Master Dharma, with the founder of the Ch'an School, then we can infer that Bodhidharma moved to the North before 495 at the very latest, and possibly as early as 480 or so.[11] (Seng-fu will be discussed in the next section.)

3. According to the *Lo-yang ch'ieh-lan chi,* Bodhidharma was still in North China sometime during the years 516 to 526. Presumably, his wanderings were restricted to North China from the time of his first journey there until his death.

4. Information in the *HKSC* indicates that Bodhidharma's death occurred around the year 530, or after 524 and before 534.[12]

In addition to this rough chronology, a few statements can be made about Bodhidharma's personal character. He was a native of South India, a brahmin by birth, and perhaps a member of the ruling family of some unknown principality. He was a Mahāyānist and a meditation instructor who focused his proselytizing efforts on the Lo-yang area.[13]

However, it must be borne in mind that these points involve a number of unverifiable suppositions and are based on potentially incompatible sources. Although nothing else can be said about Bodhidharma with any historical certainty, perhaps this is only fitting. Without question, the hagiography surrounding Bodhidharma's role as the founder of the Ch'an tradition is much more important than any actual historical contribution he may have made.

3. Seng-fu

At this point the conventional approach would be to turn to Bodhidharma's best-known student and major successor, Hui-k'o. Instead, we will first consider the case of Seng-fu, whose entire career in Ch'an antedates that of his more famous fellow student. It is indicative of the continuing strength of the Ch'an orthodoxy that Seng-fu's life and probable relevance to the history of early Ch'an have been so rarely studied; the majority of scholarly references to him concern a later legendary fabrication in which there appears a monk with a similar name.[14]

Seng-fu's *HKSC* biography[15] occurs at the very beginning of the section on meditation specialists, before those of Bhadra (given here as Buddha), Bodhidharma, Hui-k'o, and others. Originally a resident of Ch'i-hsien in T'ai-yuan (Shansi) in the far North, Seng-fu searched far and wide for a meditation instructor before he encountered the *dhyāna* master [Bodhi]dharma. Seng-fu formally "left home" to become a monk after visiting the latter's cave residence, where the two discussed the profundities of Buddhism. After penetrating to the limits of the "principle of meditation" *(ting-hsueh tsung),* Seng-fu traveled about to various centers of scriptural learning to complete his education. During this time he realized that "learning depends only on oneself, [since] sages have no words."[16]

Sometime between 494 and 497 Seng-fu traveled to the southern capital of Chien-k'ang, where he resided at Ting-lin hsia ssu on Mount Chung, just outside the city.[17] Seng-fu is said to have loved Ting-lin's forest groves and quiet setting, living there with only the bare minimum of possessions. Although widely respected by the local monks and lay people, he steadfastly refused invitations from members of the ruling class and did not go for an interview with the famed Buddhist sovereign

Emperor Wu. This reference implies that Seng-fu stayed at Ting-lin hsia ssu until after Emperor Wu's coronation in 502.

At one point Seng-fu undertook a missionary sojourn in the Szechwan area,[18] but he soon returned to Ting-lin hsia ssu. Eventually, Emperor Wu ordered his craftsmen to build a residence for the northern meditation specialist at K'ai-shan ssu. This must have occurred sometime after the temple's founding in 515.[19] In keeping with his previous asceticism, Seng-fu did not assume residence at this monastery without at least an outward show of resistance on his part. It is said that whenever he wandered past the gate of the new temple, which was dedicated to the memory of Pao-chih, Seng-fu would lean on his staff and lament:

> A [single] room with a fence about it, a woven wormwood gate, and windows made of broken pots thrust in the walls—meditation in such a place can be quite pleasant! Why should one esteem a mansion and despise a thatched hut? One can take one's peace and depart. Why must reverence for the deceased (i.e., Pao-chih) be restricted to this [new building], which is only for the purpose of pleasing the ears and eyes?[20]

Since Seng-fu did eventually take up residence at K'ai-shan ssu, we might suspect that these sentiments were something of a pose. However, it is easy to imagine that his northerner's sensibilities were affected by the high society atmosphere of southern court Buddhism. He also demonstrated his distaste for material finery during his final illness, when he rejected all gifts and instructed that his body be thrown away on a mountainside for the benefit of the birds and beasts. Here again, his ascetic sensibilities were ignored—a stele was erected to publicize his virtue, the inscription for which was written by Prince I of Hsiang-tung, the eventual Emperor Yuan.[21]

The only indication we have of Seng-fu's religious experience and teachings comes from an event that occurred after his return from what is now Szechwan to Ting-lin hsia ssu. On a certain date in 515, a spirit appeared on a mountain in what is now Kiangsi with a copy of the *Hui-yin san-mei ching (Sūtra of the Samādhi of the* [*Tathāgata's*] *Seal of Wisdom),* which was to be used by the Prince of Nan-p'ing (476–533) to help cure his current illness. If necessary, the prince was to seek assistance in understanding the text from Seng-fu, who is said to have practiced the *samādhi* in question previously. The prince supposedly performed the requisite twenty-one days of this practice and enjoyed a speedy recovery.[22]

There is no way of knowing whether Seng-fu originally practiced this *samādhi* under Bodhidharma's guidance or influence, whether he first encountered it in the South,[23] or whether it was his idea to use it as a palliative rather than for some higher spiritual end. All that can be said is that, if Bodhidharma's teaching included some form of Mahāyāna *samādhi* practice, he could hardly have chosen a more appropriate text. The *Hui-yin san-mei ching* describes the Buddha's body as imperceptible to normal consciousness because of its fundamental "thoughtlessness, immovability, and unshakability" *(wu-nien pu-tung pu-yao)*. The "*samādhi* of the *Tathāgata*'s seal of wisdom" is recommended as a means by which one might divest oneself of all impediments and achieve the sort of wisdom that would allow one to perceive the Buddha's true being. No specific reference is made to any particular efficacy in curing physical illness.[24]

Seng-fu's biography is the basis for some tantalizing but uncertain inferences. The possibilities are as follows: Seng-fu was Bodhidharma's earliest student, antedating Hui-k'o's discipleship by thirty years or more. Early in his teaching career Bodhidharma used the *Hui-yin san-mei ching,* a conjecture that is quite consistent with his later teachings as found in the *EJSHL*. The sūtra is independent of any obvious doctrinal affiliation; i.e., it is not a derivative of the *Lotus* or Pure Land scriptures, for example. (This avoidance of scriptures closely identified with other, previously established schools or traditions is a marked characteristic of Ch'an throughout its history.) In addition, the sūtra emphasizes the transcendent nature of the Buddha, which it describes in terms that are distinctly reminiscent of later usages. (The term *wu-nien,* meaning "thoughtlessness" or "nonthought," is particularly noteworthy.) Finally, the text does little more than command its readers to practice the *samādhi* involved and achieve the indicated level of wisdom, thus leaving Bodhidharma almost complete freedom of interpretation.

Although I am inclined to accept this as a probable scenario, it is impossible to know whether Bodhidharma ever used the *Hui-yin san-mei ching*. Nor can we know for certain whether Seng-fu ever used this text for anything other than a liturgy of healing, or whether he was in fact a student of Bodhidharma of the Ch'an School rather than of some other monk named Dharma.[25]

4. *Hui-k'o*

Although we know only the barest outline of Bodhidharma's life and must question the relevance of Seng-fu's activities to the history of the Ch'an School, with Hui-k'o we begin to encounter a degree of meaningful substantiation. In one sense we know very little about Hui-k'o—his dates of birth and death, for example, can only be roughly estimated—but the *HKSC* does give a general impression of his identity as a teacher, his position within the contemporary Buddhist world, and his impact on several generations of students. Although the religious personalities of those students are often poorly known, the very fact that he was the only successor of Bodhidharma to have known successors himself is an important indication of Hui-k'o's importance.

The *HKSC* biography of Hui-k'o states that his secular surname was Chi and his birthplace Hu-lao (Ssu-shui hsien, Honan).[26] Widely read in both the Chinese classics and Buddhist scriptures, he is said to have achieved a level of enlightenment that surpassed that of his contemporaries. Even though his attainments were unassailable, he was universally criticized for not having a teacher. When at age forty he did meet Bodhidharma during the latter's missionary peregrinations around the Mount Sung/Lo-yang area, Hui-k'o realized at once that he had found his true master and studied the "one vehicle" teaching of Bodhidharma for six years. (Recall that the entry on Bodhidharma said that Hui-k'o and Tao-yü studied with the master for four or five years.)

After Bodhidharma's death an official announcement was circulated throughout the area, but when monks and laymen came to inquire after the departed master, Hui-k'o attacked the propriety of their curiosity and imparted to them his understanding of the late master's teachings:

> Therefore, even though your words spread across the entire country, the intention [of Bodhidharma] will not be fulfilled. You read widely in the mysterious writings [of Buddhism, but the truth of which they speak] has not even begun to penetrate your minds![27]

Later, during the beginning of the period 534–37, Hui-k'o moved to the new capital of Yeh, where his teaching actitivies aroused hostility from those who were "stagnated on words," i.e., involved in scriptural exegesis. We are told of an otherwise unknown meditation master named Tao-heng,[28] who before Hui-k'o's arrival had about a thousand students. Tao-heng sent his students to spy on Hui-k'o, but when they heard the latter's teachings they became overwhelmed with feelings of compassion and peaceful acquiescence to the Truth. None of them returned to their original teacher, even after repeated orders, eventually saying that he had only obscured the innate perfection of their own understanding. We are also told that Tao-heng paid money to have Hui-k'o killed, but that Hui-k'o managed to convert the attacker instead.

Perhaps the final victory was Tao-heng's, though, for Hui-k'o ultimately left the area of Yeh and Wei (i.e., modern Honan and Hopeh) and became a mendicant. Sometime before Hui-k'o left Yeh the southern meditation specialist Hui-pu (518–87) visited him there and "suddenly penetrated [the hollowness of] names and views." Hui-pu also visited Hui-ssu (515–77), best known as the teacher of T'ien-t'ai Chih-i. Internal evidence suggests that these visits took place before 547; Hui-pu's date of birth suggests that they took place after 538. Therefore, Hui-k'o was still in Yeh at this time.[29] Although Hui-k'o is said to have died without any prominent successors, this assertion is contradicted by the balance of his *HKSC* biography, to be discussed in the next section of this chapter.

Hui-k'o's age and date of death are not given, but it can be inferred that he lived from ca. 485 to ca. 555 or, possibly, to sometime after 574.[30]

5. Hui-k'o's Successors

The foregoing treatment of Hui-k'o's life occupies only a third of the material presented in the *HKSC* under his name. Note the implicit conflict of the following material with Tao-hsuan's statement that Hui-k'o had no prominent successors. That is, the balance of the entry on Hui-k'o is devoted to:

1. A letter from Layman Hsiang and Hui-k'o's response. This will be discussed in Part Two along with the *EJSHL*.
2. Comments about Hua-kung, Yen-kung, and *Dhyāna* Master Ho. These men were not far removed in time from Tao-hsuan, but he knew nothing substantial about them due to a lack of written texts and funerary inscriptions.[31] Elsewhere, the *HKSC* records that *Dhyāna* Master Ho had three students: Ching-ai (534–78), Fa-k'an (524–604), and Hsuan-ching (d. 606). The two factors that unite the biographies of all three of these men and their known disciples are a devotion to meditation and an association with Mādhyamika texts and religious centers.[32]
3. A brief description and story about Dharma Master Lin, who is undoubtedly the T'an-lin remembered for his preface to the *EJSHL*. Out-of-place references to the *Laṇkāvatāra Sūtra* occur just after T'an-lin's introduction and again after the story about him.
4. A brief discussion of *Dhyāna* Master Na, who had been a popular Confucian teacher as a relatively young man before hearing Hui-k'o speak and becoming a Buddhist ascetic.
5. A longer discussion of Hui-man, a student of *Dhyāna* Master Na and an even more thoroughgoing ascetic. Another reference to the *Laṇkāvatāra Sūtra* occurs here.[33]

Tao-hsuan specifically rationalizes his coverage of Na, Hui-man, and the rest on the basis that they were "all in [Hui]-k'o's lineage *(tsung-ch'i).*" It seems significant that these men are defined according to their relationship to Hui-k'o rather than to Bodhidharma.[34]

The only one of these figures to merit individual attention is T'an-lin (fl. 506–74). His preface to the *EJSHL* describes him as a "disciple" *(ti-tzu),* presumably of Bodhidharma, but he seems to have been more closely associated with Hui-k'o. The *HKSC* describes T'an-lin as a resident of Yeh, a successful lecturer and commentator on the *Sheng-man ching (The Sūtra of* [*Queen*] *Śrīmālā),* and a protector of Buddhist scriptures and statuary during the persecution of 574. The last activity mentioned by Tao-hsuan was undertaken in concert "with fellow-students of [Hui]-k'o" *(yü K'o t'ung-hsueh),* which I believe refers to *Dhyāna* Master Ho's student Ching-ai and his followers.[35] Finally, there is a story about how T'an-lin and Hui-k'o reacted when each had one arm cut off by bandits. (With regard to Hui-k'o, this story seems eminently more plausible than that recounted at the beginning of this chapter.) While Hui-k'o maintained his composure, cauterized his wound, and went out on his round of begging as usual, T'an-lin "screamed and yelled the entire night." Although Hui-k'o's biography might be expected to favor Hui-k'o, we may infer that T'an-lin was more a scholar than a meditator. In fact, other sources record his participation in translation projects that took place during the years 525 to 543.[36]

6. Fa-chung and the Masters of the Laṇkāvatāra Sūtra

Another important source for the study of Hui-k'o's successors is the *HKSC* entry for Fa-chung (589–665?), which was added by Tao-hsuan only a short time before his death in 667.[37] Many of the details included here can be understood in traditionalistic terms—Fa-chung the talented young official who became a monk after his mother's death, Fa-chung the virtuous practitioner who defended Buddhism from both internal and external threats, and so on. However, much of his biography has a definite antiestablishmentarian cast, which is manifested most clearly in his refusal to accept official ordination, his criticism of the great translator Hsuan-tsang, and his adoption of a life of mendicancy.

Fa-chung's main area of specialization was the *Laṇkāvatāra Sūtra,* and here too both the traditionalistic and antiestablishmentarian tendencies are in evidence. He lectured on the sūtra over two hundred times and was able to quote from it at will. Although he ultimately did write a commentary on it in five fascicles, he was convinced to do so in spite of his own convictions about the utter ineffability of the Ultimate Truth.[38]

Our interest in Fa-chung derives from his emphasis on Hui-k'o's name in his own teaching of the *Laṇkāvatāra Sūtra:*

> [Fa]-chung had been immersed in [the study of] the profound scripture of Laṇkā for a long time. He traveled here and there [searching for other students of the text], without caring whether [the roads] were safe or treacherous. He met a later successor to Master [Hui]-k'o who was intensively studying this sūtra. [This later successor to Hui-k'o] then studied under the master (i.e., Fa-chung), who frequently attacked the major points [in this

successor's interpretation], so that he disbanded his following and left the propagation of the teaching [of the *Laṇkāvatāra* to Fa]-chung. [Fa-chung] lectured on [the *Laṇkāvatāra*] over thirty times in succession. He then met someone who had personally received the transmission from Master [Hui]-k'o, and [was then able to] lecture on it an additional one hundred times on the basis of the "one vehicle teaching of South India" *(nan-t'ien-chu i-sheng tsung).*

[The *Laṇkāvatāra*] *Sūtra* was originally translated by *Tripitaḳa* Master Guṇabhadra of the Sung and transcribed by Dharma Master Hui-kuan. Therefore, its text matches well with the truth and its practices correlate with reality. It emphasizes only the contemplation of wisdom, not just [beautiful] words. Later, *Dhyāna* Master [Bodhi]dharma transmitted it to [both] north and south [China. Bodhidharma's] teaching *(tsung)* was that of "forgetting words, forgetting thoughts, the true contemplation of non-attainment *(wang-yen wang-nien wu-te cheng-kuan).*" This was later practiced in the Middle Plain [of north China].

Dhyāna Master Hui-k'o was the first to receive the transmission (lit., "the rope") [from Bodhidharma. Although] most of the intellectuals of Wei were not equal to him, those who understood the teaching and its purport were at once able to achieve enlightenment. Now [Hui-k'o's] generation grows farther and farther off, causing errors among later students. This is briefly explained in the separate biography of K'o-kung (i.e., Hui-k'o). I will now relate the lineage of masters so that the succession of who studied with whom will be apparent:

[Translator's note: The list below has been reorganized somewhat for the reader's convenience. All material given in parentheses occurs in interlineal gloss form in the original text.]

I. After *Dhyāna* Master [Bodhi]dharma, there were the two persons Hui-k'o and Hui-yü (i.e., Tao-yü). [Hui]-yü received the teaching in his mind but never spoke of it.

II. After *Dhyāna* Master [Hui]-k'o:
   - A. *Dhyāna* Master Ts'an
   - B. *Dhyāna* Master Hui
   - C. *Dhyāna* Master Sheng
   - D. Old Master Na
     1. *Dhyāna* Master Shih
     2. *Dhyāna* Master Hui
     3. Dharma Master K'uang
     4. Master Hung-chih

        (Each [of these four men] resided at Hsi-ming [ssu] in the capital, but they died and the transmission of their teaching was terminated.)
   - E. *Dhyāna* Master Tuan
   - F. *Tripiṭaka* Master Ch'ang (or Master Ch'ang-tsang)

G. Dharma Master Chen
H. Dharma Master Yu
(The above all preached the mysterious principle but produced no written records.)

III. After Master [Hui]-k'o:
A. Master Shan (who produced an abstract [of the sūtra] in four fascicles)
B. *Dhyāna* Master Feng (who produced a commentary in five fascicles)
C. *Dhyāna* Master Ming (who produced a commentary in five fascicles)
1. Dharma Master Ch'ieh
2. Master Pao-yü
3. Master Pao-ying
4. Master Tao-ying
(These [four men] all successively transmitted the lamp so that it is being disseminated today.)
D. Master Hu-ming (who produced a commentary in five fascicles)

IV. Distantly succeeding to Master [Hui]-k'o:
A. Master Ta-ts'ung (who produced a commentary in five fascicles)
B. Master Tao-yin (who produced an abstract in four fascicles)
C. Dharma Master Chung (who produced a commentary in five fascicles)
D. Dharma Master An (who produced a commentary in five fascicles)
E. Dharma Master Ch'ung (who produced a commentary in eight fascicles)
F. Master Ta-ming (who produced a commentary in ten fascicles)

V. Not succeeding from Master [Hui]-k'o but relying on the *Compendium of the Mahāyāna (She lun):*
A. *Dhyāna* Master Ch'ien (who produced a commentary in four fascicles)
B. *Vinaya* Master Shang-te (who produced a commentary on the *Ju-leng-ch'ieh* [*ching*, another translation of the *Laṇkāvatāra*] in ten fascicles)[39]

At first glance, this list appears to substantiate the existence of a significant tradition of study of the *Laṇkāvatāra* beginning with Bodhidharma and Hui-k'o. A closer examination of the extant biographies of the figures listed, however, suggests that this first impression is not necessarily correct.

First, let us consider the "noncommentators," i.e., those descended through religious succession from Hui-k'o who did not produce written commentaries on the *Laṇkāvatāra Sūtra.* The first name given here, Ts'an, is presumably equivalent to the supposed Third Patriarch of Ch'an, Seng-ts'an. His biography is unknown in any source earlier than the eighth century, and even in those works it is suspiciously vague.[40] The only figure listed as a first-generation successor to Hui-k'o and known through other citations in the *HKSC* is Old Master Na, who is introduced in the entry on Hui-k'o. (See the previous section of this chapter.) Although Na's student Shih is unknown, Dharma Master K'uang is listed elsewhere in the *HKSC* as a student of Fa-lang (507–81), an authority on the San-lun School.[41]

Among the "commentators," those who produced either commentaries on or abstracts of the *Laṇkāvatāra,* we may quickly omit from consideration the two men who based their studies on the *She lun* and who had no connection with Hui-k'o. (The first of these is undoubtedly the Sui monk T'an-ch'ien of Ch'an-ting ssu,[42] but the other figure is unknown.) The only other names that are identifiable in the remainder of the list are Dharma Master Chung, who must be the Fa-chung in whose biography this list is found, and Ta-ming, a figure of some importance in the early seventh century. Although Ta-ming lacks an *HKSC* biography of his own, he was one of the teachers of Hui-hao (547–633), who was in turn one of Fa-chung's teachers.[43] The gloss following the mention of Tao-ying (III.C.4) implies that the subtradition of commentators on the *Laṇkāvatāra* remained viable longer than that of the noncommentators.

It is curious that, of the men on this list whose biographies are known, only Fa-chung had any recorded interest in the *Laṇkāvatāra.* K'uang and Ta-ming were united by a common interest in the treatises of the Chinese Mādhyamika tradition. Fa-chung was a participant in this same tradition, as were the successors to Seng-na mentioned in connection with Hui-k'o's biography. However, none of the biographies of any of these men contain any mention of the *Laṇkāvatāra Sūtra.* Since many of the figures in the list are unknown, a firm conclusion cannot be rendered; however, it would seem that the importance of this text has been misrepresented.

7. *The Possible Use of the* Laṇkāvatāra Sūtra *in Early Ch'an*

Before considering the implications of this misrepresentation, let us introduce the three references to the *Laṇkāvatāra* in Hui-k'o's *HKSC* biography. These occur (1) just after the introduction of [T'an]-lin:

> In the beginning *Dhyāna* Master [Bodhi]dharma transmitted the four-fascicle *Laṇkā*[*vatāra Sūtra*] to [Hui]-k'o, saying: "This sūtra is the only one that is suitable for China. If you base your practice on it, you will attain salvation." [Hui]-k'o single-mindedly imparted the mysterious principle [of the *Laṇkāvatāra* to his students] just as it had been explained before [by Bodhidharma].

(2) after the anecdotes about [T'an]-lin's and Hui-k'o's each losing an arm:

> At the end of each of his sermons, [Hui]-k'o said: "[The understanding of] this sūtra will become superficial after four generations. How utterly lamentable!"

and (3) after the discussion of Hui-man:

> Therefore Masters Na and [Hui]-man always carried the four-fascicle [version of the] *Laṇkāvatāra Sūtra* as the "essential [teaching] of the mind" *(hsin-yao)*. They preached and practiced it at every occasion, never varying from [the true understanding thereof] that had been bequeathed to them.[44]

Hu Shih has suggested that these three references were interpolated into the text of Hui-k'o's biography, probably at the same time that the Fa-chung biography was added to the *HKSC*. And in fact these three short statements do appear quite out of context in the *HKSC*. Even the third statement, the placement of which is less jarring than that of the other two, is preceded by doctrinal positions quite unrelated to the *Laṇkāvatāra*.[45]

Two separate issues are involved here. First, did Bodhidharma and/or Hui-k'o actually use the *Laṇkāvatāra?* Second, what was the connection between this text and the Ch'an tradition descended from Bodhidharma?

The first of these two issues cannot be definitively resolved. Other than the passages in question, there is no direct evidence to suggest that Bodhidharma and Hui-k'o did in fact use the *Laṇkāvatāra*. Indirect evidence would suggest that the impact of the *Laṇkāvatāra* was felt most strongly sometime after the study of the *She lun* had already taken hold, well after the translation of the latter text in 563.[46] Interest in the *Laṇkāvatāra* was apparently strongest right around the end of the sixth century and the beginning of the seventh, but waned after only a short period. No doubt the final blow to its popularity—and, paradoxically, the one factor that did most to make possible a nonmainstream tradition of its study—was the career of Hsuan-tsang, who attempted to establish the authority of his new translations of Yogācāra texts. The reference toward the end of Fa-chung's biography to Hsuan-tsang's refusal to permit lecturing on previously translated scriptures should be understood as referring specifically to the *Laṇkāvatāra*.[47]

Although Bodhidharma and Hui-k'o flourished slightly before the *Laṇkāvatāra Sūtra* was most popular, they may have been among the first Buddhists in China to make use of this text. This hypothesis would fit with the later proclivity of the Ch'an School to use texts not closely connected with other Buddhist factions and with Chih-i's statement that *dhyāna* masters of the North used this scripture as a justification for the idea of sudden enlightenment. Although the *EJSHL* lacks any explicit dependence on the *Laṇkāvatāra*, there may in fact be a doctrinal relationship between the two.[48]

A real connection between the *Laṇkāvatāra* and the later Ch'an tradition is only slightly less possible. Fa-chung's connection with the tradition of Bodhidharma and Hui-k'o was quite tenuous, and his interest in the text in question derived from a faction of Mādhyamika that was not connected with the Bodhidharma tradition. The superficiality of the link between the tradition of Bodhidharma and the *Laṇkāvatāra* is indicated by the fact that, even in the description of Fa-chung's study of that scripture, Bodhidharma's teaching is described as that of "forgetting words, forgetting thoughts, the correct contemplation of nonattainment." This terminology does not come from the *Laṇkāvatāra Sūtra,* but from the Mādhyamika tradition.[49]

Although Fa-chung was the only major living exponent of the *Laṇkāvatāra* at the time of Tao-hsuan's writing, even he apparently dropped out of sight after leaving Ch'ang-an sometime between 656 and 661. Whatever the reasons behind this departure (such as his conflict with Hsuan-tsang), Fa-chung's attempts to disseminate his own understanding of the *Laṇkāvatāra* were abortive. The prediction that the understanding of this text would become superficial after four generations was probably related to the frustration of Fa-chung's mission. Although the true meaning and implications of this prediction may never be known, there is no reason to correlate it with the orthodox lineage of Tao-hsin and Hung-jen.[50]

As we shall see in Chapter IV, Section 13, the connection between the *Laṇkāvatāra Sūtra* and the Northern School during the early eighth century was equally tenuous. Although this scripture apparently had some kind of mysterious appeal to the followers of early Ch'an, there is no evidence that its contents had any particular impact on the development of the school.

CHAPTER II

From Provincial China to Lo-yang and Ch'ang-an

1. Bodhidharma and the East Mountain Teaching

The phase of early Ch'an known as the East Mountain Teaching was a long period of quiet growth. For almost exactly a half century, from Tao-hsin's entry into Huang-mei in 624 until Hung-jen's death in 674, the Ch'an School existed in a quiet alpine monastery in central China. If we add to this the quarter century that Shen-hsiu spent at Yü-ch'üan ssu in Ching-chou, then Ch'an spent fully three-quarters of a century preparing for its explosion onto the national scene at the very beginning of the eighth century. The historical records indicate that the number of students interested in Ch'an grew steadily during these seventy-five years: Only five or so students can be associated reliably with Tao-hsin's name, some twenty or twenty-five with Hung-jen, and over seventy with Shen-hsiu (although many of these students may have joined him after his entry into Lo-yang in 701). In other words, we can trace the growth of Ch'an from Tao-hsin to Shen-hsiu and beyond in an unbroken line.

Unfortunately, we cannot do the same with the transition from Bodhidharma and Hui-k'o to Tao-hsin. In seventh-century sources the succession from Bodhidharma tapers off into a set of names of questionable relevance to the Ch'an tradition, as we have seen in the previous chapter. Seng-ts'an, the man who supposedly transmitted the teachings of Ch'an from Hui-k'o to Tao-hsin, is a complete unknown, and one wonders whether his name was introduced into the developing Ch'an orthodoxy solely on the basis of its occurrence in the *HKSC* entry for Fa-chung.[51] The *HKSC* contains the earliest biography of Tao-hsin, but it contains no mention of Seng-ts'an or, in fact, any indication of a connection between Tao-hsin and Bodhidharma.

The fact that the *EJSHL* was used in the compilation of the *Chin-kang san-mei ching (Sūtra of the Adamantine Samādhi)* has been taken as evidence of the influence of Bodhidharma's work, but there is no a priori reason to suggest that such influence was extended from the mountains of Huang-mei rather than from some other location.[52] In short, no explicit early evidence connects the East Mountain Teaching with the tradition of Bodhidharma. Such a connection may well have existed, but we would have to look to a text written in or near Lo-yang in the last decade of the seventh century to find it confirmed.[53]

2. *Tao-hsin's Biography in the* Hsü kao-seng chuan (HKSC)

The earliest source for the biography of Tao-hsin is the *HKSC,* which lists him as a resident of Mount Shuang-feng ("Twin Peaks Mountain") in Ch'i-chou, or Huang-mei. This biography reads as follows (for modern geographical equivalents, see the subsequent discussion):

> Shih Tao-hsin: Of the lay surname Ssu-ma, birthplace unknown. From the age of seven he studied under a single teacher, [a man whose] moral conduct was impure. [Tao]-hsin's repeated remonstrations went unheeded, [so he took to] secretly maintaining the chaste standards [of Buddhist morality on his own]. This went on for five years without the teacher's knowledge.
>
> When he heard that two monks of unknown origin had entered Mount Huan-kung in Shu-chou for the peaceful practice of meditation, [Tao-hsin] went and received the teachings from them. He followed and studied under them for ten years, but was not allowed to accompany his teachers when they went to [Mount] Lo-fu, [since they knew that] if he remained behind he would definitely be able to benefit great [numbers of sentient beings].
>
> When the government then granted ordinations to the wise and virtuous, [Tao-hsin] was registered as a resident of Chi-chou ssu. [When he went to take up residence there (?), the city of Chi-chou] had been surrounded by rebels for more than seventy days. Water was scarce within the city and the people were in great distress. When [Tao]-hsin entered [the city] the springs flowed once again. The prefectural magistrate bowed to the ground [before him and inquired]: "When will the rebels disperse?" [Tao]-hsin said: "Just recite the [*Perfection of*] *Wisdom,*" so [the magistrate] ordered the entire city to join voices [in recitation]. Instantly, the rebels outside [the city] saw awesome, gigantic warriors on all the four walls of the city . . . The magistrate announced to [the rebels]: "You may [go right ahead and] enter the city if you want to meet these giants!" The band of rebels dispersed and peace returned [to the area].
>
> Wanting to go to Moung Heng (i.e., Nan-yueh) [Tao-hsin took the] road through Chiang-chou. The monks and laypeople [of that region] made him stop at Ta-lin ssu on Mount Lu, where he stayed for ten years in spite of [problems with] rebels and bandits. The monks and laypeople of Ch'i-chou invited him to come to Chung-tsao ssu in Huang-mei hsien, to the north of the [Yangtze] River. [Tao-hsin wanted to] continue his mountain practice, and when he saw the excellent springs and rocks of [Mount] Shuang-feng, he took up permanent residence there. That night a great number of fero-

cious beasts came and surrounded him, but they all left at his command after he administered the precepts to them.

During the more than thirty years after [Tao-hsin] entered the mountain, students of Buddhism came from all over the country, no matter what the distance. The prefectural magistrate Ts'ai I-hsuan heard about this and came to pay his respects.

Just before his death, Tao-hsin said to his disciple Hung-jen: "You can make a stūpa for me [now]." Not long after giving this command he urged them to finish it quickly. He was asked: "Will you enter [the stūpa now] or not?" [Tao-hsin] answered: "I am about to enter." The congregation [of his students] said: "Are you not going to make a deputation [of your successor]?" He said: "I have made many deputations during my life." He died peacefully just after saying this.

At that time the more than five hundred people in the mountain [community], who were monks and laypeople from all over China, suddenly witnessed heaven and earth go dark. The leaves on all the trees for three *li* around turned white, and the branches of the pawlonia on either side of [Tao-hsin's] room bent their branches toward the room. Even today all [the trees] thereabout are withered. [Tao-hsin's death occurred on the] fourth day of the intercalary ninth month of the second year of the Yung-hui [period, or 651], at the age of seventy-two. In the third year [of the same period, or 652], the disciple Hung-jen and others proceeded to the stūpa, opened it, and saw [Tao-hsin's body] sitting erect as of old. They then moved it to its present location, where it still exists today.[54]

It is very interesting to notice what Tao-hsuan did and did not know about Tao-hsin. The most glaring omission, as mentioned earlier, is any reference to Bodhidharma, Hui-k'o, or their teachings. The only specific indication of any possible connection with the Ch'an tradition is the discussion between Tao-hsin and his disciples that took place just before his death, when they urged him to select a successor. Their interest seems to have been focused on the need for a managerial figurehead for the ongoing guidance of the East Mountain community. Tao-hsin's response, on the other hand, was meant to indicate that the true meaning of the transmission or "deputation" (as the term *fu-chu* has been translated here) was not based on the needs of the community but on the intimate relationship between master and disciple. During his life Tao-hsin had had many such relationships as spiritual compatriot to individual religious seekers, the lofty purity of his religious ideals being indicated by his total disinterest (or, perhaps, his feigned disinterest) in appointing a titular successor. Later on in this book I will discuss the development of the "transmission of the lamp" theory of the history of Ch'an; this *HKSC* anecdote is an important indication of the lack of any such doctrine around the year 660[55] and, at the same time, the existence of the popular expectations that helped bring such a doctrine into being.

Since Tao-hsin died in 651, Tao-hsuan must have added this entry after his first redaction of the *HKSC* in 645. However, internal evidence does not suggest any connection with the entry for Fa-chung or the references to the *Laṇkāvatāra Sūtra* discussed in the previous chapter (see Sections 6 and 7). In fact, there is no real indication of Tao-hsin's teaching; the anecdote concerning the *Perfection of Wisdom* is entertaining, but it cannot be taken seriously for this purpose. There is also no mention of scriptural study or lecturing. This absence may of course be taken as a positive indication of Tao-hsin's single-minded devotion to the practice of meditation.

It is also interesting that the only names included here are those of Tao-hsin's disciple Hung-jen and the local magistrate, Ts'ai I-hsuan (586–656). Other *HKSC* entries discussed earlier—those for Seng-ch'ou, Hui-k'o, and Fa-chung, for example—contain much larger numbers of names. As Professor Yanagida points out, Ts'ai I-hsuan was a prominent military figure from North China who was active in support of the founding of the T'ang and Empress Wu's initial rise to power.[56] From the very first, then, the East Mountain Teaching was associated with a supporter of Empress Wu.

3. An Outline of Tao-hsin's Career

The other major early source for Tao-hsin's biography is the *Ch'üan fa-pao chi (Annals of the Transmission of the Dharma-treasure,* hereafter abbreviated as *CFPC),* which was written around the year 712 on behalf of members of the Northern School. As the earliest extant "transmission of the lamp" text, the *CFPC* links Tao-hsin with Seng-ts'an and has Tao-hsin appoint Hung-jen as his successor (albeit with a curious lack of enthusiasm).[57] Since the *CFPC* is introduced in English translation in the Appendix, its entry on Tao-hsin need not be reproduced here. The following outline of Tao-hsin's life is based on both the *HKSC* and the *CFPC.* Note the comparative vagueness of the earlier source:

Birthplace: The *CFPC* states that Tao-hsin was born in Ho-nei, which refers to that part of Honan Province lying to the north of the Yellow River and centered on Ch'in-yang hsien. Given the *HKSC* alone, we might have assumed that Tao-hsin's birthplace was in or near Shu-chou (Huai-ning hsien, Anhwei)—otherwise, how could he have heard of two meditation masters taking up residence at a mountain near there?

Early training: The *CFPC* has the same story of Tao-hsin maintaining his own moral purity without the knowledge of his undisciplined teacher but gives the term as six years.

Meditation practice: In the *CFPC* Tao-hsin is described as proceeding to Mount Huan-[kung] (Ch'ien-shan hsien, Anhwei) to study under Seng-ts'an. In the section on Seng-ts'an in the same work the master's companion at that mountain retreat is listed as *Dhyāna* Master Ting, whose full name is given in later sources as Shen-ting but whose biography is completely unknown. In a further contrast with the *HKSC,* both men are said to have been in residence there beginning in 581 or shortly thereafter. As if to compensate for the addition of a year to the length of time Tao-hsin concealed his moral purity from his first teacher, here he is said to have studied with Seng-ts'an for eight or nine years, as opposed to the ten years given in the *HKSC.*[58]

After being refused permission to accompany Seng-ts'an to Mount Lo-fu in the South (Tseng-ch'eng hsien, Kwangtung), Tao-hsin is described by the *CFPC* as traveling about in order to teach the Dharma. In view of the gap in the *HKSC* biography, which fails to account for about a decade of Tao-hsin's life, this assertion should probably be accepted. Tao-hsin's period of study under Seng-ts'an or the unnamed meditation masters, whichever was actually the case, thus began around 591 or 592 and lasted until the very end of the sixth century.

Official ordination: The *CFPC* specifies that the national ordination program under which Tao-hsin officially became a monk occurred in 607, shortly after the accession of Emperor Yang of the Sui, when each prefecture was ordered to ordain a thousand monks.

Salvation of Chi-chou from rebels: In the *HKSC* this incident is presented as if it occurred at the time of Tao-hsin's official ordination and his ensuing journey to Chi-chou (Chi-an hsien, Kiangsu) to take up residence there. The *CFPC,* however, states that it occurred at the end of the Sui—Yanagida suggests that a rebellion that swept the area in 613 may be the event in question.[59]

Residence at Ta-lin ssu on Mount Lu: The *CFPC* omits this for no apparent reason. Ta-lin ssu, incidentally, was founded by Chih-k'ai (533–610), a student of Fa-lang of the San-lun School and of T'ien-t'ai Chih-i. If the suggested date of the incident at Chi-chou is to be accepted, there is no reason to assume that Tao-hsin and Chih-k'ai ever met.[60]

Residence at Mount Shuang-feng in Huang-mei: If we accept the date 613 or shortly thereafter for the incident at Chi-chou, then the *HKSC* and *CFPC* are in substantial agreement as to the timing of Tao-hsin's move to Huang-mei. The *CFPC* asserts that this occurred in 624, which is about ten years (the period of residence at Ta-lin ssu) after the Chi-chou incident. The only problem with this date is that it was only twenty-seven years until Tao-hsin's death, not the thirty or more than thirty years given in the *CFPC* and *HKSC,* respectively. (Exaggerations such as these, involving round numbers, occur several times in medieval Chinese Ch'an texts; in the face of specific dates, such as that of Tao-hsin's entry into Huang-mei, the less precise figures must be discounted.)

Tao-hsin's lesser students: In addition to Hung-jen, the *CFPC* mentions Fa-hsien of Ching-chou and Shan-fu of Ch'ang-chou. Fa-hsien (577–653) studied under at least two meditation instructors, one of them T'ien-t'ai Chih-i, before traveling to Huang-mei. We are told that Tao-hsin "further clarified the waters of [Fa-hsien's] meditation," which may be a euphemism for the final experience of enlightenment.[61]

Shan-fu (d. 660) studied under a number of different masters in central and south-central China, from whom he learned Mādhyamika doctrines, Pure Land visualizations, and other types of meditation. In the course of his travels, Shan-fu visited Huang-mei, where Tao-hsin taught him the "expedient means of entering the path" *(ju-tao fang-pien).* Although this is an interesting hint as to the nature of Tao-hsin's doctrines—the first encountered so far—it is difficult to understand why the *CFPC* denigrates Shan-fu as having the disposition of a *pratyekabuddha,* unable to understand the Mahāyāna.[62]

Another monk, Hsuan-shuang (d. 652), is mentioned in the *HKSC* but not in the *CFPC* as a student of Tao-hsin's.[63] The only other names associated with Tao-hsin are Fa-jung of the Ox-head School and Yuan-i, who was supposedly the disciple ordered to build the master's stūpa. There is no reason to believe that Tao-hsin and Fa-jung ever met.[64] The assertion regarding Yuan-i occurs for the first time in two mid-eighth century sources; its accuracy cannot be verified.[65]

Tao-hsin's death: Nothing is known of Tao-hsin's life from the time he took up residence at Huang-mei until his death in 651.

(General comments on Tao-hsin's historical significance will be deferred until the end of the following discussion of Hung-jen's life and students. See Section 6 of this chapter.)

4. Hung-jen's Life and Legendary Character

We are able to draw on only a few sources in reconstructing Hung-jen's biography: the *CFPC;* the *LCJFC* and *LCSTC;* an account by Shen-hui; the *LTFPC;* and, for only a few additional details, the *Sung kao-seng chuan (SKSC).*[66] The following is the bare outline of his life as contained in these sources, which all agree except in certain minor details:

Birth: Hung-jen was born in Huang-mei in or about the year 600, the uncertainty arising from minor discrepancies as to his date of death. His ancestors had originally lived in the northern part of Huang-mei, where his grandfather was a recluse.[67]

Youth: The *LCJFC* says that Hung-jen's father abandoned his home and family, but that the child supported his mother with exemplary filiality. Nevertheless, he too left home to become a monk while very young, at the age of either seven or twelve. The *CFPC,* which cites the latter age, has Hung-jen beginning his studies under Tao-hsin at this age. This would have been during the elder monk's period of official residence in Chi-chou.[68] (It is possible that Tao-hsin did not remain in Chi-chou throughout this period.) Hung-jen presumably remained by Tao-hsin's side at Chi-chou and at Ta-lin ssu on Mount Lu until his master moved to Huang-mei in 624.

Teaching career and death: At Tao-hsin's death in 651 Hung-jen took over leadership of the Huang-mei community. Later tradition has it that he moved the community's mountain center from its original location to Tung-shan, or "East Mountain," the easterly of the "twin peaks" of Mount Shuang-feng. Only one early source records this move explicitly, whereas early texts commonly use the term "East Mountain Teaching" in reference to both Tao-hsin and Hung-jen.[69] Nothing is recorded about Hung-jen's life for the years from his assumption of leadership of the Huang-mei community until his last words and death, probably in 674. After his death his private residence was made into a monastery.[70]

More than the details of Hung-jen's life, his personal character as depicted in the *CFPC* and other works is the most intriguing aspect of his biography. He is represented as a quiet youth of diligent filiality and an inoffensive, self-effacing worker who was completely uninterested in anything other than his own spiritual training. After his own selection as successor to Tao-hsin, the previously silent Hung-jen was immediately able to understand the problems of his students and teach them with a fluid, spontaneous style that combined an appreciation of the Ultimate Truth with complete expertise in the expediencies of religious practice.

One may readily conclude of Hung-jen's legendary image that it formed the basis of the peculiarly Ch'an hagiography of Hui-neng. Indeed, the story of Hui-neng's life as it occurs in the *Platform Sūtra* and the very closely contemporaneous *Ts'ao-ch'i ta-shih chuan (Biography of the Great Master* [*Hui-neng*] *of Ts'ao-ch'i)*[71] can be approached as a more advanced, more concrete version of the same idealized image. Hui-neng's youthful filiality, inherent insight, functional illiteracy, capacity for menial labor, dedication to his master, and style of teaching are all taken directly from the example of Hung-jen.

5. Hung-jen's Lesser Students

Except for a few tidbits of information to be gleaned from the accounts of his students, the *LCJFC* contains the only other information we have about Hung-jen's life. After giving the bare details of Hung-jen's biography, describing his teaching in suitably profound terms, and pointing out that he never wrote any explanation of the teaching but always understood the mysterious principle, Hsuan-tse, the author of the *LCJFC,* writes:

> At the time *Dhyāna* Master Shen-hsiu of Ching-chou had incorporated the lofty Truth within himself and had personally received the transmission (*fu-chu,* translated earlier as "deputation"). [I], Hsuan-tse, arrived at Mount Shuang-feng in 670, reverentially received the [master's] instructions, and served as his personal attendent for five years, being in his presence all of that time . . .
>
> In the second month of the Hsien-heng [period, or 674, Hung-jen] ordered myself and others to build him a stūpa, so with [his other] followers I transported naturally square rocks and fitted them together in a beautiful and imposing manner. On the fourteenth day of the month he asked whether or not it was finished. When I respectfully replied that it was, he said: "I cannot [die on] the same day as the Buddha's nirvāṇa (i.e., the fifteenth day of the second month)." Thereupon his house was made into a monastery.
>
> [Hung-jen] also said: "I have taught countless people during this life, but my favorites have all died. Only ten [are left] to transmit my teaching to later [generations]. I have explained the *Laṇkāvatāra Sūtra* to Shen-hsiu, who has a brilliant understanding of its mysterious principle and will certainly be of benefit to a great [number of people]. Chih-shen of Tzu-chou and the scribe Liu of Mount Pai-sung both have literary abilities. I remember Hui-tsang of Hua-chou and Hsuan-yueh of Sui-chou but do not know anything about their [current activities]. The religious practice of Lao-an of Mount Sung is profound, [while] Fa-ju of Lu-chou, Hui-neng of Chao-chou, and the Koguryŏ monk Chidŏk (Chih-te in Chinese) of Yang-chou are all capable of teaching people but are figures of only local prominence. I-fang of Yueh-chou is a lecturer."
>
> He also said to me: "Maintain your combined practice [of meditation and scriptural studies] with care. After my nirvāṇa you and Shen-hsiu shall make the sun of Buddhism shine once again, the lamp of the mind illumine once again."
>
> On the sixteenth day of the month [Hung-jen] asked: "Do you understand your mind now or not?" I respectfully replied: "I do not understand." The Great Master then pointed in all ten directions with his hands and minutely explained the mind as realized by him. Then, at noon on the sixteenth, he faced south in seated meditation, closed his eyes, and passed away. He was seventy-four years old.[72]

Hsuan-tse goes on to mention Hung-jen's stūpa, a portrait of the master on the wall of a monastery at An-chou (Hsuan-tse's place of residence), and a brief eulogy by a prominent former official who, like the magistrate Ts'ai I-hsuan mentioned in Tao-hsin's biography, was a supporter of Empress Wu.[73] Although the connection with Empress Wu is hardly surprising, clearly Hsuan-tse's reportage relates more closely to the time of its writing than to Hung-jen's own memories and opinions. Thus Shen-hsiu is conceded the position of Hung-jen's most prominent disciple and designated successor, and Hsuan-tse's references to Shen-hsiu and himself are a bald attempt to appropriate some of the recently deceased monk's glory. Similar inferences may be drawn about Hung-jen's supposed loss of contact with Hui-tsang and Hsuan-yueh and his sympathetic but unenthusiastic endorsement of Hui-neng and others. That is, these men were known as Hung-jen's disciples, but they had no personal reputation or status within Buddhist circles in the two capitals during the second decade of the eighth century.

Five slightly different versions of this list of Hung-jen's major disciples are included in the *LTFPC* (two variants) and Tsung-mi's works (three variants).[74] The individuals mentioned in these and other sources and for whom some biographical information is available are as follows:

1. Shen-hsiu: Already mentioned frequently in this study, this man's biography will be considered in detail shortly. (See Sections 8 through 13 of this chapter.)

2. Chih-shen (609–702) of Tzu-chou (Tzu-chung hsien, Szechwan): Chih-shen was the first member of two important lineages of Ch'an in the Szechwan area; the Pure Land figure Nan-yueh Ch'eng-yuan (712–802) and the great Ch'an master Ma-tsu Tao-i (709–88) were both his second-generation successors. According to his biography in the *LTFPC*, he was born in that area of parents originally from Ju-nan (Ju-nan hsien, Honan). He studied first under the famous translator and Yogācāra scholar Hsuan-tsang, then with Hung-jen at Huang-mei. His later activities centered on Te-chun ssu in Tzu-chou.[75]

Chih-shen was the author of three works: the *Hsü-jung kuan (Contemplation on the Empty Coalescence)* in three fascicles, *Yuan-ch'i (Causality)* in one fascicle, and *Po-jo hsin* [*ching*] *shu (Commentary on the Heart of Wisdom* [*Sūtra*]*)* in one fascicle. The last of these has been discovered among the Tun-huang manuscripts and published by Professor Yanagida. The *LCJFC* statement that Chih-shen possessed literary ability was undoubtedly based on an awareness of works such as these.[76]

3. Lao-an (584?–708) of Mount Sung: Also known as Hui-an, this very important Northern School figure will be covered later. (See Section 14 of this chapter.)

4. Fa-ju (638–89) of Lu-chou (Ch'ang-chih hsien, Shansi): Another important monk to be considered separately. (See Section 7 of this chapter.)

5. Hui-neng (638–713) of Chao-chou (Ch'u-chiang hsien, Kwangtung): It is noteworthy but not too surprising that Hui-neng's name is included here, since, just as with Chih-shen, the distinction between his

lineage and the Northern School did not become apparent until well after the compilation of the *LCJFC*. Although we obviously cannot consider his biography in detail here, one fact deserves immediate mention: Hui-neng's name appears in two additional Northern School texts, which implies that he was considered a member of that loosely-knit confraternity until at least the second or even the fifth decade of the eighth century.[77]

6. Hsuan-tse: Hsuan-tse's name is added to the list in the *LTFPC*, which removes Hui-neng for special treatment. Hsuan-tse's biography will be considered in Section 15 of this chapter.

7. Hsien of Ch'i-chou: Added by Tsung-mi, Fa-hsien (643–720) became prominent for a time in the capitals. His biography will be considered along with Hsuan-tse's in Section 15.

8. *Vinaya* Master Chih-hung: This monk is not mentioned in any of the lists cited earlier but is described as Hung-jen's student in the *Ta-T'ang hsi-yu ch'iu-fa kao-seng chuan (Biographies of Eminent Monks* [*Who Traveled from the*] *Great T'ang to the Western Regions in Search of the Dharma)*. One of Shen-hsiu's major successors, P'u-chi, is also mentioned as his teacher.[78]

9. Tao-shun of Pi-chien ssu in Ching-chou: Tao-shun was a native of Chih-chiang (Chiang-ling hsien, Hupeh) who studied the "teaching of birthlessness of East Mountain" *(tung-shan wu-sheng fa-men)*, which is explicitly identified with Tao-hsin and Hung-jen. Tao-shun practiced diligently for forty years, never leaving his monastery and never speaking to anyone. He was eventually invited to court in 707 or 708 along with Heng-ching (634–712), a *Vinaya* specialist and T'ien-t'ai monk. Emperor Chung-tsung favored Tao-shun with a poetic composition on his departure from court. Since this occurred on the same day as Lao-an's death (or, alternatively, exactly a year later) in 709, we may infer a relationship of some kind between the two men. Chih-chiang, to which Tao-shun returned and later died, was also Lao-an's native place.[79]

10. Yin-tsung (627–713) of Miao-hsi ssu in K'uai-chi: Yin-tsung is best known for his role in the legend of Hui-neng, and it is difficult to judge the accuracy of the statement in the *SKSC*, a late source, that he studied under Hung-jen. (Note the reference to Yin-tsung in the biography of Seng-ta, discussed immediately below.) Although he was primarily a *Vinaya* expert, Yin-tsung compiled a comprehensive record of Buddhist sages from the Liang to the T'ang dynasties. This was probably a Ch'an-style work, as may be inferred from its title, *Hsin-yao chi (Anthology of the Essentials of the Mind)*; its reported emphasis on oral sayings; and the fact that it began in the Liang, with which Bodhidharma is associated in slightly later legends. Judging solely from the location of the reference to this work within Yin-tsung's biography, we may conclude that it was

probably compiled during his sojourn in Ch'ang-an at the very end of the seventh century.[80]

11. Seng-ta (638–719), also of Miao-hsi ssu in K'uai-chi: Seng-ta was a native of K'uai-chi and a member of the Wang family—very probably related in some way to the two laymen of this surname mentioned in the biography of Yin-tsung. When Seng-ta met Hung-jen, it was "like a dry sprout getting rain." He then took up the intensive practice of meditation and later met Yin-tsung and was able to even further "polish the mirror of his mind." Seng-ta followed in Yin-tsung's footsteps by also studying the *Vinaya* (under a student of Yin-tsung's) and may have been a devotee of the *Lotus Sūtra.*[81]

The names of fourteen other students of Hung-jen are known, but their biographies are obscure.[82]

6. Hung-jen and the Nature of the East Mountain Community

We have yet to consider Hung-jen's most important disciples—Fa-ju, Shen-hsiu, and others—but at this point we should stop and consider the individual roles played by Tao-hsin and Hung-jen and the general character of the religious community on East Mountain.

Clearly, Hung-jen's personal brilliance must have been a significant factor in the development of Ch'an. That Hung-jen had many more students than Tao-hsin has already been mentioned at the beginning of this chapter. In addition, certain less-than-prominent details of Hung-jen's biography imply that he was the primary force behind the community at Huang-mei from its founding in 624 until his death a half century later. Although this hypothesis cannot be proven, note the following:

1. Huang-mei was Hung-jen's native place, to which Tao-hsin was invited by local supporters of Buddhism. These local patrons certainly included Hung-jen's family, which had a tradition of eremitism.

2. After his death, Hung-jen's residence was converted into a monastery. The mere mention of such a fact implies that Hung-jen's family was wealthy enough to be very prominent locally. In addition, the statements that he labored long and hard and lowered himself before others could only have had impact to the extent that such actions were contrary to expectations, i.e., that he was of upper-class birth and had no reason to exert himself in this way.

3. Hung-jen may have had students of his own before Tao-hsin's death, although the evidence is definitely suspect.[83]

4. After Hung-jen's death, the community at Huang-mei sank into almost complete oblivion for a long period of time. Only one other early

Ch'an monk (Fa-hsien, a minor figure to be discussed in Section 15) is listed as a resident of Huang-mei.

The Ch'an legend, and Buddhist hagiography in general, would have us conceive of Hung-jen as a completely spiritual being, thoroughly divorced from the social realities of this world. It seems more probable that he sought and found an appropriate tutor in Tao-hsin and invited him to Huang-mei in order to lay the foundation of a very successful training center. (No doubt Hung-jen received some guidance from a parent or guardian in his first contact with Tao-hsin.) Tao-hsin's apparent lack of conviction in his deputation of a successor (see Section 2 of this chapter and Section K of the translation of the *CFPC* in the Appendix) and the description of Hung-jen as meek and self-effacing may be understood as reactions to the reality of Hung-jen's status. This interpretation of Hung-jen's relative importance fits well with the esteem in which he was held by Shen-hsiu and other Ch'an figures in the capitals in the early eighth century.

In addition to this interpretation of Hung-jen's importance within the history of the Ch'an School, several inferences can be made about the East Mountain community in general. First, *Hung-jen taught meditation and nothing else.* In all the references to him, sūtra recitation, doctrinal study, and Pure Land practices are never mentioned—students only went to him to learn the practice of meditation. Second, *Hung-jen had many students.* Even if he did not teach a thousand new students every month, or eight or nine out of every ten spiritual aspirants in China, as the biographies suggest, the actual number of those who did study under him was no doubt many times greater than the twenty-five names presented earlier. Third, and in direct contrast to the Hung-jen's single-minded dedication to meditation, *his students included individuals of various interests: Vinaya* specialists, devotees of the *Lotus Sūtra* and Pure Land practices, monks with experience in the translation of Indian scriptures, and minor bureaucrats. Finally, as far as we can tell, *Hung-jen's disciples stayed with him for limited periods of time.* Fa-ju's tenure of sixteen years was the exception (see Section 7 of this chapter), for Hung-jen's other students seem to have stayed for only a few years at most. Perhaps Huang-mei simply did not appeal to most Chinese monks as a permanent residence. In any case, Hung-jen did not pin his hopes for the future of his school on a single mountain center, as Chih-i had done in grand fashion some years before, but sent his students out to spread their message across the face of China.

Ui Hakuju has suggested that the East Mountain community of Tao-hsin and Hung-jen was the locus for the origination of a unique style of monastic life later codified in the "pure regulations" (*ch'ing-kuei* [*shingi* in Japanese]) of Ch'an. Specifically, he makes the following observations:

1. Tao-hsin and Hung-jen spent sixty years in the same location.
2. Their community always numbered over five hundred persons.
3. The community was entirely dependent on its own resources and efforts for food and the other necessities of life.
4. All productive labor and even miscellaneous tasks were taken as the religious practice of Ch'an.
5. All activities (walking, standing, etc.) therefore came to be equivalent to such practice, and even to Ch'an itself.
6. The Ch'an practiced on East Mountain was spiritually pure and oriented toward the "mind nature" (*hsin-hsing* [*shinshō*]).
7. Ch'an was not designated for any special group, but for all.
8. The scriptures were not understood literally, but were approached spiritually in order to reach their deeper meaning and at times even interpreted arbitrarily in order to express the teaching of Ch'an.
9. Rules and ceremonies must have existed that were appropriate to such a style of practice in a community of such size.[84]

Although some of Ui's conclusions (e.g., 6, 7, and 8) require no real comment or criticism, in the main he has overstated his case in two ways. First, the community at Huang-mei was probably not as large as its chroniclers claimed. The figures of five hundred and a thousand given in the early texts are obviously pious exaggerations.[85] If we assume that Hung-jen's students stayed an average of five years and were distributed evenly over the quarter century of his teaching career—both arbitrary assumptions, of course—then only five of his known students would have been present at any one time. The community would have included a large number of students whose names are no longer known, not to mention lay members and temple functionaries, but it is difficult to believe that the average size of the entire group came even close to five hundred or a thousand. These figures should rather be interpreted as probably inflated estimates of the numbers of community members and interested citizenry who attended the funeral services for Tao-hsin and Hung-jen.

Second, there is absolutely no evidence that the Huang-mei community was totally self-supporting, as Ui suggests. It probably enjoyed roughly the same level and type of financial support as other contemporary institutions.[86] Ui's basis for such a suggestion is apparently the story of Hui-neng threshing rice for eight months after his arrival in Huang-mei,[87] but the real implications of this story are exactly opposite from Ui's interpretation. The *Platform Sūtra,* in which this story appears, intentionally emphasizes Hui-neng's identity as an illiterate barbarian from the South. His relegation to the threshing room is an indication of his complete lack of status in terms of conventional social, educational, and religious standards. Because the entire purport of the legend of Hui-neng was to show that true religious understanding lay outside of all such conventions, which were the normal appurtenances of the highly cultured monks who formed the cream of the Chinese Buddhist *saṁgha,* that the barbarian layperson Hui-neng was made to do physical labor is an irrefutable indication that the monks of the day were exempt from such requirements.

Moreover, the story in question can be traced back no further than the first compilation of the *Platform Sūtra* around the year 780, not to the actual events of Hui-neng's life, as Ui surmised. Hence, the conclusion just made regarding the implications of the *Platform Sūtra* story is relevant to Buddhism in the latter part of the eighth century, rather than the latter part of the seventh. Presumably, during that earlier period the Ch'an School had distinguished itself even less than in the following century from the general practice of Buddhism in China. Since the "pure regulations" cannot actually be documented until the beginning of the eleventh century, it would be unreasonable to conclude that they had already assumed their basic form in the seventh.[88]

7. Fa-ju

The first of Hung-jen's disciples to make his mark in the Chinese capitals was Fa-ju (638–89), originally of Lu-chou (Ch'ang-chih hsien, Shansi) and, at the very end of his life, a resident of the famous Shao-lin ssu on Mount Sung. Fa-ju's biography is known from the *CFPC* and from an anonymous epitaph that contains the earliest statement in any Ch'an text of the "transmission of the lamp" doctrine. Professor Yanagida has studied these two works closely and has concluded that Fa-ju was a figure of considerable importance during his own lifetime, but was intentionally slighted and eventually forgotten within just a few decades of his death.[89]

Fa-ju's first known Buddhist teacher was Hui-ming, a meditator with Mādhyamika affiliations also known as Ch'ing-pu Ming, or "Blue-robed Ming." Hui-ming was noted for his vigorous ascetic practices and had just finished his own studies under Fa-min (579–645) and Chih-yen (577–654) when Fa-ju most probably joined him, during the years 655–59. Fa-min emphasized "nonattainment" *(wu-te),* and Chih-yen taught the contemplations of impurity, compassion, and birthlessness. This combination of teachings no doubt filtered down through Hui-ming to Fa-ju, even though the two men were together only briefly.[90]

Soon after Fa-ju left home to become a monk, at age nineteen (= 658), he went to study under Hung-jen. Thus the epitaph accurately points out that, when Hung-jen died in 674, Fa-ju had been with him for sixteen years. Fa-ju's whereabouts for the next eight or nine years, i.e., from 674 to 683, are unknown, but he must have spent at least the latter part of this period in Ch'ang-an and/or Lo-yang. This inference is based on the *CFPC*'s information that his name was advanced for a position in the official *saṁgha* administration after Emperor Kao-tsung's death at the very end of 683. Fa-ju avoided official appointment by moving to Shao-lin ssu on Mount Sung, where he stayed for several years without being recognized.

Fa-ju began to teach the Dharma in 686 after a concerted request from *Dhyāna* Master Hui-tuan of Lo-yang and the entire community of Shao-lin ssu. From this beginning until his death three years later, Fa-ju taught constantly, always responding quickly to the doubts of his many students. Just before his death he is supposed to have said (according to the *CFPC*): "After this [students of Ch'an] should study under *Dhyāna* Master [Shen]-hsiu of Yü-ch'üan ssu in Ching-chou." The reader should remember this instruction, as well as Hui-tuan's request, when we discuss the biographies of Shen-hsiu's disciples I-fu and P'u-chi.[91]

Fa-ju's prominence was short-lived, however. He is treated as a major figure in the *CFPC* but listed as a teacher of only local prominence in the *LCJFC*. Yanagida suspects that the description of Fa-ju in the latter text as a resident of far-off Lu-chou rather than of the famous Shao-lin ssu was intended as a deliberate slight. Certainly Shen-hui's attacks on P'u-chi and the Northern School betray a complete ignorance of Fa-ju's significance.[92] Although Fa-ju had no known disciples of any prominence,[93] he was important as an early exponent of the new religious message of Ch'an in the area of the Chinese capitals. Since he was almost certainly the originator of—or, at least, the first to disseminate—the transmission theory that occurs in his epitaph (and that will be discussed in Chapter IV, Section 9), Fa-ju should be remembered as a significant figure in the history of Ch'an.

8. Shen-hsiu: Biographical Sources

Shen-hsiu (606?–706) was the preeminent figure of the Northern School. Without him the Northern School would not have existed, and no record of the East Mountain Teaching would have survived. Without him the development of the Ch'an School itself would have been long delayed—for decades, at the very least. For Shen-hsiu's spiritual training earned him the strong personal support of an empress, the enthusiastic adulation of the populace, and the religious dedication of a large number of disciples. Of aristocratic and perhaps even royal heritage himself, Shen-hsiu represented the ultimate amalgam: consummate scholar; outspoken and uncompromising supporter of Buddhism; and ardent practitioner and teacher of meditation, the epitome of Buddhist spiritual crafts. His stature is confirmed by the presence of his biography in the official histories of the T'ang Dynasty, an honor accorded to only two other Buddhist monks: Shen-hsiu's second-generation disciple I-hsing, an authority on esoteric Buddhism and astronomy, and Hsuan-tsang, the famous pilgrim, translator, and Yogācāra scholar.[94]

In spite of his great importance, Shen-hsiu is usually remembered by later Buddhists and modern scholars according to the fictional account contained in the *Platform Sūtra* introduced at the very beginning of this book. This account, though not entirely unsympathetic to Shen-hsiu, was designed to debase his reputation as an inspired master relative to that of the so-called Sixth Patriarch, Hui-neng, and must therefore be disregarded. As it happens, the present study of Shen-hsiu's life will help us understand the reasons behind his eventual demotion to a decidedly subordinate role within the annals of the Ch'an School.

The sources for Shen-hsiu's biography are listed here in roughly chronological order (the two sources to be used frequently in the discussion that follows are listed first by abbreviated titles):

1. *Memorial:* A memorial to the throne by Sung Chih-wen (d. 713), probably written just a few months before Shen-hsiu's death, which offers an interesting insight into the great *dhyāna* master's stature within court society and the religious life of the two capitals.[95]
2. An anonymous inscription no doubt written soon after Shen-hsiu's death and occurring at the end of, or just after, the *CFPC* in one Tun-huang manuscript.[96]
3. The entry on Shen-hsiu and other information in the *CFPC,* written about 712 but apparently not known to the authors of the following two works.[97]
4. Material from the *LCJFC* quoted in the *LCSTC.*[98]
5. Other information in the *LCSTC,* including several short imperial proclamations issued just before and just after the great monk's death.[99]
6. *Epitaph:* A long and detailed epitaph written by the prominent official and poet Chang Yueh (667–731), probably composed within a few years after Shen-hsiu's death but apparently unknown to the authors of the *CFPC, LCJFC,* and *LCSTC.* Other prominent individuals are known to have written eulogies for the departed monk, but only this one survives.[100]
7. A flowery, contentless notice by Chang Yueh on the presentation to Shen-hsiu's monastery of a plaque bearing an inscription of the deceased monk's posthumous title done in the imperial hand.[101]
8. Anecdotal material in the *T'ai-p'ing kuang chi (Extended Accounts*

of the Great Peace) depicting feats of supernormal perception and premonition on Shen-hsiu's part.[102]

9. An entry in the *Chiu T'ang shu (Older Chronicles of the T'ang [Dynasty])*, written between 936 and 946, based on the *Epitaph*.[103]

10. Fully three entries in the *SKSC:*

A. Under the name Shen-hsiu, found in the section on meditators, and combining information from the *Chiu T'ang shu* with apocryphal stories concerning Shen-hsiu and Hui-neng.

B. Under the name Wei-hsiu, occurring at the very beginning of the section on defenders of the faith, and containing an account of his efforts in this regard in and around the year 662. (The identification of Wei-hsiu with Shen-hsiu will be discussed in Section 10.)

C. Under the name Hui-hsiu, located in the section on thaumaturges, and including stories of precognition and nonconformist spontaneity.[104]

11. A short entry in the *CTL*, which includes only one item of any interest that is not found elsewhere.[105]

Although there are some very long gaps in Shen-hsiu's biography—details are lacking for over half of his life—the manner in which these sources can be pieced together makes the study of his life especially interesting and rewarding. Because of his pivotal importance, we will focus on his biography in much greater detail than we have for previous figures.

9. Shen-hsiu's Early Life and Training

Shen-hsiu was born in or around the year 606 in the Li family of Ch'en-liu wei-shih (Wei-shih hsien, Hunan), which is about fifty kilometers south of the modern K'ai-feng and about one hundred kilometers east of Mount Sung.[106] The aristocratic or perhaps even royal nature of Shen-hsiu's family is apparent in the notices about Pao-en ssu, the "home of [Shen-hsiu's] predecessors in Wei-shih," which was converted into a monastery after his death. The *LCSTC* cites an imperial edict that ordered the conversion of Shen-hsiu's "place of birth, the great Li village," into Pao-en ssu.[107] The *Chiu T'ang shu* identifies Pao-en ssu as the former residence of Prince Hsiang, the adolescent Emperor Jui-tsung. Whether or not Shen-hsiu was actually a member of the T'ang imperial family, whose surname he shared, his ties to and rapport with Emperor Jui-tsung and especially Empress Wu were very close.

After the obligatory praise of Shen-hsiu's innate mental capacities and exceptional physical appearance, the *Epitaph* says that as a youth he wandered about the area to the south of the Yangtze River. In many ways, this area was the heartland of Chinese Buddhism. Shen-hsiu's erudition was exceptionally broad:

> He could converse in the [southern] dialects of Wu and Chin and was thoroughly versed in the exegesis of the mysterious principle of Lao and Chuang (i.e., philosophical Taoism), the great truths of the *Shu*[*ching*] and *I*[*ching*] (i.e., the Chinese classics), the sūtras and *śāstra*s of the Three Vehicles, and the rules of the *Four-part* [*Vinaya*].[108]

The *CFPC* describes the circumstances under which Shen-hsiu became a Buddhist: When he was thirteen years old, in 618, the areas of Honan and Shantung suffered famines and epidemics as a result of the decline and fall of the Sui Dynasty. Shen-hsiu went to the official granaries in Ying-yang (K'ai-feng hsien, Honan) to ask for the release of grain to the populace. While doing so he met a "spiritual compatriot" *(shan chih-shih,* or *kalyāṇamitra)* and was inspired to become a Buddhist monk.[109] It is significant to find Shen-hsiu connected so early in his biography with humanitarian activities and, even in this second-hand fashion, with the social and political conditions that led to the founding of the T'ang Dynasty.

After choosing the homeless life, Shen-hsiu first traveled to Eastern Wu (Kiangsu), then to Min (Fukkien), and eventually to all the famous mountain centers of China. Mentioned by the *CFPC* are Mounts Lo-fu (Kwangtung), Tung, Meng, T'ien-t'ai (all in Chekiang), and Lu (Kiangsi). Shen-hsiu's learning is praised in much the same way as in the *Epitaph,* whose discussion of his studies no doubt refers to the period after as well as before his renunciation of the life of householder. Shen-hsiu took the full precepts at age twenty (= 625) at a monastery in Lo-yang named T'ien-kung ssu. This monastery had been the T'ang Emperor Kao-tsu's residence before his coronation but was only converted to religious use in 632.[110] Shen-hsiu was eventually to pass away at the same location.

The *CFPC* says that, following his ordination, Shen-hsiu devoted his primary energies to learning the *Vinaya* regulations and ceremonies and then moved on to the practice of meditation and the development of wisdom. Thus he is supposed to have studied all three of the basic components of traditional Buddhist training: *śīla, dhyāna,* and *prajñā.* Aside from this information, the following quarter century of his life is a complete blank.

The next known event in Shen-hsiu's life was his journey to Huang-mei in 651 to study under Hung-jen. The *CFPC* claims that Hung-jen discerned his new student's abilities at a single glance and taught him for several years. The *Epitaph*'s version of this is more explicit and may be paraphrased as follows:

> [Shen-hsiu] worked day and night for six years. Great Master Hung-jen sighed and said: "Shen-hsiu has completely mastered the East Mountain Teaching." Hung-jen [then] ordered his student to wash his feet and take his seat alongside [of the master]. At this point Shen-hsiu broke into tears, left East Mountain, and secreted himself.[111]

If we are to accept the notion that Shen-hsiu studied with Hung-jen for six years—and this figure is suspiciously reminiscent of Hui-k'o's period of training under Bodhidharma and, to cite the ultimate model, Śākyamuni's period of asceticism—this means that Shen-hsiu left Huang-mei around the year 657. This date is important only in that it renders the story of the exchange of "mind-verses" between Shen-hsiu and Hui-neng chronologically impossible.[112]

10. The Identification of Shen-hsiu with Wei-hsiu

The next period in Shen-hsiu's life must be extrapolated from a combination of direct and indirect evidence. The first clue occurs in the *CFPC*, which includes the following statement:

> Later [Shen-hsiu] was banished and assumed layman's garb as a disguise. He lived at T'ien-chü ssu in Ching-chou for over ten years without anyone recognizing him.[113]

The *CFPC* goes on to say that Shen-hsiu was returned to public status sometime during the years 676–679. Since he remained incognito for over ten years, his banishment therefore occurred sometime in or before 668, at the very latest—probably before 665.

The question is why Shen-hsiu was banished in the first place. A brief glance at the history of church-state relations during this period reveals two possible reasons: (1) the Buddhist-Taoist debates intended to determine the validity of the T'ang ruling house's ranking of the native religion over the foreign one and (2) the attempt to alter the traditional status of Buddhism by forcing the members of the *saṁgha* to do obeisance to both the emperor and their own parents. These two issues were closely related to each other, but both were legitimate causes for the involvement of a prestigious cleric with extremely good political connections. Shen-hsiu was apparently involved in the second of the two disputes.

On the fifteenth day of the fourth month in 662 an edict was issued in Kao-tsung's name ordering that all Buddhist monks and nuns reverence their parents and the emperor according to the customs previously maintained only by laypeople. Just six days later, one Wei-hsiu of Ta-chuang-yen ssu proceeded to P'eng-lai Palace in Ch'ang-an in the company of over two hundred monks and submitted a memorial opposing the attempt to restrict the traditional Buddhist prerogatives. The ensuing debate—between Wei-hsiu's supporters and opponents among the officials involved—came to no immediate conclusion, so he and the other monks left to regroup at Hsi-ming ssu.

On the twenty-fifth day of the same month, Tao-hsuan, a resident of Hsi-ming ssu known to posterity as the compiler of the *HKSC,* sent an essay defending the Buddhist position to a prince who was the fourth son of Emperor Kao-tsung. On the twenty-seventh, similar requests were sent to the mother of the current empress and to all those in the very highest stratum of official service. On the fifteenth day of the next month, Wei-hsiu, Tao-hsuan, two other similarly prominent clerical associates, and more than three hundred other monks presented the case on behalf of the Buddhist *saṁgha* before an assembly of over one thousand officials.

Unfortunately, this large meeting did not produce any consensus, and the final resolution of the dilemma is unclear. About two months after the initial decree, the emperor rescinded the requirement that monks and nuns reverence his person, but it is uncertain when, if ever, the requirement that monks reverence their parents was formally withdrawn.[114]

My hypothesis is that "Wei-hsiu of Ta-chuang-yen ssu" refers to Shen-hsiu of the Northern School of Ch'an. Wei-hsiu's entry in the *SKSC* contains no biographical information whatsoever, mentioning only that his place of birth was unknown. Other than praise of his erudition, his ability to explain Buddhism both orally and in writing, and his efforts to disseminate the teachings in his lectures, the only subject discussed in the entire entry is the dispute just summarized. This absence of biographical information for a monk prestigious enough to spearhead the opposition to an imperial edict seems unusual and leads me to visualize the following scenario:

1. Wei-hsiu was the monk described in the preceding pages, i.e., extremely well-educated and having close connections to the imperial family.

2. After his studies under Hung-jen, Shen-hsiu née Wei-hsiu moved to Ch'ang-an, where he took up residence at Ta-chuang-yen ssu and began to actively disseminate the teachings of Buddhism.

3. Stating his case on behalf of the traditional rights of the *saṁgha* too forcibly, he aroused the ire of either the emperor himself or, more likely, those officials most closely associated with the anti-Buddhist decree. As a result, he was banished from the capital and had to bide his time among his supporters at Ching-chou before resuming public activities.

4. At the time of his return to public life (676–79), Wei-hsiu changed his name to Shen-hsiu to avoid any residue of opposition to his former

stand. The *SKSC* would thus be unable to include anything about Wei-hsiu's biography, since the *Epitaph* avoids the entire incident and was written under the name Shen-hsiu.

This hypothesis not only fills a gap in the middle of Shen-hsiu's biography but also provides a partial explanation of this monk's extreme prominence at the very end of his life. That is, Shen-hsiu was welcomed by Empress Wu into Lo-yang amid such incredible fanfare not only because he was a venerable teacher of meditation, but also because he was remembered as a champion of Buddhism in its travails of four decades before. It seems likely that Empress Wu orchestrated his magnificent arrival in Lo-yang and his subsequent career as a demonstration of her support of Buddhism and her position as just heir to the T'ang realm. She no longer had need to commission such patently contrived supports to her reign as the *Ta-yün ching (Sūtra of the Great Cloud [of the Dharma]),* which was construed to predict the advent of a female bodhisattva to rule China. Rather, the imperial support of Shen-hsiu was designed both as a spectacular embellishment to her reign and as a public demonstration of the importance of Buddhism within her regime. It is also doubly significant that (as we shall see) Empress Wu bowed to him on his entrance into the capital, rather than requiring that gesture of respect from him.[115]

11. Shen-hsiu at Yü-ch'üan ssu

The *CFPC* claims that, during the years 676–679, several tens of virtuous monks from what is now Hupeh and Hunan sponsored Shen-hsiu's official ordination and residence at Yü-ch'üan ssu in Ching-chou.[116] The *Epitaph* describes Shen-hsiu's selection of a site for his own headquarters as follows:

> Seven *li* to the east of [Yü-ch'üan ssu] the land was broad and the mountains mighty. Upon seeing this, [Shen-hsiu] said: "This is truly the solitary peak of Laṇkā, [and the fitting site for the] Monastery of the [Six] Perfections. I shall grow old among its shaded pines and tangled grasses.[117]

There is no doubt that Tu-men ssu, or the "Monastery of the [Six] Perfections," was built specifically for Shen-hsiu.[118] Although the passage just quoted suggests that he picked the specific location for Tu-men ssu because of its idyllic or geomantically advantageous setting, clearly more was involved in his choice of Yü-ch'üan ssu and Ching-chou in general. T'ien-t'ai Chih-i's residence at Yü-ch'üan had helped to make it a prominent monastic establishment, and Ching-chou had been an important center of meditation practice for several centuries. In addition, Empress

Wu's personal connections with this general location may have had some influence on Shen-hsiu's choice of a safe refuge from the dangerous legacy of political activism.[119]

Whatever the circumstances, Shen-hsiu spent the next quarter century in Ching-chou. Although there are some indications that he was influenced by the example of Chih-i during his stay there—viz., his authorship of a text that used the same title as one of Chih-i's works and the Northern School's appropriation of a letter apparently written by Chih-i himself[120]—Shen-hsiu's exact activities and personal religious development while in Ching-chou are obscure. The *CFPC*'s claim that Shen-hsiu refrained from teaching until 689 out of deference to Fa-ju cannot be accepted.[121] Judging from the year of the founding of Tu-men ssu, it seems more probable that Shen-hsiu moved immediately after Hung-jen's death to assume the mantle of the East Mountain Teaching.[122]

Shen-hsiu's residence at Tu-men ssu in Ching-chou extends the East Mountain Teaching's period of quiet incubation in provincial retreats to fully three-quarters of a century, from Tao-hsin's arrival in Huang-mei in 624 to Shen-hsiu's journey to Lo-yang in 701. Unlike the community at Huang-mei, however, the community at Ching-chou continued to be a viable Ch'an School training center after Shen-hsiu's departure and eventual death. This is known from a letter from I-hsing to Shen-hsiu's epigrapher, Chang Yueh, which says that the departed master's students (I-hsing was actually Shen-hsiu's second-generation successor) were still practicing with all possible intensity and sincerity at Yü-ch'üan ssu.[123] Presumably, Shen-hsiu left some of his students there when he traveled to Lo-yang.

12. Shen-hsiu in Lo-yang and Ch'ang-an

The *CFPC* describes Shen-hsiu's entry into and activities in the two capitals in greater detail than the *LCJFC.* According to the *CFPC,* in the latter part of the year 700

> [Empress Wu] Tse-t'ien sent a palace messenger to escort [Shen-hsiu] to Lo-yang. Monks and laypeople spread flowers in his path, and the banners and canopies [on the vehicles of the wealthy and prestigious] filled the streets. He entered the palace riding on a litter (of a type reserved for members of the imperial family) and decked with palm leaves. [Empress Wu], following him, touched her forehead to the ground and knelt long in a spirit of reverent dedication and chaste purity. When [Shen-hsiu] administered the precepts to the court ladies, all the four classes [of Buddhists] took refuge in him with the same feelings of veneration that they had for their own parents. From princes and nobles on down, everyone [in the capital] took refuge in him.[124]

Other than the slight conflict concerning the date of these events, which can be resolved by noting that the *CFPC* refers to Shen-hsiu's invitation in 700 and the *LCJFC* to his actual entry into Lo-yang the following calendar year, all sources agree on the exceptional nature of the aged monk's reception. Both the *Epitaph* and the *Chiu T'ang shu* emphasize that he was carried into the palace on a litter to meet a kneeling and reverential Empress Wu.[125] The *Epitaph* defends this event, which was clearly extraordinary in the context of the T'ang, with the statement that "he who transmits the Holy Truth does not face north; he with abundant virtue does not follow the protocol of a subordinate."[126]

Shen-hsiu spent the last five years of his life traveling back and forth between the two capitals of Ch'ang-an and Lo-yang. Although his specific activities cannot be known in their entirety, we can imagine that he spent a substantial percentage of his time lecturing, administering the precepts, and performing other teaching and clerical functions. Although he was probably not directly involved in the work of translation, the *SKSC* states that he functioned as a "verifier of the Ch'an meaning" *(cheng ch'an-i)* of newly-translated scriptures.[127] As we will see in Part Two, Chapter III, Sections 5 and 6, it is very easy to imagine Shen-hsiu suggesting some unique interpretations of the terms and concepts found in such texts. The third *SKSC* biography listed earlier and the *T'ai-p'ing kuang chi* entry contain anecdotal material indicating the extent to which Shen-hsiu's activities, or his imperial support, resulted in the adulation of the Chinese public.

While in Lo-yang Shen-hsiu spent at least part of his time at T'ien-kung ssu, where he was first ordained and eventually passed away. In Ch'ang-an he probably stayed at Tzu-sheng ssu, with which he is associated in the *T'ai-p'ing kuang chi* and *SKSC* entries just mentioned. It cannot be coincidental that one of Shen-hsiu's epigraphers, who was the fourth son of Emperor Jui-tsung, owned residences that were contiguous with both of these monasteries.[128]

One of the more interesting documents pertaining to Shen-hsiu's life and impact is the *Memorial* by Sung Chih-wen, a noted poet who was in official service during the reigns of Empress Wu and Emperor Chung-tsung. More than any other source, it gives us an insight into Shen-hsiu's extraordinary status and activities at the imperial court. The author seems concerned, in fact, that the attention given to the aged monk was disrupting the functioning of government itself. The following is a rough paraphrase of the entire text:

Memorial on Behalf of the Saṁgha *of Lo-yang Requesting That* Dhyāna *Master* [*Shen*]*-hsiu Be Welcomed with* [*All Due*] *Religious Ceremony*

Various monks have said: "We have heard that the support of the True Teaching [of Buddhism] depends first of all on the power of the emperor to attract capable teachers from far and wide." I am humbly aware that on a certain date a messenger was sent by edict to escort the monk Tao-hsiu (= Shen-hsiu) of Yü-ch'üan ssu [to court]. In Your Majesty's support of Buddhism You have dreamt of this person and his words and teachings, You have had him come to the palace morning and night. This monk embodies the Ultimate Principle of birthlessness (i.e., nirvāṇa) and transmits the Wonderful Teaching of East Mountain. He lives in an open cave [at Yü-ch'üan ssu], even though he is over ninety years of age. His physical beauty grows richer day by day, his teaching ever deeper.

Students of Buddhism from the two capitals and the faithful from all areas of China all come to the Five Gated [Entrance to the Imperial City to hear his teaching]. They come from a thousand *li* away without any hesitation! [The mendicants with their] robes and begging bowls crowd into newly built halls like schools of jumping fish; their huts cover the hillside like lines of geese. Gathering like clouds and free as the dew, they go [to Shen-hsiu] empty-handed and return fulfilled.

[Shen-hsiu] was a recluse among the deep forests of the Three Ch'u who is carrying on the teaching of the One Buddha. He enjoyed living in the distant mountains, having resided for a long time in Ching-nan. Having a (karmic? kinship?) relationship with the state, he has now returned to Yü-pei (i.e., Lo-yang).

The monks and laypeople of the Nine Rivers love him as they love their parents; the men and women of the Three Rivers look up to him as to the very mountains. It is proper that the mendicants should camp in the fields, that Buddhist activities should be encouraged on the outskirts of the city. [But] if they are allowed to come into the capital, they shall lose their perspective [as to the function of temporal government. This is especially true insofar as] Tao-hsiu has forgotten (i.e., transcended) all worldly preferences and protocol.

The community of monks wishes to show reverence to this marvelous personage. To burn incense and scatter flowers while following the King of the Teaching into the hall of spiritual training—the four groups of Buddhists would all feel gratitude, a myriad people would become joyous! This would be the ultimate [experience of] overwhelmining religious sincerity.

I respectfully proceed to the Palace and offer up this memorial requesting that [Your Royal Highness] and the faithful from the city proceed with due religious ceremony to Lung-men to listen to Tao-hsiu's [teaching].

In rashly touching on the awesomeness of [the Son of] Heaven, I have been deeply presumptuous.[129]

The most striking impression given by this *Memorial* is of the public response to Shen-hsiu. Even allowing for the literary exaggeration of mendicants gathering "like schools of jumping fish," their huts covering the hillsides "like lines of geese," Sung Chih-wen's *Memorial* is an incontrovertible testimonial to the fervor with which Shen-hsiu's teachings were received in early eighth-century Lo-yang. No doubt the *Chiu T'ang shu*'s claim that ten thousand people visited Shen-hsiu every day is grossly inflated, but his popularity is indisputable.

Although the *Memorial* itself is not dated, it is possible to suggest a specific context for its composition and submission to the throne. The *LCSTC* records an edict by Emperor Chung-tsung issued in 705 that praises Shen-hsiu's religious attainments and refuses his request to return home to Ching-chou. The aged Empress Wu, who had already been quietly displaced from her former position of complete authority, was to die at the very end of this year, Shen-hsiu a few months later. Shen-hsiu's interest in returning home must have been fueled both by a wish to spend his final hours in the relative quiet of Ching-chou and by a sense of deference to Emperor Chung-tsung, who had only been returned to the throne less than two months before the edict in question was issued. Shen-hsiu was thus offering Chung-tsung the opportunity to repudiate or revise governmental support of his East Mountain Teaching.

Out of his own personal feelings of reverence for Shen-hsiu and in conjunction with the generally smooth transition that characterized the reestablishment of the T'ang after Empress Wu's short-lived Chou regime, Emperor Chung-tsung refused Shen-hsiu's request. Sung Chih-wen's *Memorial* thus made possible a course of action by which the political and religious functions of the court could be smoothly separated without implying any lessening of interest in or support for Shen-hsiu and the "Northern School" that had developed around him. In fact, Chung-tsung did travel to Lung-men late in 705—and is it not possible that he went to hear Shen-hsiu preach?[130]

13. Shen-hsiu's Death and Its Aftermath

Shen-hsiu died while sitting quietly in meditation posture at T'ien-kung ssu in Lo-yang on the twenty-eighth day of the second month of the Shen-lung period, or 706. The *Epitaph* claims that he died during the night; the *CFPC*'s description of the events surrounding his death can be found in the Appendix. The *CFPC* and the *Epitaph* both say that Shen-hsiu was over one hundred years old, but that no one had ever asked him his true age.

The *LCSTC* concurs on the date and location of Shen-hsiu's death, adding that his last words were the three characters *ch'ü ch'ü chih*. These three characters, which mean "bent over," "curved," and "straight," respectively, might refer to some progressive perfection Shen-hsiu felt he had achieved. Or, taking the first two characters as a compound, one could read the statement as "the vagaries of the world are now straightened [in the state of nirvāṇa to come]."

Perhaps the best interpretation of Shen-hsiu's last words is given by Professor Yanagida, who notes that *ch'ü-ch'ü chiao* is a *p'an-chiao,* or "doctrinal classification," term for an indirect method of teaching by which the Buddha brought his listeners to the ultimate truth in a step-by-step or even roundabout fashion. According to this interpretation, Shen-hsiu's last words would mean something like "the teachings of the expedient means have been made direct."[131] This would accord with the Northern School's well-known emphasis on expedient means. Whatever the original intent of this statement, Shen-hsiu's teaching style involved the use of perplexingly enigmatic questions, as we shall see, so there is no doubt that his last words were chosen to inspire earnest reflection among his followers.[132]

By correlating data from the biographies of Shen-hsiu and other Northern School monks, we can adumbrate an extensive program of funerary and commemorative observations that followed his death. The existence of this program not only substantiates Shen-hsiu's prestige among his contemporaries, but also indicates certain aspects of the institutional development of the Northern School.

According to the *Epitaph,* the emperor sent a messenger to convey his condolences as soon as he heard of Shen-hsiu's death. The lords and princes all sent appropriate gifts. Just a few days after his death (on the second day of the third month), Shen-hsiu was given the title Ta-t'ung ch'an-shih ("Greatly Penetrating *Dhyāna* Master"). This was only the second such imperially granted posthumous title in the history of Chinese Buddhism, and the first since the very beginning of the fifth century.[133]

Emperor Jui-tsung donated 30,000 cash for the refurbishment and enlargement of Tu-men ssu, which was

> decorated lavishly with money from the state, the bequests exceeding a million [cash]. The massive bell had been forged by the former emperor [Chung-tsung]; the collection of Buddhist sculpture was a gift of the latter emperor [Jui-tsung]. The gold plaque [bearing the name of the monastery] was written by the emperor [Chung-tsung, and the] banners decorated with flowers were made within the palace. The stūpa and monastery [as a whole] were most awe-inspiring and gained a wide reputation for having set a new standard [of beauty].[134]

Three days after the bestowal of the posthumous title Ta-t'ung (on the fifth day of the third month), Shen-hsiu's body was placed temporarily at Lung-men, the burial site of a number of other eminent Buddhist monks. The emperor, princes, and nobles formed a procession that accompanied the remains from Lo-yang as far as the I River, which flows between the cave temples of Lung-men, while a group of high officials proceeded on to the interment site itself.

The final burial services were begun on the sixteenth day of the seventh month, when an edict was issued authorizing Shen-hsiu's return to Tu-men ssu in accord with his last wishes. The chief of ceremonies of the imperial palace led the procession, followed by musicians and the head palace gatekeeper, who acted as a ceremonial guard. The emperor himself went to Lung-men to "weep over the coffin," after which Shen-hsiu's body was dispatched to Ching-chou. On the seventeenth day of the tenth month Shen-hsiu's body was finally laid to rest in an open stūpa located at a site previously selected by him behind his former residence at Tu-men ssu.

At the end of the mourning period, in the tenth month of the same year, a great assembly was held at Lung-hua ssu, a large nunnery in Ch'ang-an. Eight thousand people were in attendance for these ceremonies, which included the official ordination of fourteen of Shen-hsiu's disciples. The first and second annual observances were held at Hsi-ming ssu, with similar numbers of people present. Other services were held in the palace and at Mount Chung-nan outside of Ch'ang-an.[135]

The ordination ceremony held in conjunction with the first memorial service for Shen-hsiu at Hsi-ming ssu tells us a great deal about the contemporary state of the Northern School. The *Epitaph* says only that fourteen persons were ordained one hundred days after the funeral. While there are some discrepancies in the date as reported in various sources, these ordinations are probably the same as those mentioned in connection with Lao-an.[136]

The implications of this coincidence are as follows: Through this ordination ceremony, the titular leadership of the Northern School was transferred from Shen-hsiu to Lao-an. The latter monk maintained this position until his own death only two or three years later, after which another successor to Hung-jen, Hsuan-tse (the author of the *LCJFC,* already discussed in Sections 5 and 15), assumed or attempted to assume the same position. Whatever the degree of Hsuan-tse's success in the attempt to advance his own cause on the basis of his association with the heroes of the past—this is an admittedly cynical interpretation of his motives—eventually the mantle was passed on to the next generation. In this next generation, generally counted as the seventh from Bodhidharma, Shen-hsiu's disciple P'u-chi was the most prominent and outspoken representative of early Ch'an.

14. Lao-an and His Disciples

To achieve the proper perspective on the events immediately following Shen-hsiu's death, we must consider what little evidence is available about the life of Lao-an. This monk, originally called Hui-an, is known primarily from a very badly preserved funerary inscription and two entries in the *SKSC.*[137] He was born in Chih-chiang, Ching-chou (Chiang-ling hsien, Hupeh), in 581, 582, or sometime between 581 and 600, depending on the source. (Later sources claim that he lived to the age of 128.) In 597 he is supposed to have entered the forests to escape a Sui Dynasty campaign against those without official ordinations. During the hardships accompanying canal construction during the years 605 to 616, he traveled about collecting food for the sick and poor. After rejecting an invitation to court, in 616 he ascended Mount Heng (= Nan-yueh) to practice meditation.

According to the *SKSC,* Lao-an went to Huang-mei to study under Hung-jen sometime between 627 and 649. If this chronology were accurate, it would mean that Hung-jen accepted a student before Tao-hsin's death—and a man allegedly as old or older than Tao-hsin himself! It is unclear how long Lao-an is supposed to have studied under Hung-jen. The funerary inscription includes a reference to Shen-hsiu, Lao-an, and the "eight teachers" who "received the essentials of Ch'an" from Hung-jen. This passage obviously relies on Hsuan-tse's assertions in the *LCJFC,* as introduced earlier in Section 5. Even more interesting, when Lao-an left Huang-mei he is supposed to have recommended that students go to Shen-hsiu—a statement just as obviously modeled on the *CFPC*'s assertion about Fa-ju.

Although the funerary inscription is marred by long lacunae, Lao-an seems to have stayed at Yü-ch'üan ssu for several years. According to the *SKSC,* he took up residence in the caves at Mount Chung-nan near Ch'ang-an in 664. In 683 he moved to what is described as a rude hut in Hua-t'ai (Hua hsien, Hunan)[138] and later to a monastery named Chao-t'i ssu built there by imperial edict. After an unknown length of time at Hua-t'ai and possibly a period of wandering, Lao-an moved to Shao-lin ssu on Mount Sung. When he arrived there, he said: "This is my stopping place." Students of Ch'an gathered there "like spokes around a hub."

It is not clear when Lao-an first gained access to the imperial court. The early sources mention invitations made and spurned between 605 and 616 and again in 664, and two Sung Dynasty texts state that he first went to court in 695 or 696. Even the *LTFPC,* which is of all the eighth-century texts the most prone to exaggeration and fabrication, dates his entry to court as occurring in the year 700.[139] Whether or not the Sung figures are correct, Lao-an's presence at Shao-lin may quite possibly have attracted official attention and thus contributed to the eventual invitation of Shen-hsiu.

Although it is thus not out of the question that Lao-an's career contributed to Shen-hsiu's rise to prominence, in general the relationship between the two men seems to have been just the opposite. What little is known about Lao-an's biography seems suspiciously reminiscent of Shen-hsiu's—so much so that it is impossible to avoid the impression that Lao-an's was directly modeled on and even designed to outdo that of his more famous associate. Thus Lao-an was older than the venerable Shen-hsiu, achieved greater recognition for his humanitarian efforts at the end of the Sui, joined Hung-jen earlier, advanced Shen-hsiu's name on his own departure from Huang-mei, and cut a more exotic figure than the obviously distinguished Shen-hsiu.[140] Because of this impression, the veracity of the details of Lao-an's early biography are open to considerable doubt.

This is not to deny that Lao-an was a prominent figure in the two capitals after Shen-hsiu's death. He is known to have received valuable gifts from the emperor on several occasions. Not only did he oversee the ordination of fourteen disciples, as mentioned in connection with Shen-hsiu, but he also may have accompanied Shen-hsiu's body back to Ching-chou in the funeral procession described earlier. Lao-an himself died in 708 or 709, depending on the source. The first of these two dates fits better with other information to be considered later.[141]

Lao-an is known to have had several disciples. One of these, Chih-ta or Hui-ta, who also studied under Shen-hsiu, is remembered as the author of an interesting Northern School text. This is the *Tun-wu chen-tsung chin-kang po-jo hsin-hsing ta pi-an fa-men yao-chueh (Essential Oral Teaching of Sudden Enlightenment to the True Teaching and Attainment of the Other Shore* [*of Nirvāṇa Through the*] *Cultivation of Adamantine Wisdom).*[142]

The *Tsu-t'ang chi (Anthology of the Patriarchal Hall,* hereafter cited as *TTC)* of 952 mentions two students of Lao-an's, one of whom was the author of a short work recorded in the *CTL*. If this attribution is accurate—and I know of no reason to question it—then this short work is a very important one because of its early provenance and similarity with other mid-eighth-century works attributed to members of the Southern School. Unfortunately, no significant biographical information is available about its author. Another monk, Tao-shun, may have been associated with Lao-an, even though the association is not explicitly mentioned in his biography.[143]

The only students of Lao-an's whose biographies are known from reliable sources are Yuan-kuei (644–716)[144] and Ching-tsang (675–746). The second of these is definitely the more interesting. Ching-tsang studied for more than ten years with Lao-an, or until the master's death, and then for five years or less with Hui-neng. Ching-tsang finally received certification of his enlightenment *(yin-k'o)* and "transmission of the Dharma and the lamp" *(fu-fa ch'üan-teng)* after five years of additional practice under an unnamed teacher in Ching-nan, the general location of Yü-ch'üan ssu. Well after this experience, in about 730, Ching-tsang took up residence at a chapel dedicated to Lao-an near a stūpa at Hui-shan ssu on Mount Sung. (Coincidentally, a picture of Ching-tsang's own stūpa occurs in Tokiwa Daijō's monumental set of plates on the cultural legacies of China.[145]) In spite of his contact with Hui-neng, Ching-tsang's epitaph notes that the teaching was "transmitted directly through seven patriarchs, having arisen on Mount Sung"; the sixth and seventh generations are presumably Lao-an and Ching-tsang himself.[146]

15. Hsuan-tse and Fa-hsien

Lao-an was not, of course, the only student of Hung-jen's to be active in the two capitals after Shen-hsiu's death. In addition to the minor figure Tao-shun mentioned in passing in the previous section, Fa-hsien (643–720) of the Lung-hsing ssu in Ch'i-chou (Huang-mei) must also be cited in this regard. This monk was invited to court during the years 705–7 and was active there until his death in 720. Although Fa-hsien was a relatively unimportant figure, his epitaph by Li Shih-chih is interesting in two ways.[147]

First, one of the hagiographical anecdotes recounted in this epitaph bears evidence to the growing strength of the Ch'an legend. As the story goes, when Fa-hsien was struggling with massive rocks at the construction site of his mother's grave, a man approached him, bowed, and pulled out a book. Giving it to Fa-hsien, he said: "This is in order to help you dig the grave." The book was a "treatise of Bodhidharma's" *(P'u-t'i-ta-mo chih lun);* the grave was finished in two days.

Second, although Fa-hsien died in 720 and his epitaph was not written until 740, the only master mentioned is Hung-jen. In other words, fully sixty-five years after Hung-jen's death, the memory of his name was still strong enough to serve as a monk's sole source of religious identification. This evidence is not only a testimonial to Hung-jen's importance: Unless the absence of the names of Shen-hsiu and P'u-chi is taken as an intentional avoidance of the "Northern School," this epitaph of the year 740 evinces no indication whatsoever of any impact of the campaign launched a decade earlier by Shen-hui.[148]

In 708, either the same year or the year before Lao-an's death, another student of Hung-jen's—Hsuan-tse, the author of the *LCJFC*—received an invitation to court. Earlier in his career Hsuan-tse had assisted in Hsuan-tsang's translation work. In 667 he attended the formal establishment of an ordination platform on Mount Chung-nan. Tao-hsuan's list of those attending this ceremony identifies Hsuan-tse as a Dharma master of Wu-liang ssu in Ching-chou, a monastery whose name evokes the Pure Land tradition. These details, however scanty, corroborate Hung-jen's description of Hsuan-tse (as reported by Hsuan-tse himself) as a man accomplished in the "combined study" of several facets of Buddhist academic and spiritual learning.[149]

According to his own account (reproduced in Section 5), Hsuan-tse studied under Hung-jen from 670 to 674. His activities from the end of this discipleship until 708 are largely unknown, but he spent at least part of this period practicing meditation on Mount Shou in An-chou (Ying-shan hsien, Hupeh). It is impossible to say how long, if at all, he maintained his position in the capitals after 710.[150] The lack of information implies that his activities did not attract as much interest or attention as those of Shen-hsiu or even Lao-an. Hsuan-tse died sometime before 727, leaving his robe, bowl, and staff to his only known disciple, Ching-chueh. This reference to the bequest of robe and bowl is the first in Ch'an literature, which just a few decades later is filled with different claims about the disposition of a robe supposedly given by Hung-jen to Hui-neng.[151]

Hsuan-tse's brief success in Lo-yang and Ch'ang-an after 708 and his authorship of the *LCJFC* suggest that he attempted unsuccessfully to follow in the footsteps of Shen-hsiu and Lao-an. Since the timing of Hsuan-tse's invitation to court may have been determined by the date of Lao-an's death, we may infer a horizontal succession within a single generation of early Northern School masters after Hung-jen's death: from Shen-hsiu to Lao-an and then to Hsuan-tse. (Fa-ju's name should perhaps be placed before that of Shen-hsiu.) Although Shen-hsiu's students P'u-chi, I-fu, and Ching-hsien may have been just as prominent as Hsuan-tse, this apparently horizontal line of succession—i.e., from one member of the sixth generation after Bodhidharma to another—has interesting implications for the development of the "transmission of the lamp" theory. This subject will be taken up in some detail in Chapter IV; at present, however, we should complete the historical narrative of the development of Northern Ch'an.

CHAPTER III

The Seventh Generation and Beyond

1. The Contour of Later Northern Ch'an History

The major dimensions of the Northern School's rise to prominence should now be clear, but its subsequent history is not necessarily confined to the details of its decline and disappearance. On the contrary, the composition of the Northern School after the deaths of Shen-hsiu and Lao-an, the status claims and doctrinal statements made by P'u-chi and his successors, and the extension of Northern School proselytizing into Tibet are all subjects of great importance in their own right. In fact, several issues fundamental to the study of the Northern School and early Ch'an in general can only be addressed on the basis of an accurate understanding of this period:

1. What was the nature of the Northern School's contemporary success and the extent of its impact on the subsequent development of Chinese Ch'an?
2. What effect did Shen-hui's campaign have on the Northern School and, once again, on the subsequent development of Ch'an?
3. In what sense was the Northern School a religious "school" of Chinese Buddhism, and why did it cease to exist as such?

The traditional view, of course, is that the Northern School had little or no impact on subsequent periods of Ch'an history; that after Shen-hui's campaign the membership of the Northern School was fatally depleted as Hui-neng's swelled; and that the Northern School disappeared because of the inherent inferiority of its own teachings, its influence in the long run being essentially nil. Our review of the relatively abundant evidence for this phase of the history of early Ch'an will show that all these assertions are completely incorrect.

I have already mentioned how first Lao-an and then Hsuan-tse attempted to fill the vacuum left by Shen-hsiu's death. In addition to their own personal influence—Lao-an's deriving from his advanced age and Hsuan-tse's from the very diversity of his experience in several areas of Buddhist endeavor—the primary reason for each man's prestige was the connection with Hung-jen.[152] Sooner or later, however, the mantle of Ch'an had to be passed on to the next generation, the seventh from Bodhidharma. Here the importance of Shen-hsiu's role becomes all the more evident, for, although the students of Lao-an and Hsuan-tse were not completely unknown, those of Shen-hsiu—P'u-chi, I-fu, Ching-hsien, Hsiang-mo Tsang, and others—dominated the world of Ch'an during the second, third, and fourth decades of the eighth century.

In contrast to the serial order apparent in the careers of Fa-ju, Shen-hsiu, Lao-an, and Hsuan-tse, the men of the seventh generation seem to have coordinated their activities. Just after Shen-hsiu's death and during Lao-an's brief heyday, I-fu and P'u-chi were both in residence at the same monastery on Mount Sung. Afterward, they effectively divided the responsibilities for maintaining the glory of the Northern School between themselves, I-fu moving to Mount Chung-nan and P'u-chi staying at Mount Sung. P'u-chi thus retained control of the Northern School's long-held training center outside Lo-yang, while I-fu established a new base of operations near the much more important metropolis of Ch'ang-an.

Whether by design or by accident, I-fu seems to have become primarily a pastor to the imperial court. After fifteen or twenty years on Mount Chung-nan, he set up residence in Ch'ang-an itself and then followed the emperor back and forth between that city and Lo-yang. P'u-chi also spent time in each of these cities, but the large number of his known successors suggests that he was the Northern School's chief instructor of spiritual trainees. P'u-chi also had the dubious distinction of being singled out for attack by Shen-hui, which may be taken as a testament to his greater public stature. P'u-chi's epitaphs contain almost fantastic claims of his significance, and his name seems to rival that of Shen-hsiu himself in certain documents dating from the 760s. Finally, although no epitaphs remain for any of I-fu's students, those that exist for P'u-chi's first- and second-generation successors contain enough doctrinal information to suggest not only that P'u-chi's lineage continued on but also that it was the most philosophically dynamic sublineage of Northern Ch'an.

Shen-hsiu is credited with having had as many as seventy students.[153] Although biographical information exists for many of these figures, I will discuss only four of his most important disciples: Hsiang-mo Tsang, Ching-hsien, I-fu, and P'u-chi.

2. Hsiang-mo Tsang

Hsiang-mo Tsang, or "Demon-subduing Tsang," is mentioned in the *SKSC* and various other sources.[154] On the basis of provenance rather than content, the most interesting of these sources come from Tibet, where he evidently achieved a degree of individual prominence.[155] His early studies in Buddhism included the recitation of the *Lotus Sūtra* and emphasis on the *Vinaya.*

At one point Tsang reached the very brink of a great enlightenment experience while either giving or, more likely, listening to lectures on the "theory of the Southern School" *(nan-tsung lun).* This theory, also mentioned in the biography of one of Shen-hsiu's lesser-known students, can only be understood as a reference to the Mādhyamika.[156] At any rate, this experience led Tsang to forgo scriptural studies and travel to all the holy sites of China. During the course of his travels Tsang met Shen-hsiu, whom he accepted as his teacher.

The first encounter between Hsiang-mo Tsang and Shen-hsiu is described in the *SKSC* as follows:

> [Shen]-hsiu asked: "Your name is 'Demon-subduer.' At my place there are no mountain or tree spirits, so will you turn around and become a demon [yourself]?"
>
> [Tsang] said: "[If] there is a Buddha, there are demons."
>
> [Shen]-hsiu said: "If you are a demon, then you must reside in an inconceivable realm."
>
> [Tsang] said: "This Buddha is also nonsubstantial. What is the inconceivable [realm of] being?"

The sophistication of this dialogue suggests that it was not actually uttered and recorded at the time of the encounter. Nevertheless, even if it is in fact a much later fabrication, the very existence of this dialogue indicates that interest in or respect for Shen-hsiu and the members of the Northern School was great enough that someone took the trouble to ornament Hsiang-mo Tsang's biography with the usual trappings of later Ch'an texts.[157]

3. Ching-hsien

Ching-hsien (660–723) is not mentioned in the *SKSC* or *CTL,* but his epitaph is still extant.[158] His first teacher, an otherwise unknown figure, supposedly told Ching-hsien that Shen-hsiu was the lineal transmitter of the Dharma-treasure, a status equivalent to that of a Buddha. Ching-hsien immediately went to study under Shen-hsiu at Yü-ch'üan ssu, where he was taught with "expedient means" *(fang-pien)* and achieved a first taste of enlightenment that was like an instantaneous flood of cleansing light. Thereafter he lived alone amidst wolves, tigers, poisons, and pestilence on a mountain near Pa-hsia (Hupeh), the very famous and beautiful narrows along the Yangtze. After at least a summer of meditation, Ching-hsien's enlightenment became great and perfect. When he conveyed this new development to Shen-hsiu, the latter happily "conferred the transmission of the treasure-store" upon him *(fu pao-ts'ang chuan),* so that the succession of the lamp would not be broken.

It is unclear whether Ching-hsien accompanied Shen-hsiu to Lo-yang in 701, but some five years or so later he was ordained at court at the behest of Emperor Chung-tsung. He may have been one of the fourteen students of Shen-hsiu and Lao-an who received official ordination in 706.[159] Sometime between 716 and 723 he had an encounter with the esoteric Buddhist master and translator Śubhākarasiṁha. The text of this encounter, in which Ching-hsien is introduced as a resident of Hui-shan ssu on Mount Sung, is still extant. Ching-hsien died in 723 at Hui-shan ssu. The names of four of his students are known, but their biographies are obscure.[160]

4. I-fu

I-fu (661–736)[161] practiced the recitation of the *Lotus, Vimalakīrti,* and other standard Mahāyāna texts while still a boy. At some point he went to Fu-hsien ssu in Lo-yang, where he studied under Dharma Master Fei. This monk is probably identical to the Tu Fei who compiled the *CFPC.* (See Chapter IV, Section 10 of this part.) Probably at Fei's instigation, I-fu then went to study under Fa-ju, but was disappointed to discover that the noted Ch'an teacher had just passed away. (I-fu's birthplace and first place of scriptural study both appear prominently in Fa-ju's biography.[162])

After taking the full precepts in the first half of the year 690, I-fu traveled to Shen-hsiu's center in Ching-chou. Shen-hsiu taught I-fu according to the latter's own dispositional needs, causing his defilements to disperse and his thoughts to become concentrated; training him in the basics of meditation;[163] and impressing upon him the hollowness of worldly success or failure. I-fu responded by seeking the great goal of enlightenment with unflagging zeal. He maintained his efforts for ten years without cease—but also without achieving the ultimate success.

I-fu accompanied Shen-hsiu to court in 701 and acted as personal attendant during his teacher's final illness at T'ien-kung ssu. I-fu's enlightenment must have occurred during this time, for we are told of a "secret transmission" that occurred before Shen-hsiu's death. As mentioned earlier, I-fu stayed for a time on Mount Sung but then moved to

Hua-kan ssu on Mount Chung-nan. He lived in the Dharma hall of that monastery,[164] where he was visited by a great number of people—sincere aspirants, recluses, nobles, and literati—some for spiritual and others for worldly benefit.

In 722 I-fu moved at popular request to Tz'u-en ssu in Ch'ang-an, but three years later he accompanied Emperor Hsuan-tsung back to Lo-yang, where he stayed at Fu-hsien ssu. In 727 he returned to Ch'ang-an, only to go by imperial order to Lo-yang once again in 733. On this occasion he stayed at Nan lung-hua ssu. I-fu's health began to deteriorate in the fall of 735, and he died in the summer of the following year. At least one of I-fu's disciples may have been a prominent figure in the religious world of the 760s, but no biographical information is available.[165]

5. *P'u-chi*

P'u-chi (651–739) was the most important of Shen-hsiu's successors and perhaps the most provocative figure in Northern Ch'an history. For much of his later career he shared the limelight with Lao-an, Ching-hsien, and I-fu. That P'u-chi survived these other figures must have helped to assure his ultimate place in history; more important, he taught so many students that his own following assumed a semi-independent status in some late eighth-century descriptions of Ch'an lineages.[166]

Like his associates in the Northern School, P'u-chi referred to himself—or allowed himself to be referred to publicly—as the seventh-generation representative of the Ch'an tradition. He did not stop there, however. The following passages from P'u-chi's epitaphs indicate the full extent of his claim to individual religious authority:

> Only Heaven is great, and Yao alone modeled himself on this; only the Buddha is sagely, and the Ch'an [School] alone succeeds to this. Therefore, the five suns of the transmission in India in the West illuminated the ancient day; the seven patriarchs of the transmission of the lamp in China in the East are refulgent upon the imperial weal. [The memory of] our Seventh Patriarch and National Teacher to three courts, Preceptor Ta-chao (the "Greatly Illuminating," i.e., P'u-chi) . . . has led the emperor to bequeath a posthumous title.[167]

> The great master of the four seas—this is an appellation of our Sagely Literate and Divinely Martial Emperor [Hsuan-tsung] of the K'ai-yuan [Period]. He who has entered into the wisdom of buddhahood and gloriously become the lord of the myriad dharmas—this is an appellation of the seventh generation of our Ch'an School *(ch'an-men),* Preceptor Ta-chao.[168]

This hyperbole indicates that P'u-chi politicized the originally religious rationale for his own status in order to achieve the highest possible measure of acclaim for himself and the Ch'an School. In comparing himself (or in being compared, since P'u-chi may have inspired but obviously did not write his own epitaphs) to the Chinese emperor, P'u-chi may have accurately captured the flavor and extent of early Northern School prominence and success. Nevertheless, he also ensured the school's eventual demise by attaching its fortunes so closely to the imperial court.

Not only was Emperor Hsuan-tsung not personally disposed to Buddhism, but the An Lu-shan rebellion that occurred at the end of his reign signaled a change in the process by which Chinese Buddhist schools developed and achieved prominence.[169] Although imperial support was by no means completely irrelevant after the debacle of 755, the very success of the Southern School of Ch'an signifies the radically increased importance of tendencies that can only be termed populist. None of these populist tendencies, which are represented most clearly in the legendary image of Hui-neng, can be detected in P'u-chi's biography.[170]

Just as with Hung-jen and I-fu, P'u-chi's secular family had a tradition of eremitism. P'u-chi himself is described in the usual fashion as having great innate ability and zeal in his studies of traditional Chinese subjects. His Buddhist studies began at Ta-liang (Shen-hsiu's native place), with special attention to the *Lotus Sūtra,* Yogācāra theories, and the *Awakening of Faith* and other treatises. Later he took the precepts under Preceptor Tuan of Lo-yang, after which he studied the *Vinaya* under Preceptor Ching of Nan-ch'üan (Kuei-ch'ih hsien, Anhwei). P'u-chi's full ordination occurred in 688 at the age of thirty-eight. The Preceptor Ching who performed the ceremony was probably Heng-ching (634–712), a monk with *Vinaya* and T'ien-t'ai School affiliations.[171]

After deciding to undertake the study of meditation and practicing for a time on his own, P'u-chi sought out Fa-ju of Shao-lin ssu. When he found that Fa-ju had already died, P'u-chi went the next day to Shen-hsiu of Yü-ch'üan ssu. Several metaphors are used to describe P'u-chi's ability and speed of progress, such as the smooth gait of a thoroughbred and the easy cultivation of good land. "When the precious mirror is polished, it reflects (*ch'eng,* lit., "offers") the myriad images; when the pearl clarifies the water, visibility [extends to a depth of] a hundred rods." Later on in the epitaph we find the following passage:

> When [P'u-chi] wanted transmission of the essentials of the teaching before he had recited the precept sūtras, Ta-t'ung (= Shen-hsiu) made him discard his personal views with general examples and abuse.[172]

P'u-chi then spent five years studying under Shen-hsiu, during which time he was made to concentrate first on the *Ssu-i ching (Sūtra of [the God] Ssu-i)* and then on the *Laṇkāvatāra.* After an additional two years as Shen-hsiu's messenger, in or around 696 he went to reside at

Mount Sung. P'u-chi's official ordination occurred sometime during the years 701–5, after which he was registered at Sung-yueh ssu on Mount Sung.

After Shen-hsiu's death, P'u-chi was offered an official appointment as the leader of Shen-hsiu's disciples. News of this imperial nomination was conveyed to P'u-chi by an official named Wu P'ing-i, who was later to become an object of Shen-hui's criticism.[173] P'u-chi supposedly declined the position (the long statement on the matter attributed to him is of some doctrinal interest), but the large number of students he later attracted implies that he eventually assumed the position in fact, if not necessarily in name.

In 725 P'u-chi took up residence at Ching-ai ssu in Lo-yang. At this time both I-fu and Emperor Hsuan-tsung were also present in the same city. Two years later the emperor returned to Ch'ang-an, accompanied by I-fu. P'u-chi was installed at the Hsing-t'ang ssu in Lo-yang at this time so that the "cloud of the Dharma would rain everywhere"—or at least in both Chinese capitals. In 735 P'u-chi traveled to Ch'ang-an, where he ministered to great numbers of the nobility and presumably visited I-fu in his final hours. In 739 we find P'u-chi back at the Hsing-t'ang ssu in Lo-yang, where he spent the last days of his own life.

P'u-chi's death was followed by the appropriate bequests and other observances. For our purposes, the most interesting event was the behavior of P'u-chi's lay supporter P'ei K'uan, who joined the funeral procession in robes associated with a three-year mourning period and walked among P'u-chi's disciples. The *SKSC* says that P'ei K'uan's behavior was roundly criticized by his peers as being too extreme and marked the beginning of his fall from official favor. Tsan-ning, the compiler of the *SKSC,* defends P'ei K'uan's actions by pointing out that he was extremely close to P'u-chi and only walked barefoot, not going so far as to dishevel his hair. Such behavior may well have been commonplace during the reigns of Empress Wu and the pious Emperor Chung-tsung, but in the middle of Hsuan-tsung's reign the attitude of the court toward Buddhism had become noticeably cooler.[174]

6. P'u-chi's Disciples

P'u-chi taught an exceptionally large number of disciples during the more than three decades of his teaching career. One source written in the year 772 claims that his followers numbered as many as ten thousand, of which sixty-three were major disciples who had "ascended into the hall" to hear the master's teachings, while one had achieved a spontaneous and complete mastery of True Wisdom.[175] Information survives for roughly a third of these major disciples, although in some cases only the individual's name and a few stereotyped details are known. The following is a summary of some of the more interesting and informative biographies:

1. Hung-cheng: This monk is the one disciple of P'u-chi's supposed to have achieved perfect control of religious wisdom *(tzu-tsai chih)* according to the document just cited. Another epitaph, this one written about 760, refers to Hung-cheng as the most prominent representative of the Northern School and to another monk, perhaps a student of I-fu's, as the representative of the "single fountainhead of the Northern School." Hung-cheng is also mentioned in several other sources, but the only biographical detail known about him is his monastery of residence: Sheng-shan ssu in Lo-yang. Although the epitaphs for two of his students are still extant, unfortunately no epitaph exists for him. The fact that he is not mentioned in P'u-chi's epitaph is curious.[176]

2. I-hsing (685–727): I-hsing was clearly one of the most important monks of the entire T'ang Dynasty. He began his Buddhist career as a student of P'u-chi's, also studied the *Vinaya* and T'ien-t'ai doctrine, and became best known for his participation in the translation of various esoteric Buddhist scriptures. His twenty-fascicle commentary on the *Vairocana Sūtra* is one of the most important texts of the East Asian esoteric tradition. Nevertheless, it is I-hsing's scientific genius that has captured the greatest modern attention and that has led to his elevation to the status of popular hero by the leaders of the modern Chinese government. Briefly, he was responsible not only for the compilation of new Chinese calendars based upon the accurate observation and understanding of astronomical phenomena, but also for the construction of an armillary sphere that included within its workings the mechanical foundation of the modern clock.[177]

3. Ling-cho (691–746): This man was no doubt typical of many who became known as P'u-chi's students. A mature *Vinaya* master and *Nirvāṇa Sūtra* exponent, he only encountered the teachings of the great Ch'an master in the last fifteen years of his own life, or sometime after 730. He was active thereafter in propagating the teaching of Ch'an from his residence in Ch'ang-an, where he died at a part of Ta-an-kuo ssu named Shih-leng-ch'ieh-ching yuan, or "Chapel of the Stone-[engraved] *Laṇkāvatāra Sūtra*." We will see later that Ching-chueh, the author of the *LCSTC,* resided at the same monastery, although there is no evidence linking the two men. Ling-cho had at least four disciples, none of whom is mentioned in other sources.[178]

4. Ming-ts'an: This man's biography is important for several reasons: He is remembered as the author of a short piece recorded at the end of the *CTL;* he was perhaps the earliest and certainly the most important of the Northern School's representatives at Mount Heng or Nan-yueh in the

far South; and he had a unique and unconventional style of behavior that engendered a reputation similar to that of the legendary Pao-chih of the Liang.[179]

After becoming a mendicant and mastering the teachings of P'u-chi, his first and only teacher, Ming-ts'an then repaired to Nan-yueh. He became known as Lan Ts'an, or "Lazy Ts'an," because of his refusal to participate in monastic affairs. He was also summoned occasionally as "Leftovers" (this was also a pun on his name) because of his habit of eating food remaining after the other monks had finished. Nevertheless, in spite of his unusual ways, on the rare occasions when Ming-ts'an chose to speak, his utterances were always in complete accord with the principles of Buddhism. In the same vein, the *SKSC* goes on, his actions were not incorrect but merely incomprehensible to the unenlightened observer.

In 742, or three years after P'u-chi's death, a great change took place in Ming-ts'an's life. For reasons that are now unknown, he proceeded to Nan-yueh ssu and assumed monastic duties—supposedly operating the entire monastery during the day and staying with the cattle at night. He continued this behavior for twenty years without ever tiring, sometimes amazing his observers by moving a giant rock with a light touch of the foot or dispersing a pride of tigers with nothing more than a riding crop. Such feats were witnessed by a personage of some importance in the civil realm, Li Mi (722–89), whose appointment as prime minister during the reign of Emperor Su-tsung (r. 756–62) Ming-ts'an is supposed to have made possible through prescient augury and advice.[180]

Ming-ts'an's status in and around Nan-yueh is corroborated in other sources.[181] In considering the details of his biography, one cannot help but wonder whether the radical transformation in his behavior in 742 might not represent a Northern School victory in some sort of power struggle on Mount Heng. According to this hypothesis, Ming-ts'an's early behavior was designed to show his disrespect for the current leadership. As I shall remark in the next section, the number of Northern School figures associated with this important outpost in the Southeast grew in the wake of Ming-ts'an's example.

5. Tao-hsuan (702–60): This monk is often mentioned in modern studies because of his mission to Japan and his status as a second-generation predecessor to Saichō, the founder of the Japanese Tendai School.[182]

7. Comments on P'u-chi's Later Successors

Little would be gained from including biographical details for any of P'u-chi's second- and third-generation successors.[183] Instead, I will limit myself to the following points concerning the Northern School's longevity, strength, demography, and creative energy.

First, rather than fading away after the commencement of Shen-hui's attack on it in 730, the Northern School actually grew in membership throughout the eighth century and continued, as far as we know, until the beginning of the tenth century. This constitutes a history of over 150 years from the date of P'u-chi's death, or fully 275 years from Tao-hsin's entrance into Huang-mei. Since the several generations of Shen-hsiu's disciples include at least 125 individuals whose names are known,[184] the Northern School was clearly not short-lived, as most people have thought.

Second, in purely numerical terms the peak of Northern School strength occurred during the second half of the eighth century, probably during the 770s. No doubt the great numbers who studied Northern School doctrines and meditation techniques were a result of the momentum established during Shen-hsiu's productive career, but the school was still quite strong long after that master's death. The activities of Northern School monks in Tun-huang and Tibet, to be discussed briefly in the next section, indicate that the School was still strong enough to be chosen by the political authorities as the representative of the Chinese religious position in a strategically important set of outlying regions.

Third, although the major strongholds of the Northern School were in and near Ch'ang-an and Lo-yang, its strength in the South increased as time went on. Of P'u-chi's immediate disciples, only Ming-ts'an, of Nan-yueh, and Tao-hsuan, a temporary resident of Wa-kuan ssu in Chin-ling, were active in the South. In the next generation fully nine out of fourteen monks for whom information is available were associated with Nan-yueh and other southern locations.[185] Thus the Northern School was not entirely absent from the area of south-central China generally considered to be the site of Ch'an's most typical and creative developments. Actually, this spread of Northern School activities should not be viewed as a new development, since the original source of the school's religious energy was its period of incubation and growth in Huang-mei and Ching-chou.

Fourth, whereas the numerical strength of the Northern School is relatively easy to chart, measurement of its creative energy is more difficult. The existing evidence is inconclusive, or even self-contradictory. The remaining epitaphs that exist for monks who died in the late eighth century and beyond do not impart any sense of great religious ferment, although they do occasionally indicate a change in the style of Ch'an practice and religious dialogue. (See Chapter IV, Sections 14 and 15.) On the other hand, materials deriving from the expansion into Tibet imply that some doctrinal development was taking place.

However, another indicator of an entirely different sort does exist—the fact that so much material about the Northern School found its way into the *SKSC* and *CTL*. Much of this material is probably fabricated, and the remainder contains some chronologically impossible assertions—the most frequent being the statements that men of the late eighth and early ninth centuries studied under Shen-hsiu and P'u-chi. This material is not particularly inspiring, for the most part, but the very fact that it exists is extremely important.

Although broad generalizations are always dangerous, it would appear that, excluding comparisons with Hui-neng, all references to Shen-hsiu in Ch'an literature are positive. Clearly, some group of later successors to Shen-hsiu and P'u-chi remembered them with great reverence and backed the inclusion of Northern School-related material in Sung Dynasty texts. If Shen-hui's campaign and the *Platform Sūtra* had the net effect of tarnishing the Northern School's image, as I believe they did, then the persistent occurrence of such Northern School material in the face of that negative influence becomes even more significant.

8. The Northern School in Tibet

One of the most exciting events connected with the Northern School is the encounter that took place during the next-to-last decade of the eighth century at Bsam-yas Monastery near Lhasa, Tibet. The chief protagonists in this encounter, which seems to have been an extended series of debates, were Kamalaśīla and Mo-ho-yen (Mahāyāna). The former was an Indian monk who defended the "gradual teaching" on the basis of traditional Indian Buddhist exegetics, the latter a Chinese monk who advocated the "sudden teaching" of Ch'an. Their debates have attracted a great deal of scholarly interest, and the entire question of Ch'an activity in Tibet and other nearby regions has become one of the most interesting and promising areas of modern Buddhist studies.[186]

The historical outline of the spread of Ch'an into Tibet is still far from clear. The first contact between the Tibetans and the fledgling Chinese religious movement occurred in 751 or shortly thereafter, when the ruler of Tibet sent a delegation off to China in search of the Dharma. This delegation met and received instruction from the Korean preceptor Kim (Chin in Chinese) or, to use his Chinese religious name, Wu-hsiang of I-chou (Ch'eng-tu, Szechwan). The Tibetan party also received three Chinese texts from Kim before returning to their homeland.

When this delegation returned to Tibet in 759, the political situation there had changed. Power had shifted temporarily to a faction that supported the native Bön religion and opposed Buddhism. The proscription of Buddhism was lifted in 761, at which time the Chinese leader of the earlier expedition became abbot of Bsam-yas Monastery, where he translated and no doubt taught on the basis of Preceptor Kim's sayings.

In 763 a Tibetan minister of the pro-Buddhist emperor Khri-sron-lde-btsan went to China, this time studying under a Chinese Ch'an master in I-chou named Wu-chu. The details of the encounter between these two men are unknown; indeed, the Tibetan records mention only the name of the already deceased preceptor Kim in this regard. Nevertheless, the frequent mention of Wu-chu's name and citation of his sayings in early Tibetan religious literature, not to mention the existence of a Tibetan translation of the *LTFPC,* prove that the Pao-t'ang School was very effectively and energetically represented in contemporary missionary activities. In fact, some of the basic assertions made by the Pao-t'ang School about its own background may have been influenced by the prospect of proselytizing in Tibet.[187]

The transmission of Ch'an to Tibet that is of greatest interest here occurred after the Tibetan takeover of Sha-chou (Tun-huang), which probably took place in 781. Shortly after this temporary extension of Tibetan civil power toward China, the monk Mo-ho-yen traveled on invitation from the Tibetan emperor from Sha-chou to Lhasa. Mo-ho-yen's religious background is subject to some doubt. Even though he is routinely described with reference to Preceptor Kim, Wu-chu, and other figures quite outside his genealogy, his only known teachers were Northern School figures.[188]

Mo-ho-yen apparently returned to Sha-chou after the debates mentioned earlier, sometime during the 790s. According to Tibetan sources of the eleventh century he left in utter defeat at the hands of his Indian counterpart, but Tun-huang manuscripts in both Chinese and Tibetan indicate a more complex situation. Rather than defeat and the immediate expulsion of Chinese Buddhism from Tibetan soil, Mo-ho-yen's mission to Tibet left behind a continuing legacy of interest in Chinese-style approaches to religious practice. Since Northern School and other early Ch'an texts were translated into Uighur, Hsi-hsia, and presumably other Central Asian languages, we may infer that Chinese political interests—as well as pure religious zeal—were fueling the dissemination of Ch'an across vast areas of Asia.

CHAPTER IV

The Development of the "Transmission of the Lamp" Histories

1. Legend and Encounter Dialogue in Ch'an Literature

The Introduction to this study included a brief comment on the differing values of history and legend in the study of Chinese Ch'an. Up to this point, however, we have been concerned almost entirely with history. Having finished our historical narrative, we may now turn to the development of the "transmission of the lamp" theory and the appearance of the texts in which it first appears.

In many ways, the most significant feature of the Northern School phase of early Ch'an history is not the set of achievements of individual masters, but the veritable flood of literature intended to explain the origins and meaning of the new religious message. Since it was during the Northern School's heyday that Ch'an first achieved a sense of its own identity as a single, unified entity within the framework of Chinese Buddhism, we need to learn as much as possible about both the origins and the implications of the "transmission of the lamp" theory, which constitutes the school's statement of its own history.

Rather than begin with the various sources of this theory in Indian and Chinese Buddhist literature, we can achieve greater focus by first outlining the general place of the transmission texts within the greater context of Ch'an literature. These texts constitute only one of three distinct major genre of that massive body of literature, the other two being the "recorded sayings" *(yü-lu)* texts and the "public case" *(kung-an)* anthologies.[189]

Although not necessarily the oldest genre, the "recorded sayings" are the most fundamental of the three in that they are straightforwardly devoted to the spoken and literary output of individual Ch'an masters. Although they often contain poetry, short essays, and details about the lives of their subjects, recorded sayings texts are primarily devoted to the transcription of oral exchanges between masters and disciples. These exchanges include both verbal and nonverbal forms of communication—question and answer, silence, shouting, oral vilification, physical abuse, laughter, gesturing, and so on. Even though the reportage fails to make each and every vignette come completely alive, the "encounter dialogue"[190] recorded in these texts was clearly a unique and spirited form of communication aimed at the ultimate achievement of the religious quest, the realization of enlightenment. The master poses a question or paradox and the students struggle to understand it. Or, just as often, the students state the questions and the master tries to force them beyond the limitations of their own misconceptions. Occasionally an exegete or a devotee of Pure Land practices or scriptural recitation will appear to serve as a foil for the iconoclastic arguments of the Ch'an master, but there are also occasions when the master is surprised by an unexpectedly brilliant parry and thrust from a previously unnoticed student or visitor.

The "public case" anthologies are also composed primarily of encounter dialogue, but the format differs in that these texts contain short selections of encounter dialogue supplemented with commentary by one or more later masters. This different format reveals the extent to which the spontaneous examples of the Ch'an masters of the T'ang and Five Dynasties periods had been transformed into classical precedents to be studied and emulated in a ritualized process of meditation and religious inquiry. The ultimate aim of these anthologies, of course, was to provide a set of subjects for meditation that would enable the student to achieve his own complete self-realization. But notice what was required: At a time when traditional Buddhist education was being continually undercut by the relative decline of the religion in China, Ch'an masters composed anthologies of forty-eight or a hundred or more subjects of meditation that could only be understood by those conversant with conventional Buddhist concepts—and, even more specifically, with the use of those concepts within the Ch'an tradition. Although ultimately the student had to transcend conceptualized expressions of Buddhism in order to achieve the supreme goal, he first had to understand those expressions before being able to achieve that transcendent experience. The public case anthologies were, in a word, pedagogic tools of the most basic order.[191]

2. The Structure and Function of the "Transmission of the Lamp" Texts

Just as with the "recorded sayings" texts and "public case" anthologies, the basic ingredient of the "transmission of the lamp" texts or transmission histories is the transcription of encounter dialogue. Here, however, the overall framework in which such transcription appears is all-important. Rather than being the sum of all the known sermons, dialogues, and verses, etc., of a single master, or a selection of short individual encounters drawn from the entire lore of such dialogues, the transmission histories include the most representative teachings of all the recognized Ch'an masters known at the time. Since each master is considered within the context of his own religious generation, the result is a complex genealogical tree that is heavily annotated with encounter dialogue.

The greatest of all these works, the *Ching-te ch'üan-teng lu (CTL),* devotes an entry to the lives and teachings of each of the following overlapping groups of individuals:

1. Seven Buddhas of the past, culminating in Śākyamuni
2. Twenty-eight Indian Patriarchs, beginning with Śākyamuni and ending with Bodhidharma (These two men receive only one entry apiece, of course.)
3. Six Chinese Patriarchs, from Bodhidharma to Hui-neng
4. Numerous subsequent Chinese masters descended from Hui-neng and other early figures, listed according to religious generation and extending to the period just before the compilation of the *CTL*[192]

Where the *HKSC* and other works of the "biographies of eminent monks" genre strive to embrace the entire panorama of Buddhist activity by including translators, exegetes, meditators, thaumaturges, and so on, the *CTL* and other similar texts limit themselves to cataloguing all the various expressions of the one Ultimate Truth of Buddhism. The followers of Ch'an were certainly not unaware of the activities of translation and exegesis, sūtra recitation, and thaumaturgy, but to them only those who experienced transmission of the true teachings and enlightenment to the "Mind Nature" actually participated in the Buddhist religion per se.

The transmission histories, like all other Ch'an works, were intended to function as catalysts for the enlightenment of the readers by exposing them to examples of true religiosity and perfected behavior. In addition to this lofty goal, these texts had two other purposes of a propagandistic and quasi-historical nature: (1) to glorify the sages of the past and thereby legitimize the status of their living disciples and (2) to rationalize the origins and existence of the Ch'an School itself. The latter is of greater importance here, since one of the tasks undertaken by the Northern School was to establish Ch'an as a legitimate—in its own eyes, *the* legitimate—school of Chinese Buddhism.

This task was rendered difficult by the fact that Ch'an lacked any single underlying scriptural tradition from which it could trace its descent. Unlike the T'ien-t'ai School, for example, which used the *Lotus Sūtra,* or the Pure Land School, which revered the three Pure Land scriptures, the Ch'an School did not have any specific canon that might provide the answers to its particular religious dilemmas. On the contrary, the very existence of Ch'an was based on a reaction against the excessive reliance on scriptural study, and the school seems to have purposely avoided identification with any specific scriptural tradition. Instead, Ch'an presented itself as a "separate transmission outside the teachings" and cautioned its followers "Do not rely on words!" True, as a meditation school, Ch'an grew out of centuries of Chinese Buddhist religious practice, but as a school, nonetheless, it had to establish its own identity separate from—and yet somehow superior, in its own terms, to—the other Chinese Schools. It did this by formulating the "transmission of the lamp" theory.

3. The Theoretical Basis of the "Transmission of the Lamp" Texts

Either in spite of or because of the effort required to overcome the problems just mentioned, the Ch'an School achieved an astonishing degree of success in carving out its own unique niche within Chinese Buddhism. The primary means by which Ch'an succeeded in this task was the creation of a long series of transmission texts, beginning with the Northern School works of the early eighth century and culminating, but not ending, with the *CTL* at the beginning of the eleventh. These texts are generally constructed of the following four elements:

1. The ineffable teaching: Ch'an is more emphatic than any other Buddhist School in its position that the ultimate goal of religious practice cannot be understood with words. Elsewhere this ineffability is taken to mean that the words of the scriptures point at some higher, more abstract truth, but in Ch'an those very words are perceived as impediments to understanding. At the very least, one must not cling to the doctrinal formulations of the sūtras or turn them into unalterable dogma. Although Ch'an texts would deny its existence as a cognitively conceivable entity, they all point to some central teaching, some Ultimate Truth to which each of the masters of Ch'an become enlightened one after another.

2. The enlightened master: A buddha, patriarch, or Ch'an master is someone who has achieved the experience of enlightenment, someone who completely and perfectly embodies the ineffable truth. Because of his status as the embodiment of ultimate reality, his every action and word becomes the expression of that reality. Each and every moment of his life is a simple and direct statement of the highest Buddhist doctrine, each pronouncement the perfect response of enlightenment to a specific situation. Thus the method by which he teaches is not the logical exposi-

tion of Buddhist doctrine, but the perfect and immediate response to the needs of his students—needs that are often so well hidden by their preoccupation with traditional Buddhist doctrines that he must resort to extraordinary methods of instruction. In addition, because of his wisdom and ability as a teacher, the enlightened master is the administrative head of his own religious community and even the guardian of Buddhism during his lifetime.

3. The gifted successor(s): Although each master may have many students, only one, or perhaps a few, has a special aptitude for his teachings. The gifted successor's biography, to the extent that it is given, is made to indicate his instinctual affinity for the ineffable truth. He may be uninterested in the usual children's games and given to strange pronouncements and quiet meditation as a youth. He may be totally uninterested in scriptural study or, alternatively, a brilliant student who eventually burns his books and turns to meditation. The decision to strive for enlightenment, once made, is pursued with uncommon zeal. He may encounter incredible obstacles and be on the very point of giving up his quest entirely, but eventually he achieves the ultimate goal and becomes an enlightened master in his own right. Even so, the first inspiration does not mean that all becomes easy for him, for the complete internalization of the truth often takes years of additional effort.

4. The succession of enlightened masters: As each individual successor achieves his own realization of perfection, his master grants him "authorization" or "certification" (*yin-k'o,* or *inka* in Japanese). This constitutes permission to embark on an independent teaching career. Each student who receives such authorization and embarks on a teaching career of his own immediately assumes the role of successor and community leader within the framework of his own activities. Since each generation of students is thus related through religious genealogy to those preceding and following it, the result is an unbroken chain of enlightened masters and their communities of students beginning with Śākyamuni and the other Buddhas of the past and extending down to the present.

4. The Origin of the Transmission Theory

Now that we have taken a brief look at the "transmission of the lamp" theory as it existed at the beginning of the eleventh century, let us turn to the relevant antecedents to this theory in Indian and Chinese Buddhist literature. Obviously, space does not permit a full treatment of this subject here; the comments pertaining to Indian Buddhism will be especially brief.

Not surprisingly, the ideal image of the enlightened master and the prototype of the religious succession were derived from the biography of the historical Buddha. The story of his life was well known to Chinese Buddhists and formed the basis for numerous hagiographical embellishments found within the epitaphs and biographical statements for members of the Ch'an School. (See, for example, the account of Tao-hsin's death given in Chapter II, Section 2.) Therefore, it would not be unreasonable to suppose that events in the Buddha's legendary biography were used as justifications for the validity of the transmission theory. Actually, in some ways just the opposite seems to have been the case, since the Chinese theory was designed to overcome the influence of the orthodox Indian Buddhist tradition.

Many of the same elements used in the creation of this important theory of Chinese Ch'an were present during the formative years of primitive Indian Buddhism, but generally with a distinctly different cast. First, the Buddha's ultimate teaching was certainly considered ineffable. Note, for example, his refusal to define the state of nirvāṇa or to discuss issues such as the existence or nonexistence of the enlightened sage after death (the so-called *avyākṛta* issues).[193] Second, the sermons of the Buddha that were so diligently preserved through memorization and oral repetition might be considered his "recorded sayings," as they were in later Ch'an. Nevertheless, the type of theoretical analysis to which these sermons were subjected was radically different from the methodology of Chinese Ch'an. The Buddha's personal example was an extremely important factor in the success of his order, but there is little indication that he taught with the same demonstrative repartee used by the Ch'an masters.

In addition, the historical Buddha's refusal to select a successor to assume his position after his own passing was one of the most important determinants of the ultimate course of Indian Buddhism.[194] This refusal is thought to have enhanced Buddhism's ability to expand beyond the confines of a single religious community; in any case, the role of administrative and spiritual figurehead that the Buddha specifically refused to fill was essentially identical to the role of the patriarch or Ch'an master in later Chinese Buddhism.

The Mahāyāna reaction against early Buddhist sectarianism included certain attitudes similar to those expressed in the transmission theory. Much as exegetes and rigid theoreticians are mocked in Ch'an texts, Ānanda was caricatured within the *Perfection of Wisdom* literature and other scriptures as capable of rote memorization but no real understanding. Interestingly, some of the early versions of the transmission idea begin with similar descriptions of Ānanda's role and personality.

The emphasis on the importance of *prajñā* in the Mahāyāna has frequently been correlated, quite legitimately, with the type of understanding sought in Ch'an.[195] It can also be argued that the grandiose metaphysical imagery of the Mahāyāna scriptures made the goal of enlightenment appear substantially less rationalistic and more profound —if more distant—than in Hīnayāna texts. Finally, the redefinition of the Buddha's identity as one in a long series of perfectly enlightened sages opened the door to the Ch'an idea of a succession of equally qualified masters.

The most important factor in the development of the transmission of the lamp theory, however, was equally operant in both Hīnayāna and Mahāyāna Buddhism: the passage of time. As every student of Buddhism knows, the more time elapsed after the death of the Buddha, the more uncertain his followers became about whether they had access to the true, unalloyed teachings. In the last analysis, the councils and schisms that occurred were all based on the problem of maintaining an understanding and practice of Buddhism that was true to the teachings of the religion's founder. The occasional persecution of Buddhism by unsympathetic potentates made the situation even worse: Not only anxious about whether their understanding was accurate and complete, the followers of Buddhism were struck as well with a kind of crisis consciousness. The fear of repeated persecution induced them to take special steps to preserve the Dharma, including the first written transcription of the scriptures in Sri Lanka and the compilation of meditation sūtras in Kashmir.[196]

5. The Transmission Theory in Early Chinese Buddhism

Although the transmission theory had a number of antecedents in Indian Buddhism, only those known to the Chinese tradition will be discussed here. The most elementary prototypes of the theory occur in lists of orthodox successions from the Buddha found in *Vinaya* and meditation texts.

The motive for the Chinese *Vinaya* lists was clearly to maintain authenticity of textual reproduction within a tradition that was originally oral, not written. Two such lists exist, containing the names of twenty-seven and twenty-four men, respectively, who either "heard" *(wen)* or "transmitted" *(fu)* the *Vinaya.* With the exception of the first figure listed, Upāli, who was chosen to recite the Buddha's pronouncements on the *Vinaya* at the First Council, the two lists are completely different. These lineages, by the way, were probably recorded not for their general interest, but because they defined the religious heritage of the translators of the texts in question.[197]

The earliest comparable lists from the meditation tradition are found in Seng-yu's (438–518) *Ch'u san-tsang chi chi (Collection of Notes* [*Concerning the*] *Translation of the Tripiṭaka),* which was compiled in 515 and revised shortly thereafter. This text contains two lists (or two variants of the same list) of Sarvāstivādin masters beginning with the Buddha and ending with the names of several important Kashmiri figures. These lists include either fifty-three or fifty-four names, each of which is given a number and, generally, either the title *bodhisattva* or *arhat* (for example, "Arhat Kumārajīva, number twelve" or "Dharmatrāta Bodhisattva, number fifty-three"). The portions of these two lists that are relevant to our discussion are as follows:

Mahākāśyapa	—
Ānanda	Ānanda
Madhyāntika	Madhyāntika
Śaṇavāsa	Śaṇavāsa
Upagupta	Upagupta
* * *	* * *
Prajñātāra (?)	Prajñātāra
Puṇyatāra	Buddhasena
Buddhasena	Dharmatrāta
Dharmatrāta	* * *[198]

The first four or five names on these lists (before the three asterisks, which mark the omission of names irrelevant to our discussion) are identical to those found in the *A-yü wang chuan* or *(Legend of Emperor Aśoka).* Excerpts of this account are found in several other early works included in the Chinese canon. The last three or four names imply that these lists were originally intended to describe the religious heritage of Buddhabhadra, a student of Buddhasena known as both a meditation master and translator.[199] Thus they are obviously related to the *Ta-mo-to-lo ch'an ching (Meditation Sūtra of Dharmatrāta)* and its prefaces.

6. The Ta-mo-to-lo ch'an ching (Meditation Sūtra of Dharmatrāta) *and Its Prefaces*

Buddhabhadra's *Ta-mo-to-lo ch'an ching* and its prefaces by Hui-yuan and Hui-kuan constitute a very important source for the development of the Ch'an transmission theory. These documents give us an impression of Buddhabhadra's conception of his own religious background that is more clear than the lists just mentioned. In addition, the contents of this sūtra and its prefaces were explicitly mentioned by at least two major innovators of the Ch'an tradition.[200] One of the reasons this sūtra and its prefaces were so utilized, no doubt, is that their description of the transmission of the Dharma is more profound than the description in the *A-yü wang chuan,* where religious transmission is described very simply and on a purely verbal level. In addition, the *Ta-mo-to-lo ch'an ching* is, as its title indicates, a meditation sūtra.

The sūtra and its prefaces include the following lists of names, which are obviously truncated versions of the Sarvāstivādin lists given earlier:

Sūtra	*Hui-yuan*	*Hui-kuan*
Mahākāśyapa	———	———
Ānanda	Ānanda	Ānanda
Madhyāntika	Madhyāntika	Madhyāntika
Śāṇavāsa	Śāṇavāsa	Śāṇavāsa
Upagupta	Upagupta	———
Vasumitra	(five schools of *Vinaya)*	Puṇyamitra
Saṁgharakṣa	Dharmatrāta and Buddhasena	Puṇyalāta (?)
Dharmatrāta		Dharmatrāta and Buddhasena
Puṇyamitra		Buddhabhadra[201]

The reader cannot fail to notice the many variations among these three lists and between these lists and those introduced earlier from the *Ch'u san-tsang chi-chi.* In addition, the contemporaries Dharmatrāta and Buddhasena are listed as if they were master and disciple in the *Ch'u san-tsang chi-chi* lists. The sheer number of these anomalies implies an inconsistency in Buddhabhadra's reportage of his own religious background. Perhaps the very notion of defining one's religious identity by a genealogy of masters was only beginning to emerge in Buddhabhadra's native Kashmir.

In spite of these inconsistencies, the motives within the Kashmiri tradition for producing the *Ta-mo-to-lo ch'an ching* and for devising such lineage descriptions were identical to the motives behind the development of the Ch'an lineage theory in China. Hui-yuan's preface reads:

> Ānanda received the complete [transmission of the Buddha's] oral teachings, but he always concealed this within his own mind from those who were not [fit to receive them] . . . Shortly after the *Tathāgata* entered into nirvāṇa, Ānanda transmitted [the teaching] to his fellow disciple Madhyāntika. Madhyāntika transmitted it to Śāṇavāsa . . . The achievement [of enlightenment by Ānanda, Madhyāntika, and Śāṇavāsa] transcended words and was not described in the sūtras, being [furthermore] not the least bit different from [that of the *Tathāgata*]. Afterward came Upagupta . . .
>
> From the time [of the five schools of *Vinaya* onward, everyone] worried about the ancient texts each time there was any worldly disturbance. Each of the schools' students included those who were [fit to transmit the teaching]. They were all fearful that the great Dharma might come to an end. How profound was the basis for their sorrow! Therefore, they each wrote meditation sūtras in order to promote the practice [of meditation]. . . .
>
> Further, [the sages of the five schools] were able to respond perfectly and

> without restriction to the [needs of the] times. They concealed their names and activities so that no one knew of them. Such persons [fit to transmit the teaching] cannot be defined by sectarian labels. Being undefinable by sectarian labels, neither do they produce any teaching outside [of the True Dharma]. . . .
>
> The present translation is derived from [the teachings of] Dharmatrāta and Buddhasena. These men were the paragons of the Western realm, the patriarchs of the meditation teaching.[202]

It is instructive to note the following aspects of Hui-yuan's explanation, some of which also apply to the later Ch'an theory of the transmission of the lamp: (1) the transmission of the true teachings of Buddhism occurred unbeknownst to the majority of the religion's followers and without any reference to its occurrence in any prior written record; (2) the true teaching that was transmitted was accessible to adherents of all schools of Buddhism, according to their own individual capacity; (3) the true sages of these schools all wrote meditation sūtras so that the teachings of Buddhism would survive any eventuality; and (4) the *Ta-mo-lo-to-lo ch'an ching* contained the accurate teachings of Buddhism because its author was a direct lineal descendant of the Buddha. Of course, a contradiction exists between the implicit assumption that the transmission transcended words and the assertion that the sūtra in question contained the true teachings of Buddhism.[203]

7. Other Evidence Related to the Provenance of the Transmission Theory

Ch'an was not the only school of Chinese Buddhism to include a statement of religious genealogy in its literature. The T'ien-t'ai School justifies its own version of the Buddhist teachings on the basis of two different definitions of religious transmission. In one version Hui-wen's mastery of the *Ta chih-tu lun* is presented as evidence of his status as a direct religious descendant of Nāgārjuna. In another version Hui-ssu and Chih-i are said to have been present in former lifetimes at the exposition of the *Lotus Sūtra,* thus giving them a direct connection to the Buddha himself.[204]

The best-known T'ien-t'ai reference to a lineage scheme—and the one that has generated the greatest interest in relation to the study of Ch'an—is that based on the *Fu fa-tsang yin-yuan chuan (History of the Transmission of the Dharma-store).* This text, which appeared in the latter half of the fifth century, lists twenty-three lineal successors from the Buddha to one Siṁha Bhikṣu, who died without religious issue at the hands of an anti-Buddhist monarch in Kashmir. Since the succession was thus cut off long before it reached China, the T'ien-t'ai School masters postulated the successions from Nāgārjuna and Śākyamuni just mentioned.[205] This reference to a lineal succession is a certification of the growing strength of the idea of religious genealogy at the end of the sixth century.

Since I have just mentioned the *Ta chih-tu lun,* it may be appropriate to consider the following passage:

> Although Ānanda was very gifted he was inclined to be a *śrāvaka,* only seeking his own emancipation. Therefore, [the Buddha] informed [Ānanda of his duties vis-à-vis the transmission] three times, so that the transmission would prevent Buddhism from ever coming to an end. [The Buddha said]: "You should teach a disciple. Your disciple should then teach another person, and so on, each teaching [the next]. This is like one lamp lighting other lamps, so that the light becomes greater and greater. Do not be the last person [in this succession], the one with no seed!"[206]

Although this passage does not refer explicitly to any ineffable teaching outside the scriptures, once again there is an obvious effort to remake Ānanda's image as the devoted but uncomprehending recorder of the Buddha's words. The metaphor of the lamp and related terms do occur frequently in the biographies of pre-Ch'an School meditation specialists in the *HKSC.* Not only are a number of monks described as having individually "transmitted the lamp" of their predecessor's teachings, but the following account also appears in the biography of the eccentric religieux Pao-chih:

> When he was about to die, [Pao-chih] lit a single lamp in order to depute [the responsibility for matters] after [his own death] to the official Wu Ch'ing. When [Wu] Ch'ing heard of this he said with a lament: "The Great Master is going to remain no longer. Is the lamp to indicate that the subsequent affairs are consigned to me?"[207]

Certainly this graphic demonstration can leave no doubt that the symbolism of the lamp and the responsibilities of the duly selected religious successor were well known in the Chinese Buddhist tradition long before the advent of the Ch'an School.[208]

8. Hints of the Transmission Theory in an Early Ch'an Text

Several references occur in Northern Ch'an literature to "one lamp lighting many lamps."[209] Nevertheless, no explicit statement of the transmission theory is made in any of the earliest "transmission of the lamp" texts themselves. In addition, whereas virtually all of the information cited in previous sections relates to the transmission of the teachings in India and the "western regions," the primary focus of the earliest Ch'an texts is the sequence and definition of the transmission that occurred on Chinese soil. In fact, only three references are made in Northern

Ch'an literature to the Indian patriarchs. Two of these are based on Hui-yuan's preface to the *Ta-mo-to-lo ch'an ching* and will be discussed presently.

The third such reference occurs in an intriguing but patently contrived work entitled *Hsien-te chi yü shuang-feng shan-t'a ko t'an hsuan-li—shih-erh (Twelve Previous Worthies Gather at the Stūpa on Mount Shuang-feng to Discuss the Mysterious Principle).*[210] Although not the oldest manifestation of the transmission theory in Ch'an literature, in some ways this text is the most primitive. As is partially apparent from the work's title, the following masters are transported out of time and space to Hung-jen's burial site to present comments on the practice of meditation (only their names are of interest at the moment):

1. Pārśva: An early second-century Indian monk remembered as the compiler of the *Mahāvibhāṣa,* a massive *Abhidharma* compendium. He also figures in Kumārajīva's *Tso-ch'an san-mei ching* and both of the Sarvāstivādin lineage lists discussed earlier.[211]

2. Aśvaghoṣa: This man was an important author of Mahāyāna Buddhist literature, best known in China for the *Ta-sheng ch'i-hsin lun (Awakening of Faith in the Mahāyāna).* His verses also occur in the *Tso-ch'an san-mei ching* and his name in the Sarvāstivādin lists cited earlier, where he is listed immediately after Pārśva.[212]

3. Chao: This could be Fa-ju's student Hui-chao, known only as a resident of Shao-lin ssu, but the identification is uncertain.[213]

4. Buddha: Also known as Bhadra, this is the famed teacher of Seng-ch'ou and first resident of Shao-lin ssu.

5. K'o: The conjunction of the names *Buddha* and [*Hui*]-*k'o* makes one wonder whether there may have been some confusion about the distinction between the names Buddha and Bodhidharma.

6. Chiung (= Ming): The same unusual character also occurs elsewhere as a mistake for Dharma Master Ming, or Ta-ming ("Big Ming"), of the San-lun School.[214]

7. Min: This man is probably the teacher of Hui-ming, or Ch'ing-pu Ming ("Blue-robed Ming"), another San-lun School figure already mentioned earlier with regard to Fa-ju.[215]

8. Neng: This can only be Hui-neng, the legendary figurehead of the Southern School.

9. Hsien: This could be Fa-hsien (discussed earlier in Chapter II, Section 15), but the identification is uncertain.[216]

10. Tao: Unknown.

11. Tsang: This may be Hui-tsang of Hua-chou, an obscure figure listed as one of Hung-jen's ten major disciples, but the identification is uncertain.[217]

12. Hsiu: Here we find the name of Shen-hsiu, the major figure of the Northern School.

That all these individuals are portrayed in a gathering at Hung-jen's stūpa on Mount Shuang-feng is an important indication of his importance in the collective memory of the members of the Northern School. Moreover, this fanciful gathering represents the germ of the transmission concept: Although there is no explicit statement of a lineal succession from one to the next, they are listed in roughly chronological order and include both Indian and Chinese figures. The identity of the twelve worthies included here—which include two important Indian figures, one of the most famous adepts ever to carry the teaching of meditation to China, and at least two San-lun School authorities, not to mention Hui-k'o and the other explicitly Ch'an figures—indicates the breadth of the Northern School's sense of its own background.

9. Fa-ju's Epitaph

The earliest statement of the "transmission of the lamp" theory in any Ch'an text occurs in an epitaph for Fa-ju, who has been discussed in Chapter II, Section 7 as a long-time student of Hung-jen's and one of the first Ch'an monks to be active in the cultural and administrative center of China. The epitaph, which was no doubt written shortly after Fa-ju's death in 689, includes the following:

> The transmission [of the teaching] in India was fundamentally without words, [so that] entrance into this teaching is solely [dependent on] the transmission of the mind. Therefore, the preface to the *Meditation Sūtra of Dharmatrāta* by Dharma Master [Hui]-yuan of Mount Lu says:
>
> Ānanda received all the oral teachings [of the Buddha, but] he always concealed them in his heart when in contact with those unfit [to receive them] . . . Shortly after the *Tathāgata*'s nirvāṇa, Ānanda transmitted [the oral teachings] to Madhyāntika and Madhyāntika transmitted them to Śāṇavāsa . . . The achievement [of Ānanda, Madhyāntika, and Śāṇavāsa] was beyond words and is not discussed in the sūtras, but was exactly and without the slightest difference as pre-ordained by the Original Master (i.e., the Buddha). They were able to respond perfectly to any occasion, concealing their identities and accomplishments so that no one knew of them. These men cannot be distinguished according to school because they taught a truth separate [from sectarian doctrines].
>
> It was the *Tripiṭaka* master of south India, Dharma Master Bodhidharma, who inherited this teaching *(tsung)* and marched [with it to this] country in the East. The *Biographies (? chuan)* say:

> His inspired transformation [of sentient beings] (i.e., his ability as a teacher) being mysterious and profound, [Bodhidharma] entered the Wei [regime of north China] and transmitted [the teachings to Hui]-k'o, [Hui]-k'o transmitted them to [Seng]-ts'an, [Seng]-ts'an transmitted them to [Tao]-hsin, [Tao]-hsin transmitted them to [Hung]-jen, and [Hung]-jen transmitted them to [Fa]-ju.
>
> [These masters all] transmitted [the teachings] but could not speak of them—if a person were not fit [to comprehend the teachings], who could possibly transmit them to him?[218]

It is a pity that more is not known about Fa-ju's teachings, for this is a tantalizing passage indeed. Basically, the anonymous author of this epitaph combined two types of information in developing a unique, even epochal, theory. The first source was Hui-yuan's preface to the *Ta-mo-to-lo ch'an ching*. One passage in this preface, which claimed that the best masters of all the schools were privy to the Ultimate Truth, was altered ever so slightly to imply that the teachings of Ch'an existed completely apart from the sectarian traditions of Buddhism. The epitaph thus firmly avows the idea that the teaching of Ch'an was a "tranmission outside the teachings," as it was put in later texts.[219]

The second type of information used in the epitaph may derive in part from the *HKSC* and other written works, but ultimately it consists of the oral tradition of Ch'an as it was known to Fa-ju and his survivors. It is interesting that this oral tradition introduces Bodhidharma as the true successor to the tradition of the Buddha, Ānanda, *et al.,* completely ignoring Hui-yuan's focus on Kashmir.[220]

The description of the succession from Bodhidharma to Fa-ju is interesting for two reasons. First, it is the earliest explicit indication of any link between the Bodhidharma tradition and the East Mountain Teaching. Second, the epitaph still leaves a great deal unsaid. Although the listing of six generations of lineal predecessors was a novelty in Chinese religious literature,[221] Fa-ju's epitaph does not number or specifically identify the figures listed as "patriarchs," nor is the nature of the transmission from one to the other described. These details were only clarified in later works.

10. The Author of the Ch'üan fa-pao chi (Annals of the Transmission of the Dharma-treasure, *or* CFPC)

Fa-ju was eventually forgotten by the Ch'an tradition, but his teachings as contained in the epitaph (we can only assume that they are his rather than those of his anonymous eulogist) had a very substantial influence on the later development of the school's awareness of its own identity. This influence was felt through the *Ch'üan fa-pao chi (CFPC),* the entire format of which depends on the passage from Fa-ju's epitaph quoted in the previous section.

Not only is the *CFPC* the single most important source for the study of the development of the "transmission of the lamp" theory in the Northern School, it also contains valuable documentation of the state of Ch'an in the two capitals shortly after Shen-hsiu's death, anecdotal evidence of the hagiographical image of the ideal Ch'an master, and hints as to the status of factional distinctions within the Northern School. Shen-hui's mention of the *CFPC* in his attack on P'u-chi and the "Northern School" is further evidence of its importance.[222]

Professor Yanagida's analysis of the identity of the author of the *CFPC* has yielded helpful insights into the background of the text.[223] The author was a layman named Tu Fei, a figure almost certainly identical to the Dharma Master Fei who was an early teacher of I-fu.[224] Tu Fei's statement that he was commissioned to write the *CFPC* by "friend(s) from the past"[225] must refer to I-fu and, perhaps, to P'u-chi. That historical reality was apparently distorted to make Fa-ju appear to have received the transmission from Hung-jen earlier than did Shen-hsiu (see Chapter II, Section 11) is an indication of Tu Fei's earlier association with Fa-ju.

A few plausible inferences can be made about Tu Fei's attitudes toward the Ch'an of his day. First of all, his was an elitist view. He believed that only a few gifted individuals were capable of understanding Ch'an. He sharply criticized some of his ordained contemporaries who, solely in order to satisfy their own personal ambitions, falsely claimed spiritual experience and even transmission of the teachings to themselves.

This indignant posture toward the attitude of his contemporaries is in direct contrast with the reasons for which he was commissioned to write the *CFPC:* Whereas P'u-chi and I-fu undoubtedly wanted to glorify Shen-hsiu's successes and legitimize their own positions as successors to a lengthy line of enlightened masters, Tu Fei clearly placed the responsibility for the situation he criticizes squarely on the shoulders of the later patriarchs. These later patriarchs had decided to make Ch'an available to greater and greater numbers of people, instead of limiting its availability to the few individuals Tu Fei felt were motivated and gifted enough to understand it. At one point in the *CFPC* Tu Fei states his own belief that the adoration of former worthies might "in some cases" inspire spiritual awakening in his future readers—a pointedly lukewarm endorsement of the value of his own efforts.[226]

11. The Contents of the Ch'üan fa-pao chi (CFPC)

The *CFPC*'s understanding of the transmission idea is obviously based on the epitaph for Fa-ju, but Tu Fei quotes even less of Hui-yuan's preface to the *Ta-mo-to-lo ch'an ching* than did the epitaph. The *CFPC* includes no explicit definition of or commentary on the meaning of the religious succession. Like the epitaph, it lacks any description of or even a name for the role fulfilled by the seven masters to which the book is devoted: Bodhidharma, Hui-k'o, Seng-ts'an, Tao-hsin, Hung-jen, Fa-ju, and Shen-hsiu. These masters are neither numbered nor referred to explicitly as "patriarchs," as is the case in later texts. Instead, Tu Fei draws on a number of sources to develop colorful portraits of those individual masters.

The most heavily used source is, not surprisingly, the *HKSC,* but Tu Fei's attitude toward this text is decidedly negative. In the section on Bodhidharma, the *HKSC* is indirectly criticized for including part of the *Treatise on the Two Entrances and Four Practices.* Tu Fei admits that Bodhidharma may have used this text in the course of his instruction, but only as a provisional guide for beginning students. By the time the *CFPC* was written, the increasingly sophisticated image of the Ch'an master did not allow for such straightforward and simplistically organized doctrinal statements. In the same section on Bodhidharma, Tu Fei writes that Hui-k'o cut off his arm to prove his religious sincerity and expressly denies the "false version" in the *HKSC* involving mutilation by rebels.

These and other differences of detail between the *HKSC* and the *CFPC* may be understood when we consider the basic theoretical difference between the two works. Whereas the *HKSC* is a comprehensive collection of biographies and comments intended to document the breadth of the entire Buddhist tradition in China, the *CFPC* presents itself as the history of the true teachings of Buddhism through seven generations of enlightened masters. Even more than other works written about the same time and deriving from other subtraditions of Chinese Buddhism, the *CFPC* is dedicated to the revision of the encyclopedic tendencies of the *HKSC:* For Tu Fei and the followers of Ch'an, their school was not just a subtradition, but the mainstream of the Buddhist religion.[227]

12. Ching-chueh and the Leng-ch'ieh shih-tzu chi (Records of the Masters and Disciples of the Laṇkā[vatāra], *or* LCSTC)

The biography of Ching-chueh (683–ca. 750), the compiler of the *LCSTC,* is unique in the history of early Ch'an.[228] He was a younger brother of Emperor Chung-tsung's consort and eventual empress, the ill-fated Wei-shih (d. 710), and his family was repeatedly beset with tragedy because of this association. Ching-chueh's parents were assassinated when he was only one year old and his brothers put to death eight years later;[229] it is difficult to understand how he himself survived. He must have entered the priesthood while very young, but there no information exists about his early years.

In 705 (at age twenty-three), while in residence at Mount T'ai-hang north of the Yellow River (Shansi/Honan), Ching-chueh wrote his own commentary on the *Diamond Sūtra.*[230] Shortly thereafter he must have traveled to Ch'ang-an and Lo-yang, where he studied under Shen-hsiu and, possibly, Lao-an.[231] His most intimate religious relationship, however, was with Hsuan-tse. Ching-chueh became Hsuan-tse's student immediately after the latter's invitation to court in 708 by Emperor Chung-tsung, who was Ching-chueh's uncle. Hsuan-tse probably wrote the *LCJFC* sometime during the years 708–10.[232]

Ching-chueh no doubt left the two capitals after his elder sister Wei-shih's disastrous misadventure of 710, when she attempted to assume power as Empress Wu had done some years before. He wrote the *LCSTC* sometime during the years 713–16 at his previous mountain retreat on Mount T'ai-hang. His ignorance of the *CFPC* was no doubt the result of his absence from Ch'ang-an and Lo-yang after 710. Ching-chueh's commentary on the *Heart Sūtra* (this and the *LCSTC* are the only texts of his to survive) was written in a far-off corner of what is now Shensi Province. Sometime before his death he may have returned to Ch'ang-an, where he resided at Ta-an-kuo ssu, but this cannot be known for certain.[233]

We do not know the full extent of Hsuan-tse's *LCJFC,* but it was presumably dedicated to the major figures of the East Mountain Teaching/Northern School: Hung-jen, Shen-hsiu, Lao-an, and—by inference at the very least—Hsuan-tse. The *LCJFC* may have contained sections devoted to Bodhidharma, Hui-k'o, Seng-ts'an, and Tao-hsin, but it probably did not; in any case, Ching-chueh does not quote the *LCJFC* in the early passages of the *LCSTC.* It is possible to infer that Hsuan-tse implicitly accepted the *HKSC* as the authoritative source for the biographies of the earlier masters. Another notable difference between this work and Tu Fei's *CFPC* is the omission of any emphasis on Fa-ju's role. Because of his claim as the recorder of Hung-jen's last words, Hsuan-tse could not have admitted Fa-ju's importance without implicitly undermining his own.[234]

Although Ching-chueh's *LCSTC* evolves from the same general religious environment and utilizes the same conceptual framework as the *CFPC,* the two works could hardly be any more different. Where the *CFPC* almost completely ignores the actual teachings of its subjects in favor of their biographies and the teacher-student relationships between them, the *LCSTC* refers to the religious succession from one master to the next in most matter-of-fact terms and concentrates instead on those masters' doctrines. (One notable exception to this is the *LCSTC*'s quotation of Hung-jen's alleged last words, introduced in Chapter II, Section 5.) The succession schema posited by the *CFPC* and the *LCSTC* also differ: Where the former discusses seven masters from Bodhidharma to

Shen-hsiu, never once mentioning any of their disciples, the latter places Guṇabhadra before Bodhidharma, ignores Fa-ju, and refers to a total of twenty-four men who received transmission of the teachings of Ch'an. The treatment of Guṇabhadra, which was based on his role as the translator of the most commonly used version of the *Laṇkāvatāra Sūtra,* is an extraordinary anomaly among Ch'an historical texts. Even though the *CFPC* and the *LCSTC* derive from the same religious milieu, neither displays any knowledge of the other. Clearly, they were completely independent works.

13. The Leng-ch'ieh shih-tzu chi (LCSTC) *and the* Laṇkāvatāra Sūtra

Although Ching-chueh claimed to be writing a history of the "teachers and disciples of the *Laṇkāvatāra,*" he failed utterly at the documentation of his position.[235] The only quotations from this scripture found in the *LCSTC* are commonplace slogans unrelated to the major doctrines of the scripture. On several occasions Ching-chueh states that a given master's teachings were based on the *Laṇkāvatāra,* only to follow with an explanation of those teachings that completely ignores the sūtra. (See especially the sections on Tao-hsin and Shen-hsiu.) Even the section devoted to Guṇabhadra, which is included only because of his status as translator of the *Laṇkāvatāra,* lacks any particular emphasis on this text. In other words, Ching-chueh accepted the identification of Ch'an and the *Laṇkāvatāra*—either out of deference to Hsuan-tse or for some unknown reason—but was unable or unwilling to explicate that identification in any meaningful way.

Even more than the *CFPC,* the *LCSTC* draws on a wide variety of different source materials. In fact, the *LCSTC* suffers from a lack of internal balance due to the heterogeneity of these sources and the great disparity in the amount of space the text devotes to the different masters. The sources used by Ching-chueh, in some cases surreptitiously, are as follows:

1. Numerous quotations from several sūtras, the *Awakening of Faith,* the writings of Seng-chao, the *HKSC,* and material found in other Northern School Tun-huang manuscripts.
2. Several passages from the *Hsiu-hsin yao lun (Essential Treatise on the Cultivation of the Mind,* or *HHYL),* which is generally attributed to Hung-jen.
3. Bodhidharma's *EJSHL,* including the preface by T'an-lin.
4. A fragment from a commentary to Hui-ming's *Hsiang-hsuan fu (Ode on the Elucidation of the Mysterious),* attributed here to Seng-ts'an.

5. Probably the entire text of a work attributed here to Tao-hsin, the *Ju-tao an-hsin yao fang-pien fa-men (Essential Teaching of the Expedient Means of Pacifying the Mind and Entering the Path,* or *JTFM).*
6. Hsuan-tse's *LCJFC,* either in its entirety or nearly so.
7. Several imperial proclamations relating to Shen-hsiu, perhaps first included in the *LCJFC.*
8. An unknown source, perhaps the oral tradition, for questions and paradoxical statements attributed to Guṇabhadra, Bodhidharma, Hui-k'o, and Shen-hsiu.[236]

Some of the ways in which Ching-chueh uses these sources indicate the true extent and purpose of his efforts. He uses the *HHYL,* for example, but not for his exposition of Hung-jen's teachings and without mentioning it by name. Instead, he makes a thinly veiled reference to the illegitimacy of its popular attribution to Hung-jen and plagiarizes it to fill out his sections on Guṇabhadra and Hui-k'o.[237] The use of the commentary fragment found in conjunction with Seng-ts'an's name (item 4 in this list) is even more egregious. Although it is of course impossible to prove that Seng-ts'an did not write the commentary in question, the most reasonable interpretation is that Ching-chueh knew absolutely nothing about the teachings of Hui-k'o's successor and arbitrarily inserted part of an anonymous commentary.

Therefore, if Ching-chueh had wished to make more of a case for the identification of Ch'an with the *Laṇkāvatāra Sūtra,* he did not fail because of a lack of effort or ingenuity. Either he did not feel moved to do so, or he did not have sufficient source material to support such a position.

14. The Northern School and Encounter Dialogue

In the description of the three major genres of Ch'an literature in Section 1 of this Chapter I stated that the primary ingredient of the "transmission of the lamp" texts is the transcription of encounter dialogue. At first glance, this does not seem to be true of the Northern School texts under consideration here. These texts contain a number of stories intended to illustrate the inspired and unconventional behavior of the Northern School masters, not to mention several references to their spontaneous and intuitive teaching styles, but there are no actual dialogues between these teachers and their students. Must we therefore refrain from considering the *CFPC* and *LCSTC* as full-fledged transmission texts?

The *LCSTC,* at least, may contain a partial transcript of prototypical encounter dialogue exchanges. This text includes an intriguing set of rhetorical questions and short doctrinal admonitions, which it refers to as "questions about things" (literally, "pointing at things and asking the meanings," *chih-shih wen-i*). Such questions and admonitions are attributed to several of the early masters, as shown by the following examples:

(Guṇabhadra)

When [Guṇabhadra] was imparting wisdom to others, before he had even begun to preach the Dharma, he would assess [his listeners' understanding of physical] things by pointing at a leaf and [asking]: "What is that?"

He would also say: "Can you enter into a [water] pitcher or enter into a pillar? Can you enter into a fiery oven? Can a stick [from up on the] mountain preach the Dharma?"

He would also say: "Does your body enter [into the pitcher, etc.,] or does your mind enter?"

He would also say: "There is a pitcher inside the building, but is there another pitcher outside the building? Is there water inside the pitcher, or is there a pitcher inside the water? Or is there even a pitcher within every single drop of water under heaven?"

He would also say: "A leaf can preach the Dharma; a pitcher can preach the Dharma; a pillar can preach the Dharma; a building can preach the Dharma; and earth, water, fire, and wind can all preach the Dharma. How is it that mud, wood, tiles, and rocks can also preach the Dharma?"

(Bodhidharma)

The Great Master [Bodhidharma] also pointed at things and inquired of their meaning, simply pointing at a thing and calling out: "What is that?" He asked about a number of things, switching their names about and asking about them [again] differently.

He would also say: "Clouds and mists in the sky are never able to defile space. However, they can shade space [so that the sun] cannot become bright and pure . . ."

(Hung-jen)

The Great Master [Hung-jen] said: "There is a single little house filled with crap and weeds and dirt—what is it?"

He also said: "If you sweep out all the crap and weeds and dirt and clean it all up so there is not a single thing left inside, then what is it? . . ."

Also, when he saw someone light a lamp or perform any ordinary activity, he would always say: "Is this person dreaming or under a spell?" Or he would say: "Not making and not doing, these things are all the great *parinirvāṇa*."

He also said: "When you are actually sitting in meditation inside the monastery, is there another of you sitting in meditation in the forest? Can all the mud, wood, tiles, and rocks also sit in meditation? Can mud, wood, tiles, and rocks also see forms and hear sounds, or put on robes and carry a begging bowl?"

(Shen-hsiu)

[Shen-hsiu] also said: "Is this mind a mind that exists? What kind of mind is the mind?"

He also said: "When you see form, does form exist? What kind of form is form?"

He also said: "You hear the sound of a bell that is struck. Does [the sound] exist when [the bell] is struck? Before it is struck? What kind of sound is sound?" He also said: "Does the sound of a bell that is struck only exist within the monastery, or does the bell's sound also exist [throughout] the universe [in all the] ten directions?"

Also, seeing a bird fly by, he asked: "What is that?"

He also said: "Can you sit in meditation on the tip of a tree's hanging branch?"

He also said: "The *Nirvāṇa Sūtra* says: 'The Bodhisattva with the Limitless Body came from the East.' If the bodhisattva's body was limitless in size, how could he have come from the East? Why did he not come from the West, South, or North? Or is this impossible?"[238]

Sekiguchi Shindai has already suggested that these "questions about things" resemble the "public cases" of later Ch'an. Unfortunately, his analysis was so superficial and unconvincing that it inspired unusually harsh criticism from Yanagida, who accused him of approaching the issue with an incorrect preconception of public cases.[239] I would suggest that, rather than being correlated with the public case anthologies of the eleventh century and beyond, this Northern School material should be compared to the idiosyncratically Ch'an style of encounter dialogue that developed before the end of the eighth century. These "questions about things" represent the earliest recorded phase in the development of this type of religious dialogue.

15. Encounter Dialogue, Ma-tsu Tao-i, and the Northern School

At this point the skeptical reader may be thinking: Encounter dialogue developed in the Hung-chou School of Ma-tsu Tao-i, which flourished more than a half century after the Northern School in an area of south-central China far removed from Ch'ang-an and Lo-yang. Ma-tsu was a religious descendant of Hui-neng through Nan-yueh Huai-jang (677–744) and thus a member of the Southern rather than the Northern School. If anything, the use of encounter dialogue by Ma-tsu and his associates derives from his close association with Ch'an in Szechwan rather than from the practices of Shen-hsiu and the other members of the Northern School.

This view rests on a set of widespread but untenable preconceptions. First, a connection between Ma-tsu and the Northern School cannot be uncontestably denied. The claim that Huai-jang studied with Hui-neng cannot be proven and may have derived from competition with Shen-hui's faction. Huai-jang is also supposed to have studied for a time under Lao-an (recalling the career of Ching-tsang, who also studied under Lao-an and Hui-neng) making Ma-tsu's relationship with the Northern School at least as strong as that with Hui-neng.[240]

Second, it is erroneous to use the term "Southern School" to refer to some dominant trend beginning with Hui-neng and devolving eventually to Ma-tsu. The historical Hui-neng cannot be described as a member of the Southern School. Further, the "Southern School" of Shen-hui was not the only influence on the later Ch'an tradition; even the *Platform Sūtra,* which has long been considered the most characteristic Southern School work, is now thought to have been compiled by a member of the Ox-head School, which defined itself as separate from the schools of North and South.[241]

Third, it would be unwise to suggest that Ma-tsu's Hung-chou School of the late eighth century could have developed in ignorance of events that took place in the two capitals only a few decades earlier. Indeed, even though the Northern School achieved its greatest success in Lo-yang and Ch'ang-an, it never lacked at least a foothold in the provinces to the South.

Finally, it would be incorrect to suggest that the Northern School had no influence on the Szechwan factions of Ch'an. The *LTFPC,* which derives from one of those factions, contains exchanges that are very much like encounter dialogue, but it also displays marked deference to and influence by the Northern School.[242]

Obviously, this study cannot include a thorough investigation of the origins of encounter dialogue, for such an investigation would have to include reference to the antecedents of the practice in the Chinese classics and the salon dialogue of the Six Dynasties Period (*ch'ing-t'an* or "pure conversation"), not to mention a stylistic and doctrinal analysis of Hung-chou School texts. At this point I will limit the discussion to one issue: If the "questions about things" derive from prototypical encounter dialogues, why do Northern School texts fail to transcribe the entirety of those exchanges? This issue may be restated as follows: Why do the "questions about things" include only the teachers' questions and comments, but nothing from the students? When posed in this fashion, the problem becomes relatively simple, for one of the most important differences between traditional Chinese Buddhism and Ch'an is the attention devoted by the latter to the needs of the individual spiritual aspirant.

In other, earlier schools of Chinese Buddhism the universal cynosure was the gifted exegete, the inspired and saintly master. In the writings of such eminent figures (and their emulators) the problems of the religious training of individual practitioners merit only theoretical treatment. Such writings may contain impressive analyses of Buddhist doctrine, elaborate definitions of different types of meditation and the various approaches to practice, and so on, but they yield little or no concrete information about how the students of the day were led to achieve their own liberation.

In Ch'an texts of the ninth century and later, the master can hardly be perceived as an isolated entity. Instead, he is defined almost entirely by the kind of interaction he had with his students. These texts do indeed contain examples of the independent literary creativity of their subjects, but these examples are overshadowed by—and derive their validity from —the surrounding reams of extemporaneous dialogue.

The transition from traditional Buddhist custom to Ch'an was therefore a literary as well as a religious development. We can easily imagine that the chroniclers of early Ch'an simply did not realize the magnitude of the change that was taking place. Tu Fei, Ching-chueh, Chang Yueh, and Li Yung were all extremely well-educated members of the very highest social class, who wrote their texts with a full awareness of traditional literary form. The inherent conservatism of such figures must have been especially strong in the composition of epitaphs and eulogies, works that were intended to dispatch their subjects in a last flurry of elegant prose rather than break any new doctrinal or religious ground. To include the confused questions and misguided statements of students would have hindered the glorification of the recently departed subjects of these texts.

One clue to the nature of the literary development under discussion here occurs in I-fu's epitaph by Yen T'ing-chih. The author says that he and Tu Yü, another of I-fu's epigraphers, collected the departed master's sayings as they were remembered by his students. The two men were apparently unable to write down all of those sayings, presumably because of their great number. Even though they recognized the value of these sayings, neither of their epitaphs for I-fu contain anything that might correspond to the object of such a search.[243]

As time went on, the epitaphs of members of the Northern School and other figures important in the development of Ch'an began to include precisely this sort of material. For example, note the following exchange and commentary from the epitaph for P'u-chi's student Fa-yun (d. 766):

> "Has the Buddha's teaching been transmitted to you?"
> "I have a sandalwood image [of the Buddha] to which I pay reverence."
> [This reply was] profound yet brief, and those listening felt chills of lone-

> liness. The day after [the questioner, a prominent official,] left, Fa-yun died without illness while sitting cross-legged on his chair.[244]

After all the hyperbole about Shen-hsiu's being equivalent to a buddha and P'u-chi's being the religious ruler of the universe, it is perfectly natural to find a slightly later master deflating the idea of the transmission entirely.

The epitaph for Hui-chen (673–751), who was more closely affiliated with the T'ien-t'ai and *Vinaya* Schools than with Ch'an, includes a more explicit reference to and several examples of encounter dialogue:

> "When people do not understand, I use the Ch'an [style of] teaching *(ch'an-shuo).*"
>
> QUESTION: "Are not the teachings of the Southern and Northern [Schools] different?"
>
> ANSWER: "Outside the gates of both houses is a road to everlasting peace."
>
> QUESTION: "Do the results of religious practice vary according to the extent [of realization]?"
>
> ANSWER: "When a drop of water falls from the cliff, it knows the morning sea."
>
> QUESTION: "How can one who is without faith achieve self-motivation [in spiritual endeavor]?"
>
> ANSWER: "When the baby's throat is closed (i.e., when choking), the mother yells to frighten it [loose]. Great compassion is unconditioned, but it can also cause [a student to] whimper."[245]

A confirmed skeptic might suggest that Hui-chen is merely answering in easily understood metaphors, rather than in some really new "Ch'an [style of] teaching." If this is the case, it is clear that a new type of metaphorical usage became the vogue in Chinese Buddhism during the second half of the eighth century, for such usage is also apparent in the biographies of Fa-ch'in and Hsuan-lang, well-known representatives of the Ox-head and T'ien-t'ai Schools, respectively.[246]

Of course, the members of the Northern School were not necessarily the "inventors" of encounter dialogue, nor was their use of it identical to that of Ma-tsu and his followers. Indeed, the practice may have had a much wider currency than the extant body of literature suggests, and the members of the Northern School may have only been the first to legitimize its use in the Ch'an tradition. Until we have a better understanding of the transition from early Ch'an to the "golden age" actitivies of Ma-tsu, Lin-chi, and their colleagues, we cannot even evaluate the true significance of the Northern School's contribution in this area.

Nevertheless, in addition to the evidence introduced here, the biographies of Northern School masters contained various references to spontaneous and intuitive styles of teaching. Also, the *SKSC* and *CTL* contain several examples of encounter dialogue involving Northern School figures (as mentioned in Chapter III, Sections 2 and 7). Even though these examples may be fabricated, it seems likely that the members of the Northern School practiced some form of prototypical encounter dialogue.

Part Two

DOCTRINE

CHAPTER V

The Earliest Teachings of Ch'an

1. Introductory Remarks

Only one work, it is generally agreed, can legitimately be attributed to Bodhidharma: the *Erh-ju ssu-hsing lun (Treatise on the Two Entrances and Four Practices,* or *EJSHL).* D. T. Suzuki has suggested that certain of the numerous works from Tun-huang and elsewhere that bear Bodhidharma's name are also legitimately his, but Suzuki's arguments are based more on hope than on reason and have been thoroughly confuted.[1] After decades of discoveries in the collections at London, Paris, and Peking and after much research in Japan, China, and elsewhere on the meaning of the Tun-huang finds, our best and almost only source for the earliest teachings of Ch'an remains, ironically, the one text that has been available all along.

It is uncertain, of course, whether the *EJSHL* was actually written by Bodhidharma. The literary elegance of the text suggests that it was neither a product of his hand alone nor a simple translation from Sanskrit. Some native figure must have been responsible for putting Bodhidharma's ideas into Chinese, and it is quite possible that those ideas were transformed somewhat, either consciously or unconsciously, for presentation to the Chinese readership. It is quite possible that Hui-k'o summarized Bodhidharma's teachings for T'an-lin, who then compiled the text and added the preface, but this is, of course, pure speculation. What is known is that the *EJSHL* was distributed under Bodhidharma's name during the second half of the seventh century. At that time it was already accompanied by a certain amount of miscellaneous material, some of which is translated here. The Tun-huang manuscripts of the *EJSHL* contain a great deal of such miscellaneous material, some of which must date from the early part and middle of the eighth century.[2]

The following is a translation of the *EJSHL* and its preface by T'an-lin, plus two letters and a reply by Hui-k'o. Except for Hui-k'o's reply, all of this material has been taken from the Tun-huang manuscripts of the *EJSHL* and its appended miscellaneous material. I have used only that portion of the miscellaneous material that appears to be of arguably early vintage. The second part of the second letter translated here occurs both in the Tun-huang text and in the *HKSC*, where it is presented as having been written to Hui-k'o at the beginning of the T'ien-pao period (550–59) by one Layman Hsiang. Hui-k'o's response to this letter is found only in the *HKSC*. It is not known whether the first letter in the Tun-huang manuscript was also addressed to Hui-k'o.[3]

The earliest known title to this work is *Lueh pien ta-sheng ju-tao ssu-hsing, ti-tzu T'an-lin hsü (A Brief Exposition of the Mahāyāna* [*Teaching*] *of the Four Practices of Entering into Enlightenment, with Preface by the Disciple T'an-lin).* This title occurs in the *LCSTC* and, with the addition of Bodhidharma's name at the beginning *(P'u-t'i-ta-mo lueh pien . . .),* in the thirtieth fascicle of the *CTL*. Actually, other titles were also in use for this text during the eighth century and earlier. The abbreviated title used, *Treatise on the Two Entrances and Four Practices,* is that generally used by modern scholars.[4]

2. *Treatise on the Two Entrances and Four Practices (Erh-ju ssu-hsing lun, or EJSHL)*

Preface by the Disciple T'an-lin[5]

The Dharma Master [Bodhidharma] was from a country in south India in the western region, the third son of a great brahmin king. He was naturally brilliant and understood everything he heard. His aspirations were for the path of the Mahāyāna, so he discarded the white [garb of a layman] and assumed the black [robes of a Buddhist monk] in order to transmit the sagely tradition. He effaced his mind in the serene and had a penetrating understanding of the affairs of the world. Wise in both the internal and external, his virtue exceeded the standard of the age. Feeling compassionate sorrow as a result of the decline of the True Teaching in this obscure corner [of the Buddhist world], he crossed the mountains and oceans to proselytize in the far-off land of the Han and Wei.

Those who could overcome [the preconceptions and obstacles within] their own minds did not fail to place their faith in [Bodhidharma], but those who grasped at appearances and held [incorrect] views reviled him. At the time Tao-yü and Hui-k'o were his only [students]. These two *śramaṇa*s, having lofty aspirations that belied their youth and the good fortune to meet the Dharma Master, served him for several years. They reverentially inquired of the teaching and instilled in themselves the spirit of the master's [teaching].

The Dharma Master responded to their innate sincerity by teaching them the True Path: "Such is the pacification of the mind, such is the generation of practice, such is accordance with convention, such are expedient means.

This is the teaching of the pacification of mind in the Mahāyāna—make certain [that it is understood] without error." Such is the pacification of the mind—wall contemplation; such is the generation of practice—the four practices; such is accordance with convention—defense against calumnification; such are expedient means—the avoidance of attachment to those [means].

The above is a brief summary of the origins of the ideas expressed in the text that follows.

[Text]

There are many ways of entering into enlightenment *(ju-tao),* but all of them may effectively be subsumed under two categories: the "entrance of principle" *(li-ju)* and the "entrance of practice" *(hsing-ju).*

The entrance of principle is to become enlightened to the Truth on the basis of the teaching. [One must have a] profound faith in [the fact that] one and the same True Nature is possessed of all sentient beings, both ordinary and enlightened, and that this [True Nature] is only covered up and made imperceptible [in the case of ordinary people] by false sense impressions. If one discards the false and takes refuge in the True, one resides frozen in "wall contemplation" *(pi-kuan),* [in which] self and other, ordinary person and sage, are one and the same; one resides fixedly without wavering, never again to be swayed by written teachings. To be thus mysteriously identified with the [True] Principle, to be without discrimination, serene and inactive: This is called the entrance of principle.

The entrance of practice refers to the "four practices" [listed below], which encompass all other practices. They are the "practice of the retribution of enmity," the "practice of the acceptance of circumstances," the "practice of the absence of craving," and the "practice of accordance with the Dharma."

What is the practice of the retribution of enmity? When the practitioner of Buddhist spiritual training experiences suffering, he should think to himself: "For innumerable eons I have wandered through the various states of existence, forsaking the fundamental *(pen)* for the derivative *(mo),* generating [in myself] a great deal of enmity and distaste and [bringing] an unlimited amount of injury and discord [upon others]. Although I have not committed any offense in this [lifetime, my present suffering constitutes] the fruition of my past crimes and bad karma, rather than anything bequeathed to me by any heavenly or nonhuman being. I shall accept it patiently and contentedly, completely without enmity or complaint." The sūtra says: "Do not be saddened by the experience of suffering. Why? Because your mind (*shih,* "consciousness") penetrates the fundamental [nature of things]." When you react to events in this fashion (lit., "generate this [state of] mind"), you can be in accord with the [Absolute] Principle as you progress upon the path [toward enlightenment] through the experience of [the results of your past] enmity. Therefore, this is called the practice of the retribution of enmity.

The second is the practice of the acceptance of circumstances *(yuan,* "conditions"). Sentient beings have no [unchanging] self *(wu-wo, anātman)* and are entirely subject to the impact of their circumstances. Whether one experiences suffering or pleasure, both are generated from one's circumstances. If one experiences fame, fortune, and other forms of superior [karmic] retribution, [one should realize that this is] the result *(kan,* "response") of past causes. Although one may experience [such good fortune] now, when the circumstances [responsible for its present manifestation] are exhausted, it will disappear. How could one take joy in [good fortune]? Since success and failure depend on circumstances, the mind should remain unchanged. It should be unmoved even by the winds of good fortune, but mysteriously in accordance with the Tao (i.e., the Path, or enlightenment). Therefore, this is called the practice of the acceptance of circumstances.

The third is the practice of the absence of craving. The various kinds of covetousness and attachment that people experience in their never-ending ignorance are referred to as craving *(ch'iu).* The wise man is enlightened to the Truth, the [essential] principle of which is contrary to human convention. He pacifies his mind in inactivity *(an-hsin wu-wei)* and accepts whatever happens to him (lit., "[allows his] form to be transformed in accordance with fate"). [Understanding that] all existence is nonsubstantial, he is without desire. [The two sisters of good and bad fortune named] Merit and Darkness always travel together. The triple world, this home you are long accustomed to living in, is like a burning house! Suffering is an inescapable fact of corporeal existence—who could possibly [have a body and be at] peace? If you understand this, you will cease all [wrong] thinking and be without craving, [no matter which of the] various states of existence [you may experience]. The sūtra says: "To have craving entails suffering; to be without craving means joy." Understand clearly that to be without craving is equivalent to the true practice of the Path.

The fourth is the practice of accordance with the Dharma. The [absolute] principle of essential purity *(hsing-ching chih li)* is called Dharma. According to this principle, all characteristics are nonsubstantial and there is no defilement and no attachment, no [distinction between] "this" and "that." The [*Vimalakīrti*] *Sūtra* says: "There are no sentient beings in this Dharma, because it transcends the defilements of 'sentient being.' There are no selves in this Dharma, because it transcends the defilements of 'self.' " If the wise man can accept and understand this principle, he should practice in accordance with the Dharma.

Since this Dharma is fundamentally without parsimony, he should practice [the perfection of] charity *(dāna),* giving of his body, life, and possessions without any regret in his mind. Thoroughly understanding the three nonsubstantialities [of recipient, donor, and gift], he neither swerves [from his course] nor becomes attached [to anything], but merely rids himself of his own defilements and aids in the salvation of other sentient beings—all without grasping at characteristics (i.e., without conceptualizing the existence of self and sentient beings, etc.). In this way he benefits himself as well as others; he ornaments the path of enlightenment. Charity is [to be undertaken] as above; the other five [perfections are performed] in the same manner. To eradicate wrong thoughts and practice the six perfections—but while being without any "practice"—this is the practice of accordance with the Dharma.

[Appended Material]
[The First Letter]

I have always revered the previous sage (i.e., the Buddha). I have extensively cultivated all the practices, have always taken joy in the Pure Land, and have valued the legacy of his teaching like a thirsty man in need of water. There are many millions who realized the great enlightenment and innumerable ones who attained the four fruits[6] through their encounter with Śākyamuni. I truly believed that heaven was a separate country and hell another place and that, upon achieving enlightenment and attaining the [ultimate] fruit, one's body became changed, one's form different. [Thinking thus, I] opened the scriptures seeking blessings and [sought to make the] motivation of my practice pure. In a confused whirl of activity I practiced as I might, thus passing many years with never a moment of rest.

Eventually, though, I sat upright in serenity and fixed my attention on my mind. Having long cultivated false thoughts, however, I perceived forms on the basis of my feelings (i.e., experienced hallucinations), the transformations of which seemed never-ending. Eventually I penetrated the Dharma Nature *(fa-hsing)* and crudely cultivated Suchness *(chen-ju),* so that for the first time I understood that there was nothing that did not exist within the square inch [of my own mind]. The bright pearl penetrated brilliantly, mysteriously attaining the Profound Truth. From the Buddhas above to the squirming insects below, there is nothing that is not identified according to [the criteria of our own] minds [and that is not] a separate name of [our own] false thoughts.

Therefore, I have poured my deepest feelings into the composition of a modest verse on the expedient means of entering into enlightenment, which I address to those of a common background and like inclinations. If you have the time, please read this. If you practice seated meditation, you will surely perceive the Fundamental Nature *(pen-hsing).*

If you can meld the mind and make it pure,
then [you will realize that] a split second of discriminative consciousness is saṁsāra.
Mentation undertaken within [saṁsāra results in] the creation of wrong livelihood.[7]
If you search for the Dharma with a calculating [mind], your karma will not change.

[The Second Letter]

In its ever-increasing defilement, the mind is difficult to [bring to the] ultimate. When the Sage heard the eight words [of the verse "All things are impermanent; this life is saṁsāra" (?)], he instantly realized for the first time that his six years of asceticism had been wasted effort.

The world is universally entangled with demons who pointlessly argue and fight. They make incorrect interpretations [of Buddhism, by which they] teach sentient beings. They speak of remedies, but they have never cured a single illness.

Serene, serene—from the beginning there have fundamentally never existed any ascriptive views and [superficial] characteristics (?), so how can there be good and evil, false and true? Birth is also nonbirth, extinction also nonextinction. Motion is equivalent to nonmotion, meditation equivalent to nonmeditation.

[The following is represented by the *HKSC* as a letter from Layman Hsiang to Hui-k'o.]

Shadows are generated by forms, and echoes follow voices. Toying with shadows and belaboring their forms, [foolish practitioners] do not understand the identity of the two. Raising the voice to stop the echo, [such persons] do not understand that their voice is the basis of the echoes. Striving for nirvāṇa by eradicating the illusions is like eliminating forms and searching for shadows. Striving for Buddhahood by transcending [one's status as a] sentient being is like silencing one's voice and listening for an echo.

Know therefore that ignorance and enlightenment are identical, stupidity and wisdom not separate. [People] arbitrarily posit names where there are no names, and these names lead to the generation of [distinctions between] "this" and "not-this." [They also] arbitrarily formulate principles [explaining this reality] where there are no principles, and these principles lead to the occurrence of disputation. The phantasmagorical transformations [of phenomenal reality] are not real, so who can say "this" and "not-this"? [All is] false and without reality, so what are "being" and "non-being"?

Not having been able to go and discuss [Buddhism with you], I have written these few phrases. [Even so,] who could [ever truly] discuss the mysterious principle!

[Hui-k'o's Reply]

Your discussion of the True Dharma is completely accurate.

There is ultimately no difference between it and the true and abstruse principles.

Originally deluded, one calls the *maṇi*-pearl[8] a potsherd.

Suddenly one is awakened—and it is [recognized as] a pearl.

Ignorance and wisdom are identical, not different.

One should understand that the myriad *dharma*s are all "suchlike."

Having compassion for those who hold such discriminating views
you have taken your brush to write this letter.

Contemplating one's body and the Buddha [and seeing that they] are not different,
why should one further seek for that remainderless state [of nirvāṇa]?

3. The Message of the Letters

Taken together, the two letters attached to the *EJSHL* describe the following three states of religious consciousness:

1. Mundane striving: The author of the first letter offers a long confession of his former addiction to traditional sorts of Buddhist religious activity—scriptural study, recitation, and the like—all of which were undertaken in order to bring him closer to enlightenment, which he perceived to be a total transformation of his entire being. The Buddha's six years of asceticism mentioned in the second letter are essentially identical in that they were a period of goal-oriented behavior predicated on ascriptive views about the nature of reality. Both letters elaborate on the implications of such fundamentally false conceptions and distinctions: descriptions of reality using inherently inaccurate and misleading names or definitions of things; dichotomies between good and evil, true and false, etc.; doctrinal disputes and destructive argumentation in general; and—most important of all—the deluded notion that one could attain nirvāṇa by destroying one's illusions. In short, in this sort of consciousness one is fundamentally ignorant of the truths of *śūnyatā* and the existence of the Buddha Nature within oneself.

2. Correct religious practice: In contrast to the attempt to make progress toward a goal, which typifies religious practice in the limited sense as described in the preceding paragraph, here one dispenses with all false dualism and fixes one's attention on the mind. The proper approach to practice is described only briefly in the first letter, but at least we know that a special form of seated meditation is implied. This practice has no stages or technical progressions; somehow one must achieve one's goal without positing any goal.

3. Realization: The onset of realization occurs all of a sudden. Hui-k'o's reply refers to a sudden switch from the limited consciousness of the normal, ignorant state to the expansive openness of enlightenment. The poem at the end of the first letter refers to "melding the mind and making it pure," i.e., to dissolving the mind's tendencies to false discrimination and conceptualization, which form a barrier to the realization of the absolute realm of *śūnyatā*. We may infer that the historical Buddha instantly understood not only the vanity of his six years of asceticism, but also the identity of saṁsāra and nirvāṇa, the identity of the illusions and enlightenment. At that point his mind penetrated the fundamental reality of the universe and achieved a complete, unqualified identification with the timeless serenity of the absolute. According to the verse at

the end of the first letter, at the moment of enlightenment one realizes that saṁsāra is created by ordinary sentient beings during each and every moment of discriminative consciousness—the implication being that one thereby makes the decision to dispense with such discrimination in order to escape the suffering of saṁsāra.

The first and third of these states of religious consciousness are actually standard Buddhist fare; the second, in contrast, is distinctively Ch'an. The earliest exponents of Ch'an were apparently devoted to a style of meditative practice—not very clearly defined in these letters—that somehow dispensed with all stages of progress and lesser sorts of self-improvement and went straight to the heart of the matter of human ignorance by focusing directly on the mind itself.

4. The Meaning of the Four Practices

Now, then, to the *EJSHL* itself. The basic distinction in this text, of course, is between the entrance of principle and the entrance of practice. The term *ju* (entrance) may be easily understood in terms of the compounds *ju-tao,* "to enter the Path" or "to enter into enlightenment," and *wu-ju,* "to enter into a state of enlightenment." The character *li,* which has been translated in this context as "principle," refers to the ultimate reality or abstract principle underlying all phenomena. The entrance of principle, then, is the "entrance into enlightenment on the basis of the comprehension of the fundamental Truth about human reality." It could just as well be translated as the "entrance of the absolute," or, from another perspective, the "entrance of understanding."

Hsing-ju has been translated as the "entrance of practice," in the sense of spiritual practices aimed at the attainment of enlightenment. As we shall see, *hsing* refers not to contemplative practices per se, but to the entire spectrum of daily activity *qua* religious endeavor.[9]

For the sake of convenience, let us first consider the "four practices." The practice of the retribution of enmity is to be undisturbed by unfavorable circumstances or suffering *(k'u, duḥkha)* in one's life in the realization that they are but the karmic retribution of all enmity and ill will expressed by oneself in the past. It is best to think of enmity as representative of the basic causes of suffering, i.e., the illusions or afflictions *(fan-nao, kleśa),* which are themselves based on ignorance *(wu-ming, avidyā).* The choice of the term "enmity" *(yuan)* as the basic cause of one's present plight is apparently occasioned by a compound found in the *Tao-te ching.*[10] Although this practice is but the first and most rudimentary of the four, to successfully maintain the proper attitude in the face of diversity is to be in complete accord with the Absolute Principle, i.e., the Dharma.

In the practice of the acceptance of circumstances, one is to remain unmoved by either good or bad fortune due to an awareness of one's own lack of permanent existence *(wu-wo, anātman)* and of the incessant changes that occur in one's being and the conditions of one's life. Where the first practice is applicable only in times of explicit personal suffering, here the sphere of relevance is widened to include both good and bad karmic rewards. Suffering and impermanence are perceived to be inherent even within the experience of good fortune. However, the basic attitude enjoined by this practice is no different from that of the previous one.[11]

The practice of the absence of craving is to be without attachment or desire for any thing or circumstance within one's experience, whether favorable, unfavorable, or neutral. The word *ch'iu* has been translated here as "craving" in the sense of the Sanskrit word *tṛṣṇā,* the concept of craving referred to in the second of the Four Noble Truths as the cause of all human suffering. Although this is not a standard equivalent for this Chinese character, the text states that "the various kinds of covetousness and attachment that people experience in their never-ending ignorance are referred to as *ch'iu.*"[12] As in the case of the first practice, to accomplish this practice is to be in accord with the Absolute Principle, or the truth that is "contrary to human convention."

The last of the four practices is to govern the entirety of one's actions according to an understanding of the emptiness or nonsubstantiality of all things. The very first lines of this section define the Dharma of *śūnyatā* as equivalent to the principle *(li)* referred to in the first of the two entrances. That principle transcends defilement, attachment, characteristics, and dualistic distinctions. The practice of accordance with the Dharma is defined according to the example of the perfection of charity. Just as this perfection requires that one perceive the emptiness or nonsubstantiality of recipient, donor, and gift, so does this Ch'an treatise require that one eliminate false thoughts and cultivate the six perfections without conceptualizing anything as a "practice."

It should be obvious that the four practices form a very simple progression from the forbearance of suffering, through the rejection of craving, to a thorough realization of the nonsubstantiality of all things.[13] Actually, the four practices do not represent a series of different modes of practice, but four progressively more profound expressions of one and the same mental attitude of nonattachment. The succession of the four practices is best understood as a didactic conceit, useful in the correct orientation of new students into the practical application of the doctrine of *śūnyatā*. The implications of this observation will become apparent after we have considered the entrance of principle.

5. The Entrance of Principle

As stressed by previous commentators, the entrance of principle is undoubtedly the more important of the two entrances. Because of its importance, this part of Bodhidharma's treatise is offered here in outline form. The order of the last sentence is altered slightly for convenience of presentation:

1. The entrance of principle is to become enlightened to the Truth on the basis of the teaching.
2. [One must have a] profound faith [in the fact that]
   A. one and the same True Nature is possessed of all sentient beings, both ordinary and enlightened
   B. and that this [True Nature] is only covered up and made imperceptible [in the case of ordinary people] by false sense impressions.
3. If one discards the false and takes refuge in the True,
   A. one resides frozen in "wall contemplation," [in which] self and other, ordinary person and sage are one and the same;
   B. one resides fixedly without wavering, never again to be swayed by written teachings.
4. This is called the entrance of principle:
   A. to be mysteriously identified with the [True] Principle;
   B. to be without discrimination, serene and inactive.

Sentence 1 is obviously an introduction to the entrance of principle as a whole. The "teaching" referred to here is to be differentiated from the "written teachings" mentioned in 3B, which refers to a limited, conceptualized understanding of the Buddhist scriptures as presented by exegetes and doctrinal specialists. In this case the reference is to Bodhidharma's oral instructions or to the essential message of Buddhism per se —the fundamental truth of the scriptures as opposed to their verbal formulations.[14] Sentences 2 and 3 constitute the main part of the passage, the first explaining the essential article of religious faith according to Ch'an and the second defining the natural consequences of that faith in one's individual religious training. The last sentence, number 4, represents the passage's conclusion.[15]

Since sentences 1 and 4 obviously constitute introduction and conclusion to the entrance of principle as a whole, our main interest here is in sentences 2 and 3. The first is a straightforward statement of the idea of the Buddha Nature, the enlightened aspect or potentiality for achieving buddhahood that is inherent within all sentient beings, regardless of their level of religious insight. The unavoidable corollary of the idea of the Buddha Nature is that its presence is obscured by human illusion, discriminative thinking, and emotional activity. For all but a very few living beings—the Buddhas and sages—the Buddha Nature does not immediately reveal itself to the introspective searcher. However often or insistently we are told that we bear the seed of enlightenment within, there is simply no plain indication that this is actually so.[16]

For practicing Buddhists such as the members of the earliest Ch'an lineage, the initial invisibility of the Buddha Nature leads to the following question: How can one change oneself so that one becomes able to perceive the Buddha Nature within? At this point the testimony of the letters appended to the *EJSHL* becomes relevant. What was needed was not some form of personal transformation that would destroy or render ineffective the illusions obscuring one's view of the Buddha Nature and distinguishing one so utterly from the ranks of the enlightened. Rather, what was needed was the realization that no such transformation was required. By recognizing the unreal quality of one's illusions and rejecting the temptation to tamper with them for the purpose of some preconceived notion of spiritual progress, one attained a state of perfect enlightenment. This attainment may in fact constitute a very important type of transformation, but it would not require the replacement of one's own mundane personality with the transcendent identity of a buddha or celestial bodhisattva.

By means of the word *tan,* "only," the *EJSHL* proper clearly indicates the relative importance of the Buddha Nature and the illusions and false thinking that obscure it. But this word is apt to be overlooked by the inattentive reader. Professor Yanagida writes:

> In the present example, true spiritual practice, as well as the fundamental principle of Buddhism, is the profound conviction that all living beings possess the same one True Nature, whether they are enlightened or not. Sensory impressions are ultimately falsely arisen entities, false coverings. This is the meaning of the word "only."
>
> If one places excessive emphasis on the sensory impressions predicated by this word "only" and thinks of spiritual practice as the rejection of the false and the return to the True, then one fails to understand the entrance of principle. The True Nature is naturally clear and pure—it does not become so merely by virtue of the eradication of sensory impressions . . . If one reads carefully, this usage of "only" appears quite frequently in the texts of the early Ch'an School.[17]

In other words, the existence of an absolute or enlightened aspect within human beings is fundamentally more significant than the existence of illusions and false thoughts that obscure that enlightenment.

What does the *EJSHL* advocate as a response to this existential situation of a Buddha Nature obscured by a veil of human illusion? The first part of this response is the eminently simple concept indicated in sentence 2: profound faith. As is well known, in Buddhism faith is not an emotional commitment or outpouring of devotion, but rather an unswerving conviction, a total absence of even the slightest doubt about the nature of reality as described by the Buddhist teachings. The Chinese character for faith, *hsin,* connotes the acceptance or of reliance on something. In this case it is the complete acceptance of the existence of the Buddha Nature within the veil of illusions, or even the decision to rely on the existence of that Buddha Nature as the guiding principle of all one's actions.

The adoption of this "profound faith" in the existence of the Buddha Nature marks the initiation of the uniquely Ch'an type of religious practice that is only imprecisely indicated by the letters discussed earlier. According to the *EJSHL,* faith leads on to abide in a state described as "frozen," "fixed," "unwavering," and "without discrimination, serene and inactive."[18]

Where other Buddhist texts might describe the victory over human illusions in terms of cutting them off at the root, here we find described a position of invincible solidity in which one (a) realizes the identity of ordinary person and sage and (b) is never again swayed by written teachings. The term "written teachings" refers, of course, to the verbalized imitations of truth, rather than to the true teachings of Buddhism mentioned in sentence 1.

6. The Practice of "Wall Contemplation"

How did Bodhidharma and his followers develop the state of invincibility described in the previous section? Did they use some kind of yogic technique in which all the normal transformations of consciousness were intentionally brought to a stop? Did they somehow manage to paralyze their minds and at the same time achieve a realization of the ultimate truth of *śūnyatā?* Or is some other meaning of residing "frozen" and "fixed" implied here?

The crux of the entrance of principle is of course the troublesome term *pi-kuan,* or "wall contemplation." This term is without precedent in prior texts and, as may be seen from the following list, subject to a number of interpretations by later Chinese authorities:

1. T'an-lin's preface to the *EJSHL* refers to *pi-kuan* as Bodhidharma's teaching of the "pacification of the mind" *(an-hsin),* which is one of the most common terms for spiritual endeavor and meditation practice in early Ch'an.
2. The *HKSC* states that "the achievements of [Bodhidharma's] Ma-

hāyāna wall contemplation are the very highest," but no specific definition is given.

3. The *CFPC,* the earliest of the Ch'an transmission histories, rejects the authenticity of "wall contemplation and the four practices" as Bodhidharma's ultimate teachings. This position was repeated by a Sung Dynasty scholar of Ch'an, Ch'i-sung (1007–72).

4. The Hua-yen School's Chih-yen (602–68) lists wall contemplation in a list of eighteen types of meditation suitable for use by beginners for the treatment of different dispositional problems or spiritual ills.

5. Tsung-mi refers to this term in two different ways. In his discussion of the teachings of the Northern School, he writes:

> Bodhidharma taught people pacification of the mind through wall contemplation, in which externally one ceased discrimination and internally one made one's mind free of 'gasping' (i.e., free of impediments and attachments?). When the mind is like a wall one can enter into enlightenment *(ju-tao)*—truly, is this not a method of meditation?

In another location Tsung-mi refers to wall contemplation as an allegory for Bodhidharma's unverbalized teaching of mind and its essence of "knowing" *(chih),* a concept that Tsung-mi claimed was the quintessential aspect of the teachings of his own favorite, Shen-hui.

6. Huang-po Hsi-yun (d. 850) refers to Bodhidharma's practice as one of physically facing a wall in meditation. The *CTL* states that Bodhidharma "always sat in silence facing the wall, so people called him the 'wall-contemplating Brahmin.' "

7. A thirteenth century T'ien-t'ai work, the *Shih-men cheng-t'ung (True Succession of the House of Śākya),* defines a wall in this context as the "nonentrance of sensory data and the false."[19]

Modern interpretations of this term have been similarly diverse, if cautiously hesitant. Ui Hakuju's only comment on the subject, for example, is his definition of *pi-kuan* as "pacification of the mind in which the mind is mysteriously united with tranquillity."[20] T'ang Yung-t'ung is only slightly more explicit, saying that "the mind is like a wall, forgetting words and extirpating conceptualization." T'ang apparently understands the wall as a metaphor for unshakable solidity, rather than as a vertical surface dividing two regions of space. In addition, he interprets the compound *pi-kuan* as a verb with a preceding modifier ("to contemplate like a wall" or "wall-like contemplation"), rather than as an inverted verb-object ("to contemplate a wall"). The latter grammatical interpretation is implicit in the image of Bodhidharma "facing a wall" *(mien-pi)* in meditation, but this is clearly a later construction.[21]

Professor Yanagida has offered two interpretations of the term *pi-kuan* that are categorically different from those just given. Although they occur in separate contexts and contain assertions that are anything but conservative, their presentation together here will prove to be remarkably helpful in the understanding of the *EJSHL* as a whole:

> It is a fact that Tao-hsuan characterized [Bodhidharma's teaching] in comparison to those of [the Hīnayānist] Seng-ch'ou, writing that "the merits of Mahāyāna wall contemplation were the very highest." It is to be expected that "wall contemplation" in itself constituted the Mahāyāna contemplation of nonsubstantiality . . . Actually, the metaphor of the wall had already appeared in the *Ta chih-tu lun*'s passage on the mindfulness of the body . . . It was a metaphor for the inanimate, the unconscious (*mushin,* or *wu-hsin* in Chinese).
>
> In essence, *pi-kuan* means "the wall contemplates," not "one contemplates a wall." One becomes a wall and contemplates as such. What does one contemplate? One contemplates *śūnyatā.* One gazes intently at a vibrantly alive *śūnyatā.*[22]

The more controversial of these two interpretations is unquestionably the latter. Yanagida explicates it with reference to the figures painted on the walls of Chinese burial tumuli, figures that steadfastly view the ghastly scenes in front of them with complete detachment and aplomb. The passage occurs in a short summary of early Ch'an history aimed at a popular audience, a context that allowed for an unusually picturesque interpretation. Yanagida continues as follows:

> In general, the caves at Yun-kang and Lung-men that were created from the Northern Wei onward had countless numbers of buddhas and bodhisattvas carved into all four walls. The eyes of the buddhas and bodhisattvas were also carved into the floors and ceilings. These stone images witnessed (*miru,* using the Chinese character *kuan,* meaning "to see" or "to contemplate") the history of the people that entered and left such caves.
>
> When Bodhidharma first arrived in the Northern Wei, he presumably sat alone in meditation in such a cave. His was not a practice of "facing a wall," but of becoming a wall and witnessing himself and the world. He saw the emptiness of history, he saw the truth of the identity of unenlightened person and sage. I believe that this was the origin of the word "wall contemplation."
>
> At the same time "wall contemplation" includes the idea of "turning back the brilliance in counterillumination" (*ekō henshō,* or *hui-kuang fan-chao* in Chinese), the wonderfully bright radiance of the setting sun. Or the inconceivable function of the mirror, which illuminates each and every thing in existence . . . It is well to point out that [such ideas] begin in the Ch'an of Bodhidharma along with this difficult yet strangely appealing expression, "wall contemplation."

I suspect that it would be very difficult to defend the translation of *pi-kuan* as "the wall contemplates" before a hypothetical sixth-century audience of native Chinese speakers. Yet the line between "contemplating like a wall" and "a wall contemplating" is very fine: To achieve the former would be tantamount to achieving the latter. Although it may seem questionable at first glance, this interpretation of *pi-kuan* is helpful in understanding the *EJSHL* as a whole.

The key phrase in this passage describes Bodhidharma's practice "of becoming a wall and witnessing himself and the world." At this point we must recall Yanagida's earlier, less adventurous interpretation, in which he equates *pi-kuan* with the Mahāyāna contemplation of nonsubstantiality. According to these interpretations, *pi-kuan* involves two separate aspects, static and dynamic. These two aspects may be correlated with the two entrances of the *EJSHL:* The entrance of principle is to achieve and maintain a firm conviction of the immanence of the Buddha Nature within oneself and all other living beings, while the entrance of practice is to act at all times on the basis of a profound understanding of saṁsāra. Such a profound understanding is absolutely necessary for the enactment of the four practices. In order to overcome adversity, one must first perceive its impermanence. In order to help sentient beings, one must first comprehend the nature of their suffering. Whereas the firm conviction of the entrance of principle is represented within the practice of *pi-kuan* by the solidity of the wall, the dynamic capacity of understanding that underlies the four practices is embodied in the very notion of contemplation itself, the activity of "witnessing [one]self and the world."

The reader may object that these static and dynamic aspects of religious practice are not both immediately apparent in the term *pi-kuan.* I cannot deny this. I will not claim that this analysis constitutes a definitive and unchallangeable interpretation of *pi-kuan* and the entrance of principle. However, it does provide a key to the comprehensive interpretation of early Ch'an religious doctrine. The very presence of both the static and dynamic aspects of religious practice in the *EJSHL* is, I believe, an important explanation for its significance in early Ch'an.

7. Bodhidharma's Treatise and the Later Development of Ch'an Doctrine

One of the most important issues in the development of early Ch'an doctrine is the rejection of traditional meditation technique, with its emphasis on yogic concentration and gradual self-perfection, in favor of a sudden approach that was supposedly more open, spontaneous, and intuitive. Hu Shih, D. T. Suzuki, and others have described this as a transition from an intrinsically Indian style of practice to one that was just as uniquely and characteristically Chinese.[23] Although I will refrain from commenting on such interpretations at present, I do think it is important to note that the tendency to reject traditional meditative technique occurred in non-Ch'an School contexts during the second half of the sixth century. Note the following passages from the biographies of T'an-lun (d. 626) and Ching-lin (565–640), both of whom were associated with the She-lun School:

> [T'an-lun's teacher] counseled him: "If you fix your mind on the tip of your nose you will be able to achieve tranquillity." [T'an]-lun said: "If I view the mind as capable of being fixed to the tip of my nose I will fundamentally see neither the characteristic of the mind nor what it is fixed upon."
>
> At a different time [T'an-lun's master] informed him: "In sitting you must first learn to purify your clouded mentation. It is just like peeling an onion—you peel layer after layer and finally achieve purity *(te ching).*" [T'an]-lun said: "If I view it to be like an onion, then it can be peeled, but fundamentally there is no onion that can be peeled."
>
> Therefore, afterward [T'an-lun] ceased all reading of the sūtras and worship of the Buddhas, but simply shut himself in a room and did not come out, fulfilling his spiritual ambition by simply transcending thoughts *(li-nien)* in all his activities.[24]

> [Ching-lin] rejected the practice of lecturing in order to single-mindedly cultivate meditation. First, he practiced [the contemplation of physical] impurity and the [four] foundations of mindfulness. Then he became displeased at their petty complexities and [the way they] insisted on the cessation of human ratiocination. He turned to the practice of the various "contemplations of nonattainment" *(chu wu-te-kuan).* By transcending his thoughts in consciousness-only *(li-nien wei-shih)* he expanded his realization of the Truth. He comprehended every [such contemplation] that he undertook, practicing thus for ten years.[25]

The concepts of gradual spiritual progress and sudden enlightenment, so well known to modern readers, are not specifically mentioned in any of the primary sources introduced in this chapter. Nevertheless, it is clear that, in addition to the major dichotomy between scriptural study and the practice of meditation, a minor dichotomy also existed in late sixth- or early seventh-century Chinese Buddhism between two approaches to the practice of meditation itself. Although the methods of practice adopted by T'an-lun and Ching-lin did involve seated meditation and predetermined contemplative techniques, they were considered to be fundamentally different from the progressive approach of conventional Indian meditation. Similarly, the letters attached to the *EJSHL* contain specific rejections of traditional Buddhist practices—the use of scriptural recitation, repentance rituals, and contemplative techniques aimed at the inculcation of positive religious emotions and the simultaneous elimination of incorrect views and prejudices. The *EJSHL*'s references to a frozen and fixed state of being and the absence of the normally dualistic functions of cognitive activity constitute an expression of the same ideal.

Other scholars have, of course, interpreted the references to a frozen or fixed state in terms of yogic styles of mental cultivation. This observation can only be accepted with some modification: The *EJSHL* does not contain any allusion to the cultivation of yoga, but only to a final state of attainment that is quite similar to the ultimate stage of yogic achievement. It is impossible to know how Bodhidharma had his students reach this state; one wonders if he used the "*samādhi* of the seal of the *Tathāgata*'s wisdom," à la Seng-fu, or the "contemplations of nonattainment," like Ching-lin.

Actually, the language of the *EJSHL* is so terse and uninformative that a definitive interpretation would be impossible. When considered solely by themselves, the records of Bodhidharma's career and earliest impact are too scanty to yield any meaningful conclusions. The real value of these documents lies in their capacity to indicate general themes that govern the subsequent periods of early Ch'an history, and thereby help us understand a body of evidence that is both extensive and disorganized. In other words, the true teachings of the historical Bodhidharma cannot be deduced from the extant primary source material, but that material may be used as a key to the subsequent development of Ch'an thought.

With this understanding, I make the following observation: The static and dynamic motifs of Bodhidharma's two entrances seem to anticipate the two major themes of early Ch'an thought considered in this study. The entrance of principle emphasizes recognition of the existence of the Buddha Nature within oneself, which is the primary concern of the East Mountain Teaching texts attributed to Tao-hsin and Hung-jen. The entrance of practice is concerned with the active expression of the Dharma in the perfected activities of everyday life, which is the primary concern of the Northern School doctrines of Shen-hsiu and others. Only after analyzing the doctrines of these two phases of Ch'an thought will we be able to understand the relationship between these two approaches, the full implications of their rejection of traditional meditative technique, and the true significance of the sudden-gradual dichotomy in early Ch'an.

CHAPTER VI

The Basic Doctrines of the East Mountain Teaching

1. Problems in the Study of the East Mountain Teaching

In Part One we saw that there was no clear line of demarcation between the period known as the East Mountain Teaching, i.e., the careers of Tao-hsin and Hung-jen, and that known as the Northern School, i.e., the careers of Shen-hsiu and his successors. Although they appear to be two separate phases of early Ch'an history, the former is known almost solely through the texts of the latter. The same is true of the religious doctrines of the two phases: No matter how hard we might try to reconstruct the actual doctrines of Tao-hsin and Hung-jen, their "East Mountain Teaching" can only be approached through texts produced and/or edited during the later "Northern School" phase.

There are only a very few datable clues to the teachings of Ch'an during the seventh century:

1. The *HKSC* refers to Tao-hsin's teaching as the "expedient means of entering the Path" *(ju-tao fang-pien)* and depicts him as a devotee of the *Perfection of Wisdom.*[26]

2. The *Chin-kang san-mei ching (Sūtra of the Adamantine Samādhi),* a text probably written in Korea sometime between 645 and about 665, mentions both Bodhidharma's two entrances and a practice of "maintaining the one and preserving the three" *(shou-i ts'un-san).* The latter is reminiscent of the doctrine of "maintaining the One without wavering" *(shou-i pu i)* attributed to Tao-hsin.[27]

3. There exists a Tun-huang manuscript of a text entitled *Ta-mo ch'an-shih lun (Dhyāna Master* [*Bodhi*]*dharma's Treatise),* which might be taken as a guide to the teachings of early Ch'an. The text is probably relatively early, although its putative date of compilation or transcription, 681, is not reliable. Unfortunately, its contents do not lend themselves to precise dating.[28]

4. The composition of Shen-hsiu's *Kuan-hsin lun (Treatise on the Contemplation of the Mind)* may be assigned to the years 675–700. The introduction into the Ch'an tradition of Chih-i's *Ch'eng-hsin lun (Treatise on the Clarification of the Mind)* probably occurred during the same period.[29]

5. Finally, the epitaph for Fa-ju (638–89) mentions such topics as the different types of *samādhi* practiced at Hung-jen's monastery, Fa-ju's "sudden entrance into the One Vehicle," his ability to remain "motionless in the True Realm and yet know the myriad forms," and, as discussed in Part One, the fact that the transmission of the teaching was done without words.[30]

Unfortunately, these details are all too brief, too vague and/or difficult to interpret, and—in the case of those referring to Shen-hsiu and Fa-ju—too late to be of any real value.

Modern scholars generally explain the teachings of Tao-hsin and Hung-jen on the basis of two texts known chiefly from Tun-huang manuscripts. For Tao-hsin there exists a portion of the *LCSTC* that appears to be taken verbatim from a work called the *Ju-tao an-hsin yao fang-pien fa-men (Essentials of the Teaching of the Expedient Means of Entering the Path and Pacifying the Mind;* hereafter cited as *JTFM).* For Hung-jen, there exists the *Hsiu-hsin yao lun (Treatise on the Essentials of Cultivating the Mind),* which is known from a variety of sources. Since the *JTFM* teaches *shou-i,* or "maintaining the one," and the *Hsiu-hsin yao lun* teaches *shou-hsin,* or "maintaining the mind," scholars have generally argued that the latter text and teaching were more advanced than the former.[31]

I do not believe that this interpretation is acceptable. The *JTFM* is known solely through the *LCSTC.* Judging by the absence of separate Tun-huang manuscripts—admittedly an argument made *ex silentio*—one would have to conclude that the *JTFM* did not circulate independently. Even more important, no other early Ch'an text quotes from it or even alludes to it. Although there are no specific indications that it was of late composition, it uses many of the same texts and even the same passages as other Northern School texts of the early eighth century.[32] In addition, it addresses certain Taoist ideas and Pure Land practices that would have been of greater interest to an author working in the context of Buddhism in the two capitals in the early eighth century than to a retiring meditation specialist of the early seventh.[33]

Finally, although the text's explanation of *shou-i* does seem to be less advanced in some ways than the *Hsiu-hsin yao lun*'s concept of *shou-hsin,* the *JTFM* as a whole is a much more sophisticated, or at least a more complex, work. Although it would be misleading to suggest that this greater internal complexity necessarily implies a later date of composition, some of the ideas contained in the treatise usually attributed to Tao-hsin are suggestive of the most advanced teachings of the Northern School.

A text attributed to Tao-hsin could well have been written after one attributed to Hung-jen. We know that the *Hsiu-hsin yao lun* was not written by Hung-jen himself, since the text itself admits that it was compiled by his students.[34] Hung-jen was in many ways the most important figure of early Ch'an, in that he was the immediate spiritual forebear to many of the men who disseminated the teachings in Ch'ang-an and Lo-yang in the late seventh and early eighth centuries. Therefore, it is not surprising that a text like the *Hsiu-hsin yao lun* would have been composed to represent the fundamentals of his teachings. The attribution of this text to Hung-jen thus has a retrospective validity: Its contents are not an exact record of his teachings, but they are at least representative of the most fundamental doctrines of early Ch'an, a "lowest common denominator" of Ch'an theory around the year 700.

The existence of a handful of separate versions of the *Hsiu-hsin yao lun* from Tun-huang and elsewhere indicates its general acceptance by the members of the early Ch'an School as teachings appropriate to the departed sage of East Mountain. After Hung-jen was thus equipped with a suitable literary statement, the attentions of the early Ch'an authors would have turned naturally to his predecessor, Tao-hsin. The process continued in this reverse fashion with the compilation of the *Hsin-hsin ming (Inscription on Relying upon the Mind),* which is falsely attributed to Seng-ts'an, Tao-hsin's supposed teacher.[35]

Although specific proof is lacking, I suspect that the *JTFM* was only written very shortly, no more than a decade or so, before it was noticed by Ching-chueh and quoted in his *LCSTC* of 713–16. This interpretation must be considered tentative, but the reader should at least grant that it would be improper to follow the conventional approach in constructing a theory for the chronological development of early Ch'an religious thought. This problem is not limited to these two works. In fact, it is extremely difficult to assign a definite date to any of the doctrinal developments of early Ch'an.

Having found a diachronic approach to the teachings of early Ch'an untenable, we must turn to a synchronic, thematic approach. Because of the retrospective validity of the *Hsiu-hsin yao lun* and, to a lesser extent, the *JTFM,* these two texts will be our primary source of information about the basic tenets of the East Mountain Teaching. The reader should keep in mind that the "East Mountain Teaching" defined in these pages does not refer to the teachings of Tao-hsin and Hung-jen, but rather to the most basic doctrines of the Ch'an School in the early eighth century in the vicinity of the two capitals.

2. Textual Information

The *Hsiu-hsin yao lun,*[36] written as a dialogue between the master and an unnamed interrogator, may be divided into two parts of roughly equal length. The first, which includes sections A to M of the translation that follows, is a structured series of questions and answers. The second, sections N to V, contains fewer questions, longer doctrinal statements and descriptions of meditation practice, a greater amount of colloquial language, and numerous direct exhortations to vigorous practice.

Important points to notice while reading this text include the following:

1. the metaphor of the sun obscured by clouds that occurs in section D
2. emphasis on the importance of "maintaining [awareness of] the mind" throughout the text, and
3. the two types of meditation practice recommended in sections O and T

3. Treatise on the Essentials of Cultivating the Mind (Hsiu-hsin yao lun)

A. A Treatise on the Essentials of Cultivating the Mind, in one fascicle, [written by] Preceptor [Hung]-jen of Ch'i-chou[37] [in order to] lead ordinary people to sagehood and to an understanding of the basic principle of emancipation.[38]

B. If you do not take care of [this text], then all the [other] practitioners will be unable to see it. Please understand that in copying it, you should take care to make no mistakes or omissions, which might mislead those who follow.[39]

C. The essence of cultivating the Path is to discern that one's own body (mind?[40]) is inherently pure, [not subject to the laws of] generation and extinction, and without discrimination. Perfect and complete in its Self Nature,[41] the Pure Mind is the fundamental teacher. [Meditating on it] is superior to reflecting on the Buddhas of the ten directions.

D. QUESTION: How do you know that one's own mind is inherently pure?

ANSWER: The *Treatise on the* [*Sūtra of the*] *Ten Stages*[42] *(Shih-ti lun)* says:

> There is an adamantine Buddha Nature within the bodies of sentient beings.[43] Like the sun, it is essentially bright, perfect, and complete.

> Although vast and limitless, it is merely[44] covered by the layered clouds of the five *skandhas*. Like a lamp inside a jar, its light cannot shine.

Further, to use the bright[45] sun as a metaphor, it is as if the clouds and mists of this world were to arise together in [all] the eight directions, so that the world would become dark.[46] How could the sun ever be extinguished?

[QUESTION: Without the sun being extinguished,] why would there be no light?

ANSWER: The sun's light is not destroyed, but merely deflected by the clouds and mists. The pure mind possessed by all sentient beings is also like this, in simply being covered by the layered clouds of discriminative thinking, false thoughts, and ascriptive views. If one can just distinctly maintain [awareness of] the mind *(shou-hsin)*[47] and not produce false thoughts, then the Dharma sun[48] of nirvāṇa will be naturally manifested. Therefore, it is known that one's own mind is inherently pure.

E. QUESTION: How do you know that one's own mind is inherently not subject to the laws of generation and extinction?

ANSWER: The *Vimalakīrti Sūtra (Wei-mo ching)* says: "Suchness *(ju)* is without generation; Suchness is without extinction."[49] The term "Suchness" refers to the suchlike Buddha Nature, the mind which is the source [of all *dharmas*][50] and pure in its Self Nature. Suchness is fundamentally existent and is not conditionally produced. [The *Vimalakīrti Sūtra*] also says: "Sentient beings all [embody] Suchness. The sages and wise men also [embody] Suchness."[51] "Sentient beings" means us (i.e., ordinary people), and "sages and wise men" means the Buddhas. Although the names and characteristics of [sentient beings and the Buddhas] are different, the essential reality of the Suchness contained within the bodies of each is identical and is not subject to the laws of generation and extinction. Hence [the sūtra] says "all [embody] Suchness." Therefore, it is known that one's own mind is inherently not subject to the laws of generation and extinction.

F. QUESTION: Why do you call the mind the fundamental teacher?

ANSWER: The True Mind exists of itself and does not come from outside [oneself. As teacher] it does not even require any tuition fee![52] Nothing in all the three periods of time is more dear [to a person] than one's mind. If you discern the Suchness [inherent in the mind] and maintain awareness of it, you will reach the other shore [of nirvāṇa]. The deluded forsake it and fall into the three lower modes of existence (i.e., animals, hungry ghosts, and residents of the hells). Therefore, it is known that the Buddhas of the three periods of time take their own True Mind[53] as teacher.

Hence the treatise says: "The existence of sentient beings is dependent on the waves of false consciousness, the essence of which is illusory."[54] By clearly maintaining awareness of the mind, the false mind will not be activated *(pu ch'i),* and you will reach the state of birthlessness (i.e., nirvāṇa). Therefore, it is known that the mind is the fundamental teacher.

G. QUESTION: Why is the mind of ordinary people superior to the mind of the Buddhas?[55]

ANSWER: You cannot escape birth and death by constantly reflecting on buddhas divorced from yourself,[56] but you will reach the other shore of nirvāṇa by maintaining awareness of your own fundamental mind.[57] Therefore, [the Buddha] says in the *Diamond Sūtra (Chin-kang po-jo ching):* "Anyone who views me in terms of form and seeks me by sound is practicing a heretic path and is unable to see the *Tathāgata.*"[58] Therefore, it is known that maintaining awareness of the True Mind is superior to reflecting on Buddhas divorced from oneself. In addition, the word "superior" is only used as a word of encouragement in the context of religious practice. In reality, the essence of the ultimate fruit [of nirvāṇa] is uniformly "same" *(p'ing-teng)* and without duality.

H. QUESTION: If the true essence of sentient beings and the Buddhas is the same, then why is it that the Buddhas are not subject to the laws of generation and extinction, but receive incalculable pleasures and are autonomous *(tzu-tsai)* and unhindered [in their activities], while we sentient beings have fallen into the realm of birth and death and are subject to various kinds of suffering?[59]

ANSWER: All the Buddhas of the ten directions are enlightened to the Dharma Nature and distinctly illuminate the mind that is the source [of all individual *dharmas*] *(chao-liao hsin-yuan).* They do not generate false thoughts, never fail in correct mindfulness *(cheng-nien),* and extinguish the illusion of personal possession.[60] Because of this, they are not subject to birth and death. Since they are not subject to birth and death, they [have achieved] the ultimate state of serene extinction (i.e., nirvāṇa). Since they [have achieved] serene extinction, the myriad pleasures naturally accrue to them.

Sentient beings, [on the other hand,] are all deluded as to the True Nature and do not discern the fundamental mind. Because they cognize the various [*dharmas*] falsely,[61] they do not cultivate correct mindfulness. Since they do not have correct mindfulness, thoughts of revulsion and attraction are activated [in them]. Because of [these thoughts of] revulsion and attraction, the vessel of the mind becomes defiled (lit., "broken and leaky"). Since the [vessel of] the mind is defiled, [sentient beings] are subject to birth and death. Because of birth and death, all the [various kinds of] suffering naturally appear.

The *Sūtra of Mind-king* [*Bodhisattva*] *(Hsin-wang ching)* says: "The suchlike Buddha Nature is concealed by knowledge based on the senses *(chih-chien)*. [Sentient beings] are drowning in birth and death within the seas of the six consciousnesses and do not achieve emancipation."[62]

Make effort! If you can maintain awareness of the True Mind without generating false thoughts or the illusion of personal possession, then you will automatically be equal to the Buddhas.

I. QUESTION: [You say that] the suchlike Dharma Nature [is embodied by both sentient beings and the Buddhas] identically and without duality. Therefore, if [one group] is deluded, both should be deluded. If [one group] is enlightened, both should be enlightened. Why are only the Buddhas enlightened, while sentient beings are deluded?

ANSWER: At this point we enter the inconceivable portion [of this teaching], which cannot be understood by the ordinary mind. One becomes enlightened by discerning the mind; one is deluded because of losing [awareness of the True] Nature. If the conditions [necessary for you to understand this] occur, then they occur[63]—it cannot be definitively explained. Simply rely on the ultimate truth[64] and maintain awareness of your own True Mind.

Therefore, the *Vimalakīrti Sūtra* says: "[*Dharma*s] have no Self Nature and no Other Nature. *Dharma*s were fundamentally not generated [in the first place] and are not now extinguished."[65] Enlightenment is to transcend the two extremes and enter into nondiscriminating wisdom. If you understand this doctrine, then during all your activities[66] you should simply maintain awareness of your fundamental Pure Mind. Do this constantly and fixedly, without generating false thoughts or the illusion of personal possession. Enlightenment will thus occur of itself.

If you ask a lot of questions, the number of doctrinal terms will become greater and greater. If you want to understand the essential point of Buddhism,[67] then [be aware that] maintaining awareness of the mind is paramount. Maintaining awareness of the mind is the fundamental basis of nirvāṇa, the essential gateway for entering the path, the basic principle of the entire Buddhist canon,[68] and the patriarch of all the Buddhas of past, present, and future.

J. QUESTION: Why[69] is maintaining awareness of the mind the fundamental basis of nirvāṇa?

ANSWER: The essence of what is called nirvāṇa is serene extinction. It is unconditioned and pleasant. When one's mind is True, false thoughts cease. When false thoughts cease, [the result is] correct mindfulness. Having correct mindfulness leads to the generation of the wisdom of serene illumination (i.e., the perfect knowledge or illumination of all things without mental discrimination), which in turn means that one achieves total comprehension of the Dharma Nature.[70] By comprehending the Dharma Nature one achieves nirvāṇa. Therefore, maintaining awareness of the mind is the fundamental basis of nirvāṇa.

K. QUESTION: Why is maintaining awareness of the mind the essential gateway for entering the path?

ANSWER: The Buddha teaches that even [actions as seemingly trivial as] raising the fingers of a single hand to draw an image of the Buddha[71] can create merit as great as the sands of the River Ganges. However, this is just [his way of] enticing foolish sentient beings to create superior karmic conditions whereby they will see the Buddha and [become enlightened] in the future.[72] If you wish to achieve buddhahood quickly in your own body, then do nothing[73] except to maintain awareness of the True Mind.

The Buddhas of past, present, and future are incalculable and infinite [in number], and every single one of them achieved buddhahood by maintaining awareness of the True Mind.[74] Therefore, the sūtra says: "When one fixes the mind in a single location, there is nothing it cannot accomplish."[75] Therefore, maintaining awareness of the True Mind is the essential [gateway[76]] for entering the path.

L. QUESTION: Why is maintaining the True Mind the basic principle of the entire Buddhist canon?

ANSWER: Throughout the canon, the *Tathāgata* preaches extensively about all the types of transgression and good fortune, causes and conditions, and rewards and retributions. He also draws upon all the various things [of this world]—mountains, rivers, the earth,[77] plants, trees, etc.—to make innumerable metaphors. He also manifests innumerable supernormal powers and various kinds of transformations. All these are just the Buddha's way of teaching foolish sentient beings. Since they have various kinds of desires and a myriad of psychological differences, the *Tathāgata* draws them into permanent bliss (i.e., nirvāṇa) according to their mental tendencies.

Understand clearly that the Buddha Nature embodied within sentient beings is inherently pure, like a sun underlaid by clouds. By just distinctly maintaining awareness of the True Mind, the clouds of false thoughts will go away and the sun of wisdom[78] will appear. Why make any further study of knowledge based on the senses, which [only] leads to the suffering of saṁsāra?

All concepts, as well as the affairs of the three periods of time, [should be understood according to] the metaphor of polishing a mirror: When the dust is gone the Nature naturally becomes manifest *(chien-hsing)*.[79] That which is learned by the ignorant mind is completely useless. True learning is that which is learned by the inactive (or unconditioned, *wu-wei*) mind, which never ceases correct mindfulness. Although this is called "true learning," ultimately there is nothing to be learned. Why is this? Because the self and nirvāṇa are both nonsubstantial, they are neither different nor the same. Therefore, the essential principle[80] of [the words] "nothing to be learned" is true.

One must maintain clear awareness of the True Mind without generating false thoughts or the illusion of personal possession. Therefore, the *Nirvāṇa Sūtra (Nieh-p'an ching)* says: "To understand that the Buddha does not [actually] preach the Dharma is called having sufficiently listened [to the Buddha's preaching]."[81] Therefore, maintaining awareness of the True Mind is the basic principle of the entire Buddhist canon.

M. QUESTION: Why is maintaining awareness of the mind the patriarch of all the Buddhas of past, present, and future?

ANSWER: All the Buddhas of past, present, and future are generated within [one's own] consciousness. When[82] you do not generate false thoughts, [the Buddhas] are generated within your consciousness. When your illusions of personal possession have been extinguished, [the Buddhas] are generated within your consciousness. You will only achieve buddhahood by maintaining awareness of the True Mind. Therefore, maintaining awareness of the mind is the patriarch of all the Buddhas of past, present, and future.

N. If one were to expand upon the four previous topics, how could one ever explain them completely? My only desire is that you discern the fundamental mind for yourselves. Therefore, I sincerely tell you: Make effort! Make effort! The thousand sūtras and ten thousand treatises say nothing other than that maintaining the True Mind is the essential [way to enlightenment].[83] Make effort!

I base [my teaching] on the *Lotus Sūtra (Fa-hua ching),* in which [the Buddha] says: "I have presented you with a great cart and a treasury of valuables, including bright jewels and wondrous medicines. Even so, you do not take them. What extreme suffering! Alas! Alas!"[84] If you can cease generating false thoughts and the illusion of personal possession, then all the [various types of] merit will become perfect and complete. Do not try to search outside yourself, which [only] leads to the suffering of saṁsāra. Maintain the same state of mind in every moment of thought, in every phase of mental activity. Do not enjoy the present while planting the seeds of future suffering—[by doing so] you only deceive yourself and others and cannot escape from the realm of birth and death.

Make effort! Make effort! Although it may seem futile now, [your present efforts] constitute the causes for your future [enlightenment].[85] Do not let time pass in vain while only wasting energy. The sūtra says: "[Foolish sentient beings] will reside forever in hell as if pleasantly relaxing in a garden. There are no modes of existence worse than their present state."[86] We sentient beings fit this description. Having no idea how horribly terrifying [this world really] is, we never have the least intention of leaving! How awful!

O. If you are just beginning to practice sitting meditation,[87] then do so according to the *Sūtra of the Contemplation of Amitābha*[88] *(Wu-liang-shou kuan ching):* Sit properly with the body erect, closing the eyes and mouth. Look straight ahead with the mind, visualizing a sun at an appropriate distance away. Maintain this image continuously without stopping. Regulate your breath so that it does not sound alternately coarse and fine, as this can make one sick.

If you sit [in meditation] at night, you may experience all kinds of good and bad psychological states; enter into any of the blue, yellow, red, and white *samādhis*; witness your own body producing light; observe the physical characteristics of the *Tathāgata;* or experience various [other] transformations. When you perceive [such things], concentrate the mind and do not become attached to them. They are all nonsubstantial manifestations of false thinking.[89] The sūtra says: "All the countries of the ten directions are [nonsubstantial,] like space." Also, "The triple realm is an empty apparition that is solely the creation of the individual mind."[90] Do not worry if you cannot achieve concentration and do not experience the various psychological states. Just constantly maintain clear awareness of the True Mind in all your actions.

If you can stop generating false thoughts and the illusion of personal possession, [then you will realize that] all the myriad *dharma*s are nothing other than [manifestations of your] own mind. The Buddhas only preach extensively using numerous verbal teachings and metaphors because the mental tendencies of sentient beings differ, necessitating a variety of teachings. In actuality, the mind is the basic [subject] of the eighty-four thousand doctrines, the ranking of the three vehicles, and the definitions of the seventy-two [stages of] sages and wise men.

To be able to discern one's own inherent mind and improve [the ability to maintain awareness of it] with every moment of thought is equivalent to constantly making pious offerings to the entire Buddhist canon and to all the Buddhas in the ten directions of space,[91] who are as numerous as the sands of the River Ganges. It is equivalent to constantly turning the wheel of the Dharma with every moment of thought.

He who comprehends the mind that is the source of all *dharmas* always understands everything. All his wishes are fulfilled and all his religious practices completed. He accomplishes all [that he sets out to do] and will not be reborn again [in the realm of saṁsāra].[92] If you can stop generating false thoughts and the illusion of personal possession and completely discard [your preoccupation with] the body, then you will certainly achieve birthlessness (i.e., nirvāṇa). How inconceivably [wonderful]!

Make effort! And do not be pretentious![93] It is difficult to get a chance to hear this essential teaching. Of those who have heard it, not more than one person in a number as great as the sands of the River Ganges is able to practice it. It would be rare for even one person in a million billion eons to practice it to perfection.[94] Calm yourself with care, moderate any sensory activity, and attentively view the mind that is the source of all *dharmas*. Make it shine distinctly and purely all the time, without ever becoming blank.[95]

P. QUESTION: What is blankness of mind?

ANSWER: People who practice mental concentration may inhibit the True Mind within themselves by being dependent on sensory perceptions, coarse states of mind, and restricted breathing. Before achieving mental purity, [such people may undertake the] constant practices of concentrating the mind and viewing the mind. Although they do so during all their activities, [such people] cannot achieve [mental] clarity and purity, nor illumine that mind which is the source of all *dharmas*. This is called blankness [of mind.]

[People who possess such a] defiled mind cannot escape the great illness of birth and death. How much more pitiful are those who are completely ignorant of [the practice of] maintaining awareness of the mind! Such people are drowning in the seas of suffering that are concomitant with the realm of saṁsāra—when will they ever be able to escape?

Make effort! The sūtra says:

> If sentient beings are not completely sincere about seeking enlightenment, then not even all the Buddhas of the three periods of time will be able to do anything [for them, even if those Buddhas] are as numerous as the sands of the River Ganges.[96]

The sūtra says: "Sentient beings discern the mind and cross over [to the other shore of enlightenment] by themselves. The Buddhas cannot make sentient beings cross over [to the other shore]." If the Buddhas were able to make sentient beings cross over [to the other shore of enlightenment], then why—the Buddhas of the past being as incalculable as the sands of the River Ganges—have we sentient beings not yet achieved buddhahood? We are drowning in the seas of suffering simply because we are not completely sincere about seeking enlightenment.

Make effort! One cannot know the transgressions of one's past, and repenting now is of no avail. Now, in this very lifetime, you have had an opportunity to hear [this teaching]. I have related it clearly; it would be well for you to understand what I say. Understand clearly that maintaining awareness of the mind is the highest way. You may be insincere about seeking the achievement of buddhahood and become receptive to the immeasurable pleasures and benefits [that accrue from religious training. You may] go so far as to ostentatiously follow worldly customs and crave [personal] fame and gain. [If you do so you will] eventually fall into hell and become subject to all kinds of suffering. What a plight! Make effort!

Q. One can have success with minimal exertion by merely donning tattered robes, eating coarse food, and clearly maintaining awareness of the mind. The unenlightened people of this world do not understand this truth and undergo great anguish in their ignorance. Hoping to achieve emancipation, they cultivate a broad range of superficial types of goodness—only to fall subject to the suffering concomitant with saṁsāra.

He who, in [mental] clarity, never ceases correct mindfulness while helping sentient beings cross over to the other shore of nirvāṇa is a bodhisattva of great power.[97] I tell you this explicitly: Maintaining awareness of the mind is the ultimate. If you cannot bear suffering during this single present lifetime, you will be subject to misfortune for ten thousand eons to come. I ask you: Which case applies to you?

To remain unmoved by the blowing of the eight winds[98] [of good and ill fortune] is to have a truly special mountain of treasure. If you want to realize the fruit [of nirvāṇa], then just respond to all the myriad different realms of your consciousness by activating transformations as numerous as the sands of the River Ganges. One's discrimination [of each instant] is so skillful it seems to flow. Applying medicine to fit the disease, one is able to stop generating false thoughts and the illusion of personal possession. He who [can do this] has transcended the world and is truly a man of great stature.[99] Ah, the unrestricted freedom of a *Tathāgata*—how could it ever be exhausted!

Having explained these things, I[100] urge you in complete sincerity: Stop generating false thoughts and the illusion of personal possession!

R. Question: What do you mean by the "illusion of personal possession"?

Answer: When only slightly superior to someone else [in some way], one may think that this [superiority] is due to one's own achievement. To feel this way is to be sick even while in nirvāṇa. The *Nirvāṇa Sūtra* says: "This is likened to the realm of space, which contains the myriad things. Space does not think to itself, I am doing this."[101] This is a metaphor for the two teachings of [eradicating the] illness and practicing [the truth, i.e.,] the concept of extinguishing the illusion of personal possession and the "adamantine *samādhi*" *(chin-kang san-mei).*[102]

S. Question: Even sincere[103] practitioners who seek a perfect and permanent nirvāṇa [may only seek] the crude and impermanent standards of goodness and fail to take pleasure in the Ultimate Truth. [Such people may] try to have their minds operate according to [Buddhist] doctrines before they have manifested that which is true, permanent, wondrous, and good (i.e., the Buddha Nature). This leads to the activation of discriminative thinking, which constitutes a defiled state of mind. They may try to fix the mind in the locus of non-being *(wu-so).*[104] To do so is to be lodged in the darkness of ignorance and is not in accord with the [True] Principle.

They may grasp nonsubstantiality in an improper way, without trying to fix the mind [on a single object of contemplation] according to [Buddhist] doctrines. Although they have received a human body, theirs is the practice of animals. They lack the expedient means of meditation and wisdom and cannot clearly and brightly see the Buddha Nature. This is the predicament of religious practitioners [such as ourselves]. We beseech you to tell us the true teaching by which we can progress toward remainderless nirvāṇa!

Answer: When you are completely in [possession of] the True Mind, the achievement of your ultimate wish [is assured].

Gently quiet your mind. I will teach you [how to do this] once again: Make your body and mind pure and peaceful, without any discriminative thinking at all. Sit properly with the body erect. Regulate the breath and concentrate the mind so it is not within you, not outside of you, and not in any intermediate location. Do this carefully and naturally. View your own consciousness tranquilly and attentively, so that you can see how it is always moving, like flowing water or a glittering[105] mirage. After you have perceived this consciousness, simply continue to view it gently and naturally, without [the consciousness assuming any fixed position] inside or outside of yourself. Do this tranquilly and attentively, until its fluctuations dissolve into peaceful stability. This flowing consciousness will disappear like a gust of wind.[106]

When this [flowing] consciousness disappears, [all one's illusions will] disappear along with it, even the [extremely subtle] illusions of bodhisattvas of the tenth stage. When this consciousness and [false cognition of the] body have disappeared, one's mind becomes peacefully stable, simple, and pure. I cannot describe it any further. If you want to know more about it, then follow the "Chapter on the Adamantine Body" *(Chin-kang shen p'in)* of the *Nirvāṇa Sūtra* and the "Chapter on the Vision of *Akṣobhya* Buddha" *(Chien o-ch'u-fo p'in)* of the *Vimilakīrti Sūtra.*[107] Think about this carefully, for this is the truth.

T. Any person who can avoid losing [sight] of this mind during all his actions and in the face of the five desires and the eight winds [of good and ill fortune] has established his pure practice,[108] done that which must be done, and will never again be born into the realm of birth and death. The five desires are [those that arise relative to] form, sound, smell, taste, and touch. The eight winds are success and failure; defamation and praise; honor and abuse; and suffering and pleasure.

While cultivating the Buddha Nature[109] you must never worry about not achieving autonomous [mastery of the supernormal powers, etc.] in this lifetime. The sūtra says: "When there is no buddha in the world, then bodhisattvas who have [reached the ten] stages are unable to manifest the functioning [of enlightenment(?)]."[110] You must become emancipated from this retribution body. The abilities of sentient beings [as governed by the factors of the] past differ in ways that cannot be understood. Those of superior [ability can achieve enlightenment] in an instant, while those of inferior [ability take] an incalculable number of eons. When you have the strength,[111] generate the good roots of enlightenment according to [your own] nature (i.e., individual identity) as a sentient being, so that you benefit yourself and others and ornament the path of buddhahood.

You must completely [master] the four dependences[112] and penetrate the true characteristic [of all things]. If you become dependent on words you will lose the True Principle *(chen-tsung).* All you monks who have left home (i.e., to become monks) and practice some other form of Buddhism—this is the [true meaning of] "leaving home." "Leaving home" is to leave the home of birth and death. You will achieve success in the cultivation of the path when your [practice of] correct mindfulness is complete. To never fail in correct mindfulness—even when one's body is being torn apart or at the time of death—is to be a buddha.

U. My disciples have compiled this treatise[113] [from my oral teachings], so that [the reader] may just use his True Mind to grasp the meaning of its words. It is impossible to exhaustively substantiate [every detail] with preaching such as this. If [the teachings contained herein] contradict the Holy Truth, I repent and hope for the eradication [of that transgression]. If they correspond to the Holy Truth, I transfer [any merit that would result from this effort to all] sentient beings. I want everyone to discern their fundamental minds and achieve buddhahood at once. Those who are listening [now] should make effort, so that you can achieve buddhahood in the future. I now vow to help my followers to cross over [to the other shore of nirvāṇa].

V. QUESTION: This treatise [teaches] from beginning to end that manifesting one's own mind represents enlightenment. [However, I] do not know whether this is a teaching of the fruit [of nirvāṇa] or one of practice.

ANSWER: The basic principle of this treatise is the manifestation of the One Vehicle. Its ultimate intention is to lead the unenlightened to emancipation, so that they can escape from the realm of birth and death themselves and eventually help others to cross over to the other shore of nirvāṇa. [This treatise] only speaks of benefiting oneself and does not explain how to benefit others.[114] It should be categorized as a teaching of practice *(hsing-men)*. Anyone who practices according to this text will achieve buddhahood immediately.

If I am deceiving you, I will fall into the eighteen hells in the future. I point to heaven and earth in making this vow: If [the teachings contained here] are not true, I will be eaten by tigers and wolves for lifetime after lifetime.[115]

4. The Metaphor of the Sun and Clouds

The key to understanding the *Hsiu-hsin yao lun* is the metaphor of the sun obscured by clouds that occurs near the beginning of the text. Unfortunately, the origin of the passage containing this metaphor is obscure. The same passage is also found in Ching-chueh's *LCSTC* and Shen-hsiu's *Kuan-hsin lun,* but it is attributed in these texts to the *Shih-ti ching,* the *Sūtra on the Ten Stages,* rather than the *Shih-ti* [*ching]* lun, the treatise based on that sūtra. In fact, the passage occurs in neither. Since no scriptural precedent for this passage has ever been found, it seems best to assume that it derived from an unknown Chinese source of the late seventh century or earlier.[116]

Nowhere does the use of this metaphor occur so prominently as in the beginning of I-hsing's commentary on the *Ta-jih ching (Sūtra of the Great Vairocana* [*Buddha*]*),* one of the most important scriptures of esoteric Buddhism. I-hsing, who was at one time a student of P'u-chi, opens his commentary with an explanation of the name of the Buddha that occurs in the title of the sūtra:

> The Sanskrit word *Vairocana* is another name for the sun, having the meaning of an omnipresent brilliance that eradicates darkness. The sun of this world, however, is governed by spatial limitations. It cannot illuminate inside [a building] the same as it can outside; it can brighten one place but not another. Also, its brilliance only occurs during the daytime and does not illuminate the night. The brilliance of the sun of the *Tathāgata*'s wisdom is not like this, in that it is a great illuminating brightness that extends to every location [in the universe]. There are no spatial [limitations of] interior and exterior or distinctions of day and night.
>
> Also, as the sun travels [about] the world, the plants and trees are able to grow according to their natural allotments, so that the various tasks of this world achieve completion thereby. The brilliance of the sun of the *Tathāgata* illuminates the entire *dharmadhātu,* [so that] it is able to foster, with absolute impartiality *(p'ing-teng),* the incalculable "good roots" of sentient beings. In addition, all the excellent mundane and supramundane activities are without exception achieved on the basis of [the sun of the *Tathāgata*'s wisdom].
>
> Further, layered shadows can obscure the orb of the sun so that it is hidden, yet it is not destroyed. Violent winds can blow the clouds away so that the sun's brilliance may be seen to illuminate, yet it is not only just born. The sun of the Mind of the Buddha *(fo-hsin chih jih)* [that is within us all] is also like this: Although it may be obstructed by the layered clouds of ignorance, the afflictions, and foolish disputation, it is never decreased [by such obstructions]. Even if one achieves the ultimate [experience of the] "*samādhi* of the true characteristic of all *dharmas*," [in which] one's perfect brilliance is unlimited, [the Mind of the Buddha within] is not increased [thereby].
>
> Because of various factors such as these, the sun of this world cannot be taken as a metaphor [for the sun of the *Tathāgata*'s wisdom]. It is only by taking consideration of the small degree of resemblance and adding the word *great* that one can say: *"Mahāvairocana."*[117]

It is possible, of course, that I-hsing learned this metaphor from Śubhākarasiṁha, the esoteric Buddhist master under whom he studied the sūtra in question. However, the content and structure of the third paragraph of the statement just quoted, which discusses "layered shadows" (i.e., clouds), violent winds, and the ensuing appearance of the indestructible sun, are strikingly reminiscent of the corresponding *Hsiu-hsin yao lun* passage.[118] Whatever its origin, I-hsing's explanation of the name Vairocana utilizes the conceptual framework operant in the Ch'an School at exactly the same time.

The metaphor of the sun and clouds is used twice in the *LCSTC,* once in the entry on Guṇabhadra, and again in that on Hui-k'o. In the latter instance it appears essentially as it does in the *Hsiu-hsin yao lun*. In addition to minor variations of wording and the different attribution mentioned in the first paragraph of this section, Ching-chueh interpolates a passage from the *Avataṁsaka Sūtra* on the Buddha Nature being as vast as space. He follows the metaphor of the sun and clouds with a list of several others: ice and water, a lamp in the wind, fire within wood, gold and gangue, and water and waves. The most interesting, for our purposes, is the following:

> The Buddha Nature [exists in the] same sense as the sun and moon exist in the world (lit., "below heaven") and fire exists within wood. Within people, there is the Buddha Nature. It is also called the "lamp of the Buddha Nature" and the "mirror of nirvāṇa." Therefore, the great mirror of nirvāṇa is brighter than the sun and moon. Interior and exterior are perfect and pure, boundless and limitless.[119]

Ching-chueh's reference to the mirror is particularly interesting in light of the famous *Platform Sūtra* verses. The other reference to the metaphor of the sun and clouds in Ching-chueh's work occurs together with an allusion to the mirror that is even more apropos:

> The great path (*ta-tao,* here probably equivalent to enlightenment) is fundamentally vast. Being perfect and pure it is fundamentally existent and is not attained through causes. It resembles the light of the sun, which is underlaid by clouds. When the clouds and mists disappear, the light of the sun appears of itself. What use is it to make any further study of discriminative knowledge, to range across the written and spoken words that only lead to the path of birth and death? He who transmits oral explanations of written texts as the path [to enlightenment] is only seeking personal fame and benefit, [thereby] harming self and others.
>
> It is also like the polishing of a bronze mirror: When the dust is completely gone from the surface of the mirror, the mirror is naturally bright and pure. The *Sūtra on the Nonactivity of All* Dharmas *(Chu-fa wu-hsing ching)* says: "The Buddha does not achieve buddhahood, nor does he save sentient beings. [It is only due to] the excessive discrimination of sentient beings that [he is said to] achieve buddhahood and save sentient beings." If you do not become enlightened to this mind, you will never be certain [of its existence and function]. If you are enlightened to it, then [you will perceive] its illumination. The great function of causal generation being perfectly interpenetrating and without hindrance: This is called the "great cultivation of the path."[120]

At first glance, these references to the mirror seem to have exactly the same implication as in the *Platform Sūtra* verse attributed to Shen-hsiu. Certainly, the basic construction of the metaphor is the same: The mirror represents the fundamental mind or Buddha Nature; the dust represents the human ignorance that obscures one's True Mind. Although Ching-chueh's explicit injunction is to recognize the mind that lies beneath the obscuring dusts of the illusions, one suspects that he is also recommending that we work to rid ourselves of illusion just as one would rub dust from the surface of a mirror.

Not only is no such recommendation made in the *LCSTC,* but this metaphor is not used in the same way in the *Hsiu-hsin yao lun* and other East Mountain Teaching texts. True, the *Hsiu-hsin yao lun* does contain a reference to polishing a mirror clean of dust (see section L of the translation), but this reference is not used to exhort the student to strive for the vigorous removal of the "dust" of his own illusions. On the contrary, the implication is that the reflective or illuminative capacity of the mirror is a fundamental characteristic that is not really affected by the adventitious appearance of dust upon its surface.

Another East Mountain Teaching text, the *Liao-hsing chü (Stanzas on the Comprehension of the Nature),* puts it this way:

> Although the [Pure] Nature is without darkness, it is obstructed by the clouds of false thoughts. It is like dust on a bright mirror—how can it possibly damage the [mirror's] essential brightness (*ming-hsing,* or "brightness nature")? Although it may be temporarily obstructed, rubbing will return the brightness. The brightness [of the mirror] is a fundamental brightness, not like something appended to it. The Dharma Nature is the same.[121]

In other words, the brightness of the mirror and the existence of dust on its surface are of two fundamentally different levels of reality. The mirror is not really affected by the dust, which can be wiped off at any time. In the *Hsiu-hsin yao lun* the emphasis is placed on the sun, which is the symbolic equivalent of the mirror, rather than on the clouds or dusts of ignorance. The clouds that block our view of the sun do not destroy the sun; the winds that drive those clouds away do not thereby create the newly apparent sun. As Ching-chueh points out in the *LCSTC,* the Buddha actually neither becomes a buddha nor saves other beings—he only appears to do so to those who lack true understanding.

According to the *Hsiu-hsin yao lun,* the existence of the Buddha Nature or Fundamental Mind within all sentient beings is the single most important fact of our existence. True, that Buddha Nature may be rendered invisible or ineffective by ignorant views, dualistic conceptualization, and the karmic residue of past errors—but the important fact is that it is there. What is the appropriate religious response to this situation? Would it be to strive diligently for the annihilation of those obstacles of dualistic ignorance in order to strip away the "clouds" obscuring one's pristine internal "sun"?

No, the appropriate response is to focus on the sun rather than on one's illusions, to nurture the awareness of its existence in each and every moment, no matter what one's particular activity or situation might be. This is the meaning of the term *shou-hsin,* to "maintain [awareness of] the mind."

5. Shou-hsin *and Meditation Practice in the* Hsiu-hsin yao lun

Shou-hsin literally means "to guard the mind," or, according to a more liberal interpretation, "to maintain constant, undiscriminating awareness of the absolute mind or Buddha Nature within oneself." The word *shou* means "to protect, maintain, or uphold" and is used in other Buddhist terms in the sense of maintaining the precepts, or moral purity in general. The term *shou-hsin,* in fact, is very similar to *shou-i,* "to guard the will" or "to guard the consciousness," which is used in very early Chinese translations in the sense of "mindfulness," an important concept in Buddhist meditation theory.[122]

In the *Hsiu-hsin yao lun, shou-hsin* does not mean to guard the mind against outside influences so much as to maintain it uppermost in one's thoughts, to refrain from ever forgetting about the cardinal importance of its existence, to make its presence the dominant standard by which one orders one's life. In the strictest sense, *shou-hsin* means to simply maintain continued possession of the Absolute Mind, but this possession is treated in cognitive terms: It is the awareness of the presence of that mind that is important. Eventually, one will experience the Buddha Nature directly when one's illusions disappear.

The metaphor of the sun and clouds and the use of the term *shou-hsin* combine to indicate a very gentle approach to spiritual practice: If one maintains awareness of the mind without having any false thoughts or illusions, then the "sun of nirvāṇa" will appear naturally. In other words, one's Buddha Nature will become manifested and one will be enlightened. The insistence on maintaining awareness of the mind rather than purposefully working for and achieving enlightenment amounts to an affirmation of the ultimate perfection of the human condition just as it is, without the necessity of any adjustment or alteration.

In spite of this gentle, all-affirming attitude, the *Hsiu-hsin yao lun* is also outspoken about the need for vigorous effort in meditation. Hung-jen is frequently made to exhort his students to make effort, and enlightenment is clearly considered something to be energetically sought for and achieved, if not in this lifetime, then in the next. In the context of this treatise it is impossible to completely resolve this apparent contradiction between the passive acceptance of the ultimate perfection of the present human condition and the purposive striving for enlightenment. Quite possibly *shou-hsin* was intentionally designed to mitigate the general tendency of beginning students to grasp for an idealized and thus fundamentally misapprehended goal, i.e., the achievement of enlightenment.

Certainly, such considerations occur frequently in early Ch'an works. One important example from the letters attached to the *EJSHL,* which we discussed in the previous chapter, emphasize that the spiritual goal is not a personal transformation per se but the realization that no such transformation is required. In addition, the tension between the ultimate perfection of human existence and the need to strive diligently for self-realization is common throughout the entire Ch'an tradition. Although the *Hsiu-hsin yao lun* does not explicitly address this creative tension, the meditation techniques it suggests are in themselves functional paradigms of the importance of the Buddha Nature and the essential emptiness of the discriminative mind. Hence, the very type of practical striving advocated here is in itself an affirmation of perfection in the undisciplined human state.[123]

The first meditation technique recommended in the *Hsiu-hsin yao lun,* the visualization of the golden orb of the sun, is obviously related to the metaphor discussed earlier. (See section O of the translation.) This technique, which is loosely based on the Pure Land tradition's *Sūtra of the Contemplation of Amitābha,* is a simple concentration device for the beginning student similar to those common to all systems of Buddhist meditation and at the same time a translation of the abstract idea of *shou-hsin* and the metaphor of the sun into practical terms. That is, visualizing an image of the sun is a practical enactment of the state of enlightenment, in which the Buddha Nature has become and will remain constantly visible.

The second technique is simply to concentrate on the movement of one's own discriminative mind. (See section S.) In effect, this is to concentrate on the clouds or dusts of ignorance rather than the pure brilliance of the sun or mirror, but the overall impact is very much the same as in the former technique. Here, too, the instruction is not to wrest that ignorance from one's person, but merely to observe that ignorance until it ceases to function. In effect, this is to concentrate on one's illusions until they dissolve into nonexistence. At the point at which one's discriminative mind finally stops, one is said to have come into contact with the Absolute Mind. The meditator is not supposed to alter his practice of *shou-hsin* after achieving this contact, but rather to maintain it permanently while responding perfectly to the outside world. The difference between this new state of being and the previous, unenlightened state necessarily involves being in direct, undistorted contact with the outside world through the undeluded, Absolute Mind. Although this Absolute Mind is said to discriminate sense data, it does so perfectly and without any false conceptualization.[124]

The functioning of the enlightened mind is not discussed at length in the *Hsiu-hsin yao lun,* which describes itself as devoted solely to the benefit of self rather than others. The functioning of the enlightened mind is actually the province of the Northern School per se, but we are left to wonder just how much of the later methodology designed to explicate this issue was already in place by the time the *Hsiu-hsin yao lun* was written. As we shall see in the following section, the *JTFM* has more to say on this subject.

6. The Background of shou-i pu i *or "Maintaining the One Without Wavering"*

The most interesting subject discussed in the *JTFM* is *shou-i pu i* or "maintaining the One without wavering." Although the full four-character phrase is not found elsewhere, the term *shou-i* has a very long history in Chinese literature.[125] Yoshioka Yoshitoyo has analyzed the rich background and significance of this term in the Chinese Taoist tradition, arguing that by the beginning of the fifth century the advocates of *shou-i* assumed the status of an independent faction and that by the beginning of the sixth century this faction had developed to the point that *shou-i* had become accepted as the central element of Taoist meditation practice.[126]

The basis of the Taoist practice of *shou-i* is the emphasis on the "One" *(i),* which in the *Tao-te ching* is understood as the immediate derivative of the Tao itself and, in turn, the source of the myriad elements of phenomenal reality.[127] The term *shou-i* is used in both the *Tao-te ching* and the *Chuang-tzu,* but it is in Ko Hung's *Pao-p'u tzu* that it receives its most definitive early exposition. Here the "One" is regarded as the source of all things, including even the Tao itself, and the fundamental reason for all things being as they are. He who knows the One knows all; he who is ignorant of the One knows nothing.

The One is the source of all good fortune, as well as personal longevity, so that the Taoist scriptures teach the practice of "maintaining the One" *(shou-i).* The One is regarded as existing within the psychic centers of the body, i.e., the three "cinnabar fields" below the navel, below the heart, and behind the space between the eyes. If a practitioner could "maintain the One without tiring" *(shou-i pu t'ai),* the One would protect him from all danger.[128]

Although some of the phrases that occur in Taoist texts are very similar to the *shou-i pu i* of the *JTFM,* the explanation of the Taoist practice of *shou-i* is couched in the highly symbolic language of internal alchemy, which does not translate readily into a Buddhist context.[129] The following statement from a mid-fifth-century Taoist text, however, is unmistakably relevant to the development of Chinese Buddhism:

> The *śrāmaṇera* students of the Hīnayāna sit quietly and count their breaths. Reaching ten, they begin again, doing this all year long without forgetting it for a moment . . .

> The Taoist priests *(tao-shih),* the students of the Mahāyāna, constantly think upon the image of the true god within the body, [including] its apparel and color. They lead it going and coming *(tao-yin wang-lai),* treating it as a divine ruler, without ceasing for a moment. Therefore, thoughts do not enter from outside, the Divine and True Being descends, and the mind is without [the confusion of] excess affairs. The Mahāyāna [way of] training is to accept the pneuma and maintain the One *(shou-ch'i shou-i).*[130]

It is amusing to observe Taoists using the Buddhist terms "Hīnayāna" and "Mahāyāna" against Buddhism. For our purposes, the important implication is that the Ch'an School may have adopted use of the term *shou-i* because it represented an alternative to traditional Buddhist meditation technique that was somehow more compatible with the Chinese religious spirit. Indeed, the state in which "thoughts do not enter from the outside, the Divine and True Being descends, and the mind is without [the confusion of] excess affairs" could easily be transposed into a Buddhist idiom, with the Divine and True Being taken as an anthropomorphized Buddha Nature.

This interpretation is rendered even more plausible by the fact that another Taoist text, thought by Yoshioka to have been written around the year 700, emphasizes the importance of *shou-i* in much the same way that the *Hsiu-hsin yao lun* does *shou-hsin,* describing it as the one precept in which all others are subsumed. Not only are the terms "gradual" and "sudden" *(chien* and *tun)* mentioned, but the text recommends that one apply the precepts in one's mind, "not activating any other thought" *(pu ch'i t'a nien).*[131] "Nonactivation" *(pu-ch'i)* was an important Northern Ch'an term at the same point in Chinese religious history.

At the very least, the use of the terms *shou-i* and *shou-i pu i* in the early Ch'an School represents the borrowing or imitation of attractive Taoist terminology. Beyond this, *shou-i* may have been adopted because of its specific meaning within the Taoist tradition. That is, *shou-i* represented the quintessential element of Taoist meditation practice, a general technique that was applicable in all situations and far superior to the myriad other techniques of more specific use and elaborate description. The precipitation of *shou-i* out of the mass of Taoist spiritual technology thus resembles the quest within Buddhism for the single most important and immediately relevant religious technique, a quest that was an important factor in the development of both Ch'an meditation and the Pure Land practice of the "mindfulness of the Buddha" *(nien-fo).*

It is also possible that the Taoist practice of *shou-i* represented a sort of generalized mindfulness of one's internal harmony that appealed to the followers of early Ch'an. Thus the Buddhists overlooked the symbology of cinnabar fields and internal spirits and focused on the state achieved during the correct practice of *shou-i,* in which thoughts did not intrude on the harmonized mind. Although this interpretation seems reasonable, there is unfortunately no specific evidence to indicate the degree to which the Buddhists were aware of and indebted to the previous accomplishments of their Taoist counterparts.

7. *The Meaning of "Maintaining the One Without Wavering" in the* JTFM

The *JTFM* claims that in the practice of *shou-i pu i* "the trainee is able to clearly see the Buddha Nature and quickly enter the gateway of meditation."[132] The text describes this practice as follows:

A. First, taking the body as the fundamental [focus of one's attention], one should cultivate a detailed contemplation of the body. Also, the body is the amalgam of the four elements (i.e., earth, water, fire, and wind) and the five *skandhas* (form, feelings, perceptions, impulses, and consciousness). It is ultimately impermanent and will never achieve autonomy *(tzu-tsai).* Although it has not yet been destroyed, it is ultimately nonsubstantial. The *Vimalakīrti Sūtra* says: "The body is like a floating cloud—in an instant it disappears."[133]

Further, one should constantly contemplate one's own body to be nonsubstantial and pure[134] like a shadow, which can be seen but not grasped. Wisdom is generated from within the shadow. Being ultimately without location [of its own, wisdom] is unmoving and yet responds to things, inexhaustible in its transformations. It generates the six senses out of nonsubstantiality. The six senses are also nonsubstantial and serene, so one should realize that their six respective realms of sense perception are [illusory, like] dreams or phantasmagoria.

When the eye sees something, there is no "thing" within the eye. When a mirror reflects a face, it may be perfectly distinct, but this is an image (lit., a "shadow of the form") manifested in space, and there is not any "thing" within the mirror. You should understand that a person's face does not enter into the mirror, nor does the mirror enter into the person's face.[135] One should understand by this detailed consideration that mirror and face fundamentally do not exit or enter or go or come. This is the meaning of *Tathāgata (ju-lai,* "Thus-come One").

According to this analysis, within the eye and within the mirror there is a fundamental and constant [state] of nonsubstantiality and serenity. The illumination of the mirror and the illumination (i.e., perception) of the eye are identical. Therefore, [the eye] has been used as a comparison. The meaning of the nose, tongue, and other senses is the same. Know that the eye is fundamentally nonsubstantial and that all visible form must be understood to be "other-form" *(t'a-se).*[136] When the ear hears a sound, understand this to be an "other-sound." When the nose smells a fragrance, understand this to be an "other-fragrance." When the tongue distinguishes a taste, understand this to be an "other-taste." When the mind apprehends a *dharma,* understand this to be an "other-*dharma.*" When the body experiences a feeling, understand this to be an "other-feeling" . . .

B. To "maintain the One without wavering" is to concentrate on viewing a single thing with this eye of nonsubstantial purity, to be intent on this constantly and motionlessly, without interruption, day and night. When the mind tries to run away, bring it back quickly. Just as a line is tied to the foot of a bird to retrieve it if it tries to fly, you should view *(k'an)* [that thing] all day long, without cease. The mind will then become completely settled . . .

When studying archery, one first shoots at a large target, then a medium-sized one, then a small one then the bull's-eye, then a single hair, then one-hundredth of a hair. Then one shoots each arrow into the haft of the previous one, [each arrow] supported, haft by haft, without any of them falling. This is a metaphor for spiritual training, in which one fixes the mind [on a single object] thought after thought. Continuing this in successive moments of thought without any temporary [diversion], one's correct mindfulness is uninterrupted. One is correctly mindful of the immediate present . . .[137]

Furthermore, if the mind activates *(ch'i)* its cognitive [functions] *(chueh)* in connection with some sense realm separate from itself, then contemplate the locus of that activation as ultimately nonactivating *(pu-ch'i).* When the mind is conditionally generated, it does not come from [anywhere within] the ten directions, nor does it go anywhere. When you can constantly contemplate [your own] ratiocination, discrimination, false consciousness, perceptions, random thoughts,[138] and confused [states of] mind as nonactivated, then [your meditation] has attained gross stability. If you can stabilize the mind and be without further conditional mentation,[139] you will be accordingly serene and concentrated and will also be able accordingly to put an end to [your present] afflictions and cease the production of new ones. This is called emancipation.

If you can view the mind's most subtle afflictions, agonized confusions, and dark introspections and can temporarily let go of them and gently stabilize [your mind] in a suitable fashion, your mind will naturally attain peace and purity(?).[140] Only you must be valiant, as if you were saving your head from burning. You must not be lax! Make effort! Make effort!

C. When you are beginning to practice seated meditation and mind-viewing, you should sit alone in a single place.[141] First, sit upright in correct posture, loosen your robe and your belt, and relax your body by massaging yourself seven or eight times.[142] Force all the air out of your abdomen, so as to become like peace itself, simple and calm. By regulating the body and mind one can pacify the mind *(hsin-shen).* Therefore, being completely effaced in profound obscurity,[143] one's breathing becomes tranquil and the mind gradually regulated.[144] One's spirit *(shen-tao)* becomes clear and keen, one's mind *(hsin-ti)* bright and pure. Observing distinctly, both interior and exterior are nonsubstantial and pure,[145] so that the Mind Nature is quiescent. When it is quiescent, the mind of the sage will be manifest.

Although formless in nature, the virtuous fidelity [of the mind of the sage] is always present. The [functioning of the] abstruse numen cannot be exhausted and always maintains its brilliance: this is called the Buddha Nature.[146] He who sees this Buddha Nature transcends birth and death forever and is referred to as a person who has escaped the world. Therefore, the *Vimalakīrti Sūtra* says: "With a sudden expansiveness one retrieves the Fundamental Mind."[147] How true these words!

In contrast to the relatively straightforward manner in which different topics are introduced and discussed in the *Hsiu-hsin yao lun,* the *JTFM* is repetitive and occasionally confusing. It is much more willing than the other text to string together scriptural quotations (these have been largely excised from the passage introduced here), to make sophisticated allusions to the classics of Chinese secular and Buddhist literature, and even to state apparently self-contradictory positions. Finally, where the *Hsiu-hsin yao lun* is devoted almost entirely to static images—the existence of the Buddha Nature, maintenence of the mind, etc.—the *JTFM* mixes both the static and dynamic. In particular, it exhibits a greater interest in the ongoing functioning of the enlightened mind than in the immanence of that mind within us all.

Simply put, in the *JTFM* "maintaining the One without wavering" refers to the practice of meditation on the nonsubstantiality of one's body and the entirety of one's sensory apparatus and experience. The explanation of this practice has two different components: a definition of the nonsubstantiality of body and mind and the instruction to use that fundamentally nonsubstantial mind to contemplate a selected object of meditation.

Later in the *LCSTC,* the parent text in which the *JTFM* is found, the practitioner is advised to "sit upright in correct position on a flat [place with an unobstructed view], relax the body and mind, and distantly view the character 'one' (*i*, essentially a straight horizontal line) at the very edge of space."[148] This symbolic visualization is of much the same kind as the visualization of the sun recommended in the *Hsiu-hsin yao lun*. In this case the practitioner is identifying himself with the unity of all things. Other passages in the text, however, imply that the "One" of "maintaining the One" is equivalent to nonsubstantiality and should not be grasped too insistently.[149]

At any rate, the practical explanation of "maintaining the One without wavering" is that one is simply to contemplate every aspect of one's mental and physical existence, focusing on each individual component with unswerving attention until one realizes its essential emptiness or nonsubstantiality. The interesting aspect of this regimen is, paradoxically, its apparent conventionality. Although further examination will reveal significant differences between this and traditional Buddhist meditation practice, the description given so far would apply equally well to the most basic of Mahāyāna techniques: the insight-oriented contemplation of the nonsubstantiality of the body.

Although this type of contemplation is the common property of virtually all schools of Mahāyāna Buddhism, its presentation here differs in at least two ways from that found in more traditional texts. First, no preparatory requirements, no moral prerequisites or preliminary exercises are given. Instead, one moves directly into the practice of contemplation. Second, the technique of "maintaining the One without wavering" is in itself completely without steps or gradations. One concentrates, understands, and is enlightened, all in one undifferentiated practice. These differences may appear to be of little consequence to modern readers, whose cultures generally emphasize instant gratification and success. But it is important to remember that the traditional practice of Buddhist meditation involved a highly articulated system of moral prerequisites and contemplative techniques. Hence these two differences represent fundamental distinctions from the traditional practice of Chinese Buddhist meditation.

The *JTFM* thus contains the first explicit statement of the sudden and direct approach that was to become the hallmark of Ch'an religious practice.[150] Nevertheless, the following passage indicates that this text had a complex attitude toward meditation:

> Do not [practice] mindfulness of the Buddha, do not grasp the mind, do not view the mind, do not measure the mind, do not meditate, do not contemplate, and do not disrupt [the mind]. Just let it flow. Do not make it go and do not make it stay. Alone in a pure and ultimate location (i.e., the absolute), the mind will be naturally bright and pure.
>
> Or you can view it clearly, and the mind will attain brightness and purity. The mind will be like a bright mirror. You can [do this for] a year, and the

> mind will be even more bright and pure. Or you can do this for three or five years, and the mind will be even more bright and pure.[151]

Obviously, the *JTFM* makes allowance for both sudden apperception of the Buddha Nature and gradual improvement in the brightness and purity of the concentrated mind. As Tanaka Ryōshō has shown, the *JTFM* actually allows for a number of alternative situations: One may achieve "bright purity" of mind either with or without undertaking the extended practice of "viewing the mind." One may also achieve enlightenment either solely through one's own efforts or, conversely, with the aid of a teacher's instruction.[152] The point of these alternatives is that a true teacher must be able to understand which students are best suited for which approach and to teach them differently on the basis of that understanding. Differences of ability had long been recognized within Chinese Buddhism; P'u-chi is known to have said that enlightenment could occur either right away or only after several years of practice.[153] The orientation of the JTFM to teachers of meditation rather than to the students themselves highlights the increasing maturity of the Ch'an tradition.

8. The Metaphor of the Mirror

In the *Hsiu-hsin yao lun* the practice of meditation necessarily involves one or both of two goals: (1) intimate contact or unification with the Buddha Nature and (2) realization of the ultimate nonexistence or lack of efficacy of the illusions. The text's emphasis on maintaining a constant focus on the fundamentally pure mind is an expression of the first of these two goals; the practice of watching the discriminating mind until it naturally comes to a stop may be correlated with the second.

The description of *shou-i pu i* in the *JTFM* cannot be completely explained on the basis of the dualistic paradigm of the sun and clouds or Buddha Nature and illusions. Here the primary emphasis is on the ongoing functioning of the enlightened mind. The text mentions the inexhaustible transformation undertaken by wisdom in response to things, the nonsubstantiality of the senses and sensory phenomena, and the ultimate serenity of the apparent activity of perception. It also discusses the activation and nonactivation *(ch'i* and *pu-ch'i)* of the mind's cognitive functions.[154] The *JTFM,* therefore, posits only one comprehensive goal, the consummation of both the static realm of the perception of the Buddha Nature and the dynamic realm of the perfection of ongoing perceptual processes. The most apt paradigm for such an achievement is the metaphor of the perfectly reflecting mirror.

The metaphor of the mirror is mentioned prominently in the passages discussed in the previous section, but its most explicit statement in early Ch'an literature actually occurs even earlier in the *JTFM:*

> Truly, the *Tathāgata*'s body of the Dharma Nature is pure, perfect, and complete. All forms *(hsiang-lei)* are manifested within it, even though that body of the Dharma Nature is without any mental activity. It is like a crystal mirror suspended in an elevated building: All the various objects are manifested within it, but the mirror is without any mind that can manifest them.[155]

This is the basis for the *JTFM*'s statement that the illumination of the mirror and the illumination of the eye are identical.[156] The sun and, of course, the mind itself could also be made members to this equation. In other words, this text does not emphasize simply the immanence of the Buddha Nature, but also the activation of that Buddha Nature; not merely the recognition of the Buddha Nature as the governing principle of one's existence, but also the transformation of one's own being into an unqualified expression of that Buddha Nature.

9. The Use of the Mirror in Early Ch'an Texts

References to the mirror occur frequently in early Ch'an texts. Some of these references, such as the *Platform Sūtra* anecdote introduced at the beginning of this study—if, for the time being, we accept the traditional interpretation—use the mirror in a fashion analogous to the metaphor of the sun and clouds discussed in conjunction with the *Hsiu-hsin yao lun.* According to this usage, the "bright mirror" is equated with the constantly shining sun, and the dust that occurs on the mirror's surface, obscuring its reflective capacity, corresponds to the "clouds and mists of the eight directions" that block the light of the sun. In other instances, however, references to the mirror or the images that appear on its surface are based on a more active image of the mirror's functioning. In these instances the question of dust simply does not arise.

The mirror referred to in most Ch'an texts is an idealized version of the round metal mirrors so common in exhibitions of Chinese art (where emphasis is placed on the beautifully ornamented reverse sides rather than on the reflective surface). The difference between the real artifacts and the idealized prototype is indicated in the passage translated in the previous section, which mentions a "crystal mirror suspended in an elevated building." In other words, this mirror is made out of a special substance that lacks the metallic distortion of most ancient Chinese mirrors. Even more important than its perfectly reflective substance, however, is the fact that this mirror is mounted in a very special location where all phenomenal reality is somehow reflected on its surface. The purpose of this idealized conception of the mirror should be immediately obvious: to make the mirror a fitting match for the mind of the Buddha, whom the Chinese regarded as omniscient.

Most of the references in early Ch'an texts to the metaphor of the mirror are rather brief. Considered individually, these references are sometimes so fragmentary as to be almost incomprehensible. Taken together, however, they describe a logical or metaphorical construct that is well integrated and comprehensible. The different aspects of this extended metaphor may be explained as follows:

> The mirror functions constantly and with inherent perfection. It reflects any object that is placed before it, doing so immediately and without any distortion or fatigue. The mirror reflects images, but it does not become attached to them—when the object is no longer present, the image disappears. The images are essentially unreal, being neither part of the object nor part of the mirror. Most important, they neither interfere with each other nor exert any influence on the mirror.

In the background of this understanding of the mirror is, of course, the Yogācāra doctrine of the "great perfect mirror wisdom" *(ta yuan-ching chih,* corresponding to the Sanskrit *ādarśa-jñāna).* One of the four wisdoms possessed by enlightened beings and representing the transformation of what in unenlightened persons is the "storehouse consciousness" *(ālaya-vijñāna),* the "great perfect mirror wisdom" and the other three wisdoms are not unknown in Northern School literature. Nevertheless, most references to the mirror in the literature of this school are more general than this technical usage, referring to any perceptive function or the sage's mind in general rather than to the enlightened equivalent of one of the eight *vijñāna*s of Yogācāra philosophy.

The mirror as defined here is an apt metaphor for the mind of the sage, which is constantly functioning on behalf of sentient beings but at the same time essentially inactive. In addition, the images that appear on the surface of the mirror are used metaphorically to describe the illusoriness of phenomenal reality and the mutual noninterference or nonhindrance of its individual elements. One text describes the mirror and its images in parallel terms : "The bright mirror never thinks, 'I can manifest images;' the images never say, 'I am generated from the mirror.' "[157]

10. The Sun, the Mirror, and Bodhidharma's Treatise

These, then, are the two most important metaphors of early Ch'an: the sun and clouds and the mirror and its images. They are only rarely explained or stated completely. Instead, texts tend, especially in the case of the mirror metaphor, to mention only one aspect of the metaphor in any given context. It seems best to approach these metaphors not as rigid devices of unchanging implication, but as conceptual matrices that provide logical frameworks for the expression of several different viewpoints. Reference may be made to the unreality of the images on the mirror, for example, without any explicit mention of the mirror itself. In such fragmentary citations it is important to remember the full ramifications of the mirror as a conceptual model: The gradualistic interpretation of the *Platform Sūtra* verses should not be applied indiscriminately.

It is significant that these two conceptual matrixes of early Ch'an doctrine may be correlated so easily with the "two entrances" of Bodhidharma's *Erh-ju ssu-hsing lun.* The parallel between the "entrance of principle" and the metaphor of the sun and clouds is obvious and needs no discussion. Although the meditation practices of Bodhidharma and his immediate associates cannot be ascertained with any precision, the techniques outlined in the *Hsiu-hsin yao lun* constitute a very simple yet sophisticated response to the religious dilemma implied by the paradigm of the immanent Buddha Nature and the adventitious obfuscation caused by the illusions.

Although the similarities between the "entrance of practice" and the metaphor of the mirror are not nearly so obvious, both emphasize the active expression of one's enlightenment in the activities of daily life. The highest sense of the entrance of practice, the reader will recall, was the ability to undertake all activities in accord with the the principle of *śūnyatā.* One was to practice the perfection of charity, for example, without conceiving of the existence of recipient, donor, or gift. This approach is congruent with the mirror's ability to reflect images without becoming attached to or affected by them.

I believe that it is possible to correlate the metaphor of the sun and clouds with the simpler doctrines of the East Mountain Teaching and that of the mirror with the more complex formulations of the Northern School. This distinction is, of course, a didactic conceit of only general validity. As we have seen with the *JTFM,* the ideas that underlie both of these metaphors can occur in one and the same text. The simpler East Mountain Teaching probably antedated the ideas of the Northern School, but we cannot reconstruct the dynamics of that philosophical evolution. Nevertheless, since there are only one or two explicit instances of later doctrinal elaboration on Bodhidharma's two entrances,[158] it is interesting that his treatise contains a primitive expression of the two most important logical constructs of early eighth-century Ch'an doctrine.

CHAPTER VII

Shen-hsiu and the Religious Philosophy of the Northern School

1. Introductory Remarks

Three works merit careful study in this chapter because of their relationship to Shen-hsiu and the development of Northern School religious thought. The first is the *Kuan-hsin lun (Treatise on the Contemplation of the Mind),* a text once thought to have been written by Bodhidharma, to whom it is attributed in some manuscripts. Evidence from a contemporary T'ang manual has established beyond question that it was written by Shen-hsiu.[159]

The *Kuan-hsin lun* is generally thought to have been compiled during Shen-hsiu's period of residence at Yü-ch'üan ssu (i.e., during the last quarter of the seventh century), if only because Chih-i once lived at the same monastery and wrote a treatise by the same name. Although this argument is by no means definitive—the two treatises are not at all similar—the style and content of Shen-hsiu's text suggests that it is earlier than the other two works to be studied in this chapter. That is, the *Kuan-hsin lun* includes both a foundation of East Mountain Teaching ideas and a rough intimation of the more complex religious ideal of the Northern School.

Because of the prolixity of the *Kuan-hsin lun,* I will not translate the entire text but will limit myself, in the following analysis, to the quotation of relevant passages. The second text to be discussed here, however, can only be appreciated on the basis of a close reading of its entire contents. This text is the *Yuan-ming lun (Treatise on Perfect Illumination),* whose title originally must have been something like *Yuan-chiao fang-pien yao-chueh lun (Treatise on the Oral Determination of the Expedient Means of the Perfect Teaching).*[160]

One Tun-huang manuscript attributes the *Yuan-ming lun* to Aśvaghoṣa, the well-known author of the *Buddhacarita* (an early biography of the Buddha) and, supposedly, of the *Awakening of Faith.* This attribution is obviously spurious, and I will argue in my analysis that the *Yuan-ming lun* was probably taken from a lecture or lectures by Shen-hsiu or another prominent Northern School figure, perhaps given to introduce a written treatise or commentary. The resulting transcription does not appear to have undergone much, if any, editing for presentation in written form. Not only does it contain the repetitions, inconsistencies, and obscure pronouncements typical of oral presentations, but also the original Tun-huang manuscripts suffer from numerous lacunae. (Most of these lacunae occur at the beginning of the text; the reader is asked to perservere.) In spite of these problems, this text is the most comprehensive statement of the teachings of the Northern School.

The third text to be included in this discussion is the *Wu fang-pien (Five Expedient Means).* This simplified title is used to refer to a handful of Tun-huang manuscripts that contain similar material but different titles: in particular, the *Ta-sheng wu-sheng fang-pien men (The Expedient Means of* [*Attaining*] *Birthlessness in the Mahāyāna)* and the *Ta-sheng wu fang-pien—pei-tsung (The Five Expedient Means of the Mahāyāna—Northern School).* (In the original, the last two characters of the latter title are slightly smaller in size than the preceding five, implying that they were added as a footnote for ease of identification.) Other manuscripts bear different, less relevant titles, and the various manuscripts differ markedly in content.[161]

The English version presented here is a composite of material drawn from the various *Wu fang-pien* manuscripts. I have tried to include as much material as possible from each of the five "expedient means" without reproducing too much meaningless or repetitive detail. This composite is thus potentially misleading, in that it (1) does not include all the available material, (2) organizes the material that is included in a more coherent fashion than any single manuscript, and (3) ignores the possibility of any significant textual development within the entire group of manuscripts. These potential objections have been overlooked due to limitations of space, for the sake of the reader's convenience, and because of the lack of any generally accepted set of criteria for establishing the relative age of the various manuscripts.[162]

(For an explanation of the conventions of editing and annotation used in the following translations, please see Abbreviations and Conventions of Usage at the beginning of this study and note 224 to this part.)

2. *Treatise on Perfect Illumination (Yuan-ming lun)*

Chapter One: Elucidation of the Causes and Results of Mind and Form

Chapter Two: The Expedient Means of the Essential Teaching

Chapter Three: Elucidation of the Causes and Results of Cultivating the Path[163]

Chapter Four: Explanation of the Reverse and Direct Contemplations of the Three Vehicles

Chapter Five: Distinguishing the Conditions of Heresy and Generating the Fundamental[164]

Chapter Six: Explanation of the Causes and Results, the Correct and the False, and [the Remainder of the] Five Teachings of Entering the Path[165]

Chapter Seven: The Manifestations[166] of One's Own Mind

Chapter Eight: Distinguishing False Thoughts[167]

Chapter Nine: Elucidation of the Essence of Sound

CHAPTER ONE: ELUCIDATION OF THE CAUSES AND RESULTS OF MIND AND FORM

A. When first entering the Path,[168] one must understand[169] mind and form. Mind and form each have two types: The first is the mind [and form] of generation and extinction (i.e., impermanence; *sheng-mieh hsin*) . . . . .[170] false thoughts. Prior to this (?), the noneradication of conditional mentation *(yuan-lü)*[171] is called "false [thoughts]" . . . . . is called the ability of true enlightenment. (?)

You do not approve of this doctrine?[172]. . . . . is called "generation and extinction." If you perceive that the True Mind *(chen-hsin)* is originally without false thoughts, then you have attained the True Nature. You must constantly (?) be enlightened to [the fact that the mind of generation and extinction] is the mind of conditional transformations *(yuan-ch'üan hsin)* and that the mind is actually motionless. By accomplishing this understanding, one realizes *(ming)* that, whether walking, standing still, sitting, or lying down, one is constantly in. . . . . This is called "emancipation of the mind" *(hsin chieh-t'o)*.[173]

B. "Form" means the body. From whence are the characteristics[174] of the body generated? . . . . . First, they are generated from the beginningless influences *(chün-hsi,* or *vāsanā)* of false thoughts. Second, [they are generated] from the present causes and conditions of sensory reality (*hsiang-wei,* lit., smells and tastes). [As to] generation from the influences, those influences are the cause, and the body is the result. The influences (?) are the [cause of] the characteristic (?) of form. . . . . If the influences were without characteristics, then the body would not be the characteristic of form. Why? If the cause were without characteristics, the result would likewise (?) [be without characteristics] . . . . .

C. You do not approve of this doctrine? It is said [by some people] that the body is generated of its own Self Nature. If it arose[175] through the influences of causes and conditions, then one would know it to be [nonsubstantial. If the cause] were nonsubstantial, then the result would also be nonsubstantial. Although the inference of its existence (?) is dependent on sensory reality, there would not [really] be any body. Why is this? Form derives its sentience *(ming)* from sensory reality . . . . . food and [drink].

Also, food does not [in itself constitute] form. Just as a person's food and drink are transformed into impurities (i.e., bodily wastes) and do not become form, the least bit of sensory reality. . . . . The sensory reality of causes and conditions become the sensory reality of physical form. If "being" *(yu)* materializes[176] form, then the body is "being." Sensory reality is fundamentally nonsubstantial, [however, so] the body is also nonsubstantial. If "being" creates form, form is thus "being." If "nonbeing" *(wu)* creates form, then you should clearly understand that form is nonsubstantial.

If one contemplates (?) mind and form as nondual, their Fundamental Natures universally "same" *(p'ing-teng),* this is called Suchness *(chen-ju).* When you attain this teaching of nondual universal "sameness," you have comprehended mind and form.

Chapter Two: The Expedient Means of the Essential Teaching

A. There are many approaches to cultivation of the Path, which lead one differently to enlightenment. . . . . [To put it most succinctly,] there are three types of teaching: first, the "gradual teaching"; second, the "sudden teaching"; and third, the "perfect teaching."

You do not approve of this doctrine? Each [person] falsely grasps[177] his own place, his disposition not matching the enlightenment of others. (?) Each [person thus creates] errors and mistakes. (?) If it matched their dispositions,[178] the purport . . . . . teachings, one can distinguish the gradual, sudden, and perfect, making them separate. If one does not understand, one says they are identical. I *(yü)* now [say] that they are not identical. One must verify this by asking: The enlightened are as numerous as grains of sand,[179] so how could [their experiences] be identical?

B. I will now briefly enumerate the teachings for you, so that you will understand them to be separate. What is the gradual teaching? The understanding of ignorant people is completely dependent on the scriptures. Although the scriptures are without error, they must be understood according to one's disposition, which does not [necessarily] match the enlightenment of other people.

There are three types of dispositions: . . . . . spiritual compatriot.

According to this understanding, those who contemplate the body and mind as neither internal nor external and who achieve [understanding of the doctrine of] *anātman (?)*[180] are Hīnayānists. Realizing that dispositions are either Mahāyānist or Hīnayānist, [such people] claim that their understanding represents a Mahāyāna contemplation.

There are also those . . . . . who understand that the realms [of sensory reality] *(ching-chieh)* are all the product of one's own mind of false thoughts. If one is without false thoughts, [they feel,] then ultimately [there are no (?)] realms. When performing this contemplation, there are no limits of before and after. [Although] they do not reside in nirvāṇa, [such people] become attached to this understanding and claim that this is an understanding (?) of the sudden teaching. This is [actually] the gradual teaching, not the sudden.

C. What is the sudden teaching? The sudden teaching is to realize the locus [of origin (?)] of physical characteristics and the essence of the mind *(shen-hsiang hsin-t'i)*. Physical characteristics are originally generated from the mind of false thoughts. Those false thoughts are originally without [essence].

[QUESTION: If the mind is] said to be without essence, how can it be the fundamental source *(pen)* of the body?

ANSWER: The mind is without essence. It is also not the fundamental source of the body. Why is this? The mind does not know its own location,[181] nor does it know the generation of the body. If the mind knew its own location, then it would be able to generate itself (?) from physical characteristics.[182] Since the mind does not know its own location and does not know the locations of its going and coming, neither does it know from what location it accepts *(shou)* the body's . . . . . is generated from what location.

If the body and mind knew each other, it could be said that the body is generated from the mind. The mind could also say that it generates the body. Since the body and mind do not know each other and do not know the locations of their coming and going, then how could they generate each other? According to this understanding, whose body is the body? Whose mind is the mind? Also, if the mind does not know its own location, how can it be the fundamental source of the body?

[If] body and mind do not know each other, then they are fundamentally unable to generate each other. Why is this? The "maddening" of the eye by [hallucinations of] flowers in mid-air . . . . . the body is not the body. Understand that the eye is nonsubstantial. Because it makes being out of nonsubstantiality, being is also nonsubstantial. Therefore, to say that the eye . . . . . makes the mind [out of] nonsubstantiality, the mind is also nonsubstantial.

It is like making a vessel out of clay. The vessel is also [clay]. . . . . If the vessel were not clay, the body and mind would be "being."[183] If you now realize that there really are no three periods of time, then afterwards this. . . . . The so-called wise men and sages and [bodhisattvas of the ten] stages are all said [by me] to have been created out of nonsubstantiality. Within nonsubstantiality there is no arising and extinction [of things] *(ch'i-mieh).* Therefore, it is said [to be nonsubstantial (?)]. To achieve this understanding is called enlightenment. The mountains, forests, earth, sun, moon, stars, planets, and sentient beings . . . . . emptiness, waves [upon the (?)] Dharma Nature. Therefore, this is called sudden. The contemplation of *anātman* is therefore different.

D. I have now explained the gradual [and sudden types of] enlightenment. What about the perfect? The principle of the perfect teaching cannot be understood by foolish, ordinary people. There are ten meanings to the [perfect teaching]. What are these ten?

First, one must understand the realms of sentient beings *(chung-sheng chieh).*

Second, one must understand the worlds *(shih-chieh).*

[Third,] one must understand the meaning of the *dharmadhātu (fa-chieh i).*

Fourth, one must understand the nature of the *dharmadhātu (fa-chieh hsing).*

Fifth, one must [understand] the five oceans *(wu hai).*[184]

Sixth, one must understand the meaning of . . . . .

Seventh, one must understand the essence of the realms of sentient beings *(chung-sheng chieh t'i).*

Eighth, one must understand the essence of the worlds *(shih-chieh t'i).*

Ninth, one must understand the essence (?) of the *dharmadhātu (fa-chieh t'i* [?]).[185]

[Tenth, one must understand[186]] the essence of the expedient means of the Buddhas *(chu-fo fang-pien t'i).*

E. These ten teachings are not identical. He who distinctly comprehends [each one of] them understands the perfect teaching. . . . . In the sudden teaching, the power of meditation *(ting-li)* is great, but the function of *samādhi (san-mei yung)* is slight. In the perfect [teaching], the function of *samādhi* is great. Probably, those who do not [understand the perfect teaching (?)] cannot be said to have "comprehended the meaning" *(liao-i),* even though they possess the two teachings of meditation and practice *(ting-hsing erh men).* Such people are fools and cannot . . . . . not true. They mislead themselves and later mislead others.

This doctrine is from the *Lotus Sūtra,* [in which] the Buddha reprimanded students of the Path for [failing to] discern the meaning of the perfect teaching.[187] I *(yü)* will now explain the terms of it for you in minute detail. I will also impart its essence and cause your practices [to have] a basis. (?)[188]

F. What are the realms of sentient beings? There are three types of realms of sentient beings. What are these three? [The first is] the characteristic of sentient beings. . . . . The second is that transmigration through the three periods of time is also the characteristic of sentient beings. The third is that the sensory realms *(ching)* are also the characteristic of sentient beings. These characteristics take the Dharma Nature as their essence.

The Mind Nature of sentient beings originally has (?) the characteristics of the five *skandhas*. It arises originally from causes and conditions. When an individual sense impression (*ch'en* [?]) is conjoined [with sense organ and consciousness (?)] it has no Self Nature. When conditions have not yet conjoined [as above], fundamentally . . . . . These causes and conditions originally take the Dharma Nature as their essence. Therefore, the realms of sentient beings all arise on the basis of the Dharma, all on the basis. . . . . "being." The realms of sentient beings are originally the pneuma of nirvāṇa *(nieh-p'an chih ch'i)*.

G. [QUESTION]: If they arise on the basis of nirvāṇa, then are . . . . . essence?

ANSWER: If they are the pneuma of nirvāṇa, how can one continue to say sentient . . . . .[189] when together, this is also neither the realm of sentient beings, nor not the realm of sentient beings; neither the realm of nirvāṇa, nor not the realm of nirvāṇa. Therefore, it is said that there is no distinction between them. Therefore, which is the [realm of] sentient beings, and which is the [realm of] nirvāṇa? Therefore, I say it is neither sudden nor gradual and call it the "perfectly [accomplished]."

In the teaching of the perfectly accomplished *(yuan-ch'eng chih fa)* there ultimately is no sentient being who eradicates his afflictions *(fan-nao,* or *kleśa)*. If one is deluded as to nirvāṇa, one appears as a sentient being and possesses afflictions. If there are afflictions, then there is consciousness and the [distinction of] interior and exterior. If there are interior and exterior,[190] then there is disputation.

H. To say that the mind is within [the body] is the teaching of a fool. If it were within, it would be impermanent and equivalent to the afflictions and birth-and-death. It would also be [like a] monkey.[191] It would also be the laxity of men and gods, as well as fear. There being a past, there would be a future, there would be a present, there would be saṁsāra.

If there were saṁsāra, this would not be the Buddha Nature. The essence of the Buddha Nature is without generation and without extinction, neither transitory nor permanent, not going and not coming. [Within the Buddha Nature] there are no three periods of time, not past, not future, [not present]. Only True Suchness *(ju-ju shih-chi)* can be called the Buddha Nature—how could generation and extinction be the [Buddha] Nature?

I. I *(yü)* have achieved this understanding on the basis of the sūtras and meditation *(ching-wen chi ch'an-kuan):* To be equivalent to space, which permeates the *dharmadhātu,* is the True Nature *(chen-shih hsing).* [To say] that the mind is exterior [to the body] is an elementary teaching *(ch'u-chiao).* It is called exterior because of enlightenment to the mind of the *dharmadhātu.*[192] If it is equivalent to space, then it fills up the interior of one's [physical] form, so how could form and mind obstruct [each other]? Mind and form are non-obstructing, so how could they not penetrate space? They are the function of the *dharmadhātu.*

J. [Let me give the] interpretation of the "worlds of sentient beings" within the perfect teaching *(yuan-tsung).* The perfect teaching is based on the explanation *(fan)*[193] of the "realms of sentient beings." According to this understanding [of Buddhism] . . . . . realms of sentient beings. . . . .[194] Each sentient being is a single world. A great sentient being is a great world, and a small sentient being is a [small world. These worlds] are each different according to the allotted energies [of individual sentient beings].

It is like the [domain of a] king, the boundaries of which may be more than ten thousand *li* on all four sides. The boundaries of the provinces are within the boundaries of the king's [domain]. The boundaries of the counties are within the boundaries of the provinces. The boundaries of the towns are within the boundaries of the counties. The boundaries of the villages are within the boundaries of the towns. The boundaries of the houses are within the boundaries of the villages. The boundaries of the rooms are within the boundaries of the houses.

According to this contemplation (*kuan,* i.e., this analysis), from the [domain of the] king [on down], they are each contained within each other, each attaining the function of a [separate] world. On the basis of this understanding, [the realms of] men and gods and all sentient beings are variously dependent on each other, each attaining [a state of existence] according to one's natural allotment and without mutual interference.

K. QUESTION: What is the essence of these worlds, which are in the same locations, such that they do not obstruct each other?

ANSWER: The essence of the Great World is originally Vairocana Buddha *(Lü-she-na fo),* the ingenious expedient means of the Bodhisattvas, the strength of their vows of great compassion, and *samādhi* [itself]. *Samādhi* takes space as its essence. Because space is without obstruction, it can generate the wisdom of unobstructed *dharmadhātus*. Because the wisdom of the *dharmadhātus* is unobstructed, it can generate the wisdom of un[obstructed] *samādhi.* Because *samādhi* is unobstructed, it can generate Vairocana Buddha, whose unobstructed and limitless body is offered to all sentient beings as the basis of their existence, so that their worlds are fundamentally unobstructed. Therefore, [it is said that the worlds] are unobstructed.

The human body is also a domain on which sentient beings rely. Why? Because within each human [body] there are eighty thousand worms, and within each of these are various small worms. Each depending on the other to form its own world, each [of these worms] may be said to be a world. According to this understanding, all these are worlds—where else could the worlds of sentient beings occur?

L. All this is ultimately nonsubstantial: There are no sentient beings. If one searches for the essence [of the entire system] in one's contemplation, it is all originally the "water of the Dharma" *(fa-shui).* The separations of the flow of this water form the [various] worlds, the worlds all being the "water of the Dharma." According to this understanding, they are neither the worlds of sentient being nor not the worlds of sentient beings. They are not worlds and not not worlds. When one achieves this contemplation, one is said to have penetrated the "meaning of the worlds."

CHAPTER THREE: ELUCIDATION OF THE CAUSES AND RESULTS OF CULTIVATING [THE PATH]

A. Those who cultivate[195] the Path must understand its causes and results. If they do not understand these, they will fall into heretical views like a big, stupid fish.[196] Therefore, one must clearly understand the causes and results [of the Path].

A critic said: The preceding portion of this *Treatise on the Oral Determination of the Essential [Teaching] (Yao-chueh lun)* defined (*li,* lit., "to posit") the "worlds," each [sentient being] being a world [unto himself]. This definition was not complete—will it not be [completed] here? The essences of sentient beings and the . . . . . [essences] of the Buddhas are nonsubstantial.[197]

[The critic continued]: As defined in the preceding text, the essences of sentient beings, the essence of the *dharmadhātu,* and the essence of the expedient means of the Buddhas—all these take space as their essence. Because it is space, they must be without essence.

Therefore, know [that someone might take] the ascriptive view of a stupid and lowly person [in saying as follows]: "Space, having no cause, would have a result without a cause. How could this result possibly occur? According [to this interpretation], who is the creator of space? If space had a creator, then the myriad *dharmas* would have cause and result. If . . . . . space had no creator, then the myriad *dharmas* would be without cause and without result."

On the basis of this, the *Dhyāna* Master has (i.e., "you have") defined "essence" in such a way that someone might generate doubts [and such an] unwarranted criticism. I only beseech the *Dhyāna* Master to have great compassion and to eradicate these doubts and help us gain emancipation.

B. Answer: Such doubts are eminently worthy of hesitation (i.e., consideration). [I] always have the compassion to try to eradicate the doubts of sentient beings and will therefore explain [the answer to] this criticism for you. This essence has no fundamental *(pen)* and no derivative *(mo)*. There actually is no cause and no result. Why is this? [This statement] is based solely on the [*Perfection of*] *Wisdom Sūtra (Po-jo ching),* which says:

> Cause is also nonsubstantial, result is also nonsubstantial, practicing is also nonsubstantial, not-practicing is also nonsubstantial, and not-not-practicing is also nonsubstantial. To explain this in its entirety, the Buddha is also nonsubstantial, the Dharma is also nonsubstantial, the *Saṁgha* is also nonsubstantial, and even the sages are also nonsubstantial.[198]

On the basis of these lines from the sūtra, the preceding criticism [is answered] as follows: Although each individual sentient being has existed from beginningless time within a body of physical form, smells, and tastes, this [body] is not generated through unconditioned transformation *(wu-wei hua).* If it were generated by unconditioned transformation, then [it could be born] of a lotus flower rather than [actual human] parents. Because sentient beings are born of parents, one knows clearly that the beginningless influences have completely "perfumed"[199] that body. If the afflictions are not eradicated, the influences have not been exhausted.

In the foregoing explanation of the meaning of the essence of the *dharmadhātu* it was always held that [sentient beings] depended on buddhas other [than themselves] and the text of the [*Perfection of*] *Wisdom* in attaining enlightenment, not that they made effort and attained enlightenment on their own. If they made effort and attained enlightenment [on their own], their bodies would be like dead ashes, without the blood [of life]. Even if they had blood it would be the color of snow. Since [sentient beings] are not this way, one should clearly know that one who does not believe in cause and result is replete with afflictions.

C. [QUESTION]: At that time another person with a criticism bowed himself in elegant humility and, believing profoundly in cause and result, asked: What is the cause? What is the result?

ANSWER: One should reside in meditation and wisdom after having achieved the contemplation of nonsubstantiality *(chu ch'an pan-jo k'ung-kuan ch'eng-chiu)*. Not residing in being and nonbeing, the body and mind are universally "same," like space. Never quitting during walking, standing still, sitting, and lying down, [one should] save beings whenever possible (*sui-yuan,* lit., in accordance with conditions).[200] Saving the weak and helping the downfallen, having pity for the poor and love for the aged, one should think on the suffering of sentient beings within the three lower modes of existence and the difficulties of the poor among humankind. One should always act tirelessly to save them, [even to the point of] discarding one's own life.

One should always undertake such practices while in meditation, for the duration of three great immeasurable [eons].[201] One's vows must always be made on behalf of sentient beings rather than for oneself. One must complete these vows, not as if they are one's own vows. Such practices are called the cause.

QUESTION: What is the result?

ANSWER: The result does not transcend (i.e., is no different from) the cause. Merely reside in wisdom; do not reside in the conditioned. Therefore, in the salvation of sentient beings, never think of [your task] as finished. Just practice this practice without any period of limitation or completion. In laying down one's life to save beings, do not generate the [false] thought of self and other. Why? The *samādhi* of nonsubstantial meditation *(k'ung-ch'an san-mei)* is without any practice [that distinguishes] self and other. It is not something that bodhisattvas enter [in a preconceived fashion]. In your long eons of difficult effort, do not get any mistaken ideas! Always practice this practice without positing any thought of having completed it.

If you practice like this, the beginningless influences will be automatically extinguished. There is only the practice of nonsubstantiality *(k'ung-hsing)*. Therefore, the performance of this practice, in which the influences are all extinguished and one does not reside in [the dualism of] "other" and "self," is provisionally called the result. The result occurs automatically when the practices are fulfilled, hence the names "cause" and "result."

When the result is completely [attained], one's wisdom also fills space, one's practice also fills space, one's body also fills space, one's [buddha] realm and *nirmāṇakȳa* also fill space. Although they are [said to be] equivalent to space, they are no different from space.

D. If one generates such a body on the basis of nonsubstantiality, then that body is also nonsubstantial. If one generates such a practice on the basis of nonsubstantiality, that practice is also nonsubstantial. One's buddha realm and expedient means are also as space. Why? Because the *dharmadhātu* arises fundamentally on the basis of space, it is no different from space.

It is like waves on water. Fundamentally, the waves arise on the basis of the water. The waves actually are water and the water no different from its waves; likewise the *nirmāṇakāya.*[202] If [both] principle and practice *(li-hsing)* are realized, it is called cause and result.[203] Therefore, it is called cause and result.

E. [QUESTION]: If it is called cause and result before the influences are extinguished, how can it be called cause and result after they are extinguished?

[ANSWER]: There are no cause and result. Why? There is only the practice of nonsubstantiality and the salvation of beings, but no additional intention whatsoever. It is called result because it is like an apparition, etc. [The term] "result" is used in speaking to practitioners—the principle of this cannot be understood with the ordinary person's way of thinking or by reading a text.[204]

You must make effort for many a day, dispensing with conventional toils and sitting quietly in meditation *(ching-tso ssu-wei).*[205] You cannot understand the principle of this through an [insight] into a text [gained] during recitation. There is no mutual relationship [between that kind of insight and the realization referred to here]. This is an understanding [based on something] other than one's own efforts. This is a practice [based on something] other than one's own practice.[206] By meditating thus you will avoid such errors.

CHAPTER FOUR: EXPLANATION OF THE REVERSE AND DIRECT CONTEMPLATIONS OF THE THREE VEHICLES

A. If you want to understand the differences between the three vehicles, then you must realize that their causes and conditions *(yin-yuan)* are not the same. First, there is the direct contemplation *(shun-kuan)* of the four elements; second, the reverse contemplation *(ni-kuan)* of the four elements. Both reverse and direct [methods of contemplation can result in a] complete attainment of the principle; [practicing either one allows you to be] equivalent to space and realize the fruit of arhatship. Direct contemplation leads you directly to the fruit of arhatship. Reverse contemplation leads you through the four fruits of sagehood to the fruit of arhatship.

There are also reverse and direct [contemplations] within the contemplation of causality. Although equal to space, [those who succeeded in this contemplation] were said to have realized [the state of] *pratyekabuddha.* By this we can infer that the people of that day did not understand the doctrine [propounded here. People call] everything the Mahāyāna (i.e., the great vehicle), no matter what the size [of the vehicle] or the proximity [to the ultimate goal]. But [these doctrines] are actually not the Mahāyāna, but all the Hīnayāna (i.e., the small vehicle).

When a Hīnayānist undergoes conversion [to the Mahāyāna and decides to] enter the path of the bodhisattva, he hopes that there are "influences" stored within his eighth consciousness (i.e., the *ālaya-vijñāna*) that will generate that path of the bodhisattva [for him], as well as [enable him to] practice the six perfections. (?) When an ordinary person encounters the skilfully handled expedient means of a spiritual compatriot and, through the thirty-seven requisites of enlightenment,[207] practices the six perfections, he practices long on the basis of some teaching and achieves the enlightenment of a bodhisattva and the fruit of buddhahood.

Further, there are different [methods of] teaching, such as first explaining the cause and only afterwards the practice of the path of the bodhisattva. With the converted Hīnayānist mentioned earlier and the ordinary person who enters the Path, the cause is explained first and afterwards the result. Within this teaching, the person who has long planted the roots of goodness achieves an enlightenment that is different from that of the ordinary person. But by lengthy practice of the path of the bodhisattva, both achieve entrance [into enlightenment].

B. QUESTION: I do not understand the [cases of the] converted Hīnayānist and the ordinary person who enters the Path. I do not know on the basis of which practice someone practices long the [path of the] bodhisattva. I wonder if his long practice of the [path of the] bodhisattva is the practice of the six perfections?

ANSWER: He may either practice or not practice [anything]. Therefore, within the nonpractice of compassion he must practice the six perfections, enter into *samādhi,* and enter the teaching of the *dharmadhātu.*[208] Within these practices he cannot manifest the six perfections. If you wish to understand the teaching of the *dharmadhātu,* you must first understand the meaning of the "worlds." If you do not understand the worlds, then you will have no basis for entering the teaching of the *dharmadhātu.* Therefore, you must first understand the worlds.[209]

C. QUESTION: What is the meaning of the worlds?

ANSWER: A single sentient being is a single world. A great sentient being is a great world and a small sentient being is a small world.

Chapter Five: Distinguishing the Conditions of Heresy and Generating the Fundamental

A. Direct contemplation of the four elements is for ordinary persons of great ability who have long planted the roots of goodness and are of excellent intelligence. The Buddha preaches the teaching of causality for them, revealing to them the principle of nonsubstantiality. It is on this basis that direct contemplation is preached.

Reverse contemplation is for ordinary people who are stupid and unable. They cannot see the mysterious teaching, but only forms, smells, tastes, and tangible objects, to which they become incorrectly attached. It is for this [kind of] ordinary person that reverse contemplation is preached. If there were no gifted and unable persons, there actually would be no preaching of reverse and direct contemplation. This is doubly true for the very stupid.

The ordinary person's reverse contemplation traces sounds, smells, tastes, and tangible objects to their most minute entities *(wei-ch'en,* or *paramāṇu),* then traces that to nonsubstantiality. Generating *(ch'i)* neither form nor mind but grasping at [the status of] bodhisattva, they achieve the fruit of arhatship.

The ungifted person attains results (= fruits) such as this, but the reverse contemplation of the gifted person is different. He successively contemplates sounds, smells, tastes, and tangible objects, but rather than tracing them to their most minute entities, he [realizes them to be] manifestations of his own mind's false thoughts.

B. Question: What are these manifestations of the false thoughts of one's own mind?

Answer: All sentient beings have six senses. What are they? They are the eighth consciousness' senses of eye, ear, nose, tongue, body, and mind.

[Question]: Where do they come from? [To say] that they occur of themselves would be a heretical view and not Buddhism. But if they do not occur of themselves, then they must have some location from which they come. They must come from somewhere, but from where?

Answer: They do not occur of themselves, but all come from somewhere. They all come from within the *ālaya-vijñāna*. The *ālaya-vijñāna* is like the earth and the eye, ear, nose, tongue, body, and mind are like the seedlings of the various plants. If there were no earth, on what would the plants and trees grow? The seeds of the plants and trees are all maintained by the earth, without the exception of [a single] seed. The eye, ear, nose, and tongue are the pneuma of the *ālaya-vijñāna*.

In its Fundamental Nature the *ālaya-vijñāna* has no form, but the senses and the body do. Nowadays people do not perceive that the *ālaya-vijñāna* is their fundamental source *(pen),* but say that their parents gave birth to them. This is to falsely perform the contemplation of the physical body, tracing [its components] to their most minute entities and eventually to nonsubstantiality, falsely grasping the fruit of arhatship. If one knows that fundamentally the body is generated on the basis of the *ālaya-vijñāna,* then there are no eye, ear, nose, and tongue.

How does one know that the consciousness is originally without form and materiality? There are only the "four resemblances." What are the four resemblances? The four resemblances are the resemblance of sense organs, the resemblance of sense data, the resemblance of a self, and the resemblance of a consciousness. Searching within each of these resemblances [will show] that there fundamentally is no consciousness, no sense organ, etc.—they are all images within the *ālaya-vijñāna.*

The *ālaya-vijñāna* is in its Fundamental Nature without generation and extinction, so one must dispense with the ascriptive view of the existence of senses. Why? Because fundamentally there are no senses, because they are all objective aspects *(hsiang-fen)* of the seeds within the fundamental consciousness. As objective aspects of the fundamental consciousness, they lack the fundamental [reality] of eye, ear, nose, and tongue. Within that consciousness there is no material such as senses and consciousnesses, only the resemblance thereof. The essence of these resemblances is nonsubstantial; in tracing their [origins in meditation, they] extend into nothingness. It is only that [people] do not perceive the fundamental consciousness, but say that the eye, ear, nose, and tongue are generated of themselves.

In its essence this fundamental consciousness has only these resemblances, but is without materiality. Being without materiality, [the senses, etc.] are said to be images of one's own mind. [Since these resemblances are] images of one's own mind, how can there be a self? If there is no self, who grasps the fruit (= the result, i.e., enlightenment)? If there is no grasping of the fruit, then [one's understanding] differs from that of the ungifted ordinary people who trace the four elements into emptiness (or space) and grasp the fruit.

C. QUESTION: What is the error in grasping for the fruit?

ANSWER: Grasping for the fruit implies the error of [positing a] self. If an arhat enters *samādhi,* he is like a corpse, or like dead ashes. After a thousand eons he comes out of *samādhi* again, and after coming out of *samādhi* he is just like an ordinary person, with the same [sorts of mistaken] discrimination. This discrimination—where does consciousness come from again? A consciousness is generated, and one should clearly understand that it was maintained by the fundamental consciousness. Therefore, when he comes out of that *samādhi,* he will not have eradicated any of his afflictions at all. Such a catastrophe (i.e., the great amount of time spent without spiritual advantage) occurs because of this error, merely because he does not see that his body is an image of the fundamental consciousness.

If one realizes that the body is an image of the fundamental consciousness, then[210] one must neither eradicate the afflictions nor realize nirvāṇa. By not eradicating the afflictions one transcends the [mistaken concept of a] self. Because of this *anātman,* who is there to grasp nirvāṇa? It is only that one's "influences" are not yet exhausted. The bodhisattva knows within himself that his influences are not yet exhausted.

D. One should remember [the plight of] sentient beings [in general], who are replete with limitless fetters, and generate[211] great compassion. Because of this there is this teaching of the practice of the bodhisattva. Although one generates the practice of the bodhisattva, this is different from the practice of the ordinary person, [which is based on the] ascriptive view of a self. The *nirmāṇakāya* and *saṁbhogakāya* generated through this [teaching] are generated on behalf of ordinary people. They do not exist of themselves. If they existed of themselves, this would [imply a concept of the] self. Because they are generated on behalf of ordinary people. They do not exist of themselves. If they existed of themselves, this would [imply that they are] generated on behalf of ordinary people. They do not exist of themselves. If they existed of themselves, this would [imply a concept of the] self. Because they are generated on behalf of ordinary people, this transcends [the notion of a] self.

Chapter Six: Explanation of the Causes and Results, the Correct and the False, and [the Remainder of the] Five Teachings of Entering the Path

A. All those who undertake cultivation of the path must first learn of cause and result; second, must learn the two teachings of false and correct; third, must generate their practice on the basis of understanding; fourth, must constantly contemplate without cease; and fifth, must know the profundity or shallowness of their own stage of practice. These five teachings are cultivated by all the Buddhas of the three periods of time. They are not now preached [by me] alone.

B. First, the clarification of cause and result: You must realize that the opinions of ordinary people as to [the identity of] religious persons are [based on] conventional understanding and are thus devoid [of truth]. Those who do not understand this will often lose the path. If you understand this, then contemplate your own body from head to foot to see if you have the extraordinary marks [of a buddha]. If you live with lesser people and think of yourself as the best; if you live with people [in general] and have a standing in the marketplace; if you are an official; or if people look at you thinking that you are beautiful: know that in previous lives you cultivated forbearance and restraint from anger, and that you also decorated Buddhist statues and fulfilled all the precepts, thus achieving this [favorable] result.

If you contemplate this body from head to foot [and discover that] there is nothing at which to be looked; that people do not admire you; that you have no standing in the marketplace; that when you walk by, no one notices you, and when you sit, no one thinks you are beautiful; that your clothing does not cover your body and you have neither enough to eat, nor clothing, nor transportation: then you should know that in previous lives you did not practice forbearance but were filled with stinginess and craving and have never had good fortune. According to this contemplation, you should be deeply [ashamed] and realize your own inadequacies. You must plant [the seeds of] good fortune. This is called cause and result.

C. Second, you must understand the two teachings of false and correct.[212] The rationales used by ordinary people [as the bases of their morality] may be profound or shallow. There are those who maintain the five precepts without transgression and think that the religious merit [accruing thereby] is complete, hoping to be equal to the Buddhas. Such people, of whom there are not simply one [or two], do not go on to seek the untainted noble path. This is called "false." [Such people] are not disciples of the Buddha.

If you understand this you will realize the correct path. If you wish to realize the correct path, then you must first understand the fundamentals of the mind and second understand form. Why? Ordinary people do not attain the noble path because [they do not realize] that sentient beings are all amalgams of mind and form. They only escape their fetters by understanding this [here and] now. Therefore, you must understand the origin *(yuan)*.

There are two types of the mind's fundamentals. The first is the mind of truth *(chen-shih hsin)*. The second is the mind of false thoughts *(wang-hsiang hsin)*. The generation and extinction of ordinary people is based completely on the [mind of] false thoughts and has nothing to do with the [mind of] truth. You must understand the [mind of] false thoughts [here and] now. Ordinary people, in their stupidity, cannot comprehend the [mind of] false thoughts, but claim that mind to be real. [The mind] which is contemplated (i.e., understood) by the wise is originally without essence. If you understand, you will know its essencelessness.

D. If you wish to understand the correct and the false, then sit upright in meditation, contemplating the activity of your [mind of] false thoughts. Whether from near or far, the objects of your concentration[213] all arrive (i.e., occur) as conditions [of your mental being]. Although we say "arrive as conditions," they actually do not "arrive."[214] Therefore, [by practicing meditation] you will understand that they do not arrive.

It is truly because of not contemplating the false and true [aspects of the mind] that one says the mind is existent (*yu,* i.e., a part of being). If you contemplate the mind during its "going," then [you will realize that] if the mind were "going" the body would die. If it were "going" it would have to be conjoined with a previous [moment of] sense data. Why should [the mind] only have things of the past as its conditions and not know any new things?

If you understand this, then realize clearly that [conditions] do not arrive at one's focus of concentration. The things of the past cease because things of the past cease. Being [ultimately] without realms [of perception], the realms [of perception] are false. How can the so-called "conditions" be anything but false? Know hereby that this is the false.

E. It is also incorrect to say that the mind is within the abdomen. Why? If it were in the abdomen, it would know each and every affair of the five organs. Since it is completely ignorant [of these matters], this shows that the mind is not located within [the abdomen]. Since it is not located within, then there is no self, no "going" to external sense data, no self and other. Since self and other are nonsubstantial, the mind is said to be without [the distinctions of] "this" and "that." Therefore, this is called the "mind emancipated" *(hsin chieh-t'o).*[215] Why? Because of not residing in the two extremes [of exterior and interior]. When performing this contemplation, the mind is serene and like space. This is called "to comprehend the mind" *(liao hsin).*

F. In contemplating form, form is also of two kinds. The first is external form. The second is internal form. The mountains, rivers, and earth are external form; the five *skandha*s and four elements are internal form.

In the initial contemplation of the external four elements, the mountains, rivers, and earth which are the support of all the myriad beings, this earth is called "earth" because it is a thickly layered collection of the most minute particles [of matter]. But before those minute particles collected [to form the earth], they were fundamentally nonsubstantial. Only in response to the force of sentient beings' karma do these minute particles form from space. If that force of karma of sentient beings did not exist, those minute particles would also be nonsubstantial (*k'ung,* i.e., nonexistent). Even when collected all together [as the earth], they are still minute particles. Why? If you examine the earth you will get particles, not the earth itself. There is no earth that transcends *(li)* those particles. Realize, therefore, that prior to the aggregation of those minute particles, the earth is fundamentally nonsubstantial.

If the earth is nonsubstantial, realize also that the minute particles are nonsubstantial. Why? Space is without [any Self] Nature and [yet] generates the minute particles. The particles are without [any Self] Nature and [yet] generate the earth. If you [go from] space to earth in your contemplation[216] [you will see that] the minute particles [which form the basis of material reality] are fundamentally nonsubstantial. When performing this contemplation, you will clearly learn that the five *skandha*s and four elements are similarly [only] empty names.

As to the explanation of internal form, the generation of the internal four elements of the body is completely dependent on the external four elements. Since the external four elements are nonsubstantial, so are the internal ones. Why? People live on food, and food and clothing are generated from the earth. The earth is nonsubstantial, so food and clothing are also nonexistent. Since food and clothing are nonexistent, how could internal form exist (*li,* lit., "be posited")? Since internal form does not exist, it is obviously nonsubstantial.

Contemplation of the mind [reveals that it is] neither internal nor external. Form is also the same. That mind and form are neither internal nor external is called "serene" *(chi).* Serene, with nothing existing, it is therefore called nirvāṇa. This understanding is called "correct" (*cheng,* as in the eightfold path). It distantly transcends mistaken views and is also called the correct view, also called correct meditation, and also called correct action. Also, this teaching is called the correct teaching. All the Buddhas of the three periods of time attain the other shore [of nirvāṇa] on the basis of this teaching, which is called the correct path.

G. [Third], although you may be able to achieve this understanding, you must practice on the basis of it or else enter a heretical path or the class [of persons with] false ascriptive views. If you [decide to] practice on the basis of this understanding, [you must accept the fact that] the "perfuming" of the ordinary person's illusions is not [just] a present-day [affair, but] has been accumulating since beginningless time and so cannot be exhausted suddenly, in an instant.

Also, if you achieve enlightenment according to this understanding [you must remain] constantly aware of your present situation and not let the illusions of ignorance arise again. This is called the "practice of the cause" *(yin-hsing).* When the "influences" and illusions are all exhausted, you must not allow them to be conjoined again to the realms and data of sensory experience: Only then is this called "completely eradicated."

H. One who knows within oneself that [the illusions] are not yet exhausted must constantly [maintain] the illumination of contemplation *(kuan-hsing chueh-chao)* and [like] a bodhisattva practice the six perfections, extending the benefits of compassion everywhere, being direct with oneself and circumspect with others, allowing sufficiency to others and insufficiency for oneself. Why? In the previous contemplation [it was seen that] mind and form are nonsubstantial and without self, thus being equivalent to space. If space possessed form, then would not form have a self? Since the self is nonsubstantial, who would have whom? Since space is without self, then one must practice the compassion of nonsubstantiality *(wu-cheng tz'u).* If one does not do so, then principle and practice *(li-hsing)*[217] will be mutually contradictory. This would not be the practice of the bodhisattva. Therefore, I say to generate practice on the basis of one's understanding.

I. Fourth, you must contemplate constantly, without interruption. If you do not accomplish (i.e., make effort in) [both] principle and practice *(pu tso li-hsing),* then your associated contemplation will probably [suffer from] errors. Therefore, you must contemplate constantly, without interruption.

J. Fifth, understanding your stage of practice means that you should not immediately claim, on the basis of this interpretation [of Buddhism], that you are equal to a buddha, with whom you do not share the same realms [of existence]. The first of the stages are the wise men who cultivate faith, not persons of the ultimate [goal]. I point this out because, if you do not know your own stage [of progress], you will certainly commit the blasphemy [that Buddhism preaches] no cause and result.

Chapter Seven: The Manifestations of One's Own Mind

A. According to the *Laṇkāvatāra Sūtra,* all the *dharma*s are established [on the basis of] the principle of the self-enlightened sagely wisdom and are all the manifestations of one's own mind.[218] In explaining this idea, it is not false to say that the mountains, rivers, earth, and even one's own body are all [the manifestations of] one's own mind.

I have discussed [the fact that] the body is made up of the four elements and is a response *(kan)* to the [external] four elements. Why are there not five elements making up the world? And with regard to the four disks upon which [the world] rests, why are there not five disks? What advantage is there in this?

The commentary says: "These actually are manifestations of one's own mind. This is not mistaken."[219] Know, therefore, that [all *dharmas*] are manifested by one's own mind. I have discussed the four elements of the body because within the body there are four kinds of false thoughts. The response to these [four kinds of false thoughts molds] the four elements [into] a body, and hence there are not five elements, [but only four].

Why? The element earth exists as [part of] the body in response to the internal false thought of heaviness. The element water exists as [part of] the body in response to the internal false thought of wetness. The element fire exists as [part of] the body in response to the internal false thought of burning. The element wind exists as [part of] the body in response to the internal false thought of blowing. Therefore, it is known that these are all the manifestations of one's own mind.

B. QUESTION: The body may be understood [this way] without error, but how do you know that the mountains, rivers, and earth are [all the manifestations of] one's own mind?

ANSWER: They too depend on the internal mind. Why? The mountains, rivers, and earth are not level in response to the false thought of elevation. The earth is 360,000 *li* thick and is called the earth disk. Beneath the earth is water, also 360,000 *li* thick. This is called the water disk and is just under the earth disk. Beneath the water disk there is a great fire, which is also 360,000 *li* thick. [As with the] above, it is just under the water disk. Under this great fire [disk] is a wind disk, which is also 360,000 *li* thick. The four disks connect with each other above and below so that the earth exists [on top]. This is called the "world" *(shih-chieh)*.

Underneath the wind disk is empty space with nothing in it. Why? There are only four disks, not five or six. This is because the inner mind of sentient beings has four kinds of false thoughts. The earth disk exists in response to the internal false thought of heaviness. The water disk exists in response to the false thought of wetness. The fire disk exists in response to the false thought of burning. The wind disk exists in response to the false thought of blowing. According to this meditation, the entire [world system] is a manifestation of one's own mind. There is not a single *dharma* outside of the mind.

C. At this time a person asked: The innumerable *dharmas* of this world are based solely on one's failure to be enlightened. The various *dharmas* are [manifestations of] the mind. According to this explanation *(yin-yuan),* if there is doubt, then the various *dharma*s appear. They are existent [and then] nonexistent. This explanation thus implies the blasphemy of "being" and "nonbeing." Because it eradicates the various *dharma*s, it [also] generates the blasphemy[220] of disputation.

[ANSWER]: If you understand the responses of the mind, [the *dharma*s] are all one's own mind. Originally there are no *dharma*s. If there were *dharma*s then you could say "being" and "nonbeing," but since the *dharma*s originally are one's own mind and do not exist, how can there be any error? By this understanding one escapes the blasphemies relevant to the various *dharma*s.

D. QUESTION: The mountains, rivers, and earth are inanimate, whereas humans are animate. How can one say that all the inanimate realms are [manifestations of the human] mind? It is very difficult to believe this.

ANSWER: It is like a husband and wife, both witless fools and argumentative toward each other, who were making liquor on which to get drunk.[221] When the liquor had finished fermenting the husband went to look at it and, seeing his own reflection in the clear liquid, became angry and hit his wife. The wife [demanded] an explanation, [saying]: "What have I done?" The husband then said: "Why are you hiding another man in the [liquor] urn?" The wife did not believe him and looked in the urn herself. Seeing her own reflection, she became very angry herself and said to her husband: "Why did you hide a woman in the urn without telling me?" Then, not understanding that it was their own reflections, they began hitting each other—hitting each other with deadly intent.

When the entire village came to stop them and asked what it was all about, they explained as above. When the person who broke up the quarrel explained [about the reflections], they still did not believe, so he took the husband and wife to the urn to look at the reflections. They saw the reflections of three people, but still did not believe: "If these are reflections [of us] they should be outside of the urn [just as we are]. Why are they within the urn?" The arbitrator said: "If they are not your reflections, then you two and I are all in that urn together!"

[The arbitrator then said to the wife]: "You see [the reflections of] three people. You should realize that that is your husband's reflection." At that, the wife got even angrier and said: "There's a man bringing him a woman!" and began hitting [her husband] again and would not stop. In the end they never could believe that those were their own reflections.

E. Ordinary people are like this [in not realizing] that the mountains, rivers, and earth, sun, moon, and stars are all manifestations of the karma of their own minds, all reflected images of their own minds. Why do ordinary people not call [all this] the product of the mind and never believe? It is like the husband and wife who fought over their reflected likenesses and never believed that those [likenesses] were their own images.

The actual reflections within the urn are a metaphor for the mountains, rivers, and earth's being manifestations of one's own mind. If they were not manifestations of one's own mind, then when you see lightning and it vibrates through space and when you hear the thunder, you should realize that the sound is nonsubstantial. Further, when you see carriages on the earth, although they vibrate the earth and make a sound, you should realize that without space there would be no sound. The sound itself is also nonsubstantial. According to this understanding, all the *dharmas* are all [identical with] space.

Originally, there are no *dharmas*. It is only that ordinary people, whose false thoughts are not exhausted, see the mountains, rivers, and earth. If those false thoughts were exhausted, they would never see them. The Buddhas and Bodhisattvas, whose activities are unobstructed, do not see the mountains, rivers, and earth because their false thoughts have been exhausted. [Therefore], you should realize that the myriad *dharmas* are all manifestations of the karma of the mind.

CHAPTER NINE: ELUCIDATION OF THE ESSENCE OF SOUND

A. As for sound, the understanding of sound by people nowadays as something perceived by the ear is greatly mistaken. To say that sound arrives at the ear is also greatly mistaken.

QUESTION: How should one understand this so as to be in agreement with Buddhism?

[ANSWER]: If you wish to understand the true source of sound you must first understand the conditions *(yuan)* and essence of sound.

QUESTION: What are the conditions and essence [of sound]?

ANSWER: The bell clapper and the human effort [of striking the bell] are conditions. The spaces inside and outside the bell are its essence. In producing the sound, the essence (i.e., those spaces) sounds, not the bell.

QUESTION: The essence, [space,] is located everywhere. Why does [the sound] only extend ten *li* and not one hundred *li?*

ANSWER: The conditions may be either small or great. Although the sound does not extend through space, it is like the greatest of earthquakes, which shakes everything: Does the earth [really] flow [as it seems to]? (?) If you think about it, although the earth vibrates, it never flows. Thus it is motionless, and sound is likewise: Although conditioned by the striking of lightning, space vibrates and makes a sound, but it does not flow [anywhere itself]. Not flowing, it is motionless. It is thus not generated and not extinguished.

B. As to the doctrines of the five oceans and ten wisdoms,[222] these are the foundation of the great practice of all the Buddhas and Bodhisattvas. If you do not appreciate the doctrines of the five oceans and ten wisdoms, then you will have no way to understand the perfect teaching.

What is this perfect teaching? The perfect teaching is that sentient beings are the Buddhas and the Buddhas are sentient beings. They have always been so, not just through their present enlightenment. This is not the same as the [idea of the] bodhisattva in the three vehicles. Further, to explain the idea of the perfect teaching, [I would say that] this is not the realm of sentient beings and also not the realm of nirvāṇa.[223]

3. *The Five Expedient Means* (Wu fang-pien)

Introduction

A. Number One: Comprehensive Explanation of the Essence of Buddhahood

Number Two: Opening the Gates of Wisdom and Sagacity

Number Three: Manifesting the Inconceivable Dharma

Number Four: Elucidation of the True Nature of the *Dharma*s

Number Five: The Naturally Unobstructed Path of Emancipation (II.Int.1:167)[224]

B. Each kneel with palms together. I will now have you recite the Four Great Vows:

I vow to save the innumerable sentient beings.

I vow to eradicate the limitless afflictions.

I vow to master the infinite teachings.

I vow to realize the unsurpassable enlightenment of buddhahood.

Next request the Buddhas of the ten directions to be your preceptors.

Next request the Bodhisattvas and Buddhas of the three periods of time [to be your witnesses (?)].

Next I will ask about the five capabilities. First, can you reject all bad associates from now until the time of your enlightenment?

I can.

Second, can you become close to spiritual compatriots?

I can.

Third, can you maintain the precepts without transgression even in the face of death?

I can.

Fourth, can you read the Mahāyāna scriptures and inquire of their profound meaning?

I can.

Fifth, can you [strive] to the extent of your own power to save sentient beings from their suffering?

I can.

Next, each must say his own name and repent his transgressions, saying:

> *I now profoundly repent with all my heart all the karma of body, speech, and mind, and the ten evil transgressions [committed by me] during past, future, and present. I hope that my transgressions will be eradicated, never to occur again.*

The obstacles of the five major transgressions [should be repeated] according to the above.

It is likened to a bright pearl submerged in muddy water, the water becoming clear through the pearl's power. The virtuous efficacy of the Buddha Nature is also like this, the muddy water of the illusions being completely clarified [thereby]. Since you have finished your repentances, your three types of action (i.e., body, speech, and mind) are pure like pure lapis lazuli. The brightness [of your purity] penetrating within and without, you are now ready to take the Pure Precepts.

[To maintain] the Bodhisattva Precepts is to maintain the precepts of the mind, because the Buddha Nature is the "nature of the precepts" *(chieh-hsing)*. To activate the mind *(ch'i)* for the briefest instant is to go counter to the Buddha Nature, to break the Bodhisattva Precepts.[225] *(This [subject] is to be explained thrice.)*

Next each of you should sit in lotus postion. (II.Int.2:167)

C. QUESTION: O disciples of the Buddha, your minds are peaceful and motionless. What is it that is called purity?[226] Disciples of the Buddha, the *Tathāgatas* have a great expedient means for entrance into the Path (or into enlightenment). In one instant you can purify your mind and suddenly transcend to the stage of buddhahood.

The preceptor strikes the wooden [signal board, and everyone] contemplates the Buddha *(nien-fo)* for a time.

The preceptor says: All [phenomenal] characteristics are uniformly imperceptible. Therefore, the *Diamond Sūtra (Chin-kang ching)* says: "All that has characteristics is completely false."[227] To view the mind as pure is called "to purify the mind-ground." Do not constrict the body and mind and unfold the body and mind—view afar in expansive release. View with universal "sameness" *(p'ing-teng).* Exhaust space with your viewing.

The preceptor asks: What do you see (lit., what thing do you see)?

The disciple(s) answer: *I do not see a single thing.*

Preceptor: Viewing purity, view minutely. Use the eye of the Pure Mind to view afar without limit, without restriction.[228] View without obstruction.

The preceptor asks: What do you see?

ANSWER: *I do not see a single thing.* (II.Int.3:168)

D. View afar to the front, not residing in the myriad sensory realms, holding the body upright and just illuminating, making the true essence of reality[229] distinct and clear.

View afar to the rear, not residing in the myriad sensory realms, holding the body upright and just illuminating, making the true essence of reality distinct and clear.

View afar to both sides, not residing in the myriad sensory realms, holding the body upright and just illuminating, making the true essence of reality distinct and clear.

View afar facing upwards, not residing in the myriad sensory realms, holding the body upright and just illuminating, making the true essence of reality distinct and clear.

View afar facing downwards, not residing in the myriad sensory realms, holding the body upright and just illuminating, making the true essence of reality distinct and clear.

View in the ten directions all at once, not residing in the myriad sensory realms, holding the body upright and just illuminating, making the true essence of reality distinct and clear.

View energetically during unrest, not residing in the myriad sensory realms, holding the body upright and just illuminating, making the true essence of reality distinct and clear.

View minutely during calm, not residing in the myriad sensory realms, holding the body upright and just illuminating, making the true essence of reality distinct and clear.

View identically whether walking or standing still, not residing in the myriad sensory realms, holding the body upright and just illuminating, making the true essence of reality distinct and clear.

View identically whether sitting or lying down, not residing in the myriad sensory realms, holding the body upright and just illuminating, making the true essence of reality distinct and clear. (IIIA.Int.1:190)

E. QUESTION: When viewing, what things do you view?

[ANSWER]: *Viewing, viewing, no thing is viewed.*

[QUESTION]: Who views?

[ANSWER]: *The enlightened mind* (chueh-hsin) *views.*[230]

Penetratingly viewing the realms of the ten directions, in purity there is not a single thing. Constantly viewing and in accord with the locus of nonbeing *(wu-so),*[231] this is to be equivalent to a buddha. Viewing with expansive openness, one views without fixation. Peaceful and vast without limit, its untaintedness is the path of *bodhi (p'u-t'i lu).* The mind serene and enlightenment distinct, the body's serenity is the *bodhi* tree *(p'u-t'i shu).*[232] The four tempters[233] have no place of entry, so one's great enlightenment is perfect and complete, transcending perceptual subject and object. (IIIA.Int.2:190)

[NUMBER ONE: COMPREHENSIVE EXPLANATION OF THE ESSENCE OF BUDDHAHOOD]

A. The attainment[234] of the transcendence of thoughts in body and mind: Not perceiving the mind, the mind is suchlike, and the mind attains emancipation. Not perceiving the body, form is suchlike, and the body attains emancipation. Function like this forever, without interruption.[235] Like space, without a single thing, pure and without characteristics.

Never let there by any interruption; from now on forever transcend [all] obstacles. The eye being pure, the eye transcends obstacles. The ear being pure, the ear transcends obstacles. In this fashion, [all] six sense organs being pure, the six sense organs transcend obstacles. All [of them] are without hindrance and equivalent to emancipation. To not perceive any characteristics of the six sense organs, which are pure and have no characteristics, [and to maintain this] constantly and without interruption: this is to be a buddha.

[QUESTION]: What is a buddha?

[ANSWER]: The mind of a buddha is pure, transcending being and transcending nonbeing. With body and mind not "activating," always maintain the True Mind *(shen-hsin pu ch'i, ch'ang shou chen-hsin).*[236]

[QUESTION]: What is suchness?

[ANSWER]: If the mind does not activate, the mind is suchlike. If form does not activate, form is suchlike. Since the mind is suchlike the mind is emancipated. Since form is suchlike form is emancipated. Since mind and form both transcend [thoughts], there is not a single thing. This is the great *bodhi* tree. (II.Int.5:169)

B. "Buddha" *(fo)* is a Sanskrit word from the western country; here it is translated as "enlightenment" *(chueh).*

[QUESTION]: Where does enlightenment occur?

[ANSWER]: Enlightenment occurs within the mind.

[QUESTION]: Where is the mind?

[ANSWER]: The mind is within the body.
[QUESTION]: Where is the body?
[ANSWER]: The body occurs within false thoughts (i.e., it is a misconception with no true reality). (IIIA.1.1:191)

C. "Buddha" is a Sanskrit word from the western country; here it is translated as "enlightenment." [The *Awakening of Faith* says]:

> The meaning of "enlightenment" is that the essence of the mind transcends thoughts. The characteristic of the transcendence of thoughts is equivalent to the realm of space, which pervades everywhere. The One Characteristic of the *dharmadhātu* is the universally same *dharmakāya* of the *Tathāgata*. Inherent enlightenment is preached in relation to the *dharmakāya*.

[The same treatise also says]:

> Being enlightened to the initial activation of the mind, the mind is without the characteristic of initialness. Distantly transcending the most subtle of thoughts, one comprehensively perceives the Mind Nature. The constant maintenance (*chu*, lit., residence) of this [Mind] Nature is called the ultimate enlightenment.[237] (II.1.3:170)

D. "Buddha" is a Sanskrit word from the western country; here it is translated as "enlightenment." "The meaning of 'enlightenment' is that the essence of the mind transcends thoughts." "To transcend thoughts" is the meaning of "buddha," the meaning of "enlightenment."

Briefly, there are three senses to the meaning of "buddha." They are also called the "expedient means of the mind" *(hsin fang-pien)*.

QUESTION: What are these three meanings?

[ANSWER]: Enlightenment of self, enlightenment of others, and complete enlightenment *(tzu-chueh chueh-t'a chueh-man)*. The transcendence of mind is enlightenment of self, with no dependence *(yuan)* on the five senses. The transcendence of form is enlightenment of others, with no dependence on the five types of sensory data. The transcendence of both mind and form is to have one's practice of enlightenment perfect and complete *(chueh-hsing yuan-man)* and is equivalent to the universally "same" *dharmakāya* of a *Tathāgata*. (II.1.4:170)

E. "The characteristic of the transcendence of thoughts is equivalent to the realm of space, which pervades everywhere."

QUESTION: What is "equivalent to the realm of space, which pervades everywhere"? What is pervading and not pervading? (II.1.5:170)

[ANSWER]: Space is without generation and extinction, and the transcendence of thoughts is also without generation and extinction. Space is a characterless unconditionality, and the transcendence of thoughts is also a characterless unconditionality. Space neither increases nor decreases, and the transcendence of thoughts neither increases nor decreases. Space is without mind, and the transcendence of thoughts is without mind. Because it is without mind, it pervades everywhere. If there are thoughts, there is no pervading; if thoughts are transcended, there is pervading. (IIIA.1.3:192)

F. As to the "One Characteristic of the *dharmadhātu,*" that which the consciousness *(i,* presumably *maṇas)* knows is the *dharmadhātu,* the eighteen realms. The eye sees and the consciousness knows, and when thoughts are activated and many ideas generated, there is obstruction and no penetration. This is a defiled *dharmadhātu,* the realm of a sentient being.

When the eye sees, the consciousness knows, and thoughts are transcended, then there is no obstruction. This is a pure *dharmadhātu,* the realm of a buddha. The "One Characteristic" is without characteristics; there being no characteristics of unity or duality, this is the True Characteristic. The True Characteristic is equivalent to the "One Characteristic of the *dharmadhātu.*"[238] (IIIA.1.4:192)

G. [QUESTION]: What is a "realm of a buddha"?

[ANSWER]: As to the "One Characteristic of the *dharmadhātu,*" that which the consciousness knows are *dharma*s, the *dharmadhātu.* The eyes see forms, the ears hear sounds, the nose perceives smells, the tongue knows tastes, the body perceives tactile sensations, and the consciousness knows *dharma*s. The consciousness knows all the other five types of *dharma*s. If the mind activates in coordination with its conditions, this is equivalent to a defiled *dharmadhātu,* the realm of an [unenlightened] sentient being. If one does not activate the mind in coordination with its conditions, this is equivalent to a pure *dharmadhātu,* the realm of a buddha, the "One Characteristic of the *dharmadhātu.*"

There are two [kinds of] eighteen realms, one defiled and one pure. First [I will explain the] defiled [*dharmadhātu*] and then the pure. The eyes see forms and the consciousness knows this in coordination with its conditions. The eyes and the other five senses depend on sensory data. If defilement is activated in these five locations (*ch'u,* i.e., the five senses), then all locations are defiled (i.e., consciousness included). If all locations are included, this is a defiled *dharmadhātu,* the realm of a sentient being. (II.1.8:171)

QUESTION: What is a pure *dharmadhātu?*

[ANSWER]: A pure *dharmadhātu* is to be within the transcendence of thoughts and for the eyes to see forms without discriminating.

One thus attains emancipation of the eyes (lit., at the eye location). The other four [senses] are the same. If the five locations are emancipated, then all locations are emancipated. If all the locations are emancipated, then all the locations are pure. This is equivalent to a pure *dharmadhātu,* the realm of a buddha.[239] (II.1.9:171)

H. The interpretation of "inherent enlightenment" *(pen-chueh)* and "temporal enlightenment" *(shih-chueh):*

The transcendence of thoughts is called "inherent enlightenment" —the absolute Buddha Nature.

The transcendence of form is called "temporal enlightenment"—phenomenal Buddha Nature.

The transcendence of both form and mind, with Nature and characteristics perfectly melded and absolute and phenomena both interpenetrating without hindrance, is called the comprehensive consummation of the three meanings of enlightenment. *(The primary interpretation of the meaning* [*of this expedient means is related to*] *enlightenment. The secondary interpretation is related to the absolute and phenomena.)* (I.1.7:163)

[The *Awakening of Faith* says]:

> "Being enlightened to the initial activation of the mind, the mind is without the characteristic of 'initialness.' Distantly transcending the most subtle of thoughts, one comprehensively perceives the Mind Nature. The constant maintenance of this [Mind] Nature is called the ultimate enlightenment":

This is called the *dharmakāya* buddha.

To know the fundamental motionlessness of the six senses, one's enlightenment becoming suddenly perfect, its brilliance illuminating everywhere: This is called the *saṁbhogakāya* buddha.

To perfectly illuminate in [all] ten directions, one's sensory realms unhindered and autonomous *(tzu-tsai)* because the mind has transcended thoughts: This is called the *nirmāṇakāya* buddha.

Pure and without a single thing: This is called the *dharmakāya* buddha.

Enlightened comprehension bright and distinct: This is the *saṁbhogakāya* buddha.

Perceptive capacities autonomous: This is the *nirmāṇakāya* buddha.

The three bodies (i.e., the *trikāya*) are of one and the same essence. They are one, yet different, and incorporate, yet do not incorporate, each other. (IIIA.1.5:192ctd.)

I. [Question]: What is the *dharmakāya* buddha?

[Answer]: To cultivate morality, meditation, and wisdom while in the causal [stage] (i.e., while still nominally unenlightened), to destroy the thick and layered obstacles of ignorance within oneself (lit., "within the body"), and to create [out of this] the great refulgence of wisdom and sagacity *(chih-hui)*[240]: This is the *dharmakāya* buddha.[241] (II.1.13:171)

J. QUESTION: What is "essence"? What is "function"?

ANSWER: The transcendence of thought is the essence, and the perceptive faculties *(chien-wen chueh-chih)* are the function. Serenity *(chi)* is the essence, and illumination *(chao)* is the function. "Serene but always functioning; functioning but always serene." Serene but always functioning—this is the absolute *(li)* corresponding to phenomena *(shih)*. Functioning but always serene—this is phenomena corresponding to the absolute. Serene yet always functioning—this is form corresponding to nonsubstantiality. Functioning yet always serene—this is nonsubstantiality corresponding to form.

"Serenely illuminating, illuminating serenity." Serenely illuminating is to activate the characteristics on the basis of the Nature. Illuminating serenity is to have all the characteristics revert to the Nature. Serene illumination is the nondifferentiation of form from nonsubstantiality. Illuminating serenity is the nondifferentiation of nonsubstantiality from form.

Serenity is unfolding; illumination is constriction (lit., "rolling up").[242] Unfolded, it expands throughout the *dharmadhātu*. Constricted, it is incorporated in the tip of a hair. Its expression [outward] and incorporation [inward] distinct, the divine function is autonomous. (IIIA.1.6:192)

K. QUESTION: Body and mind being nonsubstantial, who expresses and who incorporates?

ANSWER: Body and mind being nonsubstantial, for there to be no expression and incorporation is to be united with the unconditioned *(wu-wei)*. Opening up the unconditioned, one attains the True Characteristic. Body and mind being nonsubstantial, well does one "convert" (*hui-hsiang,* or *pariṇāma,* usually "to convert [one's own merit to the benefit of others]"). One converts one's enlightenment (?) to realize the true, permanent bliss. One is forever without attachment in relationship to the sensory realms.

The dependences of defiled and pure are the two *dharma*s of body and mind: To have thoughts is the dependence on illusions as infinite as the sands of the River Ganges; to transcend thoughts is the dependence on merit as infinite as the sands of the River Ganges. (IIIA.1.7:193)

L. If one transcends the mind,[243] craving is not activated. If one transcends form, anger is not generated. If one transcends both, stupidity is not manifested.

Transcendence of the mind is escape from the realm of desire. Transcendence of form is escape from the realm of form. Transcendence of both is escape from the realm of formlessness. (I.1.7: 193ctd.)

M. Interpretation of craving, anger, and stupidity. Explanation: The meaning of enlightenment is that the essence of the mind transcends thoughts. Transcending the characteristic of craving, it is equivalent to the realm of space, which pervades everywhere. This is called enlightenment of self. Transcending the characteristic of anger, it is equivalent to the realm of space, which pervades everywhere. This is called enlightenment of others. Transcending the characteristic of stupidity, it is equivalent to the realm of space, which pervades everywhere. The single characteristic of the *dharmadhātu* is the universally "same" *dharmakāya* of the *Tathāgata.* This is called complete enlightenment. (I.1.8:164)

Interpretation of the meaning of the three realms: The meaning of enlightenment is that the essence of the mind transcends desires. The characteristic of the transcendence of the realm of desire[244] is equivalent to the realm of space, which pervades everywhere. This is enlightenment of self. The characteristic of the transcendence of the realm of form . . . *(as above. This is called enlightenment of others.)* The characteristic of the transcendence of the realm of formlessness . . . *(as above. This is called complete enlightenment.)* (I.1.9:164)

Interpretation of the three emancipations: Transcending the mind is to enter the emancipation of nonsubstantiality. Transcending form is to enter the characterless emancipation. Transcending both is to enter the emancipation of wishlessness. (I.1.10:164)

Interpretation of the three Self Natures: Transcending the mind, the Self Nature of false thoughts is not activated. Transcending form, the Self Nature of conditionality is not activated. Transcending both is the Self Nature of the perfectly accomplished.[245] (I.1.12:164)

Further, there are secondary interpretations of the three [meanings of] enlightenment, eradicating the three poisons, escaping the three realms, entering the gates of the three emancipations, transcending the three natures, attaining the two [types of] *anātman,* realizing the three [types of] birth (?), manifesting the three virtues, and completing the three bodies.

(The primary meaning and secondary interpretation of terms of

the first expedient means are now completed. This has been called the Comprehensive Explanation of the Essence of Buddhahood.) This has been called "comprehensive explanation" because everything has been interpreted according to the transcendence of mind and the transcendence of form. (I.1.18:165)

NUMBER TWO: [OPENING THE GATES OF WISDOM AND SAGACITY]

A. The preceptor strikes the wooden [signal-board] and asks: Do you hear the sound?

[ANSWER]: *We hear.*

[QUESTION]: What is this "hearing" like?

[ANSWER]: *Hearing is motionless.*

[QUESTION]: What is the transcendence of thoughts?

[ANSWER]: *The transcendence of thoughts is motionless.*[246]

This motionlessness is to develop the expedient means of sagacity *(hui fang-pien)* out of meditation *(ting)*. This is to open the gate of sagacity. Hearing is sagacity. This expedient means can not only develop sagacity, but also make one's meditation correct. [To achieve this motionlessness] is to open the gate of wisdom, to attain wisdom *(chih)*. This is called the opening of the gates of wisdom and sagacity.

If you do not achieve [mastery] of this expedient means, your correct meditation will decline into incorrect meditation, you will become attached to the "taste of *dhyāna*" (i.e., addicted to trance states), and you will fall into a Hīnayānist nirvāṇa. If you do achieve [mastery] of this expedient means, you will attain the "perfect serenity" (i.e., nirvāṇa) through your correct meditation. This is the "great nirvāṇa."

The function of wisdom is knowing *(chih)*; the function of sagacity is perception *(chien)*. This is called the opening of the knowing and perception of a buddha. Knowing and perception are *bodhi*.[247] (II.2.1:172)

QUESTION: What is motionless?

ANSWER: The mind is motionless. The motionlessness of the mind is meditation, is wisdom, is the absolute *(li)*.[248] The motionlessness of the ears is form, is phenomena *(shih)*, is sagacity. [To achieve] this motionlessness is to develop the expedient means of sagacity out of meditation, the opening of the gate of sagacity. (II.2.2:173)

QUESTION: What is the gate of sagacity?

[ANSWER]: The ear is the gate of sagacity.

[QUESTION]: How is the gate of sagacity opened?

[ANSWER]: For the ear to be motionless when hearing sounds is to open the gate of sagacity.

[QUESTION]: What is sagacity?

[ANSWER]: Hearing is sagacity. The five senses are all the gates of sagacity. (II.2.3:173)

[This expedient means] can not only develop sagacity, but also make one's meditation correct. This is to open the gate of wisdom.[249]

QUESTION: What is the gate of wisdom?

[ANSWER]: The consciousness is the gate of wisdom.

[QUESTION]: How is the gate of wisdom opened?

[ANSWER]: For the consciousness to be motionless [when knowing the *dharmas*] is to open the gate of wisdom.

[QUESTION]: How is this?

[ANSWER]: One achieves wisdom by transforming knowing into wisdom.

This is called opening the gates of wisdom and sagacity. I have now finished [explaining] for you the opening of the gates of wisdom and sagacity. (II.2.4:174)

B. [The *Lotus Sūtra* says]: "Having the power to save sentient beings."[250] The body, hands and feet [included], is serenely peaceful and motionless. (II.2.5:174)

[QUESTION]: What are sentient beings? What is power?

[ANSWER]: Motionlessness is power. False thoughts are sentient beings. For the body and mind to be motionless is called "to save sentient beings." (IIIA.2.2:194)

QUESTION: What is motionlessness?

ANSWER: The blowing of the eight winds is motionless.

[QUESTION]: What are the eight winds?

ANSWER: Success and failure, defamation and praise, honor and abuse, and suffering and pleasure.[251]

QUESTION: How many of these are unfavorable, and how many are favorable?

ANSWER: Four are unfavorable and four are favorable. Failure, defamation, abuse, and suffering are unfavorable; success, praise, honor, and pleasure are favorable. The mind of the bodhisattva is unmoving during [both] unfavorable and favorable [winds]. (IIIA.2.3:194)

C. QUESTION: How many types of people can open the gates of wisdom and sagacity?

ANSWER: There are three types of people.

[QUESTION]: Who are they?

[ANSWER]: Ordinary people, Hīnayānists, and bodhisattvas. Ordinary people hear when there is a sound, but when there is no sound or when a sound stops they do not hear. Hīnayānists never hear,

[both] whether there is a sound or no sound and when a sound stops. Bodhisattvas always hear, [both] whether there is a sound or no sound and when a sound stops.[252] (II.2.7:174)

QUESTION: Bodhisattvas should be able to hear when there is a sound, but how can they hear when there is no sound?

ANSWER: Because the essence of their hearing is constant. (IIIA.2.4:194ctd.)

QUESTION: What is the essence of hearing?

ANSWER: Motionlessness is the essence of hearing. Hearing is like the surface of a mirror, which illuminates when there is a form [in front of it] and also when there is no form. Therefore, [the bodhisattva] hears when there is a sound and also hears when there is no sound. (IIIA.2.5:194)

D. QUESTION: If these three types of people uniformly open the same gates of wisdom and sagacity, why do the Hīnayānists become attached to the taste of *dhyāna* and fall into a Hīnayānist nirvāṇa?

[ANSWER: This is because of the manner in which] the Hīnayānists open the gate of sagacity. This sagacity must be realized as the sagacity of hearing in relation to the ears. Because they now hear what they did not hear before, [the Hīnayānists] hear and generate joy in their minds. Joy is motion. Fearing motion, they grasp at motionlessness, extinguish the six consciousnesses, and realize a nirvāṇa of empty serenity. Whether there is a sound or there is no sound and when a sound stops, [since they are in this state,] they never hear. Thus they become attached to the taste of *dhyāna* and fall into a Hīnayānist nirvāṇa.

When bodhisattvas open the gate of sagacity [they realize that] hearing is sagacity. This sagacity must be realized as the sagacity of hearing in relation to the ears, [and so they] know that the six senses are fundamentally motionless. They always hear, [both] whether there is a sound or no sound and when a sound stops. Their spiritual practice is always in accord with motionlessness. By the attainment of [the mastery of] this expedient means, their correct meditation is equivalent to the attainment of "perfect serenity." This is the "great nirvāṇa." (II.2.8:175)

E. The *Nirvāṇa Sūtra* (Nieh-p'an ching) says: "Not hearing and hearing, not hearing and not hearing, hearing and hearing."[253]

QUESTION: What is "not hearing and hearing"?

[ANSWER]: Hearing what one has not heard before is "not hearing and hearing."

[QUESTION]: What is "not hearing and not hearing"?

[ANSWER]: After hearing, [the Hīnayānist] generates joy in his mind. Joy is motion. Fearing motion, he grasps at motionlessness, extinguishes the six consciousnesses, and realizes a nirvāṇa of empty serenity. He is "not hearing and not hearing," [both] whether there is a sound or no sound and when a sound stops. This is "not hearing and not hearing."

[QUESTION]: What is "hearing and not hearing"?

[ANSWER]: The Hīnayānist hears when he comes out of meditation, but within meditation he does not hear. The Hīnayānist has no sagacity when he is in meditation—he cannot preach the Dharma and cannot save sentient beings. When he comes out of meditation, he preaches the Dharma in an unconcentrated state of mind. This absence of the nurturing moisture of the water of meditation is called "meditation that is dry of sagacity." This is "hearing and not hearing."

[QUESTION]: What is "hearing and hearing"?

[ANSWER]: Ordinary people have "hearing and hearing" and bodhisattvas have "hearing and hearing." The "hearing and hearing" of the ordinary person is motion, motion in coordination with sensory data. The "hearing and hearing" of the bodhisattva is motionless, with no coordination with sensory data. The "softened refulgence" is not "coordinated with sensory data" *(ho-kuang pu t'ung ch'en).*[254] (II.2.9:175)

F. QUESTION: What is motionlessness?

ANSWER: Motionlessness is the opening of the [gates of wisdom and sagacity].

QUESTION: Who can open the gates of wisdom and sagacity?

ANSWER: The spiritual compatriot can open the gates of wisdom and sagacity. Because of the words of the spiritual compatriot, one is enlightened to the motionlessness of the six senses. This is the "external" spiritual compatriot.

[QUESTION]: Who are the "internal" spiritual compatriots?

ANSWER: Wisdom and sagacity are the "internal" spiritual compatriots.

[QUESTION]: What are wisdom and sagacity?

ANSWER: Knowing is wisdom; perception[255] is sagacity. One transforms the consciousness to create wisdom and comprehends perception (or sensory consciousness) to create sagacity. These are called the "internal" spiritual compatriots. (IIIA.2.7:195)

G. [QUESTION]: What is *bodhi?*

[ANSWER]: *"Bodhi"* is a Sanskrit word from the western country. Here it is translated "knowing and perception" *(chih-chien).* Knowing and perception are the function of wisdom and sagacity. *Bodhi* is the function of nirvāṇa. Knowing and perception are the function, wisdom and sagacity the essence. *Bodhi* is the function, nirvāṇa the essence. *(Essence and function [have now been] clarified.)* (II.2.15:177)

H. The sūtra says: "*Bodhi* cannot be attained with the body and mind. Extinction is *bodhi,* since all characteristics are extinguished."[256]

QUESTION: Why is it that this "cannot be attained with the body and mind"?

ANSWER: Since the mind is motionless and thoughts are transcended and not activated, *bodhi* cannot be attained by the mind. Since form is motionless and thoughts are transcended and not activated, *bodhi* cannot be attained by form. Body and mind both being motionless is equivalent to "extinction is *bodhi,* since all characteristics are extinguished." Also, the transcendence of both body and mind is equivalent to perfect and complete *bodhi.* (II.2.16:177)

I. QUESTION: [The sūtra says:] "Noncorrespondence *(pu-hui)* is *bodhi,* because the *āyatana*s (*ju,* i.e., the sense organs and sense data) do not correspond [with each other]."[257] Is this nonattainment in body and mind?

ANSWER: The six senses being motionless, the *āyatana*s do not correspond [with each other]. This is equivalent to perfect and complete *bodhi.* Also, the senses and sense data being undefiled, all the "locations" (*ch'u,* also equivalent to *āyatana*) are noncorresponding. (II.2.17:177)

QUESTION: Further, what about [the sūtra's line] "The impediments are *bodhi,* because they impede the desires"?[258]

ANSWER: The six senses being motionless, the desires are not generated. This is equivalent to perfect and complete *bodhi.* (II.2.18:177)

J. QUESTION: [What are] motion and motionlessness?

[ANSWER]: If one perceives that there is motion, then this is motion. If one perceives that there is motionlessness, then this is also motion. To not perceive motion and not perceive motionlessness is true motionlessness.

[QUESTION]: Can one enter into this state?

[ANSWER]: If one perceives entry, then this is motion. If one perceives nonentry, then this is also motion. To not enter and not not enter is true motionlessness.

Hīnayānists perceive motionlessness external to the mind, activate thought, and grasp that motionlessness, rendering the five senses and six consciousnesses inactive. This is the annihilatory motionlessness of the Hīnayānists. Bodhisattvas know the fundamental motionlessness of the six senses, their internal illumination being distinct and external functions autonomous. This is the true and constant motionlessness of the Mahāyāna. (IIIA.2.9:196)

[QUESTION]: What do "internal illumination being distinct" and "external functions autonomous" mean?

ANSWER: Fundamental wisdom *(ken-pen chih)* is "internal illumination being distinct." Successive wisdom *(hou-te chih)* is "external functions autonomous."

[QUESTION]: What are fundamental wisdom and successive wisdom?

ANSWER: Because one first realizes the characteristic of the transcendence of the body and mind, this is fundamental wisdom. The autonomous [quality of] knowing and perception and the nondefilement [associated with the enlightened state] are successive wisdom.[259] The first realization of the fundamental . . . . . if realization [of the transcendence of body and mind] were not first, then knowing and perception would be completely defiled. Know clearly that the autonomous [spontaneity of] knowing and perception is attained after that realization and is called successive wisdom.

When the mind does not activate on the basis of the eye's perception of form, this is fundamental wisdom. The autonomous [spontaneity of] perception is successive wisdom. When the mind does not activate on the basis of the ear's hearing of sounds, this is fundamental wisdom. The autonomous [spontaneity of] hearing is successive wisdom. The nose, tongue, body, and consciousness are also the same. With the fundamental and successive [wisdoms], the locations *(ch'u)* are distinct, the locations are emancipated. The senses do not activate, and the realizations are pure. When successive moments of mental [existence] are nonactivating, the senses are sagely *(sheng)*.

([The above is] the primary interpretation [of the second expedient means.]) (IIIA.2.10:196)

K. [The *Lotus Sūtra* says]:

> Located in the world, like space, like a lotus blossom that does not touch the water, with mind pure and transcending [the distinctions of "this" and] "that," I bow my head in obeisance to the unsurpassed Honored One.[260]

"Located in the world": What is this? The mind is the locus *(ch'u)*; the five *skandha*s are the world. The mind is located within the five *skandha*s.

"Like space": Space is the mind. The mind is thus wisdom.

"Like a lotus blossom": The lotus blossom is form. Form is thus sagacity.

["With mind pure and transcending (the distinctions of 'this' and) 'that' "]: Wisdom and sagacity pure and transcending that [set of] five senses—this is to transcend "that."

"Bow [my head]": This is respect.

"Obeisance": This is accordance *(shun).*

To always practice in accordance with wisdom and sagacity: This is the "unsurpassed Honored One."[261] (II.2.27:180)

Sūtra of the Lotus Blossom of the Wondrous Dharma (Miao-fa lien-hua ching): What is the Wondrous Dharma? The mind is the Wondrous Dharma. The mind is thus wisdom. Form is thus sagacity. This is a sūtra of wisdom and sagacity.[262]

Sūtra of the Flower Garland of the Great and Vast Buddha (Ta fang-kuang fo hua-yen ching): Great and Vast is the mind. Flower Garland is form. The mind is thus wisdom. Form is thus sagacity. This is a sūtra of wisdom and sagacity.

Diamond Sūtra (Chin-kang ching): Metal *(chin)* is the mind. Hard *(kang)* is form. The mind is thus wisdom. Form is thus sagacity. This is a sūtra of wisdom and sagacity. (II.2.28:181)

Lotus Blossom of the Wondrous Dharma: What is the Wondrous Dharma? Meditation and sagacity (*ting-hui,* usually translated as meditation and wisdom) are the Wondrous Dharma. The "lotus blossom" is a metaphor. It is as if meditation and sagacity exist in the world but are not defiled by the world. Clearly understand that meditation and sagacity are the Wondrous Dharma. The lotus blossom is located in water but is not defiled by the water. The autonomous functioning of knowing and perception is [likewise] not defiled by the six sense objects. Just as the lotus blossom opens and releases its fragrance and is enjoyed by men and gods, so does the use of this metaphor cause those who have not yet attained meditation and sagacity [now] to attain meditation and sagacity.[263] (II.2.29:181)

[The *Lotus Sūtra* says]:

> At that time, the World-honored One preached the Mahāyāna sūtra's teaching of the bodhisattva and the thoughts (*nien,* i.e., mindfulness) maintained by the Buddha. Having completed the preaching of this sūtra, he sat in lotus position and entered the *samādhi* of the locus of incalculable meanings *(wu-liang i ch'u san-mei),* with body and mind motionless.[264]

[QUESTION]: What is the [teaching of] the Mahāyāna sūtra?

ANSWER: Wisdom and sagacity are the teaching of the Mahāyāna sūtra.

"Bodhisattva": The Dharmas of wisdom and sagacity.

"Thoughts maintained by the Buddha": To maintain the original transcendence of thoughts.[265]

"Having completed the preaching of this sūtra, he sat in lotus position": Expressing the motionlessness of body and mind.

"Entered the *samādhi* of the locus of incalculable meanings": If there is mind, then there is calculation. If there is no mind *(wu-hsin),* there is no calculation.

Sam- (san): This is "correct."

-ādhi (mei): This is "mind." To practice with a correct mind and enter[266] (i.e., to be enlightened to) the meaning of the one True Characteristic—this is called "entered the *samādhi* of the locus of incalculable meanings, with body and mind motionless." (IIIA.2.20:200)

[The *Lotus Sūtra* says]:

> Then the World-Honored One arose peacefully from his *samādhi* and said to Śāriputra: "The wisdom and sagacity of the Buddhas is profound and incalculable."[267]

QUESTION: What is it for wisdom and sagacity to be "profound and incalculable"?

[ANSWER]: The *Tathagata*'s ocean of wisdom is bottomless: This is called "profound." His sagacity can transcend the six types of sense data: Therefore it is called "incalculable."

This "gate" of wisdom and sagacity is difficult to understand and difficult to enter. All the *śrāvaka*s and *pratyekabuddha*s (i.e., the Hīnayānists) are unable to recognize it.

The minds of Hīnayānists possess [the characteristics of] generation and extinction: [This is] "difficult to understand." The minds of *śrāvaka*s possess attachment and motion: [This is] "difficult to enter." The bodhisattva is without attachment and without motion and can easily understand and easily enter.

[The *Lotus Sūtra* says that] the five classes of *śrāvaka*s[268] "cannot comprehend the wisdom of the Buddha. Exhaustively thinking and calculating about it, they still cannot understand it."[269]

QUESTION: Why can they not understand?

ANSWER: They cannot understand because they have minds of desire *(ssu-ch'iu hsin).*[270]

[QUESTION]: How can they become able to understand?

[ANSWER]: They will be able to understand when they are without minds of desire.

QUESTION: What should one do with desire?

ANSWER: One should transform desire within the mind *(i)* into wisdom. (II.2.33:182)

L. *Dāna-pāramitā* is a Sanskrit word. Here it is translated as ["perfection of] charity." [To practice] charity oneself and perceive another's lack of charity is to have contempt of others. In the Supreme Teaching, one neither perceives charity nor perceives the lack of charity. When the two characteristics are equal (i.e., when both charity and noncharity go unperceived), contempt will not arise. On the basis of such *dāna* one can transcend excessive contemptuousness. This is called "excellent *dāna-pāramitā*."[271]

Śīla-pāramitā is a Sanskrit word. Here it is translated as ["perfection of] morality" . . . (II.2.35:183)

[NUMBER THREE: MANIFESTING THE INCONCEIVABLE DHARMA]

A. [In the *Vimalakīrti Sūtra*] Vimalakīrti says: "Verily, Śāriputra, the Buddhas and Bodhisattvas possess an emancipation that is called inconceivable and inexpressible *(pu k'o ssu-i.)*"[272]

QUESTION: What is "inconceivable and inexpressible" *(pu-ssu pu-i)?*

ANSWER: The mind does not conceive and the mouth does not express. When the mind does not conceive, the mind is suchlike, the mind transcends fetters, the mind attains emancipation. When the mouth does not express, form is suchlike, form transcends fetters, form attains emancipation. For mind and form both to transcend fetters is called the "inconceivable and inexpressible emancipation." (II.2.1:185)

"At that time Śāriputra":[273] The beginner.

"Saw that in this space *(k'ung)*": [The beginner's] locus of intentionality.

"There were no seats": The emptiness of the *dharma*s.

"Generating this thought": The beginner is deluded as to the principle of nonsubstantiality.

"Thinking 'Where will the congregation of bodhisattvas and great disciples sit?' ": The *dharma*s being nonsubstantial, by what can one achieve buddhahood?

"Vimalakīrti: The essence of purity *(ching-t'i).*

"Śāriputra": The beginner. The essence of purity illuminates the beginner (or the initial [activation of the] mind).[274]

"When you have come for the Dharma, why are you seeking seats?": Conceivability and inconceivability[275] manifested together.

"I have come for the Dharma, not for a seat. If one seeks the Dharma, one cannot desire [even] life.": Truly, this is the moment of the correspondence of inconceivability, when no life is manifest. No feelings, perceptions, impulses, or consciousness are manifest. No Buddha, Dharma, and *Saṁgha* are manifest. No suffering, accumulation, extinction, and path[276] are manifest. No nirvāṇa is manifest. No grasping is manifest. No attachment is manifest. (IIIA.3.2:204)

B. "Vimalakīrti said: 'Well come, Mañjuśrī!'[277]

"Vimalakīrti": The essence of purity.

"Mañjuśrī": Wondrous sagacity.

When the essence of purity and wondrous sagacity correspond, the mind does not activate. This is "well," this is meditation.

Consciousness is not generated. This is "come," this is sagacity. Therefore it is said, "Well come!"

"Characterized by noncoming, yet coming."

"Characterized by noncoming": The mind not activating, this is meditation.

"Yet coming": The [sensory] consciousnesses not being generated, this is sagacity.

"Characterized by nonseeing, yet seeing."

"Characterized by nonseeing": The mind not activating, this is meditation.

"Yet seeing": The consciousnesses not being generated, this is sagacity.

Therefore, Mañjuśrī's wondrous sagacity is sagacity developed out of meditation. *From the inner, facing the outer*[278]*—this is the teaching of serene illumination.*

"Mañjuśrī said: 'O Layman' ": When wondrous sagacity and the essence of purity correspond.

"If you complete coming (i.e., come all the way to your destination), do not come anymore; if you complete going, do not go anymore."

"If you complete coming": The consciousnesses not being generated, this is sagacity.

"Do not come anymore": The mind not being activated, this is meditation.

"If you complete going": The consciousnesses not being generated, this is sagacity.

"Do not go anymore": The mind not being activated, this is meditation.

Therefore, Mañjuśrī's wondrous sagacity develops meditation out of sagacity. *From the outer, facing the inner—this is the teaching of illuminative serenity.* Why? The previous instant introduces the succeeding instant.

"Coming, without any point of departure; going, with no destination."

"Coming": The consciousnesses not being generated, this is sagacity.

"Without any point of departure": The mind not being activated, this is meditation.

"Going": The consciousnesses not being generated, this is sagacity.

"Without any destination": The mind not being activated, this is meditation.

"Visible": The consciousnesses not being generated, this is sagacity.

"And again not visible": The mind not being activated, this is meditation. *This is when serene illumination and illuminative serenity correspond.*[279] (IV.4.3–1:222)

C. QUESTION: What is meditation? What is sagacity?

ANSWER: Not to "eye" (i.e. not to conceptualize the existence of the eye) is meditation, yet to "eye" (i.e., to allow the eye to function) is sagacity. Not to "ear" is meditation, yet to "ear" is sagacity. Nose, tongue, body, and mind; forms, sounds, smells, tastes, tangible objects, and *dharmas*; knowing and perception—all are understood as above.

Not to "eye" is sagacity, yet to "eye" is meditation. Not to "ear" is sagacity, yet to "ear" is meditation. Nose, tongue, body, and mind; forms, sounds,smells, tastes, tangible objects, and *dharmas*; knowing and perception—all are understood as above. (IV.4.3–2:224)

QUESTION: What is meditation? What is sagacity?

[ANSWER]: The nonactivation of mind is meditation; the nongeneration of the consciousnesses is sagacity.

Transcendence of the Self Natures is meditation; transcendence of the realm of desire is sagacity.

The Ultimate Truth is meditation; the provisional truth is sagacity.

Great wisdom is meditation; great compassion is sagacity.

The Absolute *(li)* is meditation; phenomenality *(shih)* is sagacity.

The Unconditioned *(wu-wei)* is meditation; the conditioned *(yu-wei)* is sagacity.

Benefit of self *(tzu-li)* is meditation; benefit of others *(li-t'a)* is sagacity.

Nirvāṇa is meditation; saṁsāra is sagacity.

The transcendence of transgression is meditation; the maintenance of the *dharmas* is sagacity. (IV.4.3–3:224)

D. [The *Vimalakīrti Sūtra* says]:

> If a bodhisattva resides in this emancipation, he can insert the broad top of Mount Sumeru into a mustard seed without any enlargement or contraction, and the original characteristics of Sumeru, the king of mountains, will be as they were before (i.e., the size of the mountain will be unchanged).[280]

QUESTION: How can Mount Sumeru be inserted into a mustard seed without any enlargement or contraction?

ANSWER: Sumeru is form, and the mustard seed is also form. When the mind does not conceive *(pu-ssu),* the mind is suchlike. Sumeru and the mustard seed are both "form being suchlike" *(se-ju).* Having exactly the same characteristic(s), they are "without any enlargement or contraction, and the original characteristics of Sumeru, the king of mountains, will be as they were before." It is only those who cross [to the other shore of nirvāṇa] who perceive Mount Sumeru to be inserted into the mustard seed without any enlargement or contraction.

[QUESTION]: What about "the original characteristics of Sumeru, the king of mountains, will be as they were before"?

ANSWER: Sumeru does not contract, and the mustard seed is not enlarged. There being no enlargement or contraction, this is called "the original characteristics of Sumeru, the king of mountains, will be as they were before." (II.3.2:186)

[QUESTION]: "If a bodhisattva resides in this emancipation, he can insert the broad top of Mount Sumeru into a mustard seed without any enlargement or contraction": What is the meaning of this?

ANSWER: If there is conceiving, then there is thought. If there is thought, then there is obstruction. If there is obstruction, then there is impediment. If there is no conceiving, then there is no thought. If there is no thought, then there is no falsity. If there is no falsity, then there is no obstruction. If there is no obstruction, then there is no impediment. If there is no impediment, then there is emancipation. With no conceiving and no nonconceiving, no thought and no nonthought, Sumeru is originally nonsubstantial and the mustard seed is originally without impediment, [so that] the eye of sagacity distinctly sees the two enter into each other without any obstruction. If there is no conceiving and no thought and the characteristics of the two [objects] are identical, then this is "inconceivable." (IIIB.32:219)

Yet the four heavenly kings and the gods of the [Heaven of the] Thirty-three are unaware of the entrance [of Sumeru, on which they reside, into the mustard seed], nor were any sentient beings [below] inconvenienced.

QUESTION: Where do the four heavenly kings live?

ANSWER: They live on Mount Sumeru.[281]

[QUESTION]: Why are they unaware of [the entrance of Sumeru into the mustard seed]?

ANSWER: Because they possess conceiving and expressing, they are unaware of it.

[QUESTION]: How can they become aware of it?

[ANSWER]: If they are without conceiving, they will become aware of it.

[QUESTION]: Who are those who have crossed [over to the other shore]?

[ANSWER]: Being without conceiving and expressing, they have crossed over (i.e., transcended) conceiving and expressing.

[QUESTION]: What about "see Sumeru enter into the mustard seed"?

[ANSWER]: If the mind does not conceive, then one does not see the characteristics of size in Sumeru and the mustard seed. One also does not see entrance, nor does one see nonentrance. To perform this kind of seeing is called "true seeing" *(chen chien).*

If there is no conceiving, then there are no characteristics. If there are no characteristics, then there is no "entrance" and no "nonentrance." Being afraid of this, *śrāvaka*s eradicate [all] mental calculation.[282] *Śrāvaka*s are not yet enlightened, so that they see the characteristics of size of Sumeru and the mustard seed. When *śrāvaka*s are enlightened, they see that Sumeru and the mustard seed are in their original nature nonsubstantial, so how can the two "enter" or "not enter"? This is to see Sumeru within the mustard seed, which is called "residing in the inconceivable emancipation." (II.3.3:186)

[NUMBER FOUR: ELUCIDATION OF THE TRUE NATURE OF THE *DHARMAS*]

A. The *Sūtra of* [*the God*] *Ssu-i (Ssu-i ching)* says: "The god Ssu-i said to Tsung-ming Bodhisattva: 'What is the True Nature *(cheng-hsing)* of the *dharma*s?' Tsung-ming said: 'Transcending the Self Natures and transcending the realm of desire are the True Nature of the *dharma*s.' "[283]

QUESTION: What are the Self Natures? What is the realm of desire?

ANSWER: When the mind activates[284] knowing and perception, the five *skandha*s each have Self Natures. When the consciousness *(shih,* or *vijñāna)* is conditioned by the eye's seeing, this is the realm of desire. When the consciousness is conditioned by the ear's sounds, the nose's smells, the tongue's tastes, and the body's tactile sensations, this is the realm of desire. If the mind does not activate, it is constantly without characteristics and is pure. This is the True Nature of the *dharma*s.

QUESTION: What is it to transcend the Self Natures and transcend the Realm of Desire?

[ANSWER]: *Preceptor* [*Bodhi*]*dharma's Explanation (Ta-mo ho-shang chieh)* says: "For the mind not to activate is to transcend the Self Natures. For the consciousness not to be generated is to transcend the Realm of Desire. For both mind and consciousness not to activate is the True Nature of the *dharmas*. Just as when a river's great flow is exhausted, waves no longer arise (*ch'i,* lit., "are activated"), so when the mind and consciousness *(i-shih,* or *mano-vijñāna)* are extinguished, the various types of [sensory (?)] consciousness *(shih)* are not generated."[285] (IV.4.2:222)

[NUMBER FIVE: THE NATURALLY UNOBSTRUCTED PATH OF EMANCIPATION]

A. Within the *dharmas* that are without characteristics, there is no differentiation and no discrimination. Because the mind is without discrimination, all the *dharmas* are without differentiation. There is no difference between long and short, self and other, ordinary person and sage, saṁsāra and nirvāṇa, emancipation and bondage, intimate and remote, suffering and pleasure, reverse and direct, the three periods of time, stupidity and wisdom—all these are without differentiation. [This is to] comprehend the path of the undifferentiated, natural, unhindered emancipation.

All the unhindered persons escape saṁsāra by one path. It is neither [for a] long nor a short [time] that the emancipated person practices.[286] (IV.5.1:228)

B. QUESTION: What is the path of nonhindrance? What is the path of emancipation? What is the path of nonabiding?

ANSWER: When the senses do not hinder the sense data, and sense data is transcended, this is the path of nonhindrance. When sense data does not hinder the senses, and the senses transcend defilements, this is the path of emancipation. Transcending sense data and transcending defilement, this is the path of nonabiding . . .

Equivalent to the mind, not the mind, and not not the mind—this is the path of nonhindrance. Equivalent to the body, not the body, and not not the body—this is the path of emancipation. Equivalent to the sense realms, not the sense realms, and not not the sense realms—this is the path of nonabiding. (IV.5.2:228)

C. Utilizing the mind *(yung-hsin)* but not postulating (*li,* the usage here being tantamount to generating) mind or mental states *(hsin hsin-so)* and contemplating neither sense realms nor the absolute—this is the *dharmakāya* buddha.

The [enlightened] perception[287] of contemplation being serene and motionless, able to be born in the Land of Motionlessness—this is the *saṁbhogakāya* buddha.

Knowing and perceiving unhindered, born out of the *dharmakāya* —this is the *nirmāṇakāya* buddha.

The *dharmakāya* has a frozen permanence[288] (*ch'ang,* elsewhere rendered as constant), the *saṁbhogakāya* has a continuous permanence, and the *nirmāṇakāya* has an uninterrupted permanence. The three permanences are one, the one permanence is threefold, neither threefold nor unitary, neither permanent nor impermanent. Frozen, continuous, and uninterrupted—these are the three permanences. (IV.5.3:230)

[QUESTION]: Why is there one [permanence]?

[ANSWER]: Because the essence of permanence is unitary.

[QUESTION]: What is the one permanence that is threefold?

[ANSWER]: The essence of permanence is the *Tathāgata*'s great *samādhi*. From this great *samādhi* is manifested inherent enlightenment. From inherent enlightenment is developed brilliant sagacity. From brilliant sagacity is realized the immediate present (i.e., phenomenal reality). This is the one permanence that is threefold.

[QUESTION]: What is the neither threefold nor unitary?

[ANSWER]: Not mind, not body, and not the sense realms—these are not threefold. Being not imperceptible is the not unitary. The not unitary is true nonsubstantiality *(chen-k'ung)*.

[QUESTION]: What is the neither permanent nor impermanent?

[ANSWER]: The nonextinction of the nature(s ?) is the impermanent. The extinguished natures' perfect melding [into the myriad *dharmas* (?)] is the non-impermanent. The non-impermanent is wondrous being *(miao-yu)*.

When the eye sees form and the mind is not activated—this is true nonsubstantiality. When form does not defile the sense organ and vision is autonomous—this is wondrous being. (IV.5.4:230)

D. When one enters meditation *(cheng-shou)* in the eye, form arises out of (i.e., leaves the state of) *samādhi*. This indicates the inconceivability of the nature of form, which [ordinary] humans and gods cannot know.[289] . . . Ear, nose, tongue, body, and mind are understood as above. (IV.5.6:231)

E. The great path of the unconditioned is level—it is only that practitioners either traverse it or not. If you desire the fruit of buddhahood, then make effort in illuminating: Investigate your sense organs, penetrate their substance! Cultivate minutely!

Cultivate, cultivate, cultivate *(yen-yen-yen)*.
Mysterious, mysterious, mysterious *(hsuan-hsuan-hsuan)*.
Wondrous, wondrous, wondrous *(miao-miao-miao)*.

There are no middle and no extremes. If you do not cultivate in this lifetime, you will not reappear [from the lower modes of existence (?)] for an [entire] eon. (IV.5.10:232)

[CONCLUSION]

A. QUESTION: Why should one study these expedient means?
ANSWER: *In order to achieve buddhahood.*

QUESTION: By what means can one achieve buddhahood?

ANSWER: *One achieves buddhahood with the Essence of the Pure Mind.*

[QUESTION]: What is the [Essence of the] Pure Mind?

[ANSWER]: The Essence of the Pure Mind is like a bright mirror. Although it has forever manifested a myriad images, it never has become attached [to any of them]. If you now wish to discern this Essence of the Pure Mind, then study these expedient means. (IV.Con.1:232)

QUESTION: What is the Essence of the Pure Mind?

ANSWER: The Enlightenment Nature *(chueh-hsing)* is the Essence of the Pure Mind. Since one has formerly not been enlightened, the mind has commanded *(shih)* enlightenment. After becoming enlightened, enlightenment commands the mind. Therefore, command [the mind so that it] views the limits [of space]. Facing forward and facing backward, above and below and in the ten directions, in quiet and confusion, light and dark, during walking, standing still, sitting, and lying down—in all cases, view. Therefore, you should understand that enlightenment is the master *(chu)* and the mind is the servant *(shih)*.

Therefore, to study these expedient means of commanding the mind, to penetratingly view the worlds of the ten directions, and to be without defilement—this is the path of *bodhi (p'u-t'i lu)*. (IV.Con.2:232)

B. The Buddha is the path of *bodhi*. Nonabiding is the seed of *bodhi*. The serenity of mind is the cause of *bodhi*. Subjugation of demons is the power of *bodhi*. The transcendence of subject and object is the progress of *bodhi*. The transcendence of *saṁsāra* is the benefit of *bodhi*. Enlightenment *(chueh)* is the master of *bodhi*. That which is equivalent to space is the essence of *bodhi*. Serene yet constantly functioning—this is the function of *bodhi*. The *samādhi* of the unconditioned True Characteristic—this is the realization of *bodhi*. (IV.Con.3-1:233)

Without the cause, the seed will not develop. Without the condition, the cause will not mature. Without the power, the condition will not grow. Without progress, the power will not harden. Without benefit, the progress will not become valiant. Without the master, the benefit will not be collected. Without the Path, the master will not get exclusive [control]. Without the essence, the Path will not penetrate [to enlightenment]. Without the function, the essence will not be bright. Without realization, the function will not be autonomous. (IV.Con.3-2:233)

C. The five teachings are:

First, Comprehensive Explanation of the Essence of Buddhahood; also called the Teaching of the Transcendence of Thoughts

Second, Opening the Gates of Wisdom and Sagacity; also called the Teaching of Motionlessness

Third, the Teaching of Manifesting the Inconceivable [Dharma]

Fourth, the Teaching of the Elucidation of the True Nature of the *Dharmas*

Fifth, the Naturally Unobstructed Path of Emancipation (IV.Con.6:235)

4. Shen-hsiu and the Teachings of the Northern School

The texts just introduced display much greater internal complexity, in both doctrinal and stylistic terms, than those presented in previous chapters. Rather than immediately grappling with the many different ideas, metaphors, and formulae contained in the *Yuan-ming lun* and the *Wu fang-pien,* I would prefer to begin with some observations about the background of these two important but difficult texts. To be specific, let me show how the appreciation of Shen-hsiu's career developed in Part One can be of help in the understanding of the doctrines of the Northern School.

We know that Shen-hsiu was the most important figure of the Northern School. What predictions about the substance and contour of his teachings can be made from our knowledge of the historical situation at the end of the seventh and very beginning of the eighth centuries? How might his teachings have contributed to some of the events that occurred after his death, i.e., P'u-chi's apparent hubris, Shen-hui's virulent anti-Northern School campaign, the attitudes and fabrications of the *Platform Sūtra* and the *LTFPC,* and the eventual demise of the Northern School? Obviously, these developments were not solely the result of Shen-hsiu's religious philosophy, but we must consider how that philosophy helped make them possible. Our knowledge of Shen-hsiu's success at court at the beginning of the eighth century is enough to yield several inferences about his teachings, even before we consider the doctrinal evidence per se.

No doubt, Shen-hsiu's teachings were true to his own conception of the East Mountain Teaching of Hung-jen and Tao-hsin. More important for this inquiry, his teachings must have conformed to certain guidelines to have gained acceptance at the court of Empress Wu. On the one hand, they must have avoided any hint of the qualities that caused the suppression of the Teaching of the Three Stages *(san-chieh chiao),* which was perceived as a challenge to the moral and economic authority of the imperial state.[290] On the other hand, Shen-hsiu must have displayed enough intellectual sophistication and conformity with the traditional perception of Buddhism to satisfy the highly literate members of the court.

Next, while meeting these basic requirements, Shen-hsiu's teachings must also have been original enough to inspire real interest and, in their own way, must have been superior to the other theories that had been presented to the court in previous years. Judging from the historical record, Shen-hsiu and his associates attempted to surround themselves with a certain mystique, an aura of supernaturalism—or, at least, this is how some of their contemporaries tended to view them. In view of the discussion of "questions about things" in Part One, Chapter V, Sections 14 and 15, and in view of Shen-hsiu's identity as the "verifier of the Ch'an meaning," it seems fair to suggest that Shen-hsiu attempted to bolster or at least match this public image in his style of teaching.

In addition, even while appearing innovative to Empress Wu and her courtiers and remaining true to his memory of the East Mountain Teaching, Shen-hsiu's teachings must have incorporated some flaw or flaws that made possible the criticisms of Shen-hui and the misrepresentations of the *Platform Sūtra*. Actually, these hypothetical flaws may not have occurred in Shen-hsiu's teachings, but only in those of P'u-chi and Hsiang-mo Tsang, who bore the brunt of Shen-hui's attacks. Nevertheless, these two students of Shen-hsiu may have only inherited and exaggerated weak points latent in their master's doctrines and style of practice.

Finally, Shen-hsiu's teachings must have somehow contributed to the development of Ch'an as a unique approach to the practice of Buddhism, independent of the "doctrinal" approach of the earlier and more conventional schools. Even though the Northern School was severely criticized by Shen-hui, that monk's innovations would have been impossible without the foundation laid by the Northern School.[291] It is important to remember that the historical importance of the Northern School does not depend on the accuracy or inaccuracy of Shen-hui's criticisms, which do not address the most important contributions of the Northern School to the subsequent development of Ch'an.[292]

According to the criteria just stated, Shen-hsiu's teachings would have to have been conventional yet original, orthodox yet iconoclastic, inspired yet flawed—an impossible list of mutually contradictory stipulations, it would seem. In fact, however, even though his teachings may have been complex or variable according to the text or teaching situation, all these conditions are satisfied by one didactic technique of the Northern School: the extensive use of metaphor or "expedient means" *(fang-pien)* in order to radically redefine the teachings of Buddhism. This technique is also referred to as "contemplative analysis" *(kuan-hsin shih)*.

5. The Use of Extended Metaphor in the Writings of the Northern School

The use of metaphor is no doubt universal within the literature of human civilizations. Certainly, the texts of both Indian and Chinese Buddhism are filled with numerous instances of this technique. Some, such as Nāgasena's analysis of the composition of a cart and the *Lotus Sūtra*'s image of the burning house, are among the best remembered passages of Buddhist literature. Hence, the mere use of metaphor, even its extensive use, is not noteworthy. Rather, it is the way in which the device is used in Northern School texts that deserves our attention.

Just as in other Buddhist contexts, the members of the Northern School considered their metaphors to be teaching devices. Although there is no single passage to prove the point, they apparently considered metaphors and other formulaic usages such as those found in the *Kuan-hsin lun* and the *Wu fang-pien* to be part of their arsenal of expedient means. (Meditation techniques and various elements of intimate, personal interaction were also subsumed under this term.[293]) An important part of the Northern School's mission was to proselytize new members, which required written explanations of the school's teachings. Although converts were no doubt welcomed from among those with little or no prior experience in Buddhism, much of the energy of early Ch'an seems to have been directed at convincing other Buddhists (or at least those with some knowledge of Buddhism) that the Northern School approach to the religion was the most, or even the only, authentic one. This task required that the Northern School trace its doctrine back to the scriptures and prove that is was the highest teaching of the Buddha. Since their message was in many ways at variance with the letter and spirit of Indian Buddhism, the members of the early Ch'an School often had not only to cite the scriptures, but also to reinterpret them to fit their own purposes. As is said in the *Yuan-ming lun,* the sūtras could not be incorrect, but one had to understand their true meaning.[294]

The metaphors found in Northern School texts are thus not quite the same as those found in earlier Buddhist scriptures. The metaphors of the sun and clouds and the mirror notwithstanding, most are intended not merely to explain some aspect of Buddhism to the listener or reader, but to redefine some component of traditional Buddhist philosophy into a statement of Northern School doctrine. In a word, the Northern School used the device of metaphor to transform all of Buddhism into an allegory for the practice of the "contemplation of the mind."

The *Kuan-hsin lun* is a very good example of this basic function of the Northern School's use of metaphor. This text does not say very much about the techniques and guidelines of mental contemplation itself. Nor is it a very well integrated text: The doctrinal statement at the beginning (see Section 8 of this chapter) is not complete in itself, and its relationship to the extensive set of metaphors that follows is not clearly indicated. Even the implications of those metaphors themselves are not always clear. For example, on the basis of this text alone, one cannot tell whether Shen-hsiu was in favor of a traditional configuration of Buddhist practice, including maintenence of the precepts, and so on, or whether he had something else in mind.[295]

In fact, the point of the *Kuan-hsin lun* was not to explain the complete ramifications of the "contemplation of the mind," only to point out that such practice was the very crux of the Buddhist religion. Thus literal readings of standard Buddhist technical terms and scriptural passages are rejected as the superficial understanding of the unenlightened, in favor of interpretations that relate solely to contemplation.

The following is a summary of the metaphors used in the *Kuan-hsin lun:*

1. The six consciousnesses associated with the different human sensory capabilities are defined as "six bandits" that cause attachment to different sensory phenomena, the creation of evil actions, and the obfuscation of Suchness.

2. The three poisons of craving, anger, and stupidity are correlated with the realms of desire, form, and formlessness, respectively. Light and heavy excesses of craving, etc., also determine one's rebirth into one of the six modes of existence, i.e., human, god, animal, and so on.

3. The three immeasurable eons during which a future Buddha strives for enlightenment are redefined as the three poisons. Eradication of those three poisons is thus the passage of the three immeasurable eons, or transcendence of infinite numbers of illusions.

4. The bodhisattva's practice of the three groups of pure precepts and the six perfections are explained as the suppression of the three poisons and purification of the six senses.

5. The "three *t'ou* and six *sheng*"[296] of milk that the historical Buddha drank before attaining enlightenment does not refer to the defiled product of this world, but to the "milk of the pure dharma of Suchness." It refers, in fact, to the three groups of pure precepts and the six perfections. In addition, the cow that produced this milk was actually Vairocana Buddha himself, who out of great compassion causes the precepts and perfections to flow out of his *dharmakāya* like milk from a cow.

6. The religious activities enjoined in the scriptures are reinterpreted as follows:

A. Temple repair: The Chinese transliteration for *saṁgha-ārāma* is defined as a "pure ground," so that the eradication of the three poisons, etc., is equivalent to the repair or "cultivation" of such a monastery.

B. Casting and painting of images: The Buddha was not interested in the creation of mundane images but was instructing the true practitioner to "make his body a forge, the Dharma its fire, and wisdom the craftsman." The three groups of pure precepts and the six perfections become the mold for casting, within the practitioner's own body, the Buddha Nature of Suchness.

C. Burning of incense: The incense referred to here is that of the true, unconditioned Dharma, which "perfumes" the tainted and evil karma of ignorance and causes it to disappear.

D. Offering of flowers: The Buddha is said never to have advocated the injury of live flowers, but refers in the scriptures to the "flowers of merit" imbued with the essence of Suchness. Such flowers are permanent and never wilt.

E. Burning of memorial lamps: The explanation of this metaphor, which is structurally similar to that of the casting of images, will be given in English translation in Section 1 of the Conclusion.

F. Circumnambulation of stūpas: The body is equated with the stūpa, and circumnambulation is defined as the ceaseless circulation of wisdom throughout the body and mind.

G. Holding of vegetarian feasts: Through the manipulation of Chinese homographs, the phrase "to hold vegetarian feasts" is interpreted as the ability to make the body and mind equally regulated and unconfused.

H. Obeisance: Through the manipulation of transitive and intransitive equivalents of the Chinese characters involved, obeisance is defined as the suppression of errors.

7. A short scriptural passage extolling the virtues of bathing[297] is introduced and reinterpreted as "burning the fire of wisdom to heat the water of the pure precepts and bathe the Dharma Nature of Suchness within one's body." The seven *dharmas* of the bath are given as follows:

A. Clean water: Just as clean water *(ching-shui)* washes away the dusts of this world, so do the pure precepts clean away the defilements of ignorance.

B. Fire: The fire that heats the bath water is actually wisdom, with which one contemplates or examines one's internal and external being.

C. Soap powder: The soap powder used to clean away dirt is actually the ability of discrimination by which one can ferret out the sources of evil within oneself.

D. Toothpicks: The "sticks of willow" used to eradicate mouth odor are nothing less that the Truth, by which one puts an end to false speech.

E. Pure ashes: The ashes or powdered incense rubbed on the body after bathing are endeavor *(vīrya),* by which one puts an end to doubt-laden ratiocination.

F. Oil: Rather than softening one's skin, the oil referred to here is meant to soften dispositional stiffness, or bad habits.

G. Underwear: The clothing worn in the bath is actually the sense of shame that inhibits evil actions.

8. The practice of "mindfulness of the Buddha" *(nien-fo)* in order to seek the Pure Land is redefined as the contemplation of mind and body. The empty recitation of the Buddha's name is specifically and emphatically rejected.

The *Kuan-hsin lun* concludes as follows:

> Therefore, know that the types of merit cultivated by the sages of the past were explained not as external [activities], but only [with respect to] the mind. The mind is the fountainhead of all goodness; the mind is the lord of the myriad evils. The permanence and joy of nirvāṇa is born of [one's own] mind; the saṁsāra of the triple realm also arises from the mind.
>
> The mind is the gateway to the transcendence of this world; the mind is the ford to emancipation. How could one who knows the gateway worry about the difficulty of success? How could one who recognizes the ford be saddened about not having attained [the other shore]?
>
> My own view is that [Buddhists] nowadays are shallow of understanding and only know the virtue of formalistic effort. They waste a lot of money and inflict injury on the countryside in their incorrect [manner of] constructing images and stūpas. They waste human labor in piling up wood and earth and in painting [their monasteries] blue and green. They expend all their mental and physical energy [in this pursuit], destroying themselves and misleading others. Having no understanding of the shamefulness [of their actions], how could they ever be enlightened? . . .
>
> If you can only concentrate the mind and illuminate your inner [being], then, with the enlightened contemplation constantly brilliant, you will extirpate the three poisons and block out the six bandits. [The three poisons will thus be] forever dissolved and [the six bandits] will never attack again. Every one of the infinite number of merits, the various ornamentations, and the innumerable doctrines will be naturally fulfilled, [including the] transcendence of the unenlightened state and realization of the state of sage. It does not take long to witness this; enlightenment is in the instant. Why worry about your white hair (i.e., about your age)?[298]

6. Northern School Metaphors as "Contemplative Analysis"

Although it is not used in the early Ch'an texts themselves, modern scholars sometimes use the term "contemplative analysis" (*kuan-hsin shih,* or *kanjin-shaku* in Japanese) to refer to the occasionally bizarre formulations of the Northern School. This term originally derives from Chih-i's four criteria for commenting on the *Lotus Sūtra.* The first three of these criteria concern the relationship between the Buddha and his audience, the doctrinal implications of a given line or term, and the alternative interpretations based on either the ultimate Mahāyāna doctrines or the more limited Hīnayāna. Contemplative analysis, the fourth of Chih-i's categories, is to approach each line of scripture as a function or component of the "contemplation of the principle of the True Characteristic of the One Mind." For example, Chih-i interprets the term "Vaiśālī" not as a place name, but as a metaphor for one's own mind.[299]

The term contemplative analysis is thus quite appropriate for Shen-hsiu, who is known to have expounded on the "Ch'an meaning" of different scriptures. Shen-hsiu may well have based his method of scriptural reinterpretation on some form of meditative intuition, but the practice of contemplative analysis seems to have involved something more than pure religious inspiration. To understand the importance of such additional factors, we will have to investigate the diversity and background of this didactic technique.

In addition to the numerous metaphors used in the *Kuan-hsin lun,* the *Wu fang-pien* contains many examples of contemplative analysis. This text frequently adverts to the definition of the Buddha as the Enlightened One in its formula "buddha is enlightenment." Through the economy of the Chinese language, the idea of enlightened *person* can be forgotten in favor of "enlightenment of self, enlightenment of other." The last part of the second expedient means includes redefinitions of the titles of several sūtras that can only be understood as forced, artificial readings. Finally, the phrase-by-phrase commentary on the *Lotus* and *Vimalakīrti* sūtras in the second and third expedient means (see sections K and A–C, respectively) interprets these texts according to typical Northern School parameters, but in a way that clearly superimposes new meaning.

In addition to these examples, another early Ch'an text deserves mention for the many metaphors and other unusual usages it contains. This is a commentary to the *Fo-shuo fa-chü ching (Sūtra of the Stanzas of the Dharma Preached by the Buddha).* This sūtra was written in medieval China but takes the translation name of a much older work: the *Dhammapāda,* a famous and oft-translated collection of Pali verses on the ascetic path. The *Fo-shuo fa-chü ching* is an interesting text in its own right, quite readable in comparison to other Buddhist texts and eloquent in its dramatic expression of the teachings of Buddhism closest to the hearts of students of Ch'an.[300] However, it is the commentary on this text that is relevant here.

Actually, two commentaries on the *Fo-shuo fa-chü ching* are known to modern scholarship, both through the Tun-huang collections. One of these (Pelliot manuscript no. 2325) is a straightforward commentary devoid of any particular importance in the present context. The second (Pelliot manuscript no. 2192) was abstracted from the great bulk of still poorly indexed Tun-huang materials by Tanaka Ryōshō. The commentary discovered by Tanaka is quite long (some 1500 lines) and contains a large amount of material not directly related to the sūtra itself. Internal evidence suggests that this commentary derives from roughly the same period of Northern School development as the *Wu fang-pien.*[301]

The following are only a few of the metaphoric constructions of the Tanaka commentary, chosen for their similarity to other examples of Northern School contemplative analysis:

1. Concerning the explanation of the character *ching* ("sūtra") in the title of the *Fo-shuo fa-chü ching,* a character that also means "the warp of a fabric," the commentary suggests:

> The body of the *skandha*s is the loom, the six senses are the warp, the six consciousnesses are the woof, the six types of sense data are the shuttle, the mental states of grasping and rejecting are the thread (?), and the conditionalities of craving are the weave. With these, each sentient being weaves his own karma of rebirth in hell or heaven. (3:20/70)[302]

2. Distinctions are made between the "exterior," or conventional, and the "interior," or intuited, definitions of terms. For example, the exterior definition of *upāsikā* is a laywoman who maintains the five precepts, etc., but the interior definition is "the sun of understanding blocked off (i.e., from outside influences [?]), the six types of sense data purified, and the attachments of craving transcended." (8:20/222) Similarly, the interior definition of a heavenly dragon *(t'ien-lung)* is given as follows:

> "Heaven" means "to purify." Disporting the mind in elevated purity and subjugating the poisons of craving, anger, [and stupidity], the dragon does not create [ordinary] rain [but rather] the rain of wisdom, which rains upon the fields of the mind so that the Dharma will grow. (8:23/225)

3. Two definitions are given for the term *ch'u-chia,* "to leave home [to become a monk]." "Superficial leaving home" is the conventional meaning of the term, whereas "mental leaving home" *(hsin ch'u-chia)* is

> to leave the home of the five *skandha*s, six consciousness, and eighteen realms. In form one may be a monk or a layperson, but one's practice is without preparation, without virtue, without advantage, and without benefit. With sensory realms and wisdom both destroyed and that destruction then destroyed, one leaves discrimination. Phenomena and principle *(shih-li)* both being purified, this is called the "essential monk." This is the unconditioned leaving of home.[303] (9:27/269)

4. A definition of nirvāṇa, which in Chinese is transliterated as *nieh-p'an,* is given as follows:

> *Nieh* is extinction (= death). *P'an* is generation (= birth). Extinguishing but not extinguishing is called *nieh.* Not generating in generation is called *p'an.* Therefore, *nieh* but not dying, *p'an* but not being born, birth-and-death (i.e., saṁsāra) and nirvāṇa serenely identical. (22:9/641)

5. On the standard Mahāyāna metaphor of an echo in an empty valley, the commentary suggests that the human form is the object of reference: "The skull is like the mountain, and the ears are empty, like the valley." (22:18/650) It goes on to say that the sounds that resonate within the head are fundamentally nonsubstantial, like those in a mountain valley.

6. A long list of metaphors for a spiritual compatriot, or *kalyāṇamitra,* is given. Many of these are quite conventional, i.e., to consider one's teacher as one's parents, one's eyes, one's feet, a ladder, or food, etc. The analogy that a spiritual compatriot is like fire, however, is made by saying that the six types of sense data are the fuel, the six consciousnesses the fire, and six perfections the flame. Similarly, in the analogy of the spiritual compatriot as a bow and arrow, meditation is the bow, wisdom is the arrow, and illumination of the mind is the action of shooting the arrow. (26:12/755)

7. The commentary defines the ten precepts in the context of a reference to a bodhisattva killing his "father," ignorance. For the sake of brevity, I will list only the first four:

> If the slightest bit of mind is generated, to illuminate and extinguish it is called "murder." To secretly practice the path without other people knowing about it is called "theft." To make good use of expedient means to penetrate the enlightenment of buddhahood is called "licentiousness." To use metaphors in preaching the Dharma, causing spiritual benefit for sentient beings is called "lying." (40:22/1184)

8. The six perfections are correlated individually with the six modes of existence (gods, humans, *asuras*, etc.), the performance of each perfection blocking off one avenue of possible rebirth. (42:21/1244)

A close examination of the metaphors given in the *Fo-shuo fa-chü ching* commentary reveals certain differences of implication from those given in Shen-hsiu's *Kuan-hsin lun.* Generally speaking, the commentary is much more inclined to use an apophatic rendering, emphasizing the fact that all instructions pertaining to religious practice must be performed without breaking the more fundamental injunction against conceptualized and willfully undertaken activity. The *Kuan-hsin lun,* in contrast, states its interpretations more emphatically and without such frequent remonstrations against false conceptualization.

In spite of the typological similarity of their metaphoric usages, the two texts do not contain identical or even overlapping sets of metaphors. At one point the commentary declines even to consider the three immeasurable eons of the Buddha's practice on the grounds that such a concept was the expression of the gradual teaching.[304] Since the redefinition of the three immeasurable eons appears prominently in the *Kuan-hsin lun*, it is clear that the process of making such metaphors was more important than any dogmatic attachment to the metaphors themselves.

7. Possible Antecedents to the Use of Contemplative Analysis in the Northern School

To understand the full dimensions of the process whereby the metaphors of Northern School contemplative analysis were generated, it is necessary to turn our attention to one of the oldest texts of Chinese Buddhism, the *An-pan shou-i ching (Sūtra on the Mindfulness of Breathing)*. This archaic document is listed as the work of the translator An Shih-kao, but a substantial amount of commentary is also included in the extant version of the text.[305] What is interesting at present is the type of effort made to explain the subject of the text. The following, which must derive from the commentator's interpolations rather than the original translation, are only some of the correspondences given in this text and in its preface by K'ang Seng-hui:

1. *An* is "body"; *pan* is "breath." (*An-pan* is a transliteration of *ānāpāna*, or "breathing.") *Shou-i* (lit., "guarding the consciousness") is "enlightenment" (*tao*, also "the Path"). *Shou* is "to prohibit" as well as "not to break the precepts." . . . *I* is the "consciousness of breathing," and also "enlightenment" *(tao)*.
2. *An* is "to be born," and *pan* is "to be extinguished (i.e., to die)." *I* is "causes and conditions." *Shou* is "enlightenment."
3. *An* is "to count," and *pan* is "to follow." *Shou-i* is "to stop" *(chih)*.
4. *An* is "to be mindful of enlightenment," and *pan* is "to release one's fetters." *Shou-i* is "not to fall into transgression."
5. *An* is "to escape transgression," and *pan* is "not to enter into transgression." *Shou-i* is "enlightenment."
6. *An-pan shou-i* means "to guide the consciousness to the attainment of the unconditioned *(wu-wei)*."
7. *An* is "being," and *pan* is "nonbeing." By being mindful of neither being nor nonbeing, one's consciousness practices in accord with enlightenment in response to the meditation of nonsubstantiality.
8. Of the six facets of the mindfulness of breathing, counting the breaths is the earth, following the breaths is the yoke, contemplating the breaths is the seed, reverting to pure mindfulness is the rain, and purify-

ing the consciousness is the furrow (*hang,* also pronounced *hsing,* meaning "practice").[306]

Many more such schema are posed in the *An-pan shou-i ching,* a good number of which are more faithful to the actual meanings of the terms involved. Nevertheless, the most apparently unreasonable of the lot are the most interesting, since they point to what may be an archetypal Chinese intellectual process. That is, such seemingly arbitrary correlations are actually a by-product of the Chinese attempt to understand this new religion from the West and are evidence of efforts to experimentally apply this new message to standard, preexistent themes of Chinese thought.

There are other indications of similar sorts of experimentation, the most famous of which is the practice of *ko-i,* or "matching the meanings." The exact dimensions of this practice are unclear, but it somehow involved the correlation of native and foreign terms and lists of terms,[307] possibly in a style similar to the examples given earlier from Northern School texts and the *An-pan shou-i ching.* Better documented is the practice of correlating the five Buddhist precepts with the five cardinal virtues of Confucianism. Although Michihata Ryōshū and Kenneth Ch'en both refer to these correlations as evidence of the sinification of the imported religion,[308] it is also valid to observe that they were more basically a means by which the foreign religion could be understood by those already steeped in Chinese culture. In other words, the apparently arbitrary use of category correlation, extended metaphor, and the interpretation of compound Chinese terms by breaking them down into their individual characters are standard concomitants of the Chinese effort to understand and assimilate new and different ideas.

Although the dimensions of this phenomenon are still quite vague—the systematization of the five elements *(wu hsing)* by the Han philosopher Tung Chung-shu and Chih-i's "ten such-likes" *(shih ju-shih)* might also be considered related sorts of conceptual manipulation and wordplay[309]—the task at hand is to determine the significance of such correlations and extended metaphors in the context of the Northern School.

My tentative conclusion is the following: Similar to the examples given from the *An-pan shou-i ching,* the use of contemplative analysis in the Northern School represents a manifestation of Ch'an's struggle to understand and express its own message. This is true not only of the more outlandish examples—for instance, the explication of the standard metaphor of a sound within an empty valley with reference to the skull as a mountain and the ears as its valleys—but also of the abundance of more reasonable doctrinal formulations that occur in early Ch'an texts.

Even from the limited sample of materials translated here, the reader should be struck by the fact that so many such formulations are posited and then forgotten almost at once. The very number of these quickly forgotten doctrinal statements implies that the Ch'an School was forced to hammer away again and again at the bulwark of traditional "doctrinal" Buddhism, stating and restating different facets of its own message in terms that were increasingly appropriate as time went on. It was impossible at the very first to step completely outside the boundaries of traditional Buddhist expression—the followers of Ch'an would not have known what to say that would have been understood and at the same time considered legitimately Buddhist. No, at the beginning it was necessary to infiltrate and erode that bulwark from within, as it were, transforming the entire realm of discourse of the current Buddhist establishment, with its emphasis on intellectual effort, material offerings, and so on, into an expression of the teaching of meditation.

Shen-hsiu's role in this effort was of paramount importance, for it was he who digested the sum of traditional Buddhist studies and developed a unique explanation for individual spiritual endeavor. Shen-hsiu's approach was at once the rationalization of a new style of religious practice and a unique and reasonable interpretation of the original intent of Buddhism. Thus his teachings could very well have been both traditionalistic and innovative at the same time.

8. The Construction of Shen-hsiu's Thought

The *Kuan-hsin lun* must be the initial focus of any discussion of the construction of Shen-hsiu's thought. This is the only text unquestionably written by him, and it may have been composed before his move to Lo-yang at the very beginning of the eighth century. The opening lines of this text read as follows:

> QUESTION: If a person wanted to seek the enlightenment of buddhahood, what would be the most quintessential *dharma* he could cultivate?
>
> ANSWER: Only the single *dharma* of contemplating the mind, which completely encompasses all practices, [may be called] the most quintessential.
>
> QUESTION: How can one *dharma* encompass all practices?
>
> ANSWER: Of [all] the myriad *dharmas*, the mind is the fundamental one. All the various *dharmas* are simply the product of the mind. If one can comprehend the mind, then the myriad practices will all be accomplished. It is like the branches, flowers, and fruit of a large tree, all of which depend on the roots for their existence. If the tree is cut down and the roots done away with [the branches, flowers, and fruit] will definitely die.
>
> If one's spiritual cultivation [aims at] comprehension of the mind, then success will occur easily and with little effort. Spiritual cultivation [not aimed at] comprehension of the mind means wasted effort and no benefit.

> Therefore, know that all good and evil derives completely from one's own mind. To seek somewhere else outside of the mind [and have any success]—this is an utter impossibility.
>
> QUESTION: How can contemplation of the mind be referred to as "comprehensive"?
>
> ANSWER: When a great bodhisattva practices the profound perfection of wisdom he comprehends that the four elements and the five *skandhas* are fundamentally nonsubstantial and without self. He comprehensively sees that his own mind has two types of different functions *(ch'i-yung)*. What are these two? The first is the Pure Mind *(ching-hsin)*. The second is the defiled mind *(jan-hsin)*.
>
> The Pure Mind is the mind of untainted Suchness *(wu-lou chen-ju)*. The defiled mind is the mind of tainted ignorance. These two types of mental *dharmas* are both naturally and fundamentally existent—although they are provisionally conjoined, they do not generate each other. The Pure Mind always desires the causes of goodness, whereas the defiled mind always thinks of evil actions. One who is himself enlightened to Suchness is unaffected by defilements and is called a sage. [Such a one] is eventually able to distantly transcend suffering and to realize the joy of nirvāṇa. One who acts in accord with the defiled is subject to its attachments and obscurations and is called an ordinary person. [Such a one] sinks helplessly within the triple realm and is subject to various kinds of suffering. Why is this? Because the defiled mind obstructs the essence of Suchness.[310]

The similarity between the *Kuan-hsin lun* and the *Hsiu-hsin yao lun* should be obvious. Just as the text attributed to Hung-jen touts *shou-hsin,* or "maintaining [awareness of] the mind," as the ultimate Buddhist endeavor, here *kuan-hsin,* or "contemplation of the mind," is represented as the "most quintessential *dharma* to be cultivated, the one *dharma* that encompasses all Buddhist practices." Shen-hsiu's text actually goes one step beyond the other by claiming that success in *kuan-hsin* is not merely tantamount to the achievement of buddhahood, but actually equivalent to the performance of *all* Buddhist practices. As Shen-hsiu says later on in the text, "Every single one of the infinite number of merits, the various ornamentations and innumerable doctrines, will be naturally fulfilled."[311]

Another similarity to the *Hsiu-hsin yao lun* is the citation of the spurious passage from the *Shih-ti ching (Sūtra on the Ten Stages)* describing the metaphor of the sun and clouds. (See the discussion of this passage in Chapter VI, Section 4.) The *Kuan-hsin lun,* however, does not attempt to advocate anything like *shou-hsin,* the unique approach to meditation that combines a gentle and energetic style of practice with symbolically sophisticated techniques. There are actually two differences between the *Kuan-hsin lun* and the *Hsiu-hsin yao lun* on this subject: (1) Shen-hsiu's text is less explicit on the actual techniques for "contemplating the mind," and (2) it emphasizes the penetration of the fundamental unreality or nonsubstantiality of the defiled mind and its attendant illusions rather than the nurturing of the Buddha Nature within oneself.

In addition, two points are stated very clearly in the *Kuan-hsin lun* that are not made in the *Hsiu-hsin yao lun.* First, the practice of the contemplation of the mind is to be maintained constantly, during all one's activities. The text reads:

> Further, "spiritual practice throughout the six periods of time" (i.e., the entire day) means to constantly practice the enlightenment of buddhahood all the time within the six senses. "Buddha" means "enlightenment" *(chueh).* Thus to cultivate the various practices of enlightenment *(chueh-hsing)* by regulating the six senses and making them pure, doing this without ceasing at all times during all activities, is called "spiritual practice throughout the six periods of time."[312]

Second, the actual achievement of enlightenment occurs instantaneously. The treatise does use language that refers to the control or subjugation of the ignorant aspects of mind, but close reading indicates that such control does not refer to the suppression or restriction of sensory activity per se. "To purify the six sense organs" means "to first subjugate the six bandits." Those bandits represent not the functions of sensory perception, but the impact of *avidyā,* or ignorance, on the senses.[313] Nor is one enjoined to progressively rid oneself of an ever-greater proportion of one's defilements or illusions. On the contrary, control of the defilements occurs suddenly and all-at-once, when the defiled mind is eradicated.

Shen-hsiu's appreciation of the instantaneous nature of ultimate realization and his emphasis on the constancy of practice are neatly expressed in the following two statements from the conclusion of the *Kuan-hsin lun:*

> How could one who knows the gateway worry about the difficulty of success? How could one who recognizes the ford be saddened about not having attained [the other shore]?
>
> It does not take long to witness this (i.e., to realize sagehood); enlightenment is in the instant. Why worry about your white hair (i.e., about your age)?[314]

These themes, then, will form the nucleus of our discussion of Northern School doctrine: the positing of defiled and pure aspects of mind, dedication to the penetration of the nonexistence or nonsubstantiality of the defiled mind and its illusions, the emphasis on constancy of practice, and the recognition of the suddenness of enlightenment.

9. The Identity of the Yuan-ming lun

The *Yuan-ming lun* is a provocative work. Its major intent is conventional Mahāyāna Buddhism—to convince its audience to train in such a way that they ensure their own enlightenment and the salvation of others. Although the general orientation of the text is beyond reproach, some of the specific declarations made are strikingly unconventional. The important ontological role played by the entity space is unparalleled in Buddhist literature, to the extent that the author felt the need to include an explicit refutation of a hypothetical accusation of heresy. In addition, the description of the world system as comprised of four disks of equal size contrasts with the orthodox system of three disks of decreasing thickness and different diameters.[315] (See Chapter Two, Section K; Chapter Three, Sections A, C, and D; and Chapter Seven, Section B, of the translation.)

It would be unfair to simply reject these peculiarities as heretical deviations from traditional Buddhist dogma. Instead, they should be approached as creative speculation combining native Chinese themes with ideas from several traditions of Buddhist doctrine. Together with the traces of Hua-yen, Mādhyamika, and Yogācāra doctrines that can be detected in this text, the peculiarities mentioned in the previous paragraph can only add to our appreciation of the manner in which one medieval Chinese Buddhist, very possibly Shen-hsiu, rationalized his own religious practice.

I have suggested that the *Yuan-ming lun* contains Shen-hsiu's teachings. In the absence of a colophon or any citation in other sources, the attribution of this text must be inferred on the basis of the following points:

1. The *Yuan-ming lun* occurs at the very beginning of an extremely important anthology of East Mountain Teaching/Northern School material that also includes the *Hsiu-hsin yao lun* and *CFPC*.[316] Hence, the author of this work was almost certainly a member of the Northern School.

2. Not only is the author or speaker of this text referred to as a *dhyāna* master, he is addressed with a measure of respect unequalled in any early Ch'an text. (See Chapter Three, Sections A and C.) If the text is the transcription of an oral presentation, as I suspect, the speaker was clearly an eminent figure rather than an anonymous idealogue.

3. The author/speaker justifies his theories by stating that they are based on his reading of the scriptures and his experience in meditation, a position identical to that known to have been held by Shen-hsiu. (See Chapter Two, Section I.)

4. Although most of the subject matter of the *Yuan-ming lun* differs from that of the *Kuan-hsin lun*—a fact that has little bearing because of the incredible fluidity of early Ch'an doctrinal formulations in general—the two texts are alike in positing pure and defiled aspects of the mind and in emphasizing the importance of constancy in religious practice.[317]

5. Similarly, in spite of the stylistic differences between this work and the *Wu fang-pien,* both contain comparable and possibly related expressions, such as those concerning space, the nature of the apprehension of sound, and the defiled and purified realms of ordinary and enlightened beings.[318]

Whether or not the *Yuan-ming lun* was transcribed directly from a lecture by Shen-hsiu, P'u-chi, or some other prominent Northern School figure, this text can legitimately be approached as a potential link between the *Wu fang-pien* and the other, earlier works of the East Mountain Teaching and the Northern School.[319]

10. The Gradual, Sudden, and Perfect Teachings in the Yuan-ming lun

One of the first surprises of the *Yuan-ming lun* is the discussion of the gradual, sudden, and perfect teachings that occurs very close to the beginning of the text. As far as I know, this is the only early Ch'an work to discuss these three teachings conjointly. As such, it is an important precursor to Shen-hui's use of the terms "sudden" and "gradual." More to the point, it is a potential indicator of the relationship between the doctrines of the Northern School and contemporary religious thought, particularly that of the Hua-yen School, which also posited definitions of these three teachings in its *p'an-chiao,* or "doctrinal classification" theories.[320]

Unfortunately, because of the severely damaged state of the *Yuan-ming lun* manuscript, the statements concerning these teachings cannot be completely deciphered. The general argument runs as follows:

1. The gradual, sudden, and perfect teachings are all different. Those who claim that they are identical do not understand them.

2. The gradual teaching seems to be limited to the doctrine of *anātman,* a basically Hīnayāna idea that its proponents mistakenly claim to be Mahāyānist in nature. (Presumably, this includes the doctrine of *anātman* as applied to individual *dharmas*, rather than to living beings only.)

3. Some people, it is alleged, believe that the sudden teaching is based on the idea that the realms of human sensory perception are the product of false thoughts, so that when one is without false thoughts one also rids oneself of the realms. The *Yuan-ming lun* treats this understanding as too facile and superficial.

4. The real sudden teaching is to achieve an understanding of "physical characteristics and the essence of the mind" *(shen-hsiang hsin-t'i).* Although this phrase seems to imply that the body is a superficial manifestation and the mind a more fundamental basis of human existence, the

text devotes quite a few lines to the refutation of this interpretation. Its ultimate resolution of the issue is that neither mind nor body can be adequately described as dependent on the other. Instead, both are nonsubstantial. Rather than the extirpation of false thoughts, then, the sudden teaching may be described as the comprehension of nonsubstantiality.

No explicit attempt is made to distinguish this correct interpretation of the sudden teaching from the more advanced perfect teaching. The latter is circumscribed by a list of ten meanings, the adumbration of which takes up the balance of the text. The fact that not all ten are explicitly defined is a measure of the informal, unedited nature of the text as it now stands.

11. Constant Practice and the Perfect Teaching

To understand the perfect teaching, we must thus understand the balance of the *Yuan-ming lun*. Perhaps it will be easiest to begin with the conventional aspect of the text's basic message, which has already been mentioned. The following is a concise statement of the text's fundamental position on religious practice, immediately recognizable as a faithful expression of the bodhisattva ideal:

> One should reside in meditation and wisdom after having achieved the contemplation of nonsubstantiality. Not residing in being and nonbeing, the body and mind are universally "same," like space. Never quitting during walking, standing still, sitting, and lying down, [one should] save sentient beings whenever possible. Saving the weak and helping the downfallen, having pity for the poor and love for the aged, one should think on the suffering of sentient beings within the three lower modes of existence and the difficulties of the poor among humankind. One should always act tirelessly to save them, [even to the point of] discarding one's own life.
>
> One should always undertake such practice while in meditation, for the duration of three great immeasurable [eons].[321]

Other passages in the *Yuan-ming lun* indicate that this description of the unflagging meditator and tireless benefactor of other living beings is predicated on the same vision of the essential emptiness or nonsubstantiality of all things as in traditional Mahāyāna writings. References to this concept occur throughout the text: the denial of the existence of sentient beings in Chapter Two, Section L; the ascription of nonsubstantiality to cause and result in Chapter Three, Sections B and E, in the latter of which the term "practice of nonsubstantiality" *(k'ung-hsing)* is used (similar terms occur scattered throughout the text); and the reference to "nonpracticing" in Chapter Four, Section B. Even the prescriptions for actual meditation practice that occur in Chapter Six, Sections D and F, are in fact methods for realizing the essential nonsubstantiality of all things.

This emphasis on nonsubstantiality may have something to do with the emphasis on performing the ultimate practice right here and now, in this lifetime, as soon as one hears and understands it. That is, since there actually are no illusions to be purified, all that is necessary is to realize this fact, cease discriminating in the manner of ordinary, unenlightened people, and initiate the practice of the bodhisattva as indicated in the text.[322] The *Yuan-ming lun* does posit certain stages of practice, which we will discuss presently, but its main purpose is to induce its audience to begin meditation practice, achieve this transformation, and continue on with the continuous activity of the bodhisattva. Its fundamental purpose is thus identical to that of the *Kuan-hsin lun*.

In the *Yuan-ming lun* the immediate goal is to achieve a transformation of one's "world" from that of a "small" sentient being to that of a "great" one. This transformation, the sudden experience of which is intimated in the *Kuan-hsin lun,* could be accomplished simply by putting an end to all one's false discrimination. This transformation differs from that indicated in the false definition of the sudden teaching given in point 3, Section 10 of this chapter in that the realms of perception are not destroyed, but transformed into a different form of reality. (Of course, ultimately neither false thoughts, the realms of perception, nor the great or small worlds of sentient beings can be said to exist in an ultimate sense.)

This transformation may be simply described, perhaps, but its accomplishment was no doubt a difficult task for real practitioners with real problems. It is thus not surprising that the *Yuan-ming lun* calls for energetic effort both before and after the moment of realization. Actually, here and in all other Northern School texts the emphasis is placed so thoroughly on the problems of initiating and continuing practice that the actual moment of realization—if such a single moment can be said to exist—is almost completely ignored. Like the *Hsiu-hsin yao lun,* this text refrains from using the promise of enlightenment as a reward to motivate its readers.

12. The Reverse and Direct Contemplations in the Yuan-ming lun

The *Yuan-ming lun* is not particularly detailed on the subject of meditation practice. Nevertheless, it does make definite statements about two contrasting approaches to meditation, which it calls the "reverse" and "direct" forms of contemplation *(ni-kuan* and *shun-kuan).*

Reverse contemplation is defined in terms reminiscent of the *Ch'eng-shih lun (Treatise on the Completion of Truth),* a text popular during the

Six Dynasties period. This text eventually fell out of favor after being criticized for its reductionist definition of *śūnyatā,* i.e., for analyzing phenomenal reality into ever-smaller conglomerations of particles until at last the very smallest of them dissolved into nothingness. This method was thought to be distinctly inferior to the Mādhyamika approach, which used a dialectical method that was not concerned with the size of the particles or their conglomerates but was based instead on the analysis of the origin, transformation, and disappearance of the particles themselves.[323] (See Chapters Four and Five of the *Yuan-ming lun.*)

It is unlikely that the *Yuan-ming lun* argues directly against the *Ch'eng-shih lun.* The argument against reverse contemplation may have been borrowed from some Chinese Mādhyamika source that made reference to the other text, but in the *Yuan-ming lun* these criticisms are directed at all traditional forms of Buddhist meditation. In general, traditional Buddhist meditation theory required the practitioner to trace each object of his contemplation back to its individual constituents. This technique requires a certain amount of analysis by the meditator, not to mention the restricted view (to borrow the early Ch'an sense of values) that the emptiness of reality can be understood only by comprehending its multiplicity and the lack of ontological integrity of any of its most basic components.

The discussion of the gradual teaching, in which the doctrinal distinctions normally thought to be Mahāyānist in nature are relegated to the province of Hīnayāna Buddhism, may have some bearing here. That is, the analysis of reality into its component parts, no matter how minute, only yields a Hīnayānist understanding similar to that indicated, for example, in Nāgasena's analysis of the cart in the *Milindapaṇha.*[324] Such a pluralistic understanding of reality, implicitly if not explicitly, still grants real existence to the components of the cart or to the most minute particles of phenomenal existence.

Direct contemplation avoids this problem completely by rejecting any suggestion that reality need be so atomized as a preliminary to understanding. Instead, nonsubstantiality is to be apprehended on the basis of a very simple analysis of human cognitive behavior: that perceptions do not actually come to the mind when they occur or go anywhere when they disappear, that the mind itself cannot be fixed in any one location, and that the mind is actually without the distinctions of "this" and "that." In one passage, the text suggests that the student could appreciate the emptiness or nonsubstantiality of all reality by contemplating the derivation from space of the infinite minute particles that comprise that reality. Although this stipulation of the role of space is exceptional in Buddhist philosophy, it is clear that the nonsubstantiality of phenomenal reality is based on the essential nonsubstantiality of its component *dharmas*, not merely because of the transitory nature of the combinations of those *dharmas*. (See Chapter Six of the translation.)

Although direct contemplation is not described with any particular eloquence in the *Yuan-ming lun,* the underlying idea of that practice is clearly stated: Contemplation of one's own cognitive existence at any given time was sufficient grounds to prove to oneself the truth of nonsubstantiality. No painstaking feats of yogic concentration and mental analysis were required, only the immediate apprehension of the underlying reality of each facet of one's normal existence. (As if this were a simple matter!)

13. Shen-hsiu's Instructions on Meditation

The following passage, found in the miscellaneous material attributed to Shen-hsiu in the anthology of East Mountain Teaching/Northern School material mentioned earlier, is much more explicit than the *Yuan-ming lun* on the practice of meditation:

> If you wish to cultivate contemplation, you must proceed first from the contemplation of the external. Why is this necessary? Because the external sensory realms constitute the causes and conditions of the generated mind, the locus of the activated illusions. Also, because ordinary people are so crude and shallow in determination, they generally have difficulty proceeding to the profound and excellent region [of the absolute, separate from sensory input]. Therefore, one enters the profound and excellent region by first undertaking contemplation of the external.
>
> [In this contemplation] one must understand that the various *dharmas* are fundamentally and in their essential nature universally "same" and without any distinctive characteristics. The various *dharmas* exist only as a phantasmagorical creation of the beginningless perfumings. They have no real essence. According to this principle of the *dharmas*' universal "sameness" and phantasmagorical creation through causes and conditions, [the *dharmas*] are fundamentally nonexistent and without birth and death, positive and negative, long and short. They are only the illusions of beginningless ignorance.
>
> Through noncomprehension of this principle, one perceives people and *dharmas* where there are no people and *dharmas*, one falsely perceives being and nonbeing where there are no being and nonbeing. One falsely generates attachment, grasping at people and grasping at *dharmas*, creating various kinds of karma and circulating through the six modes of existence. These individuals and *dharmas*, birth and death, and being and nonbeing are only the false mind. Outside of this [false] mind not a single *dharma* can be apprehended *(te)*.
>
> Understanding this principle, one must simply follow each and every [object upon which the] mind is conditioned, investigating it intimately. Know that there is only this mind and no external realms. Perform this

investigation purely and attentively, always keeping the mind focused (*yuan*, "conditioned") on this principle of the empty falsity [of all *dharmas*].

When you can maintain the mind [on this subject] for some time, then you must "countercontemplate" (*chieh-kuan*, i.e., turn around and contemplate) this false mind [itself]. Whether it is existent or nonexistent, [whether it is generated or] extinguished, [the discriminatory mind] is ultimately not apprehendable, [no matter how one may attempt] various methods of searching for it. The mind of the future is still in the future, the mind of the past is in the past, and the mind of the present is not maintained [beyond the immediate moment]. Also, because [every] two [states of] mind are dissimilar, when one realizes the generation of [one state of] mind, one does not realize the extinction [of another state of] mind (?).

In discussing the generation of the mind, one must postulate causes and conditions. Since it is only through the accumulation of causes and conditions that the mind is generated, if those causes and conditions did not accumulate, how could there be any "generation"? This "generation" is "nongeneration" (*wu-sheng*, "birthless," a synonym for *nirvāṇa*) and this "extinction" is "nonextinction." [Therefore,] one must countercontemplate this mind.

QUESTION: This mind being the mind of wisdom, the enlightened mind, why must one contemplate it?

ANSWER: Although this mind is the mind of wisdom, the enlightened mind, it is because of the flowing capacities (*liu-lei*) of the mind that there is generation and extinction and the nonannihilation of the characteristics of the sensory realms.

QUESTION: Does not this style of contemplation imply a subject and an object of contemplation (i.e., an inherent duality)?

ANSWER: What I am here calling countercontemplation is only to be constantly mindful of the contemplating mind's countercontemplation of itself —there is no subject and object. [Just as] a knife cannot cut itself and a finger cannot point at itself, the mind cannot contemplate itself [dualistically]. When there is no contemplation (i.e., when you are just trying to imagine what this practice might be like), subject and object of contemplation exist, but in actual countercontemplation there are no subject and object of contemplation. This [practice] transcends words and characteristics, the path of words being eradicated and the locus of mental activity extinguished.[325]

QUESTION: Does not the mind enter [a state of] blankness (*wu-chi*) [through this practice]?[326]

ANSWER: During [this practice the Buddha] Nature develops of itself and becomes increasingly bright and vast. How could this be blankness? What was referred to earlier as the "entrance into the profound and excellent region"[327] is a contemplation in which subject and object are both purified (i.e., rendered nonsubstantial, hence nonexistent) and which cannot be interpreted either in words or with the active mind. As just stated, the more profound and vast [one's realization of the Buddha Nature], the greater and brighter [one's contemplation] becomes.

> One who hears this and decides to cultivate enlightenment according to this principle [must realize that this point] cannot be attained through effort. How can it be reached? When the [true] practitioner hears this, he cultivates this realization through meditation.[328]

As Shen-hsiu's longest statement on the practice of meditation, this passage is interesting for a number of reasons. First, he counsels the student to begin with "external" subjects of concentration, i.e., sensory impressions of the external world. This approach is justified on the dual bases of the role played by such external sensory realms in the operation of the unenlightened mind and the lack of aptitude and determination of most meditators. Northern School literature, especially the *Wu fang-pien,* abounds in dualistic formulations. (Indeed, the writings of virtually all phases of Ch'an use the statement and resolution of dualities as a basic technique of religious expression.) When we discuss the *Wu fang-pien* in the following sections, it will be interesting to recall that Shen-hsiu defends at least this one dualism of interior and exterior on such practical grounds—and that he uses it to lead to the transcendence of subject and object.

Second, although it is fair to label Shen-hsiu's teaching of meditation as gradualistic because it requires some effort and a progression from external to internal objects of contemplation, this gradualism is mitigated by the very nature of the contemplation itself. One's object of contemplation changes, but never the goal of that contemplation. From beginning to end, the point is to comprehend the nonsubstantiality of one's object of concentration. There are no preliminary exercises required and, indeed, no specific instructions on exactly how *śūnyatā* might best be apprehended. Even the distinction between internal and external objects of concentration would be eliminated, at least in theory, were one to recall the *Yuan-ming lun*'s position that external reality is solely a manifestation of the mind. Effectively, the mind can do nothing else but contemplate itself—either directly or through the intermediary of its own manifestations.

The explicit stipulation that countercontemplation represents a form of practice lacking the subject-object dichotomy is tantamount to the position that in such a meditative state one achieves contact or identity with the ultimate, undifferentiated state of mind. Earlier, in our discussion of the *Yuan-ming lun,* it was necessary to postulate a specific moment of enlightenment, the instant in which the meditator first transformed himself by the eradication of all his illusions. In the present case the first achievement of counterillumination would have to constitute such a moment—although Shen-hsiu himself is silent on the issue.

Third, the only explicit mention of gradual improvement refers to a point after the initiation of counterillumination, when one's "[Buddha] Nature develops of itself and becomes increasingly bright and vast." This is a very pregnant assertion, in that it provides a link that joins this passage to the *LCSTC,* the *Yuan-ming lun,* and the *Wu fang-pien.* The *LCSTC,* including the portions of the *JTFM* contained in it, frequently refers to the increasingly "bright and pure" *(ming-ching)* state of the meditator's mind.[329] More significantly, the notion that the meditator's mind becomes somehow increasingly expansive in a spatial sense is distinctly reminiscent of the *Yuan-ming lun.* That text, as we have just seen, is emphatic about the importance of space as the creative substrate of all reality, suggests that the contemplation of the role of space be a part of the aspirant's meditation practice, and even outlines a system of interpenetrating "worlds" of great and small sentient beings. The significance of these positive references to space and expansive states of mind will become crystal clear when we consider passages from the *Wu fang-pien* that refer to meditation practices designed to either simulate or generate such states of mind.

14. The Construction of the Wu fang-pien

The *Wu fang-pien (Five Expedient Means)* has long been one of the most perplexing of all the early Ch'an works discovered at Tun-huang. In addition to the many textual problems alluded to in the first section of this chapter, the style of expression used in this text is very difficult to understand. This style is unique in the annals of Ch'an literature, even in the annals of Chinese religious literature as a whole—a distinction that is not necessarily to the credit of either the *Wu fang-pien* or the Northern School. Some parts of the text are clear and concise, but the bulk of it is devoted to the reproduction of endless variations on a small number of paradigmatic formulae. The repetitiveness of this material, together with the absence of any clear indication of how these formulae are to be interpreted, leads to conflicting impressions of banality and impenetrability.[330]

My own conjecture is that the *Wu fang-pien* was primarily a teachers' manual not meant for general circulation among students. Evidence for this view consists of the presence of initiation or ordination rituals at the beginning of the text and the frequent use of abbreviation throughout. Unfortunately, this hypothesis does not immediately bring us any closer to the understanding of the contents of the text. Even after several decades of scholarship on early Ch'an, many aspects of the *Wu fang-pien* still elude our comprehension.

Although the five different "expedient means" of the *Wu fang-pien* are clearly enumerated at the beginning and again at the end of the translation given earlier in this chapter, it will be convenient to repeat them here along with the titles of the scriptures on which they are said to depend:

1. Comprehensive Explanation of the Essence of Buddhahood, or Teaching of the Transcendence of Thoughts: *Awakening of Faith*
2. Opening the Gates of Wisdom and Sagacity, or the Teaching of Motionlessness: *Lotus Sūtra*
3. Manifesting the Inconceivable Dharma: *Vimalakīrti Sūtra*
4. Elucidation of the True Nature of the *Dharmas*: *Sūtra of* [*the God*] *Ssu-i*
5. Naturally Unobstructed Path of Emancipation, or Teaching of the Comprehension of Nondifferentiation: *Avataṁsaka Sūtra*[331]

This arrangement of scriptures is reminiscent of the fivefold classifications of the *p'an-chiao* ("dividing the doctrine") tradition.[332] In spite of this superficial similarity, nothing in the *Wu fang-pien* itself indicates that the five expedient means are arranged in any kind of hierarchical progression. Indeed, even a quick perusal of the text reveals that the *Lotus* and *Vimalakīrti Sūtra*s are not necessarily the sole bases of the second and third expedient means, respectively. More important, even though the *Avataṁsaka Sūtra* holds the distinction of occurring at the final and presumably highest position in such an inferred hierarchy, the *Awakening of Faith* is actually related in the most integral fashion to the construction and message of the text. According to the normal standards of the *p'an-chiao* tradition, the *Awakening of Faith* would normally be considered less important than the other four texts (at least, less important than the *Avataṁsaka*) because it stands at the very beginning of the *Wu fang-pien* and because it alone is a treatise rather than a sūtra.

We will pay close attention only to the first two expedient means. The third expedient means is merely an interesting application of the paradigms of the first two on lines from the *Vimalakīrti Sūtra,* and the fourth and fifth expedient means are represented so incompletely in the extant manuscripts, as well as in Tsung-mi's resume of the text,[333] that very little can be said about them.

15. The First Expedient Means and the Awakening of Faith

In order to understand the *Wu fang-pien* we must first consider at least part of the theoretical basis of the *Awakening of Faith.* As explained in an excellent modern commentary by Hirakawa Akira,[334] this text espouses a certain kind of idealism, the "mind-only" (*yuishin,* or *wei-hsin* in Chinese) theory, the fundamental orientation of which is different from the better-known "consciousness-only" (*yuishiki, wei-shih,* or *vijñapti-mātra* in Sanskrit) theory.

Whereas the consciousness-only theory begins with an analysis of the nature of human sensory perception and mental activity, from which it draws conclusions about human ignorance and the chain of events necessary for emancipation, the mind-only theory assumes the simultaneous existence of innate wisdom and ignorance and proceeds by analyzing the ramifications of the relationship between the two. The consciousness-only theory thus devotes a great deal of attention to the identity and interaction of the various components of human cognitive reality, i.e., the sense organs or sensory capabilities, sense data or objects of sensation, and the associated types of consciousness. Although the fundamental assumptions of the two theories are radically different, the mind-only theory of the *Awakening of Faith* in large part adopts the terminology and definitions of the consciousness-only theory, which was systematized long before this treatise appeared.

In the *Awakening of Faith* the wisdom that is innate within us all is referred to variously as Suchness *(chen-ju)*, the mind that is pure in its Self Nature *(tzu-hsing ch'ing-ching hsin)*, the *tathāgata-garbha (ju-lai tsang)*, and enlightenment *(chueh)*. The variety of names exists because of the differing ways in which the same entity may be approached. As Hirakawa explains these different terms:

> Even though Suchness does not transcend the mind, because it is the Suchness of the mind, it is described as the nature of true reality. That is, the theoretical aspect prevails in this usage. In other words, the true reality that pervades the entire universe has been expressed in the context of the mind-only theory as the Suchness of the mind.
>
> In contrast to this, the "mind that is pure in its Self Nature" may be described as the personification of Suchness. It is Suchness manifested as man. Because the Suchness of the mind is the fundamental nature of the mind, it is grasped in this instance in the context of the individual human being. In a religious sense it is quite natural that this should be the case . . .
>
> The point is that the fundamental nature of the mind is equivalent to the changeless nature of true reality. To say "Suchness" is to emphasize the aspect of principle *(li)*, whereas to say "mind" emphasizes that of wisdom *(chih)*. At the very least, it would be difficult to understand mind solely as principle. Because of this, the position of the *Awakening of Faith* may be understood as one of the nonduality of principle and wisdom. Principle is not simply principle, but necessarily becomes active as wisdom.
>
> Because wisdom is the manifestation of the principle, it cannot be thought of other than as corresponding perfectly to true reality. Therefore, wisdom is equivalent to enlightenment, the wisdom of the Buddha, and the *dharmakāya* or the *Tathāgata*. The idea that principle becomes active as wisdom is an important characteristic of the *Awakening of Faith*.[335]

Ignorance is understood within the *Awakening of Faith* as the tendency to mental dichotomization, i.e., the distinction between subject and object or between self and other. Any moment of thought, as long as it involves such preconceived dualities, is a moment of ignorance. At one point the treatise declares that "suddenly, thoughts arise" (or, to conform with the usage throughout this paper, "suddenly, thoughts are activated" [*hu-jan nien ch'i*]).[336] This is not meant to imply that an individual's ignorance may be said to have begun at a particular point in time. Rather, the term "suddenly" is used to indicate that no reason can be given for the existence of ignorance, which is referred to as beginningless. The whole thrust of the mind-only theory rests on the logically (but not temporally) prior existence of ignorance, for it is on this basis that one's entire realm of existence is manifested.

Because of the conjoint inherence of wisdom and ignorance, the *Awakening of Faith* is constrained to posit two different types of enlightenment. The first is "inherent enlightenment" *(pen-chueh),* which, as the term implies, is equivalent to the wisdom immanent within us all. This type of enlightenment exerts a constantly beneficial influence, inspiring its possessor to good works and propelling him up the spiritual ladder toward enlightenment. Because inherent enlightenment is neither fully functional nor apparent in ordinary people, the *Awakening of Faith* also posits "temporal enlightenment" *(shih-chueh).* Only through spiritual self-cultivation can one approach and finally achieve the actual experience of realization, or temporal enlightenment. At the very highest level of achievement, i.e., buddhahood, these two types of enlightenment become identical. At lower stages of progress, however, one's level of understanding may be described as either enlightenment or nonenlightenment, depending on the perspective.

Having presented some of the basic ideas of the *Awakening of Faith,* I can now introduce the passage from which the *Wu fang-pien* draws its own material. The lines actually quoted in the Northern School work are italicized in the translation that follows:

> *The meaning of "enlightenment" is that the essence of the mind transcends thoughts. The characteristic of the transcendence of thoughts is equivalent to the realm of space, which pervades everywhere. The single characteristic of the* dharmadhātu *is the universally "same"* dharmakāya *of the* Tathāgata. *"Inherent enlightenment" is preached in relation to this* dharmakāya.
>
> Why is this? The meaning of inherent enlightenment is explained in juxtaposition to that of temporal enlightenment, so that temporal enlightenment is identical to inherent enlightenment. Because temporal enlightenment is based on inherent enlightenment and because nonenlightenment exists, temporal enlightenment is explained on the basis of that nonenlightenment.
>
> Further, to be enlightened to the Mind Source (i.e., the mind that is the source of all illusions) is called ultimate enlightenment. When one is not

enlightened to the Mind Source, one has not [achieved] ultimate enlightenment.

What does this mean?

[1] An ordinary person may realize the evil activated by a previous thought, become able to calm subsequent thoughts, and make them refrain from the activation of [such evil]. Even though this is called enlightenment, this [achievement is only] based on the nonenlightenment [of the previous thought].

[2] As with the contemplative wisdom of Hīnayānists, when bodhisattvas who have only just generated the intention [to achieve buddhahood] are enlightened to the differentiation of [successive moments of] thought, their thoughts are without the characteristic of differentiation. Because they have eliminated the characteristic of the grasping of gross discrimination, this is called facsimile enlightenment.

[3] When bodhisattvas of the *dharmakāya* are enlightened to the abiding of thoughts, their thoughts are without the characteristic of abiding. Because they have transcended the characteristic of discrimination and gross thoughts, this is called partial enlightenment.

[4] Bodhisattvas who have completed the [ten] stages fulfill the expedient means and, in a single moment of correspondence, *are enlightened to the initial activation of the mind, their minds being without the characteristic of initialness. Distantly transcending the most subtle of thoughts, they attain perception of the Mind Nature. When the mind [is in a state of] constant abiding, this is called the ultimate enlightenment.*

For this reason, the sūtra says: "If a sentient being can contemplate nonthought *(wu-nien),* then this constitutes the wisdom that approaches buddhahood."

Also, to refer to the "knowledge of the characteristic of initialness" even when the activation of the mind is without any characteristic of initialness that can be known is to refer to nonthought.

Therefore, sentient beings in general are not referred to as enlightened. Because they have [experienced] a succession of thoughts since the beginning[lessness of time] and have never been able to transcend thoughts, this is called beginningless ignorance. If they can achieve nonthought, then they will know the mind's characteristics of generation, abiding, differentiation, and extinction—because these are equivalent to nonthought.

However, there actually is no differentiation of temporal enlightenment [as in the fourfold classification just given], because the four characteristics [of generation, abiding, etc.] all exist at once and are not independent. They are fundamentally equivalent; [these four constitute] one identical enlightenment.[337]

The heart of this passage is the set of four different types of temporal enlightenment achieved by different classes of practitioners. These four are correlated in reverse order with the four stages in the life of an individual *dharma,* the smallest unit of phenomenal reality in traditional Buddhist philosophy. These four stages are the generation, abiding, decay (here described by the character *i,* meaning "differentiation"[338]), and extinction. It is significant that the *Wu fang-pien* focuses solely on the stage of generation, which is correlated with the achievement of the highest level of enlightenment. As indicated earlier, the "initial activation of the mind" refers not to any temporal occurrence, but rather to the logical origin of ignorance, the root cause of the mind's innumerable cognitive aberrations.

Although in the simplest sense the practitioner perceives the crux of his own ignorance and thereby casts off that ignorance to achieve his own enlightenment, the various terms used by the *Awakening of Faith* have intriguing ramifications. Since it is axiomatic that to completely understand the problem of ignorance is to achieve emancipation from that ignorance, when the practitioner recognizes the initial activation of the mind, there no longer *is* any activation of the mind. He is then said to have "transcended thoughts" *(li-nien)* and to have entered the "realm of the transcendence of thoughts" *(li-nien ching-chieh)* or, simply, "non-thought" *(wu-nien).* The term *li-nien* can refer both to the action of transcending thoughts and, like *wu-nien,* to the subsequent state in which thoughts have been transcended. Similarly, *wu-nien* refers both to the moment at which this achievement occurs (because that single moment of thought is absolutely without anything to which it might be compared) and to the fundamental mind or enlightenment itself, which is like an ocean with no waves.

At the moment of the transcendence of thoughts, the practitioner's mental processes become entirely devoid of the subject-object dichotomy. Those processes become pure realization *(cheng)* or pure enlightenment. At the complete achievement of temporal enlightenment, the practitioner has gained complete unity with the inherent enlightenment within himself and has completely banished the taint of ignorance from his entire being.[339]

It should hardly need mentioning that the most fundamental assumptions of the *Awakening of Faith* are identical to those of Northern School doctrine. The importance of the "nonactivation" of the mind among meditation specialists in the early eighth century has already been documented,[340] and the description of the "transcendence of thoughts" as equivalent to the omnipresence of space corresponds very closely to the peculiar emphasis on space in the *Yuan-ming lun.* Clearly, the use of the terms *li-nien* and *wu-nien* in the *Awakening of Faith* should be considered the starting point for an understanding of their use in the *Wu fang-pien* and other early Ch'an texts. In particular, Shen-hui's polemical distinction between these two terms may be seen to be unwarranted, an observation already made by the Hua-yen School figure Ch'eng-kuan.[341]

16. The Unique Aspects of the First Expedient Means

In contrast to the pure and defiled aspects of mind posited in the *Kuan-hsin lun* and the *Yuan-ming lun,* the most prominent dyad in the first expedient means of the *Wu fang-pien* is that of mind and body. There are numerous passages in which first the mind, then the body, and finally both mind and body together achieve the transcendence of thoughts, or emancipation, or enlightenment. It would be useful if we had some information about the origin of this fundamental pattern of Northern School doctrine; unfortunately, the evidence I have been able to unearth is scanty and all too inconclusive. The only passages in early Ch'an literature that give any hint of the ideas contained in the *Wu fang-pien*'s dualism of mind and body are as follows:

> To know that the mind is without mind is constant *samādhi.* To comprehend that form is without form is to roam constantly in the locus of wisdom *(hui-ch'u).*
>
> [The meaning of] "buddha" is "enlightenment." To be enlightened to the nonsubstantiality of all *dharmas*, to be enlightened oneself and to enlighten others—this is called "buddha."
>
> Enlightened to the internal and external, with comprehension unhindered, and with no going and no coming—this is called *Tathāgata* (i.e., the Thus-come One).
>
> To know that the mind is without mind is for the mind to be constantly serene. To know that the realms [of perception] are without realms is for the realms to be equivalent to nonsubstantiality.[342]

These two brief passages come from a short work circulated with the *Hsiu-hsin yao lun* and other East Mountain Teaching material under the title *Ch'eng-hsin lun (Treatise on the Clarification of the Mind).* Sekiguchi Shindai has shown that this text was originally a letter written by Chih-i, and it seems likely that Shen-hsiu discovered Chih-i's letter during his quarter century of residence at Yü-ch'üan ssu.[343]

The significant aspects of these passages are (1) their explanation of the word "buddha" as enlightenment, and especially as the enlightenment of self and others, and (2) their tendency to refer to the pairs mind and body or mind and the sensory realms in extremely similar, if not identical, ways. Both of these aspects are reminiscent of the *Wu fang-pien.*

The most difficult and intriguing facet of the *Wu fang-pien* dualism is the occurrence of statements to the effect that form, the body, or the sensory realms could "transcend thoughts" and become emancipated. The only precedents to such an idea that I have been able to find also occur in the works of Chih-i:

> Because the realm is wondrous, wisdom is also wondrous.[344]

> Wisdom, which contemplates, illuminates yet is constantly serene and is called "mindfulness" *(nien)*. The realm that is contemplated is serene yet constantly illuminative and is called "foundation" *(ch'u)*. If the realm is serene, wisdom is also serene. If wisdom illuminates, the realm also illuminates . . . The suchlike realm is equivalent to the suchlike wisdom. Wisdom *is* the realm. When speaking of wisdom and the locus of wisdom (*chih-ch'u,* i.e., mindfulness and the foundation), both are called *prajñā*.[345]

Actually, the import of these brief passages is different from that of the rhetorical paradigm of the *Wu fang-pien.* Here the point is that perfect wisdom can only have a similarly perfect object, that in such a state of perfect wisdom there can be no distinction between subject and object or between the function and realm of wisdom. (A similar point regarding the *Awakening of Faith* is made by Hirakawa, as quoted earlier.)

In the *Wu fang-pien,* however, the apparent implication (please do not overlook the word "apparent") of the pattern in question is that the body is enlightened in the same sense as, but independently of, the mind. Whereas Chih-i refers to the indivisibility of the enlightened mind and its objects, thus destroying any vestige of dualism, the *Wu fang-pien* seems to be doing just the opposite by positing the independent enlightenment of mind and body.

The theoretical possibility we are faced with is that the body might be able to achieve enlightenment without the prior or accompanying enlightenment of the mind. Although the *Wu fang-pien* never considers this possibility explicitly, the implications of this apparent doctrine are so problematic that we must search elsewhere within the text for corroboration or amendment. This leads us to the second expedient means.

17. The Second Expedient Means

The major thrust of the second expedient means is to divide the compound *chih-hui,* normally translated as "wisdom," into its individual members *chih* and *hui,* each of which is then correlated with a different type of understanding. I have arbitrarily rendered *chih* as "wisdom" and *hui* as "sagacity." Several pairs of correlations are made in this part of the *Wu fang-pien.* These may be summarized as follows:

1. The function of wisdom is knowing *(chih),* whereas that of sagacity is perception *(chien* or, later in the text, *shih).* Since "knowing and perception" *(chih-chien)* is given as a translation of *bodhi,* it is also said that wisdom and sagacity are *nirvāṇa,* or the "essence" *(t'i),* whereas knowing and perception are *bodhi* or the "function" *(yung).*

2. Wisdom is the motionlessness of the mind, whereas sagacity is the motionlessness of the senses. Similarly, the mind is the gate of wisdom and the senses are the gate of sagacity.

3. Wisdom—presumably, the object of wisdom—is the absolute *(li),* whereas sagacity—or its object—is phenomenality *(shih).*

4. Wisdom is the consciousness transformed, whereas sagacity is perception made comprehensive. These two are referred to as one's "internal spiritual compatriots."

5. Although the terms "wisdom" and "sagacity" are not explicitly mentioned in the discussion of fundamental wisdom and successive wisdom, these pairs could easily be correlated.

6. Finally, some of the passages in subsequent portions of the *Wu fang-pien* refer to "meditation" *(ting)* and "sagacity" *(hui),* a pair usually rendered "meditation and wisdom" in Buddhist writings. The use of "meditation" and "sagacity" in these passages is indistinguishable from that of "wisdom" and "sagacity" earlier in the text. The later usage is continued in the third expedient means.

As with the dualism of mind and body, the origins of this inclination to split *chih-hui* into *chih* and *hui* are obscure. I have been able to find only three earlier passages of possible relevance. The first occurs in the *Hui-yin san-mei ching,* which we have already discussed briefly in relation to Bodhidharma's student Seng-fu. One of this text's verses contains references to the "gate of sagacity" *(hui-men)* and the "stage of wisdom" *(chih-ti).* Unfortunately, the distinction between these two is not clear, nor is it maintained in the other Chinese translations of the same scripture.[346]

The second relevant passage occurs in the writings of the Mādhyamika scholar Chi-tsang, whose discussion of the various Chinese translations for *prajñā* and *jñāna* contains the sentence: "The illumination of non-substantiality is sagacity *(hui);* the reflection of being is wisdom *(chih).*" The same distinction is repeated more than once, with slightly different nuances. Therefore, the logical basis of the *Wu fang-pien*'s dichotomized usage of *chih* and *hui* existed during Chi-tsang's time, even though it was stated in a manner exactly opposite to that of the *Wu fang-pien.* Other sources of the same general period are in accord with Chi-tsang rather than the *Wu fang-pien.*[347]

Although it does not specifically mention the terms *chih* and *hui,* the following passage from the commentary on the *Fo-shuo fa-chü ching* found by Professor Tanaka is very helpful in the understanding of these terms:

> Further, the Pavilion of the Superior Treasury in the Palace of the Sun and Moon refers to the pavilion [in the] palace on Mount Laṇkā where [the

> Buddha] preached the Dharma. The names "Superior Treasury" and "Sun and Moon" use the ideas of compassionate explanation to form a metaphor for the body and mind of the sage who has achieved enlightenment and attained the *dharmakāya.*
>
> When one realizes the *dharmakāya,* the *body* is like space: vast, omnipresent, containing within itself a hundred billion suns and moons. Within it thrive all the four types of living beings, as numerous as the sands of the River Ganges. There is no being not penetrated by it and no dark [corner] not illumined by it. Therefore, it is called the Palace of the Sun and Moon.
>
> "Pavilion of the Superior Treasury" refers to the realization of Suchness by the *mind* of the sage. [The sage's mind] illuminates the triple realm with the wisdom of a mirror suspended on high, which reflects the myriad *dharma*s as if storing [precious] jewels. The "superior teaching" is inexhaustible; it is given to all [living beings so that they might] transcend birth and death. It is as if a ruler residing on high were administering it to the masses below. Therefore, the sūtra says, "in the Pavilion of the Superior Treasury in the Palace of the Sun and Moon." (5:7/149)

Here the subjects being discussed are the *body* and *mind* of the true sage, but note how similar the explanation is to that of *chih* and *hui,* or wisdom and sagacity, in the *Wu fang-pien.* The sage's body is infinite in dimension and permeates all things and all living beings. In essence, the body of such an enlightened individual is the *dharmakāya* itself. The mind is described as being like a "mirror suspended on high," which illuminates the entire cosmos. Body and mind are not completely separable: There is nowhere that is not penetrated or illumined by the body, whereas the mind incorporates the myriad *dharma*s. In addition, the superior teaching, which is the source of both the body and the mind and the key to the transcendence of birth and death, is described as being given to, i.e., possessed by, all sentient beings. In other words, this is the Buddha Nature that is immanent within us all.

The dyads of the body and mind in the Tanaka commentary and of wisdom and sagacity in the *Wu fang-pien* bear an essential similarity. Although the former begins with the body as absolute, rather than with the wisdom that knows that absolute, this difference is not significant. There is of necessity a perfect correspondence between absolute reality and pure wisdom, as has been pointed out in quotations from Hirakawa and Chih-i in Sections 15 and 16 of this chapter. The second member of each dyad is defined as the ability to comprehend all phenomenal reality without any distortion or imperfection whatsoever. In other words, these two dyads are variations on those venerable mainstays of Chinese philosophy, *li* and *shih,* or the "absolute" and "phenomenality," and *t'i* and *yung* or "essence" and "function." In fact, *chih* and *hui* are correlated in the *Wu fang-pien* with each of these pairs.

The implicit correlation of the transcendence of thoughts in the mind with *chih* and the transcendence of thoughts in the body or in form with *hui* requires an unusual interpretation of the terms *shen,* "body," and *se,* "form." That is, we must infer that these do not refer merely to the physical corpus, but to that corpus plus all the sensory capacities that are the concomitants of sentient existence. Although no explicit proof of this interpretation occurs in the *Wu fang-pien,* this is the only interpretation that allows us to understand the transcendence of thoughts vis-à-vis the body in a way that relates to the spiritual experience of the practitioner. This interpretation is also the only one of which I am aware that fits with the passage from the *Fo-shuo fa-chü ching* commentary introduced earlier in this section.[348]

We must remember that a body able to transcend thoughts does not belong to just any sentient being, but rather to an enlightened person, a buddha. The body of such a being is not merely physical, but possesses the extraordinary capabilities of the *nirmāṇakāya* and the supercorporeal realities of the *saṁbhogakāya.* Although most of the formulae of the *Wu fang-pien* seem to be designed to make the grandiose terminology of Indian Buddhism more approachable, the very use of that terminology lends a greater significance to the apparent simplicity of terminology such as the transcendence of thoughts. That is, the *Wu fang-pien* is saying not only, "To become a buddha is as easy as this," but also, "By doing this you will actually become a buddha, with all that that entails."

The proof of this may be found in the text's descriptions of and statements concerning meditation practice. These descriptions and statements occur, for the most part, in the context of the ceremonial material found in the introduction and conclusion of the composite text.

18. Descriptions of Meditation Practice in the Wu fang-pien

The first question of interest in this phase of our discussion is the attitude of the Northern School authors toward the necessity of moral training as a prerequisite to meditation practice. The Northern School has a reputation in modern studies for being closely associated with Vinaya School centers, and several of its works imply an advocacy of strict maintenance of the precepts. At one point the *Wu fang-pien* advocates that the precepts should be maintained without transgression "even in the face of death."[349] Certainly, there is no indication that the members of the Northern School ever advocated anything like the institutionalized rejection of monastic convention espoused by the Chung-ching ssu faction of Ch'an in Szechwan.[350]

Nevertheless, the fundamental purpose of the ceremony found at the beginning of the *Wu fang-pien* was not to start the student off on a long career of purificatory exercises, but rather to justify the wholesale avoidance of such endeavors. Several different types of vows are included in this ceremony—the four great vows, the three refuges, the five capabilities, and the repentence of past transgressions—but all of these take up just a few lines of text and could easily have been accomplished in a half hour or so. When we recall the rejection of scriptural recitation and other forms of superficial religious practice in the *Kuan-hsin lun,* the *Yuan-ming lun,* and other texts, we must admit that this is a general characteristic of the Northern School's teachings.

After an interesting redefinition of morality as the maintenance of the Buddha Nature by the "nonactivation" of the mind, the text instructs the students in attendance to sit in lotus position, with legs crossed and each foot resting on the opposite thigh, and engage in a period of *nien-fo,* or "mindfulness of the Buddha."

The Chinese scholar Yin-shun has equated this reference to *nien-fo* with the Pure Land practice of contemplating the Buddha Amitābha—an equation that cannot be categorically denied. Some of Hung-jen's disciples were known Pure Land specialists, and the *CFPC* admits—and criticizes—the use of *nien-fo* by later patriarchs of Ch'an. Nevertheless, the *Kuan-hsin lun* specifically rejects the empty recitation of the Buddha's name, and it is difficult to believe that the practice of *nien-fo* in Ch'an would not have been redefined to accord with the particular religious outlook of the School.[351] Therefore, rather than adverting to some other source, I will define the type of meditation referred to here according to the lines immediately following in the *Wu fang-pien* itself.

These lines are emphatic on the importance of "viewing afar." The student is instructed to view in all directions during all his activities and in all situations, doing so with unremitting energy and concentration. This description should immediately remind the reader of the *Yuan-ming lun,* in which space is defined as the basis of all reality and in which the "worlds" of sentient being are described as either great or small, depending on their level of enlightenment. We can only wonder whether the "viewing afar" exercises of the *Wu fang-pien* represent instructions for the achievement of such expansive states of existence.

Although no reference is made in the *Yuan-ming lun* to such "mind-expanding" exercises, the plausibility of this hypothesis is supported by further analysis of the context and description of the *Wu fang-pien* exercises themselves. First, it is the Pure Mind, the enlightened mind, that does the viewing. This is evident from the very crucial passage contained in the conclusion to the *Wu fang-pien,* in which the enlightened state is that in which enlightenment *(chueh)* is in control of the mind, rather than vice versa. In the introduction to the *Wu fang-pien,* that which views is referred to as the "eye of the Pure Mind." In the text discussed briefly in Part One, Chapter IV, Section 8 under the title *Gathering of Twelve Departed Masters,* Shen-hsiu is quoted as saying: "In the locus of purity, view purity *(ching-ch'u k'an-ching).*"[352] "Locus of purity" is an unusual term that must refer to the mind itself, the Pure Mind. The mind that "views afar" is the essentially pure Fundamental Mind, which is equivalent to the Buddha Nature, or inherent enlightenment.

Second, although that which is viewed is all reality, the practitioner does not perceive any objects whatsoever. This is explicitly stated in the teacher-student dialogues that occur in the introduction and just before the exposition of the second expedient means. The student sees "not a single thing." Obviously, the intent is that he should see without discrimination, just as the bodhisattva operates in the world without ever conceptualizing the reality of his own existence, other beings, or his efforts of salvific assistance. That the doctrine of *śūnyatā,* which is the basis of the bodhisattva's practice, is important here is indicated by the line from the *Diamond Sūtra:* "All that which has characteristics is completely false." The same emphasis on nonsubstantiality occurs throughout the *Yuan-ming lun.*

The conjunction of the ideas of purity and nonsubstantiality, or emptiness, is in itself noteworthy. Professor Iriya Yoshitaka has shown that these two concepts were closely identified in medieval Chinese Buddhist texts. He has demonstrated that the Chinese conception of emptiness was based on the image of an empty sky, and that of purity was based on the notion of a state so clean that all objects had been completely removed—much as in an empty sky. Since most of Professor Iriya's examples are drawn from the Chinese translations of the *Laṇkāvatāra Sūtra* and the works of Ch'an figures such as Shen-hui and Huang-po Hsi-yün, it seems entirely reasonable to extend his conclusions to the texts of the Northern School.[353] Therefore, the failure to see—or, rather, the restraint from seeing—any object whatsoever means not only to perceive the nonsubstantial nature of reality, but also to perceive the ultimate purity of that reality.

As indicated by the slogan "in the locus of purity, view purity," the true meaning of the Northern School practice of viewing afar or viewing purity is thus fundamentally different from the traditional interpretation, according to which the school is criticized for positing a distinction between purity and impurity and favoring one over the other. This misinterpretation may be a natural consequence of the terminology used by the Northern School, but the original source of the misinterpretation, Shen-hui, was certainly not above intentional distortion.

19. Meditation in the Northern School

It is not immediately apparent how the practices of viewing afar and viewing purity relate to the *Wu fang-pien*'s characteristically binomial formulae of the mind and body transcending thoughts. One possibility is that viewing afar represents not the stages in which mind and body transcend thoughts individually, but the third stage, in which both body and mind achieve that state of transcendence together. Although this interpretation would provide some meaning to this otherwise redundant third stage, I can find no evidence in the text to support it. Also, the stages of the meditation techniques described by Shen-hsiu (see Section 13 of this chapter) cannot be correlated with the bipartite or tripartite formulae of the *Wu fang-pien.*

The second possibility, which I favor, is to accept as real the incongruity between the *Wu fang-pien*'s doctrinal expressions and its practical injunctions, to ponder the reasons for this lack of consistency, and to weigh the significance of viewing afar in terms of other Northern School texts and ideas. From this perspective, it is significant that viewing afar is described without any intimation of stages or levels of practice. The denial of any need for moral or practical prerequisites to spiritual practice is a frequent theme of early Ch'an texts, viz., the definition of *shou-i pu i,* or "maintaining the One without wavering," in the *JTFM.* The same theme is also expressed in the opening ceremony of the *Wu fang-pien.*

The practice of viewing afar appears to be the highest meditation practice of the Northern School. In this one exercise—or, rather, this one state of being—are subsumed all of the most important themes of early Ch'an doctrine:

1. Just as in the "entrance of principle" of Bodhidharma's *EJSHL* and the *Hsiu-hsin yao lun*'s practice of *shou-hsin,* the practice of viewing afar assumes complete realization of the presence of the Buddha Nature or Pure Mind within oneself.
2. As with the *EJSHL*'s entrance of practice and the underlying philosophy of the *Yuan-ming lun,* viewing afar is based on a full awareness of the truth of nonsubstantiality, as indicated by the fact that the practitioner sees "not a single thing."
3. Although not mentioned prominently in the *Wu fang-pien,* the ability to maintain a state of "nonactivation" *(pu-ch'i)* of mind allows the practitioner to avoid the discriminative perception of "things."
4. Viewing afar is described in terms of the perfectly reflecting mirror suspended on high, which reveals its images without distortion or attachment.

This last item, the metaphor of the mirror, constitutes the most appropriate paradigm for this Northern School practice. The mirror's innate ability to reflect is itself equivalent to the Buddha Nature or the Pure

Mind. Like the sun shining on high, the mirror can be obscured by the dusts of the illusions, but this detail is not relevant here. Rather, the illusions and the elements of phenomenal reality are the mirror's natural objects of reflection, which are seen to be nonsubstantial. Just as the passive reality of the presence of the Buddha Nature is assumed but not emphasized, the more dynamic paradigm of the mirror demands that the dusts of the illusions be recognized as nonsubstantial, unreal, and ultimately ineffectual.

The mirror's wonderful ability to reflect images without distortion and attachment is based on its ability to refrain from the activation of mind —it reflects automatically, spontaneously, without ever generating its own preferences or desires. In the terminology of the *Wu fang-pien,* when it reflects an image, it realizes that image to be an "other-image." Like space, which is the basis for the creation of all reality, it does not think, "I have created this reflection; this reflection is mine." The images, in their turn, appear on the surface of the mirror in perfect congruence with the phantasmagorical nature of phenomenal reality as we perceive it.

Finally, it is useful to consider the implications of the mirror metaphor vis-à-vis the *Wu fang-pien*'s unusual conception of the mind and body. In and of itself, the mirror is a purely cognitive entity. It reflects images perfectly and automatically, but it does not interact with them. One of the most important themes of both the *Yuan-ming lun* and the *Wu fang-pien,* however, is that true Buddhist practice should include constant activity on behalf of other sentient beings. At one point the *Wu fang-pien* redefines "sentient beings" as false thoughts, and the ability of the body and mind to be motionless is identified as the salvation of "sentient beings."[354] Is it possible that the *Wu fang-pien* reduces the function of salvation to a puerile equivalent for self-benefit? I think not.

The mirror's reflective surface represents the perfectly functioning mind of the sage. I would suggest that, at this level of sophistication, the reality that the mirror reflects is like the practitioner's body. His wisdom is perfect and unconditioned, and, as we have seen, the object of his wisdom must also be perfect and unconditioned.

The passage quoted in Section 17 from the commentary to the *Fo-shuo fa-chü ching* described the sage's body as equivalent to the *dharmakāya,* and we concluded that the usage of "body" and "form" in the *Wu fang-pien* included both the physical corpus and all human sensory functions. The concept of "sentient being" is therefore a false thought, a mistaken example of discriminative thinking, whereas the reality of "sentient being" is nonsubstantial. Each sentient being is actually a part of the whole, a part of the practitioner's own expanded being.

Although a significant gap still exists between the epistemological frame of reference of the mirror and the need for salvific activity on the part of the enlightened practitioner, the primary characteristics of each are the same: constancy of application, spontaneity and infallibility of response, and the lack of assumed dualities and individualized intentions. As it turns out, these qualities were probably those originally implied by "Shen-hsiu's" mind-verse in the *Platform Sūtra,* rather than the doctrine of gradual enlightenment. Let us return to the problem of the *Platform Sūtra* verses in the Conclusion to this study.

CONCLUSION

1. The Original Meaning of the Platform Sūtra *Verses*

This study began with a discussion of the opening narrative of the *Platform Sūtra,* in particular the "mind-verses" attributed in that text to Shen-hsiu and Hui-neng. The verse attributed to Shen-hsiu, the reader will recall, reads as follows:

> The body is the *bodhi* tree.
> The mind is like a bright mirror's stand.
> At all times we must strive to polish it
> and must not let dust collect.

In the Introduction I stated that the original meaning of this verse was not necessarily gradualistic, as the traditional interpretation would have us believe. The primary reason for this contention is the following passage from Shen-hsiu's *Kuan-hsin lun:*

> Further, lamps of eternal brightness (*ch'ang-ming teng,* i.e., votive lamps) are none other than the truly enlightened mind. When one's wisdom is bright and distinct, it is likened to a lamp. For this reason, all those who seek emancipation always consider the body as the lamp's stand, the mind as the lamp's dish, and faith as the lamp's wick. The augmentation of moral discipline is taken as the addition of oil. For wisdom to be bright and penetrating is likened to the lamp's flame (or brightness). If one constantly burns such a lamp of truly suchlike true enlightenment, its illumination will destroy all the darkness of ignorance and stupidity.[1]

Since the Northern School's emphasis on the constancy of true spiritual practice, both before and after enlightenment, has been mentioned many times in the preceding chapters, the reader should not be at all surprised to find it indicated here. Certainly, constancy is the point of both the passage just introduced and the metaphor of the mirror in the *Platform Sūtra* verse. In fact, the references to the mirror in that verse read like a truncated version of the metaphor of the lamp in the *Kuan-hsin lun* passage: The verse mentions only the mirror's stand and the dust upon it, but we can easily imagine further references—to its surface, reflectivity, and images, for example. These three components of the mirror could have been equated to the senses, wisdom, and knowledge of phenomenal reality. In this context, constantly wiping the surface of the mirror is not the key that initiates the entire process of reflection, i.e., the progressive realization of enlightenment, but rather a standard maintenence operation necessary for the ongoing functioning of the mirror. Analogous elements in the metaphor of the lamp are the addition of oil and the trimming of the wick, both of which are necessary to the continued functioning of illumination. In actual fact, medieval Chinese mirrors had to be polished frequently in order to prevent their reflective surfaces from tarnishing.

Although this was clearly the original intent of the metaphor of the mirror, I am not certain whether this interpretation was known to the compiler of the *Platform Sūtra*. He may have been using some indirect and/or corrupted source for the teachings of the Northern School. Several Northern School texts, both early and late, refer to the image of the mirror and the dust that obscures it. These references are often made in an offhand fashion or for fairly noncontroversial, laudatory purposes (e.g., "their Dharma mirrors are bright"[2]), and it is easy to imagine that a purely gradualistic usage of this popular metaphor might have occurred, even though none is recorded in the material still extant. In Part Two, Chapter II, Section 4 we noticed brief references to wiping the dust off the surface of a mirror in the *Hsiu-hsin yao lun* and one other East Mountain Teaching work, but these references fit much better with my interpretation than with the traditional one of gradualistic practice. Shen-hsiu's epitaph by Chang Yueh contains the following line: "The mirror of the mind has dust upon its external [surface]; if it is not polished, it will not reflect."[3] This passage is not a defense of gradualism either, but a manifestation of the belief that individual practice is both desirable and necessary for a true Buddhist. The same sentiment is also contained in a very short work bearing Shen-hsiu's name discovered at Tun-huang which refers to foolish sentient beings "not polishing" *(pu mo-fu)* the Buddha Amitabha within them.[4] Although these passages affirm the need for spiritual cultivation, they are not defenses of gradualism, which by the seventh and eighth centuries had been passé for much too long for anyone to argue in its defense.

Just as with the *Platform Sūtra*'s reference to the mirror, other lines in the mind-verses are distinctly reminiscent of Northern School material. One such line contains the reference to the *bodhi* tree. Recall the following lines from the *Wu fang-pien:*

Peaceful and vast without limit, its untaintedness is the path of *bodhi.* The mind serene and enlightenment distinct, the body's serenity is the *bodhi* tree.

The Buddha is the path of *bodhi.* Nonabiding is the seed of *bodhi.* The serenity of mind is the cause of *bodhi.* The serenity of body is the condition of *bodhi.* Subjugation of demons is the power of *bodhi.* The transcendence of subject and object is the progress of *bodhi.* The transcendence of *saṁsāra* is the benefit of *bodhi.* Enlightenment is the master of *bodhi.* That which is equivalent to space is the essence of *bodhi.* Serene yet constantly functioning—this is the function of *bodhi.* The *samādhi* of the unconditioned True Characteristic—this is the realization of *bodhi.*[5]

Clearly, the *Platform Sūtra* could easily have drawn its inspiration from the *Wu fang-pien.*

The other line that bespeaks Northern School influence on the mind-verses is only found in later texts of the *Platform Sūtra.* The Tun-huang version, which is the oldest still extant, actually includes two verses attributed to Hui-neng. One of these has already been introduced:

Bodhi originally has no tree.
The mirror also has no stand.
The Buddha Nature is always clear and pure.
Where is there room for dust?

The second verse reads as follows:

The mind is the *bodhi* tree.
The body is the bright mirror's stand.
The bright mirror is originally clear and pure.
Where could there be any dust?[6]

As Hu Shih first suggested, the original author must have been unsure of which verse was better—or at least unable to discard one of his own literary creations.[7] Later editions reduce Hui-neng's contribution to a single verse, with a significantly altered third line:

Bodhi originally has no tree.
The bright mirror also has no stand.
Fundamentally there is not a single thing.
Where could dust arise?[8]

D. T. Suzuki has referred to the third line of the last verse as "the first proclamation made by Hui-neng" and "a bomb thrown into the camp of Shen-hsiu and his predecessors."[9] Considering the lateness of this version of the verse in a work that was already late in itself, Suzuki's assertion is obviously incorrect.

The following dialogues and remarks from the *Wu fang-pien* seem to be related to the third line of the last *Platform Sūtra* verse:

> The preceptor asks: What do you see (lit., what thing do you see)?
> The disciple(s) answer: *I do not see a single thing.*
> Preceptor: Viewing purity, view minutely. Use the eye of the Pure Mind to view afar without limit, without restriction. View without obstruction.
> The preceptor asks: What do you see?
> ANSWER: *I do not see a single thing.*
>
> * * *
>
> QUESTION: When viewing, what things do you view?
> [ANSWER]: *Viewing, viewing, no thing is viewed.*
> [QUESTION]: Who views?
> [ANSWER]: *The enlightened mind views.*
> Penetratingly viewing the realms of the ten directions, in purity there is not a single thing.[10]

Perhaps even more significant, the commentary on the *Fo-shuo fa-chü ching* found by Professor Tanaka includes a line that reads almost exactly like that in the later versions of the *Platform Sūtra:* "Within Suchness there originally is really not a single thing." (21:16/618) The Chinese for the critical portion of this line is *yuan-lai shih wu i wu,* which is very close to the *Platform Sūtra*'s *pen-lai wu i wu.*

In other words, the three different subjects mentioned in the *Platform Sūtra* verses, i.e., the mirror, the *bodhi* tree, and the phrase "not a single thing," are *all* antedated by analogous statements in Northern School literature. Since none of this Northern School literature manifests any indication of having been influenced by Shen-hui or any other Southern School source, the only possible conclusion is that the *Platform Sūtra* was compiled in part with deliberate use of Northern School texts and doctrines.

This conclusion must be surprising, even shocking, to those who are used to approaching the *Platform Sūtra* in traditionalistic terms. Understanding the logic and ramifications of this conclusion requires a comprehensive appreciation of the history of early Ch'an doctrinal development. Accordingly, let me first recount the phases of Northern School history, then summarize some of the developments involving other factions of Ch'an during the second half of the eighth century.

2. Phases of Northern School History

We have followed the development of early Ch'an through a number of different phases: the shadowy beginnings of Ch'an under Bodhidharma and Hui-k'o, the community at Huang-mei, Shen-hsiu's residence at Yü-ch'üan ssu, the careers of Shen-hsiu and his immediate disciples in Lo-yang and Ch'ang-an, and the later Northern School. Let us briefly review each of these phases:

1. Bodhidharma, Hui-k'o, and their followers: The records for this period are too sketchy to allow real insight into the actual contributions of these very early figures. Bodhidharma is a very shadowy character, and the extent of his involvement in the writing of the *EJSHL* is unknown. Hui-k'o is depicted in the *HKSC* with somewhat greater clarity, and he seems to have supplied the real inspiration for the next generation or two of disciples, many of whom were wandering meditation practitioners. Although no clear biographical or historical link exists between these mendicants and subsequent phases of Ch'an—the lives of Bodhidharma and Hui-k'o were of course important subjects of later hagiographical elaboration—the "two entrances" and "four practices" described in the *EJSHL* define two basic logical motifs or conceptual matrixes of religious practice shared by subsequent phases of early Ch'an.

2. The community at Huang-mei: During the half-century from 624 to 674 the Ch'an School existed as a small training community in a relatively isolated location in south-central China. That the fame of this center was great enough to draw ever-increasing numbers of students is a testament to the personal charisma of Hung-jen and the appeal of the new religious message of Ch'an. The major feature of this message was an emphasis on meditation practice. However, this phase of Ch'an left no records except those edited or written during the very end of the seventh century or beginning of the eighth century, so that religious practice at Huang-mei cannot be defined with any precision.

3. Shen-hsiu's residence at Yü-ch'üan ssu: The last quarter of the seventh century was a period of continued incubation and preparation. The sojourns of Fa-ju and Lao-an at Shao-lin ssu on Mount Sung made this monastery an important staging area for the future expansion to Lo-yang and Ch'ang-an, and Fa-ju inspired the first formulation of the "transmission of the lamp" theory of the background and identity of the Ch'an School. However, it was at Yü-ch'üan ssu that Shen-hsiu developed the basics of Northern School doctrine. Shen-hsiu's *Kuan-hsin lun (Treatise on the Contemplation of the Mind),* probably written during this period, was important for its use of "contemplative analysis" to justify the status of Ch'an as the highest expression of the Buddhist teachings and, conversely, the interpretation of traditional Buddhist texts as expressions of the teaching of "contemplating the mind."

4. The careers of Shen-hsiu and his immediate disciples in Lo-yang

and Ch'ang-an: After Shen-hsiu's grand entrance into Lo-yang in 701, he and his disciples functioned in several different capacities at the imperial court: chaplains to the members of the court and the power-holding elite, to whom they administered the bodhisattva precepts and preached on the ideal deportment of sincere Buddhists; very visible foci of the religious fervor of Empress Wu and Emperor Chung-tsung; and propagandists of a new interpretation of the Buddhist faith. The label used by Shen-hsiu during this period was that of the "East Mountain Teaching," a term he used to express his respect and indebtedness to Hung-jen. (P'u-chi also used the label "Southern School.") The apparent succession from Shen-hsiu to Lao-an and Hsuan-tse and then to P'u-chi and his fellow disciples provides unusual insight into the workings of a Chinese Buddhist School. (The ideas expounded by Shen-hsiu and his disciples during this period will be discussed in Sections 5 and 6 of this Conclusion.)

5. The later Northern School: The school's membership continued to grow until it reached its peak during the 770s. Members of the school continued to make doctrinal contributions at least until the end of the eighth century, and Northern School monks were active in spreading Ch'an to Tibet, Korea, and Japan. In Tibet, a successor to Northern School teachers named Mo-ho-yen (Mahāyāna) defended the Chinese doctrine of sudden enlightenment against the gradual teaching of the Indian pandit Kamalaśīla in a famous series of debates. The Northern School may have had some impact on the development of Buddhist doctrine in Japan, where several of the school's texts were transmitted during the ninth century. In China, the Northern School lineage continued unbroken until at least the beginning of the tenth century.

3. Other Factions of Ch'an During the Late Eighth Century

After Shen-hsiu's entry into Lo-yang, Shen-hui's campaign against the Northern School was the most significant event in Ch'an history during the eighth century. The attack was initiated in 730 and was presumably carried out more or less continuously until Shen-hui's death in 758. Modern scholars have generally accepted this campaign as the proximate cause of the decline and disappearance of the Northern School, in that Shen-hui was able to demonstrate the inherent superiority of the Southern School's sudden teaching. Although this interpretation is overly simplistic and highly inaccurate, Shen-hui's campaign did act as an important catalyst for the further growth of Ch'an Buddhism.

Shen-hui created a crisis in Ch'an by his attack on the Northern School. Not only was Shen-hui extremely personal in his criticisms of P'u-chi and Hsiang-mo Tsang and apparently self-seeking in his championing of the unknown Hui-neng, but he introduced an entirely new sense of factionalism in his use of the terms "Northern School" and "Southern School." As Professor Yanagida has pointed out, the very notion of the Southern School was predicated on the existence of the Northern School. And there *was* no Northern School until Shen-hui created the label for the purpose of his own campaign. The individuals we identify with this school were loyal to the teachings and examples of their own masters. They were dedicated to a new interpretation of Buddhism, to a unique style of religious practice, but not to any sect or dogma.

Shen-hui's campaign crystallized the growing self-awareness of the Ch'an tradition into a potentially divisive factionalism, but it did not generate any overt response from the Northern School. No mention is made of Shen-hui in any Northern School text—no criticism, no admonition, no attack. This failure to rebut Shen-hui's criticisms is indicative of the fictitious nature of the entity "Northern School." In fact, Shen-hui's criticisms were restatements of basic Ch'an ideas first elaborated by Northern School authors. Ch'eng-kuan of the Hua-yen School, for example, was unable to see any significant difference between the teachings of Northern and Southern Ch'an.[11]

Shen-hui's banishment at the instigation of an unknown official has long been touted as an indication of an angry Northern School response, but this interpretation is questionable. Instead of the doctrinal content of his sermons, the reason for the accusation against Shen-hui may have been his argumentative style of lecturing or even the mere fact that he attracted large and thus potentially dangerous assemblies. It is also significant that the four different locations in which Shen-hui spent the term of his banishment are all described as Northern School strongholds (the last of them was the K'ai-yuan ssu in Ching-chou).[12] Either the Northern School would not or could not keep him out of their territory during this period. Very probably, Shen-hui continued to disseminate his own ideas during his banishment, thus turning the apparent misfortune to his own advantage.

The crisis precipitated by Shen-hui was resolved by the Ox-head School. A few statements by late eighth-century members of this faction indicate a general interest in putting to rest the divisiveness incurred by Shen-hui's activities. The *Platform Sūtra,* which was compiled by a member of the Ox-head School, presented a brilliant solution to the problem: As I pointed out in the Introduction, this text accepted and built upon Shen-hui's positions but avoided any significant reference to Shen-hui himself. The teachings of the Ox-head School were fundamentally in agreement with those of the Northern School on the subjects of mental contemplation and the necessity of constant practice, and both schools were known for their use of contemplative analysis. The major difference between the two schools lay in the Ox-head's use of a certain logical pattern that included, at one stage, the extensive use of negation. (This distinctive proclivity to negation appears prominently in the mind-verses of the *Platform Sūtra*.) Thus it is entirely reasonable that Northern School texts were influential in the composition of the *Platform Sūtra*, as suggested at the end of Section 1 of this Conclusion.[13]

4. Institutional Reasons for the Decline of the Northern School

No matter how plausible the summary just given of early Ch'an history during the latter part of the eighth century, the question still remains: Why did the Northern School disappear? One factor of major importance was the school's close identification with the imperial court. Shen-hsiu had a large number of patrons within the extended imperial family, including Empress Wu, Emperor Chung-tsung, Emperor Jui-tsung, Empress Wei-shih, Princess T'ai-p'ing, and, to a lesser extent, the eventual Emperor Hsuan-tsung. His supporters included members of factions surrounding these figures, including descendants of old aristocratic families and newly successful bureaucratic examination candidates. After Shen-hsiu's death, though, Emperor Hsuan-tsung was to feel much closer to I-hsing than to the older P'u-chi and I-fu. The emperor was profoundly affected by I-hsing's untimely death in 727. P'u-chi and I-fu were no doubt also stigmatized to some extent by their association with Empress Wu. At about the same time, Chang Yueh's final banishment in 726 and death in 731 left Yen T'ing-chih as the Northern School's most prominent supporter. But Yen was a protege of Chang Chiu-ling, whose death in 736 and the accession to power of Li Lin-fu led to important changes in the Chinese political climate. Prominent Northern School patrons forced out of power by Li Lin-fu during the mid-740's include P'ei K'uan, Li Yung, Li Shih-chih, and Fang Kuan.[14]

Even on the basis of more general considerations, it is not difficult to understand how the Northern School's support in the capital, even at social strata less rarified than those just mentioned, could have declined. The literate courtiers of Lo-yang and Ch'ang-an were always very keen on the latest intellectual and cultural trends; thus interest in the Northern School masters and their teachings could not have been maintained for more than a few decades. In fact, although we know the names of quite a few Northern School masters prominent in the second half of the eighth century, the most highly regarded Chinese meditation masters were Fa-ch'in (714–92) of the Ox-head School and Hui-chung (d. 775), an independent figure supposedly connected with Hui-neng. Even more than Ch'an masters, however, esoteric Buddhist teachers achieved the greatest support from the imperial court during this period.

The grandeur of early Northern School history soon became a thing of the past. With the erosion of imperial power after 755, the most creative factions of Ch'an—the Ox-head School and Ma-tsu's Hung-chou School—operated primarily in the provincial centers of south-central China. Although in this respect their growth paralleled that of the East Mountain Teaching a century before, the primary identity of the Northern School was based on its former success at court. Its public image ossified around the memory of that former success, and with ossification came the impression of sycophantic superficiality. That the *Platform Sūtra* could criticize the Northern School primarily for its supposed doctrinal shallowness was a function of this impression.

In addition, the unworldliness of meditation practice rendered continued intimate association with the central political system unworkable, so that the very identification of the Northern School with the imperial court was an obstacle to the school's continued success. There are examples of this incompatibility between meditation practice and political power even prior to the advent of the Ch'an School, e.g., Nan-yueh Hui-ssu's refusal to answer the summons of meditation masters to court in 552 and the abortive nature of the endeavors to create the Yun-men ssu and Ch'an-ting ssu systems of meditation centers.[15] Examples closer to our subject include Fa-ju's flight to Mount Sung to avoid appointment to a post within the official *saṁgha* administration and Sung Chih-wen's suggestion to isolate the processes of government in Ch'ang-an from the excessive religious fervor surrounding Shen-hsiu. There are, of course, extenuating circumstances to each of these examples. However, when considered together they imply a fundamental dichotomy between the goals of Buddhist meditation, an individual spiritual enterprise most naturally suited to secluded alpine retreats, and the political requirements of government, which fostered the centralization of power and culture in such cosmopolitan urban centers as Ch'ang-an and Lo-yang.

The very sophistication of life in the two capitals may have engendered a longing for the simpler virtues of the countryside. Even so, the magnificent careers of Shen-hsiu, P'u-chi, and others were simply too well known to have remained suitable material for populist glorification after their deaths. At the beginning of the eighth century Sung Chih-wen could describe the aged Shen-hsiu as a uniquely pure spiritual being who had transcended worldly protocol, but decades later the extravagant successes of Shen-hsiu's career were more readily remembered. In the second half of the eighth century, rustic purity and unlettered brilliance were more easily attributed to the relatively unknown Hui-neng—even though Hui-neng's legendary personality was based on the model of Hung-jen. Thus, paradoxically, the very success of the Northern School and the documentation of the lives of its major figures was a cause of its own supersedure by later factions of Ch'an.

Another factor that cannot be overlooked is the relative immaturity of the Northern School's contributions to the transmission of the lamp theory. To be sure, the congruence, in broad theoretical terms, between the *CFPC* and *LCSTC* is surprising for such early members of the genre. That both these texts appeared independently at virtually the same time indicates the prevalence of the transmission idea in general. Nevertheless, the fact that this theory was still far from its final form is indicated by the numerous differences in style and approach between the two works, especially the *LCSTC*'s treatment of Guṇabhadra; the lack of precise and specific terminology for the patriarchs and the act of religious transmission; and the absence of any believable list of figures to span the gap between Śākyamuni and Bodhidharma. These problems formed the basic agenda for innovations that would appear in the second half of the eighth century.

I cannot finish this discussion without posing a second question, one that is less often asked than the first: Why should the Northern School *not* have disappeared? There is no evidence that its members took any pledge of loyalty other than a personal dedication to the bodhisattva path. Each individual's affiliation was with the Dharma and with his own master, not to some institutional entity known as the East Mountain Teaching or the Northern School. In spite of the conventions adopted in this study, these terms originally had doctrinal rather than sectarian connotations.

The best model for the operation of the Northern School is that of an extended family or clan system. The religious genealogies formulated during this period corroborate this interpretation: Each monk's identity was defined on the basis of his own set of religious ancestors, and the passage of time brought with it an inevitable splintering of the clan into smaller sublineages. Just as the Ti-lun School lineages of the late sixth century blended almost imperceptibly into their She-lun School counterparts of the early seventh, the Northern School underwent a gradual and natural transformation into subsequent phases of Ch'an. The Ox-head School and Szechwan factions also had their days, as did the Yun-men, Fa-yen, and other "houses" of the ninth and tenth centuries. If any aspect of the Northern School's institutional status was most responsible for its own decline, it was the centrifugal force naturally associated with the school's continued growth.

5. Doctrinal Ramifications of the Decline of the Northern School

Thus the Northern School's demise may have been hastened by its lack of any centralized institutional structure; after Shen-hsiu's death the centrifugal forces on the school were simply too great for it to exist as a single unit. Much the same can be said of Northern School doctrine.

Although I have attempted to indicate the basic themes of early Ch'an religious theory, I have done so in spite of the multitude of different individual slogans and doctrinal formulations found in the early texts. Even more important than this heterogeneity of expression is the fact that many statements of Northern School doctrine were designed to bridge the gap between the conventional standards of traditional Chinese Buddhism and the new approach of Ch'an. Actually, they were meant not so much to bridge a preexistent gap as to create a new one.

As the discussion of contemplative analysis in Part Two, Chapter VII, Section 6 has shown, many Northern School statements weave an entirely new fabric from the threads of conventional Buddhist terminology. Although the members of the Northern School were not scholastics, they focused their attention on explaining themselves in conventional Buddhist jargon to the highly literate members of imperial court society. Their mission was not merely to state the message of Ch'an in its simplest terms, but to present that message as the quintessential truth of Buddhism. The taint of scholasticism, indirect though it was, thus became an inescapable consequence of the Northern School's historical role.

When we consider Northern School doctrine more closely, it is easy to spot the factor that allowed the school to be caricatured as philosophically backward. This is the absence of any obvious difference between the school's doctrines of constant practice and the perfect teaching and the much more elementary notion of gradual self-perfection. According to my understanding of the *Yuan-ming lun* and other Northern School texts, the perfect teaching makes allowance for gradual progress within the context of a fundamentally more significant recognition of one's present inner perfection. The recognition of that perfection and of the ultimate nonreality of the afflictions that are attendant upon ignorance results in the initiation of a type of religious practice whose quintessential characteristic is its constancy of application.

The early Ch'an masters made frequent exhortations to constant effort, but they seem to have consistently refrained from dangling the lure of the enlightenment experience in front of their students' noses. (Shen-hui was the first and most obvious violator of this convention.) Nevertheless, when taken out of context, the exhortations to greater effort and references to the constancy of practice were easily mistaken for simple gradualism. This mistaken impression was no doubt rendered more likely by the tendency of Northern School texts to use apparently sequential or progressive forms of expression, even though the doctrines themselves were essentially nonsequential, i.e., either perfect or sudden.

Just as there was no institutional reason for the Northern School not to have disappeared, so was there no doctrinal necessity for the school to have continued any longer than it did. Previous studies of early Ch'an have tended to overemphasize the supposed conflict between the Northern and Southern schools, when in fact there is no evidence that the conflict in question was not restricted to the minds of Shen-hui and his followers. None of the works studied here indicates that the participants in the early Ch'an religious movement considered themselves bound by the doctrinal formulations of their teachers. To be sure, individual allegiances between masters and disciples existed. Nevertheless, the primary characteristic of these men was not their dedication to a transmitted dogma, but rather their willingness to innovation in doctrinal expression. The disappearance of the Northern School was thus a result of the process of innovation that it began and is no more significant than the disappearance of any other Ch'an lineage. Clearly, the various contributions of the Northern School are more important than the fact of its eventual demise.

6. The Static and Dynamic Components of Early Ch'an Doctrine

The teachings of the Northern School are best approached in terms of two metaphors, the sun obscured by clouds and the perfectly functioning mirror. A brief reexamination of these metaphors will be helpful in understanding the basic themes of early Ch'an religious philosophy.

As described in the *Hsiu-hsin yao lun* and other texts, the primary emphasis of the metaphor of the sun and clouds is that the Buddha Nature is constantly present within us. The clouds of illusion that render the Buddha Nature invisible only exist adventitiously, and their negative impact is substantially less significant than the fact of the immanence of the Buddha Nature itself. This prioritization is the basis of two different meditative techniques: visualization of the sun and concentration on the activity of the discriminative mind. In each case, the instruction is not to force the manifestation of the Buddha Nature or the destruction of ignorant mentation, but to allow these events to occur naturally. Although the student is frequently encouraged to apply all his energies to his religious practice, the specific techniques recommended are apparently designed to minimize the creation of goal-oriented dualisms.

The metaphor of the mirror is not described so concisely in any single primary text, being rather a general theoretical perspective that underlies a variety of religious propositions and practical expressions. Whereas the previous metaphor describes the state of unenlightened existence, the mirror represents the mind of the fully awakened sage: It reflects its objects perfectly, immediately, and without attachment. Similarly, the sage perceives the spiritual ills of those around him and responds spontaneously and without hesitation or attachment. The religious practices based on or best explained by this metaphorical construct include "viewing afar," in which the practitioner was to mentally simulate the expansive perceptual capacities of mirrorlike wisdom; "viewing purity," in which one's entire system of cognition, both subjective and objective, was understood to be fundamentally pure and nonsubstantial; "nonactivation," in which one was to avoid willful generation of conscious and hence dualistic impulses in favor of immediate and spontaneous response; and the "transcendence of thoughts," which refers to the realization that one's entire cognitive apparatus was not intrinsically dependent on dualistically conceived entities such as thoughts and objects of perception.

Although these two metaphors could be used to support different approaches to religious practice, they are both basically congruent with the contents of the oldest text of the Ch'an tradition, the *EJSHL (Treatise on the Two Entrances and Four Practices).* This is especially true of the metaphor of the sun and clouds, which is used in the *Hsiu-hsin yao lun* to explicate the same set of religious priorities as the "entrance of principle" of the earlier text. The specific practices and formulations of the *Wu fang-pien* cannot, on the other hand, be correlated directly with the "four practices." Nevertheless, the parallel exists in that both the *Wu fang-pien* practices and formulations and the *EJSHL*'s four practices concern the outward expression of the concept of *śūnyatā* in daily life and in the activities of teaching. Where the treatise attributed to Bodhidharma enjoins one to act in accordance with the Dharma, the *Wu fang-pien* describes an ideal spiritual state in which one is constantly receptive to sensory input but completely without the tendency to attachment or conceptualization. It should be clear that both of these texts attempt to describe the bodhisattva ideal.

What is the best means for analyzing these two metaphorical constructs? The old standard of early Ch'an studies, the distinction between sudden and gradual, is no longer appropriate. The metaphor of the mirror could be used to define a gradualistic approach to the spiritual path, but such an approach is not representative of the mainstream of Northern School thought. The concept of suddenness could apply to practices based on either metaphor, i.e., one could experience a sudden vision of the Buddha Nature or an instantaneous activation of the perfect functioning of the sage. A great deal of ink has been expended in recent years by authors who did not realize that the sudden-gradual distinction is not a valid framework for historical analysis because of its originally pejorative and propagandistic intent. This fundamental methodological error is compounded by the tendency to mistakenly interpret statements based on the underlying concepts of the metaphor of the mirror in terms of the metaphor of the sun and clouds.

If the dichotomy between sudden and gradual is not an appropriate key to the teachings of early Ch'an, what is? I would like to suggest a comparison between the two metaphors just introduced and the following: (1) the two basic components or aspects of meditation practice according to Indian Buddhism, i.e., concentration and insight *(śamatha* and *vipaśyanā),* and (2) the native Chinese distinction between essence and function *(t'i* and *yung).*

To adequately understand the relevance of *śamatha* and *vipaśyanā,* we must be aware of their relative importance and understanding in Chinese Buddhism as a whole. The translations of Kumārajīva place their emphasis almost entirely on *vipaśyanā,* correlating the realizations attained through this practice with the Perfection of Wisdom and the Mādhyamika interpretation of nonsubstantiality. This emphasis continued to prevail in the theoretically oriented tradition of Buddhism in the Southern Dynasties. The Yogācāra translations of the sixth century contained a much more balanced treatment of *śamatha* and *vipaśyanā.* This is why Seng-ch'ou, the sixth-century meditation practitioner par excellence whose training was under masters of the Yogācāra tradition, appears to be so conventional in his approach.

This newfound balance between *śamatha* and *vipaśyanā* was not solely a return to some older state, since sixth century Chinese theoreticians used the newly translated Yogācāra texts as the basis for a redefinition of *śamatha.* Whereas this term originally referred to concentration on empirical objects, mental images of the elements of reality, and the generation of positive emotions such as loving kindness and faith, now it came to mean concentration on the absolute principle of ultimate reality. Both Ching-ying Hui-yuan and T'ien-t'ai Chih-i, to name two very notable examples, include references to concentration on and insight into phenomenal objects *(shih-chih* and *shih-kuan)* as well as similar operations on matters of abstract principle *(li-chih* and *li-kuan).* This development was not unprecedented in the Buddhist meditation tradition, but Chih-i's description of the preferred abstract object of meditation ("the trichiliocosm in a single moment of consciousness," or *i-nien san-ch'ien),* is certainly infinitely more complex than the concepts of impermanence, interdependence, and so on, that are associated with traditional Hīnayāna practice.[16]

How does this development relate to the doctrines of early Ch'an? Can the two basic metaphors of Ch'an, the sun obscured by clouds and the perfectly functioning mirror, be understood as abstract interpretations of *śamatha* and *vipaśyanā,* respectively? The first metaphor would represent *śamatha,* or concentration, because its emphasis is essentially static: unfailing recognition of the primacy of the Buddha Nature and cessation of the activity of the unenlightened mind. Both of the meditation techniques described in the *Hsiu-hsin yao lun*—visualizing an image of the sun and focusing on the (eventually exhausted) activity of the discriminative mind—are immediately recognizable as concentration techniques.

According to the same approach, the metaphor of the mirror would be correlated with the concept of *vipaśyanā*. Here some reservations are necessary. The mirror is an expression of wisdom because its functions are predicated on the ability to understand and identify with the fundamental nonsubstantiality of reality. The prototypical *Wu fang-pien* formula "if the mind transcends thoughts, the mind is emancipated" can only be realized in individual religious practice if one achieves understanding of the nonsubstantiality of the mind and thoughts themselves. Although in this sense the enlightened ideal typified by the mirror is dependent on the exercise of insight *(vipaśyanā)* meditation, the mirror does not define a practical technique but rather a perfected ideal.

The two components of meditation practice, *śamatha* and *vipaśyanā,* are inextricably bound together in the earlier Buddhist tradition. *Vipaśyanā* was rarely practiced without preliminary training in *śamatha,* and each step up the ladder of *śamatha* stages was occasioned by the exercise of wisdom. The Chinese Ch'an practices centered on the two metaphors discussed here are even more closely related: The mirror, or enlightened mind, is nothing other than an activated sun, or Buddha Nature. Indeed, although I have used these symbols to represent two basic logical constructs of early Ch'an, the symbols themselves can be used in either manner. That is, if one were to emphasize the sun's function of illumination, i.e., its universal, nonselective compass and salutary efficacy, one would be using this metaphor in the dynamic sense. Much more likely in the texts themselves is the other possibility: If one focuses on the mirror's reflectivity and the obscuring influence of the dust upon its surface—the traditional interpretation of the *Platform Sūtra* verses—one would be using the metaphor of the mirror in a static (but potentially progressive) sense.

The observation that the two metaphors are interchangeable, one being a static and the other a dynamic representation of one and the same Buddha Nature or enlightened mind, leads to the comparison with the Chinese concepts of essence and function. In the practice of "maintaining [awareness of] the mind" *(shou-hsin)* the emphasis is on never forgetting the primacy of the Buddha Nature's immanence, or on allowing the discriminative mind to slow down, cease to function, and thus reveal the existence of the enlightened mind within. This experience is the "seeing the Nature" (*chien-hsing,* or *kenshō* in Japanese) discussed so widely in works on Ch'an. Although these are cathartic experiences, they are described primarily as realizations of that which *exists* rather than of that which *functions.* In descriptions of such practices and experiences, static images predominate. The illuminative power of the sun is granted, but it is not analyzed.

Judging from the *Wu fang-pien*'s position that the enlightened mind should be in control of the senses, rather than vice versa, it should be obvious that the metaphor of the mirror is a dynamic version of the static image of the sun and clouds. In addition to the practices enumerated earlier, the probable Northern School use of a prototypical form of encounter dialogue and the "expedient means" of interaction between master and student may be correlated with this more dynamic emphasis.

Of the two logical constructs discussed here, the emphasis on essence *(t'i)* was more widely accepted by members of the early Ch'an School, as indicated by the popularity of the *Hsiu-hsin yao lun* and the ideas it contained. At least, the ideas of the Buddha Nature and the ultimate identity of the Pure Mind within all sentient beings were widely used in the introductory training manuals of early Ch'an.

Although the specific formulation of the function *(yung)* of enlightenment described in Part Two, Chapter VII of this study was not so widely accepted as the general understanding of the Buddha Nature and the illusions that obscure it, this area of speculation was in some ways more important than the other. It would of course be impossible to prove that any one specific doctrine of the operation of the enlightened mind was generally accepted by the followers of early Ch'an. The incredible variety of slogans and formulae that occur in the literature would prohibit the isolation of such a single interpretation. Although I have attempted to explain the basic elements of the Northern School position, one of the most important aspects of the teachings of this phase of Ch'an is their very heterogeneity. The specific formulations of the Northern School texts were often absent from later texts, but it is clear that the creative energy of early Ch'an was directed primarily at the elucidation of the more dynamic aspects of the doctrine.

The Northern School set a precedent for subsequent phases of Ch'an in its emphasis on the dynamic aspects of religious practice. The growing interest in the problems of religious trainees, rather than in the doctrinal pronouncements of gifted individuals; the apparent use of a kind of intimate religious dialogue and interaction between teachers and students; the oft-mentioned ability of teachers to intuit and respond to the underlying needs of their students; and even the emphasis of the *Yuan-ming lun* and *Wu fang-pien* on the benefit of other sentient beings—all these are evidence of the Ch'an School's movement away from meditation as trancelike contemplation and toward the practice of meditation in all phases of daily life.

7. Final Reflections on the Northern School and the Study of Ch'an

I hope that this study of the Northern School and the formation of early Ch'an will have two types of impact on subsequent research. First, there should be a more sophisticated appreciation of doctrinal and historical interrelationships in the development of Chinese Ch'an Buddhism. We must discard the old stereotypes of gradualism versus subitism, North versus South, and the *Laṇkāvatāra Sūtra* versus the *Diamond Sūtra*. In their place must be a deeper understanding of the contributions made by men who were not necessarily lionized by the orthodox tradition of Ch'an, as well as greater attention to innovations contained in texts that were not necessarily cherished within the most popular canons of the school. Although this study has been devoted to the Northern School, I believe its findings require a reevaluation of the Southern School as well. Presumably, future work will refine, modify, or even refute some of the conclusions of this research, but I hope to have outlined the most basic aspects of the historical and doctrinal development of early Chinese Ch'an.

Without question, the next major issue in Ch'an studies is the examination of the transition from early Ch'an to the classical style of practice exemplified by Ma-tsu Tao-i (709–88) and his Hung-chou School. In spite of the major stylistic differences between early Ch'an and Hung-chou School texts, the present research may be useful in understanding the encounter dialogue practiced by Ma-tsu and his students. Another obvious future task is the comparison between Northern School doctrine and the theories of the Japanese Zen master Dōgen, which emphasize similar concepts of inherent enlightenment and the constancy of religious practice.

Although the recognition of the Northern School's role in the development of Ch'an Buddhism should thus foster new vistas in research, the second area of potential impact of this study is actually the more important one: a greater awareness of the obligation to approach the study of Ch'an in a methodologically more sophisticated fashion. No matter what the specific topic within Ch'an studies, we must strive to understand the contribution and relative significance of four categories of data: history, legend, doctrine, and propaganda. Each of these four has its own distinctive value, confusion regarding which has led to gross distortions in the understanding of our subject by previous scholars.

On the most basic level, we must learn to avoid the uncritical acceptance of Ch'an legends as historical accounts. With the increased sophistication that has been achieved in the past several decades—chiefly through the prodigious and meticulous efforts of Japanese scholars—this would not seem to be that great a problem. Nevertheless, the recent work of many scholars is still hampered by the unconscious acceptance of traditional accounts and images. For example, scholars have long known that the Northern School did not teach a simple gradualism, but this traditional position continues to creep into scholarly writings on the subject, as if the actual teachings of the inferior schools did not really matter. Doctrinal pronouncements cannot be immediately accepted at face value, but must be analyzed in terms of any polemical or propagandistic intent. We should pay close attention to our own presuppositions and examine where we are unconsciously adopting the originally propagandistic positions of the orthodox tradition. In addition, in order to truly understand doctrinal interrelationships, we must consider not only the individual terms of doctrinal propositions, but also their logical configurations.

We should also be careful to avoid the tendency to use modern scholarly techniques to generate a more accurate rendition of the orthodox version of the Ch'an tradition. We must recognize when the available data is either not sufficient or not conducive to historical analysis and refrain from misrepresenting our sources to satisfy a desire for completeness. In other words, we should avoid the distorting influence of the "string of pearls" approach to Ch'an studies. Scholarship that too clearly echoes the contour of the orthodox tradition is not likely to be analytically reliable, let alone innovative or inspired.

On a more sophisticated level, we must be prepared to examine the dynamics of the Ch'an legends themselves. A great deal of work has already been done in this area, e.g., studies in the development of legends concerning Bodhidharma and the variant lists of Indian patriarchs connected with the transmission of the lamp theory. Concerning Bodhidharma, it would be quite easy to argue that his actual historical role in the creation of the Ch'an School was far less significant than his role as a legendary model. In fact, the few details known about him were not recorded for their historical value in modern terms, but as part of the early legend. The same is even more true of Hui-neng: Whereas Hui-neng's actual biography and historical role are almost entirely unknown, his legendary image was extremely important in the development of Ch'an. These are actually only the most prominent examples; virtually all of our data was compiled for purposes different from our own.

I have taken a rather simplistic approach to the analysis of early Ch'an in this study due to the lack of sophistication of most English-language works on the subject, but I hope that future studies will be spared this requirement. That is, at this point it has been necessary to distinguish between history and legend and between doctrine and propaganda. Future studies will hopefully be able to assume a greater understanding of these distinctions on the part of the reader and should thus be able to consider the different types, uses, and implications of legends, for example. Obviously, a clear sense of historical detail is necessary to avoid the vagueness, sweeping generalities, and inconsistencies of past work.

With regard to doctrine, in this study I have suggested two basic motifs or conceptual matrixes that may be useful in the future as templates for the evaluation of other Ch'an and Zen doctrines. One possibly fruitful area of inquiry is the relationship between these two basic motifs of early Ch'an thought and the subsequent distinction between "silent illumination" (*mo-chao,* or *mokushō* in Japanese) and the "contemplation of topics" *(k'an-hua,* or *kanna)* in later Ch'an. In addition, I look forward to the possibility that other scholars might evaluate the relationship between these conceptual matrixes and both Indian Buddhist doctrine and traditional Chinese philosophy, subjects that I have intentionally avoided due to considerations of space.

The use of the two conceptual matrixes has been expedient at this stage of study. In order to proceed further, we will have to consider the ways in which they fail to adequately represent the contents of the original texts. Is there any better set of organizing principles for understanding early Ch'an doctrine, i.e., an analytic approach that is somehow more accurate, more comprehensive, and more productive of useful insights? Or is it possible to achieve some of these goals while at the same time reducing the weight and extent of the interpretive framework, which tends to separate us from and color our encounter with the original texts? Since learning often involves the formulation, application, modification, and replacement of analytical theories, the process of scholarship will be well served by considering these questions. The process of inquiry will no doubt lead to greater insight and is clearly more important than the specific theories involved.

Appendix

Annals of the Transmission of the Dharma-treasure
(Ch'üan fa-pao chi, or *CFPC)*[1]

COMPILED BY TU FEI, STYLED FANG-MING, OF CH'ANG-AN

A. I prostrate myself to the spiritual compatriots who have had me safeguard my fundamental mind which is itself like the pearl that, though immersed in muddy water, suddenly appears clearly through its own power.

B. Preface: The True *Dharmakāya* [that is within all of] us is something that is perceived by the *Dharma*[*kāya*] Buddha and that transcends the oral and written teachings of the *Nirmāṇa*[*kāya*] Buddhas. Therefore, this teaching of the absolute can only be transmitted on the basis of [the disciple's] own enlightenment and realization of the [fundamental] mind. Therefore, the *Treatise* [*on the Awakening of Faith*] says:

> All the *dharma*s fundamentally transcend the characteristics of mentation and are ultimately universally "same" *(p'ing-teng),* being unchanging and indestructible. They are none other than the one mind [possessed of all sentient beings], which is thus called Suchness *(chen-ju).*

[The same treatise] also says:

> The *bodhicitta* of realization (i.e., that which occurs after realization of Suchness) obtains from the stage of the Pure Mind through the ultimate [stage] (i.e., throughout all the ten stages of the bodhisattva's progress). What realm is it that is realized? It is Suchness. Although this is described as a realm on the basis of the "transforming consciousness" (*ch'üan-shih,* i.e., the subjective aspect of the mind), this realization is actually without any "realm." It is simply the wisdom of Suchness, being called the *dharmakāya.*[2]

Also, as the [*Laṇkāvatāra*] *Sūtra* says:

> The bodhisattva, the great being, secludes himself in a quiet place for his own self-realization and the examination [of reality]. Not depending on any method other [than the One Vehicle], he transcends views and false thoughts and makes regular progress and advancement until he enters the stage of *tathāgata*. This is called [the characteristic of] the sagely wisdom of self-realization.[3]

Therefore, without achieving [realization according to] the Supreme Vehicle and transmission of the "mind-ground," how could anyone possibly enter into the True Realm?

C. The preface to the *Meditation Sūtra (Ch'an-ching hsü)* by [Hui]-yuan, the former worthy of Mount Lu, says: "The Buddha transmitted [the True Teaching] to Ānanda, Ānanda transmitted it to Madhyāntika, and Madhyāntika transmitted it to Śāṇavāsa."[4] After this [the teaching] did not fail to be transmitted on, but was maintained by the appropriate persons. This was the ultimate [state of affairs]! How could those who cling to cause and effect [in their understanding of spiritual practice] and those who research the literal meaning [of the scriptures] possibly gain entrance [to this teaching]?

Therefore, the [*Laṇkāvatāra*] *Sūtra* describes the "penetration of the teaching" *(tsung-t'ung)* as being dependent on one's own experience and advancement toward the stage of realization of the remainderless realm (i.e., nirvāṇa).[5] It completely transcends the false thoughts [incurred by] verbal and written [explanations of Buddhism], as well as all the [various] forms of false understanding. It defeats all the non-Buddhist [teachings] and the many demons [of temptation]. That which leads one toward the radiant generation of the illumination [of wisdom] based on one's own realization is called the "penetration of the teaching." This, the ultimate stage [of Buddhist endeavor], is not attainable on the basis of logical explanation. This is the truth!

It was Bodhidharma who appeared [as a sage] in India and came to this country. At that time there were men of superior wisdom in China, so that [Bodhidharma's teaching might be said to have been like] the indication of the True Realm in silent transmission, or the causation of the prodigal son's sudden return home, or the ignition of a great, bright torch in a dark room. [Even so, his teaching was something that] could not possibly be described. Afterwards, however, since human dispositions differ, there were few men of towering excellence. [Those interested in Buddhism merely] toyed with what they had already learned without seeking for superior wisdom, so that those who radically changed their lives to accept [Bodhidharma's teaching] were few indeed. Only Hui-k'o of the Eastern Wei was willing to risk his own life in search of [the teaching].

The Great Master [Bodhidharma] transmitted it to [Hui-k'o] and left [to return to India]. Hui-k'o transmitted it to Seng-ts'an, Seng-ts'an transmitted it to Tao-hsin, Tao-hsin transmitted it to Hung-jen, Hung-jen transmitted it to Fa-ju, and Fa-ju ceded it to Ta-t'ung (i.e., Shen-hsiu). From Bodhidharma onward, teacher and disciple alike made effective use of expedient means to induce realization of [the nature of the fundamental] mind. In their [activities of] guiding and teaching [sentient beings, these men] spoke only as appropriate to the situation, avoiding complicated explanations. At present there is a text in circulation known as the *Treatise of Bodhidharma (Ta-mo lun)*.[6] This is presumably [the work of] some earlier student(s) who wrote down what they heard and treasured it as an authentic treatise [of Bodhidharma's]. Nonetheless, it is replete with error.

D. This transcendent enlightenment is transmitted by the mind [in a process that] cannot be described. What spoken or written words could possibly apply? For those who have not perceived the Ultimate, we must point at the small in order to illuminate the large. For example, even in the refinement of cinnabar [as a means of achieving immortality], one must obtain the personal instruction of an immortal in order to create [real] cinnabar. Although one may be able to ascend heaven in broad daylight [by this method], if one relies [only] on the blue words of the jade-[encrusted] books, [one's efforts] will ultimately come to naught. This is merely one conditioned activity of this world, and even here [personal instruction is absolutely] necessary. How much more so the unsurpassable, true teaching [of Bodhidharma]—how could it possibly be explained in words?

Because this teaching is subtle and mysterious, it is only rarely mastered. Although the Dharma does not depend on men and the Truth does not depend on words, how could I, [Tu Fei,] be content just to know of these spiritual compatriots? If it were not for the guidance of these perfect ones, it would be difficult to identify [the content of this teaching]. I believe that in the future, spiritual awakening will in some cases be based on the adoration [of former worthies].

Therefore, I have now prepared these brief annals of the transmission of the Dharma from Bodhidharma onward, which follow here [under the title] *Annals of the Transmission of the* [*Dharma*]*-treasure,* in one fascicle.[7] I will do no more than thread together [details of these masters'] celebrated feats and places of teaching [to the extent that these] were witnessed by people or described in writing. [These masters] being united with the unconditioned and having very simple biographies, it will be impossible to explicitly verbalize their enlightenment to the sagely teaching. In addition, there are [lineage] diagrams (?) that were utilized in compiling these annals. [There are those who,] after [achieving enlightenment,] transmit this teaching, being at peace within the *dharmadhātu,* serenely located within True Nonsubstantiality *(chen-k'ung),* their "form and traces" vanishing naturally. Since they live an [apparently] normal life, without displaying anything strange or wondrous, [their cases] have been omitted here. [This omission makes me so sad that] I hold my sleeve to my eyes [to wipe away the tears] but still cannot dry my face.

From the time of Bodhidharma until the Sui and T'ang Dynasties, there have been those whose exalted enlightenment lifted them mysteriously [beyond their contemporaries]. What age is without those who achieve a profound [mastery] of the perfect and sudden? However, since they are not involved in the lineal transmission [of this teaching], their biographies are recorded elsewhere. [The existence of such biographies] illustrates the fact that there are many masters of this teaching.

E. Shih P'u-t'i-ta-mo (Bodhidharma) of Shao-lin ssu on Mount Sung, of the Eastern Wei [Dynasty]

Shih Hui-k'o of Shao-lin ssu on Mount Sung, of the Northern Ch'i

Shih Seng-ts'an of Mount Huan-kung, of the Sui

Shih Tao-hsin of Tung-shan ssu on Mount Shuang-feng, of the T'ang

Shih Hung-jen of Tung-shan ssu on Mount Shuang-feng, of the T'ang

Shih Fa-ju of Shao-lin ssu on Mount Sung, of the T'ang

Shih Shen-hsiu of Yü-ch'üan ssu in Tang-yang, of the T'ang

F. Shih P'u-t'i-ta-mo (Bodhidharma) was the offspring of a great brahmin [family], the third son of the king of a principality in southern India.[8] Having great natural insight, he [achieved] the transcendent enlightenment and [received] transmission of the great Dharma-treasure. He utilized his own sagely wisdom to [help] many human and heavenly beings open themselves to the functional wisdom of buddhahood [that is innate to all sentient beings].

In order [to help] us Chinese, he traversed the ocean and came to Mount Sung. At the time few people knew of him, and only Tao-yü and Hui-k'o, who discovered [in Bodhidharma the answer to their most] intimate, long-held aspirations, sought [his teaching] in complete earnest. They studied under him for six years in order to achieve enlightenment.

Once [after those six years of training] the master (i.e., Bodhidharma) quietly said: "Would you give up your life [in order to receive] the Dharma?" Hui-k'o then cut off his arm to prove his sincerity. *(Another text says that [Hui-k'o's] arm was cut off by bandits. This is presumably a false version [that was circulated] at one time.)*[9] Only after this did [Bodhidharma teach Hui-k'o] personally with a revelation [of the Dharma that involved the use of] expedient means. *(The expedient means that are used to bring about awakening are entirely [within the domain] of the secret interaction* (yung) *between master and disciple. Therefore, they cannot be described.)* [Bodhidharma] suddenly caused [Hui-k'o's] mind to enter directly into the *dharmadhātu.*

Four or five years later, after searching for textual corroboration [of his teachings, Bodhidharma] gave [Hui]-k'o the *Laṇkāvatāra Sūtra* and said: "According to my observation of the teaching of Buddhism [here] in China, this sūtra is the only one that is appropriate." Having some students who were not ready [to achieve enlightenment, Bodhidharma] personally transmitted [the sūtra] (i.e., explained it) several times, saying: "This will form the basis for [enlightenment] in the future." *(Another text refers to "wall contemplation"* (pi-kuan) *and the "four practices"* (ssu-hsing), *which were presumably partial, provisional teachings used at one time. These may have been recorded by followers [of Bodhidharma], but they are not his ultimate doctrines.)*

G. Thereafter, the number of [Bodhidharma's] students grew day by day, [so that] the famous monk(s) of that time were deeply jealous of him. Long unable to satisfy their [evil] intentions, they eventually were able to poison his food. *(The names of these evil person(s) are well known. Since [it is not my purpose to] expose the transgressions of others, it seems best to [leave the details] secret. On the other hand, it might be better to reveal the details on behalf of a more complete understanding of [what transpired]—I am not quite sure.)* The master ate [the food] knowingly, but the poison did not harm him. He was fed poison many times after this.

[Bodhidharma] said to Hui-k'o: "I came [to China] on behalf of the Dharma, which I have transmitted to you. There is no use in my staying here any longer, so I am going to go." He then assembled his students and explained the Ultimate Teaching once more, after which he ate the poisoned food in order to manifest the transformation [of death]. *(In the transmissions [of the teaching] after this, [the master] always explains the True Teaching one more time just before his death. [Bodhidharma's action] thus became the model for later [practice].)*

[Bodhidharma] once said that he was 150 years old. On the day [of his death] Sung-yun, the emissary of the Eastern Wei, was returning from the West and met the master at [the border outpost of] Ts'ung-ling. [Bodhidharma], who was returning to the West, said: "Your country's ruler died today." [Sung]-yün then asked the master what would happen to his own teaching. He replied: "Forty years (i.e., one generation) from now there will be a Chinese monk who will disseminate and transmit it." When [Bodhidharma's] students heard this, they opened up and examined his [grave], only to find an empty coffin.

H. Shih Seng-k'o, also called Hui-k'o, was from Wu-lao (Ssu-shui hsien, Honan). His lay surname was Chi. In his youth he was a Confucian and studied widely, especially in the [*Book of*] *Odes* and the [*Book of*] *Changes.* He left home [to become a Buddhist monk] when he realized that the secular classics did not contain the ultimate teachings. At age forty he met Master [Bodhi]dharma and [undertook] a profound quest for the ultimate enlightenment. He labored vigorously and sincerely for six years, always with the singleminded zeal of the beginning student.

[At one time] the master said: "Would you be willing to give your life for the Dharma?" [Hui-k'o] then cut off his own left arm. There was no change in his countenance—even [in spite of the pain], his determination [to gain the truth] remained. Realizing that [Hui-k'o] was fit to hear the teaching, the master divulged it to him through the use of expedient means. Thus did [Hui-k'o's] mind enter directly into the *dharmadhātu.* After four or five years of supreme effort [Hui-k'o's] understanding was complete. After the master manifested his return to the West, [Hui-k'o] took up residence at Shao-lin ssu.

During all his activities [Hui-k'o's] mind remained united with the True Realm. He taught Buddhism as the situation arose, like an echo responding to a sound (i.e., teaching exactly according to students' needs). His interaction with others served to point out the truth [of the teachings], his own actions inspiring understanding in others. Therefore, some of his students secretly made a record [of his teachings and activities].

Later, during the T'ien-p'ing period of the Wei [Dynasty, or 534–38, Hui-k'o] wandered around Yeh, [the capital, and the surrounding area of] Wei[10] teaching Buddhism to many people. There were monks who secretly poisoned Hui-k'o because of their deep envy of him, but the poison was unable to harm him, even though he knowingly ate it. At that time [his students included] Layman Hsiang and Ch'an Masters Hua and Liao, all of whom had achieved [understanding of] the Fundamental Mind through [Hui-k'o's guidance] and were laboring on behalf of Buddhism. After [Hui-k'o's move to Yeh] the number of his students grew steadily, and those who achieved enlightenment [under his guidance] were extremely numerous.

At the time of his death [Hui-k'o] said to his disciple Seng-ts'an: "I have received the transmission in a manner befitting the Dharma. I now bequeath it to you, so that you may help many people achieve their own salvation." He also personally transmitted the *Laṅkāvatāra Sūtra* to people, saying with a sigh: "After four generations [the study of] this scripture will become quite superficial. How unfortunate!"[11]

I. Shih Seng-ts'an's place of birth is unknown. In his studies under Ch'an Master [Hui]-k'o, he was able to become enlightened to the perfect and sudden and developed into [one of Hui-k'o's] most trusted students. Later, during the persecution of Buddhism [ordered by Emperor] Wu of the Chou [Dynasty, Seng-ts'an] passed more than ten years as a mountain hermit.

At the beginning of the K'ai-huang [period of the Sui Dynasty, 581–600, Seng-ts'an] and his fellow student, Ch'an Master Ting, [moved their place of] hermitage to Mount Huan-kung. *(This is in Shu-chou (Ch'ien-shan hsien, Anhwei), also being called Mount Ssu-k'ung.)* Previously there had been many ferocious beasts on this mountain that always attacked anyone who lived there, but they all left the area after [Seng]-ts'an's arrival. On the western foot of the mountain lived one Ch'an Master Pao-yueh. He had lived there for a long time and was known as a holy monk. As soon as he heard that [Seng]-ts'an had taken up residence there, [Pao-yueh] came to see him with all the joy of an old [friend]. [Pao]-yueh was the teacher of Ch'an Master [Chih]-yen.[12]

[Seng]-ts'an's own profound understanding [of the Dharma] grew every day on the basis of his *dhyāna* and *prajñā,* which were equally coalesced [in his own practice]. When his teaching activities came to their natural end, he turned to his disciple Tao-hsin and said: "The Dharma has been transmitted from Patriarch [Bodhi]dharma to me. I am going to the South and will leave you [here] to spread and protect [the Dharma]." He then explained the Ultimate Principle again, after which he retired to the South along with [Ch'an Master] Ting. No one ever knew where he ended up.

J. Shih Tao-hsin was from Ho-nei (Ch'in-yang hsien, Honan) and of the surname Ssu-ma. He left home [to become a monk] at age seven. Although his teacher was unrefined [in his own behavior, Tao]-hsin secretly maintained [his own standards of moral] purity for six years without the teacher ever knowing about it. During the K'ai-huang [period, 581–600,] he went to Mount Huan-[kung] and accepted *Dhyāna* Master [Seng]-ts'an as his teacher. He labored as diligently as he possibly could, [so that his wisdom] illuminated everything.

After eight or nine years [Seng]-ts'an went to [Mount] Lo-fu (Tseng-ch'eng hsien, Kwangtung), and [Tao]-hsin wanted to go along. [Seng]-ts'an said: "You shall remain [here] so that you might benefit many [sentient beings]." [Tao-hsin] thus wandered around teaching and was highly regarded wherever he went.

At the time of the official ordinations of the Ta-yeh [period in 607, Tao-hsin] took up residence at Chi-chou ssu (Chi-an hsien, Kiangsu). During the chaos surrounding the end of the Sui [Dynasty], rebels surrounded the city. After more than seventy days [of siege] the wells [within the city] all went dry, but when [Tao]-hsin arrived from elsewhere, water flowed in abundance once again. The local magistrate prostrated himself [before Tao-hsin and] inquired as to when the rebels might leave. [Tao-hsin replied: "If everyone] merely recites the [*Perfection of*] *Wisdom* [*Sūtra*], then there will be nothing to worry about." When [the people so chanted], the rebels saw giant soldiers all around them, [which caused them all to] retreat pell mell, so that the city was saved.

K. In the seventh year of the Wu-te [period, 624, Tao-hsin] went to Mount Shuang-feng in Ch'i-chou (Huang-mei hsien, Hupeh). When he saw [the beauty of] its forests and valleys, he decided to make it his residence for the rest of his life. He stayed there for [almost] thirty years, teaching the great Dharma [to a multitude of] followers. Fa-hsien of Ching-chou (Chiang-ling hsien, Hupeh) and Shan-fu of Ch'ang-chou (Pi-ling hsien, Kiangsu) both "faced north" to receive the teaching. [Tao]-hsin said: "Shan-fu has the temperament of a *pratyekabuddha* and will never be able to hear the great teaching."

[Tao-hsin] always exhorted his students by saying: "Make effort and be diligent in your sitting [meditation], for sitting is the fundamental [part of your training]. If you can do so for three or five years, getting a mouthful of food to stave off starvation and illness (lit., "boils"), then just close your doors and sit! Do not read the sūtras or talk to anyone. If you can do this, then sooner or later it will be of use. To strive for [enlightenment] while sitting [as diligently] as a monkey trying to get the meat out of a chestnut—such persons are very rare!"

In the eighth month of the second year of the Yung-hui [period, 651, Tao-hsin] ordered his disciples to build his crypt. Realizing that he was about to die, his students began to argue excitedly, each vying with the other for the transmission of the Dharma. When they asked him who would receive [the transmission, Tao]-hsin paused and said with a sigh: "Hung-jen is a bit better [than any of the others]." He then instructed [Hung-jen on the obligations of] the transmission and once again explained the abstruse principle. When he heard that his crypt was ready, he sat [in meditation position] and died peacefully. At the moment [of his passing into nirvāṇa] the earth shook mightily and mists arose all around. He was seventy-two years old.

On the eighth day of the fourth month (i.e., the same day as the Buddha's *parinirvāṇa*) of the following year the stone doors [of his crypt] opened by themselves to reveal that his countenance looked just as dignified as it had been in life. His students then wrapped [his body] with lacquered cloth and left the doors of the vault open. They cut a stele and had it inscribed with a eulogy written by the Secretariat Director *(chung-shu-ling)* Tu Cheng-lun.

L. Shih Hung-jen was from Huang-mei (Huang-mei hsien, Hupeh) and of the lay surname Chou. He left home [to become a monk] at a young age, becoming a student of *Dhyāna* Master [Tao]-hsin at age twelve. He was quiet and withdrawn by nature, so that even though his fellow students often made fun of him, he always kept silent and never responded. He was always diligent at menial labor, thus physically humbling himself before other people. [Tao]-hsin thought especially highly of him. He mixed in among the common servants during the day and sat in meditation all night long. He kept this up year after year without ever getting tired.

[Tao]-hsin always guided [Hung-jen] with care, so that [the student] became discerningly enlightened himself. Although he never looked at the Buddhist scriptures, he understood everything he heard. Because of his reputation, after he received the transmission the number of noblemen who gathered around him doubled every day. After a little more than ten years, eight or nine of every ten ordained and lay aspirants in the country had studied under him. No one had ever reached more [students] than this, ever since the *dhyāna* masters transmitted [the teaching] to China.

Uninterested in general pronouncements [about Buddhism, Hung-jen] observed the propriety of his students' [practice] and responded spontaneously, as an echo [follows a sound. His teaching] always proved to be mysteriously and profoundly effective.

During the eighth month of the second year of the Shang-yuan [period, 675, Hung-jen] showed increasing signs of infirmity. On the eighteenth day [of that month], having already transmitted [the teaching] personally to his disciple Fa-ju, [he realized that any final] explication [of the teaching would be] exactly the same as that which had been received by [Fa]-ju. Therefore he said nothing but died quietly while sitting. He was seventy-four years old.

M. Shih Fa-ju was from Shang-tang (Ch'ang-chih hsien, Shansi) and of the surname Wang. In his youth he accompanied his maternal uncle when the latter was given an official post in Li-yang (Li hsien, Hunan). In this way [Fa-ju was able to meet and] become a student of Ch'ing-pu ("Blue-robed") Ming. [Fa-ju] left home [to become a monk] at age nineteen, after which he made extensive studies in the Buddhist scriptures and traveled to [the various famous] locations in his quest for enlightenment. As soon as he heard that *Dhyāna* Master [Hung]-jen of Mount Shuang-feng had activated the functional wisdom of a buddha [latent within all sentient beings, Fa-ju] went and became his student. He purified himself diligently for sixteen years, until [his wisdom] perfectly illuminated the *dharmadhātu.*

Once [Fa-ju was on a] riverboat that capsized. He was carried downstream for several *li,* but his mind became neither agitated nor confused. When he was pulled out [of the river], his expression was the same as always.

After receiving personal transmission of the Dharma, [Fa-ju] taught Buddhism in various places. At the time of the official ordinations in commemoration of [Emperor] Kao-tsung's death [in 683], the *saṁgha* recommended him for appointment in the [official *saṁgha*] administration. [He avoided this by] going to Shao-lin ssu on Mount Sung, where he stayed for several years without anyone knowing [who he was]. After [his identity and/or accomplishments were discovered], those who sought the benefit of his illuminating [wisdom] arrived daily, but he rigidly excused himself [from all such entreaties].

During the Ch'ui-kung [period, 685–88], the famous worthy of the capital Hui-tuan[13] and others all went to Shao-lin and repeatedly asked [Fa-ju] to preach the Dharma. Unable to decline [any longer], he revealed the great expedient means in the manner established in the [previous generations of] master and disciple. He caused [his listeners'] minds to enter directly [into the *dharmadhātu*] without any extraneous instructions.

[Fa-ju] was simple and direct by nature and merely responded to people in such a way that, even if he reprimanded someone, it was "like [one's own boat] being struck by an empty boat." Hence no one ever resented him. His students grew in number day by day, coming from over a thousand *li* away.

In the seventh month of the first year of the Yung-ch'ang [period, 689], he commanded his students to quickly ask all the questions they might have, after which he manifested the signs of illness. One evening while sitting in meditation under a tree he addressed his students with his final instructions. [His students were] thereby able to activate the radiant wisdom [present within themselves, since it had] thus been properly transmitted to them. He also said: "After [my death] you should go study under *Dhyāna* Master Shen-hsiu of Yü-ch'üan ssu in Ching-chou." He then died serenely in sitting position. He was fifty-two years old.

N. Shen-hsiu was from Ta-liang (Shang-ch'iu hsien, Honan) and of the lay surname Li. He was exceptionally bright as a child and showed his great virtue by not being especially interested in [the usual children's] games. He was thirteen when the rebellion of Wang Shih-ch'ung occurred [in 618]. Because of the famines and epidemics that [spread over] Ho-nei and Shan-tung, [Shen-hsiu] went to the public [emergency] storehouses at Ying-yang (west of modern K'ai-feng) to petition [for the distribution] of grain [to the populace. While doing so he] met a spiritual compatriot and left home [to become a monk].

[Shen-hsiu] then traveled around the Tung-wu [region] (modern Kiangsu and Chekiang), then turned [south] to Min (Fukkien). He visited the famous mountains—Lo-fu, Tung (Shang-yü hsien, Chekiang), Meng (Hsiang-shan hsien, Chekiang), [T'ien]-t'ai (T'ien-t'ai hsien, Chekiang), and Lu (Chiu-chiang hsien, Kiangsi)—not missing a single [well-known] hermitage. His studies were done in breadth and earnest, including the *[Book of] Changes,* the [teachings of] the Yellow [Emperor] and Lao-[tzu] *(Huang-Lao),* and the Buddhist scriptures and biographies. From the philosophies of the three ancient ages there was nothing he did not learn completely. He took the full precepts at age twenty, after which he [applied his] insightful determination [to the mastery of] the rules of deportment of the *Vinaya* and the gradualistic cultivation of meditation and wisdom.

When he was forty-six [years old, Shen-hsiu] went to East Mountain to become a student of *Dhyāna* Master [Hung]-jen. [The master] realized his worth at a single glance. He taught [Shen-hsiu] for several years, guiding him to entrance into the True Realm so that his realization [enabled him to] know all.

Later, following his banishment, [Shen-hsiu] assumed secular garb to hide his identity. He lived for more than ten years at T'ien-chü ssu in Ching-chou without anyone knowing who he was. During the I-feng [period, 676–79,] several tens of very meritorious [monks] of Ching-ch'u (the general area of Hupeh and Hunan) petitioned that he be given official ordination and made to reside at Yü-ch'üan ssu in Tang-yang (Tang-yang hsien, Hupeh).

When *Dhyāna* Master [Hung]-jen died, [Shen-hsiu] said: "There is a previous transmission." Therefore he did not transmit the Dharma for over ten years. After *Dhyāna* Master [Fa]-ju's death, students did not consider even ten thousand *li* too far to come to "take refuge" at his Dharma platform. He therefore began to teach and was able to help many [students achieve their] salvation by responding to their needs. All the spiritual aspirants in the whole country came to study under him.

O. During the Chiu-shih period, [700, Empress Wu] Tse-t'ien dispatched a palace messenger to welcome [Shen-hsiu] to Lo-yang. [When he arrived], laymen and monks scattered flowers [in his path], and the sunshades and banners [of the people's vehicles] overflowed the road. [Shen-hsiu] entered [the palace] on a palanquin shaded with palm fronds, followed by [Empress Wu who,] having purified herself in mind and body, bowed her head to the floor and knelt to wait upon [the master. Shen-hsiu] administered the [bodhisattva] precepts to the palace ladies. All the people of the four directions revered him as they did their own parents—from the princes and officials on down, everyone alike took refuge in him. [Emperor Chung-tsung] Hsiao-ho repeatedly sought [the teachings from him, but even so Shen-hsiu wished to] return home [to Yü-ch'üan ssu]. Because of the emperor's firm requests, [Shen-hsiu] never was able to return home.

Through their own private observations, [Shen-hsiu's] disciples realized that he was about to die. A secret transmission [of the teaching took place] at a certain time.[14] On the twenty-eighth day of the second month of the second year of Shen-lung, (706,) he died peacefully while sitting upright at T'ien-kung ssu in Lo-yang. [His remains] were returned to Yü-ch'üan [ssu], where a stūpa was built. Out of respect for a teacher who valued the Way, no one had ever asked his age. However, since he left home [to become a monk] at the end of the Sui, he must have been over a hundred years old.

When he was living at his monastery at Yü-ch'üan [ssu] in Tang-yang, he once said to his disciples: "After I die, you should bury me here." A few days before he died, scores of white lotus blossoms sprang up on the flat area surrounding where he wanted his stūpa to be built. Afterwards, the oak tree in front of the stūpa produced several fruit that were as flavorful as plums. [Emperor Chung-tsung] Hsiao-ho established the site of the stūpa as Tu-men ssu and bestowed the title of Preceptor Ta-t'ung. [Emperor] Jui-tsung also donated thirty thousand cash for [temple] construction.

P. Comment: This world is the world of words! Therefore, the sages cannot but use words to lead us to the realm where there are no words. For this reason our fundamental teacher [Śākyamuni Buddha] said: "To say that there is a teaching that the *Tathāgata* has preached is to defame the Buddha." Confucius also said: "I will not talk." And Chuang-tzu said: "Once you've got the meaning, you can forget the words."[15] Therefore, the *Book of Changes* says about the divided top line of the hexagram *hsien:* "Responding to chin, cheeks, and tongue." The *Hsiang* [commentary on the explanations of the hexagrams] says: "[Responding to chin, cheeks, and tongue] is to bubble forth with speech." These statements are at the end of the section on [the hexagram] *hsien.* Therefore, to "grasp the Way by responding" [to things, i.e., to achieve enlightenment through spontaneous interaction with the world,] has nothing to do with speech (lit., "nothing to do with the divided top line of this hexagram").

In the past, when our fundamental teacher [Śākyamuni Buddha] appeared in the world to teach the Dharma, he always [taught] in accordance with the basic nature of those being taught. However, when [his students] achieved enlightenment, [the Buddha's] words would automatically be forgotten. After the Buddha's nirvāṇa the Arhats gathered together and wrote down in the form of the sūtras all the teachings the Buddha had uttered during his lifetime. Although [even such sublime texts as the] *Comprehensive* [*Sūtra*] *on Perfect Enlightenment (Yuan-wu liao-i* [*ching*]*)* are among these [scriptures copied down by the Arhats], the ordinary person [who strives for enlightenment on the basis of such texts] without direct contact with a sage will [only] get further and further away from the truth.[16]

After the sūtras began to be translated into Chinese during the Han and Wei Dynasties, scholars have depended greatly on the words [of the teachings. They have] dissected sentences, analyzed words, and [devised] categories and doctrines that are like decorations [rather than aids to enlightenment. Since they make an ornament of their knowledge, overly elegant prose pervades [their writings]. Because they are chasing after something that is limited, none of them ever [perceives] the ultimate nature of Suchness or opens the enlightened eye of the perfect and sudden *dharmakāya.*

Those who approach the lecturer's seat with splendor to sit and manipulate profundities attract great numbers of students and wealthy followers. [Those followers] labor ceaselessly, reverentially —and pointlessly, since none of them ever understands the teachings or becomes enlightened to the [true] principle [of Buddhism].

Q. Therefore, when [Bodhi]dharma set out to lead the ignorant [people of China to enlightenment], he ceased the use of words and dissassociated himself from the scriptures. His teaching was subtle and insightful, and his practice was expeditious and comprehensible: Not to move is meditation; not to grasp is wisdom. The eradication of the false is the True (*chen,* as in *chen-ju,* "suchness"); one's coalescence with the [Buddha] Nature is Suchness (*ju,* as before). Realization is a function of the One Essence, and [even though] its accomplishment depends on becoming enlightened oneself, there is not the slightest bit of [one's being] that can go into or out of [enlightenment], not the most transitory bit of matter that separates [enlightenment and ignorance].

Vast and without boundaries, empty and without a thing: This is called the "wondrous thing." I do not know why it is called this. Is it the *Dharmakāya,* or is it Nonsubstantiality, or is it the Real Characteristic, or is it Suchness, or is it Enlightenment? This is the pure taste of Truth [that is savored] during the consummation of silent illumination *(mo-chao).* After [achieving enlightenment] one can read the scriptures and be able to understand the most excellent expressions therein through the insight of one's illumination. One will be tranquil and without "activation" *(wu so ch'i)* with relation to all [elements of] conditioned reality.

Therefore, Hui-k'o and Seng-ts'an [forewent all self]-benefit and attained the True. Their practice left no traces; their actions left no record. The master taught inconspicuously; his students practiced in silence. Tao-hsin, however, selected a site and established a permanent residence, a residence [large enough to fit even] the heavenly bodies. [Although] his life did leave its mark (lit., "traces"), [and although] his fame was known [throughout China], he refused to transmit the great teaching to his ordinary lot of students—[even if] they were able to hear it. Therefore, Shan-fu went on to Mount Heng (= Nan-yueh), where he attained a [state of] profound *samādhi.* How much more so the ordinary, shallow-minded [students]—how could they possibly understand [the profound teachings]?

R. During the lifetimes of [Hung]-jen, [Fa]-ju, and Ta-t'ung (= Shen-hsiu), the teachings were opened up to great [numbers of students] without regard to abilities. [These students] were all immediately made to recite the name of the Buddha *(nien fo-ming).* [Those who could be] made to demonstrate [the nature of] the Pure Mind in intimate [conference with the master] were thus qualified to receive transmission of the Dharma, but this [was an eventuality] to be treasured in secret by both master and disciple. [Such transmissions] were never publicly announced. If a student were not fit [for enlightenment], he would [simply] never perceive the ultimate truth [of the teachings].

Students nowadays say questionable things to make their ignorance out to be understanding and their spiritual inexperience to be accomplishment. They mix up different methods of practice (*fang-pien,* lit., "expedient means") of the remembrance of the Buddha *(nien-fo)* and purification of the mind *(ching-hsin),* so how can they have even the vaguest idea as to the ultimate [teaching] of Suchness and the *Dharmakāya?* It is really lamentable! How can they possibly understand the operation of thought *(nien)* [when they do not understand that] thought itself is fundamentally nonsubstantial? [Or, since] the Pure Nature is already tranquil, why should we [strive to] purify the mind? [In truth,] when "thoughts" and "purity" are both forgotten, [the mind] will illuminate [all things] fully of its own accord. Seng-k'o (= Hui-k'o) once said: "After four generations, [the study of the *Laṇkāvatāra Sūtra*] will become superficial." Ah, how true![17]

However, I have not studied [Buddhism] in this way; I am not of the type [just described]. If I may venture an opinion, their transgressions are egregious. Did not P'i-sou say, "[It is as pointless as] trying to block [the flow of the Yellow River] at Meng-chin with a single cupful of soil from Wang-wu [Mountain]"?[18]

S. I have been induced to prepare this history by [two (?)] intimate friend(s) from long ago. I now lift my brush after the concluding comments [just given]. As the [*Laṇkāvatāra*] *Sūtra* says: "Only make direct progress with the mind."[19] Would "direct" mean to transcend the two extremes? Would "progress" mean to not abide in the three vehicles?

Today Ta-t'ung's (i.e., Shen-hsiu's) following is unyieldingly strong. If you learn [the teachings] well, how can [realization] be far away? If you tie [your sandals] onto your feet, you should set out on your journey. Be diligent, students! Do not waste time![20]

T. *Annals of the Transmission of the* [*Dharma*]*-treasure Through Seven Patriarchs,* in one fascicle.

Notes

INTRODUCTION

1. The *Platform Sūtra* purports to contain the oral teachings of Hui-neng (638–713), but it was actually composed around the year 780. The oldest extant version of the text is from Tun-huang and is considerably different in content and length from later editions. For an analysis of the book's original contents and authorship, see Yanagida Seizan, *Shoki Zenshū shisho no kenkyū* (Kyoto: Hōzōkan, 1967), pp. 148–212. Philip B. Yampolsky, *The Platform Sūtra of the Sixth Patriarch* (New York: Columbia University Press, 1967), contains a critical edition of the Chinese text, a discussion of its background and significance, and an English translation. The Chinese text also occurs in the *Taishō shinshū Daizōkyō,* vol. 48, pp. 337a–45b, i.e., *T*48.337a–45b. (See Abbreviations and Conventions of Usage at the beginning of this book.) For a summary of the text's history and a discussion of its English translations, see Carl Bielefeldt and Lewis Lancaster, "*T'an ching* (Platform Scripture)," *Philosophy East and West,* 25, no. 2 (April 1975): 197–212.

2. This translation is taken from Yampolsky, p. 129. The original text occurs in Yampolsky, pp. 2–3 (from the back), or *T*48.337b.

3. My translation is slightly different from that of previous scholars, the reasons for which will become apparent in the Conclusion. See the Chinese text in Yampolsky, p. 3 (from the back), or *T*48.337c.

4. Yampolsky, pp. 58–88, contains an excellent summary of the development of Hui-neng's legendary biography.

5. *Ibid.,* p. 4 (from the back), or *T*48.338a.

6. The legendary status of Hung-jen in early Ch'an will be discussed in Part One, Chapter II, Section 4.

7. Hu Shih, D. T. Suzuki, and others have associated the *Laṇkāvatāra Sūtra* and the *Diamond Sūtra* with the Northern and Southern Schools, respectively. As indicated by Yanagida, *Shoki Zenshū shisho,* p. 73 n. 30, these simplistic associations can no longer be accepted.

8. The most convenient discussion of Shen-hui's role is in Yampolsky, pp. 23–38. As Professor Yampolsky notes on p. 24, Shen-hui's importance was first real-

ized by Hu Shih. Briefly, Shen-hui studied under Shen-hsiu and Hui-neng (there is some doubt about the first), in 730 initiated a vigorous campaign against the disciples of Shen-hsiu—to whom he applied the term "Northern School"—and was active in Lo-yang and several other areas from about 745 on. The dates given here for his life are based on information published in Japan just as this study goes to press. I will consider Shen-hui's life in greater detail in a paper to appear in a volume on the sudden/gradual problem, edited by Peter Gregory and to be published by the University of Hawaii Press in association with the Kuroda Institute.

9. Shen-hui's historical contributions were overlooked by the later Ch'an School. Although he was supposedly recognized by the imperial court in 796 as the Seventh Patriarch of Ch'an, his name does not figure in either of the two orthodox lineages of the school. His own lineage came to an end with Kuei-feng Tsung-mi (780–841), whose works contain the only references to the imperial conferral of official status upon Shen-hui just mentioned. See the sources listed in Hu Shih's biographical study of Shen-hui found in the *Shen-hui ho-shang i-chi —fu Hu hsien-sheng tsui-hou-te yen-chiu,* Ma Chun-wu, ed. (Taipei: Hu Shih chi-nien kuan, 1968), pp. 70–71.

10. Ui Hakuju, *Zenshūshi kenkyū,* vol. 2 (Tokyo: Iwanami shoten, 1941), 79. Yampolsky, p. 32, points out that Shen-hui never quotes directly from the writings or sayings by Hui-neng, the verses from the *Platform Sūtra* included.

11. This set of four phrases occurs first in Shen-hui's *P'u-t'i-ta-mo nan-tsung ting shih-fei lun (Treatise on the Definition of the Truth about Bodhidharma's Southern School),* the purported text of his anti-Northern School presentation of 732. His *Nan-yang ho-shang tun-chiao chieh-t'o ch'an-men chih liao-hsing t'an-yü (The Preceptor* [*Shen-hui*] *of Nan-yang's Platform Sermon on the Direct Comprehension of the* [*Buddha*] *Nature and the Ch'an Teaching of Sudden Enlightenment and Emancipation),* which is generally considered to antedate the work just mentioned, contains the same four phrases, although the first occurs somewhat apart from the other three. See Hu, *Shen-hui ho-shang i-chi,* pp. 287 and 239.

12. This is not limited to the work cited just below; Tsung-mi apparently never mentions the *Platform Sūtra* and does not cite "Hui-neng's" verse in any of his works.

13. See the original text in Kamata Shigeo, *Zengen shosenshū tojo,* Zen no goroku, no. 9 (Tokyo: Chikuma shobō, 1971), pp. 86–87, or *T*48.402b–c. Tsung-mi classifies the different factions of early Ch'an according to their understanding of the Buddha Nature.

Chih-shen (609–702) was a student of Hung-jen's important within the lineages of Ch'an in Szechwan; Pao-t'ang Wu-chu (714–74) was one of his successors and the individual most closely associated with the *Li-tai fa-pao chi (Record of the* [*Transmission of the*] *Dharma-treasure through the Generations,* hereafter abbreviated *LTFPC).* Hsuan-shih was also a student of Hung-jen's. He was apparently involved with Pure Land practices, but next to nothing is known about him. See the discussion of Hung-jen's disciples in Part One, Chapter II, Section 5 and in the *LTFPC* in Yanagida's *Shoki no zenshi, 2—Rekidai hōbō ki,* Zen no goroku, no. 3 (Tokyo: Chikuma shobō, 1976), pp. 163–72, or T51.185c–

87c. (The editing of the *Taishō* versions of Tun-huang manuscripts is notoriously bad, but that of the *LTFPC* is egregious.)

The Ox-head School is traditionally thought of as an offshoot of Ch'an beginning with Niu-t'ou Fa-jung (594–657), but its greatest activity occurred during the middle and latter part of the eighth century. This school will be mentioned again in the Conclusion. The T'ien-t'ai School should need no introduction here. Seng-ch'ou (480–560) was an important meditation specialist; his *Hsü kao-seng chuan (Continued Lives of Eminent Monks,* hereafter cited as *HKSC)* biography is at *T*50.553b–55b. Guṇabhadra (394–468) is remembered in Ch'an literature principally as the translator of the *Laṇkāvatāra Sūtra,* which is discussed tangentially in Part One, Chapter I, Sections 6 and 7, and Part One, Chapter IV, Section 13. For his biography, see the *Kao-seng chuan (Lives of Eminent Monks,* hereafter cited as *KSC), T*50.344a–45a.

14. In addition to the work just quoted, also see Tsung-mi's *Chung-hua ch'üan hsin-ti ch'an-men shih-tzu ch'eng-hsi t'u (Lineage Chart of the Masters and Students of Ch'an in the Transmission of the Mind-ground in China)* in Kamata, pp. 274–76, 298–307, and 322–25, or *Z*2B, 1, 433d, 435c–d, and 436c–d (*H*110:866b, 870a–b, and 872–b). (All citations from the *Zoku-zōkyō,* or *Z,* have been cross-referenced to the Taiwan reprint, the *Hsü tsang-ching,* or *H.*)

15. Tsung-mi identifies the teachings of the Northern School with those of the Fa-hsiang School and applies the same critique to both. See, for example, the *Hua-yen ching hsing-yuan p'in shu-ch'ao, Z,* 1, 7, 4, 399c (*H*7:798a).

16. For example, D. T. Suzuki quotes the *Platform Sūtra* verses in his "History of Zen Buddhism from Bodhidharma to Hui-neng (Yenō)," *Essays in Zen Buddhism (First Series)* (New York: Grove Press, 1961), pp. 206–7. This article was written in 1926. Suzuki's weak disclaimer as to the verses' reliability may be found on p. 208. *A History of Zen Buddhism* by Heinrich Dumoulin, S.J., (Boston: Beacon Press, 1969), pp. 81–82 and 83, contains a similar recounting and disclaimer. Both Suzuki and Dumoulin accept the general notion that the Northern School was overwhelmed and superseded by the innately superior Southern School.

Among Chinese scholars, Hu Shih seems to have ignored the verses completely, which is consistent with his rejection of all fabricated material. Nevertheless, he frequently refers to the Northern School as "gradualistic." On the other hand, Yin-shun's *Chung-kuo Ch'an-tsung shih* (Taipei: Hui-jih chiang-t'ang, 1971), p. 209, contains the assertion and attempted proof that the verse attributed to Shen-hsiu accurately represented his teachings.

In Japanese, Ui, *Zenshūshi kenkyū,* vol. 1 (Tokyo: Iwanami shoten, 1939), 275 and 346–56, rejects the verses' authenticity as well as the notion that the Northern School taught a strictly gradualistic doctrine. Sekiguchi Shindai also rejects the validity of the verses and, in striking contrast to Yin-shun, finds evidence that Northern School doctrine actually agreed with the several different versions of Hui-neng's verse. He concludes that Shen-hsiu's teaching was thoroughly subitist, not gradualistic. See Sekiguchi's *Daruma daishi no kenkyū* (Tokyo: Shunjūsha, 1969), pp. 218–19 and 226, and *Zenshū shisōshi* (Tokyo: Sankibō busshorin, 1964), p. 103.

Yanagida suggests, first, that the verses attributed to Hui-neng are not substantially different from that attributed to Shen-hsiu and, second, that they may be further developments on a theme stated in Shen-hui's works. See his *Shoki Zenshū shisho,* pp. 262–63. In a later work oriented to a popular audience, Yanagida also uses the verses to draw some very interesting inferences about Shen-hsiu and Hui-neng. See his *Zen shisō—sono genkei o arau,* Chūkō shinsho, no. 400 (Tokyo: Chūō kōron sha, 1975), pp. 87–89.

17. Unquestionably, the one scholar whose work has caused the greatest confusion over the years is D. T. Suzuki. Although his worldwide efforts are in large part responsible for the unusually high level of interest in Ch'an, or Zen, it is unfortunate that the misconceptions and inaccuracies regarding the history of Chinese Ch'an contained in his very first article on the subject were never corrected in the half century of creative scholarly effort that followed. See "The Zen Sect of Buddhism," first published in the *Journal of the Pali Text Society,* 1906–1907, and reprinted in *Studies in Zen,* Christmas Humphreys, ed. (New York: Dell, 1955), pp. 15–17. Suzuki's last significant contribution was *The Zen Doctrine of No-mind* (London: Rider, 1949). Suzuki's tendency to accept the *Platform Sūtra* as an accurate historical document and Hui-neng and Shen-hsiu as the actual representatives of two distinct tendencies within the Ch'an School involves so many problems that it renders his writings on the teachings and history of early Ch'an almost entirely useless.

18. See Part One, Chapter II, Section 9. Also see n. 77 to Part One.

19. See Part Two, Chapter II, Section 1.

20. Hu, *Shen-hui ho-shang i-chi,* pp. 288–89.

21. *Ibid.,* p. 260. Although the *Ting shih-fei lun* is based on a presentation given by Shen-hui in 732, the preface to the text says that similar presentations occurred in 730 and 731.

22. The term *nan-tsung* appears in a commentary on the *Heart Sūtra* by Ching-chueh, whose biography will be discussed in Part One, Chapter IV, Section 12. The citation in question may be found in Yanagida, *Shoki Zenshū shisho,* pp. 69 and 396. The term *pei-tsung* ("Northern School") is attached to two Tun-huang manuscripts, but these were copied near the end of the eighth century or later. These manuscripts are the *Ta-sheng pei-tsung lun* (S2581; see Ui, 1:447–48, or *T*85.1281c–82a) and the *Ta-sheng wu fang-pien—pei-tsung* (P2058; see Ui, 1:468, and the *Suzuki Daisetsu zenshū,* vol. 3 [Tokyo: Iwanami shoten, 1968], 190). One of the other *Wu fang-pien* manuscripts bears cyclical characters equivalent to 787, 847, or 907, etc. The correct date is probably the first of these. See Ui, 1:515, or *T*85.1293a, and Ui's comments on p. 427.

23. See Yanagida, *Shoki no zenshi, 1—Ryōga shiji ki-Den'hōbōki,* Zen no goroku, no. 2 (Tokyo: Chikuma shobō, 1971), p. 298, and *T*85.1290a–b. The name "*Dhyāna* Master Shen-hsiu" has been moved to its present location from slightly below in the original text, in order to make the English version read more smoothly.

24. See Part One, Chapter IV, Section 12.

25. See Yanagida, *Shoki no zenshi, 1,* p. 268, or *T*85.1289b; Sung Chih-wen's memorial translated in Part One, Chapter II, Section 12; and Chang Yueh's epitaph for Shen-hsiu, as quoted in Part One, Chapter II, Section 9.

26. See Yanagida's discussion of the origins of the term "Southern School" in

Shoki Zenshū shisho, pp. 117–26. Yanagida concludes that Shen-hui's use of the term constituted a creative rediscovery of it, rather than a purely original innovation, and that both the name and identity of his "Southern School" were dependent on the prior existence of the "Northern School." I might add that the pejorative origins of the term "Northern School" resemble those of the term "Hīnayāna."

27. See Li Hua's epitaph for Huai-jen (669–751), *Ch'üan T'ang-wen (Complete Writings of the T'ang* [*Dynasty*]; hereafter cited as *CTW), Ch'in-ting ch'üan T'ang-wen,* Tung Kao *et al.*, eds., (1,000 fascicles; Taipei: Wai-wen shu-chü, 1961), fascicle 320, p. 10a–b, as quoted in Shiina Kōyū, "Tōzan hōmon keisei no haikei," *Shūgaku kenkyū,* 12 (March 1970): 176 n. 20. The epitaph reads: "The concentration and insight of T'ien-t'ai constitutes the meaning of all the scriptures; the East Mountain Teaching is the vehicle of all the Buddhas." The next line contains a reference to the conjoint illumination of meditation and wisdom, and the parallelism between these two concepts and the T'ien-t'ai and Ch'an Schools is implicit. "East Mountain" *(Tung-shan)* refers to part of "Twin Peaks Mountain" *(Shuang-feng shan).* Although Tao-hsin's monastery was apparently not at the same location as Hung-jen's and possibly not on Tung-shan, the term "East Mountain Teaching" is used in the primary sources without regard for this distinction. See n. 79 to Part One.

28. I will argue later that Shen-hsiu was active in Ch'ang-an in cooperation with Tao-hsuan in the early 660s. See Part One, Chapter II, Section 10, including n. 115.

29. The *LTFPC* may be found at *T*51.179a–96b or in Yanagida, *Shoki no zenshi, 2—Rekidai hōbō ki.*

30. Alas, there is just such a scholar—Nakagawa Taka, who is always ready to defend the traditional interpretation of Ch'an history. See her "Sōsan daishi no nendai to shisō," *Indogaku Bukkyōgaku kenkyū* 6, no. 1 (1958): 229–32 and "Zenshū dai sanso Sōsan daishi to *Shinjimmei*," *Tōhoku Yakka Daigaku kiyō,* 4 (November 1957): 159–66. It would also be possible to mention D. T. Suzuki in this regard, but his work on Ch'an falls into rather a separate category of semischolarly interpretation.

31. I plan to publish a study on the background of the meditation tradition in China sometime in the near future.

PART ONE

1. The account summarized here is based on the *Ching-te ch'üan-teng lu (Records of the Transmission of the Lamp* [*Recorded during the*] *Ching-te* [*Period*], hereafter cited as *CTL), T*51.217a–21c, especially pp. 219a–20b.

2. For a convenient English summary of Emperor Wu's activities, see Kenneth K. S. Ch'en, *Buddhism in China: A Historical Survey* (Princeton, N.J.: Princeton University Press, 1964), pp. 124–28.

3. Shao-lin ssu was originally built by Emperor Hsiao-wen of the Wei Dynasty for *Dhyāna* Master Bhadra. The *Shao-lin ssu pei (Inscription for Shao-lin ssu)* by P'ei Ts'ui, written in 728, is devoted to the history of this monastery. See the

CTW, fascicle 279, pp. 16b–22a, or Washio Junkei's *Bodaidaruma Sūzan shiseki taikan* of 1932.

4. *CTL, T*51.219b.

5. Sekiguchi's *Daruma no kenkyū* (Tokyo: Iwanami shoten, 1967) conveniently charts the development of the Bodhidharma legend. (This book should not be confused with his similarly titled *Daruma daishi no kenkyū* [Tokyo: Shōkokusha, 1957].) Although *Daruma no kenkyū* is very useful in its synoptic presentation of primary sources, Sekiguchi's analysis must be read with some caution. In addition, he failed to check the accuracy of the *Taishō* editions of the Tun-huang manuscripts that he used. See Yanagida's sharply critical review reprinted in *Yaburu mono* (Tokyo: Shunjūsha, 1970), pp. 226–39.

6. *T*51.1000b. Compare this rendition with that in that in Yi-t'ung Wang's recent translation, *A Record of Buddhist Monasteries in Lo-yang* (Princeton, N.J.: Princeton University Press, 1984), pp. 20–21. Whereas Wang translates *po-ssu* as "Persia," Ui, 1:7–8, identifies this as a small Central Asian country. Yanagida, *Daruma no goroku—Ninyū shigyō ron,* Zen no goroku, no. 1 (Tokyo: Chikuma shobō, 1969), p. 27, has noticed that many of the foreign monks appearing in the *Lo-yang ch'ieh-lan chi* are listed as being from *po-ssu,* so that the specific relevance of this statement regarding Bodhidharma is questionable.

7. Yanagida, "Daruma-zen to sono haikei," in Ocho Enichi, ed., *Hokugi Bukkyō no kenkyū* (Kyoto: Heirakuji shoten, 1970), pp. 118–19.

8. See Hu's "Development of Zen Buddhism in China," *The Chinese Social and Political Science Review,* 15, no. 4 (1932): 486–87, reprinted in *Ko Teki zengaku an,* Yanagida Seizan, ed. (Kyoto: Chūbun shuppansha, 1975), pp. 710–709 (sic). I have attempted to use the evidence Hu cites more rigorously than he did. Yung-ning ssu was damaged by winds in 526 and occupied by the military in 528; Hu mentions only the latter. Although he is aware that this monastery was built in 516, Hu infers that Bodhidharma must have been in the North until about 520. This is correct, but only on the basis of other evidence. See n. 12 below.

9. *T*50.551b–c. The bracketed interpolation beginning in the first line is based on T'an-lin's preface, which Tao-hsuan is obviously paraphrasing. See Yanagida's *Daruma no goroku,* p. 25; *Shoki no zenshi, 1,* p. 128; or *T*51.458b. The term "accordance with convention" translates the compound *shun-wu.* See Yanagida's explanation in *Daruma no goroku,* p. 29.

10. I believe that the *HKSC* is the most reliable source on the matter of Bodhidharma's arrival in China. The *Lo-yang ch'ieh-lan chi* contains only a very stereotyped image of Bodhidharma, while T'an-lin's preface to the *EJSHL* says only that Bodhidharma crossed "mountains and oceans" *(shan-hai)* on his way to China. This should be taken as a general expression of the distance between India and China, rather than a specific description of Bodhidharma's journey. See the translation of the *EJSHL* and T'an-lin's preface in Part Two, Chapter V, Section 2. John Alexander Jorgensen, *The Earliest Text of Ch'an Buddhism: The* Long Scroll (M.A. dissertation, Australian National University, 1979), pp. 158–60, adduces some interesting background information on the relative importance of the land and sea routes to China at this time. T'ang Yung-t'ung considers much of the same information given in the timetable I have presented in his "P'u-t'i-ta'mo," reprinted in *Ch'an-tsung shih-shih k'ao-pien,* Shih Tao-an, ed.,

Hsien-tai Fo-chiao hsueh-shu ts'ung-k'an, no. 4 (Taipei: Ta-sheng wen-hua ch'u-pan she, 1977), pp. 141–52.

11. Dumoulin is the only scholar of whom I am aware who has considered the implications of Seng-fu's biography in this way. See his "Bodhidharma und die Anfänge des Ch'an-Buddhismus," *Monumenta Nipponica,* 7 (1951): 75 and 79–80. Jorgensen, pp. 156–57 and 161, builds upon an observation by Yanagida to suggest that Bodhidharma first lived in the vicinity of P'ing-ch'eng after moving to the North and only went to Lo-yang after the capital was moved there in 494.

12. In the article listed above in n. 8, Hu Shih argues that since Bodhidharma arrived in South China before the fall of the Sung and witnessed the splendor of Yung-ning ssu in the North, he must have been in China from 470 to 520, a total of fifty years. I am puzzled by Hu's failure to use the more accurate years 479–516, a span of only thirty-seven years. His apparent goal was the contradiction of a story that Bodhidharma arrived in Canton in 520 or 530, which should be rejected for other reasons.

Hui-k'o's *HKSC* biography refers to Bodhidharma's burial on the bank of the Lo River. (*T*50.552a) According to a note in Jorgenson, p. 118, this location is mentioned elsewhere (*T*50.683a) as the place where Chih-ming was executed. Satomichi Tokuo, "Bodaidaruma to sono shūhen (ichi)," *Tōyō Daigaku tōyōgaku kenkyū kiyō,* 12 (1978): 117–20, apparently thinks that because of this reference Bodhidharma may have been executed during the late Wei or Ho-yin massacre of 508. I have not seen Satomichi's article and am skeptical of this argument.

13. The *HKSC, T*50.550a, lists Bodhidharma as a resident of the "environs of Yeh, capital of Ch'i." This must be an error based on his association with Hui-k'o.

14. See Sekiguchi's *Daruma no kenkyū,* pp. 159–67, for the development of this anecdote. In addition to Dumoulin's article, already mentioned in n. 11, see Kawashima Jōmyō, "Sōfuku ni tsuite," *Indogaku Bukkyōgaku kenkyū,* 25, no. 2 (1977): 146–47, and Yanagida's "Daruma-zen to sono haikei," pp. 134–36.

15. *T*50.550a–c.

16. *T*50.550b.

17. This was an important early meditation center. One of its early residents was Dharmamitra (356–442), a native of Kashmir and former resident of Kucha and Tun-huang. See the *KSC, T*50.342c–43a.

18. This occurred sometime during the years 502–509, when Liang forces pacified the area.

19. K'ai-shan ssu was built by Emperor Wu in 515. See Mochizuki Shinkō, *Mochizuki Bukkyō daijiten* (10 vols.; Tokyo: Sekai seiten kankō kyōkai, 1933–36), 1:389a–b and 3:2614b–c.

20. *T*50.550b.

21. See the *Liang shu,* fascicle 5, *Erh-shih-wu shih,* Erh-shih wu-shih k'an-hsing wei-yuan hui, ed. (9 vols. plus biographical index; Shanghai: K'ai-ming shu-tien, 1935; reprint Taipei, 1962), 2:1775a–77d. This individual, whose personal name was Hsiao I, was an avid supporter of Buddhism and a prolific author.

22. In addition to the *HKSC,* see the *Ch'u san-tsang chi-chi, T*55.50b–51b, and

Kawashima, p. 146. The prince's illness, which began in 508 and became severe in 514, was also reported as "cured" in 516 through the efforts of Seng-yu, the author of the *Ch'u san-tsang chi-chi.* This is recorded in the *KSC, T*50.412a–b. The prince's biography may be found in the *Liang shu,* fascicle 22, *Erh-shih-wu shih,* 2:1797a–b.

23. The *Hui-yin san-mei ching* was translated by a southerner, Chih Ch'ien, but it is associated in the *Ch'u san-tsang chi-chi* with Dharmarakṣa, a northerner.

24. The Chinese text of the *Hui-yin san-mei ching* may be found at *T*15.460c–68a. The phrase *wu-nien pu-tung pu-yao* occurs at *T*15.461b.

25. It is possible that Seng-fu's role as a follower of Bodhidharma active in the South at this time contributed in some way to the famous story of the encounter between Emperor Wu and Bodhidharma. (See the beginning of this chapter.) This hypothesis cannot be corroborated, but it recalls Kawashima's plausible suggestion that Seng-fu's activities in Szechwan were the basis of the inclusion of the name Tao-fu in an anecdote that first appears in a text from Szechwan.

26. *T*50.551c–52c. Hui-k'o's name is actually given here as Seng-k'o, also known as Hui-k'o, but it is *Hui*-k'o that is used in Bodhidharma's *HKSC* biography. Hui-k'o's birthplace is given in the *CFPC* and *LCSTC* as Wu-lao because of a ritual avoidance associated with the T'ang ruling family. See Yanagida's *Shoki no zenshi, 1,* p. 145.

27. *T*50.552a.

28. Ui, 1:40, mentions a story concerning a monk of this name. However, it only appears much later and is irrelevant to the events in question here.

29. *T*50.480c–81a. On the impact of Hui-k'o's teachings on Hui-pu, see Yanagida, *Shoki Zenshū shisho,* p. 29 n. 5.

30. According to Hui-k'o's *HKSC* biography, he had passed the age of forty when he met Bodhidharma around the year 525, hence the birthdate of ca. 485. Yanagida, "Daruma-zen to sono haikei," p. 139, suggests that the specific age of forty is an allusion to the statement by Confucius that at age forty he no longer had doubts. (See the "Wei-cheng" section of the *Lun-yü.)* The point of the reference would thus concern Hui-k'o's firm conviction, rather than his specific age. Even so, I believe the allusion would not have been made were Hui-k'o not middle-aged when he met Bodhidharma. The reference in Bodhidharma's *HKSC* biography to Hui-k'o and Tao-yü being "younger" refers, I think, to their being younger than Bodhidharma.

Hui-k'o's date of death has been deduced on the basis of the following: (1) Layman Hsiang's letter to Hui-k'o, to be discussed in Part Two, Chapter V, was written and presumably answered at the beginning of the years 550–59. Hence Hui-k'o was still alive in 550. (2) Hui-k'o's biography precedes that of Seng-ta, who died in 556. Because Tao-hsuan lists his subjects according to the chronological order of their deaths, Hui-k'o therefore died in or before 556. (In this particular fascicle, the respective dates of death of the primary subjects of each entry are 524, 524, unknown, unknown, ca. 530 [Bodhidharma], Hui-k'o, 556, 560, 559 [following one textual tradition], 571, etc. There is only one minor discrepancy in this sequence.

Most scholars interpret a line in the *HKSC* to imply that Hui-k'o was still alive in 574. At *T*50.552b, the text says that T'an-lin protected the scriptures and statuary during the persecution of 574 "together with the fellow student(s) [of] Hui-k'o *(yü K'o t'ung-hsueh).*" I interpret this as a reference to T'an-lin's cooperation with his fellow students under Hui-k'o, rather than to his fellow student Hui-k'o. Hui-k'o's second-generation successor Ching-ai is in fact described as a protector of the Dharma during the period in question. (See n. 32 below.) The modern position that Hui-k'o lived long enough to experience the persecution of 574 is no doubt influenced by the epitaph for him contained in the *Pao-lin chuan.* Since this text was written in 801, its contents cannot be considered historically reliable.

Jorgensen, pp. 130–32 and 165, identifies Hui-k'o with a monk named Hui-ko, whose name is written with an unusual second character similar to that in the name of Bodhidharma's student. Hui-ko originally lived in north China, but moved to the South after the persecution of 574 and became a member of Paramārtha's following. The reasons Jorgensen identifies this monk with Hui-k'o of the proto-Ch'an School are apparently (1) the similarity of their names, (2) Hui-ko's residence in north China until 574, (3) the tentative identification of Hui-ko's teacher Pa-mo-li with Bodhidharma, and, possibly, (4) Hui-ko's supposed use of T'an-lin's commentary on the *Nirvāṇa Sūtra.* I see no reason to assume that Pa-mo-li is a "mistake or another name for Bodhidharma." More important, nowhere is Hui-ko identified as a meditation specialist. There is also an implicit contradiction between Hui-ko's flight south after 574 and the traditional interpretation that Hui-k'o (of Ch'an) cooperated with T'an-lin in the protection of Buddhism after this date. That is, either Hui-k'o was already dead in 574, as I believe, or he stayed in the North to defend Buddhism. Finally, the reference to T'an-lin's commentary on the *Nirvāṇa Sūtra* is not mentioned specifically with regard to Hui-ko. See *T*50.431c.

Kamata Shigeo's "Hokushū haibutsu to Zen," *Shūgaku kenkyū,* 6 (April 1964): 60–65, attempts to find evidence for the influence of this persecution on Hui-k'o's thought. While I accept neither the assertion that Hui-k'o lived until after 574 nor the attribution of passages in early Ch'an literature to Hui-k'o, Kamata's conclusions may still be relevant for the Ch'an School as a whole.

31. *T*50.552b.

32. Ching-ai and his students were active in defense of the Dharma during the persecution of 574. He and his seven known students were involved, collectively, in the study of the *Vinaya,* Mādhyamika treatises and the *Ta chih-tu lun,* the *Avataṁsaka Sūtra,* and other Mahāyāna texts. See *T*50.625c–28a, 433c, 434a, 488a–89c, 516c–17b, 578b–c, 586c–87a, 626c, and 628a–30b. Fa-k'an, a devoted meditator, was also a follower of the Mādhyamika—or at least is known to have visited the San-lun School center on Mount She. The most interesting facet of his *HKSC* biography is a quotation that links his teacher, *Dhyāna* Master Ho, to the *Shou-leng-yen ching,* the Chinese translation of the *Śūraṁgama-samādhi Sūtra.* See *T*50.652b–c. Hsuan-ching was a resident of [Ta]-chuang-yen ssu in Ch'ang-an. (This is the former Ch'an-ting ssu and future residence of Shen-hsiu, née Wei-hsiu, as discussed in Part One, Chapter II, Section 10.) He was also an expert in the *Perfection of Wisdom Sūtras* associated with Mañjuśrī. Since Shen-hsiu cites one of these sūtras as the scriptural basis of the East Mountain Teaching, Hsuan-ching may have constituted an important link between the Bodhidharma tradi-

tion and the Northern School. Unfortunately, he had no known successors. See *T*50.569b–c for Hsuan-ching's biography and Yanagida, *Shoki no zenshi, 1,* p. 298, or *T*85.1290b, for Shen-hsiu's reference. (The passage in which this reference occurs has been presented in the Introduction, Section 6, albeit with the reference itself omitted for the sake of brevity.)

33. These interpolated references to the *Laṇkāvatāra Sūtra* will be introduced and discussed in Section 8 of this chapter.

34. This conclusion is shared by Jorgensen, p. 173.

35. On Ching-ai, see n. 32. Mizuno Kōgen, "Bodaidaruma no ninyūshigyō-setsu to *Kongō zammai kyō," Komazawa Daigaku Bukkyō Gakubu kenkyū kiyō,* 13 (1955): 57, points out that there is no direct evidence that T'an-lin studied under Bodhidharma. Although Mizuno accepts the description of T'an-lin as a fellow student of Hui-k'o's, he suggests that T'an-lin later studied under Hui-k'o.

36. See Yanagida, *Daruma no goroku,* p. 27. The beginning date of T'an-lin's known translation activities implies that he was born no later than 506. Jorgensen, p. 142 n. 25, points out that the earliest dated work by T'an-lin is from 538. The *Ta T'ang nei-tien lu* mentions T'an-lin's many prefaces (*T*55.269c–70a), a complete list of which is given in Walter Liebenthal's "Notes on the *Vajrasamādhi," T'oung Pao* 44 (1956): 384f. See also Sekiguchi, *Daruma no kenkyū,* p. 155–56 and 159 nn. 2, 3, and 4, which list some of Chi-tsang's citations of T'an-lin as a linguistic authority for the understanding of the Sanskrit terminology of the *Śrīmālā-siṁha-nāda Sūtra.* Jorgensen gives all fifteen citations: *T*37.21c, 22a, 22b (twice), 29b, 38b, 39b, 43a, 45b, 52c, 54b, 55a, 58b, 73a, and 89c. The issues involved here are discussed in Hanazuka Hisayoshi, "*Shōmangyo* Donrin-chū to Kichizō," *Shūgaku kenkyū* 23 (March 1981): 236–40. Also see Yanagida, "Daruma-zen to sono haikei," p. 140f.

37. *T*50.666a–c.

38. Yanagida, *Shoki Zenshū shisho,* p. 119, suggests that Fa-chung's style of lecturing was more intuitive than the traditional practice of doctrinal exposition.

39. *T*50.666b. Yagi Shinkei, "Ryōgashū kō," *Bukkyōgaku seminā,* 14 (October 1971): 58, suggests that the "later successor" to Hui-k'o mentioned in the first paragraph of this passage was Hui-hao (547–633), under whom Fa-chung is known to have studied sometime within a span of six years around the second decade of the seventh century. Yagi traces the line of succession as follows: Hui-k'o—Hui-pu—Fa-lang—Ta-ming—Hui-hao. Note that all four of these successors to Hui-k'o were associated with the Mādhyamika. See a similar analysis in Hirai Shun'ei, *Chūgoku hannya shisōshi kenkyū—Kichizō to Sanron gakuha* (Tokyo: Shunjūsha, 1976), pp. 333–34. The last sentence of the translation before the list is a paraphrase and involves a minor repunctuation, omitting the first period in line 13 of the Chinese. As to my reordering of the list, nos. 1–4 below II.D and nos. 1–4 below III.C actually occur at the very end, after V.B, in the original. The gloss after II.D.4 begins with the character *ming,* "name," which Yanagida has suggested is an error for *ko,* "all." See *Shoki Zenshū shisho,* p. 22.

40. The presence of *Dhyāna* Master Ts'an's name in this list has long been a problem in the study of early Ch'an. Eighth-century Ch'an sources are obviously ignorant of the biography of Seng-ts'an, and it is possible that he came to be con-

sidered the Third Patriarch solely because of the appearance of his name at the head of this list. A monk named Seng-ts'an is mentioned briefly in the *HKSC* in connection with a Mount Tu in Lu-chou, which is near where the *HKSC* says Tao-hsin met two unnamed meditation masters. Beginning with the *CFPC*, later sources identify this Seng-ts'an as the Third Patriarch and as one of Tao-hsin's unnamed teachers. See *T*50.510c. There was, however, a figure named Seng-ts'an who lived at about the same time (529–613), but he was an exegete and debater, a very prestigious personage in the Sui capital. Although the anecdotes contained in his biography surround this Seng-ts'an with an almost occultish charisma that would have been more appropriate for a meditator than an exegete, the only explicit similarity to the biographies of the other figures listed here is his association with the San-lun School. See *T*50.500a–1a, 514b, 527b, and 546a. Both eighth-century Ch'an authors and modern scholars refrain even to consider the possibility that this Seng-ts'an might be connected with the Ch'an School. However, it is still quite possible that he is the individual listed in Fa-chung's biography as a student of the *Laṇkāvatāra*.

41. *T*50.547b. See also Hirai, pp. 292 and 340. The *HKSC* contains the biography of a monk named Hung-chih, but he died on Mount Chung-nan in 655, before Hsi-ming ssu was founded.

42. T'an-ch'ien was a specialist in the *She-lun* who was mentioned in an edict establishing Ch'an-ting ssu as the headquarters of a national system of meditation centers. It is unknown whether this edict, which was issued in 602, was ever carried out. T'an-ch'ien's biography is in the *HKSC* at *T*50.571b–74b. See n. 13 to the Conclusion.

43. Kamata Shigeo's "Shotō ni okeru Sanronshū to Dōkyō," *Tōyō Bunka Kenkyūjo kiyō*, 46 (March 1968): 59–62, contains a convenient compilation of the references to Ta-ming and a discussion of his Mount Mao San-lun School faction.

44. *T*50.552b–c.

45. See his "Leng-ch'ieh tsung k'ao" in the *Hu Shih wen-ts'un*, (Shanghai: Ya-tung t'u-shu kuan, 1930), 4:212, or *Ko Teki zengaku an*, p. 172. The character *ku*, "therefore," is used to conjoin the doctrinal statements and the reference to the *Laṇkāvatāra*. D. C. Lau, *Tao-te ching* (Baltimore, Md.: Penguin Books, 1963), p. 172, points out that this character is often used "precisely where the logical link is weakest," thus indicating an artificial attempt to connect otherwise unrelated material.

46. "Shina yuishiki gakushijō ni okeru ryōgashi no chii," *Shina Bukkyō shigaku*, 1, no. 1 (1937): 21–44. One of Yūki's points is the explanation of an apparent difference between the theories of early and later *She lun* School figures as a result of the study of the *Laṇkāvatāra*.

47. *T*50.666c. Interest in the *Laṇkāvatāra* among students of the Yogācāra tradition may have declined also because of the rise in popularity of the *Ch'i-hsin lun* or *Awakening of Faith*.

48. For Chih-i's characterizations of Northern *Dhyāna* Masters, see n. 25 to Part Two. As to the question why the devotees of Ch'an might have been interested in the *Laṇkāvatāra*, D. T. Suzuki's observations are relevant. In his *Essays in Zen Buddhism (First Series)*, pp. 87–88, Suzuki describes this sūtra as a

rambling collection of notes, lacking in supernatural phenomena and mystical formulae, but filled with a deep philosophical meaning and presented in terms of dialogues between the Buddha and a single bodhisattva, rather than between the Buddha and a number of other figures. It is difficult to say how significant these characteristics were to the earliest Ch'an figures.

Perhaps the best modern interpretation of the import of this scripture is that it sought to unite two basic strains of Mahāyāna thought, those of the *ālaya-vijñāna,* or "storehouse consciousness," and the *tathāgata-garbha,* or "matrix of the Buddha." This interpretation has been suggested by Shimizu Yōkō, "*Nyūryōgakyō* no shiki no sansōsetsu ni tsuite—nyōraizō to ārayashiki no dōshi o megutte," *Indogaku Bukkyōgaku kenkyū,* 25, no. 1 (1976): 162–63. See also Yin-shun's "Sung-i *Leng-ch'ieh ching* yü Ta-mo-ch'an" in the *Ch'an-tsung shih-shih k'ao-pien,* pp. 211–22.

49. *T*50.666b. The term "correct contemplation of nonattainment" *(wu-te cheng-kuan)* occurs in Chi-tsang's *San-lun hsuan-i, T*45.10c. See Kuno Hōryū's "Gozu Hōyū ni oyoboseru Sanronshū no eikyō," *Bukkyō kenkyū,* 3, no. 6 (1939): 51–88, and "Ryōgazen," *Shūkyō kenkyū,* 1, no. 3 (1939): 548–60. The problems of Fa-chung and the early Ch'an and Mādhyamika Schools have been discussed briefly by Hirai Shun'ei in his "Shoki Zenshū shisō no keisei to Sanronshū," *Shūgaku kenkyū,* 5 (April 1963): 77–79.

50. See Yanagida, *Shoki Zenshū shisho,* pp. 26–28.

51. See n. 40.

52. Mizuno Kōgen's "Bodaidaruma no ninyūshigyō-setsu to *Kongō zammai kyō*" discusses the origins of the *Chin-kang san-mei ching.* Mizuno's textual comparison of this Chinese sūtra, the *HKSC,* and the *EJSHL* implies that the sūtra borrowed from the *EJSHL* itself and not from (or, at least, not only from) the *HKSC.* See pp. 54–56. Robert Buswell, a graduate student at the University of California, Berkeley specializing in Korean Buddhism, is writing his Ph.D. dissertation on "The Korean Origins of the *Vajrasāmadhi-sūtra.*" Buswell will argue that the sūtra, which is known in Korean as the *Kŭmgang sammae-kyŏng,* was written in Korea about 685 by a student of Tao-hsin's named Fa-lang, or Pŏmnang.

53. See Chapter IV, Section 9.

54. *T*50.606b. I have rendered Tao-hsin's unknown teachers consistently in the plural, although the Chinese lacks any specific indicators of number. Later tradition identifies Seng-ts'an as one of these. In the third paragraph of the translation, three periods mark the omission of the four characters *ssu-yü te chien,* "if you wish to see" (p. 606b, line 12), which are superfluous. In the following paragraphs I have rendered the characters *chung-tsao ssu* as the proper name of a monastery. Whether or not this is a proper name, the meaning is "monastery constructed by the congregation." Shiina, "Tōzan hōmon keisei no haikei," p. 179, for example, interprets these three characters in the declarative sense, but in an epitaph introduced on the following page in his article they occur in nominal form. Shiina also notices that this epitaph, which includes information about the history of the monastery in question, implies that Tao-hsin only entered Huang-mei in or after 627, when the monastery was allegedly built. Although the epitaph in question seems to contain early information, its date of construction is late

enough (1019) that we cannot use it to overturn the evidence of the *CFPC*. See the original text in Shiina, p. 180.

55. See Chapter II, Section 10 and n. 115 for a hypothesis on the origins of Tao-hsuan's information regarding Tao-hsin that would give the date 660 a more specific validity.

56. See Yanagida, *Shoki no zenshi, 1,* pp. 17–18, and the primary sources mentioned there, and Shiina, "Tōzan hōmon keisei no haikei," pp. 178–79. Shiina suggests that Ts'ai first visited Tao-hsin at Huang-mei in 650, at the time of his official appointment to a post in what is now Chekiang Province. Since Tao-hsin died in 651, Ts'ai no doubt continued his religious affiliation with (and, presumably, financial support of) Hung-jen after this date.

57. See Yanagida, *Shoki no zenshi, 1,* pp. 376 and 386, as well as section K of the translation in Appendix A. One source of Tao-hsin's biography that is no longer extant is an epitaph by Tu Cheng-lun. See Yanagida's note on pp. 385–86. Tu Cheng-lun is mentioned in the *HKSC* entry for Fa-chung, *T*50.666c. Yanagida, *Shoki Zenshū shisho,* pp. 83–84, suggests that this epitaph was not actually written by Tu, although it was probably composed by the early eighth century. Since the *CFPC* account of Tao-hsin's life contains so little that does not also occur in the *HKSC,* it is possible that this epitaph contained no new substantive information. See Yamazaki Hiroshi, *Chūgoku Bukkyō—bunkashi no kenkyū* (Kyoto: Hōzōkan, 1981), pp. 163–83, for a study of Tu Cheng-lun's Buddhist activities.

58. The *LCSTC* gives Tao-hsin's term of study under Seng-ts'an as twelve years, the basis of which is unknown. See *Shoki no zenshi, 1,* p. 167, or *T*85.1286b.

59. *Shoki no zenshi, 1,* pp. 379–80. If this anecdote is to be taken seriously, one can only wonder how Tao-hsin could have entered a city under siege. Perhaps the rebels were unconcerned about one seemingly harmless monk.

60. Sekiguchi Shindai makes much of this possible meeting between Chih-k'ai and Tao-hsin, using it as an argument for the connection between early Ch'an and the T'ien-t'ai School. See *Daruma daishi no kenkyū,* p. 274. Shiina points out that three or four different monasteries on Mount Lu had the name Ta-lin ssu, so that Chih-k'ai and Tao-hsin may not have even resided at the same location. See "Tōzan hōmon keisei no haikei," p. 184.

Whether or not the two ever met and whether or not Tao-hsin imbibed heavily of Chih-k'ai's religious spirit while at Ta-lin ssu may be immaterial to the issue of T'ien-t'ai/Ch'an interaction, because Chih-k'ai was more of a San-lun than a T'ien-t'ai figure (see his *HKSC* biography at *T*50.570b–c). A closer and more fertile contact between the two schools must have occurred during Shen-hsiu's period of residence at Yü-ch'üan ssu, where Chih-i once lived. In addition, Nakagawa Taka has shown that even where "Tao-hsin" uses T'ien-t'ai sources, the ideas most characteristic of his thought do not occur in the original versions of those sources themselves. See her "Zenshū dai shiso Dōshin zenji no kenkyū," *Bunka,* 20, no. 6 (1956): 893–96.

61. *T*50.599c–600a. The reference to all sentient beings possessing the "first taste of *dhyāna*" *(ch'u-ti wei ch'an)* is reminiscent of the words of encouragement spoken by an unnamed monk to Seng-ch'ou. See *T*50.553c.

62. *T*50.602c–603b. Shan-fu studied under Fa-min, Chih-yen, and other masters whose names are unknown. Fa-min's *HKSC* biography occurs at *T*50.538b–39a. For Chih-yen, see *T*50.602a–c. Chih-yen is remembered as the second patriarch of the Ox-head School, a status of questionable historicity. See Sekiguchi's "Gozu-zen no rekishi to Daruma-zen," *Zenshū shisōshi,* pp. 251–58, and my "The Ox-head School of Chinese Buddhism: From Early Ch'an to the Golden Age," R. M. Gimello and P. N. Gregory, eds., *Studies in Ch'an and Hua-yen,* Studies in East Asian Buddhism (Honolulu: University of Hawaii Press in association with the Kuroda Institute, 1983), pp. 176–78. Yanagida discusses both Famin and Chih-yen briefly on p. 36 of *Shoki Zenshū shisho.* The criticism of Shanfu as a *pratyekabuddha* is unusual. The only other similar usage of which I am aware was directed at the Japanese Zen master Dōgen in the thirteenth century. See Imaeda Aishin, *Chūsei Zenshūshi no kenkyū* (Tokyo: Tōkyō Daigaku shuppan kai, 1970), p. 37.

63. *T*50.600a–b.

64. The inaccuracy of the traditionally accepted meeting between Tao-hsin and Fa-jung is discussed by Sekiguchi in his *Daruma daishi no kenkyū,* pp. 111–20.

65. One reference to Yuan-i occurs in Shen-hui's writings, for which the reader must refer to Suzuki's now rare *Tonkō shutsudo Kataku Jinne zenji goroku* (Tokyo: Morie shoten, 1934), p. 58. The *LTFPC* includes another reference, Yanagida, *Shoki no zenshi, 2,* p. 86, or *T*51.181c–82a.

66. For the *CFPC* and *LCSTC* accounts, see *Shoki no zenshi, 1,* pp. 386 and 268–88, or *T*85.1289b–90a (for the *LCSTC).* The *LTFPC* account is based very closely on these, containing only a few fanciful additions and one or two details from Shen-hui's account. See *Shoki no zenshi, 2,* pp. 92–93, or *T*51.182a–b, and pp. 59–60 of Suzuki's edition of Shen-hui's "recorded sayings" mentioned in the previous note. The *SKSC* biography occurs at *T*50.754a–b.

67. This detail is stated at the beginning of Hung-jen's *SKSC* biography.

68. Ui, 1:139, suggests that Hung-jen met Tao-hsin at Ta-lin ssu. Ui counts backward from Tao-hsin's date of death the number of years the two men are supposed to have spent together, but such figures are prone to exaggeration.

69. Shen-hui's account implies such a move by saying that Tao-hsin taught at Mount Shuang-feng and Hung-jen at Mount P'ing-mu "to the east of Mount Shuang-feng." The move is perhaps also implied by Tao-hsuan's statement that well after Tao-hsin's death Hung-jen and others examined the departed master's physical remains and removed them to their "present location." See *T*50.606b. Shiina discusses this issue in some detail in his "Tōzan hōmon keisei no haikei," pp. 173–74, concluding that near the end of his life Hung-jen may have moved in order to accommodate a growing congregation. Whatever the original validity of this move may be, it is reflected in the modern placement of monasteries and ruins on Mount Shuang-feng. See Tokiwa Daijō and Sekino Tadashi, *Shina Bukkyō shiseki hyōkai* (Tokyo: Bukkyō shiseki kenkyūkai, 1927), 4:154–59.

70. *Shoki Zenshū shisho,* pp. 55–56, includes a discussion of the various dates given for Hung-jen's death. The fact that his residence was made into a monastery is stated in the *LCJFC, Shoki no zenshi, 1,* p. 273, or *T*85.1289c.

71. The *Ts'ao-ch'i ta-shih chuan* was written about 782 and taken to Japan by Saichō, where the manuscript is now officially recognized as a National Treasure.

See Yanagida's "Zenseki kaidai," p. 469, and Yampolsky, pp. 70–77. The text occurs at *Z*2B, 19, 483a–88d (*H*146:965a–75b). The character *pieh* ("separate") given in the title of the printed text does not occur in the original manuscript.

72. *Shoki no zenshi, 1,* p. 273, or *T*85.1289c. The notion of a list of ten disciples is no doubt borrowed from the traditional biography of Confucius, just as the idea that all Hung-jen's favorites had died recalls that sage's grief over Yen-hui's untimely death.

73. See Yanagida's note in *Shoki no zenshi, 1,* p. 286. Shiina, p. 182, points out that the eulogy was probably written at the very beginning of the eighth century, rather than just after Hung-jen's death.

74. The most convenient reference for these lists is Ui, 1:140–41.

75. See *Shoki no zenshi, 2,* p. 137, or *T*51.184b–c.

76. Yanagida's "'Shishū Sen zenji sen, *Hannya shingyō so'* kō," *Yamada Mumon rōshi koki kinen shū: Hana samazama,* Yanagida Seizan and Umehara Takeshi, eds. (Tokyo: Shunjūsha, 1972), pp. 145–77, contains the text of Chih-shen's commentary and, on p. 148, a brief discussion of Chih-shen's life. Chih-shen's studies under Hsuan-tsang are supposed to have taken place in 621, at the famous translator's age of twenty-two. Yanagida suggests that the link between these two men was fabricated because of the existence of Chih-shen's commentary on the *Heart Sūtra (Hannya shingyō* in Japanese), which Hsuan-tsang translated.

77. The two Northern School texts that mention Hui-neng are the epitaph for Lao-an's student Ching-tsang (see Section 14 of this chapter) and a curious work to be discussed in Chapter IV, Section 8.

The early sources for Hui-neng's biography are actually not in agreement about the date of his studies at Huang-mei. Wang Wei's inscription for Hui-neng, which was commissioned by Shen-hui and thought to have been written around the year 740, gives no date for these studies. See Yampolsky, pp. 66–67, for a convenient synopsis of this epitaph. The *Shen-hui yü-lu* and *LTFPC* have Hui-neng going to Huang-mei at age twenty-two and departing eight months later, in 659 or 660. See Suzuki's *Kataku Jinne goroku,* p. 62, and *Shoki no zenshi, 2,* p. 98, or *T*51.182b. Fa-hai's preface to the *Platform Sūtra* dates the event at 661. The sūtra itself lacks any such reference, although it agrees with Shen-hui's account in having Hui-neng at Huang-mei for eight months. The *Ts'ao-ch'i ta-shih chuan,* which was written in 782 or 783, uses the year 674. See Yampolsky, pp. 60 and 72. In general, the later the text, the later were Hui-neng's supposed dates of study under Hung-jen. Ui, 1:161, inverts logic when he argues that, because of the *Platform Sūtra* story, Shen-hsiu must have been at Huang-mei when Hui-neng received his religious confirmation from Hung-jen. It is more reasonable to deny the historicity of the Hui-neng myth. The conclusion that Shen-hsiu and Hui-neng did not study under Hung-jen at the same time was first mentioned to me by Robert Zeuschner. The issue is discussed by Bernard Faure, *La Volonte d'Orthodoxie: Généalogie et doctrine du bouddhisme Ch'an et l'école du Nord—d'après l'une de ses chroniques, le* Leng-chia shih-tzu chi *(début du 8è s.)* (Ph.D. dissertation, University of Paris, 1984), pp. 36–37.

78. See Ui, 1:143, and *T*51.8c. Chih-hung was born in Lo-yang, lived for a time at Shao-lin ssu, and studied under Hung-jen at Huang-mei and, eventually,

under P'u-chi. He is known to have written odes on the events of his travels, but none of them survive. His dates may have been approximately 650–730.

79. See *T*50.758a and Ui, 1:158–59. Heng-ching is also known as Hung-ching; see *T*50.732b–c and *Shoki Zenshū shisho,* p. 210 n. 16. The date of Tao-shun's departure from court is given in the *SKSC* biography of an associate; see Ui, 1:158.

80. *T*50.731b. The name "Yin-tsung" is based on this monk's lay surname ("patriarch Yin"), just as in the cases of Ma-tsu Tao-i of the Hung-chou School and the Ox-head School monk Ho-lin Hsuan-su, who was also known as Ma-tsu or Ma-su. Yin-tsung's reputation was based primarily on his construction of ordination platforms and the ordination of thousands of people in the Chiang-tung area. He also supervised the construction of a massive image of Maitreya in or near the capital, probably sometime during the years 689–95. If Yin-tsung did in fact study with Hung-jen and Hui-neng, it is possible that he helped popularize the East Mountain Teaching and the figure of Hui-neng. Yin-tsung's *Hsin-yao chi* may have been the source of some of Shen-hui's anecdotes.

81. See *T*50.889b, *Shoki Zenshū shisho,* pp. 226 and 259, and Yampolsky, pp. 112–13, 120, and 165–68.

82. Hung-jen's lesser disciples are discussed by Ui, 1:149–50 and 153–58. Two of these figures, Hsuan-shih and the nun I-sheng, are listed in separate locations by Tsung-mi as representatives of the "Pure Land Ch'an of South Mountain" *(Nan-shan nien-fo men ch'an).* See Kamata Shigeo, *Zengen shosenshū tojo,* pp. 48 and 87, or *T*48.400c and 402c. These two figures are discussed by Sekiguchi, *Daruma daishi no kenkyū,* pp. 303–4 and 310. One figure of some importance who is supposed to have studied under Hung-jen is Fa-ch'ih (635–702), who was associated with the rise of the Ox-head School. See his biographies at *T*50.757c *(SKSC)* and *T*51.228c *(CTL).* Also see the discussions in *Shoki Zenshū shisho,* p. 130, and McRae, "The Ox-head School," p. 179.

83. The *SKSC* claims that Fa-ch'ih, just mentioned in the previous note, began his studies under Hung-jen at the age of thirteen, or in 647. The *CTL* biography gives the more likely age of thirty (664). The latter figure cannot be immediately accepted, however, since it does not fit well with the rest of Fa-ch'ih's biography.

84. Ui, 1:86–87.

85. The *HKSC* account of Tao-hsin's life refers to the "more than five hundred people in the mountain [community]" at the time of the master's death. (See the translation at the beginning of this chapter.) The figure of one thousand members of Hung-jen's congregation occurs in the *Platform Sūtra.* See Yampolsky, p. 127.

86. Shiina discusses this issue on the basis of information regarding the lay supporters of Tao-hsin and Hung-jen and statements regarding the remarkable industry of Hung-jen and some of his students (Shen-hsiu, for example). Shiina's conclusion is that the monks at Huang-mei were diligent in the operation of their monastery and that this characteristic may have led eventually to the spirit of self-reliance typical of the later Ch'an School. Nevertheless, it is likely that the East Mountain community received financial support from Ts'ai I-hsuan and others and equally *unlikely* that the monks there maintained an agricultural operation of any significant size. See "Tōzan hōmon keisei no haikei," pp. 176–78. For a discussion of the economic foundation of Buddhist monasteries during the T'ang, see Ch'en, pp. 261–73, and the studies he lists on pp. 523–26.

87. See Yampolsky, p. 128.

88. Ui's study of the *Platform Sūtra* may be found in the second volume of his tryptich on Ch'an, or *Zenshūshi kenkyū*, vol. 2 (Tokyo: Iwanami shoten, 1941), 1–116. His theory on the origin of the text is stated on pp. 100–9. (See especially pp. 103–5.) The innovation of the "pure regulations" is traditionally attributed to Po-chang Hui-hai (720–814), but there is no contemporary evidence with which to substantiate this claim. The *CTL* contains brief hints as to the existence of some type of Ch'an monastic regulations, but the oldest extant version of any complete set of them is the *Ch'an-yuan ch'ing-kuei*, which may have been written in 1103. See *T*51.250c–51b and the prefatory analysis in Kagamishima Genryū *et al.*, *Yakuchū Zennon shingi* (Tokyo: Sōtō shūmuchō, 1972), pp. 1–3.

Martin Collcutt includes a concise and well-stated account of the problem of the Po-chang code in his *Five Mountains: The Riuzai Zen Monastic Institution in Medieval Japan* (Cambridge, Mass.: Harvard University Press, 1981), pp. 136–45.

89. See *Shoki Zenshū shisho*, pp. 35–41 and 487–96, for a discussion of Fa-ju's life and an annotated edition of the epitaph in question. For the *CFPC* biography, see *Shoki no zenshi, 1*, p. 390, and section M of the translation in the Appendix.

90. Fa-min and Chih-yen have already been mentioned with regard to Tao-hsin's student Shan-fu. See n. 62.

91. See the discussion of the biographies of I-fu and P'u-chi in Chapter III, Sections 4 and 5. The Hui-tuan of Lo-yang who was involved in Fa-ju's resumption of teaching was probably P'u-chi's initial preceptor.

92. *Shoki Zenshū shisho*, p. 51.

93. Only one man is known to have been a disciple of Fa-ju. This is Hui-chao, who is mentioned in the *Shao-lin ssu pei*, *CTW*, fascicle 279, p. 20b. Hui-chao may be identical to a *Dhyāna* Master Chao mentioned in Chapter IV, Section 8.

94. See the *Chiu T'ang shu*, fascicle 191, *Erh-shih-wu shih*, 4:3592b–c. Lo Hsiang-lin has commented on this biography in his "*Chiu T'ang shu* Shen-hsiu chuan shu-cheng," *T'ang-tai wen-hua shih* (Taipei: Shang-wu Shu-chü, 1955), pp. 105–10.

95. *Wei Lo-hsia chu-seng ch'ing fa-shih ying Hsiu ch'an-shih piao*, *CTW*, fascicle 240, pp. 11b–12b, and reproduced in *Shoki Zenshū shisho*, p. 507.

96. *Chung-nan shan kuei ssu Ta-t'ung Tao-*[*hsiu*] *ho-shang t'a-wen*, in *Shoki no zenshi, 1*, pp. 426–27. Also see p. 430n. The relationship of this inscription to the *CFPC* is not clear. Also, the characters *kuei* and *tao* in the title are problematic, the latter being almost illegible. Although it is quite possible that a stūpa was built for Shen-hsiu on Mount Chung-nan outside of Ch'ang-an, there is no record of such a memorial. On the other hand, Emperor Chung-tsung did construct a thirteen-story stūpa for the departed master at Nan-p'u shan on Mount Sung. One wonders if this was the actual location indicated. See Mochizuki, 3:2880b, and Faure, p. 75 n. 98.

97. *Shoki no zenshi, 1*, pp. 396 and 403.

98. *Ibid.*, pp. 295 and 298, or *T*85.1290a–b.

99. *Shoki no zenshi, 1*, pp. 302, 306–7, and 312–13, and *T*85.1290b–c.

100. *Ching-chou Yü-ch'üan ssu Ta-t'ung ch'an-shih pei-ming ping hsü*, *CTW*, fascicle 231, pp.1a–4b. An annotated edition of this text occurs in *Shoki Zenshū*

shisho, pp. 497–516. Shen-hsiu's other eulogists are recorded in the *LCSTC* and *SKSC* (the first of the three *SKSC* entries listed in item 10).

101. *Hsieh hsi yü-shu Ta-t'ung ch'an-shih pei-e chuang, CTW*, fascicle 224, pp. 5b–6a, reproduced in *Shoki Zenshū shisho*, p. 502.

102. These occur in fascicles 94 and 97, respectively. See the *T'ai-p'ing kuang chi*, Li Fang *et al.*, eds. (10 vols.; Peking: Chung-hua shu-chü, 1961) 2:624–25 and 645. These stories are the basis of part of the material in the third of Shen-hsiu's *SKSC* biographies listed in item 10.

103. See n. 94.

104. *T*50.755c–56b, 812b–c, and 835b–c. The last of these includes a reference to Emperor Hsuan-tsung, which must be an error for Chung-tsung if the identification of Hui-hsiu and Shen-hsiu is to be accepted.

105. *T*51.231b. The item found here and nowhere else is a verse attributed to Shen-hsiu on the foolishness of seeking enlightenment outside one's own mind. This verse may be authentic, but it is not very significant. Shen-hsiu is also mentioned in the *Tsu-t'ang chi (Anthology of the Patriarchal Hall*, hereafter cited as *TTC)*, pp. 34a, 34b, 35a, 42b, 43b, 44b, and 50a, but these references lack historical value.

106. There are several different names given for Shen-hsiu's birthplace in the primary sources, but with one minor exception they all refer to the same location. See *Shoki Zenshū shisho*, pp. 502–3.

107. *Shoki no zenshi*, p. 302, or *T*85.1290b.

108. *Shoki Zenshū shisho*, p. 498.

109. *Shoki no zenshi, 1*, p. 396. Shen-hsiu's spiritual compatriot cannot be identified. Both Ching-ai and Hui-man, who are associated with the early Bodhidharma lineage, came from Ying-yang. See Chapter I, Section 5, items 2 and 5, and the *HKSC*, *T*50.625c and 552c. Shen-hsiu's spiritual compatriot may have been Lao-an, who is said to have traveled about performing humanitarian services during and after the Sui Emperor Yang's canal construction projects. It is possible, however, that this assertion about Lao-an was made on the basis of Shen-hsiu's biography. See the discussion of Lao-an in Section 14 of this chapter.

110. See the *Epitaph, Shoki Zenshū shisho*, p. 499. For information about the monastery, see pp. 510–11n. Yanagida points out that a monastery by this name existed as early as the year 467. It is mentioned as the residence of several T'ang Dynasty monks but eventually came to be associated principally with Shen-hsiu.

111. *Shoki Zenshū shisho*, p. 498. Yanagida points out on p. 505 that the washing of feet indicates acceptance of a teacher and transcendence of the affairs of the world.

112. See n. 77.

113. *Shoki no zenshi, 1*, p. 396. The name T'ien-chü ssu may be an error for T'ien-kung ssu, since the latter occurs in the *HKSC* and the former does not.

114. These events are summarized in Michihata Ryōshū, *Tōdai Bukkyōshi no kenkyū* (Kyoto: Hōzōkan, 1957), pp. 335–41. A better discussion occurs in Stanley Weinstein, "Buddhism under the T'ang," forthcoming in the second volume of the *Cambridge History of China: The T'ang Dynasty*. Incidentally, the *SKSC* (*T*50.812b) states that the original edict enjoining parents to reverence both the emperor and their own parents was withdrawn, but no date is given.

115. A corollary to this hypothesis is that Shen-hsiu was in Ch'ang-an in the early 660s and well-enough acquainted with Tao-hsuan to provide the information for the *HKSC* entry on Tao-hsin. For another example of multiple biographies for one individual, see Arthur Wright, "Seng-jui Alias Hui-jui: A Biographical Bisection in the *Kao-seng chuan,*" *Liebenthal Festschift,* pp. 272–93.

116. *Shoki no zenshi, 1,* p. 396.

117. *Shoki Zenshū shisho,* p. 498.

118. Mochizuki's chronological table asserts that the *Chiu T'ang shu,* fascicle 95, and the *SKSC,* fascicle 8, indicate that Tu-men ssu was founded in 675. I do not find any such reference in the former, and the latter only mentions "Shen-hsiu of Tu-men," without specifying a date. If the establishment of this monastery did take place in 675, this would imply that Shen-hsiu's ordination was the consummation of an extended local campaign.

119. Empress Wu's father, Wu Shih-huo, was once the military governor of Ching-chou. His entrée into political power came from an association with Emperor Kao-tsu. If this were a factor in Shen-hsiu's choice of residence, an interesting parallel would exist between his life and that of the Northern Ch'i meditation specialist Seng-ch'ou. That is, both of them were closely associated with the eventual wielders of imperial power long before their successful careers at court.

120. See n. 29 to Part Two.

121. The *CFPC* claim occurs in *Shoki no zenshi, 1,* p. 396, or section N of the translation in the Appendix.

122. It is possible that the timing of Shen-hsiu's resumption of public activities was more closely related to political developments than to Hung-jen's death. Lao-an's disciple Yuan-kuei was ordained during the amnesty that followed the assassination of Crown Prince Li Hung by the future Empress Wu in 675. Since she was able to consolidate her power at this time, Shen-hsiu may have benefitted from this even more than Yuan-kuei. See n. 144.

123. See I-hsing's letter in the *CTW,* fascicle 914, pp. 16b–17b. Yanagida translates the critical lines of this letter in *Shoki no zenshi, 1,* p. 311. During the last two decades of the seventh century the Northern School established, in addition to Tu-men ssu in Ching-chou, a strong center at Shao-lin ssu and other monasteries on Mount Sung. Yet another center was established on Mount Chung-nan in the second decade of the eighth century. See Chapter III, Section 1.

124. *Shoki no zenshi, 1,* p. 403. The *Fo-tsu t'ung-chi (T*49.369c*)* claims that Shen-hsiu entered the capital in 690, but the source of this information is unknown. Even the *LTFPC,* the early source most prone to inaccurate exaggerations, confirms his invitation in 700. See *Shoki no zenshi, 2,* p. 129, or *T*51.184a.

125. This is also corroborated in a work by Saichō, the founder of the Japanese Tendai School. See *Shoki Zenshū shisho,* p. 507.

126. *Ibid.,* p. 499.

127. *T*50.724c.

128. *Shoki no zenshi, 1,* p. 306.

129. See n. 95. This is actually the oldest extant work to refer to the East Mountain Teaching, which is given here (near the end of the first paragraph) as *tung-shan miao-fa.* Note the finely wrought parallelism in the third and fourth

paragraphs between south and north (Ching-*nan* and Yü-*pei*) and the Nine Rivers (Chiu-chiang) and Three Rivers (San-ho). Chiu-chiang is a city in what is now Kiangsi Province, while San-ho refers to the general area south, east, and north of the Yellow River in northern China.

130. The *LCSTC* edict occurs on p. 302 of *Shoki no zenshi, 1,* or *T*85.1290b. Chung-tsung's progress to Lung-men is mentioned in Mochizuki's chronological table; the original source is the *Chiu T'ang shu,* fascicle 7, *Erh-shih-wu shih,* 4:3078a. (The progress is given as having occurred in the tenth month of the year in question.) The *Epitaph, Shoki Zenshū shisho,* p. 499, states that at one point Shen-hsiu was given permission to return to Tu-men ssu but that this favor was rescinded before he could take advantage of it. As to the limited impact of Sung's *Memorial,* the *Chiu T'ang shu* states that the reverence accorded Shen-hsiu during Chung-tsung's reign was even greater than before. More specifically, a Sung Dynasty commentary on the T'ang translation of the *Śūraṁgama-samādhi Sūtra* states that Shen-hsiu obtained a copy of the text at the training center within the imperial palace, copied it, and took it back to Tu-men ssu in Ching-chou. Although this story is suspect because Shen-hsiu did not return to Tu-men ssu until after his death, it suggests that Shen-hsiu was active in the palace at Lo-yang at least until the year 705, when this translation was completed. See Tzu-hsuan's (964 or 965–1038) *Shou-leng-yen i shu-chu ching, T*39.825c. The fact of Shen-hsiu's acquisition of this text is also mentioned in the *SKSC, T*50.738c.

131. See *Shoki no zenshi, 1,* p. 305. Nakamura Hajime, *Bukkyōgo daijiten,* (3 vols.; Tokyo: Tōkyō shoseki, 1975), 1:287b, cites a commentary on the *Avataṁsaka Sūtra* by Ch'eng-kuan as the locus classicus of the term *ch'ü-ch'ü chiao.*

132. Shen-hsiu's last words should be considered along with the "questions about things" introduced in Chapter IV, Section 14.

133. See the *Ta-Sung seng-shih lueh, T*54.252c.

134. *Shoki Zenshū shisho,* p. 500.

135. See the *Eulogy* and n. 96 above.

136. The *Fo-tsu t'ung-chi* refers to these ordinations as occurring under Lao-an in the fifth month of the Shen-lung period (706). See *T*49.372b. Lao-an's *SKSC* biography has the seventh month. (*T*50.823c.) See the discussion of his biography in Section 14 of this chapter.

137. See Sung Tan's *Sung-shan Hui-shan ssu ku ta-te Tao-an ch'an-shih pei-ming, CTW,* fascicle 396, pp. 12a–14b, and the *SKSC, T*50.823b and 829c. Lao-an is also mentioned in the *LCSTC* (*Shoki no zenshi, 1,* pp. 273 and 295, or *T*85.1289c and 1290a) and the *LTFPC (Shoki no zenshi, 2,* pp. 92, 122, and 129, or *T*51.182b, 183c, and 184a) and receives historically useless entries in the *TTC,* p. 55b (he is also mentioned on p. 35a), and the *CTL, T*51.231c.

138. Hua-t'ai was associated with Li Yung (678–747), an important epigrapher of Northern School figures. It was also the eventual scene of Shen-hui's attack on P'u-chi and the Northern School in 732. See *Shoki Zenshū shisho,* p. 114 n. 3.

139. The two Sung Dynasty sources are the *Fo-tsu t'ung-chi, T*49.370b, and the *Fo-tsu t'ung-tsai, T*49.584b. For the *LTFPC,* see *Shoki no zenshi, 2,* p. 129, or *T*51.184a.

140. Although not necessarily intended to belittle Shen-hsiu, a story in the *Tsu-t'ing shih-yuan,* a Sung Dynasty text, demonstrates this implicit one-upsmanship. While residing in the palace, on one occasion Shen-hsiu and Lao-an

were assisted into the bath by female attendants. Hearing that only Lao-an went about taking his bath in complete composure, Empress Wu sighed in amazement and said: "Only through seeing him enter the bath have I learned of the existence of a superior man *(ch'ang-jen).*" Implicitly, Shen-hsiu comes out second-best in this observation. See *Z*2, 18, 8b (*H*113:15b).

141. The *SKSC* states that Lao-an returned to Yü-ch'üan ssu briefly after Shen-hsiu's death. The earlier date for Lao-an's death fits better with the timing of Hsuan-tse's invitation to court, as discussed in the next section of this Chapter. One aspect of Tao-an's death that deserves at least passing notice is that the eccentric monk Wan-hui (632–711) clutched the dying monk's hands, stared at him crazily, and talked on and on incomprehensibly. As with Pao-chih and Fu Hsi of an earlier era, eccentricity was appreciated at court under the guise of religious inspiration. Wan-hui had supervised some of the services following Shen-hsiu's death and was officially ordained by imperial edict in 706. (See *Shoki Zenshū shisho,* p. 513a.)

142. See Yanagida's *Zenseki kaidai,* p. 458, and Ueyama Daishun, "Chibetto-yaku *Tongo shinshū yōketsu* no kenkyū," *Zenbunka kenkyūjo kiyō,* 8 (1976): 33–103.

143. See the *TTC,* pp. 55b–56a, and the *CTL, T*51.461b. For Tao-shun, see Section 5 of this chapter.

144. Yuan-kuei's very brief epitaph occurs in the *CTW,* fascicle 914, p. 20a–c. His *SKSC* biography, which is not very informative, is at *T*50.828b–29b. The most interesting feature of this biography is a story about the conferring of the Buddhist precepts on the spirit of Mount Sung. A similar story occurs in the *SKSC* biography of Lao-an. Ui, 1:340, mentions a disciple of Yuan-kuei's named Ling-yun (d. 729) who resided at Hui-shan ssu on Mount Sung, but the source of this information is unknown. (Yuan-kuei was a resident of Hsien-chü ssu, also on Mount Sung.) Yuan-kuei is listed as a student of Lao-an's in the *CTL, T*51.224b.

145. Tokiwa Daijō and Sekino Tadashi, *Shina bunka shiseki* (Tokyo: Hōzōkan, 1939–41), 2, plate 113.

146. Ching-tsang's biography is known through an anonymous epitaph found in the *CTW,* fascicle 997, pp. 10a–11a; the *Chin-shih ts'ui-pien,* fascicle 87, compiled by Wang Ch'ang (4 vols.; Taipei: Kuo-lien t'u-shu ch'u-pan yu-hsien kung-ssu, 1964), 3:1524a–25a; and Tokiwa, *Shina bunka shiseki* 2, plate 114 (1). Ching-tsang's native place was Chi-yin, the same as that of a student of Shen-hsiu's named Hsiang-yü. (See n. 163.) Ching-tsang received official ordination in 708 and Hui-neng died in 713; thus the two were together for five years or less—four years or less if Lao-an died in 709.

147. See the *Ta-T'ang Ch'i-chou Lung-hsing ssu ku Fa-hsien ta ch'an-shih pei-ming, CTW,* fascicle 304, pp. 12b–16b, and Ui, 1:154. Fa-hsien is probably identical to the individual named Hsien who is listed by Tsung-mi as one of Hung-jen's disciples. See Ui, 1:141.

148. That Fa-hsien is identified with Lung-hsing ssu in Ch'i-chou (1) verifies the approximate provenance of the epitaph, since this national monastic system was only established in 738, and (2) underscores the apparent demise of the center on Mount Shuang-feng, for which we have absolutely no information after Hung-jen's death.

149. *Shoki no zenshi, 1,* p. 273, or *T*85.1289c.

150. Hsuan-tse's fortunes may have been affected by those of his student Ching-chueh. See Chapter IV, Section 12.

151. See the preface to Ching-chueh's commentary on the *Heart Sūtra, Shoki Zenshū shisho,* p. 597.

152. Hung-jen's importance is demonstrated by Fa-hsien's epitaph (as discussed in Chapter II, Section 15), by the continuity between his legendary image and that of Hui-neng, and by the existence of the *Hsiu-hsin yao lun* (as discussed in Part Two, Chapter VI, Section 1).

153. The figure of seventy major students is given in the *Epitaph, Shoki Zenshū shisho,* p. 499. See the *CTL, T*51.224a–b for a list of nineteen of his students. Ui, 1:275–95, discusses the biographies of fourteen of Shen-hsiu's students. The following is a brief resume of the lives of Shen-hsiu's lesser students:

A. Chü-fang (647–727) is given a biography in the *SKSC, T*50.759b–c, and the *CTL, T*51.232a–b, but he is not mentioned in earlier sources. (See Ui, 1:284–85.) Early in his career he lectured on the "theory (or treatise[s]) of the Southern School" *(nan-tsung lun),* which must be a reference to the Mādhyamika. (*Shoki Zenshū shisho,* p. 122.) Soon, however, he became aware of the importance of meditation and sought out Shen-hsiu. The first meeting between the two men is described in classical encounter dialogue style. Chü-fang's teaching supposedly emphasized both sudden enlightenment and gradual practice, with many of his students actually achieving the former. He taught in Han-ling in Shang-tang (a general location already mentioned with regard to Fa-ju) and An-kuo yuan in Yun-chou, then spent more than twenty years on Mount T'ai, where he died.

B. Chih-feng's biography is appended to that of Chü-fang in the *SKSC, T*50.759c. See also the *CTL, T*51.232b, and Ui, 1:286. There are several minor similarities between the biographies of these two men, but nothing of real interest here. Chih-feng gave up the study of the Yogācāra in order to devote himself to meditation.

C. Hsiang-yü's biography also occurs in the *SKSC, T*50.759c–60a. He is listed in the *CTL, T*51.224b, and discussed by Ui, 1:286–87. Hsiang-yü first studied the Taoist classics, then switched to Buddhism. He studied the *Vinaya* and visited numerous holy sites before becoming a student of Shen-hsiu. Hsiang-yü died at the age of seventy-three at Mount Ta-fo in Ying-chou (Chung hsien, Hupeh), but no date is given.

D. Ssu-heng (651–726) is known solely from an epitaph and a note of praise by Emperor Chung-tsung on his portrait. See Ui, 1:289–90. This monk was primarily an expert in the *Vinaya* who studied for a time under Shen-hsiu.

E. Hu-lei Ch'eng is known through a comment made by the compilers of the *CTW* and prefixed to a very brief epitaph written by Hu for Hsiao-liao, a student of Hui-neng. (See fascicle 913, p. 6a.) In this comment Hu is identified as a student of Shen-hsiu active during the period 705–706. The *CTL* lists him as a student of Shen-hsiu with the title of *Dhyāna* Master, so that he must have been a monk. (*T*51.224b.) The *CTW*'s source of information was probably the *CTL* entry for Hsiao-liao, *T*51.237c. This individual may have been identical to the Hsiao-liao listed as a disciple of Wu-hsiang of Szechwan (*T*51.224c). The word "hu-lei," incidentally, is a synonym for *p'i-pa,* the Chinese lute.

F. Ch'ung-shen: Ui, 1:291, mentions the existence of a very tattered epitaph for this individual.

G. Tz'u-lang is listed in the *CTL* as a student of Shen-hsiu's who had three students of his own. See Ui, 1:291–92. Of Tz'u-lang's three students, only one is known: Hsuan-tsung (682–767) of Mount Tzu-chin in Shou-chou, whose biography occurs in the *SKSC* (*T*50.838b). Based on this biography, Ui infers that Tz'u-lang remained in Ching-chou to teach when Shen-hsiu went to Lo-yang in 701.

H. Hui-fu is listed in the *LCSTC* as one of four major successors, but his biography is unknown. See *Shoki no zenshi, 1,* p. 320, plus Yanagida's note on p. 324, or *T*85.1290c, and Ui, 1:290. The *LCSTC* identifies Hui-fu as a resident of Mount Yü in Lan-t'ien, just to the east of Ch'ang-an. Ui suggests that he may be identical to the Hsiao-fu, or "Little Fu," listed in the *CTL, T*51.224b, for whom three otherwise unknown disciples are listed. (One of these disciples is listed as a resident of Lan-t'ien, which bolsters the probability of this identification.) There is a Hsiao-fu listed as one of the teachers of Mo-ho-yen, the famous Ch'an emissary to Tibet, but minor problems are connected with this identification, as will be mentioned in Section 8 of this chapter. (See n. 188.)

I. Ta-fu (655–743) is known through an epitaph, as discussed by Ui, 1:375. Ta-fu, or "Big Fu," was a *Vinaya* specialist who became a student of Shen-hsiu at Yü-ch'üan ssu. He accompanied Shen-hsiu to court in 701 and in 707–10 was made abbot *(shang-tso)* of T'u-shan ssu, then Shan-fu ssu, Ching-shan ssu, and Lung-hsing ssu. The second and fourth of these in particular were important monasteries, so that Ta-fu must have played an important role in the Northern School's extension of power throughout the Ch'ang-an religious establishment. In 738 he was made the abbot of the newly established K'ung-chi ssu, where he died five years later. A Ta-fu is also listed as a teacher of Mo-ho-yen. Yanagida, *Shoki Zenshū shisho,* pp. 459–60 n. 20, identifies this Ta-fu as I-fu, who was one of Shen-hsiu's most prominent students.

154. See the *SKSC, T*50.760a, the *CTL, T*51.232b, and Ui, 1:287–89. Hsiang-mo Tsang is also listed as one of Mo-ho-yen's teachers.

155. Some of Tsang's sayings became well known in early Tibetan Buddhism. Hsiang-mo Tsang may also be the author of short doctrinal pronouncements in the miscellaneous material appended to the *EJSHL* (Yanagida, *Daruma no goroku,* p. 239) and in a curious text discussed briefly in Chapter IV, Section 8. Finally, he is listed in a pseudolineage of early Tibetan Ch'an in the Tun-huang manuscript P. tib. 116. See Ueyama Daishun, "Tonkō shutsudo Chibetto-bun Zen-shiryō no kenkyū—P. tib. 116 to sono mondaiten," *Bukkyō Bunka Kenkyū-jo kiyō,* 13 (June 1974): 9.

156. See the discussion of Chü-fang, including the reference to Yanagida's comment, in n. 153, item A.

157. With regard to the possible fabrication or ornamentation of Hsiang-mo Tsang's biography, note the similarity between it and the two previous entries in the *SKSC.* These are devoted to Chü-fang, Hsiang-yü, and Chih-feng. These entries contain several similar names of monasteries and teachers, dialogues, sponsorship by locally prominent figures, and long periods of alpine retreat at the end of each subject's life, etc. Comparison with another set of entries occur-

ring only a few pages below in the *SKSC,* at *T*50.765a–66a, may indicate the provenance of the entries for Chü-fang *et al.* The second group of entries covers Tao-shu (734–825), Huai-k'ung (705–87), Yuan-kuan (752–830), Ch'ung-kuei (756–841), and Ch'üan-chih (752–844). The first two of these monks are said to have been associated with Shen-hsiu and P'u-chi, respectively; in the case of Tao-shu, this assertion is chronologically impossible. Yuan-kuan's father held the same official status in the same location as that mentioned in the biographies of Chih-feng and Hsiang-yü, while Ch'üan-shih is supposed to have had an oral exchange with a local governor named Wei Wen-ch'ing. Chih-feng and Chü-fang each took part in similar dialogues, that of the former being with the governor Wei Wen-sheng. (*T*50.759c.) Although these coincidences are each trivial individually, taken together they imply that Shen-hsiu and P'u-chi were still remembered with reverence during the late eighth and early ninth centuries.

158. See the *CTW,* fascicle 362, pp. 6b–8a. A partial rubbing is reproduced in Tokiwa, *Shina bunka shiseki,* 2, plate 115 (2).

159. Ching-hsien's epitaph has a lacuna at this critical point, so we know only that he was ordained in 705, 706, or 707.

160. The text of Ching-hsien's encounter with Śubhākarasiṁha is the *Wu-wei san-tsang shou-chieh ch'an-hui wen chi ch'an-men yao-fa, T*18.942b–46a. A short passage from this work is translated in n. 340 to Part Two. See Yanagida's "Zenseki kaidai," p. 468. Ui, 1:284, gives slightly different dates for the events connected with Ching-hsien's biography, even correcting a number given in the epitaph. His basis for these dates is unknown, although he may have used a different text for the epitaph than that in the *CTW.*

161. See the *SKSC, T*50.760b–c, and the epitaph for him by Yen T'ing-chih, *CTW,* fascicle 280, pp. 11b–16a. Other sources for his biography include a notice by Yang Po-ch'eng, *CTW,* fascicle 331, p. 8a–b; a stūpa inscription by Tu Yü, *T'ang-wen shih-i,* fascicle 19, Lu Hsin-yuan, ed. (72 fascicles; originally published 1888, reprint Taipei: Wen-hai ch'u-pan she, 1962), 1:298a–99b; and information in the entry for Shen-hsiu in the *Chiu T'ang shu.* Yanagida, *Shoki no zenshi, 1,* p. 324, notes that Yen T'ing-chih's epitaph is generally considered to be the very best of such T'ang Dynasty works, from both calligraphic and literary standpoints.

162. The locations in question are Lu-chou (Ch'ang-chih hsien, Shansi) and Ju-nan (Ju-nan hsien, Honan), respectively. See *T*50.760b, *CTW,* fascicle 280: 12a, and Chapter II, Section 7.

163. The epitaph refers to "cultivating the "five teachings" *(wu men)* and entering the "seven purities" *(ch'i ching).*" These may be equivalent to the "five types of inhibitory contemplation" *(wu t'ing-hsin kuan)* and these five plus two other stages of the *darśanamārga.* See Mochizuki, 2:1258c and 2:1890c. Of course, the "five teachings" could also be a reference to the five expedient means *(wu fang-pien)* of the Northern School, which will be discussed in Part Two, Chapter VII.

164. As noted in Section 1 of this chapter, both I-fu and P'u-chi were on Mount Sung for a time after Shen-hsiu's death. That I-fu lived in the Dharma hall (*fa-t'ang,* or *hattō* in Japanese) at Hua-kan ssu may have some relationship to the configuration of later Ch'an monasteries, which were built with

Dharma halls but without pavilions of the Buddha *(fo-tien)*. This innovation reflects Ch'an's rejection of religious devotionalism in favor of meditation practice.

165. See Ui, 1:296 and Yampolsky, pp. 38–39. The only student of I-fu's for whom some information is available is Ssu-jui, but even this man's biography is suspect. He supposedly studied with I-fu for five years sometime between 713 and 732 at Shao-lin ssu. I-fu was in the Lo-yang area during this period only from 725–727; there is no record of his being on Mount Sung during this period and no reference to his ever being at Shao-lin ssu. See *T*51.226b and Ui, 1:295.

166. See the epitaph by Li Hua discussed in Yampolsky, pp. 38–39. The number of monks listed in the *SKSC* and elsewhere as successors to P'u-chi, rather than as successors to Shen-hsiu or members of the Northern School in general, may also be taken as evidence of this point. (Two examples of this are discussed in n. 176.) In this regard, P'u-chi's role seems parallel to that of Hui-k'o. (See Chapter I, Section 5, including n. 34.)

167. This passage occurs in the Tun-huang manuscript S2512. See Tanaka Ryōshō's "Hokushū-zen no seiten sotō-setsu—*Daishichi-so Daishō oshō jakumetsu nissai sambun* (gi) o meguru ichi shiron," *Komazawa Daigaku Bukkyō Gakubu kenkyū kiyo* 26 (March 1968): 90–102.

168. This passage occurs in Li Yung's epitaph for P'u-chi, *CTW*, fascicle 262, p. 3b.

169. This fact is implicit in Weinstein's analysis of the Sui-T'ang Schools in "Imperial Patronage in T'ang Buddhism," p. 268f.

170. In addition to the sources already listed in notes 167 and 168, see the *SKSC*, *T*50.760c–61a, and the *Chiu T'ang shu* entry for Shen-hsiu. Also see Ui, 1:279–83, Yanagida, *Shoki no zenshi, 1*, pp. 322–23, and Tanaka Ryōshō, "Daishō zenshi Fujaku ni tsuite," *Indogaku Bukkyōgaku kenkyū*, 16, no. 1 (March 1967): 331–34.

171. For Heng-ching, see n. 79. Preceptor Tuan is probably the monk mentioned in the *CFPC* with regard to Shen-hsiu's return to public activities in 675.

172. See p. 9a of the epitaph.

173. The *Chiu T'ang shu* and *SKSC* have this appointment occurring during Shen-hsiu's life in respect for his advanced age, although contextual clues in the latter text imply that it actually occurred after Shen-hsiu's death. Tanaka, "Daishō zenji Fujaku ni tsuite," p. 332, discusses the accounts of this attempted appointment and decides that it occurred after Shen-hsiu's death and was not accepted by P'u-chi. I suspect that P'u-chi chose to defer to Lao-an. For a discussion of Wu P'ing-i's biography and the background of Shen-hui's criticism, see Yanagida, *Shoki Zenshū shisho*, pp. 111 and 116 n. 14.

174. P'ei K'uan is known to have been in conflict with the very powerful Li Lin-fu around this time. He was not, however, the only high-ranking official associated with the Northern School to run afoul of this powerful politician. In 747 Li Yung was put to death, Li Shih-chih committed suicide after having been stripped of office the previous year, and Fang Kuan was banished. These men were associated with P'u-chi, Fa-hsien, and I-fu, respectively. See the chronological table in *Tōdai no shijin—sono denki*, Ogawa Tamaki, ed. (Tokyo: Daishukan shoten, 1975), p. 692.

175. This is Tu-ku Chi's epitaph for Seng-ts'an, *CTW,* fascicle 390, pp. 21b–24b, mentioned by Ui, 1:296.

176. The epitaph that refers to "single fountainhead of the Northern School" is mentioned in n. 165. Some of the references to Hung-cheng are listed by Ui, 1:310. The epitaph for Hung-cheng's student Ch'i-wei (720–81), *CTW,* fascicle 501, pp. 13a–15a, was written by Ch'üan Te-yü (759–818), who also wrote the epitaph for Ma-tsu Tao-i. See *Shoki Zenshū shisho,* p. 354, for comments on this epigrapher's importance. Ch'üan Te-yü was Ch'i-wei's great-nephew. Ch'i-wei's career was unique in that at age nine he studied Esoteric Buddhist practices under Vajrabodhi and later studied Ch'an under a nun before becoming Hung-cheng's disciple. Ch'i-wei's epitaph is interesting for (1) its reference to P'u-chi as the seventh generation from Bodhidharma and complete omission of Shen-hsiu's name; (2) its numerous references to Ch'i-wei's family, which obviously derive from the relationship between him and his epigrapher; and (3) its extensive but unimaginative use of standard Ch'an plattitudes and cliches. See Ui, 1:325–26.

The other epitaph to which I have alluded in the text is by Li Hua for Ch'ang-chao (705–63), *CTW,* fascicle 316, pp. 17a–18a. See Ui, 1:325–26. This monk actually studied under P'u-chi, Hung-cheng, and an unknown master named Ching-shou. Ui suggests that this may be a mistake for Ching-ai [ssu], so that the individual in question is actually T'an-chen (704–63) of that monastery. (Ui also mentions Fa-yuan of the same monastery, but T'an-chen's date of birth makes him a more likely candidate.)

177. The most complete study on I-hsing is Osabe Kazuo's *Ichigyō zenji no kenkyū* (Kobe: Kōbe Shōka Daigaku Keizai Kenkyūjo, 1963). Ui, 1:299–300, discusses the general outline of I-hsing's biography. A passage from I-hsing's commentary on the *Vairocana Sūtra* will be introduced in Part Two, Chapter VI, Section 4.

178. See the *SKSC, T*50.761b–c, and Ui, 1:300–301.

179. See the *SKSC, T*50.834a–b, Ui, 1:305–306, and Ming-ts'an's work in the *CTL, T*51.461b–c.

180. As a precocious youth, Li Mi was favored by Chang Chiu-ling, Chang Yueh, and Yen T'ing-chih, all of whom were associated with the Northern School. See his biography in the *T'ang shu,* fascicle 139, and the *Chiu T'ang shu,* fascicle 130.

181. See Ui, 1:306.

182. See Ui, 1:307–8, and Mochizuki, 4:3883a–c. Tao-hsuan's dates are from the latter source. Faure, *La Volonte d'Orthodoxie,* pp. 233–45, discusses the legacy of the Northern School in Japan, a subject which is outside the scope of this study.

183. See Ui, 1:295–315. There is a certain parallelism in the tendencies to cite Hui-k'o and P'u-chi in lineage descriptions, rather than Bodhidharma and Shen-hsiu, respectively.

184. Ui, 1:329, lists the 126th and final known member of the Northern School, beginning with Shen-hsiu. This number does not include Chih-hung, who studied under Hung-jen and P'u-chi.

185. Those with some experience in the South include Tao-shu, Ch'ung-kuei, Ch'üan-chih, Yuan-kuan, Ch'eng-hsin, Jih-chao, Fa-jung, Ch'ung-yen, and

Chen. Those without such experience are Heng-cheng, T'an-chen (d. 791), Ch'i-wei, Ch'ang-chao, and Shen-hsing (in the Chinese pronunciation).

186. The landmark study in this field is Paul Demieville's *Le Concile de Lhasa: Une controverse sur le quiétisme entre bouddhistes de l'Inde et de la Chine au ville siècle de l'ère chrétienne,* Bibliotheque de l'Insitut des hautes etudes chinoises, vol. 7 (Paris: Impr. nationale de France, 1952). Substantial additional work has been done in Japan, principally by Ueyama, Obata, and Okimoto. Their findings are summarized in Jeffrey Broughton, "Early Ch'an Schools in Tibet," R. M. Gimello and P. N. Gregory, eds., *Studies in Ch'an and Hua-yen,* pp. 1–68. I have relied heavily on Broughton's article in the preparation of Section 8 of this chapter. With regard to the debates themselves, Okimoto Katsumi, "Tonkō shutsudo Seizōbun Zenshū bunken no kenkyū (1)," *Indogaku Bukkyōgaku kenkyū,* 26, no. 1 (March 1977): 460, has suggested that they should not be treated simplistically in terms of the victory and defeat of two separate schools of thought. The English reader may wish to consult Joseph F. Roccasalvo, "The Debate at bSam yas: A study in religious contrast and correspondence," *Philosophy East and West,* 30, no. 4 (December 1980): 505–20. Unfortunately, Roccasalvo attempts to explain the Chinese position on the basis of the works of Suzuki and Dumoulin.

187. For example, the patently absurd link between Preceptor Kim (Wu-hsiang) and Wu-chu in the *LTFPC* could have been motivated by the prestige of the former in Tibet.

188. Mo-ho-yen is listed in the Tibetan pseudolineage mentioned in n. 155. His actual teachers are listed in the *Tun-wu ta-sheng cheng-li chueh,* Demieville, plate 156b, and repeated and discussed in Yanagida, *Shoki Zenshū shisho,* pp. 459–60 n. 20. In addition to Hsiang-mo [Tsang], whose identity is certain, the text lists "Hsiao-fu Chang ho-shang" and "Ta-fu Liu ho-shang." These may be I-fu and Hui-fu. As Yanagida notes, Jao Tsung-i has argued, based on the occurrence of the name Mo-ho-yen in a list in one of Tsung-mi's works, that the Ch'an emissary to Tibet was also a student of Shen-hui. However, it is possible that Tsung-mi added Mo-ho-yen to his list of Shen-hui's successors because of an inferred relationship between the teachings of the two men. Yanagida also notes the occurrence of the same name in an Esoteric Buddhist context, and it is impossible to know whether all these citations refer to the same individual. See Jao, "Shen-hui men-hsia Mo-ho-yen chih ju-Tsang, chien lun ch'an-men nan-pei tsung chih t'iao-ho wen-t'i," *Hsiang-kang Ta-hsueh wu-shih chou-nien chi-nien lun-wen chi,* vol. 1 (Hong Kong: Hong Kong University, 1964), 173–78.

Whatever Mo-ho-yen's true background, the two most influential Ch'an groups in Tibet at this time were apparently the Pao-t'ang faction of Wu-chu and the Northern School. This conclusion is made by Obata in his "Chibetto no Zenshū to *Rekidai hōbō ki,*" (in Yanagida, *Shoki no Zenshi, 2,* pp. 325–37) and reiterated, with additional information, in his "Chibetto no Zenshū to zōyaku gikyō ni tsuite," *Indogaku Bukkyōgaku Keukyu,* 23, no. 2 (1975): 667. In another article, "Chibetto-den Bodaidarumatara zenji kō," *Indogaku Bukkyōgaku kenkyū,* 24, no. 1 (1975): 232, Obata suggests that Mo-ho-yen's description as the successor to the Seventh Patriarch of Ch'an makes him, in effect, an extension of Wu-chu's Pao-t'ang faction. (Were the materials in question in Chinese rather than Tibetan, I would have assumed that the term "Seventh Patriarch" was a reference to Hsiang-mo Tsang.)

189. The term "transmission history" or "transmission text" is an adaptation of the compound *tōshi* (*teng-shih* in Chinese; lit., "lamp history") used by Yanagida, which is itself adapted from the various titles including or implying the three characters *ch'üan-teng lu,* or "records of the transmission of the lamp," as in the title of the *CTL.* Well-known examples of the other two genre of texts would be the *Lin-chi lu* (*The Records of Lin-chi; Rinzai-roku* in Japanese) and the *Pi-yen lu (Blue Cliff Records; Hekigan-roku).* The English terminology used here was developed in the course of preparing "The Development of the 'Recorded Sayings' Texts of the Chinese Ch'an School" (a translation of Yanagida Seizan, "Zenshū goroku no keisei"), Whalen Lai and Lewis Lancaster, eds., *Early Ch'an in China and Tibet,* Berkeley Buddhist Studies Series, no. 5 (Berkeley, Calif: Asian Humanities Press, 1983), pp. 185–205.

190. This term refers to the dialogue *(wen-ta)* resulting from the encounters *(chi-yuan)* between master and disciple.

191. This interpretation of the public case anthologies is my interpretation of comments made in private conversation by Professor Yanagida in 1975.

192. *T*51.196–467. See Yanagida's "Zenseki kaidai," p. 478, for information about this important text. Although the *CTL* was presented to the throne in the year 1004, the text may have undergone some revision shortly after this date.

193. See T. R. V. Murti, *The Central Philosophy of Buddhism* (London: George Allen and Unwin, 1955), pp. 36–54; K. N. Jayatilleke, *Early Buddhist Theory of Knowledge,* pp. 470–76; and Mochizuki, 3:2268b–69a.

194. See Étienne Lamotte, *Histoire du bouddhisme indien—des origines à l'ère Śaka,* Bibliothèque du *Museon,* vol. 43 (Louvain, Belgium: Institut Orientaliste, Universite de Louvain, 1958), 69–71.

195. See, for example, Dumoulin, *A History of Zen Buddhism,* pp. 36–38, and Suzuki, *Essays in Zen Buddhism, (First Series),* p. 73.

196. Kumārajīva's *Tso-ch'an san-mei ching, T*15.269c–86a, was compiled from the teachings of a number of Kashmiri masters. Buddhabhadra's *Ta-mo-to-lo ch'an ching, T*15.300c–25c, contains the teachings of the Kashmiri meditation master Buddhasena. The same translator's *Kuan-fo san-mei hai ching, T*15.645c–97a, is devoted to exercises of meditative visualization. Buddhabhadra arrived in Ch'ang-an in 406, stayed at Hui-yuan's monastery on Mount Lu for a short while, and then moved to Chien-k'ang in 412. See the *HKSC, T*50.334b–35c, and the *Ch'u san-tsang chi-chi, T*55.103b–4a. Also see *T*50.339a–c, 400b, and *T*55.112b–13a.

197. The first of these lists (*T*22.492c–3a) occurs in the Mahāsaṁghika *Vinaya,* which was translated in 416–18 by Fa-hsien and Buddhabhadra. The second (*T*24.684b–85a) is found in a Chinese commentary to a work found in the Pali canon of the Theravādins. This text, known as the *Shan-chien lü pi-po-sha,* describes the importation of the *Vinaya* to Sri Lanka and the international *Vinaya* campaign carried out by Moggaliputta-tissa. The translator of this work, Saṁghabhadra, defines his own religious ancestry according to the first five names given in the list in question. (See the *Li-tai san-pao chi, T*49.95b.) This and some of the following information is discussed by Mochizuki, 4:3067b–68a.

198. The first list, which ends in the name Dharmatrāta, occurs at *T*55.89a–b. The transcription given here as Prajñātāra (?) could indicate Paratāra; the Chinese is Po-lo-to-lo. The second list, which includes three irrelevant names after Dharmatrāta, is located at *T*55.89c–90a. The asterisks indicate the occurrence of irrelevant names.

199. See Lamotte, *Histoire du bouddhisme indien,* pp. 223–30, which includes references to the various Chinese works and a summary of the account in question. The two Chinese translations of the *A-yü wang ching* contain slightly different statements of the transmission. The earlier text, which may have been translated as early as 306 (but see Mochizuki, 1:93a), presents a somewhat disorganized set of transmission anecdotes (*T*50.114a–16b) involving the Buddha, Mahākāśyapa, Ānanda, and Śāṇavāsa. The later translation, which was done by Saṁghabhadra in 512, includes a straightforward statement of the transmission scheme and is in part organized into chapters on the basis of this version of the transmission. (The lineage is listed at *T*50.152c and repeated in its entirety at the end of the text, *T*50.169c.) Although the two Chinese translations may simply represent variant originals of comparable antiquity, it seems likely, in view of the other material introduced here, that the theory of the transmission per se was developing in Kashmir over the course of the fourth and fifth centuries. For further information on the legend of Aśoka, see John S. Strong, *The Legend of King Aśoka: A Study and Translation of the* Aśokāvadāna (Princeton, N.J.: Princeton University Press, 1983).

200. These two innovators were Fa-ju—or, rather, his anonymous epigrapher —and Shen-hui. See Section 9 of this chapter.

201. The list of masters given in the sūtra itself may be found at *T*15.301c. The list in Hui-yuan's preface occurs just above, at 301a–b, as well as in the *Ch'u san-tsang chi-chi, T*55.65c–66a. Hui-kuan's preface occurs only in the latter work, the names in question being found at *T*55.66c–67a. The contents of the two prefaces are so nearly identical that they must have been prepared on the basis of the same lectures by Buddhabhadra. It is difficult to understand how the sūtra and its two prefaces could contain different versions of the transmission, even allowing for the problems of interpreting Buddhabhadra's lectures. The Chinese for Puṇyalāta (?) is Fu-jo-lo, possibly identical to the Prajñātāra (?), or Po-lo-to-lo, mentioned in n. 197.

202. *T*15.301a–b or *T*55.65c–66a.

203. Note that the schools of Buddhism referred to here were distinguished on the basis of the *Vinaya,* rather than doctrinal interpretations. Also, if we read the text very precisely, we find that what is actually referred to here is not the inability of the scriptures to describe the Buddha's teachings, but only the fact that Ānanda's special relationship to the Dharma is unmentioned in the scriptures.

204. See Chan-jan's commentary on the *Mo-ho chih-kuan* (*T*46.147c) and the *HKSC* (*T*50.564b). The latter version actually includes references to two other individuals named Chien and Tsui. Perhaps because the latter of these two definitions of the transmission fails to mention Hui-wen, it goes largely unnoticed by the later T'ien-t'ai tradition.

205. See the *Mo-ho chih-kuan, T*46.1a–b. In traditional T'ien-t'ai exegetics, the transmission from the Buddha to Siṁha *Bhikṣu* is referred to as the *chin-k'ou*

hsiang-ch'eng, or "transmission of the golden mouth," and that from Nāgārjuna to Hui-wen, Hui-ssu, and Chih-i is known as the *chin-shih hsiang-ch'eng,* or "transmission of the present teachers." See Andō Toshio, *Tendaigaku—kompon shisō to sono tenkai* (Kyoto: Heirakuji shoten, 1968), p. 7, or Fukuda Gyōe, *Tendaigaku gairon* (Tokyo: Bun'ichi shuppan, 1954), pp. 14–16. For information on the *Fu fa-tsang yin-yuan chuan,* see Mochizuki, 5:4493c–94b.

206. *T*25.755b. Yanagida mentions this and other related passages in *Shoki Zenshū shisho,* pp. 611–12.

207. *T*50.394c.

208. The reader should recall the dialogue recorded in the *HKSC* between Tao-hsin and his disciples on the subject of the transmission, which suggests that the practice of choosing a single successor was known during the 660s. See Chapter II, Section 2.

209. See, for example, Shen-hsiu's *Kuan-hsin lun, T*85.1272a or *Suzuki Daisetsu zenshū,* suppl. vol. 1 (Tokyo: Iwanami shoten, 1971), 623.

210. This text occurs in the Tun-huang manuscript P3559 at (607/26:2), just after the *CFPC.*

211. See Mochizuki, 1:559b–60a. Part of the *Tso-ch'an san-mei ching* translated by Kumārajīva was written by Pārśva. See Mochizuki, 2:1440c–41a, and Ono Gemmyō, *Bussho kaisetsu daijiten* (13 vols.; Tokyo: Daitō shuppan sha, 1933), 4:7a–b.

212. The transliterations of non-Chinese names here are taken from Mizuno, "Zenshū seiritsu izen no Shina no zenjō shisōshi josetsu," p. 23.

213. See n. 93.

214. See Hirai, p. 326.

215. See Chapter II, Section 7.

216. See Chapter II, Section 15. There is no obvious relationship between the two passages attributed to Hsien here and in *Daruma no goroku,* p. 239.

217. See the list of Hung-jen's disciples included in the passage from the *LCJFC* introduced in Chapter II, Section 5.

218. See the text in Yanagida's *Shoki Zenshū shisho,* pp. 487–88, and the Japanese translation on pp. 37–38.

219. This interpretation is stressed by Yanagida, pp. 38–39.

220. There is a parallel of sorts between this oversight and the Chinese adaptation of theories about the demise of Buddhism, which are generally subsumed under the term *mo-fa,* or "final [period of] the Dharma." In both cases statements and ideas originally referring to Kashmir and/or the western regions in general were reinterpreted to refer specifically to China.

221. The emergence of the San-lun School is considered to have been an important development in the growth of sectarian consciousness in Chinese Buddhism. Nevertheless, even though Chi-tsang and his contemporaries in this school were also very conscientious in recording several generations of their own religious predecessors, I am not aware of any statement of theirs extending to the sixth generation. See Leon Hurvitz, "Chih-i (538–597): An Introduction to the Life and Ideas of a Chinese Buddhist Monk," *Melanges chinois et bouddhiques,* 12 (1960–1962), 79–80, citing T'ang Yung-t'ung, *Han-Wei liang-Chin nan-pei ch'ao Fo-chiao shih* (Ch'ang-sha: Shang-wu yin-shu kuan, 1928), p. 758f, and

Itō Ryūjū, "Sanron gakuha ni okeru shiji sōjō to Zenshū," *Shūgaku kenkyū* 14 (March 1947): 117–22.

222. See the *Ting shih-fei lun* in Hu Shih's *Shen-hui ho-shang i-chi,* p. 284.

223. See *Shoki Zenshū shisho,* p. 48, and *Shoki no zenshi, 1,* pp. 25–26.

224. See *Shoki Zenshū shisho,* pp. 48 and 57 n. 2, for the background of this observation. The secondary source Yanagida cites was in error; the epitaph for I-fu mentions Dharma Master Fei as a teacher but says nothing of Fei referring I-fu to Fa-ju, while the epitaph for P'u-chi does not mention Fei at all. Tu Fei's biography of Hui-ssu is listed in the catalogues of two Japanese pilgrims to China, *T*55.1075b and 1077c.

225. See *Shoki no zenshi, 1,* p. 424, or section 19 of the translation in the Appendix.

226. See *Shoki no zenshi, 1,* pp. 346 and 420, or sections 4 and 18 of the translation. I cannot help wondering if Tu Fei was not paid a commission for writing the *CFPC.*

227. The title of the *CFPC* uses the character *chi,* "annals," rather than the modern homophone meaning "records". (Shen-hui's *Ting shih-fei lun* corroborates this usage.) Yanagida comments on the significance of this choice in *Shoki no zenshi, 1,* p. 328, and on the general attitude of the *CFPC* to the *HKSC* in *Shoki Zenshū shisho,* p. 54. Incidentally, the transmission statement included in P3559 and mentioned in n. 328 to Part Two is obviously based on the *CFPC.*

228. See *Shoki Zenshū shisho,* pp. 87–100, and *Shoki no zenshi, 1,* pp. 31–34.

229. The graves of one of Wei-shih's brothers and her daughter, Princess Yung-t'ai, have been two of the most spectacular archeological discoveries of modern Chinese history.

230. This work is mentioned in Li Chih-fei's preface to Ching-chueh's commentary on the *Heart Sūtra, Shoki Zenshū shisho,* p. 597.

231. See the *LCSTC, Shoki no zenshi, 1,* pp. 52–53 (this passage is lacking in *T*85).

232. Yanagida, *Shoki Zenshū shisho,* p. 58, suggests that the *LCFJC* was written after Hsuan-tse's entry into the capital in 708. It is also probable that he transmitted it to Ching-chueh before that monk's presumed departure from the capital in 710. If Ching-chueh received materials from the capital much after this date, he would have learned of the compilation of the *CFPC,* which does not seem to have been the case.

233. On this monastery, see *ibid.,* pp. 90–91 and 98 n. 11. Another Northern School monk named Ling-cho was also associated with the same monastery, as mentioned already in Chapter III, Section 6, no. 3.

234. Yanagida has suggested that Hsuan-tse's inclusion of Fa-ju in the list of Hung-jen's disciples as a resident of Lu-chou rather than Shao-lin ssu represents an attempt to deny his influence as a founder of Ch'an in the two capitals (*Shoki no zenshi, 1,* p. 284). On the probable contents of the *LCJFC,* see *Shoki Zenshū shisho,* pp. 59–60. Hsuan-tse's attitude toward the *HKSC* may be attributable to his earlier personal association with Tao-hsuan.

235. *Shoki Zenshū shisho,* pp. 64, 66–70, and 74.

236. The scriptural quotations, etc., mentioned in item 1 are two numerous to be listed here; see Yanagida's notes in *Shoki no zenshi, 1.* The passages based on

the *Hsiu-hsin yao lun* are mentioned in the notes to the translation of that work in Part Two, Chapter II. Also see the discussion in Section 4 of the same chapter. The material mentioned in items 3-8 occurs in the sections of the *LCSTC* devoted to the individuals involved.

237. On the relationship between the *Hsiu-hsin yao lun* and the *LCSTC,* see Yanagida's *Shoki Zenshū shisho,* pp. 79-82.

238. See Yanagida, *Shoki no zenshi, 1,* pp. 122, 140–41, 287–88, and 312–13, or *T*85.1284c, 1285b, 1289c–90a, and 1290b–c.

239. See Sekiguchi, *Daruma no kenkyū,* pp. 335–43, and Yanagida, *Yaburu mono,* p. 236.

240. See Yanagida, *Shoki Zenshū shisho,* pp. 335–40.

241. This is a major thesis of *ibid.,* pp. 181-209. Also see McRae, "The Ox-head School," pp. 189-91 and *passim.*

242. For example, although the *LTFPC* includes a prominent reference to Shen-hui's sermon at Hua-t'ai in order to bolster its own specious claims to the succession from Hui-neng, it omits any mention of the fact that the sermon in question was delivered as an attack on the Northern School. See Yanagida, *Shoki no zenshi, 2,* pp. 154–55, or *T*51.185b–c.

243. The epitaphs by Yen and Tu are listed in n. 171. See p. 15b of the former. One anecdote involving I-fu is included in the *T'ai-p'ing kuang chi,* fascicle 97, 2:645–46.

244. See the epitaph by Li Hua in the *CTW,* fascicle 320, pp. 4b–8a. Fa-yun's biography is summarized in Ui, pp. 298–99.

245. See the epitaph, also by Li Hua, *CTW,* fascicle 319, p. 12b. On the following page of the epitaph (13c), Hui-chen is quoted as teaching that one should be "without practice [as such] but never ceasing. Transcending mind, form is pure. When both are pure, they have been transcended. With transcendence comes birthlessness (i.e., nirvana) . . ." These ideas are reminiscent of the *Wu fang-pien,* which makes the passages quoted from this epitaph even more significant.

246. On Hsuan-lang, see the epitaph by Li Hua, *CTW,* fascicle 320, pp. 1a–4b. Obviously, it is quite possible that the primary reason prototypic encounter dialogue material found its way into these three epitaphs may have been their common authorship. On Fa-ch'in, see the discussion of his biography in McRae, "The Ox-head School," pp. 191–95.

PART TWO

1. Suzuki felt that Bodhidharma wrote the *EJSHL* and its miscellaneous appended material; the *Chueh-kuan lun* of the Ox-head School and the closely related *Wu-hsin lun;* and Shen-hsiu's *Kuan-hsin lun.* On the accretions to the *EJSHL,* see his *Kōkan Shōshitsu issho oyobi kaisetsu* (Osaka: Ataka Bukkyō bunko, 1936), pp. 10 and 14. Suzuki is very explicit about accepting all traditional material at face value, except where there is definite evidence of misrepresentation. For his views on the other works mentioned, see his studies in the *Suzuki Daisetsu zenshū,* 2:108–41, 161–87, and 209–10, plus suppl. vol. 1:576–89. For more accurate attributions and other useful textual information, see Yanagida's "Zenseki kaidai," pp. 454–57, and the sources listed there.

2. Okimoto discusses certain Tibetan translations of some of this miscellaneous material in his "Chibetto-yaku *Ninyū shigyō ron* ni tsuite," *Indogaku Bukkyōgaku kenkyū,* 24, no. 2 (1976): 999–992 (sic). Jorgensen, *The Earliest Text of Ch'an,* contains an annotated translation and study of the entire manuscript version of the *EJSHL* and the miscellaneous material that accompanies it. See pp. 248–49 for an English rendering of the Tibetan translation of the *EJSHL* proper. On pp. 379–80, Jorgensen argues that the entire manuscript of the "long scroll" was compiled by the end of the seventh century, probably by 645. On pp. 380–89, he discusses the authorship of the text and concludes that T'an-lin was probably the compiler. Although Jorgensen skilfully counters earlier suggestions by Sekiguchi and Nakagawa as to the provenance of the text, his own conclusions are based on circumstantial evidence and are far more specific than is justified. I see no reason why the compilation of the "long scroll" did not take place over a period of time extending well into the eighth century.

3. There has been considerable disagreement over the years about the authorship of this miscellaneous material. Some have considered the section translated here under the provisional title "Second Letter" to be the preface to some longer work—perhaps the subsequent portion of the Tun-huang manuscript—rather than simply to the brief verse included here. I do not believe there is any conclusive argument for attributing different portions of the manuscript to Bodhidharma, Hui-k'o, or other early figures. For the present purposes, I have followed the usage in Yanagida's *Daruma no goroku.* For a convenient review of the positions taken by different scholars, see Tanaka Ryōshō, "*Shigyōron* chōkansu to *Bodaidaruma-ron,*" *Indogaku Bukkyōgaku kenkyū,* 14, no. 1 (1965): 217–20. Cf. Jorgensen, pp. 381–84. For the portions of the translation here taken from the *HKSC,* see *T*50.552b–c.

4. See the *CTL, T*51.458b–c. Yanagida, *Daruma no goroku,* pp. 15–21, contains a discussion of the details of manuscripts, titles, and textual history, plus a list of important secondary studies.

5. The title and reference to the preface by T'an-lin do not occur in the Tun-huang manuscript, but are added by Yanagida on the basis of the *LCSTC.* See his *Shoki no zenshi, 1,* pp. 127–32. I have omitted the customary annotation for the balance of this translation in deference to Yanagida's *Daruma no goroku,* pp. 27–31 and 36–47. My interpretation of the text does not differ substantially from Yanagida's.

6. These are the four stages of attainment in the Hīnayāna, beginning with the "stream-winner" and culminating with the arhat.

7. This is a reference to the fifth member of the Noble Eightfold Path.

8. A *maṇi*-pearl is a wish-giving gem. The allusion here is to something that is valuable but not recognized as such. In other contexts, the ability of Inherent Enlightenment to cleanse away the spiritual impurities of its possessor is described as the hypothetical ability of a pearl to clarify the water in which it is submerged.

9. Suzuki offers the following translations for these terms: "entrance by reason" or "entrance by higher intuition," and "entrance by conduct" or "entrance by practical living." See his *Manual of Zen Buddhism* (New York: Grove Press, 1960), p. 73.

10. See *Daruma no goroku,* p. 41, or the *Tao-te ching,* 63, and the *Lun-yü,* 14.

11. Many years later Huang-po Hsi-yun (d. 850) was to say something quite reminiscent of this practice: "Just utilize your old karma according to the consequences of your conditions *(sui-yuan),* and don't make any new transgressions." Huang-po's student Lin-chi I-hsuan alludes to both this and the following practice when he says: "Utilize your old karma according to the consequences of your conditions, spontaneously *(jen-yun)* putting on your clothing, walking when you want to walk, sitting when you want to sit, without ever activating *(ch'i)* a single moment's desire *(ch'iu)* for enlightenment." See Yanagida's *Zen shisō,* p. 55.

12. The *Bukkyōgaku jiten,* Taya Raishun *et al.,* eds. (Kyoto: Hōzōkan, 1955), p. 87, has a good definition of *ch'iu* as "seeking after something without cease." Nakamura's *Bukkyōgo daijiten* does not give *tṛṣṇa* as an equivalent for the single character *ch'iu,* but note the compound *ai-ch'iu* (*aigu* in Japanese), which is given as such on 1:15c.

13. See n. 332 for another comment on the internal structure of the *EJSHL.*

Yanagida has suggested that the four practices may constitute a reinterpretation of the four foundations of mindfulness along Mahāyānist lines, specifically those of the Perfection of Wisdom. This possibility is interesting in view of the importance of the four foundations in the thought and practice of Seng-ch'ou, a contemporary of Bodhidharma and Hui-k'o. The correspondences would be developed as follows:

A. Mindfulness of the body: The first practice of the *EJSHL* is based on the direct, personal experience of suffering. It would not be too extreme to suggest that such suffering was primarily physical—i.e., lack of food, water, and shelter, as well as various forms of vilification and abuse by others.

B. Mindfulness of feelings: Rather than just emotional responses, this refers to any impression or perception experienced *(shou)* by one's physical/sensory apparatus, including the mind. The second practice refers to all good and bad eventualities.

C. Mindfulness of the mind: Craving, the subject of the third practice, is the single most important obstacle to a perfectly functioning mind and, at the same time, the quintessential feature of the unenlightened mind.

D. Mindfulness of *dharmas*: Whereas the feelings of the second foundation of Mindfulness refer to all sensory and emotive impressions, "*dharmas*" refers here to all the fundamental building blocks of an individual sentient being's physical and psychological existence: sensory capabilities, feelings, perceptions, memories, physical form, etc. This is entirely different from the definition of Dharma *(fa)* used in the fourth practice. One could argue that the fourth practice describes the ability to act in accord with the Dharma of *śūnyatā* with respect to all *dharmas*, but this interpretation is somewhat forced.

14. This idea is similar to the *Laṇkāvatāra Sūtra*'s concept of *tsung-t'ung,* or "penetration of the truth," i.e., the true inner understanding of the ultimate message of the scriptures, as opposed to *shuo-t'ung,* or "penetration of the preaching," a conceptualized understanding of the words and formulae of the text and nothing more. See Yanagida's *Shoki Zenshū shisho,* p. 52, for the importance of this idea in the Northern School, and his *Zen shisō,* pp. 17–18, for its relevance here. The term *tsung-t'ung* occurs in Section C of the *CFPC.*

15. The *HKSC* version reads simply: "To be mysteriously identified with the Tao (= enlightenment?), serene and inactive, is called the entrance of principle."

16. See the discussion of the concept of Buddha Nature in the *Hōbōgirin*, Sylvain Lévi and J. Takasusu, eds. (Tokyo: Maison franco-japonaise, 1929–37), 2:185–87.

17. "Hokushūzen no shisō," *Zenbunka Kenkyūjo kiyō*, 6 (1974): 71–72. The word *tan* occurs again, with a similar meaning, in the fourth practice.

18. On the subject of faith, note Tanaka's observation that a pair of terms related to this concept in the *EJSHL* also occur in esoteric Buddhist texts translated into Chinese in the early eighth century. As Tanaka himself admits, the inverted temporal sequence mitigates against any conclusion concerning Bodhidharma's identity in terms of Indian religious developments, but perhaps there is some relationship between the Ch'an and esoteric traditions in China. The two terms are *shen-hsin* ("profound faith") and *hsin-chieh* ("accept and understand"), occurring in the first entrance and the fourth practice, respectively. Similar usages occur in the *Ch'an-men ching* and *Sheng-chou lu*. See Tanaka's "Daruma-zen ni okeru shin ni tsuite," *Shūkyō kenkyū*, 38, no. 2 (1965): 84–85.

Another speculative suggestion that should be introduced here is T'ang Yung-t'ung's opinion that the language of the *EJSHL* is reminiscent of the *Upaniṣads*, specifically, the *Maṇḍūkya Upaniṣad* and commentary by Gauḍapāda. I cannot accept the accuracy of this comparison. See T'ang's *Fo-chiao shih*, p. 791. T'ang also wrote in a letter to Hu Shih, his teacher, that Bodhidharma's treatise resembled Brahmanist and Upaniṣadic writings. Hu's reply includes the suggestion that the *Laṇkāvatāra Sūtra*, on which Bodhidharma supposedly based his teachings, was a product of Buddhism's spread to South India and its admixture with non-Buddhist elements. T'ang's letter and Hu's reply were written in July 1928. See the *Ko Teki zengaku an*, pp. 235 and 239.

While these specific speculations are now clearly obsolete, one can still wonder whether non-Buddhist thought had any influence on the *EJSHL*. It is possible that sentences 3A–B of the entrance of principle may be taken to describe a type of meditation very much like the "cessation of the transformations of consciousness" that constitutes the classical definition of yoga *(yogaś citta vṛtti nirodhāḥ)*. In addition, the distinction between the two entrances could be interpreted to resemble the distinction between *jñāna* and *karma* yoga.

19. Most of the citations listed here are discussed in Yanagida, *Shoki Zenshū shisho*, pp. 423–29. For no. 2, see *T*50.596c. For no. 3, see Yanagida, *Shoki no zenshi, 1*, p. 356, or section F of the translation in Appendix A, and *T*51.743c (mentioned by Ui, 1:14). For no. 4, see Chih-yen's *K'ung-mu chang*, *T*45.559a–b. For no. 5, see *T*48.403c and 405b and Kamata, *Zengen shosenshū tojo*, pp. 116 and 141. For no. 6, see *T*48.387a and Iriya Yoshitaka, *Denshin hōyō—Enryōroku*, Zen no goroku, no. 8 (Tokyo: Chikuma shobō, 1969), p. 135. (Professor Iriya comments on p. 147 that *mien-pi* does not necessarily mean physically sitting before a wall.) For the *CTL* reference, see *T*51.219b. For no. 7, see *Z*2B, 3, 454a (*H*130:907a).

20. Ui, 1:21.

21. T'ang, pp. 784–85. Other scholars who discuss "wall contemplation" are Lü Ch'eng, Masunaga Reihō, Suzuki Kakuzen, Takamine Ryōshū, and John

Alexander Jorgensen. Lü, in his "T'an-t'an yu-kuan ch'u-ch'i Ch'an-tsung ssu-hsiang te chi-ko wen-t'i," *Ch'an-tsung shih-shih k'ao-pien,* Shih Tao-an, ed., Hsien-tai Fo-chiao hsueh-shu ts'ung-k'an, no. 4 (Taipei: Ta-sheng wen-hua ch'u-pan she, 1977), pp. 202, suggests a connection with the "totality-sphere" techniques of meditation (*kṛtsna-āyatana,* or *kasiṇa-āyatana* in Pāli). Lü's idea is that in order to contemplate the element earth one begins with a disk of mud erected on a frame in front of oneself, rather in the form of a wall. In a similar vein, Masunaga has compared the same technique of early Buddhism to the visualization of the sun or the character "one" *(i)* in the East Mountain Teaching. See his "Zenshisō no Chūgokuteki keitei," *Bukkyō no kompon shinri—Bukkyō ni okeru kompon shinri no rekishiteki keitai,* Miyamoto Shōson, ed. (Tokyo: Sanseido, 1957), p. 795. Suzuki's comments are extensive but inconclusive. See his "Hekikan shiron (I)" *Komazawa Daigaku Bukkyō Gakubu kenkyū kiyō,* 33 (March 1975): 23–39 and "Hekikan shiron (II)," 34 (March 1976): 26–46. His musings are summarized in his " 'Hekikan' to 'kakukan' ni tsuite," *Indogaku Bukkyōgaku kenkyū,* 24, no. 1 (1975): 124–129.

Takamine's brief comments, which refer to the *Chin-kang san-mei ching* and the writings of Li T'ung-hsuan, occur in his *Kegon to Zen to no tsūro* (Nara: Nanto Bukkyō kenkyūkai, 1956), pp. 11–12. Note that Takamine also published an earlier version of this study under the same title in *Nihon Bukkyō gakkai nempō,* 18 (1952): 39–58. See pp. 49–52.

Jorgensen's rambling comments on "wall contemplation" include an interesting reference to a line in Ssu-ma Ch'ien's *Shih-chi* about "looking from on top of a wall" *(ts'ung pi-shang kuan),* which Jorgensen glosses as "to be an onlooker, to be uninfluenced by what is going on around you." See Jorgensen, p. 196, and the biography of Hsiang Yü in the *Shih-chi.* The implication is that Bodhidharma's wall contemplation might involve a similar sense of detachment from the world. Even more significant, Jorgensen, p. 194, cites an "adamantine wall *samādhi*" in the *Sui-tzu-i san-mei,* which is attributed to Hui-ssu. According to this text, when Śāriputra was once in the *samādhi* in question, a demon hit him so hard with a club that the reverberations were felt in all the worlds and times. Śāriputra, however, was unaware of the blow, and after coming out of *samādhi* knew only that the skin on the top of his head felt a bit unusual. (*Z*1, 98, 350d–51a [*H*98.700b–1a]) The power of this *samādhi* is reminiscent of the frozen solidity referred to elsewhere in the *EJSHL.*

22. The first of the passages introduced here is from "Shoki Zenshū to shikan shisō," pp. 261–62. The second passage, as well as that given just below, is from *Zen shisō,* pp. 29–30.

23. Hu understood the history of early Ch'an as a transition from an essentially Indian level of complexity to the intrinsically simple approach that suited the Chinese so much better. See his "Development of Zen Buddhism in China," *Chinese Social and Political Science Review,* 15, no. 4 (1932): 475–505, reprinted in the *Ko Teki zengaku an,* 722–691 (sic). Suzuki was more inclined to believe that the heart of Zen (to use the Japanese pronunciation which he preferred) was shared by Indian Buddhism and even other non-Buddhist religious systems, but that the mode of expression changed according to variations in time and place.

See, for example, his "The Historical Background of Zen Buddhism," *Zen Buddhism,* William Barrett, ed. (Garden City, N.Y.: Doubleday, 1956), pp. 48–58 and 74.

24. *T*50.598a–b, introduced in Yagi, "Ryōgashū kō," p. 61. T'an-lun was born no later than 547, and the events described here took place after he became thirteen. Yagi suggests that T'an-lun's teacher was Ching-tuan (543–606), a successor to Ratnamati and Seng-shih. (He is identified here only as *Dhyāna* Master Tuan.)

25. *T*50.590a. The experiences described here probably occurred in or before 595.

In addition to the evidence introduced here regarding T'an-lun and Ching-lin, it is instructive to consider Chih-i's comments regarding two teachings held by "northern *dhyāna* masters." One of these, the tenth of his three southern and seven northern *p'an-chiao* schema, is that there is "only One Vehicle, not two and not three. With one sound is the Dharma preached; according to the identity (of the listener) is it understood differently." (*T*33.801b) This "teaching of the one sound" *(i-yin chiao)* is directly opposed to the orthodox Ti-lun School position regarding the three vehicles. (See Ōchō, *Hokugi Bukkyō no kenkyū,* pp. 41–42.) Since Hui-k'o is said to have learned the One Vehicle from Bodhidharma, it might be possible to associate this teaching directly with these early Ch'an figures. Unfortunately, Chih-i's rebuttal of this teaching yields no further information about it. (*T*33.805a–b)

The ninth of the three southern and seven northern schema, which is also attributed to northern *dhyāna* masters, elucidates two types of Mahāyāna teachings, the "Mahāyāna with characteristics" *(yu-hsiang ta-sheng)* and the "Mahāyāna without characteristics" *(wu-hsiang ta-sheng).* The former teaches the progression of the bodhisattva through the ten stages, whereas the latter holds that "the True Dharma is without graduated distinctions [and that] all sentient beings constitute the characteristic of nirvāṇa." This teaching is said to be based on the *Laṇkāvatāra Sūtra* and the *Sūtra [of the Questions] of Ssu-i [Bodhisattva] (Ssu-i ching).* (Also *T*33.801b) Yagi, "Ryōgashu kō," p. 52, shows that the "Mahāyāna without characteristics" is also based in part on the *Vimalakīrti Sūtra* and introduces evidence from Chih-i's writings to the effect that this teaching was basically no different from the doctrine of sudden enlightenment expounded by Tao-sheng in the fifth century. That is, since the True Characteristic of the *dharmakāya* is without characteristics and undifferentiated, realization thereof occurs completely and all at once, in a sudden flash, without admitting to any stages of partial realization.

Yagi, pp. 53–54, also observes that Tao-hsuan's *HKSC* essay on exegetes refers pejoratively to those who studied the *Laṇkāvatāra* and *Abhidharma* literature, broke the precepts, became attached to eating and drinking, and "took false knowledge as true understanding and confused consciousness to be perfect wisdom." (*T*50.549b) Yagi feels that this last phrase is reflective of the northern *dhyāna* masters mentioned by Chih-i; I suspect that Yagi interprets such behavior as an antecedent to the eccentricity and iconoclasm of later Ch'an masters. Unfortunately, there is no direct proof that any of this evidence relates directly to the members of the early Ch'an School.

26. *T*50.603a.

27. *T*9.369c and 370a. See the discussion of *shou-i ts'un-san* and *shou-i pu i* in Chapter VI, Section 2 of this part.

28. This treatise was introduced by Sekiguchi in his *Daruma daishi no kenkyū,* pp. 49–81. A transcription of the text may be found on pp. 463–68 of that work. Sekiguchi accepts the date 681, then makes the incredible assertion that the text may actually be a valid work of Bodhidharma's. My own reaction is that, even if this were one of the texts referred to in the *LCSTC* and *CFPC* as circulating under Bodhidharma's name, as Sekiguchi suggests, that would not be enough to prove the accuracy of such an attribution.

I also find Sekiguchi's interpretation of the relationship between this text and the *EJSHL* unconvincing. (See pp. 69–81.) The text seems much more closely related to the *Hsiu-hsin yao lun,* since it contains the phrase *shou pen-ching hsin,* "maintain the originally pure mind." (Sekiguchi, p. 465.) *Shou-hsin* is without question the most distinctive slogan of the *Hsiu-hsin yao lun.* (See section I of the translation in Section 3 of this chapter for the four-character version of this slogan.) The treatise in question also contains other phrases and topics of discussion similar to those found in the *Hsiu-hsin yao lun* and Northern School works in general, but I cannot discern any criteria for determining the exact provenance of the text.

29. Sekiguchi, *Daruma daishi no kenkyū,* pp. 246–70, analyzes the relationship between the *Ch'eng-hsin lun* and ideas generally attributed to Tao-hsin. I believe it is much more likely that Shen-hsiu discovered this work during his quarter century of residence at Yü-ch'üan ssu, the monastery of its author Chih-i, rather than that Tao-hsin found it during his brief stay at a former residence of a sometime student of Chih-i's. (See Sekiguchi, pp. 272–73.) An alternate title for this work is *Cheng-hsin lun (Treatise on the Realization of the Mind).*

30. See the text in Yanagida, *Shoki Zenshū shisho,* pp. 487–89, and Part One, Chapter IV, Section 9.

31. See the following two sections of this chapter for textual information and an English translation of the *Hsiu-hsin yao lun.* For the *JTFM,* see Sections 6, 7, and 8. The position that there is a developmental relationship between *shou-i* and *shou-hsin* and/or the texts in which they are explained is held by Sekiguchi, *Zenshū shisōshi,* p. 85; Yin-shun, *Chung-kuo Ch'an-tsung chih,* p. 80; Suzuki, "Zen shisōshi kenkyū, dai-ni—Daruma kara Enō ni itaru," *Suzuki Daisetsu zenshū,* vol. 2 (Tokyo: Iwanami shoten, 1968), 272; Masunaga, "Zen shisō no Chūgokuteki keitai," p. 794; and Yanagida, "Chūgoku Zenshū shi," *Zen no rekishi—Chūgoku,* Kōza Zen, no. 3, Suzuki Daisetsu and Nishitani Keiji, eds. (Tokyo: Chikuma shobō, 1967), pp. 26–27. (Both Suzuki and Masunaga devote closer attention to the practice of "viewing a single thing" [*k'an i-wu*] than to *shou-i* and *shou-hsin.*)

32. See Yanagida Seizan, *Shoki no zenshi, 1,* pp. 213 and 263–64, or *T*85.1287c and 1289b.

33. See Yanagida, *Shoki no zenshi, 1,* pp. 263–64, or *T*85.1289b.

34. See section V of the translation.

35. It is impossible to determine the exact date of compilation of the *Inscrip-*

tion on Relying on the Mind. Yanagida, *Shoki Zenshū shisho,* p. 266 n. 17, lists the early ninth century works in which it first appears or is mentioned.

36. The *Shinsen zenseki mokuroku* compiled by the Komazawa University Library (Tokyo: Komazawa toshokan, 1962) contains detailed information about the various editions of the *Hsiu-hsin yao lun* under the headings *Ichijō kenjishin ron* (*I-sheng hsien tzu-hsin lun* in Chinese; p. 6a), *Saijōjōron* (*Tsui-shang sheng lun;* p. 139a), and *Shushin yōron* (*Hsiu-hsin yao lun;* p. 173a). Also see Tanaka Ryōshō's useful guide to Tun-huang materials pertaining to Ch'an, "Tonkō Zenshū shiryō bunrui mokuroku shokō," *Komazawa Daigaku kenkyū kiyō,* 29 (March 1971): 11–16, and Yanagida's "Zenseki kaidai," p. 455. The following summary combines information from all three of these sources.

The *Hsiu-hsin yao lun* was published in Korea in 1570 under the title *Choesangsŭng'non (Tsui-shang sheng lun* in Chinese, or *The Treatise on the Supreme Vehicle).* This was republished several times, one edition of which (first printed in Japan in 1716) is reprinted in *Z*2A, 1, 415a–17b (*H*110:829a–33b) and *T*48.377a–79b. It is also included in the *Sŏnmun ch'waryo* printed in Korea in 1907, an anthology often used by Japanese scholars earlier in this century (the Japanese pronunciation is *Zemmon satsuyō*). One of these earlier scholars was Nukariya Kaiten, who argued that the *Tsui-shang sheng lun* did not represent Hung-jen's true teachings. See his *Zengaku shisōshi,* vol. 1 (Tokyo: Genkōsha, 1923) 371–74. The discovery of this text and other Ch'an-related materials among the Tun-huang manuscripts has rendered Nukariya's position obsolete, even though some of his observations about the text itself are still valid.

The first notice of any of the Tun-huang manuscripts of the *Hsiu-hsin yao lun* was apparently that in Ch'en Yuan's *Tun-huang chieh-yü lu* (6 vols.; Peking: Kuo-li Chung-yang Yen-chiu-yuan li-shih yü-yen yen-chiu-so, 1931), in which it is listed as manuscript *chou*-04. Because the beginning of this Peking manuscript was damaged, Ch'en used the title *I-sheng hsien tzu-hsin lun (Treatise on the One Vehicle of Manifesting One's Own Mind).* This title is based on material at the end of the treatise itself. (See section W; also note the alternate titles occurring at the ends of certain manuscripts mentioned in n. 103.) The identity and significance of this Peking manuscript were confirmed by Suzuki during his visit to Peking in 1934. He published a collotype facsimile of this manuscript in his *Tonkō shutsudo Shōshitsu issho* (Osaka: Ataka Bukkyō bunko, 1935) and a printed edition in his *Kōkan Shōshitsu issho oyobi kaisetsu,* pp. 41–55.

In the meantime Tokushi Yūshō announced the existence of the *Hsiu-hsin yao lun* among the Tun-huang manuscripts in the possession of the library of Ryūkoku University in Kyoto. See his "*Shōshitsu rokumonshū* ni tsuite," *Ryūkoku gakuhō,* 309 (June 1934): 316–18. Suzuki published synoptic transcriptions of the Korean, Peking (edited and augmented on the basis of the Korean text), and Ryūkoku manuscripts in his *Kōkan Shōshitsu issho oyobi kaisetsu,* pp. 41–52. In 1938 Suzuki visited England, where he discovered three additional manuscripts in the Stein collection (S2669, S3558, and S4064). Around 1941 he edited these three manuscripts together with the Korean and Peking versions, the result of which was published in 1951 in his *Zen shisōshi kenkyū, dai-ni.* This is contained in the *Suzuki Daisetsu zenshū,* 2:303–309. According to a note on p. 270 of this volume, Suzuki does not seem to have used the Ryūkoku manuscript for this edition. He also failed to distinguish between the three Stein manuscripts, referring to them all as the "original text" *(gembon).*

All the other known manuscripts of the *Hsiu-hsin yao lun,* i.e., S6159, P3559, P3434, and P3777, were discovered by Yanagida Seizan on the basis of information in various catalogues and through an examination of microfilm copies of the British collections. Tanaka, p. 11, also notes the existence of a Tun-huang manuscript of this text in Leningrad, unavailable to Western scholars.

At present there are nine different manuscripts and one printed of this text: P3434, P3559, P3777; S2669, S3558, S4064, S6159; Peking *chou*-04; Ryūkoku University Library No. 122 (the *Kammon daijō hōron* manuscript); and the printed Korean edition. S6159 is fragmentary, being incomplete at both beginning and end, and has not been consulted in the course of this study. Since Suzuki's editions suffer from problems of inaccuracy and because they were done without knowledge of some of the most important manuscripts, I have compiled a new edition for the purposes of this study. Fortunately, I have had access to Professor Yanagida's handwritten synoptic transcription of all the extant versions of the text, which I have double-checked against photocopies of the original manuscripts. There are significant differences between some of the different versions of the *Hsiu-hsin yao lun.* The Korean text has obviously been edited to make certain passages more readable and the terminology a little more positive and complex. This editing, as well as the retitling of the text, probably occurred in China—an inference based on the similar, if less extensive, editing of P3559. The other manuscripts contain numerous minor differences but resemble each other in using consistently simpler terminology than P3559 and the Korean version.

The textual environment of the *Hsiu-hsin yao lun* in P3559 is also quite different from that in the other unprinted manuscripts. This extremely important manuscript includes the following material:

A. The *Yuan-ming lun,* which will be presented in translation in Chapter VII

B. A brief statement on Ch'an that is heavily laden with Yogācāra and *tathāgata-garbha* theory terminology

C. The *Hsiu-hsin yao lun* itself

D. Some 55 lines of miscellaneous material preceded by the heading *Hsiu ho-shang chuan (Transmission of Preceptor* [*Shen*]*-hsiu),* part of which will be introduced in translation in Chapter VII, Section 13

E. The *Ch'üan fa-pao chi (CFPC),* already discussed in Part One, Chapter IV, Sections 10 and 11, and presented in translation in the Appendix

F. The *Ch'ou ch'an-shih i (The Intention* [*Mind ?*] *of Dhyāna Master* [*Seng*]*-ch'ou),* an interesting text in spite of the obvious falsity of its attribution to Seng-ch'ou

G. The *Ch'ou ch'an-shih yao-fang (The Prescription of* Dhyāna *Master* [*Seng*]*-ch'ou),* also spurious

H. The *Ta-sheng hsin-hsing lun (Treatise on the Practice of Mind in the Mahāyāna),* also supposedly by Seng-ch'ou

I. A verse by P'u-chi (different from that contained in Suzuki's *Shōshitsu issho*)

J. A few lines of miscellaneous material

K. The *Chin-kang wu li (Five Obeisances of the Vajra)* by Preceptor Yao, an unknown figure

L. Some fifty lines of miscellaneous "contemplative analysis" material (see Chapter III, Section 6 for a definition of this term) related to the recitation of the *Great Perfection of Wisdom Sūtra*

Although some of the individual works just listed are represented in other Tunhuang manuscripts, i.e., items B, C, E, and K, this is the only manuscript to contain two or more, let alone all of them. The reverse side of this manuscript was copied in 751, the obverse probably in the same year or shortly thereafter. (See n. 160.) For a discussion of the manuscript as a whole, see Yanagida Seizan, "*Den'hōbōki* to sono sakusha—Perio 3559-gō bunsho o meguru Hokushūzen kenkyū no sakki, jo no ichi," *Zengaku kenkyū,* 53 (July 1963): 45–71. Jan Yünhua, "Seng-ch'ou's Method of *Dhyāna,*" Lai and Lancaster, eds., *Early Ch'an in China and Tibet,* pp. 51–63, accepts the attributions of works F, G, and H to Seng-ch'ou. I consider them spurious because of (1) the absence of any reference to them with regard to Seng-ch'ou, (2) the lack of any obvious relationship with what little is known about Seng-ch'ou's meditation practice, and, conversely, (3) the clear relationship between the content of these works and other doctrines of the early Ch'an. P3559 (more accurately, P3664/P3559; see n. 160) represents an anthology of East Mountain Teaching/Northern School works, in which the legendary figure of Seng-ch'ou was used in name only.

In contrast to the composition of P3559, seven different manuscripts contain some or all of the following works, always in the same order:

A. The *Ssu hung shih-yuan (The Four Great Vows),* apparently first used by Chih-i

B. The *Ta-mo ch'an-shih kuan-men* (Dhyāna *Master [Bodhi]dharma's Teaching of Contemplation*), which describes seven different types of meditation (see Sekiguchi, *Daruma daishi no kenkyū,* pp. 295–316)

C. An essay provisionally entitled by Suzuki the *Fa-hsing lun (Treatise on the Dharma Nature),* which manifests probable influence by Shen-hui (see the *Suzuki Daisetsu zenshū,* 2:444–45)

D. The *Liao-hsing chü (Stanzas on Comprehending the Nature),* which will be quoted in Section 4 of this chapter (see the *Suzuki Daisetsu zenshū,* 2:450–52, but note that Suzuki was unaware of P3777 and another Peking manuscript to contain this work, *sheng* 生-67)

E. The *Ch'eng-hsin lun (Treatise on the Clarification of the Mind),* which was written by Chih-i but transmitted within the Ch'an tradition, rather than the T'ien-t'ai School (see the *Suzuki Daisetsu zenshū,* 2:443–44, and Sekiguchi, *Daruma daishi no kenkyū,* pp. 246–94)

F. Two *mantra*s for warding off sleepiness and entering into *samādhi* (attributed to the esoteric Buddhist master Śubhākarasiṁha, who arrived in Ch'ang-an in 716) plus a line from the *Nirvāṇa Sūtra*

G. The *Hsiu-hsin yao lun*

H. Some "contemplative analysis" material provisionally titled *San-pao wen-ta (Dialogues on the Three Jewels)* and reproduced in the *Suzuki Daisetsu zenshū,* 2:445–46

I. Shen-hsiu's *Kuan-hsin lun (Treatise on the Contemplation of the Mind),* which will be discussed in Chapter VII, Sections 5–8.

Excluding S2583 and the Peking manuscript *sheng*-67, which contain only the single items B and D, respectively, the contents of each manuscript are as follows:

	P3434	Peking	S4064	S3558	P3777	S2669	Ryūkoku
A)						X	X
B)						X	X
C)						X	X
D)			X	X	X		
E)	X	X		X	X	X	X
F)	X	X	X	X	X	X	X
G)	X	X	X	X	X	X	X
H)						X	X
I)							X

For detailed information regarding the contents and physical descriptions of the various manuscripts, see Nakata Banzen, "Tonkō bunken no saikentō—toku ni Kōnin no *Shushin yōron* ni tsuite," *Indogaku Bukkyōgaku kenkyū,* 17, no. 2 (1969): 714–17. The Ryūkoku Library manuscript is in Tibetan booklet form, but all the others are conventional Chinese rolls. S2669 actually begins with some irrelevant material on military strategy and warfare. Finally, P3434 bears cyclical characters corresponding to the year 893 on its reverse side, which could represent its approximate date of transcription.

The only modern translation of the *Hsiu-hsin yao lun* other than the one presented here is an English rendition by W. Pachow in "A Buddhist Discourse on Meditation from *Tun-huang,*" *University of Ceylon Review,* 21, no. 1 (1963): 47–62, reprinted in his *Chinese Buddhism: Aspects of Interaction and Reinterpretation* (Lanham, Md.: University Press of America, 1980), pp. 35–54. Pachow's translation is generally quite accurate, but it suffers from a tendency to interpret the text in terms of Sri Lankan Buddhism, a small number of questionable English constructions, and a complete lack of annotation. In addition, it was based on only one manuscript, S4046, with some reference to S2669 and S3558. I have consulted Pachow's translation frequently in the compilation of the one presented here, but I have been influenced more strongly by the recommendations of Professor Yanagida, with whom I had the privilege of discussing this text during several private meetings in Kyoto in 1976–77.

The edited text found at the end of this book has been compiled with reference to all the manuscripts and printed versions discussed here. Textual variants have been recorded in the notes only when absolutely necessary. A bold dot has been placed in the text to mark the location of any such variants; specification of the length of the phrase involved has been done in Chinese and is inclusive of the character so marked.

37. Huang-mei hsien, Hupeh.

38. The Ryūkoku manuscript has only the last five characters of this title, which is presumably due to an error of transcription. Other titles for the text were mentioned in n. 36. Some of these occur at the end of the text, as mentioned in n. 115.

39. The phrasing of this section is a bit jumbled and repetitive. This is also true of other sections of the text, especially the questions. The term *hu-ching* (lit. "to protect purity," i.e., "to take care of") also occurs in the *Ch'an-men ching (Sūtra of Ch'an)* and the poetry of Han-shan. See Yanagida's "*Zemmonkyō* ni tsuite," *Tsukamoto hakase juju kinen Bukkyō shigaku ronshū* (Tokyo: Tsukamoto hakase juju kinen kai, 1961), p. 880, and Iritani Sensuke and Matsumura Takashi, *Kanzanshi,* Zen no goroku, no. 13 (Tokyo: Chikuma shobō, 1970), p. 11.

40. Both the immediate context and the overall intent of the *Hsiu-hsin yao lun* imply that the word *shen,* "body," is a mistake for *hsin,* "mind." Nevertheless, all versions have the former, including the long passage based on this and the succeeding sections of the text quoted in the *Tsung-ching lu, T*48.588b. The same substitution of *shen* for *hsin* may be found on occasion in other early Ch'an documents and may represent more than an error of transcription.

41. The Chinese for "[not subject to the laws of] generation and extinction" is simply *pu sheng pu mieh.* Hereafter this phrase will be translated without brackets.

42. This passage does not occur in any of the Chinese translations of the *Sūtra* and *Treatise on the Ten Stages,* or in the section of the *Avataṁsaka Sūtra* corresponding to the former. See Yanagida, *Shoki no zenshi, 1,* p. 152. The passage does occur in Shen-hsiu's *Kuan-hsin lun* (see the analysis in the next section of this chapter); the *TCL* (in part; *T*48.858b); and, inexplicitly, at the end of the Tun-huang manuscript of a commentary (*Z*1, 41, 206a [*H*41:424b]) on the *Heart Sūtra* attributed to Hui-ching (578–645). This last would be the earliest known appearance of the passage in question, but it may have been added by a later copyist. The passage in question is not integrally related to the commentary itself. In addition, the authorship of the commentary is in itself problematic, since Hsuan-tsang only translated the very short sūtra in question some four years after Hui-ching's death. See Mochizuki, 5:4266a.

The passage in question also occurs in the *LCSTC, Shoki no zenshi, 1,* p. 146, or *T*85.1285c. The following textual evidence implies that the *LCSTC* is quoting the *Hsiu-hsin yao lun,* rather than vice versa:

A. The *LCSTC* adds explicatory material throughout, including a supporting quotation from the *Avataṁsaka Sūtra.* This line from the *Avataṁsaka Sūtra* does not occur in the *Hsiu-hsin yao lun,* but Ching-chueh quotes it in his commentary on the *Heart Sūtra.* See Yanagida, *Shoki Zenshū shisho,* p. 609.

B. The *LCSTC* substitutes the more explicit "How could the sun's light achieve brightness and purity?" for the the *Hsiu-hsin yao lun*'s short and ambiguous "How could the sun ever be extinguished?" Because of multiple meanings of the character *lan* 爛, the *Hsiu-hsin yao lun* question could also be read "How could the sun ever shine [through the clouds]?" This reading is acceptable, but the *LCSTC* makes the question more explicit. In addition, the *LCSTC* removes the phrase "the answer says" *(ta yueh),* which occurs in the other text without the necessary "the question says" *(wen yueh).* (See section D, of the *Hsiu-hsin yao lun.*)

C. The *LCSTC* uses the term *ming-ching* ("bright and pure") in the rhetorical question just cited and two other times in this section. This term is used nine other times in the *LCSTC* (five of these are in the *JTFM* attributed to Tao-hsin), but not once in the *Hsiu-hsin yao lun.*

D. The *LCSTC* adds the phrase "sitting quietly and purely" *(mo-jan ching-tso),* which, as Yanagida notes in *Shoki no zenshi, 1,* pp. 152–53, is one of Ching-chueh's special points of emphasis.

E. Finally, shortly after this passage in the *LCSTC* occur a few lines that are also found in section O of the *Hsiu-hsin yao lun.*

43. Section F has a similar phrase, *shen-chung chen-ju* ("Suchness within the bodies [of sentient beings and Buddhas]").

44. See Yanagida's comments on the significance of this usage, which are introduced in Chapter V, Section 5,

45. The original manuscripts all have the character *chi* 即, "namely," which has been amended to *lang* 郎, "bright," on the suggestion of Professor Iriya Yoshitaka.

46. The concept expressed here is identical to that in the metaphor used to describe the meaning of the "untainted" *(wu-jan)* in the *Ta-sheng fa-chieh wu ch'a-pieh lun.* See Ui Hakuju, *Hōshōron kenkyū* (Tokyo: Iwanami shoten, 1979), p. 396, and Yanagida, *Shoki no zenshi, 1,* p. 154.

47. Hereafter *shou-hsin* is translated without the aid of brackets.

48. See the term "sun of wisdom" *(hui-jih)* in section L.

49. The *Hsiu-hsin yao lun* abbreviates the passage in question. See *T*14.542b. The same passage also occurs in the miscellaneous material attached to the *EJSHL,* the *Chueh-kuan lun* of the Ox-head School, and the *Tun-wu yao-men* attributed to Hui-hai. See Yanagida's *Daruma no goroku,* p. 246, and Tokiwa Gishin and Yanagida Seizan, *Zekkanron: Eibun yakuchū, gembun kōtei, kokuyaku* (Kyoto: Zen Bunka Kenkyūjo, 1976), p. 91, or the *Suzuki Daisetsu zenshū,* 2:191; and Hirano Sōjō, *Tongoyōmon,* Zen no goroku, no. 6 (Tokyo: Chikuma shobō, 1969), p. 51.

50. The locus classicus for the term *hsin-yuan* is the *Awakening of Faith,* where it refers to the mind as the source of illusion and hence of all *dharmas*. More specifically, it is the point at which ignorance begins to operate within one's *tathāgata-garbha,* when the *tathāgata-garbha* switches from being the one Pure Mind to the mind of illusion. The infinite *dharmas* that comprise phenomenal reality are said to "exist" solely on the basis of the ignorant mind—the Pure Mind is nondiscriminating and thus does not recognize their existence. The transformation that occurs within the *tathāgata-garbha* is not a temporally definable event but is only an expedient explanation of the present state of being of ordinary, unenlightened people. See Hirakawa Akira, *Daijō kishin ron,* Butten kōza, no. 22 (Tokyo: Daizō shuppan sha, 1973), p. 109. The *Hsiu-hsin yao lun* seems at times to confuse this first arising of the ignorant mind with the Pure Mind that constitutes the Buddha Nature.

51. Also *T*14.542b.

52. *Shu-hsiu* originally referred to dried meat offered to a teacher upon one's first application for instruction. It is thus an application or matriculation fee, but I have rendered it as "tuition fee" in order to make the passage more readable.

53. The True Mind is so named because it is part of the perfect realm of the absolute, or Suchness.

54. Unidentified. Śikṣānanda's translation of the *Awakening of Faith* contains a vaguely similar line, as has been pointed out to me in a personal communication by Tokiwa Gishin of Hanazono College. See *T*32.585b, lines 7–8. However, the two passages are not similar enough to be used as evidence that the *Hsiu-hsin yao lun* was written after Śikṣānanda's translation, which was done in 695.

55. This section is obviously directed against the Pure Land practice of *nien-fo* ("mindfulness of the Buddha"). The term *nien-fo* is used in the *Wu fang-pien (Suzuki Daisetsu zenshū*, vol. 3 [Tokyo: Iwanami shoten, 1968], 168, and section Intro.:C of the translation in Chapter VII, Section 3) and in the *Ta-mo ch'an-shih kuan-men* (*T*85.1270c). The *Kuan-hsin lun* emphasizes the importance of actual contemplation, rather than the mere oral recitation of the Buddha's name. See *T*85.1273a.

Certain of Hung-jen's students were Pure Land practitioners, and the Szechwan lineages that claimed descent from him had very distinctive approaches to *nien-fo* that were influenced by Ch'an doctrine. See Tsukamoto Zenryū, *Tō chūki no Jōdokyō* (Kyoto: Hōzōkan, 1975), pp. 307–11. The *JTFM* shares the anti-Pure Land bias of this text. See Yanagida, *Shoki no zenshi, 1*, pp. 213–14, or *T*85.1287c.

56. Similar usages of the word *t'a* ("other") occur in a translation by Chu Fa-hu (d. ca. 308), *T*12.149c, and in Chih-i's *Fa-hua hsuan-i*, *T*33.766c. Also see the *JTFM* in Yanagida, *Shoki no zenshi, 1*, p. 226, or *T*85.1288b.

57. The term *pen-hsin* ("fundamental mind") occurs in the *Vimalakīrti Sūtra*, *T*14.541a.

58. *T*8.752a.

59. This question has interrogative particles at both beginning and end. Similar redundancies occur in sections B and I. The compound *sheng-ssu* has been translated as either "birth and death" or "saṁsāra."

60. *Cheng-nien* ("correct mindfulness") is the seventh member of the Noble Eightfold Path. The formula "to not generate false thoughts and extinguish the illusion of personal possession" *(wang-nien pu sheng wo-so-hsin mieh)* occurs nine times in this text. Except where the two phrases thereof are separated by a third phrase, it has been translated simply as "to not generate false thoughts or the illusion of personal possession." The translation of *wo-so-hsin* is based on the *Ta chih-tu lun:* "The self *(wo)* is the basis of all illusions. First one becomes attached to [the belief that] the five *skandha*s constitute the self. Then one becomes attached to external things as one's possessions *(wo-so).*" (*T*25.295a.) *Wo-so-hsin* is thus the belief that things external to the self belong to the self, a sort of compounded ignorance. This usage occurs in the *Wu-liang-shou ching* and the *Chin-kang san-mei ching*, *T*9.373b. See the definition in section R of the translation.

61. Literally, "having various false conditions" *(chung-chung wang-yuan).*

62. This probably refers to a sūtra of Chinese authorship listed as the *Hsin-wang p'u-sa shuo t'ou-to ching (Sūtra on Austerities Preached by the Bodhisattva [Named] Mind-king).* See the *K'ai-yuan shih-chiao lu, T*55.677b. Shen-hui quotes from what is presumably the same text in his *Wen-ta tsa ch'eng-i.* See the *Suzuki Daisetsu zenshū,* 3:285. The only other known reference to the *Hsin-wang ching* is a quotation from it in Tsung-mi's commentary to a portion of the *Avataṁsaka Sūtra,* the *Hua-yen ching hsing-yuan p'in shu-ch'ao, Z*2, 7, 409d (*H*7:818b).

63. Literally, if the conditions are "conjoined" or "coincide" *(ho).*

64. Because of the verbal usage of *hsin* here, I have translated it as "to rely on." The idea here is related to that of "faith" or "conviction," another meaning for the same character, since one must first accept the reality of the Fundamental Mind and then make a firm commitment to depend on its guidance at all times. In a private conversation, Professor Yanagida pointed out to me that in the compound *hsin-hsin,* the character in question has a meaning very similar to *chen,* "true," and should be translated along the lines of "perfected." *Hsin-hsin,* a term which occurs at the beginning of the answer in section S, refers to the enlightened state of mind that constitutes the actualization of the ultimate within one's own person. Hence the famous work attributed to Seng-ts'an, the *Hsin-hsin ming,* should be rendered as either *Inscription on Relying on the Mind* or *Inscription on the Perfected Mind.*

65. *T*14.540b. The wording of the original is slightly different.

66. Literally, during "walking, standing still, sitting, and lying down" *(hsing-chu-tso-wo).*

67. A paraphrase of a lengthy section of the *Hsiu-hsin yao lun* beginning with this line occurs in the *TCL, T*48.426a, where it is attributed to a "former worthy." The same work also includes this line in its description of Hung-jen's teachings, *T*48.940a.

68. Literally, the "twelve divisions of the canon" *(shih-erh pu ching).* The emphasis is not on the fact that the scriptures are traditionally divided into twelve sections, but on the fact that *shou-hsin* is the basic teaching of all the scriptures. The same term occurs in sections L and O.

69. Many of the questions in this text contain the word *chih,* "to know," and should be translated as "How is it known that . . . ?" or "How do you know that . . . ?" This is almost always matched with *ku chih,* "Therefore, it is known that . . . ," at the end of the answer that follows. This pattern has been translated faithfully so far but will now be dropped for reasons of simplicity. As in this section, the logic of the text's argumentation is often more apparent than real. See n. 45 to Part One.

70. The logical series of A implies B, B implies C, and so on, has been abbreviated somewhat. Similar abbreviations occur in the original manuscripts.

71. See the *Lotus Sūtra, T*9.9a. The impact of the doctrine of expedient means contained in this important scripture is very strong in this and the following sections. The phraseology here has been modified somewhat in the process of translation.

72. The point of seeing the Buddha is to be able to receive his teachings directly rather than through the secondhand authority of written scriptures and later

teachers. The advantage of the Pure Land teachings, which were quite popular at this time, was that they enable devotees to be reborn in a situation where they can hear the Buddha's teachings directly and become enlightened more easily than while alive. This line could also be understood as "to see one's own identity as a Buddha."

73. In Ch'an texts the term *wu-wei* often has the connotation of "not doing anything." This depends on context, of course, as the term can also mean "inactive," in the Taoist sense, or "unconditioned." See section L of the translation.

74. A very similar statement occurs in the *LCSTC,* in which the Buddhas achieve enlightenment through "seated meditation" *(tso-ch'an).* See Yanagida, *Shoki no zenshi, 1,* p. 143, or *T*85.1285c.

75. See the *I-chiao ching (Sūtra of the Bequeathed Teaching), T*12.1111a, where the exact wording is a little different. The original manuscripts of the *Hsiu-hsin yao lun* differ on which character to use as the verb, "to fix" or "to regulate." All the three variants, *chih* 止, *cheng* 正, and *chih* 制, have the same meaning in this situation: to seize control of the mind and subdue its hyperactive tendencies. As Yanagida points out in *Shoki no zenshi, 1,* p. 245, this line is quoted very frequently in Ch'an texts.

76. The word *men* ("gate" or "doctrine") is absent from the original at this point but has been added on the basis of usages in section I and the question in section K.

77. The phrase *shan ho ta-ti,* "mountains, rivers, and the great earth," occurs here as a single unit for the first time in any Ch'an text. Also see the *Wu fang-pien, Suzuki Daisetsu zenshū,* 3:220 (IIIB.38).

78. The term *hui-jih,* "sun of wisdom," also occus in Wang Wei's (700–61) epitaph for Hui-neng. See Yanagida, *Shoki Zenshū shisho,* p. 541. Note the similar terms *fa-jih* ("Dharma-sun") in section D and *fo-jih* ("sun of Buddhism") in the *LCSTC,* Yanagida, *Shoki no zenshi, 1,* p. 273, or *T*85.1289c.

79. The *LCSTC* contains a passage that is clearly an exegesis of this part of the *Hsiu-hsin yao lun.* See Yanagida, *Shoki no zenshi, 1,* p. 112, or *T*85.1284b. The original manuscripts differ on the last part of this line. Suzuki, who believed firmly that *chien-hsing,* "to see the [Buddha] Nature," was an innovation of Hui-neng's, has suggested that P3559 maintains an older and more reliable reading with its *tzu-jan ming hsien,* "naturally the brightness is manifested." The Korean text has the similar *ming tzu-jan hsien.* However, if one takes the character *chu* 住, "to reside," in S2669 as a mistake for *hsing* 性, "nature," then fully six out of eight texts containing this section have the compound *chien-hsing.* Even P3559 and the Korean edition have this compound in other sections, the latter even including it in a part of section O where it does not belong. Hence it can hardly be said that either of these texts was unaware of this compound or avoided it on principle. In fact, the concept of seeing or manifesting one's Buddha Nature is a central thesis of the *Hsiu-hsin yao lun.*

80. The same compound, *fa-t'i,* "Dharma-essence," occurs near the end of section E, where it is rendered "essential reality."

81. The original is slightly different. See *T*12.520b.

82. The rest of this section is problematic. At one point the original manuscripts (excluding the Korean edition) have *hsin* 心, "mind," where they should have

sheng 生, "to generate." The Korean edition is considerably simplified at this point, while P3559 omits two characters, resulting in its own unique but quite acceptable reading: "When you do not generate false thoughts, [the Buddhas] are generated within your consciousness and the illusion of personal possession is extinguished. Within this consciousness (i.e., within the Buddha Nature ?) one should first maintain awareness of the True Mind. You will achieve buddhahood upon doing so."

83. See a similar statement in section O. The phrase *ch'ien ching wan lun* occurs with roughly the same usage in the *Chin-kang san-mei ching, T*9.367a; the *Tun-wu yao-men,* Hirano, p. 99; and the *TCL, T*48.943ab. The *Chin-kang san-mei ching* passage is quoted in the *Chu-ching yao ch'ao, T*85.1196b.

84. This passage does not occur as such in the *Lotus Sūtra.* See *T*9.12bff for the general context.

85. This logic embodies the assumption of gradualism, or at least of the need for religious effort prior to the sudden experience of enlightenment.

86. This passage is from the *Lotus, T*9.15c–16a. The original is slightly different. The same passage is also used in the *Lin-chi lu,* where it is interpreted as an expression of enlightenment. That is, the enlightened person has the fortitude to exist in hell without any discomfort at all. See Yanagida Seizan, *Rinzai-roku,* Butten kōza, no. 30 (Tokyo: Daizō shuppan sha, 1972), p. 135, or *T*47.500a.

87. Similar phrases occur in Chih-i's *Hsiu-hsi chih-kuan tso-ch'an fa-yao, T*46.465c and 466c. Also see the *JTFM,* Yanagida, *Shoki no zenshi, 1,* pp. 248 and 255, or *T*85.1288c and 1289a.

88. The description of meditation that follows here is noticeably different from that contained in the sūtra itself. There the contemplation on the setting sun, which is the first of sixteen different techniques, is described in part as follows:

> Sit upright facing the West and clearly contemplate the sun. Keep the mind still and think of it singlemindedly. Visualize the sun as it is about to set, in the form of a hanging drum. Having done so, you should become able to see it brightly, whether your eyes are open or closed . . . (*T*12.342a)

The reader has no doubt noticed that very few of the scriptural citations in the *Hsiu-hsin yao lun* follow their respective originals precisely.

89. Similar material occurs in the *Tun-wu chen-tsung chin-kang po-jo hsin-hsing ta pi-an fa-men yao-chueh* (hereafter abbreviated as *Tun-wu chen-tsung yao-chueh),* which is a product of the Northern School. See Ueyama Daishun, "Chibetto-yaku *Tongo shinshū yōketsu* no kenkyū," p. 99.

90. The first of these lines resembles a passage in the *Avataṁsaka Sūtra, T*9.395a, while the second is taken, with slight changes in wording, from the *Awakening of Faith.* See Hirakawa, p. 170, or *T*32.577b.

91. This could also be read "to all the scriptures [preached by] all the Buddhas in the ten directions of space."

92. The preceding statements about those who "comprehend the mind" occur, with one phrase omitted, in the *LCSTC,* Yanagida, *Shoki no zenshi, 1,* p. 146, and *T*85.1285c. The last phrase may also be found in the *Tun-wu yao-men.* See Hirano, p. 89.

93. The text has *tsao-ta* 造大, "to make great." A similar compound, *tsao-tz'u* 造次, occurs in the Korean edition and in the *JTFM,* Yanagida, *Shoki no zenshi, 1,* p. 241, and *T*85.1288c. Another related term, *tsao-tso* 造作, occurs in the *Lin-chi lu,* Yanagida, *Rinzairoku,* p. 92. See Yanagida's explanation on the same page.

94. A similar passage occurs in the *JTFM,* Yanagida, *Shoki no zenshi, 1,* p. 146, or *T*85.1285c.

95. The term *wu-chi* (*avyākṛta* in Sanskrit) is used in *Abhidharma* and other types of Buddhist literature to refer to states of mind that have neither good nor bad influence on one's subsequent condition. In Ch'an texts it refers to a dull state of trance or mental stupor, as the section that follows describes.

96. The source of this citation and the one that follows is unknown. They occur together, without attribution, in the same passage of the *LCSTC* already mentioned in n. 94. As Yanagida observes (*Shoki no zenshi, 1,* p. 157), the term *ching-ch'eng,* "sincerity," probably occurs on the basis of influence from T'an-lin's preface to the *EJSHL,* where it is used in reference to Hui-k'o. It also occurs with reference to Hui-k'o in the *LCSTC,* p. 128, or *T*85.1285a. The topic of the second scriptural quotation is also discussed in the *Tun-wu yao-men,* Hirano, p. 99.

97. This name appears in the *Tun-wu yao-men,* Hirano, p. 11.

98. The eight winds are listed in section T below. They also occur in the *Wu fang-pien, Suzuki Daisetsu zenshū,* 3:174 and 194, and section II:B of the translation in Chapter VII, Section 3. Also see the *Tun-wu yao-men,* Hirano, p. 11.

99. See the *Tun-wu yao-men,* Hirano, p. 11. The fact that this one section of the *Tun-wu yao-men* contains three items also found in this section of the *Hsiu-hsin yao lun* (see the previous two notes) cannot be coincidental. The same section of this supposedly Southern School text also contains the four characters *wang-nien pu sheng,* "to not generate false thoughts," one of the catchword phrases of the *Hsiu-hsin yao lun.* See n. 59.

100. "Hung-jen" tends to use *wu* 吾 in reference to himself alone and *wo* 我 in reference to himself and people in general.

101. The most similar line in the *Nirvāṇa Sūtra* refers not to space but to bodhisattvas. See *T*12.520b.

102. It might be better to revise this passage to read "the two teachings of meditation and practice" *(ting-hsing erh men)* or "the two teachings of principle and practice" *(li-hsing erh men).* Although I have chosen to avoid such editorial intervention, by any reading this passage implies a recognition of the two teachings referred to here as the East Mountain Teaching and the Northern School. See n. 217.

103. *Chih* 至, "utmost," has been taken as an error for *chih* 志, "ambition." The same substitution occurs in the second question of section S.

104. The two characters *wu-ch'u* are used as a compound in the *Tun-wu chen-tsung yao-chueh,* where they figure prominently in the explanation of a famous line from the *Diamond Sūtra.* See Ueyama, p. 96 (P2799, lines 22–23).

105. One of the textual variants, *yeh-yeh,* means "to be in constant motion." See the *Lien-mien tzu-tien,* Fu Ting-i, ed. (Taipei: Taiwan Chung-hua shu-chü, 1969), 3:2187.

106. Similar descriptions of meditation occur in the *Wo-lun ch'an-shih k'an-fa*

(Dhyāna *Master Wo-lun's Method of Contemplation*) and the *JTFM*. For the former, see the *Suzuki Daisetsu zenshū*, 2:452; for the latter, see Yanagida, *Shoki no zenshi, 1*, p. 249, or *T*85.1288c–89a.

107. See *T*12.382c–84c and *T*14.554c–55c. The *Nirvāṇa Sūtra* chapter mentions Akṣobhya Buddha and contains some material on morality vaguely reminiscent of that in the *Vimalakīrti Sūtra* chapter, but it is difficult to imagine why they should be cited together here. The latter is quoted in the *Tun-wu yao-men*, Hirano, p. 18.

108. The Sanskrit term *brahmacarya* refers to the practice of transcending desires and maintaining the precepts. It is also translated as *ching-hsing.*

109. The compound *mo-lien,* "to polish and train," hence, "to cultivate," also occurs in section O. It is very suggestive of the concept of polishing dust and tarnish off of a mirror, but the immediate context here does not imply the removal of the dusts of illusion (the five desires and the eight winds of good and ill fortune), but development of the ability to remain unaffected by them even in their presence. Like the lotus blossom, which rises unsullied out of the mud, the bodhisattva is supposed to operate within this world without being defiled by it. "Cultivating the Buddha Nature" is synonymous with "cultivating the mind," as in the title of this treatise.

110. The sūtra has not been identified. The precise meaning and extent of the quotation are uncertain.

111. There is a vernacular usage, *te-li,* "to receive the benefit" of someone else's advice, teaching, or efforts. Following this, "Hung-jen" would be saying: "Now that you have had the good fortune to hear this teaching . . ." See Iriya Yoshitaka, *Hō koji no goroku,* Zen no goroku, no. 7 (Tokyo: Chikuma shobō, 1973), p. 68.

112. The dictionaries list four different sets of "four dependences" *(ssu i),* but the reference here is probably to the "four dependences of the Dharma" *(fa ssu i)* mentioned without explication in the *Ta chih-tu lun, T*25.195b. These are the dependences on (1) the Dharma rather than on people, (2) sūtras that contain the complete Buddhist teaching rather than only a portion thereof, (3) ideas rather than words, and (4) wisdom rather than knowledge. See Ui Hakuju, *Bukkyō jiten* (Tokyo: Daitō shuppansha, 1938), p. 393.

113. The inference that Hung-jen had nothing to do with the compilation of the *Hsiu-hsin yao lun* has been mentioned in Section 1 of this chapter. Possibly, the treatise referred to here is not the entire *Hsiu-hsin yao lun,* but only the essay-like first part. According to this interpretation, Hung-jen's disciples wrote sections C through M on the basis of his previous teachings and presented the result to him for his personal comments and additions, which are recorded in sections N through W. If this interpretation were correct—and I am not at all certain that it is—then the present text would resemble the Tun-huang version of the *EJSHL* in being composed of a preconceived doctrinal statement and the records of oral comments on that statement. The *Hsiu-hsin yao lun* differs in only recording the comments of one individual, more like a traditional recorded sayings text.

114. This appears at first glance to be an admission that "Hung-jen" was not concerned with helping others. It seems better to assume that such endeavors were simply left uncovered in this one text. The avoidance of this topic is one of

the characteristics that distinguish the East Mountain Teaching from the Northern School. The *Wu fang-pien* never mentions "benefit of self" without also referring to "benefit of others," and the *JTFM* is directed not only at students but also at the teachers of Ch'an.

115. This could also be read, "If you do not believe me, you will be eaten . . ." P3559 punctuates after the character *wo,* "I," which implies that its Tun-huang reader followed this reading. The Ryūkoku manuscript has *che,* "one who . . . ," instead of *wo,* also indicating the variant reading. However, the *Tun-wu yao-men* contains a much more explicit version of the same passage that substantiates the reading followed in the translation, a reading that makes better sense as Hung-jen's own vow. See Hirano, p. 117.

Immediately following the text as given here, P3559 includes an eighty-character passage attributed to Shen-hsiu. This passage is reproduced in Yanagida's "*Den'hōbōki* to sono sakusha," p. 48, and translated in part in Chapter VII, Section 13. This is followed by an alternate title for the *Hsiu-hsin yao lun: Tao fan ch'ü sheng hsin-chueh (Oral Determination of the Mind that Leads Ordinary People to Sagehood).*

P3777 concludes by listing a totally obscure year period and copyist's name; S2669 and the Ryūkoku manuscript repeat the title as found in section A, excluding only Hung-jen's name and place of residence. S4064 and the Peking manuscript have no closing title, and the other Tun-huang manuscripts lack the end of the text itself, including the title. The Korean version has a postscript the mentions some of the persons involved in the text's printing and dissemination. See *T*48.379b.

116. See n. 42. The inference that this passage and its metaphorical construction derived from a late seventh-century Chinese source is mine, but I believe this represents Professor Yanagida's position as well.

117. *T*39.579a, recapitulated briefly on p. 746c–47a.

118. *T*39.579b contains the *Diamond Sūtra* line *ying wu-so-chu erh sheng ch'i hsin* (the *Taishō* edition of I-hsing's work has . . . *erh chu ch'i hsin*). This line is most often associated with Hui-neng but was first noticed within the Ch'an School in the *Tun-wu chen-tsung yao-chueh,* written in 712. See the text in Ueyama, p. 96. I-hsing's commentary must be placed at the very end of his life, since it was apparently edited immediately after his death by two other monks. Therefore, it was written well after the *Hsiu-hsin yao lun.* See Mochizuki, 4:3376b. Finally, the specific imagery of floating clouds blocking off the sun occurs in Chinese texts of the Han Dynasty and before. See the first poem in Sui Shu-shen, ed., *Ku-shih shih-chiu shou chi-shih* (Peking: Chung-hua shu-chü, 1955), p. 2.

119. Yanagida, *Shoki no zenshi, 1,* pp. 146–47, and *T*85.1285c.

120. See *Shoki no zenshi, 1,* p. 112, or *T*85.1284b. On the *Chu-fa wu-hsing ching,* see Yanagida's note in *Daruma no goroku,* p. 79.

121. See the *Suzuki Daisetsu zenshū,* 2:450. The text uses the terms *ching-hsing,* "Pure Nature;" *fa-hsing,* "Dharma Nature;" *hsin-hsing,* "Mind Nature;" and *fo-hsing,* "Buddha Nature." The subject of the opening clause of the passage introduced here could be any of these.

122. The most prominent example of the use of *shou-i,* "guarding the will," in the sense of Buddhist mindfulness is the *An-pan shou-i ching.* The subject of this

work is *ānāpāna-smṛti,* the mindfulness of breathing. See *T*15.163a-73a. In view of the assertions made in the Conclusion, Section 6, it is also relevant that Ching-ying Hui-yuan uses the term *shou-hsin* in his definition of *śamatha.* See his *Ta-sheng i-chang, T*44.665c, as cited in Fukushima, "Jōyōji Eon no shikan kenkyū," p. 6.

123. As mentioned in n. 50, the *Hsiu-hsin yao lun* seems at times to confuse the "mind source" *(hsin-yuan),* the primary function of delusory consciousness responsible for the appearance of the myriad *dharmas*, with the "pure mind" *(ching-hsin),* or Buddha Nature. Thus, even more than in other texts like the *Kuan-hsin lun* that posit a sharp dichotomy between the pure and defiled aspects of mind, in the *Hsiu-hsin yao lun* the importance of the Buddha Nature and the emptiness of the discriminative mind are only two sides of the same coin.

124. See section R, which briefly describes the ability to "respond to all the myriad different realms of . . . consciousness by activating transformations as numerous as the sands of the River Ganges."

125. One of the oldest occurrences of the term in reference to Buddhism is in a memorial submitted in the year 166 to Emperor Huan of the Han Dynasty by Hsiang K'ai. The relevant passage is translated in E. Zürcher, *The Buddhist Conquest of China* (2 vols.; Leiden, Belgium: E. J. Brill, 1959), p. 37. On p. 333 n. 104, Zürcher glosses *shou-i* as a "Taoist technical expression which in archaic Buddhist translations is sometimes used to render *samādhi,*" citing Maspero and T'ang Yung-t'ung. On p. 435 n. 96, Zürcher further suggests that *shou-i* was also used in early translations as an equivalent for *dhyāna* and notes its probable derivation from lines in the *Tao-te ching* and *Chuang-tzu.* (See n. 127 to this Part.) *Shou-i* also occurs in the Chinese translation of the *Dhammapāda,* i.e., the *Fa-chü ching,* as well as in other early translations and the *T'ai-p'ing ching.* See T'ang, pp. 110–11. Other such citations are listed and commented on in Yanagida, *Shoki no zenshi, 1,* pp. 234–35. Finally, for the background of *shou-i* in Taoist literature, see Yoshioka Yoshitoyo, "Bukkyō no zenpō to Dōkyō no shuichi," *Chisan gakuhō,* 27–28 (November 1964): 109–25.

126. See Yoshioka, pp. 119–20.

127. See the *Tao-te ching,* 10 and 42, and the *Chuang-tzu,* 11 (twice).

128. For the *Pao-p'u tzu,* see Yoshioka, pp. 110–12, or James R. Ware, trans., *Alchemy, Medicine, Religion in the China of A.D. 320: The Nei P'ien of Ko Hung (Pao-p'u tzu)* (Cambridge, Mass.: M.I.T. Press, 1966), pp. 301–8.

129. See the descriptions of *shou-i pu t'ai* ("maintaining the one without tiring") in the *Pao-p'u tzu* and *shou-i pu shih* or ("maintaining the one without losing [it]") quoted in Yoshioka, p. 114.

130. See Yoshioka, p. 116.

131. *Ibid.,* p. 124.

132. See *Shoki no Zenshi, 1,* p. 225, or *T*85.1288a. For an analysis and complete translation of the *JTFM,* see David Chappell's "The Teachings of the Fourth Ch'an Patriarch Tao-hsin (580–651)," in Lai and Lancaster, eds., *Early Ch'an in China and Tibet,* pp. 89–129.

133. *T*14.539b.

134. This is an excellent example of the type of equivalence discussed in Iriya Yoshitaka's "Kū to jō," *Fukui hakase juju kinen tōyō bunka ronshū* (Tokyo:

Waseda University Press, 1969), pp. 97–106. In the following lines of this passage, it is difficult to distinguish the idea of empty space from that of nonsubstantiality.

135. See the *Pan-chou san-mei ching, T*13.899b and 905c.

136. See section G of the *Hsiu-hsin yao lun* and n. 56. Chappell, p. 115, translates *t'a* as "objectified," which accurately indicates the importance of the subject-object dualism here.

137. The use of archery practice as a metaphor for meditation occurs in many texts, but Yanagida suggests that the specific language of hitting successively smaller targets was an innovation of the *JTFM*. See his note in *Shoki no zenshi, 1,* pp. 246–47.

138. The term "discrimination" here represents *chueh-kuan,* or *vicāra,* the ability of the mind to discriminate and understand anything. "Perceptions" is a translation of *ssu-hsiang,* which has a meaning quite different from that in modern Chinese usage. In archaic Chinese Buddhist terminology it refers to the third of the five *skandha*s, *saṁjñā,* which takes as its object the second *skandha, vedanā* or "feelings." See Yanagida's note, *Shoki no zenshi, 1,* p. 254, and his article " 'Shisō' to iu go o megutte," *Indogaku Bukkyōgaku kenkyū,* 8, no. 1 (1960): 206–11.

139. According to Kamata, *Zengen shosenshū tojo,* p. 74, the term *yuan-lü hsin,* "the mind of conditional mentation," refers to the mind's activity of sensory and conceptual discrimination. Kamata points out that the Yogācāra tradition used the term to refer to all eight *vijñāna*s and that the term *yuan-lü* was derived from the compounds *p'an-yuan* and *ssu-lü.*

140. The first part of this sentence is only a tentative translation of the Chinese.

141. My impression is that "Tao-hsin" uses the term "single place" *(i-ch'u)* in a more profound sense than simply a single physical location. Rather, he is referring to a state of mind that is existentially solitary in its purity. Earlier in the text there occurs the line "alone in a pure and ultimate location" *(tu i ch'ing-ching chiu-ching ch'u).* See *Shoki no zenshi, 1,* p. 205, or *T*85.1287b.

142. Yanagida, *Shoki no zenshi, 1,* p. 256, translates this as "to sway the upper body back and forth seven or eight times," which is in accord with contemporary practice in Ch'an and Zen meditation halls. The original text reads *an-ma,* for which Nakamura, 1:27a, gives the Sanskrit equivalents *paripīḍana* and *prapīḍana* and the definitions "to press everywhere" and "to massage the hands and feet."

143. The English phrase "completely effaced in profound obscurity" is an interpretive paraphrase of the four characters *yao-yao ming-ming,* which refer to a realm of mysterious darkness with which the meditator becomes united. The term *yao-ming* is found in the *Tao-te ching,* 21, and the *Chuang-tzu,* 11. It also occurs in Seng-chao's *Nieh-p'an wu ming lun, T*45.157b.

144. Yanagida, *Shoki no zenshi , 1,* p. 258, equates the otherwise unknown term *lien-hsin,* "to regulate the mind," with *shou-hsin,* "to maintain the mind," and *she-hsin,* "to concentrate the mind."

145. The conjunction of the terms for nonsubstantiality and purity is reminiscent of Iriya's argument cited in n. 134.

146. The "mind of the sage" *(sheng-hsin)* is a term associated with Seng-chao.

See his *Po-jo wu chih lun, T*45.154b. The term *chih-chieh,* "virtuous fidelity," is apparently used in order to represent the purity and constancy of influence of the Buddha Nature within sentient beings. The sentence regarding the functioning of the "abstruse numen" *(yü-ling)* is based loosely on Seng-chao's *Nieh-p'an wu ming lun, T*45.157c. I have followed the translation in *Jōron kenkyū,* Tsukamoto Zenryū, ed. (Kyoto: Hōzōkan, 1972), p. 61. See Yanagida, *Shoki no zenshi, 1,* p. 258.

147. *T*14.541a. The term *huo-jan* refers to the sudden experience of a very expansive, unimpeded state of consciousness. My own interpretation is that it resembles the overwhelming feeling one experiences on reaching the top of a tower, when after a long climb one is suddenly able to see great distances all around. The phrase quoted here occurs in sections 19 and 30 of the *Platform Sūtra.* See Yampolsky, pp. 141 and 151.

148. *Shoki no zenshi, 1,* p. 287, or *T*85.1289c.

149. For a discussion of these remarks, which constitute criticism of Taoist positions, see Kamata Shigeo, "Shoki Zenshū no rōsō hihan," *Shūgaku kenkyū,* 10 (March 1968): 58–64.

150. It is significant that the *JTFM,* and early Ch'an in general, arrives at its sudden teaching by identifying itself with the most profound understanding of conventional Mahāyāna Buddhism and simply omitting the traditional preconditions to that understanding.

151. *Shoki no zenshi, 1,* p. 205, or *T*85.1287b.

152. Tanaka Ryōshō, "Dōshin-zen no kenkyū," *Komazawa Daigaku kenkyū kiyō,* 22 (March 1964): 145–47.

153. P'u-chi's epitaph contains an interesting quotation of his teachings, which is relevant to the topic at hand and to other issues to be introduced later:

> By concentrating the mind on a single locus, one ceases thinking about the myriad conditions. One may achieve penetration in an instant, or one may gradually achieve realization over [a period of] months and years—[but in either case] one illuminates the essence of buddhahood *(fo-t'i).* This [teaching] has been transmitted to me: Point directly at the *dharmakāya.* Maintain your mindfulness naturally, like filling a vessel with drops of water or walking on frost or ice. By doing so one will be able to "open the gate" of expedient means. By directly indicating its precious characteristic, one enters deeply into the original treasury. By comprehending the pure cause, one's ears and eyes are no longer sense organs; sound and form are not sensory realms . . . (*CTW,* fascicle 362, pp. 6b–7a)

154. *Pu-ch'i* is an important term within Northern School doctrine. See the occurrence of *ch'i* in the *Wu fang-pien,* section Intro:B, and n. 340.

155. Yanagida, *Shoki no zenshi, 1,* p. 199, or *T*85.1287b.

156. Yanagida, *Shoki no zenshi, 1,* p. 226, or *T*85.1288b.

157. See the *Ta-sheng k'ai-hsin hsien-hsing tun-wu chen-tsung lun* (hereafter abbreviated *Chen-tsung lun), Suzuki Daisetsu zenshū,* 3:327. The same text, pp. 326–27, discusses the four wisdoms of Yogācāra philosophy, which culminate in the wisdom likened to a great mirror.

158. The most explicit example of the influence of the *EJSHL* of which I am

aware occurs in the *Ta-sheng hsin-hsing lun* attributed to Seng-ch'ou in the Tun-huang manuscript P3559. (See n. 36 above for discussion of the occurrence of this text in P3559.) Near the beginning of this text (678/29:3) occurs the statement that one "first enters the 'gate' of principle from the outside, and second activates the 'gate' of function from principle" *(i ts'ung wai ju li-men, erh ts'ung li ch'i yung-men).* The ideas expressed in this sentence, and the terminology with which they are expressed, constitute a link between the *EJSHL* and the doctrines of Shen-hsiu and the Northern School, as discussed in Chapter VII. (See Section 13 in particular.)

159. The *Kuan-hsin lun* is represented in quite a few manuscripts: seven from Tun-huang (S646, S2595, S5532, P2460, P2657, P4646, and another at the Ryūkoku University Library); a Korean printed edition in the same anthology mentioned earlier regarding the *Hsiu-hsin yao lun* (see n. 36); two manuscripts at the Kanazawa Bunko, which were copied in 1201 and 1252 (the latter was apparently copied from the former); and a Japanese printed version contained in the *Shōshitsu rokumonshū (Anthology of Six Texts from Bodhidharma's Cave).* In Korean and Japanese printed versions the text occurs under the name *P'o-hsiang lun (Treatise on the Destruction of Characteristics).* (See *T*48.366c–69c.)

The *Kuan-hsin lun* was one of seven Ch'an-related texts discovered by Yabuki Keiki in the Stein collection in London and displayed in Japan in 1917. (See n. 161.) In 1932 Kamio Isshun published an article showing that the version contained in the Korean and Japanese editions, which attributed the text to Bodhidharma, was actually a work of Shen-hsiu's known as the *Kuan-hsin lun.* His evidence came from Hui-lin's (750–820) *I-ch'ieh ching yin-i,* a non-Ch'an School and thus a relatively reliable source first compiled in 788 and put in its final form in 806 or 807. See Kamio's "*Kanjinron* shikō," *Shūkyō kenkyū,* n.s. 2, no. 5 (1932): 98–104. This article was an important stimulus to the modern study of early Ch'an.

In 1934 Tokushi Yūshō published an analysis of the entire *Shōshitsu rokumonshū* that expanded on Kamio's findings. This was his "*Shōshitsu rokumonshū* ni tsuite;" see especially pp. 221–28. Also in 1934, D. T. Suzuki published a collated edition of all four manuscripts known at the time: S2595 (Suzuki used the printed edition in *T*85.1270c–73b, a less-than-reliable source); the Kanazawa Bunko manuscripts, which he edited as one; and the printed Korean and Japanese editions. In 1936 Suzuki republished this collated edition in his *Kōkan Shōshitsu issho oyobi kaisetsu,* adding the Ryukoku Library manuscript. See the *Suzuki Daisetsu zenshū,* suppl. vol. 1:576–645, for this final edition, and p. 647 for bibliographical information supplied by Furuta Shōkin.

Yanagida's *Zenseki kaidai,* pp. 456–57, mentions the occurrence of the title *Kuan-hsin lun* and quotations from the text in certain Chinese and Japanese works, details of the Kanazawa Bunko version's transmission to Japan, and the existence of a translation of the text into Uighur. For a recent analysis of the *Kuan-hsin lun,* see Sengoku Keishō, "*Kanjinron* no shisō to tokushitsu ni tsuite," *Shūgaku kenkyū,* 23 (March 1981): 237–40.

160. The most comprehensive discussion of this work to date is Tanaka Ryōshō's "Tonkōbon *Emmyōron* ni tsuite," *Indogaku Bukkyōgaku kenkyū,* 18, no. 1 (1969): 204–7. As Tanaka notes, the earliest known reference to this text is

in Ch'en Yuan's catalogue of Tun-huang materials remaining in China, the *Tun-huang chieh-yü lu,* 5:441b, which contains a brief description of Peking manuscript *fu* 符-6. Kanda Kiichirō's "*Den'hōbōki* no kanchitsu ni tsuite," *Sekisui sensei kakōju kinen ronsan* (Tokyo: Sekisui sensei kakōju kinen kai, 1942), pp. 145–52 (plus 8 double plates of the manuscript), was the first article to describe the opening section of P3559, in which the text in question is found. Unfortunately, the first part of this manuscript was then unknown. This led Kanda to misconstrue the title *Yuan-ming lun* as referring to the immediately following 45 lines of text, rather than to the preceding 217. Kanda noted the existence of the Peking manuscript and P3664, but he must not have seen the latter of these himself; his listing of the chapter titles of the text includes only those that occur in P3559. From the contents of the opposite side of P3664, we now know it to be the beginning of P3559. Since the opposite side of P3018, the continuation of P3559, bears the date 751, this is the *terminus ad quem* for all the material in these three manuscripts. See Tanaka, p. 207. Incidentally, P3018 is one of the manuscripts containing a portion of the miscellaneous material attached to the *EJSHL.* It bears the title *P'u-t'i-ta-mo lun (Treatise of Bodhidharma).* Yanagida's *Daruma no goroku,* p. 15, indicates that P3018 is only a partial record of this material.

Yanagida's important "*Den'hōbōki* to sono sakusha," pp. 47–48, summarizes Kanda's analysis—including the error regarding the application of the title *Yuan-ming lun*—and adds the suggestion that the material in question was written by some Northern School figure. Yanagida also mentions the existence and presumed wartime destruction of a manuscript owned by Ishii Mitsuo (Sekisui), the existence of which was mentioned previously by Suzuki in his comments on the *Chueh-kuan lun,* an Ox-head School text occurring in the same manuscript. (Suzuki's observation occurs in his and Furuta Shōkin's edition of the *Chueh-kuan lun,* i.e., *Zekkanron* [Kyoto: Kōbundō, 1935], a rare volume which I have not been able to consult. This reference is drawn from Yanagida, p. 47.) Yanagida laments the loss of the Ishii manuscript, since it might have included the eighth chapter of the text, which is inexplicably missing in P3559. As it turns out, the Ishii manuscript is still in existence, but it too lacks this chapter.

Tanaka's article mentioned at the beginning of this note corrects the error concerning the application of the title *Yuan-ming lun* and summarizes all known bibliographic information about the text. Tanaka's new findings were made possible by his examination of a newly discovered manuscript, S6184. This manuscript is only a few lines in length, but it includes the title and some of the chapter headings of the text. Tanaka also notes that the Peking manuscript contains the same title and headings, differing only in the addition of an attribution to Aśvaghoṣa. (The Chinese reads *Ma-ming p'u-sa tsao.*) P3664, as mentioned earlier, consists of the opening section of P3559 and also includes the same title and chapter headings, although without any attribution of authorship. The evidence of these three manuscripts was enough to show conclusively that the title *Yuan-ming lun* refers to the nine-chaptered treatise, rather than the forty-five lines following that title in P3559.

Finally, Okabe Kazuo's very brief resume of these matters, *"Emmyōron,"* in *Tonkō Butten to Zen,* Shinohara Toshio and Tanaka Ryōshō, eds., Kōza Tonkō, no. 8 (Tokyo: Daitō shuppan sha, 1980), pp. 344–49, includes the information that the Ishii manuscript is now at the Tōyō Bunko in Tokyo. It is apparently not available in microfilm or published form, or even for inspection on a regular basis. Nevertheless, Okabe reports that Tanaka was able to see it in a special viewing in July 1973. At this time Tanaka observed the title for the eighth chapter and the fine print annotation "included in the above two chapters" *(i-shang erh-p'in t'ung-shuo)*. Evidently, the *Yuan-ming lun* contains no independent eighth chapter.

The translation below is based solely on P3664 and P3559. (See n. 189 for the juncture between the two.) The former, which I have transcribed from photocopies of the microfilm, is difficult to read because of shoddy calligraphy and the extremely poor condition of the manuscript. For P3559 I have had the benefit of Professor Yanagida's transcription (mentioned already in n. 36), which I have checked against the photocopies of the microfilm. Obviously, the Ishii manuscript would have been of use in this study, but it is apparently not available. However, since this manuscript is apparently limited to the titles for Chapters Eight and Nine, the text of Chapter Nine, the title *Yuan-ming lun,* and the forty-five lines that also follow the *Yuan-ming lun* in P3559, the loss is probably not that significant. (See Tanaka, pp. 204–5.) In the same sense, the Peking manuscript would also have been useful, but apparently only the first half of it (120 lines) is devoted to this treatise, the latter half being an abbreviated transcription of the *Awakening of Faith*. Even these 120 lines might not have been that useful, since they apparently abbreviate the P3664/P3559 version throughout. (The combined length of this version is 277 lines.) Also, 84 lines of the Peking manuscript are said to be damaged, although the extent of this damage and its distribution throughout the manuscript is unclear. Therefore, the inability to consult the Peking and Ishii manuscripts has been only a minor impediment to the preparation of the English translation.

My reconstruction of the original title of the text is based on material found in the text itself. See the reference to a topic of discussion in the "*Yao-chueh lun* above" found in Chapter Three. The topic actually occurs in the earlier part of the text. The term *yuan-ming* does not occur in the text, unlike terms such as the *yuan-chiao fang-pien* in the reconstructed title.

See n. 163 for remarks concerning my edition of the Chinese text, which is found at the end of this book.

161. The *Wu fang-pien* was one of the very first set of Tun-huang manuscripts, Ch'an material included, to be published in Japan. In May 1917 an exhibit of "rotograph" reproductions was held at Shūkyō University (now Taishō University) in Tokyo. The organizer of this exhibit, Yabuki Keiki, had examined the collection in London the previous summer and had selected a total of 132 items for display. Among these were six Ch'an texts, plus a seventh whose relationship to Ch'an tradition was yet to become known:

C-16: *Ta-sheng wu-sheng fang-pien men* (three plates)
C-17: *Kuan-hsin lun* (one plate)
C-18: *Lun* (one plate)
C-19: *Ta-sheng pei-tsung lun* (one plate)
C-23: *O-mi-t'o tsan-wen, P'u-t'i-ta-mo ch'an-shih kuan-men*

C-24: *Ch'eng-hsin lun*
A-7: *Ch'an-yao ching, Ch'an-men ching ping hsü*

The numbers given are from Yabuki's original catalogue, the *Shutain-shi* [=*Stein*] *shūshū Tonkō chihō-shutsu ko shahon Butten rotogurafu kaisetsu mokuroku* (Tokyo: Shūkyō Daigaku, 1917). I have used Chinese transliterations for convenience.

Yabuki must have felt that the first work listed was particularly important, since he included three plates of it in his exhibit, or about four feet five inches of the original manuscript. Although Yabuki defined the text only as a Ch'an dialogue, he did point out that the manuscript (S2503) included a "poem in praise of Ch'an" *(Tsan ch'an-men shih),* a thirteen-character colophon, and the *Ta-sheng wu-sheng fang-pien men* itself. (The plates were taken from this last work.) The poem and colophon are printed at *T*85.1291c–93a; the other text occurs at *T*85.1273b–78a. (A brief concordance to *Wu fang-pien* texts is given at the end of this note.)

Of the other texts displayed in 1917, the second was Shen-hsiu's treatise (Yabuki knew only that it was not Chih-i's work of the same name); the third was a portion of the material appended to the *EJSHL* (S2715) rediscovered in 1936 by D. T. Suzuki; the fourth was a brief homiletic that may be found at *T*85.1281c–82b; the fifth was identical to a text later to become better known through a manuscript owned by the Ryukoku University Library (see item B in n. 36); the sixth was eventually to be recognized by Sekiguchi Shindai as a product of T'ien-t'ai Chih-i (see n. 29); and, finally, the seventh has come to be recognized as having been written by members of the early Ch'an School. For the last work, see Yanagida, "*Zemmonkyō* ni tsuite," *Tsukamoto hakase juju kinen Bukkyō shigaku ronshū* (Tokyo: Tsukamoto hakase juju kinen kai, 1961), pp. 869–82.

For reasons unknown, Yabuki only included two of the seven items (C-17 and C-23) in his *Meisa yoin* (Tokyo: Iwanami shoten, 1930). The contents of this work derived from his second sojourn in London in 1922–23, when he was apparently unable to reexamine some of the manuscripts he had seen before. Yanagida, who has been my source for most of the information given here, suggests that the problem may have been a lack of manuscript numbers in 1916. He also speculates that the manuscripts printed in the *Taishō tripiṭaka* were based on plates sent to Japan after Yabuki's 1922–23 visit. Yabuki's commentary on the work just mentioned, the *Meisa yoin kaisetsu,* was published in 1933, also by Iwanami. Thus he was able to include references to text in vol. 85 of the *Taishō* canon, which had appeared the year before. See Yanagida's "Tonkō no zenseki to Yabuki Keiki (1)," *Sanzō,* 54 (April 1972): 1–4.

In 1936 Kuno Hōryū discovered two new manuscripts of the *Wu fang-pien* in Paris: P2058, entitled *Ta-sheng wu fang-pien—pei-tsung* and (at the end) *Pei-tsung wu fang-pien men,* which Kuno describes as very clearly written but incomplete; and P2270, which he deemed complete but was very pale and difficult to read. At least the second of these two manuscripts was written by a well-known copyist named San-chieh ssu Tao-chen. Kuno made various comments on the content of the *Wu fang-pien* manuscripts and included a printed edition at the end of his article "Ryūdōsei ni tomu Tōdai no Zenshū tenseki—Tonkō shutsudo hon ni okeru Nanzen Hokushū no daihyōteki sakuin," *Shūkyō kenkyū,* n.s. 14, no. 1 (1939): 117–20 and 123–36.

Ui Hakuju included editions or reprintings of some of the manuscripts of the *Wu fang-pien* at the end of the first volume of his *Zenshūshi kenkyū,* which was also published in 1939. The *Ta-sheng pei-tsung lun* (Ui's text no. 5, pp. 447–48) was taken directly from *T*85.1281–82a and reflects the minor errors of that edition of S2581. (Ui and the Taishō editors included only about half of the contents of the manuscript. I have not used it here, since it has little or no relationship to the *Wu fang-pien.*) The *Ta-sheng wu-sheng fang-pien men* (no. 6, pp. 449–67) was apparently based on a comparative study of *T*85.1273b–78a and S2503, since Ui occasionally indicates misprints in the former. Nevertheless, my own comparison with photocopies of the Tun-huang manuscript indicates numerous errors remaining in Ui's text. Ui's edition of the *Ta-sheng wu-sheng fang-pien—pei-tsung* (no. 7, pp. 468–510) was based on plates of the Pelliot collection manuscripts borrowed from Kuno. The untitled work published along with the *Ta-sheng wu fang-pien—pei-tsung* (no. 8, also pp. 468–510) was based on hitherto unpublished plates of S2503 acquired from Yabuki. Although Ui's decision to print edited synoptic versions of the Pelliot and Stein collection manuscripts was an important innovation, his work is not free from error. (I have cross-checked only the manuscripts from London.) Finally, the untitled work on pp. 511–15 (his no. 9) occurs at *T*85.1291c–93c under the title *Tsan ch'an-men shih,* but Ui notes that this title refers only to the poem found at the end of this textual unit. Ui apparently used the *Taishō* edition. (See his bibliographic comments on pp. 424–27.)

The last major contributor to the textual understanding of the *Wu fang-pien* was D. T. Suzuki, whose comments and editions were published posthumously in the third volume of his complete works. The actual work of editing was done sometime prior to June 1949. (See Furuta Shōkin's note, *Suzuki Daisetsu zenshū,* 3:562.) Suzuki focused on the three most important manuscripts of the *Wu fang-pien* material: S2503, P2058, and P2270. From these manuscripts he isolated the following texts:

I (pp. 161–67): from S2503, plates 15–17, equivalent to Ui's untitled text no. 9, pp. 511–15, and the *Tsan ch'an-men shih, T*85.1291c–92c. Suzuki omits the poem from which the *Taishō* title derives.

II (pp. 167–89): from S2503, plates 18–28, entitled *Ta-sheng wu-sheng fang-pien men,* equivalent to Ui's text no. 6, pp. 449–67, and *T*85.1273b–78a

IIIA (pp. 190–212): based initially on P2058 and (from p. 199) on P2270 and equivalent to Kuno's text and Ui's text no. 7, pp. 468–510, with the exception noted in the following

IIIB (pp. 213–20): based on P2270 and equivalent to pp. 132.10–136.10 of Kuno's text and pp. 498.2–509.13 of Ui's text no. 7

IV (pp. 220–35): based once again on S2503, plates 9–14, and equivalent to Ui's text no. 8, pp. 468–510

With the exception of his hypothesis that the fourth of his texts was the latest of the *Wu fang-pien* material (as discussed in the following note), Suzuki offers no rationale for his isolation of these texts from the three manuscripts in question. Certainly, we must question the validity of the removal of some three thousand characters just before the final headings and title of text IIIA to create an independent text IIIB. In spite of these reservations, I have used Suzuki's editions because they are more accurate, more comprehensive, and more widely available than any other source. (I have spot-checked Suzuki's texts against the photographs of S2503 and found them generally accurate.) See n. 224.

162. The order of texts in vol. 3 of the *Suzuki Daisetsu zenshū* was apparently intended to reflect the internal development of the *Wu fang-pien*. Suzuki felt that the pinnacle of the *Wu fang-pien*'s philosophy was related to the *Avataṁsaka Sūtra,* which is more apparent in his text no. IV. See p. 152. In private conversations in May 1974, Professor Yanagida suggested to me that Suzuki's text no. I, although shorter and more fragmentary, may have been the last of the group because of its use of the word *t'ung* 通, "penetration" or "interpretation." See Takeda Tadashi's "*Daijō gohōben* no shohon no seiritsu ni tsuite," *Indogaku Bukkyōgaku kenkyū* 19, no. 1 (1960): 262–66, for a statement on the difficulties of establishing developmental relationships between the various manuscripts. Takeda feels that the *Wu fang-pien* existed in basic form during Shen-hsiu's life and that any variations or additions occurred within twenty years or so after his death.

163. P3559 lacks the character *tao* in its title for this chapter, but it occurs in P3664 and S6184. It is unfortunate that Tanaka did not list the titles as given in the Peking manuscript. (See p. 206 of the article mentioned in n. 131.)

The nature of the *Yuan-ming lun* manuscripts has necessitated editorial conventions somewhat different from those used in the case of the *Hsiu-hsin yao lun.* Except where absolutely necessary I have not indicated obvious errors of orthography. Common Buddhist abbreviations, such as those for *bodhisattva* and *nirvāṇa,* have been converted to standard forms. Typesetting has required the use of conventional forms rather than the cursive forms commonly used in Tunhuang manuscripts. Punctuation has been added roughly in keeping with that in the original. Lacunae at the top or bottom of the line have been marked consistently with three boxes, whereas those occurring mid-line have been marked by one or more boxes in proportion to the size of the hiatus. P3664 is sixty-one lines in length; line numbering begins again at 1 for P3559.

164. This title is partially obscured in P3664 and is therefore taken from the body of the treatise in P3559. It could be understood as "Distinguishing Heresy and Thereby Generating the Fundamental."

165. Here P3664 lacks the character *tao.* The translation is based in part on the contents of the chapter in question.

166. The compound translated here as "manifestations" is *hsien-liang.*

167. This title occurs only in the Ishii manuscript and P3664 and is partially obscured in both. The chapter itself does not occur in any of the extant manuscripts. See n. 131.

168. Elsewhere in this paper the term *ju-tao* has been translated as "entering into enlightenment," but in this text it has the meaning of "first undertaking spiritual practice."

169. The character *ming* is used in at least two ways in this text. Here and in lines 72 and 82 (both Chapter Four), for example, it occurs with the unambigu-

ous meaning of "to understand." In line 46 (Chapter Two), it is used with the meaning of "to explain." For an example of its use which could be interpreted in either way, see the very end of Chapter Four and n. 209.

170. Throughout this translation, words may be enclosed in brackets for either of two reasons. They may represent added material necessary for presentation in English, or they may indicate my reconstruction of the text where damage to the manuscript has resulted in lacunae. Five periods are used to indicate these lacunae, which almost always occur at the top and bottom of the lines in question.

171. See n. 139.

172. This phrase occurs several times in this text, with the connotation "What do you think about that?" At the very end of the text it is used in a longer construction with the meaning "If you do not appreciate" (i.e., "understand"). Prior to this phrase (line 7/1:7 of the Chinese manuscript) occur four extraneous characters, one of them of indecipherable form.

173. This term occurs again in Chapter Six (line 74 of the manuscript). It is also reminiscent of passages in the *Wu fang-pien,* which refer to the emancipation of the mind and then the body.

174. The text has *hsiang* 想, "thoughts," a copyist's error for *hsiang* 相, "characteristics." Such mistakes are very common throughout this and other Tun-huang manuscripts, including the line below that reads, "If the influences were without characteristics . . ." There the character for "thoughts" or false conceptualization occurs, rather than that for "characteristics." The two characters differ only by the presence or absence of one four-stroke element. I will not annotate such errors of transcription in the pages that follow.

175. The character is *ch'i,* "to arise"; "to generate," or "activate." In some Northern School contexts the idea of *pu-ch'i,* "nonactivation," is very important; see n. 340. Since this particular connotation is absent in the present text, I have translated the character *ch'i* variously according to context.

176. The phrase is *jo yu shih se,* the meaning of the third character apparently being "to invest with materiality." See n. 199.

177. The character missing here is probably *tso,* "to make." Compare P3559, line 99.

178. I find the wording of this line to be incomprehensible, including that part of the line corresponding to the previous sentence of the translation. I have tried to capture the general import.

179. The word "verify" is a tentative translation of *shih,* normally meaning "real" or "truly." I have taken it in a transitive sense. Unfortunately, the character in the manuscript is itself unclear. The Chinese for "numerous as grains of sand" is also problematic, being *kao ch'en sha chieh shu.* The first character, as it is, refers to a river in Shensi Province. This would be an interesting touch, if it were intentional. A more conventional phrasing would have been simply *wei-ch'en shu.*

180. This translation is tentative because of the obscurity of the second character, but it fits the context. See line 44 of the Chinese manuscript.

181. It is a common injunction of Buddhism that the mind resides in none of the three locations relative to the body: interior, exterior, and intermediate.

182. I am unaware of any precedent for this logic.

183. Perhaps the logic is that body and mind could be termed "being" if they were totally unrelated entities, rather than different aspects of the same reality.

184. At the very end of the text is a reference to the "five oceans and ten wisdoms" *(wu-hai shih-chih),* which presumably refers to this item and the list in which it is contained. The meaning of the "five oceans" is unknown.

185. The last of these three characters is only partially legible.

186. There does not appear to be enough room for this part of the title, but consistency would require its presence.

187. The *Lotus* uses the term "teaching of the One Vehicle" rather than "perfect teaching." The *Yuan-ming lun* probably refers to the admonition in the sūtra's chapter on expedient means. See *T*9.13cff.

188. This is a tentative reading.

189. The last line of P3664 and the first line of P3559 are identical. I find it difficult to understand how such a repetition could have occurred. Perhaps the separation of the two pieces took place during the very act of copying, and the line in question was repeated to show how the two pieces fit together. Line numbering in the transcribed text found at the end of this book has been initiated once again at this point.

190. Here I have used the terms "interior" and "exterior." Elsewhere I have used "within" and "without" and other similar equivalents, depending on the English context.

191. The allusion is probably to the metaphor of the mind being like a monkey that hops from one sensory window onto the world to another in an undisciplined, hyperactive fashion.

192. Judging from the context, the point must be that this is a mistaken apprehension of or attachment to the *dharmadhātu.*

193. Rather than "explanation," this could refer to the "transformation" of an unenlightened person's realm into that of an enlightened person.

194. The redundant characters *shih-chieh,* "world," occur here. The previous ellipses indicate three missing characters.

195. *Shou* 受, "to receive," is taken as an error for *hsiu* 修, "to cultivate."

196. The reference is to a *mahāllaka,* an immense fish used as a metaphor for something stupid. See Nakamura, 2:1278a–b.

197. A tentative reading. An alternate interpretation would be: "Within this teaching there appears no essence of sentient beings, and the . . . . . of the Buddhas are completely nonsubstantial."

198. I have been unable to find the exact source of this quotation. It may be only a rough paraphrase.

199. The term used is *chun-shih,* "perfumed and materialized."

200. See the occurrence of this term in the *EJSHL,* translated in the preceding chapter of this part.

201. This would seem to be in direct conflict with Shen-hsiu's *Kuan-hsin lun,* which interprets the three immeasurable eons of practice necessary to become a buddha in a nontemporal fashion. I do not believe this apparent contradiction is significant; see the discussion of "contemplative analysis" in Section 6 of this chapter. In the present context the connotation of the term is simply that one should practice constantly and without cease.

202. This is reminiscent of the metaphor of waves and water found in the *Awakening of Faith.* See Hirakawa, *Daijō kishin ron,* pp. 119 and 125–27 or *T*32.576c.

203. *Li-hsing* could be translated simply as "ideal practice." However, the emphasis on the necessity of achieving a balance of both understanding and practice occurs throughout this text. "Practice," in fact, seems to refer to activities undertaken on behalf of sentient beings, rather than meditative endeavors. This distinction, not to mention the specific term used here, is clearly reminiscent of the *EJSHL.* See the end of Chapter Six of the translation below and n. 217.

204. It is significant that a distinction is made between practitioners and nonpractitioners—all that is necessary is to undertake and continue spiritual practice. The *Hsiu-hsin yao lun* contains a similar injunction that its message cannot be understood with the ordinary mind. See section I of the translation in Chapter VI.

205. Here occur four characters that are indecipherable in the immediate context.

206. This is a paraphrase. The text has, literally: "This is an other-understanding, not a self-understanding. This is an other-practice, not a self-practice."

207. The Chinese translation for the term that is used here, *san-shih-ch'i chu-tao fa-men,* is not one of the several conventional ones. The thirty-seven requisites include the four foundations of mindfulness, four kinds of exertion, four bases of power, five faculties, five strengths, seven constituents of enlightenment, and the Eightfold Path. See Nakamura, 1:472b–d.

208. The negative of "nonpractice" is partially obscured, and the syntactical relationship between the phrases is in doubt.

209. This could be rendered equally well as, "Therefore, I first had to explain the worlds." On the different meanings of the character *ming,* see n. 169.

210. The character *wu* 無, "not," has been taken as *i* 亦, "also," to avoid a double negative.

211. *Sheng* 乘, "vehicle," is presumably an error for *sheng* 生, "to generate."

212. There are not false and correct in the sense of truth value, but in that of being in opposition to or accord with the spirit of Buddhism.

213. Here *ch'ien ching* is used to mean a previous moment of mentation, rather than an object of concentration physically in front of one.

214. Two very similar characters, *chih* 至 and *tao* 到, meaning "to come" and "to arrive," respectively, are used here. It is uncertain whether they were meant to have identical or slightly different connotations in this instance.

215. See Chapter One, line 10, and n. 173.

216. Literally, "If from space you next contemplate the earth."

217. The compound *li-hsing* occurs again a few lines below in the *Yuan-ming lun.* The correlation of such terminology with the two basic ideas of the East Mountain Teaching and Northern School should be obvious. See nn. 102 and 203.

218. The topic of "self-enlightened sagely wisdom" *(tzu-chueh sheng-chih)* is mentioned at least five times in the *Laṇkāvatāra Sūtra.* See *T*14.485a, 486c, 491b, 506c, and 510b. In the third and fourth instances there is also reference to the elements of phenomenal reality being the "manifestations of one's own mind," as in

the *Yuan-ming lun*. Incidentally, the first and second instances utilize the metaphor of the mirror, which suddenly reflects reality without any false thoughts.

219. I cannot find this statement at the corresponding locations of any of the readily available commentaries on the *Laṇkāvatāra Sūtra*. The commentary referred to here may have been one by Shen-hsiu or P'u-chi, which was being introduced and summarized in the lecture(s) that became the *Yuan-ming lun*. In addition, I cannot find any other references to a world system constructed on the basis of four disks, rather than three. See n. 315.

220. The term used here means "to revile the Dharma," although heresy seems to be the real problem, not blasphemy.

221. According to Tanaka, "Tonkōbon *Emmyōron* ni tsuite," p. 207, the Peking manuscript includes this anecdote in Chapter Six. I have taken several small liberties with the text in order to present a smoother translation.

222. See the list of ten items given in Chapter Two.

223. This ending is very abrupt, as if the original conclusion of the text has been omitted or lost.

224. The peculiar character of the *Wu fang-pien* has required the use of two special conventions. First, since this composite version is based on the text in the *Suzuki Daisetsu zenshū,* I have included specification of the manuscript, section, and page number for each segment. The first number, in Roman numerals, represents the manuscript number in Suzuki's edition. ("IIIA" and "IIIB" refer to Suzuki's first and second sections of his third manuscript.) Then follows the major section of that manuscript from which the segment in question was taken, i.e., "Int" for the Introduction, "Con" for the Conclusion, and nos. 1–5 for each of the five expedient means. The next number, that just before the colon, represents the segment number as given by Suzuki. (Some of these segment labels are hyphenated numbers, such as "3–1.") Finally, the number after the colon is the page number in the *zenshū* edition. Hence the present example, "II.Int.1: 167," means that the segment in question occurs on p. 167 in the *Suzuki Daisetsu zenshū* edition and that it is the first one in the Introduction of Suzuki's second manuscript. The second special convention is that liturgical *responses* are given in italics, while glosses and liturgical *instructions* in the text, which usually occur in smaller Chinese characters in the original manuscripts, are indicated by the simultaneous use of both parentheses and italics. Liturgical *queries* preceding the responses are not italicized.

225. The distinction between "going counter to" and "being in accord with" the Buddha Nature *(wei* and *shun)* resembles the *Yuan-ming lun*'s notion of "reverse" and "direct" types of contemplation *(ni* and *shun)*. I wonder if Suzuki has erred in the transcription of the *Wu fang-pien* manuscripts; I have not been able to check his version against the microfilms in this case. The sentence included here in underlined form occurs in the text in slightly smaller characters. The same convention is followed below.

226. This could be read, "When your minds are peaceful and motionless, what is it that is called purity?"

227. See *T*8.749a.

228. The characters *ho yen wen,* "the preceptor asked," occur here but have been overlooked for reasons of simplicity.

229. Nakamura, 2:1006c, says the following about *tang-t'i* (*tōtai* in Japanese): "The true nature of things as they are. A word that directly indicates their fundamental essence. Fundamental essence. The thing itself." According to this definition, *tang-t'i* refers to the true reality of Suchness itself, or the true reality of a specific object of contemplation. Since no such specific object is mentioned, I have chosen the more general alternative.

230. The term *chueh-hsin* is not very common in the *Wu fang-pien*. See the use of *chueh-hsing*, "enlightenment nature" at the end of the composite text (Conclusion, section A).

231. This term occurs prominently and repeatedly in the *Tun-wu chen-tsung yao-chueh*.

232. See similar terms at III.B.1:213 and IV.Con.3–1:233 (Conclusion, section B, of the composite text).

233. The text goes on to define these as the tempter of the afflictions, that of thinking and mental confusion; the tempter of the heavens, that of exterior limits and sensory realms; the tempter of the *skandha*s, that of physical laziness; and the tempter of death, that of the interruption of effort.

234. I have omitted an exchange which equates the Buddha with the "three sixes" *(san-liu)*. Suzuki edits this to read "three points" *(san-tien)*, which are the three dots used to make the character *i* in the Siddhaṁ version of the Sanskrit syllabary. In esoteric Buddhism these dots are equated with the *dharmakāya*, *prajñā*, and *mokṣa*. This usage is attested as early as the ninth century and may well have been in use as early as the period in question. See Nakamura, 1:483a. However, it seems better to leave the text as it stands and interpret the "three sixes" as a reference to the eighteen *āyatana*s or the capabilities, data, and consciousnesses associated with the six types of sensory awareness.

235. Here occur the smaller characters *ju yen*, "entered [and] said," the meaning of which is unclear. (Could they be some kind of stage direction?)

236. *Pu-ch'i*, "nonactivation" is mentioned in Section 19 of this chapter. On "maintain[ing] the True Mind," see the *Hsiu-hsin yao lun*.

237. See Hirakawa, pp. 102 and 105, or *T*32.576b. These passages are discussed in Section 15 of this chapter.

238. Suzuki's text I.1.4:163 includes an abbreviated version of this material. Following this occurs a citation from a work called the *Liu-ken chieh-t'o men (Teaching of the Emancipation of the Six Senses)*, otherwise unknown. The passage cited defines each sense organ as nonsubstantial and without self, etc.

239. Suzuki's text II.1.10:171 relates different portions of the *Awakening of Faith* line quoted here to "self" and "other," but this subject is not continued elsewhere in the *Wu fang-pien*.

240. We will see subsequently that this compound must be translated using two synomyms.

241. Suzuki's text I.1.5:163 contains an explanation of five different kinds of *dharmakāya*. These are based, the text tells us, on the *Ta t'ung fang-kuang ching (Sūtra on the Penetration of the Great Expanse)*, a Six Dynasties work probably composed in China. The relevant portion of this text is reproduced at *T*85.1348c, but its explanation of the five kinds of *dharmakāya* differs from that found here in the *Wu fang-pien*. The definitions given in the Northern School text contain

two interesting points: (1) the term "merit" *(kung-te)* is defined in terms of contemplative analysis, so that *kung* refers to the transcendence of thoughts and *te* to the manifestation of the absolute, and (2) there is a reference to the *dharmakāya* of space, "which is equivalent to the realm of space," a concept that is reminiscent of the *Yuan-ming lun.*

242. The terms "unfolding" and "constriction" seem at first glance to be related to breathing meditation, but the usage here actually refers to the passive realization and active expression of enlightenment.

243. *Li-hsin,* "to transcend the mind," may be an abbreviation for *hsin li-nien,* "the mind transcends thoughts." The same would be true of "transcend[ing] form."

244. I am adding *chieh hsiang* 界相, not just *chieh* 界, as Suzuki does.

245. The three self natures that occur here are the older Chinese equivalents for the three *svabhāva* of the Yogācāra tradition, as found in the Chinese translations of the *Laṇkāvatāra Sūtra.* See Nakamura, 1:113c and 1364a. I have taken the character *shih* 是 in the definition of the third self nature as an error for *yuan* 圓.

246. This opening dialogue is a composite of material from Suzuki's texts II.2.1:172, II.2.38:184, and IIIA.2.1:193. A different version occurs at what evidently corresponds to the same location in another manuscript, IIIB.1:213. This other version goes as follows:

> Do you perceive (*chien,* "to see") your body?
> *No.*
> Do you perceive your mind?
> *No.*
> Not perceiving the body, the body is emancipated. Not perceiving the mind, the mind is emancipated. Emancipation has the meaning of autonomous spontaneity *(tzu-tsai).*
> The characteristic of not perceiving the body and mind is without going and without coming. Vast and without a single thing, the gate of *bodhi (p'u-t'i men)* opens of itself.

247. *Chih-chien* is translated either as "knowing and perception" or "perceptive faculties," depending on the need for binominal symmetry.

248. The *Wu fang-pien*'s penchant for symmetry suggests that we should interpolate at this location a statement about the gate of wisdom and the sentence, "The senses are motionless."

249. Suzuki actually includes these two sentences in segment II.2.3.

250. Although Suzuki indicates that this is a quotation from the scriptures, its exact source has not been identified.

251. See the *Hsiu-hsin yao lun,* section T, and n. 108.

252. These three types of hearing seem to correspond with the differences in brainwave activity of nonmeditators and experienced practitioners of different types of meditation. That is, whereas nonmeditators habituate quickly to a repeated auditory stimulus, experts in Indian yogic meditation enter a state in which they never respond to the sound at all, and Zen meditators hear the sound each time in exactly the same way, without habituation. Although the case of the nonmeditator does not quite fit the *Wu fang-pien*'s statement about ordinary,

unenlightened people, it is still possible to infer that early Ch'an strove to define a type of meditative endeavor substantially different from traditional Indian practices. Unfortunately, it is impossible to determine whether the dichotomy implied here is completely culture-bound, i.e., Indian vs. Chinese approaches to meditation, or whether some precedent to this "constant practice" occurred in Indian Mahāyāna Buddhism.

253. This passage has not been located in the *Nirvāṇa Sūtra.*

254. This contradicts a well-known line in the *Tao-te ching,* 4.

255. Here the character for "perception" is *shih,* not *chien.*

256. *T*14.542b.

257. *T*14.542c.

258. *T*14.542b.

259. At roughly this point in the corresponding passage, Suzuki's text II.2.20: 178 has the following: "With fundamental and successive [wisdoms], all locations (i.e., all types of sensory activity) are clearly distinct, all locations are emancipated, all locations are [engaging in] spiritual practice."

260. Although this metaphor is common in Buddhist literature, it does not occur in the *Lotus* as given here.

261. Suzuki's text IIIA.2.16:199 adds the concept of motionlessness to its answers regarding space and the lotus blossom. It also closes with the following line about the "unsurpassed Honored One": "Always in accordance with the characterless principle, illuminating the source of the fundamental mind."

262. Suzuki's text IIIA.2.17:199 has added the idea of motionlessness, as just above, plus an interesting additional line. It has, in total:

> The mind's being motionless is the "wondrous Dharma." The body's being motionless is the "lotus blossom." When body and mind are motionless, one enters the "*samādhi* of the locus of incalculable meanings." This is called the *Sūtra of the Lotus Blossom of the Wondrous Dharma.*

A reference to the *samādhi* in question occurs in the *Lotus* and is quoted in the *Wu fang-pien* just below.

263. Suzuki's text IIIA.2.18:200 adds the phrases "open the gate of expedient means, manifest the path of truth *(chen-shih lu).*" The latter term also occurs in IIIA.2.19:200.

264. This is abbreviated very slightly from the original, which occurs at *T*9.2b and again on p. 4a.

265. It is interesting to see *li-nien* occur so explicitly as a substantive compound. The same usage occurs in the corresponding passage at II.2.31:181.

266. Suzuki's text II.2.32:182 has *shun,* "to be in accord," instead of *ju,* "to enter."

267. *T*9.5b.

268. Also *T*9.5b.

269. *T*9.6a. As Suzuki suggests, I am omitting the character *wen,* "question," that precedes this phrase.

270. It is tempting to correlate this statement with the third of Bodhidharma's four practices. See the translation of the *EJSHL* in Chapter V.

271. The text continues on to treat all the six perfections in the same manner.

Suzuki's text IIIA.2.25:202 includes the same passage but abbreviates all but the first perfection. I have included only enough of this material to indicate the pattern.

272. *T*14.546b. Like *chih-hui, pu k'o ssu-i* must be broken up for translation here. The reason for this will be apparent in the dialogue just below.

273. *T*14.546a. The phrases below are from the same source.

274. In this line I have translated both *ch'u-hsin jen* and *ch'u-hsin* as "beginner."

275. Here I have left *ssu-i* and *pu ssu-i* undivided, in order to yield a more fluid English rendition.

276. These are, of course, the Four Noble Truths.

277. *T*14.544b.

278. The reciprocal position occurs shortly below. I have used bold print to help the reader distinguish the key sentences.

279. Note that this is not just the correspondence of serenity and illumination, but the correspondence of the two expressions of their correspondence.

280. See *T*14.546b. "Enlargement or contraction" is only "increase or decrease" in the original, the volumetric nature of this change being understood.

281. Suzuki's text III.3.5:207 correlates the gods of the Heaven of the Thirty-three with the five sense organs and five sensory consciousnesses. The scriptural passage just above is abbreviated from *T*14.546b–c.

282. That is, they eradicate all mental activity, rather than just the dualistic discrimination that is the real problem.

283. *T*15.36b–c.

284. I have followed Suzuki in taking *ch'i* instead of *chih*.

285. This text is otherwise unknown. Although the contents of the quotation from it are somewhat more annihilatory than the *Wu fang-pien* in general, its use here substantiates the fact that the members of the Northern School were circulating their own teachings under Bodhidharma's name.

286. The first of these quotations is from Śikṣānanda's translation of the *Avataṁsaka, T*10.68c. The second is presumably from the same source.

287. The interpretation that this is an enlightened perception is a concession to the occasional use of *chueh-hsin* in the *Wu fang-pien*. Here the text has only *chueh*.

288. The *dharmakāya* has a "frozen" permanence because it is unrelated to the realm of activity, I believe.

289. See Buddhabhadra's translation of the *Avataṁsaka, T*9.438c. Śikṣānanda's wording, *T*10.77c-78a, is different but more explicit. The lines quoted here were apparently fairly popular, even though their interpretation among members of the Northern School is not certain. They also occur in a fragmentary manuscript of the *Wu fang-pien* (S2503) reprinted in the *Taishō tripiṭaka*. See *T*85.1292c and n. 161.

290. The fundamental study of the Teaching of the Three Stages is Yabuki Keiki's *Sankaikyō no kenkyū* (Tokyo: Iwanami shoten, 1927).

291. See Yanagida's discussion of the origins of the Southern School in *Shoki Zenshū shisho*, pp. 101–102. Yanagida begins this discussion with the statement, "The Southern School is predicated on the Northern School. Without the Northern School there could not have been any Southern School."

292. Unfortunately, in the present context I will be unable to consider Shen-hui's historical role and his criticisms of the Northern School. On the latter subject, see Robert Zeuschner's doctoral dissertation, *An Analysis of the Philosophical Criticisms of Northern Ch'an Buddhism* (University of Hawaii, 1977).

293. In some cases the Sanskrit term *prayoga* seems a better equivalent than *upāya* for the Chinese term *fang-pien*.

294. See Chapter Two, section B of the translation.

295. The general thrust of the *Kuan-hsin lun* is that one should eradicate the three poisons of craving, anger, and stupidity. This would seem to imply a conservative approach to religious practice, i.e., one of self control, etc. However, the eradication of the three poisons is not presented as synonymous with but rather as sharply different from traditional moral and spiritual training. The eradication of the poisons is contrasted with the tradition of the Buddha's three immeasurable eons of training, a tradition that is then itself redefined. (See item 3 in the list that follows in the text.) Exactly the same observation holds true for the *Kuan-hsin lun* as has already been made about the concept of mindfulness in the *JTFM:* The most important innovation is that the recommended practice included no prerequisites or preparation but could be accomplished immediately. (See Chapter VI, Section 7.)

296. This would be equivalent to about six liters by Han Dynasty measures (when the Buddha's biography first became known in China) and twenty-one liters during the T'ang Dynasty (when Shen-hsiu was writing). In either case, a substantial volume of milk.

297. The quotation is from the *Wen-shih ching (Sūtra on the Bath-house)*. The original translation of the sūtra itself is attributed to An Shih-kao and bears the full title *Fo-shuo wen-shih hsi-yü chung-seng ching*. See *T*16.803a for the list of seven items used here. A commentary on this scripture was discovered at Tun-huang, but it contains nothing like the material found in the *Kuan-hsin lun*. See *T*85.536c–40a.

298. The *Kuan-hsin lun* occurs in printed form at *T*85.1270c–73b and in the *Suzuki Daisetsu zenshū*, suppl. vol. 1:592–643. The former is based on only one Tun-huang manuscript and lacks the opening passage cited below (see n. 310), whereas the latter is a synoptic transcription of three versions of the text, each representing the edition of two manuscripts.

299. The term *kuan-hsin shih* derives originally from Chih-i's four criteria for commenting on the *Lotus Sūtra*. These are: *yin-yuan shih* ("conditional analysis"), which concerns the relationship between the Buddha and sentient beings; *yueh-chiao shih* ("doctrinal analysis"), which begins with the correlation of the particular scriptural line or term with one of Chih-i's four teachings (*Tripiṭaka*, common, unique, or perfect); *pen-chi shih* ("truth-level analysis"), in which individuals or doctrines are approached in either their "fundamental" *(pen)* Mahāyāna or their "manifested" *(chi)* Hīnayāna, i.e., their ultimate or literal, identities; and *kuan-hsin shih* ("contemplative analysis"), which approaches each line from the scripture as a function or component of the "contemplation of the principle of the true characteristic of the one mind." See Nakamura, 2:983a–b, or Andō, *Tendaigaku*, pp. 43–45. Ui was the first to use the term in reference to the Northern School. This is one of the meanings of *fang-pien*, "expedient means," in early texts; I will use "contemplative analysis" in order to avoid confusion. Faure, *La*

Volonte d'Orthodoxie, pp. 102–3, defines *upāya* in the Northern School as not simply a means, but "an attempt to transcend the dualistic distinction between ends and means. It is (or claims to be) the Ultimate Truth, the Truth that is manifested in all 'fashions of a certain fashion.' "

300. See *T*85.1432b–35c and Yanagida, "Zenseki kaidai," p. 463. The name *Dhammapāda,* or *Dharmapāda* in Sanskrit, actually refers to an entire genre of texts. See Mizuno Kōgen, *Hokkukyō no kenkyū* (Tokyo: Shunjūsha, 1981).

301. P2325 is reproduced at *T*85.1435c–45a. Although P2192 cannot be dated precisely, it betrays no influence from Shen-hui's Southern School and no knowledge of the *Yuan-ming lun, Wu fang-pien,* or even the *LCSTC.* On the other hand, it does contain references to principle *(li)* and practice *(hsing)* and a statement on there "fundamentally not [being] a single thing." (See the Conclusion, section 1 of the composite text.) The general outlook and style of metaphoric construction in this text implies a provenance similar to that of the *Wu fang-pien.*

302. The format used here for citations from microfilms of Tun-huang manuscripts is explained in Abbreviations and Conventions of Usage.

303. See similar sentiments expressed in the *Ta-mo ch'an-shih lun,* Sekiguchi, *Daruma daishi no kenkyū,* pp. 467–68.

304. This statement occurs at line 22:11/643.

305. The *An-pan shou-i ching* occurs at *T*15.163a–73a. Ui Hakuju's study of this text, which was published posthumously, attempts to separate the original scripture from the interpolated commentary. Unfortunately, no explanation of the criteria used in this process is either given or apparent. See his *Yakkyōshi kenkyū* (Tokyo: Iwanami shoten, 1971), pp. 201–44. A better attempt at deciphering at least the opening portion of the text is made by Aramaki Noritoshi, "Indo Bukkyō kara Chūgoku Bukkyō e—*Amban shui kyō* to Kō Sōe - Dōan - Sha Fu jo nado," *Bukkyō shigaku,* 15, no. 2 (1971): 1–45. Also see Kawashima Jōmyō, "*Amban shui kyō* ni tsuite," *Indogaku Bukkyōgaku kenkyū* 24, no. 2 (1976): 750–53.

306. *T*15.163c–64b.

307. The term *ko-i* is often used by modern students of Chinese civilizations as a catchword for an entire early phase of Buddhist-Taoist syncretism. The original meaning of the term was much more narrowly restricted, however. See Zürcher, p. 184.

308. See Michihata, *Tōdai Bukkyōshi no kenkyū,* pp. 357–76, and Kenneth K. S. Ch'en, *The Chinese Transformation of Buddhism* (Princeton, N.J.: Princeton University Press, 1973), pp. 55–60.

309. For a convenient summary of Tung's ideas and works, see Li Wei-hsiung, *Tung Chung-shu yü Hsi Han hsueh-shu* (Taipei: Chung-wen chih ch'u-pan she, 1979). Pages 66–73 deal specifically with his theories on *yin-yang* and the five elements. Andō, *Tendaigaku,* p. 45, mentions the *shih ju-shih* of the T'ien-t'ai tradition in the context of his explanation of "contemplative analysis." Also see Andō, pp. 139–41.

310. See the *Suzuki Daisetsu zenshū,* suppl. vol. 1:592–95. (The *Taishō* edition lacks this opening passage.)

311. This passage occurs at *T*85.1273c or *Suzuki Daisetsu zenshū,* suppl. vol. 1:641–42.

312. *T*85.1272b or *Suzuki Daisetsu zenshū,* suppl. vol. 1:624–25.

313. See *T*85.1270c or the *Suzuki Daisetsu zenshū,* suppl. vol. 1:598.

314. *T*85.1273a–b or *Suzuki Daisetsu zenshū,* suppl. vol. 1:640 and 642. The second of these two statements has already been included in the passage translated at the very end of Section 5 of this chapter.

315. The *Wai-tao hsiao-sheng nieh-p'an lun,* a brief text translated by Bodhiruci and comprised of material associated very closely with the *Laṇkāvatāra Sūtra,* contains the following description of a non-Buddhist school known as the "mouth-power teachers" *(k'ou-li lun-shih):*

> Space is the cause of the myriad things. At the very beginning is born space. From space is born wind. From wind is born fire. From fire is born smoke. [From] smoke is born water. The water then freezes solid and forms the earth. From the earth is born the myriad plants. From the myriad plants are born the five grains. From the five grains is born sentience. Therefore, in our treatise it says: "Sentience is food; afterward, it is again no more. (?) Space is called nirvāṇa. Therefore, the heretical "mouth-power teachers" say that space is permanent and is called the cause of *nirvāṇa.* (*T*32.158a)

This is by no means identical to the teaching found in the *Yuan-ming lun,* but the similarity is striking. See Mochizuki, 1:735c–36a and 915c. In contrast to the *Yuan-ming lun*'s four disks (see Chapter 7), the traditional Buddhist orthodoxy posits only three (wind, water, and metal). See *T*29.57af, de La Vallée Poussin, *L'Abhidharmakośa,* 2:138f, or Mochizuki, 2:1696a–b.

316. See n. 36.

317. For the treatment of these subjects in the *Kuan-hsin lun,* see Section 8 of this chapter. Also see Chapters Six and Three of the *Yuan-ming lun.* (The critical passage in the latter chapter is discussed in Section 11 of this chapter.)

318. The *Yuan-ming lun* refers to the penetration of space by mind and body (Chapter Two, eight paragraphs from the end), to one's wisdom, practice, and body, etc., filling space when the goal is achieved (Chapter Three, five paragraphs from the end), and to the equivalence of mind and form with space (Chapter Six, three paragraphs from the end). The *Wu fang-pien* discusses space in sections I.A, I.E, I.M, and II.K. In addition, one of the short works bearing Shen-hsiu's name discovered at Tun-huang refers to "body and mind pervading the *dharmakāya.*" See the *Ta-t'ung ho-shang ch'i li-wen (Shen-hsiu's Seven Ritual Statements),* S1494 or Yanagida, "*Den'hōbōki* to sono sakusha," p. 50 n. 3. Interestingly, this work also contains a reference to the "ordinary original mind within the body" *(t'i-chung p'ing-teng pen-lai hsin),* which evokes Ma-tsu's famous references to the ordinary mind. The *Yuan-ming lun*'s discussion of sound may be found in Chapter Nine. In the *Wu fang-pien,* see sections II.A and II.C–E. Concerning the realms, see the latter part of Chapter Two and the very end of Chapter Five in the *Yuan-ming lun* and sections I.E–F in the *Wu fang-pien.*

319. An additional reason to associate the *Yuan-ming lun* with Shen-hsiu might have been the similarity between its emphasis on the "perfect teaching" *(yuan-tsung)* and the "perfectly accomplished" *(yuan-ch'eng)* and the title of a lost work attributed to Shen-hsiu in a Korean catalogue. (The catalogue also lists

a thirty-fascicle commentary on the *Avataṁsaka*.) The title of this work is *Miao-li yuan-ch'eng kuan (Contemplation of the Wondrous Principle and the Perfectly Accomplished)*. However, there is no further similarity between the contents of the *Yuan-ming lun* and the few excerpts of the *Miao-li yuan-ch'eng kuan* that survive and, more important, the latter text is now considered to have been written by another monk named Shen-hsiu who died about 770 (as is the sūtra commentary). The passages in question were discovered by Ōya Tokujō and were published in Kim Ji-gyŏn, "Kōchū *Hokkaizu entsū ki,*" *Shiragi Bukkyō kenkyū,* Kim Ji-gyŏn *et al.*, eds. (Tokyo: Sankibō Busshorin, 1973), pp. 380–84. One of the passages in question (p. 383) incorporates material attributed to Shen-hsiu in the *TCL* (*T*48.943a–b). See Yanagida's "Zenseki kaidai," p. 468. Additional passages of similar attribution are introduced by Yoshizu Yoshihide, "Jinshū no *Kegon kyōsho* ni tsuite," *Shūgaku kenkyū,* 24 (March 1982): 204–9. See Sakamoto, *Kegon kyōgaku no kenkyū* (Kyoto: Heirakuji shoten, 1956), p. 56, and *T*55.1166a and c. Bernard Faure provides a comprehensive analysis of the entire issue in "Shen-hsiu et l'*Avataṁsaka-sūtra,*" *Zinbun: Memoirs of the Research Institute for Humanistic Studies,* 19 (1983): 1–15, as well as in his dissertation, *La Volonte d'Orthodoxie,* pp. 118–28.

320. The most convenient reference in English for the *p'an-chiao* theories of the Hua-yen School is Weinstein, "Imperial Patronage in T'ang Buddhism," p. 304. For a more extensive treatment, see Sakamoto, *Kegon kyōgaku no kenkyū,* pp. 149–265. The list of ten meanings given in Chapter Two of the *Yuan-ming lun* is reminiscent of the Hua-yen School's predilection to categories of ten, but this similarity is of little measurable significance.

321. See Chapter Three, section C, of the translation.

322. Professor Yanagida, in his "Shoki Zenshū to shikan shisō," p. 264, asserts that the principle of nonsubstantiality was fundamental to the development of the Ch'an School from its very inception. This is in contrast to the traditional view, of course, which identifies the Northern School with the *Laṇkāvatāra Sūtra* and the Southern School with the *Diamond Sūtra* and a newfound emphasis on the Perfection of Wisdom.

323. See Ch'en, *Buddhism in China,* pp. 129–31, for a brief discussion of the *Ch'eng-shih lun.* Mibu Taishun, "*Jōjitsuron* ni okeru shikan," *Shikan no kenkyū,* Sekiguchi Shindai, ed. (Tokyo: Iwanami shoten, 1975), pp. 139–45, contains a discussion of this text's doctrine of meditation.

324. See T. W. Rhys Davids, trans., *The Questions of King Milinda,* Part I, Sacred Books of the East, no. 35 (Oxford: Clarendon Press, 1890), pp. 43–45.

325. This saying ("The path of words . . .") occurs first in the *Ta chih-tu lun,* *T*25.71c. (The two phrases occur here in opposite order from the later conventional usage.) See Nakamura, 1:429a.

326. The connection with the *Hsiu-hsin yao lun,* section P, is obvious.

327. See the end of the first paragraph of this translation.

328. See P3559, 17:9/391f, or Yanagida, "*Den'hōbōki* to sono sakusha," p. 49. It is possible that the passage introduced here is not specifically attributable to Shen-hsiu. The heading "transmission of Preceptor [Shen]-hsiu" occurs shortly above in the manuscript (17:3/385). This is followed by a three-line exhortation to vigorous exertion in meditation, a space of one character, the heading "Oral Determination of the Mind that Leads Ordinary People to Sage-

hood" *(tao-fan ch'ü-sheng hsin-chueh),* two spaces, a statement on the transmission of the teaching from Bodhidharma to Hung-jen's disciples, and, finally, the passage in question. The second heading and transmission statement clearly refer to the *Hsiu-hsin yao lun* and, in my opinion, should be placed just after that text. (The transmission statement is clearly related to the *CFPC,* as has already been noted.) This leaves the passage in question directly after Shen-hsiu's exhortation.

329. See n. 42, item C, for a comment on the occurrences of the term *ming-ching* in the *LCSTC.*

330. Suzuki's short introduction to his edition of the *Wu fang-pien* manuscripts in the third volume of his complete works (pp. 141–52) contains several references to the lack of clarity of the text. At one point, he even suggests that one of the text's position's was "irritating" *(modokashii)* to Shen-hui. Although we cannot accept Suzuki's preconceptions, it is understandable that the style of the *Wu fang-pien* offered him little reason to challenge them.

331. This list includes the variant titles that occur in the manuscripts, plus the scriptural correspondences as given by Tsung-mi. For the latter, see Kamata, *Zengen shosenshū tojo,* pp. 301–302, and Z1, 14, 277c–78b (*H*14.554a–55b).

332. I believe that the explication of five expedient means, rather than four, six, or some other number, is a reflection of the *p'an-chiao* tradition. Although this is only a superficial relationship, it is consistent with the Northern School's adaptation of traditional Buddhist motifs to its own purposes. This is not the only early Ch'an work that may be compared with *p'an-chiao* schema: The structure of the *EJSHL* attributed to Bodhidharma seems even more organically related. That is, the entrance of principle and the four practices constitute a five-fold progression similar to that found in some *p'an-chiao* theories. For ease of reference, we may recall the "five periods" of the T'ien-t'ai system. Immediately after his enlightenment, the Buddha is supposed to have taught the *Avataṁsaka Sūtra,* which contained an unsimplified statement of the highest truth. Seeing that his message was not being communicated, the Buddha changed his approach and taught the very simple Hīnayāna teachings, progressively more sophisticated Mahāyāna doctrines, and eventually the most profound ideas of the *Lotus Sūtra.* Although this scheme was developed after the composition of the *EJSHL* (even if the *EJSHL* were written well after Bodhidharma's death) the notion of beginning with the unadulterated truth and then progressing from the simplest to the most profound of religious doctrines is apparent in other, much earlier *p'an-chiao* schema, viz., Hui-kuan's theory, which is summarized in Hurvitz, "Chih-i," pp. 219–24. This comparison suggests that the logical structure, if not necessarily its content, is thoroughly Chinese.

333. This resume is mentioned in n. 331.

334. See Hirakawa, *Daijō kishin ron,* pp. 57–61 and 95–101. Also see Yoshito S. Hakeda, trans., *The Awakening of Faith—Attributed to Aśvaghosha, Translated, with Commentary* (New York: Columbia University Press, 1967), pp. 12–15.

335. See Hirakawa, pp. 99–100. The fact that the *Wu fang-pien* prefers the "matrix of buddhahood" over the "consciousness-only" theory fits with the rejection of the false view of the sudden teaching and reverse contemplation in the *Yuan-ming lun.* (See Chapters Two and Five of the translation.)

336. *Ibid.,* p. 182, or *T*32.577c.

337. Hirakawa, pp. 102–6, or *T*32.576b. The reader may also consult Hakeda, pp. 37–40. The differences between my translation and the late Professor Hakeda's are due to the particular usage of terminology in this paper.

338. The idea referred to here is not that of decay into nonexistence or unmanifestness, but differentiation from successive thoughts.

339. See Hirakawa's commentary, pp. 109–112.

340. See the end of section IV.C of the *Wu fang-pien* translation.

The esoteric Buddhist master Śubhākarasiṁha criticizes the practice of meditation by students in Ch'ang-an as follows:

> You beginners are [in such] great fear of activating the mind and the motion of thoughts that you cease to make spiritual progress. In singlemindedly maintaining "nonthought" *(wu-nien)* as the ultimate, the [longer you] search, the more unattainable [is your goal]. (*T*18.945a)

(The text in which this passage occurs has been mentioned in n. 160 to Part One.) It is noteworthy that this criticism, which was addressed to a congregation led by Shen-hsiu's disciple Ching-hsien, certifies the popularity of both *pu ch'i* ("nonactivation") and *wu-nien* ("nonthought") a decade before the initiation of Shen-hui's anti-Northern School campaign in 730. Also, the phrase "not a single thing" *(wu i wu)* occurs on p. 945b.

341. See Kamata's discussion of Ch'eng-kuan's comments in *Chūgoku Kegon shisōshi no kenkyū* (Tokyo: Tōkyō Daigaku shuppan kai, 1965), pp. 486–91. Also see Yoshizu Yoshihide's discussions of Ch'eng-kuan's view of Ch'an in "Chōkan no Zenshū-kan ni tsuite," *Shūgaku kenkyū,* 22 (March 1980): 206–11, and "Tonkyō ni okeru Chōkan no kaishaku ni tsuite," *Shūgaku kenkyū,* 23 (March 1981): 209–14. Sengoku Keishō reviews issues related to *li-nien* in "Hokushū-zen ni okeru mushin to rishin ni tsuite," *Shūgaku kenkyū,* 22 (March 1980): 221–24. For an occurrence of *li-hsin* (*rishin* in Japanese), see section I.L of the translation and n. 243.

342. See the *Ch'eng-hsin lun* in the *Suzuki Daisetsu zenshū,* 2:443–44.

343. See n. 29.

344. *T*33.697c. Also see p. 707a and Mochizuki, 1:606a–b.

345. *T*46.578a.

346. See *T*15.462c, 469c, and 479a.

347. See Chi-tsang's *Ta-sheng hsuan lun, T*45.49b, and Oda Tokunō, *Bukkyō daijiten* (Tokyo: Daizō shuppan kabushiki kaisha, 1954), p. 1210c. Sasaki Genjun's "Chie," *Indogaku Bukkyōgaku kenkyū,* 2, no. 2 (1954): 84–86, contains a concise definition of the background of the two types of wisdom in Indian Buddhism.

348. Obviously, physical objects might be said to "transcend thought" in the sense that they are in and of themselves unrelated to thought, but it is only the practitioner's awareness of this fact that would have any real significance. Actually, to talk of "physical objects" or a reality that exists external to the practitioner is to miss the point of Buddhist philosophy in general, in which the only "form" that is actually encountered by any individual being occurs as *dharmas* of cognition.

349. The *Wu fang-pien* statement occurs at Intro.B of the composite text.

Other evidence of Northern School maintenance of the precepts occurs in the *Ta-sheng pei-tsung lun,* T85.1281c–82a. For a discussion of the Northern School's identification with *Vinaya* centers, see Shiina, "Hokushū-zen ni okeru kairitsu no mondai," *Shūkyō kenkyū,* 11 (March 1969): 139–59.

350. The example of Ming-ts'an is the exception that proves this rule: His radical reform after 742 implies that his behavior was a calculated response to a specific situation at Nan-yueh ssu rather than a general rejection of monastic discipline.

351. See Yin-shun's *Chung-kuo Ch'an-tsung shih,* pp. 166–68. The *Kuan-hsin lun*'s comments on *nien-fo* are mentioned in point 8 of the list included in Section 5 of this chapter. See T85.1273a or the *Suzuki Daisetsu zenshū,* suppl. vol. 1:636–40. The *CFPC* (section S) uses the term *nien fo-ming* ("remembrance of the name of the Buddha"). This implies oral recitation, but the reference is to a shallow practice given to large numbers of beginning students. Faure, *La Volonte d'Orthodoxie,* p. 213, comments insightfully on the ambiguous relationship between the interiorization and ritualization of meditation practice, using the *Wu fang-pien* reference to *nien-fo* as an example of the latter. Finally, Shen-hsiu's reference to sentient beings' foolishly "not polishing" the Buddha Amitābha within them, to be mentioned in the Conclusion, Section 1, implies a contemplative and (at least primarily) nonrecitative interpretation of *nien-fo.* See n. 4 to the Conclusion.

352. See P3559, 26:9/614.

353. See Iriya, "Kū to jō," pp. 97–106.

354. See section II.B of the translation.

CONCLUSION

1. *Suzuki Daisetsu zenshū,* suppl. vol. I, pp. 622–24, or T85.1272a.
2. See the *LCSTC, Shoki no zenshi, 1,* p. 321, or T85.1290c.
3. See Yanagida, *Shoki Zenshū shisho,* p. 501.
4. The work is called the *Hsiu ch'an-shih ch'üan-shan wen (Shen-hsiu's Homiletic).* See S5702 or Yanagida, "*Den'hōbōki* to sono sakusha," p. 50 n.3. See n. 351 to Part Two.
5. See sections Intro.E and Concl.B of the translation in Part Two, Chapter VII, Section 3.
6. See Yampolsky, p. 132, or T48.338a.
7. See his "An Appeal for a Systematic Search in Japan for Long-hidden T'ang Dynasty Source-materials of the Early History of Zen Buddhism," *Bukkyō to bunka,* Yamaguchi Susumu, ed. (Kyoto, 1960), pp. 20–21, as cited in Yampolsky, p. 132 n. 39.
8. See T48.349a. Yampolsky, p. 94 n. 9, suggests that this form of the verse probably appeared around 850. Also see T85.1206c for an interesting variation on "Shen-hsiu's" verse and the following elaboration: "There is no tree, but [its] image does exist. *(This is a metaphor for being in space.)* Streets in the wind [are marked by (?)] the tracks of birds." The specific meaning of this passage is far from clear, but at least this much is certain: The verse in question occurs in conjunction with reference to the nonexistence of the tree—as in one of "Hui-

neng's" retorts—in a text that is obviously closer to Northern School writings than it is to the *Platform Sūtra.* That is, the manuscript in question (it is only a fragment) uses a style of allegorical symbolism that is very similar to the "contemplative analysis" of the Northern School. Shen-hsiu used a similar reference to the "tracks of birds" in one of his "questions about things;" see Part One, Chapter IV, Section 14. Finally, it uses the phrase "nonactivation" *(pu ch'i)* in a manner that is based on the *Awakening of Faith* and identical to Northern School usage (also p. 1206c).

9. *The Zen Doctrine of No-mind* (London: Rider and Company, 1949), p. 22. Yampolsky, p. 94, also cites this passage and notes its inaccuracy.

10. See sections Intro.C and Intro.E in Part Two, Chapter VII, Section 3. The phrase "not [without] a single thing" also occurs in the *Wu fang-pien* at IIIB.1:213; see the translation in n. 246. For two additional occurrences of the same phrase, see line 27:1/636 of P3559 (attributed without basis to Seng-ch'ou) and the text mentioned in n. 160 to Part One and n. 340 to Part Two.

11. Ch'eng-kuan sees little difference between the terms *li-nien* and *wu-nien,* which are associated with the Northern and Southern Schools, respectively. See *T*36.62a–b, 261b, and 262a. Additional comments by Ch'eng-kuan on the ideas of the Northern School may be found on p. 274c. Kamata, *Chūgoku Kegon shisōshi no kenkyū,* p. 487f, believes that Ch'eng-kuan may have been influenced on this point by the Ox-head School monk An-kuo Hsuan-t'ing. See n. 341 to Part Two.

12. On Shen-hui's banishment, see Hu Shih's biographical study of Shen-hui in the *Shen-hui ho-shang i-chi,* pp. 64–66, and the sources mentioned there. I am now working on a comprehensive reappraisal of Shen-hui.

13. For further information on this subject, see my article "The Ox-head School."

14. See Yamazaki Hiroshi, *Zuitō Bukkyō no kenkyū* (Kyoto: Hōzōkan, 1967), pp. 191–98, Faure, *La Volonte d'Orthodoxie,* pp. 162–69, and n. 174 to Part One.

15. Hui-ssu, the well-known teacher of T'ien-t'ai Chih-i, left north China in 552 after Emperor Wen-hsuan of the Northern Ch'i issued a summons for all meditation teachers to come to court in 552. This summons was part of the preparation for the establishment of a national system of meditation centers staffed by specially selected "liberated and wise" monks as teachers. The main hub of this system was Yun-men ssu on the slopes of Mount Lung, about thirty-five kilometers from the capital at Yeh. This monastery was established for Seng-ch'ou (480–560), an important early meditation specialist. Seng-ch'ou's biography is in the *HKSC* at *T*50.553b–55b. Yun-men ssu is described on p. 555a.

16. See Fukushima, "Jōyōji Eon no shikan shisō," pp. 4–8.

APPENDIX

1. The following translation is based on Yanagida's critical edition and Japanese translation of the *CFPC,* which may be found in his *Shoki no zenshi, 1,* pp. 327–435. For textual information, see pp. 38–39 of the same work. Because of the existence of Professor Yanagida's commentary, which is both copious and

masterful, I have limited the annotation here to the bare minimum necessary for the English reader.

2. See Hirakawa, *Daijō kishin ron,* pp. 72 and 323, or *T*32.576a and 581a.

3. *T*16.497b. The first sentence of this section of the *CFPC* is also adapted from the same scripture, *T*16.507a.

4. See the discussion of this passage in Part One, Chapter IV, Sections 6, 9, and 11.

5. Yanagida explains this term on the basis of its occurrence at *T*16.499b.

6. Yanagida suggests that this refers to the *EJSHL* and its appended material.

7. Note the occurrence of a slightly different title at the very end of this work.

8. Even though the *CFPC* is critical of the *EJSHL* and *HKSC,* the influence of these two sources is quite evident in its treatment of Bodhidharma's biography.

9. Interlineal glosses in the text are indicated by the conjoint use of italics and parentheses.

10. Note that the characters for the Wei 魏 Dynasty and the area of Wei 衛 are not identical.

11. This prediction, which occurs in the *HKSC, T*50.552b–c, is repeated in section R of the *CFPC.*

12. Chih-yen is mentioned in reference to Fa-ju in Part One, Chapter II, Section 7. Yanagida, *Shoki no zenshi, 1,* pp. 374–75, points out that the reference to Pao-yueh here involves a chronological anachronism.

13. A Preceptor Tuan of Lo-yang is mentioned with regard to P'u-chi's biography in Part One, Chapter III, Section 5. See nn. 91 and 111 to Part One.

14. I-fu's epitaph refers to a "secret transmission" from Shen-hsiu to I-fu that occurred just before the death of the former. See Part One, Chapter III, Section 4.

15. See the *Diamond Sūtra (Chin-kang pan-jo ching), T*8.751c; the *Lun-yü,* 17; and the *Chuang-tzu,* 26.

16. My interpretation of this passage differs from that of Professor Yanagida, who feels that the *CFPC* is rejecting the *Yuan-wu liao-i ching* as an inferior expression of the Buddhist teachings.

17. This prediction, which occurs first in the *HKSC,* has already been introduced in section H of the *CFPC.* See n. 50 to Part One and the discussion in Part One, Chapter I, Section 7.

18. As Yanagida points out, this metaphor is based on a line in the *Hou Han shu,* 33, *Erh-shih-wu shih,* 1:769b.

19. This phrase occurs in a quotation from the *Laṇkāvatāra* found in the *TCL, T*48.844b. Yanagida quotes at length from the passage in which it occurs in the sūtra itself.

20. Here occurs the stūpa inscription listed in Part One, Chapter II, Section 8 as one of the sources of Shen-hsiu's biography. Its relationship to the *CFPC* is uncertain.

Bibliography

DICTIONARIES AND COLLECTIONS

Bukkyō daijiten 仏教大辞典, Oda Tokunō 織田得能 (Tokyo: Daizō shuppan kabushiki kaisha 大蔵出版株式会社, 1954).

Bukkyō jiten 仏教辞典, Ui Hakuju 宇井伯寿 (Tokyo: Daitō shuppan sha 大東出版社, 1938).

Bukkyōgaku jiten 仏教学辞典, Taya Raishun 多屋頼俊 *et al.* (Kyoto: Hōzōkan 法蔵館, 1955).

Bukkyōgō daijiten 仏教語大辞典, Nakumura Hajime 中村元 (3 vols.; Tokyo: Tōkyō shoseki 東京書籍, 1975).

Bussho kaisetsu daijiten 仏書解説大辞典, Ono Gemmyō 小野玄妙 (12 vols.; Tokyo: Daitō shuppan sha, 1932–36).

Ch'in-ting ch'üan T'ang-wen 欽定全唐文, Tung Kao 董誥 *et al.*, eds. (1,000 fascicles; Shanghai, 1814; reprint Taipei: Huai-wen shu-chü, 1961).

Dai Kan-Wa jiten 大漢和辞典, Morohashi Tetsuji 諸橋轍次 (13 vols.; Tokyo: Daishukan shoten 大修館書店, 1955–60).

Dai Nippon zokuzōkyō 大日本続蔵経 (150 vols.; Kyoto: Zōkyō shoin 蔵経書院, 1905–12; reprint Taipei: Shin wen-feng ch'u-pan kung-ssu 新文豊出版公司, 1968–70).

Erh-shih-wu shih 二十五史, Erh-shih wu-shih k'an-hsing wei-yuan hui 二十五史刊行委員會, ed. (9 vols. plus biographical index; Shanghai: K'ai-ming shu-tien 開明書店, 1935; reprint Taipei, 1962).

Lien-mien tzu-tien 聯緜辭典, Fu Ting-i 符定一, ed. (3 vols.; Taipei: Taiwan Chung-hua shu-chü 台灣中華書局, 1969).

Hōbōgirin—dictionnaire encyclopédique du bouddhisme d'après les sources chinois et japonaises, Sylvain Lévi and J. Takakusu, eds. (4 vols. plus appendixes; Tokyo: Maison franco-japonaise, 1929–37).

Mochizuki Bukkyō daijiten 望月仏教大辞典, Mochizuki Shinkō 望月信亨 (10 vols.; Tokyo: Sekai seiten kankō kyōkai 世界聖典刊行協会, 1933–36).

Shinsen Zenseki mokuroku 新選禅籍目録, Komazawa University Library (Tokyo: Komazawa Daigaku Toshokan 駒沢大学図書館, 1962).

T'ai-p'ing kuang chi 太平広記, Li Fang 李昉 *et al.*, eds. (10 vols.; Peking: Chung-hua shu-chü 中華書局, 1961).

Taishō shinshū daizōkyō 大正新修大蔵経, Takakusu Junjirō 高楠順次郎, ed. (100 vols.; Tokyo: Daizō shuppan kai 大蔵出版会, 1922–33).

T'ang-wen shih-i 唐文拾遺, Lu Hsin-yuan 陸心源, ed. (72 fascicles, 1888; reprint Taipei: Wen-hai ch'u-pan she 文海出版社, 1962).

SECONDARY WORKS

Andō Toshio 安藤俊雄, "Rozan Eon no zenshisō" 廬山慧遠の禅思想, Kimura Eiichi 木村英一, ed., *Eon kenkyū: kenkyū hen* 慧遠研究: 研究篇 (Kyoto: Sōbunsha 創文社, 1962), pp. 249–85.

———, *Tendaigaku—kompon shisō to sono tenkai* 天台学—根本思想とその展開 (Kyoto: Heirakuji shoten 平楽寺書店, 1968).

Aramaki Noritoshi 荒牧典俊, "Indo Bukkyō kara Chūgoku Bukkyō e—*Amban shui kyō* to Kō Sōe – Dōan – Sha Fu jo nado" インド仏教から中国仏教へ—安般守意経と康僧会・道安・謝敷序など, *Bukkyō shigaku* 仏教史学, 15, no. 2 (1971): 1–45.

Bielefeldt, Carl, and Lancaster, Lewis, "*T'an ching* (Platform Scripture)," *Philosophy East and West*, 25, no. 2 (April 1975): 197–212.

Broughton, Jeffrey, "Early Ch'an Schools in Tibet," R. M. Gimello and P. N. Gregory, eds., *Studies in Ch'an and Hua-yen*, Studies in East Asian Buddhism, no. 1 (Honolulu: University of Hawaii Press, 1983), pp. 1–68.

Buswell, Robert, *The Korean Origins of the* Vajrasamādhi Sūtra (Ph. D. dissertation, in progress, University of California, Berkeley).

Chappell, David, "The Teachings of the Fourth Ch'an Patriarch Tao-hsin (580–651)," Whalen Lai and Lewis Lancaster, eds., *Early Ch'an in China and Tibet*, Berkeley Buddhist Studies Series, no. 5 (Berkeley, Calif.: Asian Humanities Press, 1983), pp. 89–129.

Ch'en, Kenneth K. S., *Buddhism in China: A Historical Survey* (Princeton, N.J.: Princeton University Press, 1964).

———, *The Chinese Transformation of Buddhism* (Princeton, N.J.: Princeton University Press, 1973).

Ch'en Yuan 陳垣, *Tun-huang chieh-yü lu* 敦煌劫餘錄 (6 vols.; Peking: Kuo-li Chung-yang Yen-chiu-yuan li-shih yü-yen yen-chiu-so 國立中央研究院歷史語言研究所, 1931).

Collcutt, Martin, *Five Mountains: The Rinzai Zen Monestic Institution in Medieval Japan* (Cambridge, Mass.: Harvard University Press, 1981).

Demiéville, Paul, *Le concile de Lhasa: une controverse sur le quiétisme entre bouddhistes de l'Inde et de la Chine au VIIIe siècle de l'ère chrétienne*, Bibliothéque de l'Institut des hautes etudes chinoises, vol. 7 (Paris: Impr. nationale de France, 1952).

———, "Le *Yogācārabhūmi* de *Saṅgharakṣa*," *Bulletin d'Ecole Français d'Extrême Orient*, 44, no. 2 (1954): 339–436.

Dumoulin, Heinrich, S. J., "Bodhidharma und die Anfänge des Ch'an-Buddhismus." *Monumenta Nipponica*, 7 (1951): 67–83.

———, *A History of Zen Buddhism*, trans. by Paul Peachey (New York: Random House, 1963; reprint Boston: Beacon Press, 1969).

Ehara, N. R. N., Soma Thera, and Kheminda Thera, trans., *The Path of Freedom (Vimuttimagga)* (Colombo, Sri Lanka: D. R. D. Weerasuria, 1961).

Faure, Bernard, *La Volonte d'Orthodoxie: Généalogie et doctrine du bouddhisme Ch'an et l'école du Nord—d'après l'une de ses chroniques, le* Leng-chia shih-tzu chi (*début du 8è s.*) (Ph.D. dissertation, University of Paris, 1984).

———, "Shen-hsiu et l'*Avataṁsaka-sūtra*," *Zinbun: Memoirs of the Research Institute for Humanistic Studies*, 19 (1983): 1–15.

Fukuda Gyōe 福田堯穎, *Tendaigaku gairon* 天台学概論 (Tokyo: Bun'ichi shuppan 文一出版, 1954).

Fukushima Kōsai 福島光哉, "Jōyōji Eon no shikan shisō" 浄影寺慧遠の止観思想, *Tōhōgaku* 東方学, 36 (September 1968): 1–14.

Furuta Shōkin: see under D. T. Suzuki.

Gimello, R. M., and Gregory, P. N., eds., *Studies in Ch'an and Hua-yen*, Studies in East Asian Buddhism, no. 1 (Honolulu: University of Hawaii Press in association with the Kuroda Institute, 1983).

Gregory, P. N.: see under Gimello.

Hanazuka Hisayoshi 花塚久義, "*Shōmangyō* Donrin-chū to Kichizō" 勝鬘経曇林註と吉蔵, *Shūgaku kenkyū*, 23 (March 1981): 236–40.

Hattori Masaaki 服部正明, "Zen to Indo Bukkyō" 禅とインド仏教, *Zen no honshitsu to ningen no shinri*, Hisamatsu Shin'ichi and Nishitani Keiji, eds., (Tokyo: Sōbunsha, 1976), pp. 509–24.

Hei Dōki: See under Pi Tao-chi.

Hirai Shun'ei 平井俊栄, *Chūgoku hannya shisōshi kenkyū—Kichizō to Sanron gakuha* 中国般若思想史研究—吉蔵と三論学派 (Tokyo: Shunjūsha 春秋社, 1976).

———, "Shoki Zenshū shisō no keisei to Sanronshū" 初期禅宗思想の形成と三論宗, *Shūkyō kenkyū* 宗教研究, 5 (April 1963): 75–79.

Hirakawa Akira 平川彰, *Daijō kishin ron* 大乗起信論, Butten kōza 仏典講座, No. 22 (Tokyo: Daizō shuppan sha 大蔵出版社, 1973).

Hirano Sōjō 平野宗浄, *Tongoyōmon* 頓悟要門, Zen no goroku 禅の語録, no. 6 (Tokyo: Chikuma shobō 筑摩書房, 1969).

Hisamatsu Shin'ichi 久松真一 and Nishitani Keiji 西谷啓治, eds., *Zen no honshitsu to ningen no shinri* 禅の本質と人間の真理 (Tokyo: Sōbunsha, 1969).

Hu Shih 胡適, "An Appeal for a Systematic Search in Japan for Long-hidden T'ang Dynasty Source-materials of the Early History of Zen Buddhism," Yamaguchi Susumu 山口益, ed., *Bukkyō to bunka* 仏教と文化 (Kyoto, 1960), pp. 15–23; reprinted in Yanagida Seizan, ed., *Ko Teki zengaku an* (Kyoto: Chūbun shuppan sha, 1975), pp. 667–59 (sic).

———, "Development of Zen Buddhism in China," *The Chinese Social and Political Science Review*, 15, no. 4 (1932): 475–505; reprinted in Yanagida Seizan, ed., *Ko Teki zengaku an*, pp. 721–691 (sic).

———, *Ko Teki zengaku an*: See under Yanagida.

———, "Leng-ch'ieh tsung k'ao" 楞伽宗考, *Hu Shih wen-ts'un* 胡適文存, vol. 4 (4 vols., Shanghai: Tung-ya t'u-shu kuan 東亞圖書館, 1930), pp. 194–235; reprinted in Yanagida Seizan, ed., *Ko Teki zengaku an*, pp. 154–95.

———, *Shen-hui ho-shang i-chi —fu Hu hsien-sheng tsui-hou-te yen-chiu* 神會和尚

遺集—附胡先生最後的研究, Ma Chun-wu 馬君武, ed. (Taipei: Hu Shih chi-nien kuan 胡適紀念館, 1968).

Hurvitz, Leon, "Chih-i (538–597): An introduction to the Life and Ideas of a Chinese Buddhist Monk," *Mélanges chinois et bouddhiques*, 12 (1960–62).

Ikeda Rosan 池田魯參, "*Daijō shikan hōmon* kenkyū josetsu—tenseki oyobi kaisetsu" 大乗止観法門研究序説—典籍及び解説, *Komazawa Daigaku Bukkyō Gakubu kenkyū ronshū* 駒沢大学仏教学部論集, 5 (December 1974): 17–36.

Imaeda Aishin 今枝愛真, *Chūsei Zenshūshi no kenkyū* 中世禅宗史の研究 (Tokyo: Tōkyō Daigaku shuppan sha 東京大学出版社, 1970).

Iritani Sensuke 入谷仙介 and Matsumura Takashi 松村昂, *Kanzanshi* 寒山詩, Zen no goroku, no. 13 (Tokyo: Chikuma shobō, 1970).

Iriya Yoshitaka 入矢義高, *Denshin hōyō—Enryōroku* 伝心法要—宛陵録, Zen no goroku, no. 8 (Tokyo: Chikuma shobō, 1969).

———, *Hō koji no goroku* 龐居士の語録, Zen no goroku, no. 7 (Tokyo: Chikuma shobō, 1973).

———, "Kū to jō" 空と浄, *Fukui hakase juju kinen tōyō bunka ronshū* 福井博士頌寿記念東洋文化論集 (Tokyo: Waseda Daigaku shuppan bu 早稲大学出版部, 1969), pp. 97–106.

Itō Ryūjū 伊藤隆寿, "Sanron gakuha ni okeru shiji sōjō to Zenshū" 三論学派における師資相承と禅宗, *Shūgaku kenkyū* 宗学研究, 14 (March 1947): 117–22.

Jan, Yün-hua, "Seng-ch'ou's Method of *Dhyāna*," Whalen Lai and Lewis Lancaster, eds., *Early Ch'an in China and Tibet*, Berkeley Buddhist Studies Series, no. 5 (Berkeley, Calif.: Asian Humanities Press, 1983), pp. 51–63.

Jao Tsung-i 饒宗頤, "Shen-hui men-hsia Mo-ho-yen chih ju-Tsang, chien lun Ch'an-men nan-pei tsung chih t'iao-ho wen-t'i 神會門下摩訶衍之入藏, 兼論禪門南北宗之調和問題, *Hsiang-kang Ta-hsueh wu-shih chou-nien chi-nien lun-wen chi* 香港大學五十週年紀念論文集, vol. 1 (Hong Kong: Hsiang-kang Ta-hsueh, 1964), pp. 173–78.

Jorgensen, John Alexander, *The Earliest Text of Ch'an Buddhism: The* Long Scroll (M.A. dissertation, Australian National University, 1979).

Kagamishima Genryū 鏡島元隆 *et al.*, *Yakuchū Zennon shingi* 訳註禅苑清規 (Tokyo: Sōtō shūmuchō 曹洞宗務庁, 1972).

Kamata Shigeo 鎌田茂雄, *Chūgoku Kegon shisōshi no kenkyū* 中国華厳思想史の研究 (Tokyo: Tōkyō Daigaku shuppankai, 1965).

———, "Shoki Zenshū no rōsō hihan" 初期禅宗の老荘批判, *Shūgakū kenkyū*, 10 (March 1968): 58–64.

———, "Shotō ni okeru Sanronshū to Dōkyō" 初唐における三論宗と道教, *Tōyō Bunka Kenkyūjo kiyō* 東洋文化研究所紀要, 46 (March 1968).

———, *Zengen shosenshū tojo* 禅源諸詮集都序, Zen no goroku, no. 9 (Tokyo: Chikuma shobō, 1971).

Kamio Isshun 神尾弌春, "*Kanjinron* shikō" 観心論私考, *Shūgaku kenkyū*, new series vol. 2, no. 5 (1932): 98–104.

Kanda Kiichirō 神田喜一郎, "*Den'hōbōki* no kanchitsu ni tsuite" 伝法宝紀の完帙について, *Sekisui sensei kakōju kinen ronsan* 積翠先生華甲寿記念論纂

(Tokyo: Sekisui sensei kakōju kinen kai, 1942), pp. 145–52 (plus 8 double plates).

Kawashima Jōmyō 川島常明, "*Amban shui kyō* ni tsuite" 安般守意経に就いて, *Indogaku Bukkyōgaku kenkyū* 印度学仏教学研究, 24, no. 2 (1976): 750–53.

———, "Sōfuku ni tsuite" 僧副について, *Indogaku Bukkyōgaku kenkyū*, 25, no. 2 (1977): 670–71.

Kuno Hōryū 久野芳隆, "Gozu Hōyū ni oyoboseru Sanronshū no eikyō" 牛頭法融に及ぼせる三論宗の影響, *Bukkyō kenkyū* 仏教研究, 3, no. 6 (1939): 51–88.

———, "Ryōgazen" 楞伽禅, *Shūkyō kenkyū*, I:3 (1939): 548–60.

———, "Ryūdōsei ni tomu Tōdai no Zenshū tenseki (Tonkō shutsudo hon ni okeru nanzen hokushū no daihyōteki sakuhin)" 流動性に富む唐代の禅宗典籍(燉煌出土本に於ける南禅北宗の代表的作品), *Shūkyō kenkyū*, new series vol. 14, no. 1 (1939): 117–44.

de La Vallée Poussin, Louis, *L'Abhidharmakośa de Vasubandhu* (6 vols.; Brussels: Institut Belge des Hautes Études Chinoises, 1971).

Lai, Whalen, and Lancaster, Lewis, eds., *Early Ch'an in China and Tibet*, Berkeley Buddhist Studies Series, no. 5 (Berkeley, Calif.: Asian Humanities Press, 1983).

Lamotte, Étienne, *Histoire du bouddhisme indien—des origines à l'ére Śaka*, Bibliothèque du *Museon*, Vol. 43 (Louvain, Belgium: Institut Orientaliste, Universite de Louvain, 1958).

———, *La Somme du Grand Véhicule d'Asaṅga (Mahāyānasaṁgraha)*, Publications de l'Institut Orientaliste de Louvain, no. 8 (2 vols.; Louvain, Belgium: Institut Orientaliste, 1973).

Lau, D. C., *Tao-te ching* (Baltimore, Md.: Penguin Books, 1963).

Li Wei-hsiung 李威熊, *Tung Chung-shu yü Hsi Han hsueh-shu* 董仲舒與西漢學術 (Taipei: Chung-wen che ch'u-pan she 中文哲出版社, 1979).

Liebenthal, Walter, "Notes on the *Vajramādhi,*" *T'oung Pao*, 44 (1956): 347–86.

Lin Li-kouang, *L'Aide-Mémoire de la Vraie Loi (saddharma-smṛtyupasthāna-sūtra): Recherches sur un Sūtra Développé du Petit Véhicule*, Publications de Musée Guimet, Bibliothèque d'Études, no. 54 (Paris: Adrien-Maisonneuve, 1949).

Lo Hsiang-lin 羅香林, "*Chiu T'ang-shu* Shen-hsiu chuan shu-cheng" 舊唐書神秀傳疏證, *T'ang-tai wen-hua shih* 唐代文化史 (Taipei: Shang-wu shu-chü, 1955, pp. 105–10.

Lü Ch'eng 呂澂, "T'an-t'an yu-kuan ch'u-ch'i Ch'an-tsung ssu-hsiang te chi-ko wen-t'i" 談談有關初期禪宗思想的幾個問題, Shih Tao-an 釋道安, ed., *Ch'an-tsung shih-shih k'ao-pien* 禪宗史實考弁, Hsien-tai Fo-chiao hsueh-shu ts'ung-k'an 現代佛教學術叢刊, no. 4 (Taipei: Ta-sheng wen-hua ch'u-pan she 大乘文化出版社, 1977), pp. 199–204.

Magnin, Paul, *La Vie et l'Oeuvre de Huisi (515–577) (Les origines de la secte bouddhique chinoise du Tiantai)*, Publications de l'École Française d'Extrême-Orient, vol. 116 (Paris: École Française d'Extrême-Orient, 1979).

Makita Tairyō 牧田諦亮, *Tō kōsōden sakuin* 唐高僧伝索引 (3 vols.; Kyoto: Heirakuji shoten, 1973–75).

Masunaga Reihō 増永霊鳳, "*Daijō mushō hōben mon* no kenkyū" 大乗無生方便門の研究, *Indogaku Bukkyōgaku kenkyū*, 3, no. 2 (1955): 309–12.

———, "Zenshisō no Chūgokuteki keitai" 禅思想の中国的形態, Miyamoto Shōson 宮本正尊, ed., *Bukkyō no kompon shinri—Bukkyō ni okeru kompon shinri no rekishiteki keitai* 仏教の根本真理—仏教における根本真理の歴史的形態 (Tokyo: Sanseidō 三省堂, 1957), pp. 775–806.

Matsuda Fumio 松田文雄, "Bodaidaruma ron – *Zoku kōsōden* no Daruma, sono joron" 菩提達磨論—続高僧伝の達磨, その序論, *Indogaku Bukkyōgaku kenkyū*, 26, no. 2 (1978): 595–600.

McRae, John R., "The Development of the 'Recorded Sayings' Texts of the Chinese Ch'an School" (trans. from Yanagida Seizan, "Zenshū goroku no keisei"), Whalen Lai and Lewis Lancaster, eds., *Early Ch'an in China and Tibet*, Berkeley Buddhist Studies Series, no. 5 (Berkeley, Calif.: Asian Humanities Press, 1983), pp. 185–205.

———, "The Ox-head School of Chinese Buddhism: From Early Ch'an to the Golden Age," R. M. Gimello and P. N. Gregory, eds., *Studies in Ch'an and Hua-yen*, Studies in East Asian Buddhism, no. 1 (Honolulu: University of Hawaii Press in association with the Kuroda Institute, 1983), pp. 169–253.

Mibu Taishun 壬生台舜, "*Jōjitsuron* ni okeru shikan" 成実論における止観, Sekiguchi Shindai 関口真大, ed., *Shikan no kenkyū* 止観の研究 (Tokyo: Iwanami shoten 岩波書店, 1975), pp. 139–45.

Michihata Ryōshū 道端良秀, *Tōdai Bukkyōshi no kenkyū* 唐代仏教史の研究 (Kyoto: Hōzōkan, 1957).

Mizuno Kōgen 水野弘元, *Hokkukyō no kenkyū* 法句経の研究 (Tokyo: Shunjūsha, 1981).

———, "Bodaidaruma no ninyūshigyō-setsu to *Kongō zammai kyō*" 菩提達摩の二入四行説と金剛三昧経, *Komazawa Daigaku Bukkyō Gakubu kenkyu kiyō* 駒沢大学仏教学部研究紀要, 13 (1955): 33–57.

———, "Zenshū seiritsu izen no Shina no zenjō shisōshi josetsu" 禅宗成立以前のシナの禅定思想史序説, *Komazawa Daigaku Bukkyō Gakubu kenkyū kiyō*, 15 (March 1957): 15–54.

Murti, T. R. V., *The Central Philosophy of Buddhism* (London: George Allen and Unwin, 1955).

Nakagawa Taka 中川孝, "Sōsan daishi no nendai to shisō" 僧璨大師の年代と思想, *Indogaku Bukkyōgaku kenkyū*, 6, no. 1 (1958): 229–32.

———, "Zenshū dai sanso Sōsan daishi to *Shinjimmei*" 禅宗第三祖僧璨大師と信心銘, *Tōhoku Yakka Daigaku kiyō* 東北薬科大学紀要, 4 (November 1957): 159–66.

———, "Zenshū dai shiso Dōshin zenji no kenkyū" 禅宗第四祖道信禅師の研究, *Bunka* 文化, 20, no. 6 (1956): 893–96.

Nakata Banzen 中田万善, "Tonkō bunken no saikentō—toku ni Kōnin no *Shushin yōron* ni tsuite" 敦煌文献の再検討—特に弘忍の修心要論について, *Indogaku Bukkyōgaku kenkyū*, 17, no. 2 (1969): 714–17.

Nishitani Keiji: See under Hisamatsu.

Nukariya Kaiten 忽滑快天, *Zengaku shisōshi* 禅学思想史, vol. 1 (Tokyo: Genkōsha 玄黄社, 1923).

Obata Hironobu 小畠宏允, "Chibetto no Zenshū to *Rekidai hōbō ki*" チベットの禅宗と歴代法宝記, in Yanagida Seizan ed., *Shoki no zenshi, 2—Rekidai hōbō ki*, Zen no goroku, no. 3 (Tokyo: Chikuma shobō, 1976), pp. 325–37.

———, "Chibetto no Zenshū to zōyaku gikyō ni tsuite" チベットの禅宗と蔵訳擬経について *Indogaku Bukkyōgaku kenkyū*, 23, no. 2 (1975): 667–68.

———, "Chibetto-den Bodaidarumatara zenji kō" チベット伝ボダイダルマタラ禅師考, *Indogaku bukkyōgaku kenkyū*, 24, no. 1 (1975): 229–32.

Ōchō Enichi 横超慧日, *Chūgoku Bukkyō no kenkyū* 中国仏教の研究 (Kyoto: Hōzōkan, 1958).

———, "Chūgoku Bukkyō shoki no zenkan" 中国仏教初期の禅観, *Indogaku Bukkyōgaku kenkyū*, 4, no. 1 (1956): 79–82.

———, *Hokke shisō no kenkyū* 法華思想の研究 (Kyoto: Heirakuji shoten, 1971).

———, ed., *Hokugi Bukkyō no kenkyū* 北魏仏教の研究 (Kyoto: Heirakuji shoten, 1970).

———, "Hokugi Bukkyō no kihonteki kadai" 北魏仏教の基本的課題, in Ōchō Enichi, ed., *Hokugi Bukkyō no kenkyu* (Kyoto: Heirakuji shoten, 1970), pp. 3–62.

Ogawa Tamaki 小川環樹, *Tōdai no shijin—sono denki* 唐代の詩人—その伝記 (Tokyo: Daishukan shoten, 1975).

Okabe Kazuo 岡部一男, "*Emmyōron*" 円明論, Shinohara Toshio and Tanaka Ryōshō, eds., *Tonkō Butten to Zen*, Kōza Tonkō, no. 8 (Tokyo: Daitō shuppan sha, 1980), pp. 344–49.

Okimoto Katsumi 沖本克己, "Chibetto-yaku *Ninyū shigyō ron* ni tsuite" チベット訳二入四行論について, *Indogaku Bukkyōgaku kenkyū*, 24, no. 2 (1976): 999–92 (sic).

Osabe Kazuo 長部和雄, *Ichigyō zenji no kenkyū* 一行禅師の研究 (Kobe: Kōbe Shōka Daigaku Keizai Kenkyūjo 神戸商科大学経済研究所, 1963).

Pachow, W., "A Buddhist Discourse on Meditation from *Tun-huang*," *University of Ceylon Review*, 21, no. 1 (1963): 47–62, reprinted in W. Pachow, *Chinese Buddhism: Aspects of Interaction and Reinterpretation* (Lanham, Md.: University Press of America, 1980), pp. 35–54.

Pi Tao-chi 幣道紀, "Nangaku Eshi no zenkan," *Indogaku Bukkyogaku kenkyū* 南岳慧思の禅観, XVIII: 1 (1969): 217–220.

Roccasalvo, Joseph F., "The Debate at bSam yas: A study in religious contrast and correspondence," *Philosophy East and West*, 30, no. 4 (December 1980): 505–20.

Rhys Davids, T. W., trans., *The Questions of King Milinda*, Part I, Sacred Books of the East, vol. 35 (Oxford: Clarendon Press, 1980; reprint New York: Dover Publications, 1963).

Sakamoto Toshio 坂本幸男, *Kegon kyōgaku no kenkyū* 華厳教学の研究 (Kyoto: Heirakuji shoten, 1956).

Sasaki Genjun 佐々木現順, "Chie" 智慧, *Indogaku Bukkyōgaku kenkyū*, 2, no. 2 (1954): 84–86.

Satō Tetsuei 佐藤哲英, *Tendai daishi no kenkyū—Chigi no chosaku ni kansuru kiso-teki kenkyū* 天台大師の研究—智顗の著作に関する基礎的研究 (Tokyo: Hyakkaon 百華苑, 1961).

Sekiguchi Shindai 関口真大, ed., *Bukkyō no jissen genri* 仏教の実践原理 (Tokyo: Sankibō busshorin 山喜房仏書林, 1977).

———, *Daruma daishi no kenkyū* 達摩大師の研究 (Tokyo: Shōkokusha 彰国社, 1957; reprint Tokyo: Shunjūsha, 1969).

———, *Daruma no kenkyū* 達磨の研究 (Tokyo: Iwanami shoten, 1967).

———, ed., *Shikan no kenkyū* 止観の研究 (Tokyo: Iwanami shoten, 1975).

———, *Tendai shikan no kenkyū* 天台止観の研究 (Tokyo: Iwanami shoten, 1969).

———, "Tendai shikan ni okeru zazen" 天台止観における生禅, *Taishō Daigaku kenkyū kiyō* 大正大学研究紀要, 42 (March 1957): 37–81.

———, *Zenshū shisōshi* 禅宗思想史 (Tokyo: Sankibō busshorin, 1964).

Sekino Tadashi: see under Tokiwa.

Sengoku Keishō 仙石景章, "Hokushū-zen ni okeru mushin to rishin ni tsuite," 北宗禅における無心と離心について *Shūgaku kenkyū*, 22 (March 1980): 221–24.

———, "*Kanjinron* no shisō to tokushitsu ni tsuite," 観心論の思想と特質について *Shūgaku kenkyū*, 23 (March 1981): 237–40.

Shiina Kōyū 椎名宏雄, "Hokushū-zen ni okeru kairitsu no mondai" 北宗禅における戒律の問題, *Shūkyō kenkyū*, 11 (March 1969): 135–59.

———, "Tōzan hōmon keisei no haikei" 東山法門形成の背景, *Shūgaku kenkyū*, 12 (March 1970): 173–85.

Shimizu Yōkō 清水要晃, "*Nyūryōgakyō* no shiki no sansōsetsu ni tsuite—nyoraizō to ārayashiki no dōshi o megutte" 入楞伽経の識の三相説について—如来蔵とアーラャ識の同視をめぐって, *Indogaku Bukkyōgaku kenkyū*, 25, no. 1 (1976): 162–63.

Shinohara Toshio 篠原寿雄 and Tanaka Ryōshō 田中良昭, eds., *Tonkō Butten to Zen* 敦煌仏典と禅, Kōza Tonkō 講座敦煌, no. 8 (Tokyo: Daitō shuppan sha, 1980).

Shioiri Ryōdō 塩入良道, "Shoki Tendaisan no kyōdanteki seikaku" 初期天台山の教団的性格, *Nihon Bukkyō Gakkai nempō* 日本仏教学会年報, 39 (1973): 133–49.

Strong, John S., *The Legend of King Aśoka: A Study and Translation of the* Aśokāvadāna (Princeton, N.J.: Princeton University Press, 1983).

Sui Shu-shen, 隋樹森, ed., *Ku-shih shih-chiu shou chi-shih* 古詩十九首集釋 (Peking: Chung-hua shu-chü, 1955).

Suzuki, D[aisetsu] T[eitarō] 鈴木大拙[貞太郎], *Essays in Zen Buddhism (First Series)* (London: Rider, 1949; reprint New York: Grove Press, 1961).

———, "The Historical Background of Zen," *Zen Buddhism*, ed. by William Barrett (Garden City, N.Y.: Doubleday, 1956), pp. 27–80.

———, *Kōkan Shōshitsu issho oyobi kaisetsu* 校刊少室逸書及解說 (Osaka: Ataka Bukkyō bunko 安宅仏教文庫, 1936).

———, *Manual of Zen Buddhism* (Kyoto: Eastern Buddhist Society, 1935; reprint New York: Grove Press, 1960).

———, *Suzuki Daisetsu zenshū* 全集 (Tokyo: Iwanami shoten, 1968–71).

———, *Tonkō shutsudo Kataku Jinne zenji goroku* 燉煌出土荷沢神会禅師語録 (Tokyo: Morie shoten 森江書店, 1934).

———, *Tonkō shutsudo Shōshitsu issho* 燉煌出土少室逸書 (Osaka: Ataka Bukkyō bunko, 1935).

———, and Furuta Shōkin 古田紹欽, eds., *Zekkanron* 絶観論 (Kyoto: Kōbundo 公文堂, 1935).

———, *The Zen Doctrine of No-mind* (London: Rider and Co., 1949).

———, "The Zen Sect of Buddhism." *Journal of the Pali Text Society*, 1906–1907; reprinted in *Studies in Zen*, Christmas Humphreys, ed. (New York: Dell Publishing, 1955), pp. 15–17.

———, "Zenshisōshi kenkyū, dai-ni—Daruma kara Enō ni itaru" 禅思想史研究第二—達摩から慧能にいたる, *Suzuki Daisetsu zenshū*, vol. 2 (Tokyo: Iwanami shoten, 1968).

Suzuki Kakuzen 鈴木格禅, "'Hekikan' shiron (I)" 「壁観」試論(一), *Komazawa Daigaku Bukkyō Gakubu kenkyū kiyō*, 33 (March 1975): 23–39.

———, "'Hekikan' shiron (II)," *Komazawa Daigaku Bukkyō Gakubu kenkyū kiyō*, 34 (March 1976): 26–46.

———, "'Hekikan' to 'kakukan' ni tsuite" 「壁観」と「覚観」について, *Indogaku Bukkyōgaku kenkyū kiyō*, 24, no. 1 (1975): 124–29.

Takamine Ryōshū 高峰了州, "Kegon to Zen to no tsūro," 華厳と禅との通路 *Nihon Bukkyō gakkai nempō*, 18 (1952): 39–58.

———, *Kegon to Zen to no tsūro* (Nara: Nanto Bukkyō kenkyūkai 南都仏教研究会, 1956).

Takeda Tadashi 武田中, "*Daijō gohōben* no shohon no seiritsu ni tsuite" 大乗五方便の諸本の成立について, *Indogaku Bukkyōgaku kenkyū*, 19, no. 1 (1960): 262–66.

Tanaka Ryōshō 田中良昭, "Daishō zenji Fujaku ni tsuite" 大照禅師普寂について, *Indogaku Bukkyōgaku kenkyū*, 16, no. 1 (1967): 331–34.

———, "Daruma-zen ni okeru shin ni tsuite" 達摩禅における信について, *Shūkyo kenkyū*, 38, no. 2 (1965): 224–25.

———, "Dōshin-zen no kenkyū" 道信禅の研究, *Komazawa Daigaku Bukkyō Gakubu kenkyū kiyō*, 22 (March 1964): 144–59.

———, "Hokushū-zen no seiten sotō-setsu—Daishichi-so *Daishō oshō jakumetsu nissai sambun* (gi) o meguru ichi shiron" 北宗禅の西天祖統説—『第七組大照和尚寂滅日斎讃文』(擬)をめぐる一試論 , *Komazawa Daigaku Bukkyō Gakubu kenkyū kiyō*, 26 (March 1968): 90–102.

———, "*Shigyōron* chōkansu to *Bodaidaruma-ron*" 四行論長巻子と菩提達摩論, *Indogaku Bukkyōgaku kenkyū*, 14, no. 1 (1965): 217–20.

———, ed., *Tonkō Butten to Zen*: See under Shinohara.

———, "Tonkōbon *Emmyōron* ni tsuite" 敦煌本円明論について, *Indogaku Bukkyōgaku kenkyū*, 18, no. 1 (1969): 204–7.

———, "Tonkō Zenshū shiryō bunrui mokuroku shokō" 敦煌禅宗資料分類目録初稿, *Komazawa Daigaku Bukkyō Gakubu kenkyū kiyō*, 29 (March 1979): 1–18 (from the back).

T'ang Yung-t'ung 湯用彤, *Han-Wei liang-Chin nan-pei ch'ao Fo-chiao shih* 漢魏両晋南北朝仏教史 (Ch'ang-sha and Chungking: Shang-wu yin-shu kuan 商務印書館, 1928; reprint [of the Ch'ang-sha edition] Taipei: Kuo-shih yen-chiu shih 國史研究室, 1973).

———, "P'u-t'i-ta-mo" 菩提達摩, Shih Tao-an, ed., *Ch'an-tsung shih-shih k'ao-pien*, Hsien-tai Fo-chiao hsueh-shu ts'ung-k'an, no. 4 (Taipei: Ta-sheng wen-hua ch'u-pan she, 1977), pp. 141–52.

Tokiwa Daijō 常盤大定 and Sekino Tadashi 関野貞, *Shina bunka shiseki* 支那文化史蹟 (12 vols.; Tokyo: Hōzōkan, 1939–41).

———, *Shina Bukkyō shiseki hyōkai* 支那仏教史蹟評解 (5 vols.; Tokyo: Bukkyō shiseki kenkyūkai 研究会, 1925–28).

Tokiwa Gishin 常盤義伸 and Yanagida Seizan 柳田聖山, *Zekkanron: Eibun yakuchū, gembun kōtei, kokuyaku* 絶観論：英文訳註・原文校定・国訳 (Kyoto: Zenbunka Kenkyūjo 禅文化研究所, 1976).

Tokushi Yūshō 禿氏祐祥 "*Shōshitsu rokumonshū* ni tsuite" 少室六門集に就いて, *Ryūkoku gakuhō* 竜谷学報, 319 (June 1934): 211–18.

Tsukamoto Zenryū 塚本善隆, ed., *Jōron kenkyū* 肇論研究 (Kyoto: Hōzōkan, 1972).

———, *Tō chūki no Jōdokyō* 唐中期の浄土教 (Kyoto: Hōzōkan, 1975).

Ueda Yoshifumi 上田義文, "Bukkyō ni okeru 'shin' no gainen" 仏教における「心」の概念, Hisamatsu Shin'ichi and Nishitani Keiji, eds., *Zen no honshitsu to ningen no shinri* (Tokyo: Sōbunsha, 1969), pp. 525–54.

Ueyama Daishun 上山大峻, "Chibetto-yaku *Tongo shinshū yōketsu* no kenkyū" チベット訳頓悟真宗要決の研究, *Zenbunka kenkyūjo kiyō* 禅文化研究所紀要, 8 (1976): 33–103.

———, "Tonkō shutsudo Chibetto-bun Zen shiryō no kenkyū—P. tib. 116 to sono mondaiten" 敦煌出土チベット文禅資料の研究—P. tib. 116 とその問題点, *Bukkyō Bunka Kenkyūjo kiyō* 仏教文化研究所紀要, 13 (June 1974): 1–11.

Ui Hakuju 宇井伯寿, *Hōshōron kenkyū* 宝性論研究 (Tokyo: Iwanami shoten, 1971).

———, *Yakkyōshi kenkyū* 訳経史研究 (Tokyo: Iwanami shoten, 1971).

———, *Zenshūshi kenkyū* 禅宗史研究 (3 vols.; Tokyo: Iwanami shoten, 1939–43).

Ware, James R., tr., *Alchemy, Medicine, Religion in the China of A.D. 320: The Nei P'ien of Ko Hung (Pao-p'u tzu)* (Cambridge, Mass.: M.I.T. Press, 1966).

Washio Junkei 鷲尾順敬, *Bodaidaruma Sūzan shiseki taikan* 菩提達摩嵩山史蹟大観 (1932).

Weinstein, Stanley, "Buddhism under the T'ang," Denis Twitchett, ed., *Cambridge History of China: The T'ang Dynasty* (Cambridge, England: Cambridge University Press, forthcoming).

———, "Imperial Patronage in the Formation of T'ang Buddhism," Arthur F. Wright and Denis Twitchett, eds., *Perspectives on the T'ang* (New Haven, Conn.: Yale University Press, 1973), pp. 265–306.

Wright, Arthur F., "Biography and Hagiography: Hui-chao's *Lives of Eminent Monks*," *Silver Jubilee Volume of the Zinbun-Kagaku-Kenkyu-syo* (Kyoto: Jimbun Kagaku Kenkyūjo 人文科学研究所, 1954), pp. 383–432.

———, "Seng-jui Alias Hui-jui: A Biographical Bisection in the *Kao-seng chuan*, *Liebenthal Festshrift* (Santiniketan, India, 1957), pp. 272–93.

Yabuki Keiki 矢吹慶輝, *Meisa yoin—Tonkō shutsudo miden koitsu Butten kaihō* 鳴沙餘韻—敦煌出土未伝古逸仏典開宝 [English sub-title: *Rare and Unknown Chinese Manuscript Remains of Buddhist Literature Discovered in Tun-huang Collected by Sir Aurel Stein and Preserved in the British Museum*] (Tokyo: Iwanami shoten, 1930).

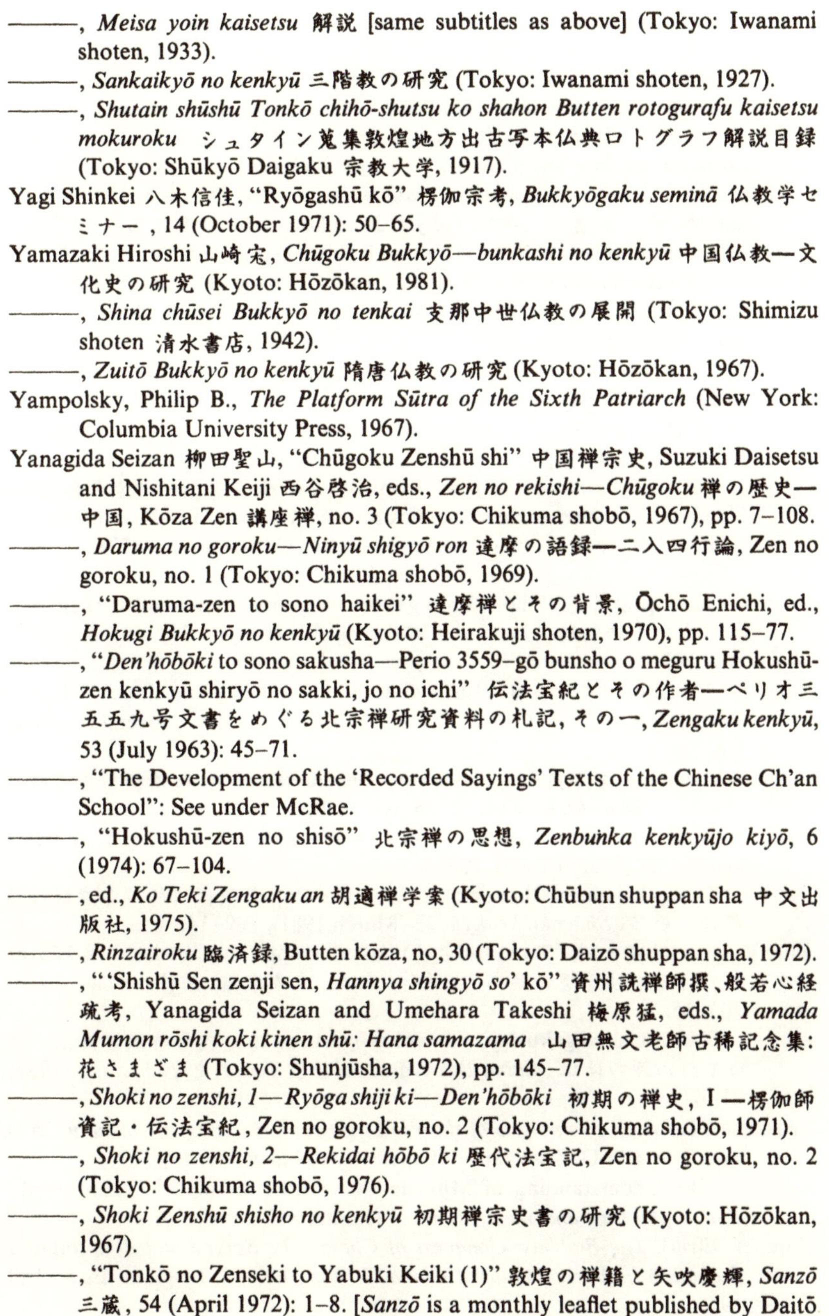

———, *Meisa yoin kaisetsu* 解説 [same subtitles as above] (Tokyo: Iwanami shoten, 1933).

———, *Sankaikyō no kenkyū* 三階教の研究 (Tokyo: Iwanami shoten, 1927).

———, *Shutain shūshū Tonkō chihō-shutsu ko shahon Butten rotogurafu kaisetsu mokuroku* シュタイン蒐集敦煌地方出古写本仏典ロトグラフ解説目録 (Tokyo: Shūkyō Daigaku 宗教大学, 1917).

Yagi Shinkei 八木信佳, "Ryōgashū kō" 楞伽宗考, *Bukkyōgaku seminā* 仏教学セミナー, 14 (October 1971): 50–65.

Yamazaki Hiroshi 山崎宏, *Chūgoku Bukkyō—bunkashi no kenkyū* 中国仏教—文化史の研究 (Kyoto: Hōzōkan, 1981).

———, *Shina chūsei Bukkyō no tenkai* 支那中世仏教の展開 (Tokyo: Shimizu shoten 清水書店, 1942).

———, *Zuitō Bukkyō no kenkyū* 隋唐仏教の研究 (Kyoto: Hōzōkan, 1967).

Yampolsky, Philip B., *The Platform Sūtra of the Sixth Patriarch* (New York: Columbia University Press, 1967).

Yanagida Seizan 柳田聖山, "Chūgoku Zenshū shi" 中国禅宗史, Suzuki Daisetsu and Nishitani Keiji 西谷啓治, eds., *Zen no rekishi—Chūgoku* 禅の歴史—中国, Kōza Zen 講座禅, no. 3 (Tokyo: Chikuma shobō, 1967), pp. 7–108.

———, *Daruma no goroku—Ninyū shigyō ron* 達摩の語録—二入四行論, Zen no goroku, no. 1 (Tokyo: Chikuma shobō, 1969).

———, "Daruma-zen to sono haikei" 達摩禅とその背景, Ōchō Enichi, ed., *Hokugi Bukkyō no kenkyū* (Kyoto: Heirakuji shoten, 1970), pp. 115–77.

———, "*Den'hōbōki* to sono sakusha—Perio 3559–gō bunsho o meguru Hokushū-zen kenkyū shiryō no sakki, jo no ichi" 伝法宝紀とその作者—ペリオ三五五九号文書をめぐる北宗禅研究資料の札記, その一, *Zengaku kenkyū*, 53 (July 1963): 45–71.

———, "The Development of the 'Recorded Sayings' Texts of the Chinese Ch'an School": See under McRae.

———, "Hokushū-zen no shisō" 北宗禅の思想, *Zenbunka kenkyūjo kiyō*, 6 (1974): 67–104.

———, ed., *Ko Teki Zengaku an* 胡適禅学案 (Kyoto: Chūbun shuppan sha 中文出版社, 1975).

———, *Rinzairoku* 臨済録, Butten kōza, no, 30 (Tokyo: Daizō shuppan sha, 1972).

———, "'Shishū Sen zenji sen, *Hannya shingyō so*' kō" 資州詵禅師撰、般若心経疏考, Yanagida Seizan and Umehara Takeshi 梅原猛, eds., *Yamada Mumon rōshi koki kinen shū: Hana samazama* 山田無文老師古稀記念集: 花さまざま (Tokyo: Shunjūsha, 1972), pp. 145–77.

———, *Shoki no zenshi, 1—Ryōga shiji ki—Den'hōbōki* 初期の禅史, I—楞伽師資記・伝法宝紀, Zen no goroku, no. 2 (Tokyo: Chikuma shobō, 1971).

———, *Shoki no zenshi, 2—Rekidai hōbō ki* 歴代法宝記, Zen no goroku, no. 2 (Tokyo: Chikuma shobō, 1976).

———, *Shoki Zenshū shisho no kenkyū* 初期禅宗史書の研究 (Kyoto: Hōzōkan, 1967).

———, "Tonkō no Zenseki to Yabuki Keiki (1)" 敦煌の禅籍と矢吹慶輝, *Sanzō* 三蔵, 54 (April 1972): 1–8. [*Sanzō* is a monthly leaflet published by Daitō shuppan sha in conjunction with the publication of the *Kokuyaku issaikyō Indo senjutsu bu* 国訳一切経印度選述部.]

———, "Tōshi no keifu" 灯史の系譜, *Nihon Bukkyō gakkai nempō*, 19 (April 1954): 1–46.

———, *Yaburu mono* 破るもの, (Tokyo: Shunjūsha, 1970).

———, "*Zemmonkyō* ni tsuite" 禅門経について, *Tsukamoto hakase juju kinen Bukkyō shigaku ronshū* 塚本博士頌寿記念仏教史学論集 (Tokyo: Tsukamoto hakase juju kinen kai 会, 1961), pp. 869–82.

———, *Zen shisō—sono genkei o arau* 禅思想—その原形をあらう, Chūkō shinsho 中公新書, no. 400 (Tokyo: Chūō kōron sha 中央公論社, 1975).

———, "Zenseki kaidai" 禅籍解, Nishitani Keiji 西谷啓治 and Yanagida Seizan, eds., *Zenke goroku* 禅家語録, vol. 2, Sekai koten bungaku zenshū 世界古典文学全集, no. 36B (Tokyo: Chikuma shobō, 1974), pp. 445–514, plus pp. 1–9 (from the back).

———, "Zenshū goroku no keisei," 禅宗語録の形成 *Indogaku Bukkyōgaku kenkyū*, 18, no. 1 (December 1969): 39–47.

Yin-shun 印順, *Chung-kuo Ch'an-tsung shih* 中國禪宗史 (Taipei: Hui-jih chiang-t'ang 慧日講堂, 1971).

———, "Sung-i *Leng-ch'ieh ching* yü Ta-mo-ch'an" 宋譯楞伽經與達摩禪, Shih Tao-an, ed., *Ch'an-tsung shih-shih k'ao-pien*, Hsien-tai Fo-chiao hsueh-shu ts'ung-k'an, no. 4 (Taipei: Ta-sheng wen-hua ch'u-pan she, 1977), pp. 211–22.

Yoshida Dōkō 吉田道光, "Shoki Jiron gakuha ni okeru shomondai" 初期地論学派における諸問題, *Indogaku Bukkyōgaku kenkyū*, 23, no. 2 (1975): 802–803.

Yoshioka Yoshitoyo 吉岡義豊, "Bukkyō no zempō to Dōkyō no shuichi" 仏教の禅法と道教の守一, *Chisan gakuhō* 智山学報, 27–28 (November 1964): 109–25.

Yoshizu Yoshihide 吉津宜英, "Chōkan no Zenshū-kan ni tsuite 澄観の禅宗観について," *Shūgaku kenkyū*, 22 (March 1980): 206–11.

———, "Jinshū no *Kegon kyōsho* ni tsuite 神秀の華厳経疏について," *Shūgaku kenkyū*, 24 (March 1982): 204–9.

———, "Tonkyō ni okeru Chōkan no kaishaku ni tsuite" 頓教に於ける澄観の開釈について, *Shūgaku kenkyū*, 23 (March 1981): 209–14.

Yūki Reimon 結城令聞, "Shina Bukkyō ni okeru mappō shisō no kōki" 支那仏教に於ける末法思想の興期, *Tōhō gakuhō* 東方学報, 6 (February 1936): 205–15.

———, "Shina yuishiki gakushijō ni okeru ryōgashi no chii" 支那唯識学史上に於ける楞伽師の地位, *Shina Bukkyō shigaku* 支那仏教史学, 1, no. 1 (1937): 21–44.

Zeuschner, Robert, *An Analysis of the Philosophical Criticisms of Northern Ch'an Buddhism* (Ph.D. dissertation, University of Hawaii, 1977).

———, "The Understanding of Mind in the Northern Line of Ch'an (Zen)," *Philosophy East and West*, 28, no. 1 (January 1978): 69–79.

Zürcher, E[rik], *The Buddhist Conquest of China: The Spread and Adaptation of Buddhism in Early Medieval China* (2 vols.; Leiden, Belgium: E. J. Brill, 1959).

Character Glossary

A-yü wang ching 阿育王經
A-yü wang chuan 阿育王傳
ai-ch'iu 愛求
aigu (= ai-ch'iu) 愛求
An 岸
An 安
An-chou (Ying-shan hsien, Hupeh) 安州(應山縣)
an-hsin 安心
an-hsin wu-wei 安心無爲
An-kuo Hsuan-t'ing 安國玄挺
An-kuo yuan 安國院
an-ma 按摩
an-pan 安般
An-pan shou-i ching 安般守意經
An Lu-shan 安祿山
An Shih-kao 安世高
An-yang hsien 安陽縣
Chan-jan 湛然
Ch'an 禪
ch'an-chiao 禪教
Ch'an-ching hsü 禪經序
ch'an-men 禪門
Ch'an-men ching 禪門經
Ch'an-men ching ping hsü 禪門經幷序
ch'an-shuo 禪說
Ch'an-tao 禪道
Ch'an-ting ssu 禪定寺
Ch'an-yao ching 禪要經
Ch'an-yuan ch'ing-kuei 禪苑清規
Ch'an-yuan chu-ch'üan chi tu-hsü 禪源諸詮集都序
Chang Chiu-ling 張九齡
Chang Yueh 張說
ch'ang 常
Ch'ang-an 長安
Ch'ang-chao 常超
Ch'ang-chou (Pi-ling hsien, Kiangsu) 常州(毘陵縣)
ch'ang-jen 長人
Ch'ang-li (Ling-yuan hsien, Jehol) 昌黎(淩源縣)
Ch'ang-sha (Hsiang-yin hsien, Hunan) 長沙(湘陰縣)
Ch'ang-sha ssu 長沙寺
Ch'ang-[tsang] 長[藏]
chao 照
Chao (= Hui-chao?) 超
Chao-chou (Ch'ü-chiang hsien, Kwangtung) 韶州(曲江縣)
chao-liao hsin-yuan 照了心源
che 者
chen 眞
Chen 甄
Chen 眞
chen chien 眞見
chen-fa 眞法
chen-hsin 眞心
chen-ju 眞如
chen-k'ung 眞空
chen-shih hsin 眞實心
chen-shih hsing 眞實性
chen-shih lu 眞實路
chen-tsung 眞宗
Chen-tsung lun 眞宗論

ch'en 塵
Ch'en-liu wei-shih (Wei-shih hsien, Hunan) 陳留尉氏(尉氏縣)
cheng (correct) 正
cheng (realization) 證
cheng ch'an-i 正禪義
Cheng-fa nien-ch'u ching 正法念處經
cheng-hsing 正性
cheng-nien 正念
cheng-shou 正受
ch'eng 呈
Ch'eng-hsin lun 澄心論
Ch'eng-kuan 澄觀
Ch'eng-shih lun 成實論
Chi 姬
chi (serenity) 寂
chi (annals) 紀
chi (records) 記
chi (namely) 即
chi (traces) 迹
Chi-chou (Chi-an hsien, Kiangsu) 吉州(吉安縣)
chi-mieh 寂滅
Chi-tsang 吉藏
chi-yuan 機緣
ch'i 起
ch'i ching 七淨
Ch'i-chou (Huang-mei hsien, Hupeh) 蘄州(黃梅縣)
Ch'i-hsien 祁縣
ch'i-mieh 起滅
Ch'i-sung 契嵩
Ch'i-wei 契微
ch'i-yung 起用
Chiang-chou 江州
Chiang-ling (Chiang-ling hsien, Hupeh) 江陵(江陵縣)
chiao-wai pieh chuan 教外別傳
Chidŏk (= Chih-te) 智德
chieh 界
chieh hsiang 界相
chieh-hsing 戒性
chieh-kuan 却觀
Ch'ieh 伽
Chien 鑒
chien (gradual) 漸
chien (perception) 見
chien-hsing 見性
Chien-k'ang 建康
Chien o-ch'u-fo p'in 見阿閦佛品
chien-wen chueh-chih 見聞覺知
Ch'ien (= T'an-ch'ien) 遷
ch'ien ching 前境
ch'ien-ching wan-lun 千經萬論
chih (wisdom) 智
chih (know) 知
chih (stop) 止
chih (ambition) 志
chih (utmost, come) 至
chih (regulate) 制
chih-chieh 志節
chih-chien 知見
Chih-chiang (Chiang-ling hsien, Hupeh) 枝江(江陵縣)
Chih Ch'ien 支謙
chih-ch'u 智處
Chih-feng 智封
Chih-hsien 智銑
chih-hui 智慧
Chih-hung 智弘
Chih-i 智顗
Chih-k'ai 智鍇
chih-kuan 止觀
chih-shih wen-i 指事問義
Chih-ta (= Hui-ta) 智達
Chih-te (= Chidŏk in Korean) 智德
chih-ti 智地
Chih-yen (Hua-yen School) 智儼
Chih-yen (San-lun School) 智巖
Chin (= Kim in Korean) 金
chin 金
Chin-kang po-jo ching 金剛般若經
chin-kang san-mei 金剛三昧
Chin-kang san-mei ching (= Kŭmgang sammae-kyŏng in Korean) 金剛三昧經
Chin-kang shen p'in 金剛身品
Chin-kang wu li 金剛五禮
chin-k'ou hsiang-ch'eng 金口相承
Chin-ling 金陵
chin-shih hsiang-ch'eng 今師相承
ching (sūtra) 經
ching (pure) 淨
ching (sensory realm) 境

Ching (= Heng-ching) 景
Ching-ai 靜藹
Ching-ai ssu 敬愛寺
ching-ch'eng 精誠
ching-chieh 境界
Ching-chou Yü-ch'üan ssu Ta-t'ung ch'an-shih pei-ming ping hsü 荊州玉泉寺大通禪師碑銘並序
ching-ch'u k'an-ching 淨處看淨
Ching-chueh 淨覺
Ching-hsien 景賢
ching-hsin 淨心
ching-hsing 淨行
ching-lin 靜林
Ching-nan 荊南
Ching-shan ssu 慶山寺
Ching-shou 敬愛
ching-shui 淨水
Ching-te ch'üan-teng lu 景德傳燈錄
ching-t'i 淨體
Ching-tsang 淨藏
ching-tso ssu-wei 靜坐思惟
ching-wen chi ch'an-kuan 經文及禪觀
Ching-ying Hui-yuan 淨影慧遠
ch'ing-kuei (= shingi in Japanese) 清規
Ch'ing-pu Ming 青布明
ch'ing-t'an 清談
Chiu 就
Chiu-chiang 九江
Chiu-shih 久視
chiu tz'u-ti ting 九次弟定
Chiu T'ang shu 舊唐書
ch'iu 求
Chiung (= Ming?) 炅
Choesangsŭng'non (= Tsui-shang sheng lun) 最上勝論
Ch'ou ch'an-shih i 稠禪師意
Ch'ou ch'an-shih yao-fang 稠禪師藥方
chu (subject, master) 主
chu (reside) 住
chu ch'an po-jo k'ung-kuan ch'eng-chiu 諸禪般若空觀成就
Chu-ching yao ch'ao 諸經要抄
Chu Fa-hu 竺法護
Chu-fa wu-hsing ching 諸法無行經
chu-fo fang-pien 諸佛方便
chu wu-te kuan 諸無得觀
Ch'u 楚
ch'u (āyatana, locus, foundation) 處
ch'u-chia 出家
ch'u-chiao 初教
ch'u-hsin 初心
ch'u-hsin jen 初心人
Ch'u san-tsang chi-chi 出三藏記集
ch'u-ti wei ch'an 初地味禪
Chü-fang 巨方
ch'ü-ch'ü chiao 屈曲教
ch'ü-ch'ü chih 屈曲直
ch'ü-ch'ü Ching-sheng 沮渠京聲
Ch'ü-lu 鉅鹿
chuan 傳
Ch'üan-chih 全植
Ch'üan fa-pao chi 傳法寶紀
ch'üan-shih 轉識
Ch'üan T'ang-wen 全唐文
Ch'üan Te-yü 權德輿
ch'üan-teng lu 傳燈錄
Chuang-tzu 莊子
chueh 覺
Chueh 覺
chueh-hsin 覺心
chueh-hsing (enlightenment nature) 覺性
chueh-hsing (practices of enlightenment) 覺行
chueh-hsing yuan-man 覺行圓滿
chueh-kuan 覺觀
Chueh-kuan lun 絕觀論
Ch'ui-kung 垂拱
chün-hsi 熏習
chün-shih 熏質
Chung 沖
Chung-ching ssu 衆淨寺
chung-chung wang-yuan 種種妄錄
Chung-hua ch'üan hsin-ti ch'an-men shih-tzu ch'eng-hsi t'u 中華傳心地禪門師資承襲圖
Chung-nan shan kuei ssu Ta-t'ung Tao-[hsiu] ho-shang t'a-wen 中南山歸寺大通道[秀]和上塔文
chung-sheng chieh 衆生界

chung-sheng chieh t'i 衆生界體
Chung-shu-ling 中書令
Chung-tsao ssu 衆造寺
Ch'ung 寵
Ch'ung-kuei 崇珪
Ch'ung-shen 崇慎
Ch'ung-yen 崇演
Crown Prince Li Hung 李弘
ekō henshō (= hui-kuang fan-chao) 廻光返照
Emperor Chung-tsung 中宗
Emperor Chung-tsung Hsiao-ho 中宗孝和
Emperor Hsuan-tsung 玄宗
Emperor Jui-tsung 睿宗
Emperor Kao-tsu 高祖
Emperor Kao-tsung 高宗
Emperor Su-tsung 肅宗
Emperor Wu 武帝
Emperor Yang 煬帝
Empress Wu Tse-t'ien 則天武后
Erh-ju ssu-hsing lun 二入四行論
erh men 二門
fa-chieh hsing 法界性
fa-chieh i 法界義
fa-chieh t'i 法界體
Fa-ch'ih 法持
Fa-ch'in 法欽
Fa-chung 法沖
Fa-hsien (student of Tao-hsin) 法顯
Fa-hsien (student of Hung-jen) 法顯 (現)
fa-hsing 法性
Fa-hsing lun 法性論
Fa-hua ching 法華經
Fa-hua hsuan-i 法華玄義
Fa-jih 法日
Fa-ju 法如
Fa-jung 法融
Fa-k'an 法侃(=侃)
Fa-lang (= Pŏmnang in Korean) 法朗
Fa-min 法敏
fa-shui 法水
fa-t'ang 法堂
fa ssu-i 法四依
fa-t'i 法體
Fa-yuan 法玩
Fa-yün 法雲
fan 翻
fan-nao 煩惱
Fang Kuan 房琯
Fang-ming 方明
fang-pien 方便
Fei (= Tu Fei) 朏
Feng 豐
fo 佛
fo-hsin chih jih 佛心之日
fo-hsing 佛性
fo-jih 佛日
Fo-shuo fa-chü ching 佛說法句經
Fo-shuo wen-shih hsi-yü chung-seng ching 法說溫室洗浴衆僧經
fo-t'i 佛體
fo-t'ien 佛殿
Fo-tsu t'ung-chi 佛祖統記
Fo-tsu t'ung-tsai 佛祖通載
fu 付
fu-chu 付囑
fu-fa ch'üan-teng 付法傳燈
Fu fa-ts'ang yin-yuan chuan 付法藏因緣傳
Fu Hsi 傅翕
Fu-hsien ssu 福先寺
Fu-jo-lo 富若羅
fu pao-ts'ang chuan 付寶藏傳
furyū monji (= pu li wen-tzu) 不立文字
gembon 原本
Han-ling 寒嶺
Han-shan 寒山
hang (= hsing) 行
hattō (= fa-t'ang) 法堂
Hekigan-roku (= Pi-yen lu) 碧巖録
Heng-ching 恆景
ho 合
Ho 和
Ho-jung 和融
ho-kuang pu t'ung ch'en 和光不同塵
Ho-lin Hsuan-su 鶴林玄素
Ho-nei (Ch'in-yang hsien, Honan) 河内(沁陽縣)
ho yen wen 和言問
Hou Han shu 後漢書
hou-te chih 後得智

Hsi-hsia 西夏
Hsi-ming ssu 西明寺
Hsiang (= Layman Hsiang) 向
Hsiang (commentary) 象
hsiang (thoughts) 想
hsiang (characteristics) 相
hsiang-fen 相分
Hsiang-hsuan fu 詳玄賦
hsiang-lei 相類
hsiang-wei 香味
Hsiang-yü 香育
Hsiao-fu 小福
Hsiao-fu Chang ho-shang 小福長和尚
Hsiao-liao 曉了
Hsieh hsi yü-shu Ta-t'ung ch'an-shih pei-e chuang 謝賜御書大通禪師碑額狀
Hsien (= Ching-hsien?) 賢
Hsien (= Fa-hsien?) 顯
hsien (hexagram) 咸
Hsien-chü ssu 閑居寺
hsien-liang 現量
Hsien-te chi yü shuang-feng shan-t'a ko t'an hsuan-li—shih-erh 先德集於雙峯山塔各談玄理十二
hsin (mind) 心
hsin (faith, rely) 信
hsin-chieh 信解
hsin chieh-t'o 心解脱
hsin ch'u-chia 心出家
hsin fang-pien 心方便
hsin-hsin 信心
Hsin-hsin ming 信心銘
hsin hsin-so 心心所
hsin li-nien 心離念
hsin-shen 心神
hsin-ti 心體
Hsin-wang ching 心王經
hsin-yao 心要
Hsin-yao chi 心要集
hsing (practice) 行
hsing (nature) 性
hsing-ching chih li 性淨之理
hsing-chu-tso-wo 行住坐臥
hsing-ju 行入
hsing-men 行門
Hsing-t'ang ssu 興唐寺
hsiu 修
Hsiu ch'an-shih ch'üan-shan wen 秀禪師勸善文
Hsiu ho-shang chuan 秀和尚傳
Hsiu-hsi chih-kuan tso-ch'an fa-yao 修習止觀坐禪法要
Hsiu-hsin yao lun 修心要論
Hsiu-hsing fang-pien ch'an ching 修行方便禪經
Hsiu-hsing tao-ti ching 修行道地經
Hsin-wang p'u-sa shuo t'ou-to ching 心王菩薩説頭陀經
hsin-yuan 心源
Hsü-jung kuan 虛融觀
Hsü kao-seng chuan 續高僧傳
Hsuan-ching 玄景
Hsuan-hsuan-hsuan 玄玄玄
hsuan-hsueh 玄學
Hsuan-lang 玄朗
Hsuan-shih 宣什
Hsuan-shuang 玄爽
Hsuan-tsang 玄奘
Hsuan-tse 玄賾
Hsuan-tsung 玄宗
Hsuan-yueh 玄約
hu-ching 護淨
hu-jan nien ch'i 忽然念起
Hu-lao (Ssu-shui hsien, Honan) 虎牢(汜水縣)
Hu-lei Ch'eng 忽雷澄
Hu-ming 胡明
Hua (= Hua-kung) 化
Hua-kung (= Hua) 化公
Hua-kan ssu 化感寺
Hua-t'ai (Hua hsien, Hunan) 滑台(滑縣)
Hua-yen ching 華嚴經
Hua-yen ching hsing-yuan p'in shu ch'ao 華嚴經行願品疏抄
Huai-jen 懷仁
Huai-k'ung 懷空
Huang-Lao 黃老
Hui 惠
Hui-chao 惠超
Hui-chen 惠眞
Hui-ching 慧淨
Hui-ch'ou (= Seng-ch'ou) 惠稠

hui-ch'u 慧處
Hui-chung 慧忠
hui fang-pien 慧方便
Hui-fu 慧福
Hui-hao 慧滈
hui-hsiang 廻向
Hui-hsiu (= Shen-hsiu?) 惠秀
hui-jih 慧日
Hui-k'o 慧可
Hui-kuan 慧觀
hui-kuang fan-chao (= ekō henshō in Japanese) 廻光返照
Hui-lin 慧林
Hui-man 慧滿
hui-men 慧門
Hui-ming 惠明
Hui-neng 惠能
Hui-pu 慧布
Hui-shan ssu 會善寺
Hui-sung 慧嵩
Hui-ssu 慧思
Hui-ta (= Chih-ta) 慧達
Hui-tsang 惠藏
Hui-tuan 惠端
Hui-yin san-mei ching 慧印三昧經
Hui-yü (= Tao-yü) 惠育
Hui-yuan 慧遠
Hung 洪
Hung-cheng 宏正
Hung-chih 弘智
Hung-chou School 洪州宗
Hung-jen 弘忍
huo-jan 豁然
i (one) 一
i (differentiation) 異
i (also) 亦
I-chiao ching 遺教經
I-ch'ieh ching yin-i 一切經音義
i-ch'ieh ch'u 一切處
I ching 易經
I-chou (Ch'eng-tu, Szechwan) 益州 (城都)
i-ch'u 一處
I-fang 義方
I-feng 儀鳳
I-fu 義福
i hsin ch'üan hsin (ishin denshin in Japanese) 以心傳心
I-hsing 一行
I River 伊水
i-shang erh-p'in t'ung-shuo 以上二品通說
I-sheng hsien tzu-hsin lun 一乘顯自心論
i-shih 意識
i sung pao-shen 以送報身
i ts'ung wai ju li-men, erh ts'ung li ch'i yung-men 一從外入理門, 二從裏起用門
i-yin chiao 一音教
Ichijō kenjishin ron (= I-sheng hsien tzu-hsin lun) 一乘顯自心論
inka (= yin-k'o) 印可
ishin denshin (= i hsin ch'üan hsin) 以心傳心
jan-hsin 染心
jen-yün 任運
Jih-chao 日照
jo yu shih se 若有實色
ju (enter, āyatana) 入
ju (Suchness) 如
ju-ju shih-chi 如如實際
ju-lai 如來
ju-lai tsang 如來藏
Ju-leng-ch'ieh ching 入楞伽經
ju-shih an-hsin wei pi-kuan 如是安心爲壁觀
ju-tao 入道
Ju-tao an-hsin yao fang-pien fa-men 入道安心要方便法門
ju-tao fang-pien 入道方便
ju yen 入言
K'ai-feng 開封
K'ai-huang 開皇
K'ai-shan ssu 開善寺
K'ai-yuan 開元
K'ai-yuan shih-chiao lu 開元釋教錄
Kammon daijō hōron (= Kuan-men ta-sheng fa lun) 觀門大乘法論
kan 感
k'an 看
k'an i-wu 看一物

kang 剛
kanjin-shaku (= kuan-hsin shih) 観心釈
kao ch'en chieh shu 隔塵沙劫數
Kao-seng chuan 高僧傳
ken-pen chih 根本智
Kim (= Chin) 金
ko 各
k'o-ch'en wei-wang pu ju yueh pi 客塵僞妄不入曰壁
Ko Hung 葛洪
ko-i 格義
K'o (= Hui-k'o) 可
K'o-kung (= Hui-k'o) 可公
kōan (= kung-an) 公案
Koguryŏ 高麗
ku chih 故知
k'u 苦
kuan 觀
Kuan-fo san-mei hai ching 觀佛三昧海經
kuan-hsin 觀心
Kuan-hsin lun 觀心論
kuan-hsin shih (= kanjin-shaku in Japanese) 觀心釋
kuan-hsing chueh-chao 觀性覺照
K'uang 曠
Kuei-feng Tsung-mi 圭峯宗密
Kŭmgang sammae-kyŏng (= Chin-kang san-mei ching) 金剛三昧經
kung 供
kung-an (= kōan in Japanese) 公案
kung-te 功德
k'ung 空
k'ung-ch'an san-mei 空禪三昧
K'ung-chi ssu 空迹寺
k'ung-hsing 空行
K'ung-mu chang 孔目章
kyōge betsuden (= chiao-wai pieh chuan) 教外別伝
lan 爛
Lan-t'ien 藍田
Lan Ts'an (= Ming-ts'an) 懶 (or 嬾) 瓚
lang 朗
Lao-an 老安
Lao and Chuang 老莊
Lao-tzu 老子
Layman Hsiang 向居士
Leng-ch'ieh jen-fa chih 楞伽人法誌
Leng-ch'ieh shih-tzu chi 楞伽師資記
li (posit) 立
li (measure of distance) 里
li (absolute, principle) 理
Li (surname) 李
Li Chih-fei 李知非
li-hsin 離心
li-hsing 理行
li-hsing erh men 理行二門
Li Hua 李華
li-ju 理入
Li Lin-fu 李林甫
Li Mi 李泌
li-nien 離念
li-nien ching-chieh 離念境界
li-nien wei-shih 離念唯識
Li Shih-chih 李適之
li-t'a 利他
Li-tai fa-pao chi 歷代法寶記
Li-yang (Li hsien, Hunan) 澧陽(澧縣)
Li Yung 李邕
liang 量
Liao 廖
liao hsin 了心
Liao-hsing chü 了性句
liao-i 了義
lien-hsin 斂心
Lin-chi lu 臨濟錄
Ling-cho 靈著
Ling-yün 靈運
Liu 劉
Liu-ken chieh-t'o men 六根解脫門
liu-lei 流類
Liu-tsu t'an ching 六祖壇經
Lo-yang 洛陽
Lo-yang ch'ieh-lan chi 洛陽伽藍記
Lu-chou (Ch'ang-chih hsien, Shansi) 潞州(長治縣)
Lü-she-na fo 盧舍那佛
Lueh pien ta-sheng ju-tao ssu-hsing, ti-tzu T'an-lin hsü 略辯大乘入道四行, 弟子曇林序
lun 論

Lung-hsing ssu 龍興寺
Lung-hua ssu 龍華寺
Ma-ming p'u-sa tsao 馬鳴菩薩造
Ma-su (= Ho-lin Hsuan-su) 馬素
Ma-tsu 馬祖
Ma-tsu Tao-i 馬祖道一
mei 昧
men 門
Miao-fa lien-hua ching 妙法蓮華經
Miao-hsi ssu 妙喜寺
Miao-li yuan-ch'eng kuan 妙理圓成觀
miao-miao-miao 妙妙妙
Miao-sheng ting ching 妙勝定經
miao-yu 妙有
mien-pi 面壁
Min (region) 閩
Min 敏
ming (name) 名
ming (sentience) 命
ming (understand, illuminate, realize) 明
Ming 明
ming-ching 明淨
ming-hsing 明性
Ming-ts'an 明瓚
ming tzu-jan hsien 明自然顯
miru 見る
mo 末
mo-chao 默照
mo-fa 末法
Mo-ho chih-kuan 摩訶止觀
Mo-ho-yen 摩訶衍
mo-jan ching-tso 默然靜坐
mo-lien 磨練
Mount Chung 鐘山
Mount Chung-nan 中南山
Mount Heng (= Nan-yueh) 衡山
Mount Huan-kung (Ch'ien-shan hsien, Anhwei) 皖公山(潜山縣)
Mount Lo-fu (Tseng-ch'eng hsien, Kwangtung) 羅浮山(增成縣)
Mount Lu (Chiu-chiang hsien, Kiangsi) 盧山(九江縣)
Mount Lung 龍山
Mount Ma-t'ou (Ch'i-yuan hsien, Honan) 馬頭山(濟源縣)
Mount Mao (Chü-kung hsien, Kiangsu) 茅山(句宮縣)
Mount Meng (Hsiang-shan hsien, Chekiang) 蒙山(象山縣)
Mount Niu-t'ou (Chiang-ning hsien, Kiangsu) 牛頭山(江寧縣)
Mount Pai-sung 白松山
Mount P'ing-mu 憑茂山
Mount She (Chiang-ning hsien, Kiangsu) 攝山(江寧縣)
Mount Shou 壽山
Mount Shuang-feng 雙峯山
Mount Ssu-k'ung 思(or 司)空山
Mount Sung 嵩山
Mount Ta-fo 大佛山
Mount T'ai 泰山
Mount T'ai-hang 太行山
Mount T'ien-t'ai (T'ien-t'ai hsien, Chekiang) 天台山(天台縣)
Mount Tung (Shang-yü hsien, Chekiang) 東山(上虞縣)
Mount Tu (Feng-yang hsien, Anhwei) 獨山(鳳陽縣)
Mount Tzu-chin 紫金山
Mount Yü 玉山
mushin (= wu-hsin) 無心
Na (= Seng-na) 那
Nan-ch'üan (Kuei-ch'ih hsien, Anhwei) 南泉(貴池縣)
Nan lung-hsing ssu 南龍興寺
nan Neng pei Hsiu 南能北秀
Nan-shan nien-fo men ch'an 南山念佛門禪
nan t'ien-chu i-sheng tsung 南天竺一乘宗
nan-tsung 南宗
nan-tsung lun 南宗論
Nan-yang ho-shang tun-chiao chieh-t'o ch'an-men chih liao-hsing t'an-yü 南陽和尚頓教解脫禪門直了性壇語
Nan-yueh (= Mount Heng) 南岳
Nan-yueh Hui-ssu 南岳慧思
Nan-yueh ssu ta ch'an-shih li shih-yuan wen (= Li shih-yuan wen) 南岳思大禪師立誓願文

Nan-yueh Huai-jang 南岳懷讓
Neng (= Hui-neng?) 能
ni 逆
ni-kuan 逆觀
nieh 涅
nieh-p'an 涅槃
nieh-p'an chih ch'i 涅槃之氣
Nieh-p'an ching 涅槃經
Nieh-p'an lun 涅槃論
Nieh-p'an wu ming lun 涅槃無名論
nien 念
nien-fo 念佛
nien fo-ming 念佛名
Northern School (= pei-tsung) 北宗
O-mi-t'o tsan-wen 阿彌陀讚文
Ox-head School (Niu-t'ou tsung) 牛頭宗
Pa-hsia 八峽
pa sheng-ch'u 八勝處
pan 般
Pan-chou san-mei ching 般舟三昧經
p'an 槃
p'an-chiao 判教
p'an-yuan 攀緣
Pao-chih 保(or 寶)誌
Pao-en ssu 報恩寺
Pao-lin chuan 寶林傳
Pao-p'u tzu 抱朴子
Pao-t'ang School 保唐宗
Pao-t'ang Wu-chu 保唐無住
Pao-ying 寶迎
Pao-yü 寶瑜
Pao-yueh 寶月
pei-tsung 北宗
P'ei K'uan 裴寬
P'ei Ts'ui 裴漼
pen 本
pen-chi shih 本迹釋
pen-chueh 本覺
pen-hsin 本心
pen-hsing 本性
P'eng-lai Palace 蓬萊宮
Pi-chien ssu 碧澗寺
pi-kuan 壁觀
Pi-yen lu 碧巖錄
p'i-pa 琵琶
pieh 别
ping (illness) 病
ping (both) 並
ping hsing erh men 並[病]行二門
p'ing-teng 平等
Po-chang Hui-hai 百丈懷海
Po-jo ching 般若經
Po-jo hsin [ching] shu 般若心[經]疏
Po-jo wu chih lun 般若無知論
Po-lo-to-lo 婆羅多羅
po-ssu 波斯
P'o-hsiang lun 破相論
Pŏmnang (= Fa-lang) 法朗
Prince Hsiang (= Emperor Jui-tsung) 相王
Prince I of Hsiang-tung 湘東王繹
Prince Li Hung (= Crown Prince Li Hung) 李弘
Prince of Nan-p'ing 南平王
Princess Yung-t'ai 永泰公主
pu ch'i 不起
pu ch'i t'a nien 不起他念
pu-hui 不會
pu k'o ssu-i 不可思議
pu li wen-tzu (furyū monji in Japanese) 不立文字
pu mo-fu 不磨拂
pu sheng pu mieh 不生不滅
pu-ssu 不思
pu ssu-i 不思議
pu-ssu pu-i 不思不議
pu tso li-hsing 不作理行
P'u-chi 普寂
p'u-t'i lu 菩提路
p'u-t'i men 菩提門
p'u-t'i shu 菩提樹
P'u-t'i-ta-mo (= Bodhidharma) 菩提達摩(or 磨)
P'u-t'i-ta-mo ch'an-shih kuan-men 菩提達摩禪師觀門
P'u-t'i-ta-mo [chih] lun 菩提達摩[之]論
P'u-t'i-ta-mo nan-tsung ting shih-fei lun 菩提達摩南宗定是非論
Rinzairoku (= Lin-chi lu) 臨濟錄
Saichō 最澄
Saijōjōron (= Tsui-shang sheng lun) 最上乘論

san 三
San-chieh chiao 三階教
San-chieh ssu Tao-chen 三界寺道真
San-ho 三河
san-liu 三六
San-lun School 三論宗
San-lun hsuan-i 三論玄義
san-mei yung 三昧用
San-pao wen-ta 三寶文答
san-shih-ch'i chu-tao fa-men 三十七助道法門
san-t'ien 三點
san-tsang 三藏
se 色
se-ju 色入
Seng-chao 僧肇
Seng-chou 僧周
Seng-ch'ou 僧稠
Seng-fu 僧副
Seng-jui 僧叡
Seng-k'o (= Hui-k'o) 僧可
Seng-na (= Na) 僧那
Seng-shih 僧寔
Seng-ta (= Hui-ta?) 僧達
Seng-ts'an (= Ts'an?) 僧璨
Seng-yu 僧祐
Sha-chou (= Tun-huang) 沙州
Shan 善
Shan-chien lü pi-po-sha 善見律毘婆沙
shan chih-shih 善知識
Shan-fu 善伏
Shan-fu ssu 薦福寺
shan-hai 山海
shan ho ta-ti 山河大地
Shan-hui 善慧
Shang-tang (Ch'ang-chih hsien, Shansi) 上黨(長治縣)
Shang-te 商德
shang-tso 上座
Shao-lin ssu (= Shōrinji in Japanese) 少林寺
Shao-lin ssu pei 少林寺碑
she-hsin 攝心
She lun 攝論
She-lun School 攝論宗
She ta-sheng lun 攝大乘論
shen 身
shen-chung chen-ju 身中眞如
shen-chung p'ing-teng pen-lai hsin 身中平等本來心
shen-hsiang hsin-t'i 身相心體
shen-hsin 深信
shen-hsin pu ch'i, ch'ang shou chen-hsin 身心不起,常守眞心
Shen-hsing 神行
Shen-hsiu 神秀
Shen-hui 神會
Shen-lung 神龍
shen-tao 神道
Shen-ting (= Ting?) 神定
shen-t'ung 神通
sheng (volumetric measure) 升
sheng (generate) 生
sheng (sage) 聖
sheng (vehicle) 乘
Sheng 盛
Sheng-chou lu 聖冑錄
sheng-hsin 聖心
Sheng-man ching 勝鬘經
sheng-mieh hsin 生滅心
shih (consciousness, perception) 識
shih (phenomena) 事
shih (verify, make real) 實
shih (command, servant) 使
Shih 實
shih-chieh 世界
shih-chieh t'i 世界體
shih-chueh 始覺
shih-erh pu ching 十二部經
shih hsiang 十想
shih ju-shih 十如是
Shih leng-ch'ieh ching yuan 石楞伽經院
shih-li 事理
Shih-men cheng-t'ung 釋門正統
Shih ti ching 十地經
Shih-ti [ching] lun 十地[經]論
shingi (= ch'ing-kuei) 清規
shinshō (= hsin-hsing) 心性
shōshitsu 少室
Shōshitsu rokumon shū 少室六門集
shou (accept, experience) 受
shou (maintain) 守
shou-ch'i shou-i 受氣守一

Shou-chou 壽州
shou-hsin 守心
shou-i (guard the consciousness) 守意
shou-i (maintain the one) 守一
shou-i pu i 守一不移
shou-i pu shih 守一不失
shou-i pu t'ai 守一不怠
shou-i ts'un-san 守一存三
Shou-leng-yen i shu-chu ching 首楞嚴義疏注經
shou pen-ching hsin 守本淨心
Shu ching 書經
Shu-chou (Huai-ning hsien, Anhwei) 舒州(懷寧縣)
shu-hsiu 束修
Shuang-feng shan 雙峯山
Shūkyō Daigaku 宗教大学
shun 順
shun-kuan 順觀
shun-wu 順物
shuo-t'ung 說通
Shushin yōron (= Hsiu-hsin yao lun) 修心要論
Sŏnmun ch'waryo (= Zemmon satsuyō in Japanese) 禪門撮要
Southern School (nan-tsung) 南宗
ssu-ch'iu hsin 思求心
Ssu hung shih-yuan 四弘誓願
ssu-i 思議
ssu-i 四依
Ssu-i ching 思益經
Ssu-jui 思叡
Ssu-heng 思恒
ssu-lü 思慮
Ssu-lun School 四論宗
Ssu-ma 司馬
ssu-yü te chien 思欲得見
Sui-chou (Sui hsien, Hupeh) 隨州(隨縣)
Sui T'ien-t'ai Chih-che ta-shih pieh chuan (= Pieh chuan) 隋天台智者大師別傳
sui-yuan 隨緣
Sun 孫
Sung 嵩
Sung Chih-wen 宋之問
Sung kao-seng chuan 宋高僧傳
Sung-shan Hui-shan ssu ku ta-te Tao-an ch'an-shih pei-ming 嵩山會山寺故大德道安禪師碑銘
Sung Tan 宋儋
Sung-yueh ssu 嵩岳寺
Sung-yün 宋雲
Ta-an-kuo ssu 大安國寺
Ta-chao 大照
Ta chih-tu lun 大智度論
Ta-chuang-yen ssu 大莊嚴寺
Ta fang-kuang fo hua-yen ching 大方廣佛華嚴經
Ta-fu 大福
Ta-fu Liu ho-shang 大福六和尚
Ta-jih ching 大日經
Ta-lin ssu 大林寺
Ta-liang (Shang-ch'iu hsien, Honan) 大梁(商邱縣)
Ta-ming 大明
Ta-mo ch'an-shih kuan-men (= Daruma zenji kammon in Japanese) 達摩禪師觀門
Ta-mo ch'an-shih lun 達摩禪師論
Ta-mo ho-shang chieh 達摩和尚解
Ta-mo lun 達摩論
Ta-mo-to-lo ch'an ching 達摩多羅禪經
Ta-sheng fa-chieh wu ch'a-pieh lun 大乘法界無差別論
Ta-sheng hsin-hsing lun 大乘心行論
Ta-sheng hsuan lun 大乘玄論
Ta-sheng i-chang 大乘義章
Ta-sheng k'ai-hsin hsien-hsing tun-wu chen-tsung lun 大乘開心顯性頓悟真宗論
Ta-sheng pei-tsung lun 大乘北京論
Ta-sheng wu fang-pien—pei-tsung 大乘五方便北宗
Ta-sheng wu-sheng fang-pien men 大乘無生方便門
Ta-Sung seng-shih lueh 大宋僧史略
Ta-t'ang Ch'i-chou Lung-hsing ssu ku Fa-hsien ta ch'an-shih pei-ming 大唐蘄州龍興寺故法現大禪師碑銘
Ta-T'ang hsi-yu ch'iu-fa kao-seng chuan 大唐西遊求法高僧傳
Ta-tao 大道
Ta-tsu 大足

Ta-ts'ung 大聰
Ta-t'ung ch'an-shih 大通禪師
Ta-t'ung fang-kuang ching 大通方廣經
Ta-t'ung ho-shang ch'i li-wen 大通和尚七禮文
Ta-yeh 大業
ta yuan-ching chih 大圓鏡智
ta yueh 答曰
Ta-yün ching 大雲經
t'a (other, objectified) 他
t'a (tread) 踏
t'a-se 他色
T'ai-p'ing ching 太平經
T'ai-p'ing kuang chi 太平廣記
T'ai-yuan 太原
Taishō Daigaku 大正大學
tan 但
T'an-ch'ien (= Ch'ien?) 曇遷
T'an-chen 曇眞
T'an-lin 曇林
T'an-lun 曇倫
tang-t'i 當體
Tang-yang (Tang-yang hsien, Hupeh) 當陽(當陽縣)
T'ang-wen shih-i 唐文拾遺
tao (arrive) 到
tao (way, enlightenment) 道
Tao 道
Tao-fan ch'ü-sheng hsin-chueh 導凡趣聖心決
Tao-fu 道副
Tao-heng 道恒
Tao-hsin 道信
Tao-hsiu (= Shen-hsiu) 道秀
Tao-hsuan (author of *HKSC*) 道宣
Tao-hsuan (student of P'u-chi) 道璿
tao-shih 道士
Tao-shu 道樹
Tao-shun 道俊
Tao-te ching 道德
Tao-yin 道蔭
tao-yin wang-lai 導引往來
Tao-ying 道瑩
Tao-yü (= Hui-yü) 道育
te 德
te ching 得淨
te-li 得利
teng-shih (= tōshi in Japanese) 燈史
Ti lun (= Shih-ti lun) 地論
Ti-lun School 地論宗
ti-tzu 弟子
t'i 體
t'i-chung p'ing-teng pen-lai hsin 體中平等本來心
t'i-hsin 體心
T'ien-chü ssu 天居寺
T'ien-kung ssu 天宮寺
t'ien-lung 天龍
T'ien-p'ing 天平
T'ien-t'ai Chih-i 天台智顗
T'ien-t'ai chih-kuan 天台止觀
T'ien-t'ai School 天台宗
ting 定
Ting (= Shen-ting) 定
ting-fa 定法
ting-hsing erh men 定行二門
ting-hui 定慧
ting-li 定力
Ting-lin hsia ssu 定林下寺
Ting shih-fei lun 定是非論
tōshi (= teng-shih in Chinese) 灯史
tōtai (= tang-t'i) 當体
t'ou 斗
Tōyō Bunko 東洋文庫
Ts'ai I-hsuan 崔義玄
Tsan ch'an-men shih 讚禪門詩
Tsan-ning 贊寧
Ts'an (= Seng-ts'an?) 粲
Tsang 藏
tsao-ta 造大
tsao-tso 造作
tsao-tz'u 造次
Ts'ao-ch'i ta-shih [pieh] chuan 曹溪大師[別]卷
tso 作
tso-ch'an 坐禪
Tso-ch'an san-mei ching 坐禪三昧經
Tsu-t'ang chi 祖堂集
Tsu-t'ing shih-yuan 祖庭事苑
Tsui 最
Tsui-shang sheng lun 最上乘論 (= Choesangsŭng'non in Korean; = Saijōjōron in Japanese)

tsung 宗
Tsung-ching lu 宗鏡錄
tsung-ch'i 宗系
Tsung-mi 宗密
tsung-t'ung 宗通
Tu Cheng-lun 杜正倫
Tu Fei (= Fei) 杜胐
tu i ch'ing-ching chiu-ching ch'u 獨一清淨究竟處
Tu-ku Chi 獨狐乃
Tu-men ssu 度門寺
Tu Yü 杜昱
T'u-shan ssu 塗山寺
Tuan (= Hui-tuan?) 端
tun 頓
Tun-huang 敦煌
Tun-wu chen-tsung chin-kang po-jo hsin-hsing ta pi-an fa-men yao-chueh 頓悟眞宗金剛般若心性達彼岸法門要決
Tun-wu chen-tsung yao-chueh 頓悟眞宗要決
Tun-wu ta-sheng cheng-li chueh 頓悟大乘正理決
Tun-wu yao men 頓悟要門
Tung Chung-shu 董仲舒
Tung-shan 東山
tung-shan ching-men 東山淨門
tung-shan fa-men 東山法門
tung-shan miao-fa 東山妙法
tung-shan wu-sheng fa-men 東山無生法門
t'ung 通
tzu-chueh chueh-t'a chueh-man 自覺覺他覺滿
tzu-chueh sheng-chih 自覺聖智
tzu-hsing 自性
tzu-hsing ch'ing-ching hsin 自性清淨心
Tzu-hsuan 子璿
tzu-jan ming hsien 自然明現
tzu-li 自利
tzu-tsai 自在
tzu-tsai chih 自在智
Tzu-chou (Tzu-chung hsien, Szechwan) 資州(資中縣)
Tz'u-en ssu 慈恩寺
Tz'u-lang 辭朗
Tzu-sheng ssu 資聖寺
Wa-kuan ssu 瓦官寺
Wan-hui 万廻
Wang 王
wang-hsiang hsin 妄想心
wang-nien pu sheng 妄念不生
wang-nien pu sheng wo-so-hsin mieh 妄念不生我所心滅
Wang Shih-ch'ung 王世充
Wang Wei 王維
Wei (dynasty) 魏
Wei (region) 衛
wei-ch'en 微塵
wei-ch'en shu 微塵數
wei-hsin (= yuishin in Japanese) 唯心
Wei-hsiu (= Shen-hsiu?) 威秀
Wei Lo-hsia chu-seng ch'ing fa-shih ying Hsiu ch'an-shih piao 爲洛下諸僧請法事迎秀禪師表
Wei-mo ching 維摩經
Wei-shih 韋士
wei-shih (= yuishiki in Japanese) 唯識
Wei Wen-ch'ing 衛文卿
Wei Wen-sheng 衛文昇
wen (ask) 問
wen (hear) 聞
Wen-shih ching 溫室經
wen-ta 問答
Wen-ta tsa ch'eng-i 問答雜徵義
wen yueh 問曰
wo 我
Wo-lun ch'an-shih k'an-fa 臥輪禪師看法
wo-so 我所
wu (pronoun) 吾
Wu (region) 吳
wu (not, non-being) 無
wu-cheng tz'u 無諍慈
wu-chi 無記
Wu Ch'ing 吳慶
Wu-chu 無住
wu-ch'u 無處
Wu fang-pien 五方便
wu hai 五海
wu-hai shih-chih 五海十智
Wu-hsiang 無相

wu-hsiang ta-sheng 無相大乘
wu-hsin (= mushin in Japanese) 無心
Wu-hsin lun 無心論
wu hsing 五行
wu i wu 無一物
wu-jan 無染
wu-ju 悟入
Wu-lao (Ssu-shui hsien, Honan) 武牢 (汜水縣)
wu-liang i ch'u san-mei 無量義處三昧
Wu-liang-shou kuan ching 無量壽觀經
Wu-liang ssu 無量寺
wu-lou chen-ju 無漏眞如
wu men 五門
wu-nien (= munen in Japanese) 無念
wu-nien pu-tung pu-yao 無念不動不搖
wu-ming 無明
Wu P'ing-i 武平一
wu-sheng 無生
Wu Shih-huo 武士彠
wu-so 無所
wu so ch'i 無所起
wu-te 無得
wu-te cheng-kuan 無得正觀
wu t'ing-hsin kuan 五停心觀
wu-wei 無爲
wu-wei hua 無爲化
Wu-wei san-tsang shou-chieh ch'an-hui wen chi ch'an-men yao-fa 無畏三藏受戒懺悔文及禪門要法
wu-wo 無我
Yang-chou (Chiang-tu hsien, Kiangsu) 揚州(江都縣)
Yang Po-ch'eng 陽伯成
Yao 堯
Yao-chueh lun 要決論
yao-ming 窈冥
yao-yao ming-ming 窈窈冥冥
Yeh 鄴
yeh-yeh 業業
Yen-kung 彥公
YenT'ing-chih 嚴挺之
yen-yen-yen 研研研
yin-hsing 因行
yin-k'o 印可
Yin-tsung 印宗
yin-yuan 因緣
yin-yuan shih 因緣釋
Ying-chou (Chung hsien, Hupeh) 郢州(鍾縣)
ying wu-so-chu erh sheng [or: chu] ch'i hsin 應無所住而生[or住]其心
Ying-yang (K'ai-feng hsien, Honan) 滎陽(開封縣)
yu (being) 有
yu (distant) 攸 or 悠
yu-ch'ueh 悠闕
yu-hsiang ta-sheng 有相大乘
yu-wei 有爲
yü (pronoun) 余
Yü 玉
Yü-ch'üan ssu 玉泉寺
yü K'o t'ung-hsueh 與可同學
yü-ling 幽靈
yü-lu 語錄
Yü-pei 豫北
yuan (enmity) 怨
yuan (origin) 源
yuan-ch'eng chih fa 圓成之法
Yuan-ch'i 緣起
yuan-chiao fang-pien 圓教方便
yuan-chiao fang-pien yao-chueh lun 圓教方便要決論
yuan-ch'üan hsin 緣轉心
Yuan-i 元一
Yuan-kuan 元觀
Yuan-kuei 元珪
yuan-lü 緣慮
yuan-lü hsin 緣慮心
yuan-ming 圓明
Yuan-ming lun 圓明論
yuan-tsung 圓宗
Yuan-wu liao-i ching 圓悟了義經
yueh-chiao shih 約教釋
Yueh-chou (Chao-hsing hsien, Chekiang) 越州(紹興縣)
yuishiki (= wei-shih) 唯識
yuishin (= wei-hsin) 唯心
Yun-chou 鄆州
Yun-men ssu 雲門寺
yung 用
yung-hsin 用心
Yung-ning ssu 永寧寺
Zemmon satsuyō (= Sŏnmun ch'waryo in Korean) 禪門撮要

Index

www.ingramcontent.com/pod-product-compliance
Lightning Source LLC
Chambersburg PA
CBHW020458100426
42812CB00024B/2708

* 9 7 8 0 8 2 4 8 1 0 5 6 6 *

 **Production Notes**

Composition and paging for this book were done on the Quadex Composing System and typesetting on the Compugraphic 8400 by the design and production staff of University of Hawaii Press.

The text and display typeface is Compugraphic Times Roman.

Offset presswork and binding were done by Vail-Ballou Press, Inc. Text paper is Writers RR Offset, basis 50.

〔A〕蘄州忍和上道凡趣聖悟解脱宗修心要論一卷

〔B〕若其不護淨、一切行者無由趣見。願知；若寫者、願用心無令脱錯、恐誤後人。

〔C〕夫言修道之體；自識當身本來清淨、不生不滅。無有分別、自性圓滿、清淨之心、此是本師、乃勝念十方諸佛。

〔D〕問曰、何知自心本來清淨。

答曰、『十地論』云、「衆生身中有金剛佛性。猶如日輪、體明圓滿、廣大無邊。只爲五陰重雲所覆、如瓶内燈、光不能照。」又以朗日爲喩、譬如世間雲霧八方倶起。天下陰暗、日豈爛也。

何故無光。

答曰、日光不壞。只爲雲霧所映。一切衆生清淨之心、亦

蘄　下十九字(朝)第五祖弘忍大師説、凡趣聖道、悟解眞宗、修心要論

忍　下五字(龍)忍大師是祖超凡

道　P3554 導

若　下二十九字 P3559 (北)欠也

知　一字(朝)善知識

體　下五字(朝)本體須識身心

重　(朝)黒〔以下同〕

照　(朝)照輝〔下六字欠〕(龍)〔下有四十三衍字〕

朗　(龍)(朝)欠也。(北) P3434 P3559 P3777 S2669 S3558 S4064 即

復如是。只爲攀緣妄念諸·見重·雲所覆。但能顯然·守心、妄念不生、涅槃法日。自然顯現。故知、自心本來清淨。

〔E〕問曰、何知自心本來不生不滅。

答曰、『維摩經』云、「如無有生、如無有滅。」如者、爲眞如佛性、自性清淨心源。眞如本有、不從緣生。又云、「一切衆生皆如也。衆聖賢亦如也。」一切衆生者、即我等是。衆聖賢者、即諸佛是。言名相雖別、身中·眞如、法體並同、不生不滅。故言「皆如也。」故知自心本來不生不滅。

〔F〕問曰、云何名心爲本師。

答曰、此眞心·者、自然而有。不從外來、不索束修。於三世中所有至親、莫過於心。若識·眞如守之、即到彼岸。迷者棄之、即墮三途。故知、三世諸佛以自心爲師。

諸　(龍)知

然　下二字(龍)照現眞

日　下三字(龍)如日照

中　P3559心

心　P3559如

識　下五字(龍)識自身心(朝)識心者守之(北)識心者眞如口P3559識者守之

故『論』云、「衆・生者、依妄識波浪而有、體是虛妄。」了然守心、妄心不起、即到無生。故知、心爲本師。

〔G〕問曰、云・何凡心得勝佛心。

答曰、常念他佛、不免生死。守我本心、得到彼岸。故『金剛般若經』云、「若以色見我、以音聲求我、是人行邪道、不能見如來。」故知、守眞・心勝念他佛。又言勝者、只是約行勸人之語。其實究竟果體平等無二。

〔H〕問曰、衆生與佛、眞體既同。何故諸佛不生不滅、受無量快樂、自在無礙。我等衆生墮生死中、受種種苦者何。

答曰、十方諸佛、悟達法性、皆自照了・心源、妄想不生、不失正念、我所心滅。故得不受生死。以不生死故、即畢究寂滅。以寂滅故、萬樂自歸。

衆 下十四字㊞朝欠也

云 下八字㊞朝何名自心勝念彼佛

眞 ㊞朝本眞 P3559 自

語 ㊞龍 S3558 義

佛 下三字㊞龍佛眞如體性 P3434 佛

性 其體

了 ㊞朝照燎

一切衆生、迷於眞性、不識本心。種種妄緣、不修正念。不正念故、即憎愛心起。以憎愛故、即心器破漏。心破漏故、即受生死。有生死故、即諸苦自現。『心王經』云、「眞如佛性沒在知見。六識海中、沈淪生死、不得解脱。」努力。會是守眞·心、妄念不生、我所心滅、故自然與佛平等。

〔I〕問曰、眞如法性同一無二、迷應俱迷、悟應俱悟。何故佛獨覺悟、衆生昏迷。因何故爾。

答曰、自此已上、入不思議分、非凡境所及。識心故悟、失性故迷。緣合即合、不可定説。但眞諦信、自守眞心。故『維摩經』云、「無自性無他性。法本不生、今則無滅。」此悟即離二邊、入無分別智。若解此義、但於行住·坐臥、恒常

心 (龍)心學法無益

力 (龍)力努力

眞 P3559欠也 (朝)本眞

等 (朝)等無二

住 下三十二字(朝)欠也

凝然守本淨心。妄念不生、我所心滅、自然證解。
更欲廣起問答、名議轉多。欲知法要、守心第一。此守心
者、乃是涅槃之根本、入道之要門、十二部經宗、三世諸
佛之祖。

〔J〕問曰、何知守心・是涅槃之根本。

答曰、言涅槃者、體是寂滅無爲安樂。我心既眞、妄想即
斷。妄想斷故、即其正念。正念具故、即寂照智生。寂照智
生故、即窮達法性。達法性故、即得涅槃。故知、守心是涅
槃之根本。

〔K〕問曰：何知守心・是入道之要門。

答曰、乃至擧一手爪甲畫佛像、或造恒沙功德者、只是

心 (朝)本眞心 (龍)S4064 眞心

曰 (龍)〔下有十衍字〕

心 (朝)本眞心 (龍)眞心

佛爲教導無智慧衆生、作當來之因、勝緣報業、及見佛之因。若願自身早成佛者、會是無·爲守眞心。三世諸佛無量無邊。若有一人、不守眞·心得成佛者、無有是處。故『經』云、「正·心一處、無事不辨。」故知、守眞·心是入道之要門。

〔L〕問曰、何知守眞·心是十二部經之祖。

答曰、如來於一切經中廣説一切罪福、一切因緣果報、或引一切山河大地草木等種種物、起無量無邊譬喩、或現無量神通種·種變化者、只是佛爲教導無智慧衆生、有種種慾、心行萬差。是故如來隨其心門、引入常·樂。既·體知衆生佛性本來清淨、如雲底日。但了然守眞·心、妄念雲盡、慧日即現。何須更多學知見、歸生死苦。

無　下五字㊀朝守本眞心　P3559守自眞心

眞　P3559欠也

正　下二字㊀朝制心　P3559 P3777止心　S4664正念

眞　㊀北P3434欠也㊀朝㊀龍本眞

門　全欠也

眞　㊀朝本眞㊀龍P3559欠也

種　下全S3558欠也

常　下二字㊀朝P3559一乘我

既　=即？

眞　㊀朝本眞

一切義理、乃三世之事、譬如磨鏡。塵盡自·然見性。即今無明心中學得者、終是無用。若能了然不失正念、無爲心中學得者、此是眞學。雖·言眞學、竟無所學。何以故。我及涅槃二皆空故、無·二無一。故無·所學、法體·非空。要須了然守眞·心、妄念不生、我所心滅。故『涅槃經』云、「知佛不說法者、是名多聞。」故知、守眞·心是十二部經之宗。

〔M〕問曰、何知守心·是三世諸佛之祖。

答曰、三世諸佛皆從識·性中生。先·守眞心、妄念不生、我所心滅、後得成佛。故知、守心·是三世諸佛之祖。

〔N〕上來四種問答、若欲廣說何窮。吾眞望得汝自識本心。是故慇懃如是。努力努力。千經萬論、莫過守眞·心是要。努力。

自　(朝)明自然現　P3559 自然明現　P3777 自明見性　S2669 自然見住

雖　下四字 P3559 欠也

無　下三字 P3559 云無學、雖言眞學、竟無所學

體　下二字 (朝)性雖

眞　(朝)本眞　P3559 其眞

眞　(朝)本眞　P3559 欠也

心　(朝)本眞心

識　(朝)心

先　下十六字 (朝)以外〔妄念不生、識性中生、我所心滅、識·性中心。先守眞心、後得成佛。〕

識　下四字 (龍)識性衆生　P3559 性中　P3777 識性亦已

吾案『法華經』云、「示汝大車寶藏、明珠妙藥等物、汝自不取不服。窮苦。奈何奈何。」會是妄念不生、我所心滅、一切功德自然圓滿。不假外求、歸生死苦。於一切處念・念齊心。莫受現在樂、種未來苦、自誑誑他、不脱生死。努力努力。今雖無用、共作當來・之因。莫使三世虚度、枉喪功夫。『經』云、「常處地獄、如遊園觀。在餘惡道、如己舍宅。」我等衆生今現如此、不覺不知、驚怖殺人、了無出心。奇哉。

〔○〕若初心學坐禪者、依『無量壽觀經』端坐正身、閉目合口、心前平視、隨意遠、作一日想守之。念念不住、即善調氣息聲。莫使乍麁乍細、即令人成病。

苦夜坐時、或見一切善惡境界、或入青黄赤白等諸三

心　㊀朝眞心

心　㊀朝心是佛

眞　P3559自心

念　下四字㊀朝正念察心㊀龍念念觀心　P3559念念察心　S4064念念齊心

來　㊀朝來成佛

之　㊀朝本眞心

昧、或見自身出入・光明、或見如來身相、或・有種種變現。知時攝心莫著。皆並是空、妄想而現。『經』云、「十方國土皆如虛空。」又云、「三界虛幻、唯是一心作。」若不得定、不見一切境界者、亦不須怪。但於行住坐臥中、恒常了・然守眞・心。

會是妄念不生、我所心即滅、一切萬法不出自心。所以諸佛廣説、若許言教譬喩者、只爲衆生行行不同、遂使教門差別。其實八萬四千法門、三乘位體、七十二賢聖行宗、莫過自心是本。

若能自識本心、念念磨練者、於念念中、常・供養十方恒沙諸佛、十二部經、念念常轉法輪。

若了心源者、一切心義無窮、一切願足、一切行滿、一切

入 (朝) P3559 大

或 下二十字 P3559 欠也

了 (龍) 凝

眞 (朝) 本眞

者 (朝) 莫住者、即自見佛性也

常 下十九字 (龍) 欠也

皆辦、不受後有。會是妄念不生、我所心滅、捨此身已、定
得無生。不可思識。
努力。莫造·大。如此要·門語、難可得聞、聞而能行者、恒沙
衆中、莫過有一。行而能到者、億億劫中、稀有一人。好好
自安靜、善調諸根、熟視心源、恒令照了清淨、勿令無記。
〔P〕問曰、云何是無記心。
答曰、諸攝心人爲緣外境、麁心少息、内縛眞心。心未淨
時、於行住坐臥中、恒徵意看心、由未能得了了清淨、獨
照心源、是名無記。
亦是漏心、猶不免生死大病。況復惣不知守心者、是人
沈沒生死苦海。何日得出。可憐。
努力。『經·』云、「衆生若不精誠、不内發者、於三世中、縦值恒

造 下二字(朝)造次 P3559 放逸

要 下三字(朝)眞實不妄語(龍)要門義 P3559 要語

記 (朝)記心王

經 下二十六字(龍)欠也

沙諸佛、無所能爲。」『經』云、「衆生識心自度。佛不能度衆生。」若·佛能度衆生者、過去諸佛、恒沙無量、何故我等不成佛也。只是精誠不内發、是故沈沒苦海。

努力。過去不知己過、悔亦不及。今身現在、有遇得聞。分明相語、快解此語、了知守心。是等一道。不肯發至心、求願成佛、受無量自在快樂、乃始轟轟隨俗、貪求名利、當來墮地獄中、受種種苦惱奈·何。努力。

〔Q〕但能着破衣、喰麁食、了然守心。最省氣力、而能有功。世間迷人不解此理。於無明心、多涉艱辛、廣修相善、望得解脫、乃歸生死苦。

了然不失正念而度衆生者、是大力菩薩。分明語汝、守

若　下六字（龍）（北）P3434 P3777 S2669 S4064 欠也　P3559 若佛度衆生

力　（朝）力、努力。勤求本心、勿令妄漏

心　（龍）眞心

奈　下四字（朝）將何所及、奈何奈何。努力努力。

心　（朝）本眞心

功　（朝）功是精進人也

心第一。不肯現在一生忍苦、欲得當來萬劫受殃。聽汝、更知何屬。

八風吹不動者、眞是殊持寶山。若欲知果者、但對於萬境起恒、沙化用、巧辨若流。應病與藥、而能妄念不生、我所心滅者、眞出世丈夫。如來自在、嘆何可盡。吾說此言者、至心勸汝、不生望=妄念、滅我所心。

〔R〕問·曰、云何是我所心。

答曰、爲有少許勝他;自念我能。如是所心、涅槃中病。『涅槃經』云、「譬如虛空能含容萬物、而此虛不自念言、我能如是。」此喩我所心滅趣、金剛三昧、病·行二門。

〔S〕問曰、諸至·行人求眞常寂滅者、但·樂無常麁善、不樂於第一義諦。眞常妙善未現、只欲發心緣義、遂思覺心

一 (朝)一若不勸學者、甚癡人也

心 (朝)心則是出世之士

問 下八字 S4064 欠也

他 (朝)他之心

病 下四字 (朝)欠也 (龍)並行二門

至 =志?

但 下二字 (朝)只樂 (龍)(北) P3434 P3777 S2669 S4064 世間

起、即是漏心。只·欲正心無所、即無明昏住、又不當理。
只欲不正·心不緣義、即妄取空。雖受人身、行畜生行。爾
時無有定慧方便、而不能得了了明見佛性。只是行人
沈沒之處。若爲進·起得到無餘涅槃。願示眞·趣。
答曰、會是信心具足、至·願成就。
緩緩靜心。更重教汝。自閑淨身心、一切無所攀緣。端坐
正身；令氣息調、徽其心不在內不在外不在中間。好好
如如、穩·熟看、即及見此心識·流動、猶如水流陽炎、葉·葉
不住。既見此識·時、唯是不內不外。緩緩如如、穩看熟；即
返覆融消、虛凝湛住。其此流動之識、颯然自滅。
滅此識者、乃是滅十地菩薩衆中障或。(二惑)此識身等滅已、
其心即虛凝恢怕、皎潔然。吾更不能說其形狀。汝若欲

只 下六字㊀朝 只欲亡心 P3559 欲止心無所
正 ㊀朝 P3559 止
進 下二字㊀龍 進去 P3559 進趣 ㊀朝 超
眞 下二字㊀朝 眞心 P3559 歸眞趣
至 ㊀朝 志
身 ㊀朝 念
穩 下三字㊀朝 穩看看熟 ㊀龍 穩穩看心 P3559 穩看熟視
識 下㊀龍〔有七十三衍字〕
葉 下二字㊀朝 曄曄 ㊀龍 葉成 P3559 業業
識 下㊀龍〔有百九十五衍字〕
熟 ㊀朝 看熟 P3559 熟視

得知者、取『涅槃經金剛身品·』乃『維摩經見阿閦佛·品。』緩
緩·尋思、此·是實語。
〔T〕能·得於行住坐臥中；及對五慾八風；不失此心者、是
人梵行已立、所作已辨、究竟不受生死之身。五欲者、色
聲香味觸。八風者、利衰毀譽稱譏苦樂。
此是行人磨練佛性處、甚莫怪今身不得自在。『經』云、「世
間無佛、住地菩薩不得現用。」要脱此報身。衆生過去、根
有利鈍、不可判。上者一念間、下者無量劫。若有力時、隨
衆生性、起菩提善根、自利利人、莊嚴佛道。
要須了四依、乃窮實相。若依文執、即失眞宗。諸比丘等、
學·他出家修道、此是出家、出生死家；是名出家。正念具

品 (朝)品第三卷中
佛 下二字 (朝)佛品第三卷
此 下四字 (朝)細心搜檢熟看
能 下二字 (朝)若此經熟實得能
中 下十九字 (龍)欠也
風 下 P3434 欠也

學 (朝) P3559 汝學

足、修道得成、乃至解身支節、臨命終時、不失正念、即是·
佛。

〔U〕第子上來集此論者、直以信心依文取義。作如是說
者、實非了了證知。若乖聖理者、願懺悔除滅。若當聖道
者、廻施衆生。願皆識本心、一時成佛。聞者努力、當來成
佛。願在前度我們徒。

〔V〕問曰、此論從首至末、皆顯自心是道。未知、果行二門、
是何門而攝。
答曰、此論顯一乘爲宗。然其至意、導迷趣解、自免生死、
乃能度人。直言自利、不說利他。約行門攝。若有人依文
行者、即在前成佛。

家 ㊀朝 P3559 枷

是 下二字 ㊀朝 P3559 得成佛 S2669 佛

徒 下 ㊀龍〔有百二十五衍字〕

若我誑汝、當來墮十八地獄。指天地爲誓、若不信、我世世被虎狼所食。

食

下(龍)以此所冀聖壽萬歲、十方法界含靈、同入如來果海爾云校正雪峇刻手一訓等二十化主印珠、慧澄、道熙、隆慶四年庚(龍)道凡趣聖悟解脱宗修心要論一卷 S2669 道凡趣聖悟解脱宗修心要門論一卷

P3664

圓明論

明心色因果品第一

要門方便品第二

辨[2]明修道釋?因果品第三

辨明三乘逆順觀品第四

簡□□緣[3]生品第五

入邪正五門辨因果品第六

自心現量品第七

簡[4]妄相(想)品第八

辨明聲體品第九

明心色因〔果品第一〕

〔A〕夫[5]入道之初、須明心色各有二種、一者生滅?心〔色〕□□□妄[6]?想前乎縁慮不斷名爲妄〔想〕□□□名[7]爲眞覺?之能。元未[=來]不善其義?□□□曰[2/8]生滅、若見眞心元無妄想、既得眞性。常須覺悟□□□乃[9]?是?縁轉心、心實不動。作此解明行住坐臥常在禪?□□□無[10]?碍?名心解脱也。

〔B〕色者即是身也。身想〔相〕從何而生、推導□□□一[11]者從無始妄想熏習而生、二者即從現在香味因縁□□□從[12]生、熏習則是因、身則是果。熏習?是色相?□□□若[13]習非有想、身亦非色相。何以故、爲因是無相、果亦?□□□

〔C〕不[14]善其義。謂身自性而生。若從因縁習氣起者、即知是虚?〔因〕既[15]是空、果亦是空。依香味中推、亦無有身。何以故。色從香味〔飲〕食[16]爲命。食又非色。如人飲食變爲垢?穢、亦非作色、細?少香〔味〕□□□因[17]縁香味爲色身香味。若有質色、身是其有、香味本作?空?□身[18]亦是空。若有作其色、色即是其有。

將無作其色、明知是空。

爲[19]〔觀〕心色無二、本性平等、名曰眞如。得此無二平等法門時、了其心色也。

〔A〕要[20]門方便品第二

夫學道多?端、趣悟不同?□□□其[21]門有其三種。一者漸教、二者頓教、三者圓教。其義不善。浪〔作?〕爲[22]各執自許。根基不會餘人所悟。各相非毀。若契會根基、趣?□門[23]者、即辯其漸頓圓、成其別也。若不解者、即言同也。余今所□不[24]同也。須實?之問、悟者即隔塵沙劫數、豈得是其同也。

〔B〕今爲略[25]簡其教、即知別也。何爲漸教。暗人解者、皆悉附經文。經文無過[26]、良爲將自根基所解、不會餘人所悟。

根其有其三、□□□及[27]善知識。取其解者、觀身心不在内外、得其無〔我〕者、是小乘人也。爲[28]自知根基大小、故便執所解、自謂名爲大乘觀也。

又復有□□□□[29]解所有境界並是自己妄想心作。若自無妄想者、畢竟□□
□境[30]界。作此觀時、即無前後際。即不住涅槃、執其所解、自謂是其?頓教[31]?所聆。乃
是漸門、非是頓也。

〔C〕云何頓教。頓教者、善知身相心體來?□□□之[32]處也。其身相者、元從妄相=想心
中生。其妄想元無有□□□
言[33]無體、云何與身爲本。

答曰、其心無體。亦不與身爲本。所以者何。心[34]自相不知處所、亦不知生身。心若
知處所、可能生於身相。以心不自知[35]其處所、及不知從何處而去來、亦不知至
何處受身□□□從[36]何處而生。

若也身心各得・相知者、可道、身從心生。心復可言生其[37]身也。身心既是不相知、
及不知來去處所者、何能相生也。作此解?者[38]、身是誰家身、心是誰家心。心復不
自知其處所、云何與身爲本。□□□

身[39]心各不相知、即是元來不能相生也。何以故。空花所誑眼□□□身[40]既非身。明眼是空。以將空作其有、有亦是其空。故說眼根□□□是[41?]空作其心、心亦是其空。

譬如依泥起其器。器亦□□□器[42]若非是泥、身心是其有。今既覺非實三世亦復此□□□所[43]言賢聖及地位者、並言空以爲作也。空中無起滅、故言□□□作[44]此解者名爲悟。所有山林土地日月星辰衆生等類□□□虛[45]空、法性波浪也。是故名頓。觀於無我故言別也。

〔D〕今顯漸□□□所[46]悟。不知若爲合其圓也。凡愚之知、不可測量圓門之理也。

〔圓〕門[47]者有十種義。云何名十。

一者、須明衆生界。

二者、須明世界。

〔三〕者[48]、須明法界義。

四者、須明法界性。

五者、須〔明〕五海。

六者、須明□□□義。[49]

七者、須明衆生界體。

八者、須明世界體。

九者、須明法界體?。

〔十者、須明〕[50]諸佛方便體。

〔E〕此十門不同。就其中了了分明者、即解圓教。□□□將?[51]頓門中、定力多、三昧用少。圓之中、三昧用多。恐?無□□□者[52]、雖有定行二門、終不名了義。其人愚性?示?既?更不□□□非?[53]眞、自悞亦後悞他。

此義是『法華經』佛己訶責學道之者〔不〕[54]簡圓門之義。余今一一爲次第釋名、又出其體也。令?諸行□憑[55]也。

P3559

云何衆生界者。有三種衆生界也。何等爲三。□□□衆[56]生相□□相?。二者、三世
流轉亦是衆生之相。三者、受用境?身[57]?亦是衆生之相。其相者、□以?法性爲體。
衆生心性元有?五[58]陰之相。元從因緣而起。一塵?合無有自性。緣未合時本□□
□此[59]因緣元將法性爲體。故〔衆〕生界量並因?法起並因?□□□有[60]。衆生之界元
是涅槃之?氣也。
若依涅槃而起?爲?□□□體[61/1]己不。
答、既是涅槃之氣、何處更言衆□□□俱[2]?時、亦非衆生界、非非衆生界、亦非涅
槃界、非非涅槃界。以故道□中[3]無二故、是誰爲衆生、是誰爲涅槃。故言無漸無
頓、號之一爲圓成。
其[4]圓成之法、是畢竟無衆生斷煩惱。若迷於涅槃、即見有衆生、即[5]有煩惱。既有
煩惱、即有心識、即有内外。既有内外、即有諍〔論〕。

〔H〕言[6]心内者、是愚人法也。若在内、即是無常、亦是煩惱、亦是生滅、亦是□[7]猿、亦是人天放逸、亦是恐怖。既有過去、即有未來、即有現在、即〔有〕[8]流轉。

既是流轉、即非佛性。佛性體者、不生不滅、不斷不常、不來不[9]去、非三世、非過去、非未來。如如實際、始名佛性。寧以生滅作其〔佛〕[10]性也。

〔I〕余依經文及禪觀得其解者、等虛空遍法界、即是眞實性。〔若〕[11?]心在外者、即初教。悟法界之心、故言外也。既等虛空、滿於色内、何〔更〕[12]有色與心爲礙。心色既是無礙、豈不遍於虛空也。即是法界之用[13]也。

〔J〕圓宗之中、通於衆生界也。翻衆生界、以爲圓宗也。依此解□□[14]□衆生界也。世界一衆生是一世界。大衆生是大世界。小衆生是〔小世〕[15]界。勢分各別。

譬如王者之界、四方數萬餘里。州郡之界、並在王者[16]之界内也。縣界復在州郡之界内。鄉界復在縣界内。村界復在鄉[17]界内。居宅之界復在村界内。房舍之界復在居宅界内。

作是觀者[18]、從王者轉轉相容、各得世界之用也。若依此解者、人天地獄一[19]切衆生、重重相依、各得勢分、不相障碍也。

〔K〕問曰、世界同處、以何爲體得[20]不相碍。

答曰、大世界元將盧舍那佛、復將菩薩巧方便、大悲願力[21]、復將三昧爲體。三昧復將虚空爲體。虚空無障碍、故能生無[22]碍法界智。法界之智無碍、故能生無〔碍〕三昧智。以三昧無碍、故能[23]生盧舍那佛。無碍無邊身、與一切衆〔生〕依止。以世界本是無碍[24]故、是以不相障碍也。

人身亦是衆生依止界。何以故。以人〔身〕中[25]有八萬户蟲。蟲中亦有諸小蟲。轉轉相依作世界、各自相名以爲〔世〕界[26]也。作此解者、種種是世界。何處更有衆生界。

〔L〕盡是畢竟空。□無[27]衆生也。尋體而觀、元是法水而流。分其水而作世界、世界還□法[28]水。作此解時、亦非衆生界、非非衆生界、亦非世界、非非世界。作[29]此觀時、名爲通於世界義也。

辨明修釋因果品第三

〔A〕彼[30]諸受=修道人等要須明其因果。若不明者、例墮摩訶羅外道見[31]見也。為此因緣要須分明。

難曰、如上『要決論』中所立世界義□並[32]是世界。此義不成就。此門中更不見。衆生體乃至諸佛□□皆[33]悉是空。

又上文中、立世界體、乃至衆生體、法界體、乃〔至〕諸?佛[34]方便體、並將虛空為體。既是虛空、即應無體。所以得知?□□如[35]愚下見、虛空無因、所以有無因果。果橫從何起。若□□□虛[36]空誰之所作也。虛空有其作者、萬法有因有果。若□□□空[37]無其作者、萬法無因復無果。

此依禪師立體而起疑?〔惑〕□□是[38]麼甲橫生難。性=唯願禪師大慈悲、為除疑惑、令得解脫。

〔B〕答曰[39]、如上所難、大有逗留。終日慈悲、欲除衆生疑惑。故作〔是〕[40]難、爲汝解釋。若依其體、無本無末。實無因果。所以者何。但[41]依『般若經』云「因亦空、果亦空、行亦空、非行亦空、非非行亦空[42]。惣而言之。佛亦空、法亦空、僧亦空、乃至賢聖亦空。」准此經[43]文、如上所難、亦復如是。雖然與一切衆生、無始已來、住於色[44]香味資身。非是無爲化起。若是無爲化起、合依蓮花、不[45]依父母。既依父母、明知無始習氣、熏資其身具足。煩惱未[46]除、習氣未盡。

如上法界體中所明義者、並是依他諸佛般若文[47]得解悟。未是自用功而得悟也。若是用功而得悟者、其身如死灰復[48]無有血。設使有血、猶如雪色。既不如是、明知具煩惱、若爲不信因果。

〔C〕余時時設難外人雅伏屈躬、深信因果、復問、若爲爲因、若·爲爲果[50]。

答曰、當須住禪般若、空觀成就、不住有無、身心平等、猶如虛空、行住[51]坐臥、無有癡息、隨緣救物、濟弱扶傾、憐貪愛老。當念衆生三塗[52]等苦、及以人間貪寒困苦、

常以捨命救之。不以辭勞。

如是？行行常[53]在禪定、經於三大阿僧祇。仍須衆願、備如衆生意、莫如己意。須滿衆[54]願、莫如己願。如斯行行、是名因。

又問、若爲爲果。

答曰、果者、不離於因。但住[55]般若、不住有爲。故度衆生、莫作盡意。但行其行、莫限了時。捨命救物、莫生自他之想。所以者何。空禪三昧、無有自他之行。即非菩薩所入。遠劫勤[56]苦、莫生顛倒之意。常行此行、不立滿足之想。

如斯行行、無始習氣[57]、自然滅盡。唯有空行。所以爲空行、習氣倶盡、不住彼我。假與立名、名[58]之爲果。行行滿足、果自然至、故名因果。

果若滿時、智亦滿虛空、行[59]亦滿虛空。國土及化身、並皆滿虛。雖然等虛空、與[60]空無別異也。

[D]依空起其身、身亦是其空。依空起其行、行亦是其空[61]。國土及方便、皆悉如虛

空。所以者何。元依虛空法界起、不異於[62]虛空。猶如水上波。波元依水起。波還即是水。水既不異波。化身亦如是[63]。理行如証、名之爲因果。故名因果。

〔E〕若習氣未盡、名爲因果。習氣[64]既盡、豈得名爲因果。不得爲因果。所以者何。唯有空行救物。更無[65]心意。猶如幻等、故名爲果。果語諸行人等、不可以將凡情、依文取[66]解。即言得其理、要須用功日久。捨俗塵勞、靜坐思惟。已送報身。莫[67]以誦得文、謂言得理。全不相關。此是他解、非是我功。此是他行、非是[68]己行也。作此思惟、得免其過也。

辨明三乘逆順觀品第四

〔A〕欲[69]明三乘差別、各須知因緣不同。一有順觀四大、二逆觀四大。逆順俱達[70]理

盡、齊等虛空、証羅漢果。順觀者、直至羅漢果。逆觀者、例[71]入四聖果、聖然後入〔羅〕漢果。

因緣觀中、亦有逆順。雖同虛空、名証辟支[72]佛。所以分別、時人不明此義。大小遠近、是以名為大乘、其實非是[73]大乘、並是小乘義也。

聲聞人廻心入菩薩道、望?八識習氣藏而得、而生[74]菩薩道、并行六波羅蜜。凡夫逢善知識方便善巧因緣、於三十七助道法門[75]而行六波羅蜜、久行復依何門、入得菩薩大行、得成佛果。

又說教不同、或[76]先說因、然後行菩薩道。上來聲聞廻心、及凡人入道者、先說因、然後說果。久[78]種善根人、於此門中得悟者不同凡夫。及久行菩薩道、並皆得入。

〔B〕問曰、上聲[79]聞廻心及凡夫入道、所以不解。未知、久行菩薩、復依何行菩薩道。未審、久行菩[80]薩、行六波羅蜜已不。

答云、行亦得、不行亦得。所以須不?行慈悲門中、中六波[81]羅蜜、入三昧門、復入法

界門。行行者、即不見六波羅蜜也。若爲是法界門[82]、若欲明者、先須明世界義。若不明世界者、無由得入法界門。是以先須明世界。

〔C〕問曰、何者名世界義。

答曰、一衆生是一世界。大衆生是大世界。小衆生是小世界也。

簡異外道縁生得根本品第五

〔A〕順[85]觀四大者、爲利根凡夫、久種善根、恵情爽達。佛即爲説縁起法[86]門。即懸見空理。就此根基爲説順觀也。

逆觀者、爲凡夫愚鈍。不[87]見玄門、唯見香味觸、妄生計着。爲此凡夫即説逆觀也。

若[88]無利鈍凡夫、實無説逆順觀。多愚有其二分。凡夫逆觀、從聲香[89]味觸推至微塵、推至虚空。色心不起、即取菩薩、是即獲得羅漢[90]果。

此是鈍根之人獲果如是。若利根凡夫逆觀者、不然。從聲[91]香味觸次第觀之、亦

非微塵、並是自心妄想現。

〔B〕問曰、若爲是自[92]心妄想現。

答曰、一切衆生具有六根。何以有之。皆八識眼耳鼻舌[93]身意等根。何處得來。若是自然而有者、即外道所見、亦非佛法。既[94]非是自然而有、即合有來處。既合有來處、未知、從何處來也。

答曰[95]、亦非是自然、並有來處。比從賴耶識中來。賴耶識猶如大地。眼耳[96]鼻舌身意等、猶如百草萌牙。若無大地、草木叢林、依何而得生[97]長。草木叢林種子、皆是地之所持。不失種子。今見眼耳鼻舌並是[98]賴耶〔識〕之氣。賴耶本性無有形質。及諸根身是有形質。今時凡夫不見[99]賴耶爲本、謂言父母能生。是以浪作色身之觀。推至微塵、乃至虚[100]空、妄取羅漢之果。若知身本來依賴耶而起者、即無眼耳鼻舌[101]。

何以得知識元無有形質。唯有四似。何者名爲四似。似根似塵似我[102]似識、此是

四似。一一似中、推覓元無有識根等、並是賴耶之中[103]影像也。但見賴耶、本性無有生滅。即捨諸根之見。何以故。元無諸[104]根識故、並是本識種子相分故。本識之相分者、即無眼耳鼻舌之根[105]本。識中先無根識之質、唯有似也。其似即體是空。推趁即無[106]。只爲不見本識、謂言眼耳鼻舌自然生。今本識體者、唯有似、無[107]有質。以質無故、名爲自心影像。既是自心影像者、何有我也。既[108]無有我、誰取果也。以不取果故、不同鈍根凡夫。推於四大、至於虛空[109]取其果。

〔C〕問曰、取果有何過也。

答曰、取果有我之過。若羅漢入定[110]、猶如死人、復如死灰。經於千劫、更復出定。出定以後、還同凡夫。分[111]別既同。分別者、何處更得識來。既有識生、明知本識所持。是以得出[112]其定、爲此無來未斷一分煩惱。有此過故、既有此患、只爲不見身[113]是本識影像。

若知身是本識之影像者、無不須斷煩惱[114]、亦不須証涅槃。不斷煩惱、故離其我也。唯有習氣[115]未盡。菩薩即自知習氣未盡。

〔D〕當念衆生具無量縛、乘[=生]起大悲[116]。因此即有菩薩行門。雖起菩薩之行、不同凡夫我見之行。所起化報之[117]身者、爲凡〔夫〕而起。非是自爲。若是自爲者、還是我也。以爲凡〔夫〕而起故、是以離其過也。

入道邪正五門辨因果品第六

〔A〕凡[119]欲修道、先須識其因果、二須識其邪正兩門、三須依解起行、四須觀[120]莫癡、五須明行位深淺。有此五門、三世諸佛之所共修。非今獨說[121]。

〔B〕第一、明因果者。凡人之言道人、須自知此是俗情、蓋亦是虛。若不自知[122]、即多失道。若自知者、先觀我身、從頭至足、相好具足已不。曰若下人[123]共叢、我身最爲第一、衆生共許、朝市有名、郡官共許、即衆人共觀[124]、坐即人皆美之、當知前業修

行忍辱不愼、兼復莊嚴尊像具[125]足衆戒、獲果如是。

若觀此身從頭至足、無所可觀、衆人不讚、朝[126]市無名、行則無人記、坐復無人美、衣不蓋形、食不充口、衣馬不具、當[127]知前身、未曾忍辱、慳貪具備、不曾爲福、如此觀者、深須慚愧、自知[128]不具足者、當須種福。是名因果。

〔C〕第二、須解邪正兩門者、凡人依有其深淺[129]。如似有人、修持五戒不犯、其人意功德具足、望與佛齊。如此意者、是[130]人悉爾、非獨一人。爲更不求無漏聖道。名爲邪、非是佛第子也。

若爲作解得[131]合?正道。若欲會其正道、先須達其心本、二須達其色。何以故。一切衆生[132]、皆以色和合、爲凡夫不得聖道。今須了達、始得出纏?。是以須達其[133]元。

若爲心本、本有二種。一者、眞實心。二者、妄想心。凡夫生滅都由妄想。不[134]關眞實。

今須達其妄想。若爲達其妄想、凡夫愚癡不了、謂心是實[135]。智者所觀、元無有體。

若爲作解、得知無體。

〔D〕若欲知虛實者、端[136]坐思惟。觀其妄念起動。所緣前境、無問遠近、皆悉緣至。雖言緣至、而[137]實不到。所以得知、不到。正由不觀其虛實、謂心是有。若觀去時心、若也[138]是其去者、身即應合死。若也是其去者、應合了前頭境界。何故唯緣[139]舊事、不知新事。若作此解、明知、不到前境。已舊事謝故、舊事既謝。即[140]是無境、境既是虛。所言緣者、豈不是妄、爲此得知、是其妄也。

〔E〕若言心在[141]腹内者、亦復不然。何以故。若在腹内、應知腹内五藏中一一事。皆悉不知、明[142]心不在内。心不在内故、即無有我、不到外塵、即無有彼我。彼我既空、名心無彼[143]此。故名心解脱。何以故。已不住二邊故。作此觀時、其心寂然猶如虛空。是名[144]了心。

〔F〕若爲觀色、觀色亦有二種。一者、外色。二者、内色。外色者、山川大地是也[145]。内色者、五陰四大是也。

先觀外四大、山川大地、萬物所依。即此大地是微塵[146]積叢厚重始名爲地。即此微塵未叢以前、元本是空。從虛空衆業[147]力所感、始有微塵。若衆生元無業力者、微塵亦空、乃至積叢竟時、亦是微[148]塵。何以故。若索地體、只得其塵、不得其地。其地若離微塵、更無大地。明知[149]、微塵未叢以前、大地既空。大地既空、明知、微塵亦空。何以故。此虛空無性、化[150]起微塵。微塵無性、化起大地。從其虛空、尋觀大地、微塵本是其空。作[151]此觀時、明知、五陰及四大、亦復如是。是名皆空也。

若爲明其內色者、其身四[152]大、皆依外四大生。外四大既是空、內亦如是。何以故。人依食而立。衣食從地而[153]生。大地既是空、衣食亦非有。衣食既非有、內色依何立。內色既不立、明[154]知、即是空。

觀心無內外、及色亦復然。色心無內外、是名爲寂。寂無所有[155]、故號爲涅槃。作此解時、是名爲正。遠離顚倒。亦名正見、亦名正定、亦名正[156]業。作此說者、亦可（一名）正說。

三世諸佛共乘此法得至彼岸。是名正道。

〔G〕雖然得[157]此解、仍須依解起其行。若不如是、即入外道邪見位中。若爲依解始[158]起其行、爲凡夫無始已來、煩惱熏習積累非今、不可一時頓盡。亦復[159]依今解悟、常覺現前、勿令無明煩惱重起、是名因行。習氣煩惱都[160]盡、更不得與色塵、境界重合、始名斷盡。

〔H〕若自知未盡者、常須觀行[161]覺照、菩薩行六波羅蜜、慈悲一切、饒益於人、推直於他、攬曲向己、計足[162]向他、欠損向己。何以如是。前觀心色、空無有我、即是虛空。虛空若有色、即[163]色有我爭。我既是空、誰有誰爭。以虛空無我、是以須行無諍慈也。若[164]不如是、即理行相乖、非菩薩之行。故言依解起行也。

〔I〕四、須常觀、莫失者[165]、若不作理行相副之觀者、恐其有失。是以須常觀莫癡。

〔J〕五、明行位[166]者、莫已得此解、現前即言共佛等。未同諸境界。約位判時、始是修信賢[167]人、非是究竟人也。若不知其位者、定入無因果謗。故以此言也。

自[168]心現量品第七

〔A〕依『楞伽經』自覺聖智宗、立一切諸佛皆是[169]自心現量義。若解者、山川大地、及以己身、並是自心、非是謬?也。且論[170]身分四大、四大所感。何無五大、天地所成。乃四輪而立、云何不說五輪而[171]成。有何所益。

『釋』曰、實是自心所現。非是謬也。所以得知、自心所現。且論[172]身四大者、爲內有四種妄想。感得四大以爲身、是以無五大。何以故。內有沉[173]重妄想故、感得地大以爲身。內有津潤妄想故、感得水大以爲身。內[174]有忿熱妄想故、感得火大爲身。內有飄動妄想故、感得風大以爲身。是[175]以得知、皆是自心現量。

〔B〕問曰、其身信知不惑、山川大地、若爲得知自心。

答曰[176]、亦由內心。何以故。已有高下妄想故、感得山川大地不平。其地下厚三百

六十萬里[177]、名爲地輪。其地下有水、得深三百六十萬里、名爲水輪。已承大地。其水輪下[178]、復有大火、復深三百六十萬里、已上衝承其水輪。其大火下、復有風輪、復深[179]三百六十萬里。上下四輪、次第相承、大地得存、名爲世界。其風輪下、即[180]是懸空、更無物也。何以故。只有四輪、而無五六．者、爲衆生内心有四種妄想[181]。還爲内有沈重妄想、故感得地輪。爲内津潤妄想、故感得水輪。爲内[182]有忿熱妄想、故感得火輪。爲内有飄動妄想、故感得風輪。以相成也[183]。作此思惟、皆是自心所現。除心以外、更無一法。

〔C〕爾時有人問言、天地萬法無[184]數者、只由未悟。諸法是其心。爲此因緣、即有疑心、即見諸法。是有是無[185]。爲此因緣、即起有無謗也。爲破除諸法、即起相違戲論謗也。

若知[186]其心所感者、惣是自心。元無諸法。若也有法、即言有無。既是自心、元無[187]諸法。何得言有過也。作此解者、即於諸法、離其謗也。

〔D〕問曰、山川大地[188]是無情、人是有情。云何忽言無情之境是其心也。若爲得信、實難[189]可信。

答曰、譬如夫妻二無智愚癡、相共平章、作酒欲沾。酒既醞?已[190]、其夫往看其酒、酒已澄清。乃見自影、即以成瞋、打其婦、婦分疏、我有[191]何事。其夫即言、你何故將一男人、藏着瓮中。其婦不信、即看瓮中、乃[192]見自影、還復大瞋即語夫言、你何將一婦女藏着瓮中、不語我知。爾[193]時夫妻相打、各不識自影。相打至死。並舍救問其所由、各如上説、其解鬬[194]人釋、亦復不信。即將夫妻就瓮看影。乃見三人影、又復不信。若其[195]是影、合在瓮外、何故在瓮裏。其解鬬人即語、若不是你影者、我[196]即共你夫妻、並在瓮中。乃見三人明知、是你夫影。爾時其婦更瞋口云[197]、有一男人、送一箇女婦來。又復相打、不知休息。畢竟不信是其影也[198]。

〔E〕凡夫亦爾、山川大地日月參辰、並是自心業所現、盡是自心影像。何以[199]凡夫

不名[=知]心作、決定不信。亦如夫妻二人諍影像相似、決定不信是自[200]影也。瓮中實影者、喻山川大地亦是自心現量。若非自心現量者[201]、既見雷車、震其虛空得作聲、明知、此聲是其空也。又見乘車在地[202]、雖震其地以作聲、若無虛空、終不出聲。明知、此聲亦是空也。作此[203]解時、一切諸法盡是虛空。元無法也。只由凡夫妄想未盡、見山川大[204]地。妄想若盡、畢竟不見也。諸佛菩薩、以去處無障碍、只由妄想盡[205]、是以不見山川大地。明知、萬法皆是心業所現也。

辨[206]明聲體品第九

〔A〕凡言聲者、時人作解、耳所得聲者、大錯。言[207]聲到耳者、亦大錯。

問曰、若爲作解、契會佛意。

若欲解聲眞源者、先[208]須識其聲緣、亦須明其聲體。

問曰、何者是緣、何者是體。

答曰、鍾杵及[209]人功用並是其緣。鍾内空及鍾外空並是其體。遂出其聲、即此聲[210]者、是其體聲、非是鍾也。

問、其體者、處處皆遍。何以只滿十里、不滿百[211]里。

答、以緣有大小。聲雖不滿虚空、猶如下震其百出、皆悉大動、其地[212]可以、有流轉以不。若審思量、其地雖震、不曾流轉。即是不動。聲亦[213]如是。雖緣擊震、虚空乃震處作聲、亦不流轉。既不流轉、即是不動[214]。即是不生、即是不滅也。

〔B〕如五海十智之義、是一切諸佛菩薩大行之根本[215]也。若不善五海十智之義者、無由得解圓門義也。

又圓教之義、是何[216]法。圓教法門者、衆生是諸佛、諸佛是衆生。舊來如是、不由今悟。不[217]與三乘菩薩同也。又圓教門中明義者、亦非衆生界、亦非涅槃界也。

圓[218]明論一卷。

CHINESE TEXTS
of the
Hsiu-hsin yao lun
and
Yuan-ming lun